LONGMAN LINGUISTICS LIBRARY

LINGUISTIC THEORY

LONGMAN LINGUISTICS LIBRARY

General editors
R. H. Robins, University of London
Martin Harris, University of Essex

A Short History of Linguistics
Third Edition
R. H. ROBINS

Structural Aspects of Language Change
JAMES M. ANDERSON

Text and Context
Explorations in the Semantics and Pragmatics of Discourse
TEUN A. VAN DIJK

Introduction to Text Linguistics
ROBERT-ALAIN DE BEAUGRANDE AND WOLFGANG ULRICH DRESSLER

Spoken Discourse
A Model for Analysis
WILLIS EDMONDSON

Psycholinguistics
Language, Mind, and World
DANNY D. STEINBERG

Dialectology
W. N. FRANCIS

Principles of Pragmatics
GEOFFREY N. LEECH

Generative Grammar
GEOFFREY HORROCKS

Norms of Language
Theoretical and Practical Aspects
RENATE BARTSCH

The English Verb
Second Edition
F. R. PALMER

Pidgin and Creole Languages
SUZANNE ROMAINE

General Linguistics
An Introductory Survey
Fourth Edition
R. H. ROBINS

A History of English Phonology
CHARLES JONES

Generative and Non-linear Phonology
JACQUES DURAND

Modality and the English Modals
Second Edition
F. R. PALMER

Linguistics and Semiotics
YISHAI TOBIN

Multilingualism in the British Isles I: the Older Mother Tongues and Europe
EDITED BY SAFDER ALLADINA AND VIV EDWARDS

Multilingualism in the British Isles II: Africa, Asia and the Middle East
EDITED BY SAFDER ALLADINA AND VIV EDWARDS

Dialects of English
Studies in Grammatical Variation
EDITED BY PETER TRUDGILL AND J. K. CHAMBERS

Introduction to Bilingualism
CHARLOTTE HOFFMANN

English Verb and Noun Number:
A functional explanation
WALLIS REID

English in Africa
JOSEF S. SCHMIED

Linguistic Theory: The Discourse of Fundamental Works

Robert de Beaugrande

LONGMAN

LONDON AND NEW YORK

LONGMAN GROUP UK LIMITED
Longman House, Burnt Mill, Harlow
Essex CM20 2JE, England
and Associated Companies throughout the world.

*Published in the United States of America
by Longman Inc., New York*

© *Longman Group UK Limited 1991*

First published 1991

British Library Cataloguing in Publication Data
Beaugrande, Robert-Alain de
Linguistic theory : the discourse of fundamental works. –
(Longman linguistics library).
1. Linguistics
I. Title
410

ISBN 0–582–08210–2
ISBN 0–582–03725–5 pbk

Library of Congress Cataloging-in-Publication Data
De Beaugrande, Robert.
Linguistic theory : the discourse of fundamental works / Robert de
Beaugrande.
p. cm. — (Longman linguistics library)
Includes bibliographical references and indexes.
ISBN 0–582–08210–2 (cased). — ISBN 0–582–03725–5 (paper)
1. Linguistics—History—20th century. I. Title. II. Series.
P77.D44 1991
410′.904—dc20 90–24332
CIP

Set in 10 on 11 pt Times
Produced by Longman Singapore Publishers (Pte) Ltd
Printed in Singapore

Contents

Graphic conventions

To conserve space, references to works by the sample linguists are made with abbreviations; note 1 to each chapter provides a key, and the general key follows (p. vii). A page reference is not shown when it is identical with the one just before it, and may thus be shared by a series of quotes (and an unmarked quote after one marked, say, '100f', might come from page 100, 101, or both); cross-references (indicated by 'cf.'), however, are not included in this tactic. A number with 'n' designates a footnote; 'f' is for a quote extending over two pages, and 'ff' is for one over three pages. Several page numbers for one quote indicate that it is a composite or that the source repeated itself in whole or in part; passages closer to the exact or complete wording of the quote are cited before looser or shorter approximations. References to other works are done with author and date; where relevant, the original publication date follows in square brackets. To avoid numerous brackets or spaced periods, I set each part of a quote in its own quotation marks ('_____'). I made some minor changes in the form of verbs (person, tense) and nouns or pronouns (number, case), but none I felt would change the meaning or intention of the quote. Linguistic examples were placed in double quotes ("_____"). 'Italics' were 'added' ('i.a.'), 'removed' ('i.r.'). or, rarely, 'shifted' in a quote ('i.s.'); otherwise, all italics here came from the original sources. My own translations into English are indicated by 'm.t.'. Thematic terms are highlighted in bold type to help direct the flow of the exposition.

List of abbreviations

AT   *Aspects of the Theory of Syntax* (Chomsky)
BL   *Language* (Bloomfield)
CG   *Course in General Linguistics* (Saussure)
EF   *Explorations in the Function of Language* (Halliday)
EL1   *Essais linguistiques* (Hjelmslev)
EL2   *Essais linguistiques II* (Hjelmslev)
IF   *Introduction to Functional Linguistics* (Halliday)
IG   *Intonation and Grammar in British English* (Halliday)
LB   *Language in Relation to a Unified Theory of the Structure of Human Behavior* (Pike)
NT   Notes on transitivity and theme in English (Halliday)
PT   *Prolegomena to a Theory of Language* (Hjelmslev)
P1   *Papers in Linguistics 1934–1951* (Firth)
P2   *Selected Papers of J.R. Firth 1952–1959*
RT   *Résumé of a Theory of Language* (Hjelmslev)
SB   *Syntax und Bedeutung* (Hartmann)
SD   *Strategies of Discourse Comprehension* (van Dijk & Kintsch)
SL   *Language* (Sapir)
SS   *Syntactic Structures* (Chomsky)
TG   *Theorie der Grammatik* (Hartmann)
TMS   *Tongues of Men and Speech* (Firth)
TS   *Theorie der Sprachwissenschaft* (Hartmann)

Mottos

We ignore the achievements of our predecessors not only to our individual detriment but greatly to the peril of our collective scientific enterprise.

Charles Hockett

Any new attempt at synthesis in linguistics must consider the origins of our theories and terminology.

J.R. Firth

The difficulty of explaining the various phases of speech is so great and there are so many sources of error, that we must be more cautious in accepting statements here than in other sciences of observation.

Samuel Stehman Haldeman

A truly creative dialogue is not at all common, even in science . . . . What is essential is that each participant is suspending his or her point of view, while also holding other points of view in a suspended form and giving full attention to what they mean.

David Bohm and David Peat

Chapter 1

Linguistic theory as discourse

1.1 'Surveys' of 'linguistic theory' have become so numerous that a new one calls for some justification. It seems to me that even though linguistics is *about* language, the major works in linguistic theory have seldom been analysed and synthesized *as* language, specifically: as a mode of discourse seeking to circumscribe language by means of language. Perhaps this lack is due in part to the limitations imposed by theorists who did not address discourse as a linguistic phenomenon, or only marginally so. Perhaps too, it was tacitly assumed that theories do not critically depend on the language in which they happen to be expounded. Today, however, discourse has become a major area of concern, and the dependence of concepts and arguments on the discourse that constitutes them is widely acknowledged.

1.2 Therefore, to examine linguistic theories as discourse constructions is by no means to discount their conceptual importance, but to insist on attending very carefully to the emergence of those conceptions within the original discourse before proceeding on to the more usual stages of abstraction and paraphrase. This insistence can be particularly instrumental in tracing the development of terminology, and the continuity, evolution, or change in the major lines of argument not merely between theorists, but within the work of an individual theorist.

1.3 On the whole, the history of the 'science of language' has not been unmanageably diffuse. Major theoretical works and frameworks have not been overly numerous. And on the whole, the discipline has been fairly parsimonious in its theorizing, indeed resolutely so in the face of the complexity of language. Yet we can certainly not claim that the problems addressed by our predecessors have by now vanished or been completely resolved. Instead, we frequently sense a need to return to those problems and re-examine the principles set forth decades ago to approach them.

1.4 In that situation, surveys of linguistic theory should be cautious about imposing an artificial, retrospective sense of order and direction on the discipline by distilling out a few main 'ideas', 'schools', 'trends', or 'paradigms'. That method can abbreviate or conceal the complexity and diversity of scientific interaction and discourse. A counterbalance could be attained by surveying linguistics as a 'model science' perpetually in the process of situating itself in respect to language.

1.5 Such a survey is a problematic and arduous project, but I hold it to be urgent for several reasons. First, many of the issues in linguistics that preoccupy linguistic theorists today were recognized and deliberated by our predecessors. We cannot get a full sense of our domain by reducing the works of the founders to a handful of precepts and slogans, without due regard for the overall argument and context, including important qualifications and reservations. That strategy tends to convert complicated, energizing research programmes too eagerly into inhibiting new orthodoxies. And in hindsight, we may get the utterly mistaken impression that linguistics did not properly appreciate the depth and difficulty of the issues.

1.6 Second, linguistic theory is essentially a domain of work in progress, a discipline always in search of itself. Leading theorists often voiced their dissatisfaction with the state of linguistics as they saw it (cf. 12.3). But if we construe their discontent as a pretext for writing off the past, we incur the risk of repeating the same shortcomings they perceived and strove to alleviate.

1.7 Third, certain signs indicate that linguistic theory has for some years been moving into a phase of stagnation and diminishing returns. Despite decades of effort, the relations between theory and practice, between model and domain, or between method and evidence have not been definitively established, and seem to be shifted once again by every new school or trend. In consequence, the history of the discipline may appear discontinuous and non-cumulative, with research projects typically clustered around sporadic bursts of theorizing. The status of theoretical entities, even such central ones as 'word' and 'sentence', remains in dispute. No consensus obtains about the future trends and modifications that linguistics should undergo. In such a state of affairs, we cannot merely wait to see what develops in day-to-day research and discussion. We need to draw up the theoretical balance sheets of past investigations. Surveying the major issues and problems of the discipline through their treatment in the discourse foundational works can be an inaugural step in planning for future research on a truly comprehensive and organized scale.

1.8 All linguists share at least one special predicament: they can get evidence only from their own *encounters with language*, with and within some mode of **discourse** (cf. 12.1, 48). The system never steps forward to be 'observed' in some concrete selfhood; and data are not data until they have been *understood as language*. In consequence, linguists deal with data in whose constitution and interpretation they are always to some degree involved, at least behind the scenes. Since language is so extraordinarily sensitive to how it is used, it may assume different appearances depending on how it is grasped. We therefore need to expand our scope from 'looking at language' to 'looking at linguists looking at language' and in particular talking or writing about it. We cannot eliminate the linguist's perspective, but we can scrutinize it by asking how human beings, whether linguists or ordinary speakers, abstract systematic knowledge from language experience and at the same time apply systematic knowledge in order to relate experience to language (cf. 12.44).

1.9 That you must 'know language' to 'understand language' and vice versa is a truism, but by no means an insignificant one. We seem to confront a peculiarly vicious circularity enshrouding the question of how we might approach language from the 'outside': how children or linguists or anybody else can reach the 'critical mass', the stage of 'knowing' the system behind or beyond the individual *uses* of language (cf. 12.38). Much of that knowledge is concealed from conscious awareness during everyday discourse, and the prospects for making it conscious and explicit are by nature precarious (cf. 12.49). To observe yourself observing language, to watch or hear yourself thinking, to grasp your own understanding – all these acts are easily beset by paradox or infinite regress. We can, however, subject the discourse of those engaged in such acts to steadily more circumspect and integrative scrutiny, thereby adding fresh emphasis to our perennial insistence on the centrality of language (cf. 12.22).

1.10 My survey accordingly proceeds by arranging and presenting the discourse, the statements and arguments, of representative theorists in linguistics of this century, sticking as close as is feasible to their actual wordings, especially where major points are expressed. By this expedient, I hoped to restrict my own role in increasing or complicating the mediation between linguistics and language, as I would have had to do had I paraphrased and summarized the sources in my own words. Though admittedly laborious, this method may help to reanimate the complex flow of the discourse in the gradually emerging discipline, to focus on characteristic moves, and to retrace the key terms as they gain or lose currency. Proceeding by author rather than by 'school' may help to accentuate individual views, voices, and personalities, and thus to re-experience some of the momentum and perplexity of repeated confrontations with the recalcitrant problems that the study of language necessarily raises.

1.11 Due to this gallery of problems, a general book on linguistics tends to have the character of a performance, raising and responding to typical questions, such as:

Where does linguistics stand among the other disciplines?
Which aspects of language deserve to be put in focus, and which ones are of lesser interest?
What means or methods are recommended or rejected?
How do linguists gather data, and how can they check their own estimation of it against other sources?
How are examples brought to bear on theoretical issues and abstractions?
What are the fundamental units and structures of language?
What is the theoretical status of traditional concepts such as 'word', 'phrase', and 'sentence'?

We shall be seeing quite a spectrum of potential answers, some explicit, others merely implicit. Few of the answers will seem definitive, since they depend on the goals and aspirations of the particular theorist, and these are by no means uniform (cf. 12.58, 60ff). Still, considering such a spectrum assembled in one volume may shed light on the nature of the questions, whatever the eventual answers we may yet select.

1.12 It was rather agonizing to decide which 'fundamental works' should be used, given the unmanageably large number worthy of inquiry. My selection was guided by two major criteria. First, these works were influential in the general development of theories or models, as attested for instance by frequent citation. Second, these works propound such a wide range of positions and issues that we can profit by bringing them into explicit interaction with each other. I do not mean to suggest that the works I selected are the only ones or even the best ones produced by each linguist, but only that they are important and rewarding examples of the discourse of linguistic theory.

1.13 My treatment is only roughly in chronological order, because the works and their spans of influence sometimes overlapped in time, and because some influences emerge more clearly through direct follow-ups, e.g. Bloomfield to Pike, Hjelmslev to Chomsky, and Firth to Halliday. However, similar arguments and conceptions also appear where we cannot trace such influences, or at least none that the authors acknowledge. Conversely, demonstrable influences do not necessarily promote agreement, and successors may differ from their predecessors or teachers on major issues.

1.14 Obviously, my selection could have been different or larger. But the approach proved to require such detailed attention to each work and theorist that I lacked the space to include more of them. For motives of size, I regretfully deleted a chapter on Terry Winograd, a major thinker both in linguistics and in artificial intelligence. I also deeply regretted not being able to deal with such undeniably influential linguists as Emile Benveniste, Dwight Bolinger, Wallace Chafe, Simon Dik, Charles Fillmore, Charles Carpenter Fries, Hans Glinz, Joseph Grimes, Z.S. Harris, Roman Jakobson, Daniel Jones, William Labov, George Lakoff, Robert E. Longacre, Aleksei Leontev, Nikolai Marr, André Martinet, Vilém Mathesius, Ivan Meshchaninov, Nikolai Trubetzkoy, or Leo Weisgerber. Also, I would have liked to include such precursors and pioneers as Franz Bopp, Jan Baudouin de Courtenay, Samuel Haldeman, Wilhelm and Alexander von Humboldt, Hermann Paul, Rasmus Rask, Henry Sweet, Dwight Whitney, etc. And major figures from neighbouring disciplines also deserve such attention: semioticians such as Julia Kristeva, Jurij Lotman, Charles Morris, Charles Peirce, Thomas Sebeok, etc.; language philosophers such as John Austin, Jacques Derrida, Michel Foucault, Paul Grice, Martin Heidegger, Alfred Korzybski, Jacques Lacan, John Searle, Ludwig Wittgenstein, etc.; logicians such as Rudolf Carnap, Max Cresswell, Richard Montague, János Petöfi, Alfred Tarski, Lotfi Zadeh, etc.; psychologists and psycholinguists like Philip N. Johnson-Laird, Alexander Luria, William Levelt, William Marslen-Wilson, George Miller, Charles Osgood, etc.; sociologists like Basil Bernstein, Erving Goffman, Harvey Sacks, Emmanuel Schegloff, etc.; anthropologists such as Edmund Leach, Bronislaw Malinowski, Claude Lévi-Strauss, etc.; or analysts of narrative and literary or poetic discourse such as Roland Barthes, Algirdas Greimas, Tzvetan Todorov, etc. Though I had to exclude all these figures, I glean some comfort from the fact that I have made use of their work in my previous writings, and from the hope that I may give them more attention in the future.

Chapter 2

Ferdinand de Saussure[1]

2.1 Ferdinand de Saussure's *Cours de linguistique générale* (*Course in General Linguistics*) is a peculiar book, not merely published but in part composed after the author's death. Since he 'destroyed the rough drafts of the outlines used for his lectures', the editors, Charles Bally, Albert Sechehaye, and Albert Riedlinger, used 'the notes collected by students' in order to 'attempt a reconstruction, a synthesis', and to 'recreate F. de Saussure's thought' (CG xviiif). To 'draw together an organic whole', the editors tried to 'weed out variations and irregularities characteristic of oral delivery', and to 'omit nothing that might contribute to the overall impression' (CG xix). Thus, the 'Saussure' of the *Cours* is a composite voice, speaking from a lecture platform between 1897 and 1911 and passing through the notebooks of followers who confess that 'the master' 'probably would not have authorized the publication of these pages' (CG xvii, 38, xviiif). Many problems with its formulation and interpretation may reflect the difficulties of its composition.

2.2 Saussure – or 'Saussure', as I should write perhaps – seems fully conscious of his role as founder of a 'science'. He constantly searches for generalities, high-level abstractions, and fundamental definitions. Over and over, he states what is 'always' or 'never' the case, what applies in 'each' or 'every' instance, what are the 'only' relevant aspects, and so on. At times, these universalizing assertions may go beyond what can be demonstrated, or conflict with each other in puzzling ways.[2] Formulating the common denominators of Saussurian 'thought' can thus be quite challenging.

2.3 His 'hesitation to undertake the radical revision which he felt was necessary' in linguistics seems to have deterred him from writing a general book; in fact, 'he could not bring himself to publish the slightest note if he was not assured first of the fundamental foundations' (Benveniste 1971: 33). In a letter to Antoine Meillet dated 4 January, 1894 he proclaimed himself 'disgusted' 'with the difficulty' of 'writing ten lines concerning the facts of language which have any common sense', and with 'the very great vanity of everything that can ultimately be done in linguistics' (*ibid.*, 33f). He lamented 'the absolute ineptness of current terminology, the necessity to reform it, and, in order to do that, to show what sort of subject language in general is'. In the *Cours*, he still finds 'current terminology' 'imperfect or incorrect at many points', and its components 'all more or less illogical' (CG 44). Still, he often proposes and defends terms with bravura, and many of these have become standard. And he 'does not hesitate to use' 'the expressions condemned' by 'the new school' he envisions (CG 5n) (cf. 2.30).[3]

2.4 Like most of the theorists in my survey, Saussure was highly discontent with the state of the discipline (cf. 12.3). He charged that 'no other field' was so beset by 'mistakes', 'aberrations', 'absurd notions, prejudices, mirages, and fictions' (CG 7, 3f, 97, 215). He deplored the 'confusion' 'in linguistic research' as well as the 'absurdities of reasoning', and the 'erroneous and insufficient notions' created by his predecessors (CG 99, 4f) (cf. 2.10). The intent to found a new direction can sharpen such polemics, especially when established 'schools' 'watch the progress of the new science suspiciously' and each 'mistrusts the other' (cf. CG 3).

2.5 'Before finding its true and unique object', 'the science that has been developed around the facts of language passed through three stages' (CG 1) (cf. 4.4ff; 8.6–9, 15; 11.22–26; 12.4–8).[4] First, the 'study' of '"grammar"' was 'based on logic', but 'lacked a scientific approach and was detached from language itself'. Preoccupied with 'rules for distinguishing between correct and incorrect forms', grammar 'was a normative discipline, far removed from actual observation'. Second, 'classical philology' was devoted to 'comparing texts of different periods, determining the language peculiar to each author, or deciphering and explaining inscriptions' (CG 3, 1). This approach 'followed written language too slavishly', 'neglected the living language', and focused on 'Greek and Latin antiquity' (CG 1f). Third, 'comparative philology' explored the relatedness of many languages, but 'did not succeed in setting up the true science of linguistics', because it 'failed to seek out the nature of its object of study' (CG 2f). Also, 'the exaggerated and almost exclusive role' 'given to Sanskrit' was a 'glaring mistake' (CG 215) (cf. 4.4, 40; 8.4f, 74, 8[6]; 11.20f).

2.6 Although (or because) he owed so much to it,[5] Saussure was especially critical of 'philology', the historical study of language. Because 'modern linguistics' 'has been completely absorbed in diachrony', (i.e., issues of 'evolution'), its 'conception of language is therefore hybrid and hesitating'; this 'linguistics' 'has no clear-cut objective' and fails 'to make a sharp distinction between states and successions' (CG 81f). In contrast, 'the "grammarians" inspired by traditional methods' at least tried to 'describe language-states'. Though 'traditional grammar neglects whole parts of language', does not 'record facts', and 'lacks overall perspective', 'the method was correct': however 'unscientific', 'classical grammar' is judged 'less open to criticism' than 'philology' (cf. 12.4). Now, 'linguistics, having accorded too large a place to history, will turn back to the static viewpoint of traditional grammar, but in a new spirit and with other procedures, and the historical method will have contributed to this rejuvenation' (CG 82f) (cf. 2.15; 6.49; 7.4; 8.38; 11.41, 88; 12.7). In effect, 'general linguistics' would become a 'true science' by supplying the theoretical and methodological framework absent from earlier approaches, while drawing freely on their findings and examples.

2.7 Saussure envisioned 'linguistics' taking its place among 'other sciences that sometimes borrow from its data, sometimes supply it with data' – e.g., 'political history', 'psychology', 'anthropology', 'sociology', 'ethnography', 'prehistory', and 'palaeontology' (CG 102f, 147, 9, 6, 224) (cf. 12.9–20). Yet 'linguistics must be carefully distinguished' from such sciences, which can contribute only to 'external linguistics', concerning 'everything that is outside' the 'system' of 'language' (CG 6, 9, 20f) (cf. 2.9; 12.9). In return, 'we can draw no accurate conclusions outside the domain of linguistics proper' (CG 228).

2.8 On a grand scale, Saussure foresaw *'a science that studies the life of signs within society'*, and called it **semiology** (CG 16). 'Linguistics is only a part of that general science' and is charged with 'finding out what makes language a special system within the mass of semiological data'. 'If we are to discover the true nature of language, we must learn what it has in common with all other semiological systems' (CG 17) (cf. 6.50–56; 11.9f). For Saussure, 'language, the most complex and universal of all systems of expression, is also the most characteristic; in this sense linguistics can become the master-pattern for all branches of semiology' (CG 68) (cf. 6.53; 12.18, 21f). Though he didn't elaborate on this future science in detail, he predicted it would establish 'laws', 'rules', and 'constant principles' (CG 16f, 88).

2.9 To explain why 'semiology' had 'not been recognized as an independent science with its own object', Saussure contends that 'heretofore language has almost always been studied in connection with something else, from other viewpoints' (CG 16) (cf. 6.5ff; 9.2). He now announces, in a much-quoted aphorism at the close of the book, that *'the true and unique object of linguistics is language studied in and for itself'* (CG 232) (cf. 6.64; 12.35). Against Dwight Whitney, he demurs that 'language is not similar in all respects to other social institutions' (CG 10). Also, 'other sciences work with objects that are given in advance', whereas in 'linguistics', 'it would seem that it is the viewpoint that creates the object' (CG 8) (cf. 12.58).

2.10 In Saussure's estimate, 'all idioms embody certain fixed principles that the linguist meets again and again in passing from one to another' (CG 99). Hence, 'the linguist is obliged to acquaint himself with the greatest possible number of languages in order to determine what is universal in them by observing and comparing them' (CG 23) (cf. 6.57; 12.18, 49, 12[4]). 'But it is very difficult to command scientifically such different languages', and 'each idiom is a closed system', so 'each language in practice forms a unit of study' (CG 99). In this connection, Saussure concedes that 'the ideal, theoretical form of a science is not always the one imposed upon it by the exigencies of practice; in linguistics, these exigencies are more imperious than anywhere else; they account to some extent for the confusion that now predominates in linguistic research' (cf. 2.4).

2.11 'Language' constitutes a 'linguistic *fact*' that, Saussure hopes, can 'be pictured in its totality' (CG 112). To do so, 'we must call in a new type of facts to illuminate the special nature of language', and must 'throw new light on the facts', whether 'static' or 'evolutionary' (CG 16f, 189f) (cf. 2.6, 36). For instance, 'concepts' are 'mental facts'; 'analogy' is 'a universal fact'; 'a phonological system' is a 'set of facts'; and so on (CG 11, 176, 171, 34).

2.12 But dealing with 'facts' may be quite problematic, since 'nothing tells us in advance that one way of considering the fact in question takes precedence over any other' (CG 8). We may have to 'sift the facts' 'many times to bring to light' the essentials (cf. CG 202). 'The most serious mistake in method' is to suppose that 'the facts embraced' by a 'law' 'exist once and for all instead of being born and dying within a span of time' (CG 146). Even where the 'facts' may suggest otherwise, 'we must defend our principle: there are no unchangeable characteristics' (CG 230f). 'Permanence results from sheer luck'.

2.13 The range or extension of a fact is also a problem. On the one hand, 'it is a serious mistake to consider dissimilar facts as a single phenomenon' (CG 146). Against the neogrammarians and philologists, who tried to show how 'a set of facts apparently obeys the same *law*', Saussure argues that such 'facts' are 'isolated' and 'accidental'; and that 'regardless of the number of instances where a phonetic law holds, all the facts embraced by it are but multiple manifestations of a single particular fact' (CG 93f).[6] He suggests that 'the term "law"' might 'be used in language as in the physical and natural sciences', but only from a timeless 'panchronic viewpoint' he opposes (CG 95) (cf. 12.11). All the same, he refers to 'laws that govern the combining of phonemes', the 'evolution' of a 'word', the 'accentuation' of 'syllables', or the status of 'initial consonants' and 'vowels' (CG 51, 86, 30f).

2.14 Evidently, Saussure couldn't quite decide whether 'the facts of language' are 'governed by laws' (CG 91) (cf. 11.22). 'The laws of language' differ from 'every social law', which is 'imperative' ('comes in by force') and 'general' ('covers all cases'). 'Like everything that pertains to the linguistic system', a 'law' 'is an arrangement of terms, a fortuitous, involuntary result of evolution' (CG 86). 'And the arrangement that the law defines is precarious precisely because it is not imperative' (CG 92). Moreover, 'laws' such as those governing 'alternation' may be 'only a fortuitous result of underlying' 'facts' (CG 159). In sum, 'speaking of linguistic law in general is like trying to pin down a [phantom]' (CG 91).

2.15 Saussure's deliberations already raise the persistent problem in modern linguistics of how to decide what is '*real*' (cf. 1.12f; 12.24f, 57). At times he seems confident: 'when we examine "abstractions" more closely, we see what part of reality they actually stand for, and a simple corrective measure suffices to give an exact and justifiable meaning to the expedients of the grammarian' (CG 184) (cf. 12.57). He chides other schools for 'notions' with 'no basis in reality', though he himself is forced on occasion (e.g., when considering 'geographical diversity', which disrupts his conception of the closed system) into a 'schematic simplification' that 'seems to go against reality' (CG 4, 196).

2.16 At any rate, 'the *concrete* entities of language are not directly accessible' (CG 110). So he would justify the thesis that 'language is concrete' with the mentalistic premise that 'associations which bear the stamp of collective approval' 'are realities that have their seat in the brain' (CG 15) (cf. 2.31, 66, 83; 12.10). 'The concrete object of linguistic science is the social product deposited in the brain of each individual' (CG 23). When 'sound and thought combine', they 'produce a **form**, not a **substance**'; 'all the mistakes in our terminology, all our incorrect ways of naming things that pertain to language, stem from the involuntary supposition that the linguistic phenomenon must have substance' (CG 113, 122) (cf. 6.28–31; 11.89, 11[14]).

2.17 Still, 'to base the classifications' 'for arranging all the facts' 'on anything except concrete entities' 'is to forget that there are no linguistic facts apart from the phonic substance cut into significant elements' (CG 110) (cf. 3.18; 12.26). Hence, in order to show that '*abstract* entities are always based, in the last analysis, on *concrete* entities', Saussure invokes the 'series of material elements' (CG 138). 'Thought' follows 'the material state of signs' (CG 228) (cf. 3.10, 12.84). 'Syntax' resides inside 'material units distributed in space'; and 'words' are situated in 'the substance that constitutes sentences' (CG 139, 172) (cf. 12.33). Despite such jarring passages, Saussure emphasizes that 'language exists independently' of 'the material substance of words'; that 'the word-unit' is 'constituted' 'by characteristics other than its material quality'; and that 'a material sign is not necessary for the expression of an idea' (CG 18, 94, 86). 'A material unit exists only through its meaning and function', just as these two require 'the support of some material form' (CG 139).

2.18 Considerations like these made Saussure uneasy about 'calling the **word** a concrete linguistic object' (CG 8) (cf. 3.31; 4.54, 60; 5.53; 6.23; 7.70, 7[19]; 8.54; 11.69, 71, 77; 12.29). 'There has been much disagreement about the nature of the word'; 'the usual meaning of the term is incompatible with the notion of a concrete unit' (CG 105).[7] Nevertheless, 'being unable to seize the concrete entities or units of language directly, we shall work with words' (CG 113). Insofar as 'the word' 'at least bears a rough resemblance' to 'the linguistic unit' and 'has the advantage of being concrete', 'we shall use words as specimens equivalent to real terms in a synchronic system, and the principles that we evolve with respect to words will be valid for entities in general' (CG 113f). After all, 'the word is a unit that strikes the mind, something central in the mechanism of language'; so 'everything said about words applies to any term of language' (CG 111, 116) (cf. 12.54).

2.19 Saussure is determined to view 'language' as 'a well-defined object in the heterogeneous mass of speech facts' (CG 14). 'We must put both feet on the ground of language and use language as the norm of all other manifestations of speech' (CG 9, i.r.) (cf. 2.8). But to do so, he drastically limits the object of study: 'the science of language is possible only if' 'the other elements of speech' 'are excluded' (CG 15) (cf. 2.7, 9). He draws a firm dichotomy between '**language [langue]**' and '**human speech [langage]**', making the former 'only a definite part' of the latter and oddly arguing that 'language' 'can be classified among human phenomena, whereas speech cannot' (CG 9, 15). 'We cannot put' 'speech' 'in any category of human facts, for we cannot discover its unity'; only 'language gives unity to speech' (CG 9, 11) (cf. 12.39). 'Speech cannot be studied, for it is not homogeneous' (CG 19). None the less, we are counselled to 'set up the science of language within the overall study of speech', and told that 'the subject matter of linguistics comprises all manifestations of human speech' (CG 17, 6).

2.20   To limit further 'the rational form linguistic study should take', Saussure makes a dichotomy between '**language**' [**langue**] and '**speaking**' [**parole**] (CG 98, 13, i.a.) (cf. 12.36). 'The two objects are closely connected' and 'interdependent', yet are 'two absolutely distinct things' (CG 18f). 'Speaking is necessary for the establishment of language, and historically, its actuality always comes first' (CG 18). But 'language' is 'passive', 'receptive', 'collective', and 'homogeneous', while 'speaking' is 'active', 'executive', 'individual', and 'heterogeneous' (CG 13, 15). Unlike 'language', 'speaking is not a collective instrument; its manifestations are individual and momentary' and 'depend on the will of speakers' (CG 19). Saussure vowed to 'deal only with linguistics of language'; even if he 'uses material belonging to speaking to illustrate a point', he 'tries never to erase the boundaries that separate the two domains' (CG 19f). Though according to his editors, he 'promised to the students' a 'linguistics of speaking' he did not live to present, the *Cours* indicates that such a 'science' wouldn't belong to 'linguistics proper'; 'the activity of the speaker should be studied in a number of disciplines which have no place in linguistics except through their relation to language' (CG xix, 20, 18) (cf. 2.7; 9.6).

2.21   In yet another trend-setting dichotomy, Saussure claimed that '**language** and **writing** are two distinct systems of signs; the second exists for the sole purpose of representing the first' (CG 23). 'The linguistic object is not both the written and the spoken forms of words; the spoken forms alone constitute the object' (CG 23f) (cf. 4.37–44; 6.50; 8.72ff; 9.42f; 11.83; 12.33). Like Bloomfield, he seems indignant about 'the tyranny' whereby 'writing' 'usurps the main role' (CG 31, 24). 'Grammarians' are chided for 'drawing attention to the written form', 'sanctioning the abuse' with 'free use' of 'pronunciation', and 'reversing the real, legitimate relationship between writing and language' (CG 30) (cf. 4.42f). For Saussure, 'writing obscures language; it is not a guise for language but a disguise [or travesty]'. At least, writing seems to confuse *him*: he calls it 'stable', then 'unstable'; he rejects 'the notion that an idiom changes more rapidly when writing does not exist' yet grants that 'spelling always lags behind pronunciation' (CG 27, 29, 24, 28).

2.22 'Spelling' annoys him particularly, being replete with 'inconsistencies', 'aberrations', 'irrational' or 'illegitimate' forms, and 'absurdities' that 'cannot be excused' (CG 28f) (cf. 4.38; 8.73ff). 'By imposing itself upon the masses, spelling influences and modifies language' (CG 31). 'Visual images lead to wrong pronunciations', 'pathological' 'mistakes', 'monstrosities', and 'deformations' – fit for 'teratological' inquiry (i.e., '"the study of monsters"') (CG 31f, 22). This irritation may have been fuelled by his native French – in contrast, say, to the 'ingenious' and 'remarkable analysis' displayed by 'the Greek alphabet', 'realizing almost completely' 'a one-to-one ratio between sounds and graphs' (CG 53, 39). Also, he saw things with the eyes of a phonetician and a historian: 'the pronunciation of a word is determined, not by its spelling, but by its history', whereas 'spelling' does not follow 'etymology' (CG 31, 28).[8] All the same, he makes no strong case for 'spelling reform' and 'hopes only that the most flagrant absurdities' 'will be eliminated' (CG 34) (cf. 2.69; 8.74).

2.23 Ultimately, he relents about writing: since 'the linguist' 'is often unable to observe speech directly, he must consider written texts' and 'pass' through 'the written form' 'to reach language' (CG 6, 34) (cf. 4.43f; 11.82). 'The prop provided by writing, though deceptive, is still preferable' (CG 32). So, 'far from discarding the distinctions sanctioned by spelling', Saussure 'carefully preserves them', e.g., because 'the opposition between implosives and explosives is crystal clear in writing' (CG 53, 62) (cf. 2.72).

2.24 A kindred reservation is raised against **'literary language'**, being here 'any kind of cultivated language, official or otherwise, that serves the whole community' (CG 195) (cf. 4.41; 6.4; 12[4]). Though this reservation is maintained more consistently than that against writing, the motives offered for it – aside from the hardly contestable provision that 'the linguist must consider not only correct speech and flowery language, but all other forms of expression' (CG 6) – are rather obscure and contradictory. For example: 'the privileged dialect, once it has been promoted to the rank of official or standard, seldom remains the same'; yet 'literary language, once it has been formed, generally remains fairly stable', and 'its dependency on writing gives it a special guarantee of preservation' (CG 195, 140). Or: 'literary language' 'breaks away from' 'spoken language' and 'adds to the undeserved importance of writing', yet does not 'necessarily imply the use of writing' (CG 21, 25, 196). Or again: 'when a natural idiom is influenced by literary language', 'linguistic unity may be destroyed'; yet 'given free reign, a language has only dialects' and 'habitually splinters' (CG 195). Whatever his motives, Saussure did set a countertrend to traditional grammar by marginalizing literary examples (cf. 3.4; 4.41; 6.4).[9]

2.25 Saussure proposed to 'localize' his restricted notion of 'language' 'in the limited segment of the speaking-circuit where an auditory image becomes associated with a concept' (CG 14). 'Language' is 'organized *thought* coupled with *sound*'; and 'each linguistic term is a member, an "articulus" in which an idea is fixed in a sound and a sound becomes the sign of an idea' (CG 111, 113) (cf. 3.11, 32, 35; 6.30f; 11.17, 22, 47, 61).

This viewpoint led to the famous thesis that the 'sign' 'results from associating' a 'signified' with a 'signifier' (CG 67) (cf. 8.20; 10.85; 11.11, 47).[10] 'The linguistic entity exists only through' this 'associating'; 'whenever only one element is retained, the entity vanishes' (CG 101f).

2.26 'Language' is thus a 'self-contained whole and a principle of classification' by virtue of being 'a system of distinct signs corresponding to' or 'expressing' 'distinct ideas' (CG 9f, 16) (cf. 3.40; 11.58). 'As in any semiological system, whatever distinguishes one sign from the others constitutes it' (CG 121). Therefore, 'language is characterized as a system based entirely on the **opposition** of its concrete units' or 'on the mental opposition of auditory impressions' (CG 107, 33). 'The general fact' is 'the functioning of linguistic oppositions' (CG 122). Saussure's most extreme formulation is also the most frequently quoted: 'in language there are only **differences** without positive terms' (CG 120). His crucial reservation, however, is seldom quoted and reinvokes the dual nature of the sign: 'the statement that everything in language is negative is true only if the signified and the signifier are considered separately' – whereby, we just saw, 'the entity vanishes'. 'The sign in its totality' of two entities 'is positive in its own class'. 'Their combination is a positive fact; it is even the sole type of facts that language has, for maintaining the parallelism between two classes of differences is the distinctive function of the linguistic institution' (CG 120f) (cf. 4.26).

2.27 Each of the 'two elements', 'the idea and the sound', 'functions' in ways which 'prove that language is only a system of pure values' (CG 111). To some extent, the two sides control each other. 'The source material of language' is 'pictured' as 'two parallel chains, one of concepts and the other of sound-images' (CG 104) (cf. 6.41; 9.3; 11.43, 69). 'In an accurate delimitation, the division' of the two 'chains' 'will correspond'. Moreover, in 'countless instances', 'the alteration of the signifier occasions a conceptual change', and 'it is obvious that the sum of ideas distinguished corresponds in principle to the sum of the distinctive signs' (CG 121) (but cf. 2.29; 5.64, 67, 75ff; 7.82; 10.36; 11.93; 12.59). 'Any nascent difference will tend invariably to become significant'; reciprocally, 'any conceptual difference perceived by the mind seeks to find expression through a distinct signifier, and two ideas that are no longer distinct in the mind tend to merge into the same signifier'. 'Thought' may be 'forced' 'into the special way that the material state of signs opens to it' (CG 228).

2.28 But the two sides do *not* control each other to the extent that 'the bond between the signifier and the signified is **arbitrary**' (CG 67) (cf. 3.3; 4.27; 9.13, 32; 10.86).[11] If the 'sign' 'results from' that bond, Saussure 'can simply say: *the linguistic sign is arbitrary*', i.e., 'it is **unmotivated**', as shown by words for the same thing ("tree") in different languages (CG 66f, 69) (cf. 4.27; 9[17]). This 'principle' 'dominates all the linguistics of language' (CG 68). Among its 'numberless' 'consequences', I mention three I think essential to Saussurian argument. First, 'the arbitrary nature of the sign explains' 'why the social fact alone can create a system' (CG 113). Second, 'arbitrary and differential are two correlative qualities': 'a segment of language can never in the final analysis be based on anything but its non-coincidence with the rest' (CG 118). Third, 'in linguistics *to explain a word is to relate it to other words*, for there are no necessary relations between sound and meaning' (CG 189). If 'the choice of a given slice of sound to name a given idea' were not 'completely arbitrary', 'the notion of value would be compromised, for it would include an externally imposed element' (CG 113).

2.29 Although 'no one disputes the principle of the arbitrary nature of the sign', and 'wholly arbitrary' 'signs' 'realize better than others the ideal of the semiological process' (CG 68), Saussure betrays some uneasiness. At one point he calls 'arbitrariness' an 'irrational principle' 'which would lead to the worst sort of complication if applied without restriction' (CG 133). He is accordingly 'convinced': 'everything that relates to language as a system' serves 'the limiting of arbitrariness' (cf. 2.56). The linguist must 'study' 'language' 'as it limits arbitrariness'. Various 'degrees' may range 'between the two extremes – a minimum of organization and a minimum of arbitrariness' (CG 131, 133). Such 'proportions' might 'help in classifying' 'diverse languages'; those 'in which there is least motivation are more **lexico-logical**, and those in which it is greatest are more **grammatical**' (CG 133; cf. CG 161) (cf. 12.59). Or, 'within a given language', we might consider how 'all evolutionary movement may be characterized by continual passage from motivation to arbitrariness' and vice versa (CG 134). Or again, we might examine how 'motivation varies, being always proportional to the ease of syntagmatic analysis and the obviousness of the meaning of the subunits present' (CG 132). 'At any rate, even in the most favourable cases motivation is never absolute; not only are the elements of a motivated sign themselves unmotivated', 'but the value of the whole term is never equal to the sum of the value of its parts' (cf. 2.27; 5.29, 67; 11.93; 12.59).

2.30 Alongside 'motivated', '**natural**' is treated as a converse of 'arbitrary' (CG 69), and here, too, Saussure is not fully consistent. He vows that 'natural data have no place in linguistics' (CG 80). Similarly, 'the traditional divisions of grammar' 'do not correspond to natural distinctions' (CG 136) (cf. 3.23; 4.71). And 'the false notion' of 'language' as 'a natural kingdom' leads to 'absurdities' (CG 4).[12] Even if 'semiology' 'welcomes' the 'natural sign, such as pantomime', 'its main concern will still be the whole group of systems grounded on the arbitrariness of the sign' (CG 132).[13] Despite this, Saussure invokes 'natural dialectal features', 'the natural fact' of 'geographical diversity', the 'two natural coordinates' of 'associative' and 'syntagmatic', and the 'natural organic growth of an idiom' (CG 201, 196, 203, 137, 21). In his view, by 'giving language first place among the facts of speech, we introduce a natural order' (CG 9). With a comparable inconsistency, he condemns the designation of language as an 'organism' or an 'organic' entity, but frequently applies these terms himself (CG 5, 231, 21f, 69, 153, 193).

2.31 The division of the sign into signified and signifier is not the same as the division of the 'speaking-circuit' into the '**psychological** parts (word-images and concepts)' and the '**physiological** (phonation and audition)' (CG 12). 'Speaking' involves the 'physiological', whereas 'language' 'is exclusively psychological' (CG 18; cf. CG 8, 12ff) (cf. 12.14). So 'both terms involved in the linguistic sign', the signified and the signifier, 'are psychological and are united in the brain by an associative bond' (CG 65f) (cf. 2.16). Even the 'material and mechanical manifestations' are 'psychological'; 'the psychophysical mechanism' is significant only for 'exteriorizing' the 'combinations' that 'express' 'thought' (CG 6, 14). The 'sound-image' 'is not the material sound, but the psychological imprint of the sound, the impression that it makes on our senses' (CG 66). Still, we have seen Saussure invoking the 'material' aspect to suggest the 'concreteness' of language (cf. 2.17, 27).[14]

2.32 In exuberant moments, Saussure pictures language as a fortunate development for the human mind, agreeing this time with traditional 'philosophers and linguists': 'without language, thought is a vague, uncharted nebula' (CG 112) (cf. 3.3; 6.2, 31; 11.17). 'There are no pre-existing ideas, and nothing is distinct before the appearance of language'. 'Psychologically, our thought – apart from its expression in words – is only a shapeless and indistinct mass', a 'floating realm' (CG 111f). 'Thought, chaotic by nature, has to become ordered in the process of its decomposition; language takes shape between two shapeless masses', namely, 'the indefinite plane of jumbled ideas and the equally vague plane of sounds'. 'Without the help of signs we would be unable to make a clear-cut consistent distinction between two ideas'. At such moments, Saussure downplays the influence of 'arbitrariness', against which 'the mind contrives to introduce a principle of order and regularity into certain parts of the mass of signs' (CG 133). 'The mechanism of language is but a partial correction of a system that is by nature chaotic'. He even says, contravening his own conception of system, that 'language' 'is a confused mass, and only attentiveness and [de]familiarization will reveal its particular elements' (CG 104) (cf. 12.42).

2.33 Signalling a mentalist orientation linguistics would later reject (cf. 4.8; 12.4f, 10f), Saussure invokes 'the sum of word-images stored in the minds of all individuals', where 'forms' are 'associated' 'through their meanings', as the basis for 'the social bond that constitutes language' (CG 13, 165). In this sense, 'linguistics has only the perspective of speakers' (CG 212).[15] But he concedes that 'we never know exactly whether or not the awareness of speakers goes as far as the analyses of grammarians' (CG 138). 'Doubtless speakers are unaware of the practical difficulties of delimiting units'; 'in the matter of language, people have always been satisfied with ill-defined units' (CG 106, 111) (cf. 12.7, 59).

2.34 Nevertheless, Saussure set yet another trend for linguistics by typically implying that the categories and notions he proposes are shared by the minds of 'speakers' (e.g., CG 138, 160, 185, 192) (cf. 12.49). He depicts the 'objective analysis based on history' and done by 'the grammarian' as 'but a modified form' of the 'subjective analysis' 'speakers constantly make'

(CG 183) (cf. 12.58). 'Both analyses are justifiable, and each retains its value', even if he can find 'no common yardstick for both the analysis of speakers and the analysis of the historian'. 'In the last resort, however, only the speakers' analysis matters, for it is based directly upon the facts of language'. Fair enough, but he stressed that the 'facts' can be elusive, even for experts (cf. 2.12ff).

2.35 A compromise would be to assign the knowledge of speakers to a level of which they are not 'conscious'.[16] In accounting for 'analogy', for example, 'no complicated operation such as the grammarian's conscious analysis is presumed on the part of the speaker'; 'the sum of the conscious and methodological classifications made by the grammarian' 'must coincide with the associations, conscious or not, that are set up in speaking' (CG 167, 137f). Or, if 'language is not complete in any speaker' and 'exists perfectly only within a collectivity', we might assign the knowledge to 'the collective mind of speakers', wherein 'logical and psychological relations' 'form a system' (CG 14, 99f). This designation would be appropriate for 'synchronic linguistics', whereas 'diachronic linguistics' would 'study relations that bind together successive terms not perceived by the collective mind but substituted for each other without forming a system' (CG 99f, i.r.).

2.36 The quest for the locus of language thus leads to Saussure's 'radical distinction between **diachrony** and **synchrony**' (CG 184). Though 'very few linguists suspect' it, 'the intervention of the factor of time creates difficulties peculiar to linguistics and opens to their science two completely divergent paths' (CG 79). Saussure now calls for 'two sciences of language', one 'static' or 'synchronic', and the other 'evolutionary' or 'diachronic' (CG 81). Because 'static linguistics' was not yet established and seemed 'generally much more difficult' (CG 101), Saussure favoured it in his own theorizing. For him, 'language is a system whose parts can and must be considered in their synchronic solidarity' (CG 87). 'Language is a system of pure values determined by nothing except the momentary arrangement of terms'; and 'a system of interdependent terms in which the value of each term results solely from the simultaneous presence of others' (CG 80, 114). Only 'synchronic facts' 'affect the system as a whole' and are therefore 'always significant' (CG 85, 87; cf. CG 95). 'In analysis, then, we can set up a method and formulate definitions only after adopting a synchronic viewpoint' (CG 185). Besides, 'the synchronic viewpoint' 'is the true and only reality to the community of speakers' (CG 90, 212).

2.37 In contrast, 'the diachronic perspective deals with phenomena that are unrelated to systems', and with 'partial facts' (CG 85, 87). 'The diachronic phenomenon' is 'the evolution of the system' through 'a shift in the relationship between the signifier and the signified' (CG 181) (cf. 2.48). 'In a diachronic succession, the elements are not delimited for once and for all'; they 'are distributed differently from one moment to the next' (CG 179). Hence, 'the units delimited in diachrony would not necessarily correspond to those delimited in synchrony' (CG 181). Moreover, 'the synchronic fact' 'calls forth two simultaneous terms', whereas 'the diachronic fact' 'involves' 'only one term': 'for the new one to appear', 'the old one' 'must first give way to it' (CG 85). These theses complicate 'the problem of the diachronic unit' and 'the essence' of 'evolution' (CG 181). 'An element taken from one period' qualifies as 'the same' as 'an element taken from another period' only if 'regular sound changes' intervene and if the 'speaker passes from one form to the other without there being a break in their common bond' (CG 181f) (cf. 2.73).

2.38 For Saussure, 'the opposition between the two viewpoints, the synchronic and the diachronic, is absolute and allows no compromise' (CG 83). 'The more rigidly they are kept apart, the better it will be', and their respective ' "phenomena" ' 'have nothing in common' (CG 22, 91). 'The synchronic law is general but not imperative' and merely 'reports a state of affairs' (CG 92). In 'diachrony, on the contrary', we find 'imperativeness' that 'is not sufficient to warrant applying the concept of law to evolutionary facts', which, 'in spite of certain appearances', are 'always accidental and particular' (CG 93) (cf. 2.47, 55; 4.75). Hence, a synchronic approach fits better the standard notion of how science works.

2.39 Elsewhere, however, he concedes that 'the system and its history' 'are so closely related that we can scarcely keep them apart' (CG 8). 'Synchronic truth is so similar to diachronic truth that people confuse the two or think it superfluous to separate them' (CG 96). 'In fact, linguistics has confused them for decades without realizing that such a method is worthless' (CG 97). The 'force of circumstances' is blamed for 'inducing' us to 'consider' 'each language' 'alternately from the historical and static viewpoints' (CG 99). Yet Saussure insists it is 'absolutely impossible to study simultaneously relations in time and relations within the system' (CG 81). 'We must put each fact in its own class and not confuse the two methods'.

2.40 He accordingly finds it 'obvious that the diachronic facts are not related to the static facts they produced' (CG 83). 'A diachronic fact is an independent event; the synchronic consequences that stem from it are wholly unrelated to it' (CG 84). Hence, 'the linguist who wishes to understand a state must discard all knowledge of everything that produced it' (CG 81). 'He can enter the mind of speakers only by completely suppressing the past; the intervention of history can only falsify his judgment' (CG 81) (cf. CG 160). Admittedly, 'the forces that have shaped the state illuminate its true nature, and knowing them protects us against certain illusions'; 'but this only goes to prove clearly that diachronic linguistics is not an end in itself' (CG 90).

2.41 This line of argument implies we can assign events or causes to a separate science or domain from their results or effects (cf. 2.74). Apparently, the key factor is that 'diachronic facts are not' 'directed toward changing the system'; 'only certain elements are altered without regard to the solidarity that binds them to the whole' (CG 84). Even when 'a shift in a system is brought about' or a 'change was enough to give rise to another system', the 'events' responsible are 'outside the system' 'and form no system among themselves' (CG 95, 85). 'In the science of language, all we need do is to observe the transformations of sounds and to calculate their effects'; 'determining the causes' is not 'essential' (CG 18).

2.42 A further problem is how to gather data 'outside the system'. If 'the linguist' 'takes the diachronic perspective, he no longer observes language, but rather a series of events that modify it' (CG 90). 'The causes of continuity are a priori within the scope of the observer, but the causes of change in time are not' (CG 77). Still, 'evolutionary facts are more concrete and striking' than 'static' ones; the 'observable relations tie together successive terms that are easily grasped' (CG 101). We are confronted with 'observable modifications'; 'innovations' 'enter into our field of observation' when 'the community of speakers has adopted them' (CG 88, 98). This 'community' cannot however be the only point of reference, since the 'succession in time' of 'the facts of language' 'does not exist insofar as the speaker is concerned' (CG 81). 'The linguist' needs 'external evidence', such as 'contemporary descriptions' (which 'lack scientific precision'), 'spelling', 'poetic texts', 'loanwords', 'puns', and 'stories' (CG 35f, i.r.).

2.43 Similarly agile manoeuvring is performed to deal with '**geographical**' 'diversity', which gets relegated to 'external linguistics', presumably for not applying to closed or uniform systems: 'it is impossible, even in our hypothetical examples, to set up boundaries between the dialects' (CG 191, 204). 'Dialectal differences' appear when an 'innovation' 'affects only a part of the territory' (CG 200). In another about-face, Saussure says 'divergences in time escape the observer, but divergences in space immediately force themselves upon him' (CG 191). 'Geographical diversity was, then, the first observation made in linguistics and determined the initial form of scientific research in language'. But to preserve the 'profound unity' postulated in his synchronic approach and 'hidden' by 'the diversity of idioms', Saussure maintains that '*time*' 'is actually the basic cause of linguistic differentiation': 'by itself, *space* cannot influence language' (CG 99, 198). If 'change itself' and 'the instability of language stem from time alone', 'geographical diversity should be called temporal diversity' (CG 198f, i.r.).[17] Here, effects get fully referred back to the events that caused them – just the reverse of the argument for keeping diachrony separated (cf. 2.40f).

2.44 Saussure implies that language changes all by itself: 'language is not controlled directly by the mind of speakers', and the 'sign' and 'language' 'always elude the individual or social will' (only 'speaking' is 'wilful') (CG, 228, 19, 17, 14). 'Speakers do not wish' or 'try to change systems', but 'pass from one to the other, so to speak, without having a hand in it' (CG 84ff). But it's hard to see how language can change at all if 'the signifier' 'is fixed, not free, with respect to the linguistic community' (CG 71). 'The masses have no voice in the matter, and the signifier chosen by language could be replaced with no other'. 'No individual, even if he willed it, could modify in any way at all the choice'; and 'the community itself cannot control so much as a single word'. 'We can conceive of a change only through the intervention of specialists, grammarians, logicians, etc.; but experience shows us that all such meddlings have failed' (CG 73) (cf. 4^{27}).

2.45 Notwithstanding, ordinary speakers do change language. 'An evolutionary fact is always preceded' by 'a multitude of similar facts in the sphere of speaking' (CG 98). 'Nothing enters language without having been tested in speaking, and every evolutionary phenomenon has its roots in the individual' (CG 168) (cf. 3.57; 4.81, 4^6). 'One speaker had to coin the new word, then others had to imitate and repeat it until it forced itself into standard usage'. So 'in the history of any innovation there are always two distinct moments: (1) when it sprang up in individual usage; and (2) when it became a fact of language, outwardly identical but adopted by the community' (CG 165). The 'distinction made' between 'diachrony' and 'synchrony' is 'in no way invalidated' by this process. But we would need, it seems to me, a reliable way, short of interviewing the entire community, for telling just when an innovation passes from one 'moment' to the other, and for (here again) separating causes from effects (cf. 4.77f).

2.46 His idea that 'evolution in time takes the form of successive and precise innovations' (CG 200) must have made Saussure uneasy about inexact improvisations of speakers. When he deals with 'folk etymology', he does just what he scolds 'grammarians' for: 'thinking that spontaneous analyses of language are "wrong"' (CG 183) (and cf. 2.49). 'This phenomenon called folk etymology' 'works somewhat haphazardly and results only in absurdities', 'mistakes', and 'deformations' (CG 173ff). During 'crude attempts to explain refractory words', the words get 'misunderstood', 'corrupted', and 'mangled'. The grounds for castigating folk etymology can only be that it is not sanctioned by historical knowledge – which, Saussure grants, ordinary speakers do not have (CG 81, 90, 100, 160, 212) (cf. 2.35, 40, 64).

2.47 One of the rare occasions[18] when his reverent editors reassure us that Saussure is not 'being illogical or paradoxical' is when he 'speaks of both the immutability and the mutability of the sign' – and assigns both phenomena the same cause, namely, 'the arbitrary nature of the sign' (CG 73ff). On the one hand, 'language always appears as a heritage of the preceding period'; 'no society' 'has ever known language other than as a product inherited from preceding generations' (CG 71). 'The arbitrary nature of the sign' 'protects language from any attempt to modify it'; 'the sign' 'follows no law other than that of tradition' (CG 73f). Also, 'society', 'inert by nature, is a prime conservative force'. 'Generations' 'fuse and interpenetrate'; 'speakers are largely unconscious of the laws of language'; and 'even their awareness would seldom lead to criticism, for people are generally satisfied with the language they have received' (CG 72). Such arguments are thought to show that 'the question of the origin of speech' 'is not even worth asking'; 'the only real object of linguistics is the normal, regular life of an existing idiom' (CG 71f) (cf. 3.11, 18; 8.6, 17).

2.48   On the other hand, 'time changes all things; there is no reason why language should escape this universal law' (CG 77). 'The arbitrary nature of the sign' is now deployed to explain why 'language is radically powerless against the forces which from one moment to the next are shifting the relationship between the signified and the signifier' (CG 75) (cf. 2.37). Those forces 'loosen' 'the bond between the idea and the sign'. A further paradox arises: 'the sign is exposed to alteration because it perpetuates itself' (CG 74).

2.49   Perhaps because such shifts disrupt Saussure's search for order, he tends to misprize language change as a matter of 'deteriorations', 'vicissitudes', 'damage', 'disturbance', 'breaking', and 'effacement', 'in spite of' which 'language continues to function' (CG 87, 152ff, 161). He envisions 'a blind force against the organization of a system of signs', and a 'great mass of forces that constantly threaten the analysis adopted in a particular language-state' (CG 89, 169) (cf. 3.13, 16). He admonishes that 'the total number of forms is uselessly increased'; 'the linguistic mechanism is obscured and complicated'; and 'phonetic evolution first obscures analysis, then makes it completely impossible' (CG 161, 155). Like those brought against folk etymology, such condemnations disrupt the descriptive, non-evaluative methodology whereby Saussure wants to overcome 'the illusion' of 'the first linguists', for whom 'everything that deviated from the original state' was 'a distortion of an ideal form' (CG 163) (cf. 4.80).

2.50   'Fortunately, **analogy** counterbalances the effects' of 'transformations' (CG 161). 'An analogical form is a form made on the model of one or more other forms in accordance with a definite rule' (i.r.). It can 'offset' 'change', 'restore regularity', and 'unify', 'preserve', or 'renew' 'forms' (CG 171f). Thus, 'analogy always plays an important role' in the 'preservation' or 'redistribution of linguistic material' (CG 173). 'The most obvious and important effect of analogy' is to 'substitute more regular forms composed of living elements for older irregular and obsolescent forms' (CG 171). To the extent that it 'always uses old material for its innovations', 'analogy' 'is remarkably conservative' (CG 172). Since it 'constantly renews' 'forms', 'analogy' is claimed to 'intervene' even 'when forms remain unchanged'. 'A form may be preserved' either by 'complete isolation or complete integration in a system that has kept the basic parts of the word intact and that always comes to the rescue' (CG 173). If change appears harmful, the system appears beneficial.

2.51   To be sure, 'analogy' 'is capricious' (CG 162) and alters as well as preserves. It 'collaborates efficiently with all the forces that constantly modify the architecture of an idiom' (CG 171). It 'reflects the changes that have affected the functioning of language and sanctions them through new combinations'. 'To analogy are due all normal non-phonetic[19] modifications of the external side of words' (CG 161). However, 'imperfect analyses sometimes lead to muddled analogical creations' (CG 171).

2.52   By showing how 'language never stops interpreting and decomposing its units', 'analogy' is a good illustration of 'the principle of linguistic **creativity**', and a 'manifestation of the general activity that singles out units for subsequent use' (CG 169, 165f). 'Any creation must be preceded by an unconscious comparison of the material deposited in the storehouse of language, where productive forms are arranged according to their' 'relations' (CG 165) (cf. 5.47; 7.76; 8.58). Hence, 'analogy' presupposes 'awareness and understanding of a relation between forms'. This 'awareness' leads to 'the chance product': 'the form improvised' by 'the isolated speaker' 'to express his thought' (CG 165f). 'It is wrong to suppose that the production process is at work only when the new formation actually occurs: the elements were already there' to guarantee the 'potential existence in language' of any 'newly formed word' (cf. 6.23f). 'The final step of realizing it in speaking is a small matter in comparison to the build-up of forces that makes it possible.' This time, effects get downplayed in favour of causes in order to give us 'one more lesson in separating language from speaking' (CG 165).

2.53 'Analogy is therefore proof positive that a formative element exists at a given moment as a significant unit' (CG 170). 'Every possibility of effective talk' has the same source as 'every possibility of analogical formations': the way 'speech is continually engaged in decomposing its units' (CG 166).[20] 'If living units perceived by speakers at a particular moment can by themselves give birth to analogical formations, every definite redistribution of units also implies a possible expansion of their use' (CG 170). 'All such innovations are perfectly regular; they are explained in the same way as those that language has accepted' (CG 168f). 'Decomposable' 'words can be rated for capacity to engender other words' (CG 166) (cf. 5.47).[21]

2.54 The question of when two forms are the same now receives a different treatment than it did in the discussion of the 'diachronic unit' (cf. 2.37). Here, 'analogical innovation and the elimination of the older forms are two distinct things' (CG 164). 'Analogical change' is an 'illusion'; 'nowhere do we come upon a transformation' of an element. The reasoning behind this claim must be Saussure's belief that 'analogy is psychological', 'grammatical, and synchronic', rather than 'phonetic' (CG 165f, 161). So 'analogy by itself could not be a force in evolution', nor be 'an evolutionary fact', even though 'the constant substitution of new forms for old ones is one of the most striking features in the transformation of language' (CG 169, 171). 'Enough' 'creations of speakers' endure 'to change completely the appearance of its vocabulary and grammar' (CG 169) (cf. 2.49).

2.55 This tricky reasoning reflects the intent to place '**grammar**' mainly on the 'synchronic' side; 'since no system straddles several periods, there is no such thing as historical grammar' (CG 134) (cf. 2.74).[22] Thus, 'all grammatical laws' 'are synchronic', even though 'grammatical classes evolve' (CG 159, 141). It would be 'radically impossible' that 'a phonetic phenomenon would mingle with the synchronic fact' in 'grammar' (CG 152) (cf. 2.51, 54). In return, 'morphology, syntax, and lexicology interpenetrate because every synchronic fact is identical' (CG 136). Correspondingly, 'morphology has no real, autonomous object'; 'it cannot form a discipline distinct from syntax' (CG 135) (cf. 3.26, 34f; 4.61f, 65; 5.51, 53f; 6.45, 49; 7.75f; 8.57; 9.31, 34, 75, 9⁵, 9¹⁵; 10.35, 40; 11.71, 75, 77; 12.28). Also, 'the lexical and the syntactic blend'; 'there is basically no distinction between' 'a phrase' and a 'word that is not a simple, irreducible unit' – 'the arrangement' of 'groups of words in phrases' 'follows the same fundamental principles' as does that of 'subunits of the word' (CG 135f) (cf. 3.26, 34f; 4.61; 5.53f; 8.57; 9.75; 10.40; 11.75).

2.56 To capture 'synchronic facts', we should recognize that 'in language everything boils down' not only 'to **differences**, but also to **groupings**' (CG 136, 128) (cf. 8.51, 78–82; 9.75–81). To study groupings, yet another major dichotomy is proposed: we should 'gather together all that makes up a language state and fit this into a theory of **syntagms** and a theory of **associations**' (CG 136). 'Each fact should' 'be fitted into its syntagmatic and associative class' (CG 137). 'Only the distinction' 'between syntagmatic and associative relations can provide a classification that is not imposed from the outside' (CG 136). 'The groupings in both classes are for the most part fixed by language; this set of common relations constitutes language and governs its functioning' (CG 127). Moreover, 'syntagmatic' and 'associative' 'solidarities' 'are what limits arbitrariness' and supplies 'motivation': '(1) analysis of a given term, hence a syntagmatic relation; and (2) the summoning of one or more other terms, hence an associative relation' (CG 132f) (cf. 2.29). So 'the whole subject matter of grammar should be arranged along its two natural coordinates'; and 'almost any point of grammar will' 'prove the necessity of the dual approach' (CG 137).

2.57 This fresh dichotomy is predictably propounded in mentalistic terms. 'Our memory holds in reserve all the more or less complex types of syntagms, regardless of their class or length, and we bring in the associative groups to fix our choice when the time for using them arrives' (CG 130). Every 'unit is chosen after a dual mental opposition' (CG 131). For instance, 'the isolated sound' 'stands in syntagmatic opposition to its environing sounds and in associative opposition to all other sounds that may come to mind'. Or, the 'parts' of 'syntagms', such as the 'subunits' of 'words', can be 'analysed' because they can be 'placed in opposition' (CG 129). Similarly, 'from the synchronic viewpoint', each word 'stands in opposition to every word that might be associated with it' (CG 95) (cf. 2.26).

2.58 These assertions fit 'the only definition' Saussure 'can give' for 'the unit' of 'language': 'a slice of sound which to the exclusion of everything that precedes and follows it in the spoken chain is the signifier of a certain concept' (CG 104, i.r.). In fact, 'almost all units of language depend on what surrounds them in the spoken chain, or on their successive parts' (CG 127). He propounds the principle that 'in the syntagm a term has value because it stands in opposition to everything that precedes or follows it, or to both' (CG 123) (cf. 11.51, 81), but he gives no demonstrations for stretches of real discourse. He is merely extending his concept of 'opposition' to cover the problem of 'the unit' in the sequence, and thereby altering the concept. In the abstract system (e.g., of phonemes or morphemes), elements must be similar in many respects (e.g., class or category) in order to give full value to their opposition. No such principle is required for successive elements in a chain or syntagm; they could differ in many diverse ways that contribute less to their value than does their manner of combination (cf. 11.50f, 56, 70).

2.59 In a Saussurian perspective, the production of discourse could be a process of 'thinking unconsciously of diverse groups of associations' and 'mentally eliminating everything that does not help to bring out the desired differentiation at the desired point' (CG 130). He envisions language units 'calling up' or 'recalling' others (CG 130, 134, 164) (cf. 10.69, 87). Such claims are unproblematic if 'the sum of the conscious and methodical classifications made by the grammarian who studies a language-state without bringing in history must coincide with the associations, conscious or not, that are set up in speaking' (CG 137f) (cf. 2.33f; 12.49). But the situation is more precarious if 'it is by a purely arbitrary act that the grammarian groups' 'words' 'in one way rather than in another' (CG 127) (cf. 3.13; 4.82; 5.30; 6.15; 9.3; 12.27). For instance, 'in the mind of speakers the nominative case is by no means the first one in the declension, and the order in which terms are called depends on circumstances'.

2.60 By definition, '**syntagms**' are 'combinations supported by linearity' and 'always composed of two or more consecutive units' (CG 123). 'Syntagmatic groupings mutually condition each other' (CG 128). Indeed, 'syntagmatic solidarities' are 'what is most striking in the organization of language' (CG 127, i.r.). Such images as 'spatial coordinations', 'two units distributed in space', or 'a horizontal ribbon that corresponds to the spoken chain' (CG 128, 136f) indicate that Saussure was influenced by the appearance of alphabetic written language (cf. 2.5, 17, 21, 23; 12.33). When 'auditory signifiers' are 'represented in writing', 'the spatial line of graphic marks is substituted for succession in time' (CG 70) (cf. 2.72).

2.61 One problem with 'the syntagm' is clearly recognized: 'there is no clear-cut boundary between the **language** fact, which is the sign of collective usage, and the fact that belongs to **speaking** and depends on individual freedom' (CG 125) (but cf. 2.20, 33, 44f). 'In a great number of instances', 'both forces have combined in producing' 'a combination of units' and have done so 'in indeterminate proportions'. Therefore, 'not every syntagmatic fact is classed as syntactical' (and pertaining to the language system), 'but every syntactical fact belongs to the syntagmatic class' (CG 137). 'The **sentence** is the ideal type of syntagm, but it belongs to speaking, not to language' (CG 124) (cf. 12.54). Only 'pat phrases in which any change is prohibited by usage' 'belong to language' (cf. 4.60; 5.32, 54; 7[34]; 9.93; 12.28).

2.62 Also, 'to language rather than to speaking belong the syntagmatic types that are built upon **regular forms**' (CG 125). One example is 'word-parts: prefixes, roots, radicals, suffixes, and inflectional endings' (CG 185).

'The **root** [racine] is the irreducible element common to all words of same family' – 'the element in which the meaning common to all related words reaches the highest degree of abstraction and generality' (CG 186). The '**radical** [radical]' 'is generally the common element' in 'a series of related words' and 'conveys the idea common to every word' (CG 185). Despite the similar definitions (and common etymology), the 'radical' differs from the 'root' – 'even when phonetically identical to it' – in being 'reducible', longer, and less 'general' and 'abstract' (CG 186). 'The **prefix** goes before the part of the word that is recognized as the radical'; 'the **suffix** is the element added to the root to make a radical' (CG 187). 'The prefix also differs from the suffix' in being 'more sharply delimited, for it is easier to separate from the word as a whole' (CG 188). 'A complete word usually remains after the prefix is removed', but not after 'the suffix' is.

2.63 Word-parts can be a problem in gathering data. Saussure enlists cases where 'the division' 'is self-evident'; where the 'radical emerges spontaneously when we compare'; or where 'the speaker knows, before he has made any comparison with other forms, where to draw the line between the prefix and what follows it' (CG 185, 188).[23] Moreover, 'the root' 'is a reality in the mind of speakers', though they 'do not always single it out with equal precision' (CG 186). 'In certain idioms', in 'German, for instance', 'definite characteristics call the root to the attention of speakers'; but 'the feeling for roots scarcely exists in French' (CG 186f). Still, 'structural rules', 'regular alternations', and 'possible oppositions' that 'single out the subunits' 'which language recognizes and the values which it attaches to them' (CG 187ff) might be grasped only by specialists.

2.64 Word-parts can start out as separate 'elements' and then get 'welded' by '**agglutination**' 'into one unit' 'which is absolute or hard to analyse' (CG 169, 176). 'The mind gives up analysis – it takes a short-cut' – and 'the whole cluster of signs' 'becomes a simple unit' (CG 177). 'The phenomenon' has 'three phases: (1) the combining of several terms in a syntagm'; (2) 'the synthesizing of the elements into a new unit'; and '(3) every other change necessary to make the old cluster of signs more like a simple word', e.g., 'unification of accent'. Saussure finds a 'striking' 'contrast': '*agglutination*' 'blends' 'units' and 'works only in syntagms', whereas '*analogy*' 'builds' 'units' and 'calls forth associative series as well as syntagms' (CG 177f). 'Agglutination is neither wilful nor active' and its 'elements' are 'slowly set'; 'analogy' 'requires analyses and combinations, intelligent action, and intention', and makes 'arrangements' 'in one swoop'. However, Saussure admits, 'often it is difficult to say whether an analysable form arose through agglutination or as an analogical construction' – 'only history can enlighten us' (CG 178f), and, we were told, ordinary speakers do not perceive diachronically (cf. 2.35, 40, 46).[24]

2.65 The counterpart of '**syntagmatic**' is, as we saw, '**associative**', a domain that would later be called '**paradigmatic**' (cf. 4.57f; 5.74; 6.34; 8.32; 9.3; 11.71).[25] 'Whereas a syntagm immediately suggests an order of succession and a fixed number of elements, terms in an associative family occur neither in fixed numbers nor in a definite order' (CG 126). In the latter 'family', then, 'a particular word is like the centre of a constellation', or 'the point of convergence of an indefinite number of coordinated terms' that 'float around' within 'one or more associative series' (CG 126, 129). 'Large' 'associations' 'fix the notion of parts of speech' by 'combining all substantives, adjectives, etc.' (CG 138). However, 'the traditional divisions of grammar' 'do not correspond to natural distinctions' (CG 136) (cf. 3.23; 4.55; 5.73; 6.49; 8.43; 12.24). 'The mind creates as many associative series as there are diverse relations', though Saussure's editors suggest that 'the mind naturally discards associations that becloud the intelligibility of discourse' (CG 125ff).

2.66 The mentalist outlook is crucial here because 'coordinations formed outside discourse' 'are not supported by linearity' or by 'the theory of syntagms' (CG 123, 136). 'Their seat is in the brain; they are part of the inner storehouse that makes up the language of each speaker' (CG 123) (cf. 2.16). 'These associations fix word-families, inflectional paradigms, and formative elements (radicals, suffixes, inflectional endings, etc.) in our minds' (CG 138). Perhaps Saussure's inclination toward mentalism on this point reflects his determination to keep his 'science' clear of 'speaking', the domain which, as we shall see with Bloomfield, Pike, and Firth, best supports a non-mentalist orientation. All the same, the 'functioning of the dual system' Saussure depicts must be inferred from actual 'discourse' (CG 129) before it can be projected into 'our minds' (cf. 12.1).[26]

2.67 Such problems are conspicuously less acute in respect to the **sounds** of language, the area which Saussure, like many of our theorists, considered most basic (cf. 2.17, 70f; 3.18, 58f; 4.30, 79; 5.42, 5^{12}; 7.20, 72; 8.66f; 11.80, 82; 12.27). In 'the domain of phonetics', the 'absolute distinction between diachrony and synchrony' is easiest to 'maintain' (CG 141). The same point could, I think, be made for the division between 'language' and 'speaking', or between 'social' and 'individual': the sounds of language possess a more reliable identity apart from any one set of occurrences than do, say, meanings (cf. 2.85; 12.27).

2.68 Saussure's assessment differs from the one favoured in later linguistics when he uses '**phonetics**' for 'the study of the evolution of sounds', and '**phonology**' for 'the physiology of sounds' (CG 33) (cf. 4.30; 6.43; 8.70; 11.80). In addition, he avers that 'phonetics is a basic part of the science of language; phonology' 'is only an auxiliary discipline and belongs exclusively to speaking'. He repeatedly warns against 'lumping together' the two 'absolutely distinct disciplines'. The 'principles of phonology' are concerned with 'the phonational mechanism' and 'mechanical' 'elements' (CG 48, 51, 38). But 'phonational movements do not constitute language'; 'explaining all the movements of the vocal apparatus' 'in no way illuminates the problem of language' (CG 33) (cf. 2.71, 77; 3.17; 4.29; 6.7).

2.69 Elsewhere, though, he uses the term 'phonology' in its later standard sense: 'the description of the sounds of a language-state' (CG 140).

'We must draw up for each language studied a **phonological system**' comprising 'a fixed number of well-differentiated **phonemes**' (CG 34) (cf. 4.29f, 33f, 45; 5.42f; 6.43; 8^{35}; 11.80, 89; 12.26). 'This system' is declared 'the only set of facts that interests the linguist'; 'graphic symbols bear but a faint resemblance to it' (CG 34f). 'Modern linguists have finally seen the light' and 'freed' 'linguistics' 'from the written word' (CG 32f), although his own exclusion of writing was not maintained (cf. 2.21ff). His 'rational method' for 'dealing with a living language' includes both '(a) setting up the system of sounds revealed by direct observation, and (b) observing the system of signs used to represent – imperfectly – these sounds' (CG 37). 'Phonology' can 'provide precautionary measures for dealing with the written form' (CG 34). He even concedes that 'the perceptible image of the written word' keeps us from 'perceiving only a shapeless and unmanageable mass'; 'apart from their graphic symbols, sounds are only vague notions' (CG 32) (cf. 2.23; 4.40; 6^8; 8.71, 8^{33}). Surprisingly, though, he recommends that 'a phonological alphabet', with 'one symbol for each element', be reserved for 'linguists only' (CG 33f) (cf. 8.75). 'A page of phonological writing' would present a 'distressing appearance' and be 'weighed down by diacritical marks'. 'Phonological exactitude is not very desirable outside science' (cf. 4.32).

2.70 Saussure advocates a 'science that uses **binary** combinations and sequences of phonemes as a point of departure' (CG 50) (cf. 5.21, 40). This 'science would treat articulatory moves like algebraic equations: a binary combination implies a certain number of mechanical and acoustical elements that mutually condition each other' (CG 51) (cf. 2.60; 12.15). 'In a phonational act', i.e., 'the production of sound by the vocal organs', the 'universal' aspect transcending 'all the local differences of its phonemes' is 'the mechanical regularity of the articulatory movements' (CG 38, 51) (cf. 3.14, 21; 4.29; 5.42; 6.43; 7.20; 8.66, 70; 11.80; 12.26). In these 'movements', 'a given sound obviously corresponds to a given act' (CG 40). 'All species of phonemes will be determined when all phonational acts are identified' (CG 43). Accordingly, 'the phonologist' should 'analyse a sufficient number of spoken chains from different languages' in order to 'identify and classify the elements', 'ignoring acoustically unimportant variations' (CG 40).

2.71 A 'natural point of departure for phonology' is to 'divide' 'the sound chain' 'into homogeneous' 'beats', 'each beat' 'corresponding' to a 'concrete irreducible unit' and 'characterized by unity of impression' (CG 38, 53) (cf. 9^{16}). 'A phoneme is the sum of the **auditory** impressions and **articulatory** movements, the unit heard and the unit spoken, each conditioning the other' (CG 40) (cf. 3.17f; 4.28ff; 5.43; 11.80f). 'The auditory beat' matches the 'articulatory beat'. In fact, 'auditory impressions exist unconsciously before phonological units are studied' and enable 'the observer' to 'single out subdivisions in the series of articulatory movements' (CG 38). So 'auditory impression' is 'the basis for any theory' and 'comes to us just as directly as the image of the moving vocal organs' (CG 38). But Saussure offers a 'classification of sounds according to their oral articulation',

even though these 'movements do not constitute language' (CG 44f, 33)
(cf. 2.68, 77; 3.21; 4.34).[27]

2.72 'The signifier, being auditory, is unfolded solely in time' and
'represents a span' 'measurable in a single dimension' (CG 70) (cf. 2.60;
12.33). In any 'grouping', a given 'sound' 'stands in syntagmatic opposition
to its environing sounds and in associative opposition to all other sounds
that may come to mind' (CG 131) (cf. 2.57). 'Phonologists too often forget
that language is made up' 'of expanses of spoken sounds', whose 'reciprocal
relations' merit 'attention' (CG 49f) (cf. 4.35; 8.65). Indeed, 'the science of
sounds becomes invaluable only when two or more elements are involved in
a relationship based on their inner dependence'. Here, 'combinatory
phonology' can 'define the constant relations of interdependent phonemes',
such as that between 'implosion and explosion' (CG 51f) (cf. 2.23).
'Freedom in linking phonological species is checked by the possibility of
linking articulatory movements'.

2.73 Whereas '**phonology** is outside time, for the articulatory mechanism
never changes', '**phonetics** is a historical science, analysing events and
changes and moving through time', and therefore 'the prime object of
diachronic linguistics' (CG 33, 140) (cf. 2.37). Though he believes 'phonetic
evolution is a disturbing force', Saussure says 'phonetic changes are
absolutely regular' in the sense that they 'result in the identical alteration of
all words containing the same phoneme' (CG 161, 153, 143; cf. CG 35).
However, 'absolute changes are extremely rare'; more often, 'what is transformed' is 'the phoneme as it occurs under certain conditions – its environment, accentuation, etc.' (CG 144). Saussure distinguishes '*spontaneous*
and *combinatory* phonetic phenomena', the former having an 'internal'
'cause', and the latter 'resulting from the presence of one or more other
phonemes'.[28]

2.74 'Phonetic changes' may seem 'unlimited and incalculable' (CG 151),
but some limits are postulated. For example, 'phonetic evolution cannot
create two forms to replace one' (CG 155). So 'phonetic doublets do not
exist; the evolution of sounds only emphasizes previous differences' (CG 157).
'The same unit cannot be subjected at the same time and in the same place
to two different transformations' (CG 155f). Every 'duality' or 'alternation'
thus gets classified as 'grammatical and synchronic', 'absolutely unrelated to
phonetic changes' (CG 156ff). Here, 'the diachronic character of phonetics
fits in very well with the principle that anything which is phonetic is neither
significant nor grammatical' (CG 141) (cf. 2.54f). If 'phonetic changes attack
only the material substance of words', 'in studying the history of the sounds
in a word we may ignore meaning' and 'consider only the material envelope
of a word' (CG 18, 141). None the less, when 'phonetic modifications'
'result in alternations' or 'oppositions', 'the mind seizes upon the material
difference, gives it significance, and makes it the carrier of conceptual
difference' or 'attaches grammatical values' (CG 159, 231). Once again,
causes and effects get put into different theoretical domains (cf. 2.41).

2.75   By dividing things up this way, Saussure provides no proper home for '**etymology**', the history of both forms and their meanings: it is 'neither a distinct discipline nor a division of evolutionary linguistics' (CG 189). 'It is only a special application of principles that relate to synchronic and diachronic facts'. 'Analogy' is called upon to 'show' that 'the synchronic relation of several different terms' 'is the most important part of etymological research'. 'Etymology is then mainly the explaining of words through the historical study of their relations with other words'. Its 'description' of 'facts' 'is not methodical, for it' 'borrows its data alternately from phonetics, morphology, semantics, etc.' (CG 190). It 'uses every means placed at its disposal by linguistics, but it is not concerned with the nature of the operations it is obliged to perform'. Besides, 'etymology' is fraught with 'uncertainty': 'words with well-established origins' are 'rare', and 'scholars' may be led into 'rashness' (CG 225).

2.76   To seek 'the causes of phonetic changes' is to confront 'one of the most difficult problems in linguistics' (CG 147) (cf. 3.54–60; 4.75). Some possibilities are rejected: 'racial predispositions', 'soil and climate', and 'changes in fashion' (CG 147, 151) (cf. 3^2; 4.80). Others are provisionally accepted, though not as complete or conclusive causes: 'the law of least effort'; 'phonetic education during childhood'; 'political instability' of a 'nation'; and the 'linguistic substratum' of an 'indigenous population' 'absorbed' by 'newcomers' (CG 148–51). Yet if we believe 'a historical event must have some determining cause' (CG 150), we will be hard put to explain why certain changes and no others occurred at just the times they did.

2.77   The programme for the study of sounds outlined by Saussure has remained a fundamental part of linguistics, though the emphasis on sound changes has receded. Having a mentalist orientation, he wanted a theory that would not depend on 'material' aspects (cf. 2.16f) and insisted 'the movements of the vocal apparatus' do not 'illuminate the problem of language' (cf. 2.68, 72). But his ultimate recourse was a 'classification' based on 'oral articulation' (cf. 2.71; 12.26).

2.78   Perhaps to offset the abstractness of language, Saussure, like many linguists, draws comparisons with more tangible entities. Though he misprizes the 'illogical metaphors' of rival 'schools', he admits that 'certain metaphors are indispensable' (CG 5). Some of his own are fairly proximate, e.g., when he compares 'language' to 'a dictionary of which identical copies have been distributed to each individual'; or 'the social side of speech' to 'a contract signed by the members of a community'; or 'the vocal organs' to 'electrical devices used in transmitting the Morse code' (CG 19, 14, 18).

2.79   Other metaphors are more remote, e.g., when the language system is pictured in terms of a 'theatre', 'a symphony', 'a tapestry', 'a garment covered with patches cut from its own cloth', or 'the planets that revolve around the sun' (CG 179, 18, 33, 172, 84f). A 'system of phonemes' is said to work like a 'piano' (CG 94). Studying 'the evolution of language' is compared to 'sketching a panorama of the Alps' and moving 'from one peak of the Jura to another' (CG 82). 'The autonomy' of 'synchrony' is analogous to 'the projection of an object on a plane surface' or to 'the stem of a plant' 'cut transversely' (CG 87). 'The word is like a house in which the arrangement and function of different rooms has been changed'; or like a 'five-franc piece' that 'can be exchanged for a fixed quantity' or 'compared with similar values' (CG 183, 115). 'A linguistic unit is like the fixed part of a building, e.g., a column' (CG 123f). 'Thought' and 'sound' resemble 'the air in contact with a sheet of water', or the 'front' and 'back' of 'a sheet of paper' (CG 112f, 115).[29] 'Trains' and 'streets' are enlisted to expound the interplay of 'differences and identities' (CG 108f). The 'analogical fact' is portrayed as 'a play with a cast of three' – the 'legitimate heir', 'the rival', and 'a collective character' (CG 163). 'The description of a language state' is modelled after the 'grammar of the Stock Exchange', which suggests a more everyday sense for the term 'values' (CG 134) (cf. 2.27ff, 36, 58).

2.80 Saussure's 'most fruitful' 'comparison' is 'drawn between the functioning of language and a game of chess' (CG 88f, 22f, 95, 107, 110) (cf. 6.51; 9[49]; 10.4). 'The respective value of the pieces depends on their position on the chessboard just as each linguistic term derives its value from its opposition to all the other terms' (CG 88) (cf. 2.26, 57f, 72). Though 'the system' 'varies from one position to the next', 'the set of rules' 'persists' and 'outlives all events' (CG 88, 95). The 'material make-up' of the pieces has no 'effect on the "grammar" of the game' (CG 110, 23). However, 'chess' is 'artificial', whereas 'language' is 'natural'; and 'the chessplayer *intends*' to 'exert an action on the system, whereas language premeditates nothing': 'the pieces' are 'modified spontaneously and fortuitously' (CG 88f) (cf. 2.52, 63, 73).

2.81 Such metaphors relieve Saussure's abstract vision of language by introducing objects or events that could be seen or felt, and whose reality admits little doubt. Yet even the most complex metaphor, the chess game, falls far short of the complexity of language. The rules and pieces of chess are known to anyone who plays the game, and disputes about them are unlikely to arise. The rules and units of language are so numerous, diffuse, and adaptable that even experts seldom agree on any large number of them. A 'linguistic term' rarely stands in such a clear and stable 'opposition to all the others' as a bishop or a knight differs from all other chess pieces.

2.82 The abstractness of language can also be offset by comparing linguistics to other 'sciences' like 'geology', 'zoology', 'astronomy', and 'chemistry' (CG 213, 53, 106f) (cf. 12.11). These sciences have reasonably concrete object domains; but Saussure's favoured model was mathematics, which does not (cf. 3.73; 4.21; 12.15). 'Language' can be conceived as 'a type of algebra consisting solely of complex terms' (CG 122) (cf. 3.72f; 5.27, 86; 6.8, 29, 51, 60; 7.40, 7[18]). 'Relations' should be 'expressed' by 'algebraic formulas', 'proportions', and 'equations', though Saussure does not expect a 'formula' to 'explain the phenomenon' (CG 122, 164f, 166f, 169). Moreover, 'studying a language-state means in practice disregarding changes of little importance, just as mathematicians disregard infinitesimal quantities in certain calculations' (CG 102).

2.83 And building a science of language was Saussure's ultimate aspiration. Presumably, the reason why he 'probably would not have authorized the publication of these pages' (cf. 2.1) was that his own conceptions seemed too unstable and unsatisfactory to fit his ideals of science. He firmly asserted categorical dichotomies, but could not always maintain them himself, e.g., 'synchronic' versus 'diachronic' (2.38f), or 'collective' versus 'individual' (2.20, 61). He emphasized that language is social and psychological, yet wanted linguistics cleanly separated from sociology and psychology (cf. 2.7, 16, 28, 31ff, 35, 78; cf. 12.14).[30] He situated language in the minds of speakers, but could not decide how far the speaker's knowledge of a language is comparable to the categorical framework of linguistics (cf. 2.33f, 36, 42, 45, 59, 63, 63).[31] He vacillated between mentalism and mechanism in appealing to notions like 'brain', 'mind', and 'thought' (cf. 2.16f, 18, 27, 31ff, 35, 40, 52, 57, 63, 65f, 74; 12.10), yet repeatedly referring to language itself as a 'mechanism' (CG 87, 103, 108, 111, 121, 133, 161, 165). Perhaps he wanted to deflect the issues of intention and will (cf. 2.20, 47, 64, 80).

2.84 Of course, the nature of language is so intricate and multiplex that its descriptions often entail inconsistencies, and a pioneering disquisition like the *Cours* is liable to be full of them. It both asserts and doubts that linguistics should involve a study of speech, pay attention to writing, and accept the word as a basic unit (cf. 2.19, 21, 23, 60, 18). Inconsistencies also beset the views that traditional grammar was a mistaken enterprise (cf. 2.5f); that grammar has a historical aspect (cf. 2.55); and that language is essentially arbitrary (cf. 2.28f). Some of these vacillations may be due to the improviso circumstances of its composition, or to the carelessness or exaggerated reverence of the editors, who do not comment upon them. But more importantly, language seems to have been resisting Saussure's determined campaign to make it hold still, to be as static, orderly and precisely circumscribed as he wanted it to be (cf. 12.52).

2.85 Some of the abstractions and dichotomies he deployed in this campaign tended to disperse the very factors that might have assisted him (cf. 12.55). His dismissal of 'speaking' and thus of actual discourse led him to inflate 'the arbitrary nature of the sign' (cf. 2.28f, 47), to fall back on 'association' and 'opposition' (cf. 2.57ff), and to neglect methods of data-gathering (cf. 12.27, 45). His turn against 'diachrony' left him deeply perplexed about 'time' and 'history' (cf. 2.12, 20, 34, 36, 39f, 42f, 45f, 55, 59f, 72f, 75f). Arguing from the neat oppositions of phonemic systems clashed sharply with the elusive, often metaphoric handling of semantics in terms of 'concepts', 'ideas', 'thoughts', and 'signifieds' (cf. 2.17, 25–28, 31f, 48, 52, 58, 62).

2.86 Many of Saussure's successors have underestimated the intricacies and qualifications within his arguments. Some of his terms, concepts, and dichotomies have been taken at face value, oversimplified, or treated as absolutes for the theory, doctrine, and organization of linguistics. This premature and selective orthodoxy has not merely misrepresented Saussure's intent to raise issues and problems rather than to resolve them, but has impeded comprehensive solutions. The reach of his vision is best revealed in the way that the same perplexities and dilemmas both explicit and implicit in his book have persisted in linguistics ever since. We are still uncertain about how a language is related to the multitude of speech events in the experience of language users, including linguists or grammarians (cf. 12.26, 49). We are still without an account of time and space in language (cf. 12.33). Disputes still rage over the status of rules or laws applying to all languages, and over the nature of linguistic units, especially in semantics (cf. 12.26ff, 60). Written language still dominates the representational methods of theories ostensibly concerned with spoken language (cf. 12.33). And little headway has been made in determining what sort of causalities apply in language, and how.

2.87 Thus, Saussure's deliberations deserve their place at the outset of 'modern linguistics' by virtue of their problematic nature as well as their monumental scope. He thought it 'evident' 'that linguistic questions interest all who work with texts' (CG 7). Consequently, 'that linguistics should continue to be the prerogative of a few specialists would be unthinkable – everyone is concerned with it in one way or another' (cf. 3.2). To be sure, Saussure's own work was a major contributor to the specializing of language models. But if read with the care they deserve, his inaugural deliberations provide both an inspiring and a sobering impetus for reconsidering how to stake out possible topographies of the discipline.

Notes

1. The *Course in General Linguistics*, translated by Wade Baskin, is cited as CG. I occasionally use square brackets to give the original French or to emend the English translation, which I found generally reliable. For a thorough exegesis of Saussure's 'manuscript sources' see Godel (1957).
2. On inconsistencies, see 2.83f, and Notes 3, 10, 12, 14, 16, 17, 20, 22, 23, 29, and 31.
3. He expressly points out such dictions as 'language does this or that' or the 'life of language' (CG 5n). Further terms he both condemned and used include 'material', 'natural', 'organism', and 'mechanism' (cf. 2.17, 30, 83).
4. Scholars cited here include: for the first stage none, for the second stage Friedrich August Wolf, and for the third stage Franz Bopp (1816), William Jones, Jacob Grimm (1822–36), August Friedrich Pott, Adalbert Kuhn, Theodor Benfey, Theodor Aufrecht, Max Müller (1861), Georg Curtius (1879), and August Schleicher (1861) (CG 1–5) (see my References for presumable source-works). Among those who 'brought linguistics nearer its true object', mention is made of Friedrich Christian Diez (1836–38), Dwight Whitney (1875), and 'the neogrammarians (Junggrammatiker) [Friedrich] K[arl] Brugmann, H[elmut] Osthoff, the Germanic scholars W[ilhelm] Braune, E[duard] Sievers, and H[ermann] Paul, and the Slavic scholar [August] Leskien' (CG 5) (again, see References). The works receive only cursory, mainly negative commentary, or none, except for Bopp's. A fuller coverage is given by Bloomfield. Firth declared homage to very early grammarians, but only to English ones (cf. 8.15, 8[12]).

5. Saussure's first major work was his *Mémoire sur le système primitif des voyelles dans les langues indo-européennes*, published in 1878 and still regarded today as a milestone in philology.

6. This abstruse argument reflects Saussure's belief that historical changes have a less systematic organization than the language at any single point in time (cf. 2.14, 19f). But elsewhere he says it is 'a serious mistake to consider dissimilar facts as a single phenomenon' (CG 146).

7. Nor is the word a reliable tool for theory: 'starting from words in defining things is a bad procedure', and 'all definitions of words are made in vain' (CG 14).

8. The study of etymology falls between the cracks in Saussure's scheme, since it is historical and yet not limited to word-sounds. See 2.75.

9. In denying 'phonetic doublets', Saussure dispatches one case because one of two forms 'is only a learned borrowing'; two more cases are passed over as 'literary French' (CG 156) (cf. 4.83). However, Saussure is not terribly well-disposed toward dialects either: because they conflict with his vision of the unified, closed system, he makes a shaky argument that diversity in space is 'actually' diversity in time and thus would fall under his exclusion of diachrony (cf. 2.43, 2^{17}).

10. In his last lectures ('from May to July 1911), de Saussure used interchangeably the old terminology ("idea" and "sign") and the new ("signifier" and "signified")' (CG 75, translator's note). The new became standard, especially among semioticians.

11. Whitney is credited with 'insisting upon the arbitrary nature of the sign', though he 'did not follow through' by making it a defining trait of language (CG 76).

12. Comparisons between 'language' and a 'plant' are also decried, though Saussure later compares the static and evolutionary versions of linguistics to cutting a plant 'transversely' or 'longitudinally' (CG 4, 87f) (2.79).

13. 'Two objections' are met by arguing that 'onomatopoeia' and 'interjections' are either outside the system, or if they do enter they become 'unmotivated' (CG 69). Compare 3^4; 8^{43}.

14. 'The sound-image is sensory, and if I happen to call it "material", it is only in that sense, and by way of opposing it' to 'the concept' (CG 66).

15. Saussure argues from here that 'linguistics' has 'only one method' (CG 212), namely the 'synchronic' one he favours (CG 212) (2.36). He did not consider that isolating an ideal, static state of the language may increase rather than reduce the number of possible methods, as the subsequent development of linguistics showed (cf. Ch. 7). On the question of whether linguistic constructs match the knowledge of speakers, compare 2.40, 42, 44, 47, 53, 59, 63, 83; 3.11, 19, 57, 2^{22}, and the passages cited in notes to 12.49.

16. See for instance CG 38, 47, 72, 118, 138, 165; and compare the passages cited in 12.49. In one passage where the translation has 'speakers are not conscious', the original French has 'the language [langue] is not conscious' (CG 47).

17. In one section, 'geographical isolation' is waved aside as an 'unsatisfactory and superficial explanation; differentiation can always be explained without it' (CG 210). But in another, 'geographical separation' is judged 'the most general force in linguistic diversity' (CG 193).

18. The other occasion is 'Saussure's treatment of holds', i.e., 'intermediate stretches' in 'spoken chains', as both 'mechanical and acoustic entities' (CG 52).

19. 'Non-phonetic' because Saussure decides to make 'analogy' 'grammatical' (2.54). In return, 'phonetics' is made the centre of 'diachronic linguistics' (2.73), befitting the preoccupation of philology with sound changes.

20. In another formulation, 'language' is claimed to do the same thing (CG 169)

(2.52). The discussion of how innovations occur (cf. 2.45) suggests that 'speech' is probably the better term.

21. Languages in which 'most words are not decomposable' are termed 'lexicological', the others being 'grammatical' (CG 166) (cf. 2.29; 3.53). Making words out of decomposable units helps 'limit arbitrariness' (CG 133) (cf. 2.29). This notion of 'lexicological' seems to befit the idea of the lexicon being a listing of irregularities (cf. 12.59).

22. Elsewhere, however, Saussure concedes that 'grammatical classes evolve', thus putting in question 'the absolute distinction between diachrony and synchrony' (CG 141). 'Once the phonetic force is eliminated, we find a residue that seems to justify the idea of a "history of grammar"'; but 'the distinction between diachrony and synchrony' is still judged 'indispensable' for reasons 'calling for detailed explanations outside the scope of this course' (CG 143).

23. But compare some formulations suggesting diversity instead: 'speakers often single out several kinds' or 'grades of radicals in the same family of words'; 'delimitations will vary according to the nature of the terms compared'; and 'the speaker may make every imaginable division' (CG 185, 188).

24. The editors comment: 'the two phenomena act jointly in the history of language, but agglutination always comes first' and 'furnishes models for analogy' (CG 178). If not followed up by 'analogy', 'agglutination' 'produces only unanalysable or unproductive words'.

25. The term 'paradigmatic' prevents confusion with the different kind of 'association' Saussure postulates between sound-image and concept, or between signifier and signified (e.g., CG 14f, 18f, 65f, 76, 102) (cf. 2.25).

26. An exception might be where 'an identical function' among various forms 'creates the association in absence of any material support' (CG 138). A case in point would be the 'zero sign' (CG 86, 186) (cf. 4^3; 5.56; 6^{16}; 7.75, 90).

27. The editors 'supplement' 'Saussure's brief description' with 'material' from Otto Jespersen, but claim to be 'merely carrying out de Saussure's intent' (CG 41).

28. 'But a spontaneous fact' 'may be conditioned negatively by the absence of certain forces of change' – an odd stipulation in a conception devised for 'the classing of changes' (CG 144f).

29. The 'sheet of paper' metaphor became the famous one in semiotics, though the 'air and water' one is probably more insightful, since one side is, as Saussure notes, more 'material' (2^{14}), and surely the two sides would be 'cut' differently in an analysis (cf. 6.47f).

30. For Saussure, 'the viewpoint of the psychologist' is to 'study the sign-mechanism in the individual' (CG 17). This is precisely *not* the view in empirical psychology, which seeks statistical significance among large populations (cf. Ch. 10). Saussure may have had psychoanalysis in mind here, as Sapir did (cf. 3.12).

31. In particular, he both claimed and denied that speakers can discern word-parts, change language, and observe language change (cf. 2.42, 44f, 63, 2^{23}).

Chapter 3

Edward Sapir[1]

3.1 Like Saussure's *Cours*, Sapir's *Language*, first published in 1921, seeks
to stake out the overall field of language study. The 'main purpose is to
show what' Sapir 'conceives language to be, what is its variability in place
and time, and what are its relations to other fundamental human interests –
the problem of thought, the nature of the historical process, race, culture,
art' (SL v).[2] He stresses that the 'content of language is intimately related to
culture', the latter defined as 'the socially inherited assemblage of practices
and beliefs that determines the texture of our lives' (SL 219, 207). 'The
history of culture and the history of language move along parallel lines'
(SL 219).[3] Indeed, 'the superficial connections' between 'speech' and 'other
historical processes' are so close that it needs to be shaken free of them if we
are to see it in its own right' (cf. 4.2; 6.6; 11.9; 12.1). 'Language' is thus an
'acquired "cultural" function' rather than 'an inherent biological function'
with an 'instinctive basis' (SL 3f) (cf. 3.15; 4.2; 8.26, 42, 44, 91; 9.1f, 6ff, 18,
22f, 107; 12.62).[4] 'Eliminate society' and 'the individual' 'will never learn to
talk, that is, to communicate ideas according to the traditional system of a
particular society'. 'Language' has an even greater 'universality' than
'religion' or 'art': 'we know of no people that is not possessed of a fully
developed language' (SL 22). Indeed, 'language' may have 'antedated even
the lowliest developments of material culture', which were 'not strictly
possible until language' 'had taken shape' (SL 23) (cf. 4.10; 8.28; 9.7).

3.2 Such theses project a vast scope for the study of language, in pointed
contrast to the narrower pursuits of the time (cf. 12.3). Sapir hopes to
provide 'a stimulus for the more fundamental study of a neglected field'
(SL vi). His book could 'be useful' 'both to linguistic students and to the
outside public that is half inclined to dismiss linguistic notions as the private
pedantries of essentially idle minds' (SL v) (cf. 2.88). 'Knowledge of the
wider relations of their science is essential to professional students of
language if they are to be saved from a sterile and purely technical attitude'.
We should avoid 'making too much of terminology', taking too much
'account of technical externals', or parading 'the technical terms' and
'technical symbols of the linguistic academy' (SL 140, 138, vi). We should
also resist such tendencies as the inclination to 'worship our schemes' as

'fetishes'; 'the strong craving for a simple formula' 'with two poles' that 'has been the undoing of linguists'; and 'the evolutionary prejudice' carried over from nineteenth-century 'social sciences' that has been 'the most powerful deterrent of all to clear thinking' (SL 122f) (cf. 3.49; 2.6; 12.14).

3.3 Sapir's characteristic stance is a striking mix of sobriety and exuberance. His portrayals of language, for example, range from staid abstractions of a Saussurian cast over to extravagant panegyrics. At the sober end, Sapir describes 'language' as a 'conventional', 'arbitrary system of symbolisms' (SL 4, 11). Or, less abstractly, it is 'a purely human and non-instinctive method of communicating ideas, emotions, and desires by means of a system of voluntarily produced symbols' (SL 8). At the exuberant end, 'language' is declared 'the most significant and colossal work that the human spirit has evolved'; 'the most self-contained' and 'massively resistant of all social phenomena'; the 'finished form or expression for all communicable experience'; and 'the most massive and inclusive art we know, a mountainous and anonymous work of unconscious generations' (SL 220, 206, 231) (cf. 6.2; 12.22). Moreover, 'language' 'is the most fluid of mediums' and 'a summary of thousands upon thousands of individual intuitions'; 'the possibilities of individual experience are infinite' (SL 221, 231) (cf. 3.13, 70; 4.31; 5.25, 28; 8.42). Hence, 'languages are more to us than systems of thought transference. They are invisible garments that drape themselves about our spirit and give a predetermined form to all its symbolic expressions' (SL 221).

3.4 In Sapir's view, quite unlike Saussure's, 'language exists only insofar as it is actually used – spoken and heard, written and read' (SL 154f) (cf. 12.36). But this claim is addressed mainly to the 'pedagogue' who 'struggles against' ' "incorrect" ' usage and insists on 'maintaining caste' and 'conserving literary tradition' (SL 156f) (cf. 2.5, 24, 2[9]; 4.40, 87; 8.26).[5] The 'logical or historical argument' of such pedagogues is often 'hollow' or 'psychologically shaky', lacks 'vitality', or promotes 'false' 'correctness' (SL 156ff). Instead, we must 'look to' 'the uncontrolled speech of the folk' and examine 'the general linguistic movement' and 'the actual drift of the English language' (SL 156, 167). 'The folk makes no apology' and feels 'no twinge of conscience' about usage, yet 'has a more acute flair for the genuine drift of the language than its students' do (SL 156, 161). So we should explore how a 'system proceeds from the unconscious dynamic habit of the language, falling from the lips of the folk' (SL 230).

3.5 However, caution is needed because 'the man in the street does not stop to analyse his position in the general scheme of humanity' and may confuse 'racial, linguistic, and cultural' 'classifications' or see 'external history' as 'inherent necessity' (SL 208). Even linguists may be 'so accustomed to our own well-worn grooves of expression that they have come to be felt as inevitable' (SL 89) (cf. 3.50; 4.4, 72; 5.11; 8.14). Hence, 'a destructive analysis of the familiar is the only method of approach to an understanding of fundamentally different modes of expression'.

3.6 In Sapir's exuberant outlook, 'the fundamental groundwork of language' 'meets us perfected and systematized in every language known to us' (SL 22). Yet he is equally impressed by the 'incredible diversity' of 'speech'. Indeed, 'the total number of possible sounds is greatly in excess of those in use' (SL 44). From among 'the indefinitely large number of articulated sounds available', each 'language makes use of an explicit, rigidly economical selection' (SL 46). In 'grammatical notions', too, 'the theoretical possibilities' 'are indefinitely numerous'; 'it depends entirely on the genius of the particular language what function is inherently involved in a given sequence of words' (SL 63).

3.7 Exuberance and sobriety are again mixed in Sapir's characterization of language as a system. An exuberant conception (just cited) is 'the **genius** of language': the 'type' or 'basic plan', 'much more fundamental, much more pervasive, than any single feature' or any 'fact' of 'grammar' (SL 120) (cf. 3.32, 46, 51, 63, 68). This 'genius' is variously claimed to affect the 'possibilities of combining phonetic elements'; the interdependence of 'syllables'; the amount of 'conceptual material' 'taken in' by the individual 'word' (cf. 3.32); the 'outward markings' of 'syntactic equivalents' with 'functionally equivalent affixes'; the 'functions' of 'sequences of words'; the selection of 'conventional interjections'; and even the 'effects' a 'literary artist' can draw from 'the colour and texture' of the language's 'matrix' (SL 54, 35, 32, 115, 63, 5, 222). Only in regard to 'race' does Sapir dismiss the notion of 'genius' as a 'mystic slogan' or a 'sentimental creed' (SL 208f, 212).

3.8 A sober conception, on the other hand, is the '**economy**' of a language. This conception is applied to the 'selection' of 'articulated sounds'; the 'alternations between long and short syllables'; the availability of 'rhyme'; and the relative importance of 'word order' versus 'case suffixes' (SL 46, 229f, 64). The 'economy' also 'irons out' the 'less frequently occurring associations' between 'radical elements, grammatical elements, words', or 'sentences' on one side, and 'concepts or groups of concepts' on the other (SL 37f). This process limits the 'randomness of association' and thereby makes 'grammar' possible (cf. 2.29). Even the single sentence is said to have a 'local economy' of 'its terms' (SL 85).

3.9 If we 'accept language as a fully formed functional system within man's psychic or "spiritual" constitution', then 'we cannot define it as an entity in psycho-physical terms alone' (SL 10f). We should 'discuss the intention, the form, and the history of speech' 'as an institutional or cultural entity' and 'take for granted' 'the organic and psychological mechanisms back of it'. Sapir is thus 'not concerned with those aspects of physiology and physiological psychology that underlie speech' (cf. 2.31). He alludes only in passing to 'the vast network of associated localizations in the brain and lower nervous tracts' (cf. 4.10, 14, 18f; 8.21, 23). 'Language' 'cannot be definitely "localized" in the brain', 'for it consists of a peculiar symbolic relation – physiologically an arbitrary one – between all possible elements of consciousness on the one hand, and certain selected elements localized in

the auditory, motor, and other cerebral and nervous tracts on the other'
(cf. 2.16, 31, 66; 7.31, 93, 7⁴³; 8¹⁶).

3.10 Although Sapir vows he has 'little to say about the ultimate
psychological basis of speech', he believes that 'linguistic forms' 'have the
greatest possible diagnostic value' for 'understanding' 'problems in the
psychology of **thought** and in the strange, cumulative drift in the life of the
human spirit' (SL vf) (cf. 5.69; 6.2, 6; 7.10; 8.24; 11.17ff, 22, 62; 12.10).[6]
'Language and our thought grooves are inextricably interrelated, are in a
sense, one and the same' (SL 217f). 'Linguistic morphology is nothing more
or less than a collective *art* of thought, an art denuded of the irrelevancies of
individual sentiment' (SL 218). Moreover, 'all voluntary communication of
ideas, aside from normal speech, is either a transfer, direct or indirect, from
the typical symbolism of language as spoken and heard, or, at the least,
involves the intermediary of truly linguistic symbolism' (SL 21). Even those
who 'think without the slightest use of sound imagery are, at last analysis,
dependent upon it', 'the auditory-motor associations' being 'unconsciously
brought into play' (SL 20). As proof, Sapir cites 'the frequent experience of
fatigue in the speech organs' after 'unusually' 'intensive thinking' (SL 19).[7]
'Gesture languages' too owe their 'intelligibility' to 'their automatic and
silent translation into the terms of a fuller flow of speech' (SL 21).

3.11 Consequently, 'the feeling entertained by so many that they can
think, or even reason, without language is an illusion' (SL 15). 'Thought
may be no more conceivable, in its genesis and daily practice, without
speech than is mathematical reasoning practicable' without a 'mathematical
symbolism'. An evolutionary connection is propounded: 'that language is an
instrument originally put to uses lower than the conceptual plane and that
thought arises as a refined interpretation of its content' (cf. 4.34; 8.6). 'The
product grows' 'with the instrument', and 'the growth of speech' is
'dependent on the development of thought' (SL 15, 17). In view of 'the
unconscious and unrationalized nature of linguistic structure', 'the most
rarefied thought may be but the conscious counterpart of an unconscious
linguistic symbolism' (SL vi, 16). The idea that people 'are in the main
unconscious' of the 'forms' they 'handle', 'regardless of the material
advancement or backwardness of the people' (SL 124) (cf. 3.61), is favoured
by other theorists as well (cf. 12.49). Sapir also surmises that the 'analysis'
of forms is 'unconscious, or rather unknown, to the normal speaker',
implying that 'students of language cannot be entirely normal in their
attitude toward their own speech' (SL 161, n) (cf. 12.1, 49).

3.12 However, 'language and thought are not strictly coterminous', and
'the flow of language itself is not always indicative of thought' (SL 14f). 'At
best language can but be the outward facet of thought on the highest, most
generalized level of symbolic expression', rather than 'the final label put
upon the finished thought' (cf. 7.25). Conversely, 'from the point of view of
language, thought may be defined as the highest latent or potential content
of speech', its 'fullest conceptual value'. Or, 'language, as a structure, is on
its inner face the mould of thought' (SL 22). Still, 'the feeling of a free, non-

linguistic stream of thought' may be 'justified' in cases wherein 'the symbolic expression of thought' 'runs along outside the fringe of the conscious mind'. This view concurs with 'modern psychology', whose 'recent literature' 'has shown us how powerfully symbolism is at work in the unconscious mind' (SL 16, 126n). Perhaps 'a more general psychology than Freud's will eventually prove' 'the mechanisms of "repression of impulse" and of its symptomatic symbolization' 'to be as applicable to the groping for abstract form, the logical or aesthetic ordering of experience, as to the life of the fundamental instincts' (SL 157n).[8]

3.13 A 'speech sound' attains 'linguistic significance' by being 'associated with some element or group of elements of **experience**'; 'this "element"' 'is the content or meaning of the linguistic unit' (SL 10). Hence, 'the elements of language' are 'symbols that ticket off experience' (SL 12). For that purpose, 'the world of our experiences must be enormously simplified and generalized' into 'a symbolic inventory'. 'The concreteness of experience is infinite, the resources of the richest language are strictly limited' (SL 84). Besides, 'the single experience lodges in an individual consciousness and is, strictly speaking, incommunicable' (SL 12). So 'we must arbitrarily throw whole masses of experience together as similar enough to warrant being looked upon – mistakenly but conveniently – as identical', 'in spite of great and obvious differences' (SL 13). 'It is almost as though at some period in the past the unconscious mind of the race had made a hasty inventory of experience' and 'saddled the inheritors of its language' with a 'premature classification that allowed of no revision' (SL 100). 'Linguistic categories make up a system of surviving dogma – dogma of the unconscious'.

3.14 Sapir thus concludes that 'the latent content of all languages' is 'the intuitive science of experience' (SL 218) (cf. 3.23; 11.12f; 12.24). 'The essence of language consists in assigning conventional, voluntarily articulated sounds' 'to diverse elements of experience' (SL 11). The ' "concept" ' serves as 'a convenient capsule of thought that embraces thousands of experiences' (SL 13). 'The single impression' enters one's 'generalized memory', which is in turn 'merged with the notions of all other individuals'. 'The particular experience' gets 'widened so as to embrace all possible impressions or images that sentient beings may form or have formed'.

3.15 Despite his reverence for Freudian ideas and his emphasis on experience, Sapir shows scant concern for 'volition and emotion', albeit 'they are, strictly speaking, never absent from normal speech' (SL 39). 'Ideation reigns supreme in language'; 'volition and emotion come in as distinctly secondary factors' (SL 38) (cf. 9.15). 'Their expression is not of a truly linguistic nature'. To support this outlook, Sapir judges the 'expression' of 'impulse and feeling' to be 'but modified forms of the instinctive utterance that man shares with the lower animals' rather than 'part of the essential cultural conception of language' (cf. 3.1). Though 'most words' 'have an associated feeling-tone' derived from 'pleasure or pain', this tone is not 'an inherent value in the word itself', but 'a sentimental growth on the word's true body, on its conceptual kernel' (SL 39f).

'Speech demands conceptual selection' and the 'inhibition of the randomness of instinctive behaviour' (SL 46n) (cf. 3.9). Besides, 'the feeling-tone' 'varies from individual to individual' and 'from time to time' (SL 40). So 'desire, purpose, emotion are the personal colour of the objective world', and constitute 'non-linguistic facts' (SL 39, 46n).

3.16 Even in its more rarefied domains, Sapir finds language far from ideal. He notes a 'powerful tendency for a formal elaboration that does not correspond to clear-cut conceptual differences' (SL 98) (cf. 2.49).[9] Instead, we run up against 'form for form's sake', and a 'curious lack of accord between function and form' (SL 98, 100, 89) (cf. 3.22, 24, 33; 4.47, 49; 7.63; 8.58; 9.19; 11.25, 27; 12.54). 'Irrational form' 'is as natural to the life of language as is the retention of modes of conduct that have long outlived the meaning they once had' (SL 98). 'Phonetic processes' favour 'non-significant differences in form'; and 'grammatical concepts' tend to 'degenerate into purely formal counters' (SL 100; cf. SL 61).

3.17 Again like Saussure (cf. 2.68ff), Sapir declares that 'the mere **phonetic** framework of speech does not constitute the inner fact of language, and that the single **sound** of articulated speech is not' 'a linguistic element at all' (SL 42) (cf. 2.68; 4.29; 6.7). 'The mere sounds of speech are not the essential fact of language' (SL 22). 'Language is not identical with its auditory symbolism', though it is a 'primarily auditory system of symbols' (SL 16f). 'Communication' 'is successful only when the hearer's auditory perceptions are translated into the appropriate and intended flow of imagery or thought' (SL 18).

3.18 Nevertheless, 'the cycle of speech' as 'a purely external instrument begins and ends in sounds' (SL 18) (cf. 2.17, 67; 12.27). 'Speech is so inevitably bound up with sounds and their articulation that we can hardly avoid' 'the subject of phonetics' (SL 42) (cf. 2.70f; 3.14, 21; 4.29; 5.42; 8.70; 12.26). 'Neither the purely formal aspects of a language nor the course of its history can be fully understood without reference' to its 'sounds'. At one point, Sapir asserts that 'auditory' and 'motor imagery' are 'the historic fountain-head of all speech and of all thinking' (SL 21) (cf. 3.10, 3[7]; 8.6).

3.19 In regard to sound systems, 'the feeling' of 'the average speaker' is not reliable but 'largely illusory', namely that a 'language' 'is built up' 'of a comparatively small number of distinct sounds, each of which is rather accurately provided for in the current alphabet by one letter' (SL 42f) (cf. 2.22f; 4.38; 6.50; 7.46, 66; 8.11, 53, 75f; 12.26). 'Phonetic analysis convinces one that the number of clearly distinguishable sounds and nuances of sounds that are habitually employed by speakers of a language is far greater than they themselves realize' (cf. 4.29).

3.20 We should rather assume that 'every language' 'is characterized' 'by its ideal system of sounds and by the underlying phonetic pattern' (SL 56).[10] 'The actual rumble of speech' must therefore be traced to an 'ideal flow of phonetic elements' (cf. 2.68; 4.30; 5.42f; 12.26). 'Back of the purely objective system of sounds', each language has 'a more restricted "inner" or "ideal" system' that can 'be brought to consciousness as a finished pattern, a psychological mechanism' (SL 55).[11] 'The inner sound-system, overlaid though it may be with the mechanical or the irrelevant, is a real and immensely important principle in the life of a language'. 'Unless their phonetic "values" are determined', 'the objective comparison of sounds' has 'no psychological or historical significance'.

3.21   For 'the organic classification of speech sounds', Sapir offers four criteria: 'the position of the glottal cords'; the passage of 'breath' through the 'mouth' or 'nose'; 'free' or 'impeded' passage; and 'the precise points of articulation' (SL 52f). This scheme should be 'sufficient to account for all, or practically all, the sounds of language'.[12] For example, 'each language selects a limited number of clearly defined positions as characteristic of its consonantal system, ignoring transitional or extreme positions'. Or, the language picks out its 'voiced sounds', which, being 'the most clearly audible elements of speech', 'are carriers of practically all significant differences in stress, pitch, and syllabication' (SL 49) (cf. 4.34). 'The voiceless sounds' serve to 'break up the stream of voice with fleeting moments of silence'.

3.22   Besides the 'system of sounds', 'a definite **grammatical** structure' 'characterizes' 'every language' (SL 56). ' "Grammatical" processes' are 'the formal methods employed by a language' (SL 57) (cf. 12.54). 'Grammar' indicates that 'all languages have an inherent economy of expression', wherein 'analogous concepts and relations are most conveniently symbolized in analogous forms' (SL 38) (cf. 3.8). 'Were language ever completely "grammatical", it would be a perfect engine of conceptual expression. Unfortunately or luckily, no language is tyrannically consistent. All grammars leak' (cf. 12.59). Hence, we should expect to find a 'relative independence', or a 'lack of accord', 'between function and form' (SL 58f, 89; cf. SL 64, 69ff) (cf. 3.16).

3.23   For Sapir, 'our conventional classification of words into "**parts of speech**" is only a vague wavering approximation of a consistently worked-out inventory of experience', 'far from corresponding' to a 'simple' 'analysis of reality' (SL 117) (cf. 2.30, 65; 3.13; 4.55; 5.72f; 9.27; 12.7, 24). 'The "parts of speech"' 'grade into each other' or are 'actually convertible into each other' (SL 118) (cf. 12.54). Hence, they 'reflect not so much our intuitive analysis of reality as our ability to compose that reality into a variety of formal patterns'. 'For this reason no logical scheme of the parts of speech – their number, nature and necessary confines – is of the slightest interest to the linguist' (SL 119) (cf. 12.7, 17).

3.24   Taken by itself, 'every language' does have 'a definite feeling for patterning on the level of grammatical formation' (SL 61). 'All languages evince a curious instinct for the development of one or more grammatical processes at the expense of others, tending always to lose sight of any explicit functional value that the process may have had' and 'delighting, it would seem, in the sheer play of its means of expression' (SL 60) (cf. 3.16).

The 'feeling for form as such, freely expanding along predetermined lines, and greatly inhibited in certain directions by the lack of controlling patterns, should be more clearly understood than it seems to be' (SL 61). Meanwhile, a strong later trend in American linguistics was foreshadowed by Sapir's recommendation that 'linguistic form may and should be studied as types of patterning, apart from the associated functions' (SL 60) (cf. 4.49; 7.63; 12.54). This counsel is ominous if 'a linguistic phenomenon cannot be looked upon as illustrating a definite "process" unless it has an inherent functional value' (SL 62).

3.25 'The various grammatical processes that linguistic research has established' 'may be grouped into six main types: word order, composition, affixation', 'internal modification', 'reduplication, and accentual differences' (SL 61).[13] Of these, **word order** is 'the most economical method of conveying some sort of grammatical notion' – 'juxtaposing two or more words in a definite sequence' (SL 62). 'It is psychologically impossible to see or hear two words juxtaposed without straining to give them some measure of coherent significance'. When 'two simple' words, or even mere 'radicals' (roots), 'are put before the human mind in immediate sequence it strives to bind them together with connecting values'.

3.26 '**Composition**' is 'the uniting into a single word of two or more radical elements' (SL 64) (compare Saussure's 'agglutination', 2.64). 'Psychologically, this process is closely allied to word order insofar as the relation between the elements is implied, not explicitly stated'. But 'it differs' 'in that the compounded elements are felt as constituting but parts of a single word-organism'. 'However, then, in its ultimate origins the process of composition may go back to typical sequences of words in the sentence, it is now, for the most part, a specialized method of expressing relations' (SL 65) (cf. 12.54).

3.27 '**Affixation** is incomparably the most frequently employed' 'of all grammatical processes' (SL 67) (cf. 2.62). A well-developed system of affixes may allow a language to be somewhat 'indifferent' about 'word order' by compensating with 'differences' that are 'rhetorical or stylistic' rather than 'strictly grammatical' (SL 63) (cf. 7.55). 'Of the three types of affixing – the use of prefixes, suffixes, and infixes – suffixing is much the commonest' and may indeed 'do more of the formative work of language than all other methods combined'. In some languages (e.g., Nootka of Vancouver Island), 'suffixed elements' 'may have as concrete a significance as the radical element itself' (SL 66; cf. SL 71n). In others (e.g., Latin and Russian), 'the suffixes alone relate the word to the rest of the sentence' by demarcating 'the less concrete, more strictly formal, notions of time,[14] person, plurality, and passivity', while 'the prefixes' are 'confined to the expression of such ideas as delimit the concrete significance of the radical element' (SL 68). Still, 'in probably the majority of languages that use both types of affixes, each group has both delimiting and formal or relational functions' (SL 69).

3.28 'Internal modification' entails 'vocalic or consonantal change', and is 'a subsidiary but by no means unimportant grammatical process' (SL 61, 73). 'In some languages, as in English', it 'indicates fundamental changes of grammatical function'. 'Consonantal change' 'is probably far less common than vocalic', but 'not exactly rare', appearing prominently in 'Celtic languages' for instance (SL 74f).

3.29 'Reduplication' is a 'natural' operation, namely 'the repetition of all or part of the radical element' (SL 76). 'This process is generally employed, with self-evident symbolism, to indicate such concepts as distribution, plurality, repetition, customary activity, increase of size, added intensity, continuance'. 'The most characteristic examples' 'repeat only part of radical element', mainly to signal 'repetition or continuance' of an action (SL 77f).

3.30 'Variations in **accent**, whether of stress or of pitch', are 'the subtlest of all grammatical processes' (SL 78f). 'Accent as a functional process' is hard to 'isolate', being 'often combined with alternations in vocalic quantity or quality or complicated by the presence of affixed elements'. Even so, 'pitch accent' in particular 'is far less infrequently employed as a grammatical process than our own habits of speech would prepare us to believe' (SL 81).

3.31 Once more like Saussure, Sapir is cautious about the status of the **word** (cf. 2.18; 4.54, 60; 5.53; 6.23; 8.54; 11.69, 71, 77; 12.29). He remarks that the word is 'roughly' 'the "element of speech"', or 'the first speech element that we have found which we can say actually "exists"' (SL 24, 27). 'Linguistic experience' 'indicates overwhelmingly' 'that there is not, as a rule, the slightest difficulty in bringing the word to consciousness as a psychological reality' (SL 33) (cf. 12.57). 'The psychological validity of the word' is strikingly revealed when 'the naive Indian, quite unaccustomed to the concept of the written word', still 'dictates a text to a linguistic student word by word' (SL 33f). Yet 'the psychological existence' of the word is not based on its outward shape, e.g., on its 'phonetic characteristics', such as 'accent' or 'cadence'; these 'at best strengthen a feeling of unity that is already present on other grounds' (SL 35). Above all, 'the word' 'cannot be cut into without a disturbance of meaning'.

3.32 Sapir predictably favours a mentalistic account, though not in terms of one-to-one correspondences between word and meaning (cf. 5.48, 64; 6.27; 9.39; 12.54). It is 'impossible' to 'define the word as the symbolic, linguistic counterpart of a single concept' (SL 32). 'Words, significant parts of words, or word groupings' can all be 'the outward sign of a specific idea' (SL 25). Conversely, 'the single word expresses either a simple concept or a combination of concepts so interrelated as to form a psychological unity' (SL 82). Hence, 'the word may be anything from the expression of a single concept – concrete or abstract or purely relational – to the expression of a complete thought' (SL 32). 'The word is merely a form, a definitely moulded entity that takes in as much or as little of the conceptual material of the whole thought as the genius of the language allows' (cf. 3.7; 11.63).

Therefore, 'the single word may or may not be the simplest significant element of speech we have to deal with' (SL 25).[15] 'The mind must rest on something; if it cannot linger on the constituent elements, it hastens all the more eagerly to the acceptance of the word as a whole' (SL 132; cf. CG 177) (cf. 12.32).

3.33 We might proceed not up from smaller units but down from larger units by stipulating that 'the word is one of the smallest, completely satisfying bits of isolated "meaning" into which the sentence resolves itself' (SL 34) (cf. 12.26). 'Radical (or grammatical) elements and sentences' 'are the primary **functional** units of speech, the former as an abstracted minimum, the latter as an aesthetically satisfying embodiment of a unified thought' (SL 32). 'The words', in contrast, are 'the actual **formal** units of speech' and 'may on occasion identify themselves with either of the two functional units; more often they mediate between the two extremes'. 'The importance' of 'methods of binding words into a larger unity' 'is apt to vary with the complexity of the individual word' (SL 109).

3.34 A parallel between word and sentence is drawn to describe 'complex words', i.e., 'firmly solidified groups of elements' (SL 111). The 'elements' 'are related to each other in a specific way and follow each other in a rigorously determined sequence' (SL 110). 'A word which consists of more than a radical element is a crystallization of a sentence or some portion of a sentence' (SL 111) (cf. 2.55; 3.26; 4.61; 5.41; 8.56; 10.40, 79f; 11.71, 75, 77, 93; 12.54). 'Speech is thus constantly tightening and loosening its sequences' (SL 112). 'Complex words' illustrate this process: 'while they are fully alive' and 'functional at every point, they can keep themselves at a psychological distance from their neighbours; as they gradually lose much of their life, they fall back into the embrace of the sentence as a whole and the sequence of independent words regains the importance it had in part transferred to the crystallized groups of elements' (SL 111f).

3.35 'Breaking down, then, the wall that separates word and sentence, we may ask': what 'are the fundamental methods' of 'passing from the isolated notions symbolized by each word' or 'element to the unified proposition that corresponds to a thought?' (SL 110). The answer is a 'venturesome and yet not altogether unreasonable speculation that sees in word order and stress the primary methods for the expression of all syntactic relations and looks upon the present relational value of specific words and elements as but a secondary condition' (SL 113). 'At some point', 'order asserts itself in every language as the most fundamental of relating principles' (SL 116) (cf. 3.25; 7.3, 55; 10.64, 86).

3.36 Along these lines, pursuing the status of the word leads to the status of the **sentence**. Sapir cheerfully says the 'definition' of the 'sentence' 'is not difficult', since it is 'the major functional unit of speech' (SL 35; cf. SL 66). Also, 'it is the linguistic expression of a proposition' (SL 35) (cf. 3.44f; 8.55; 9.72, 9[24]; 10.39–50). Just as a 'sentence' 'combines a subject of discourse with a statement in regard to this subject', a 'proposition' involves 'a subject of discourse' plus 'something' 'said about it' (SL 35, 119). 'The sentence does not lose its feeling of unity so long as each and every one' of its 'elements' 'falls into place as contributory to the definition of either the subject of discourse or the core of the predicate' (SL 36). Still, 'the vast majority of languages' 'create some formal barrier between these two terms of the proposition' (SL 119). 'The most common subject of discourse' 'is a noun' and may be either 'subject' or 'object' in the traditional 'technical sense' (SL 119, 87f, 82f, 94). The thing 'predicated of a subject is generally an activity' whose 'form' is a 'verb' (SL 119). 'No language wholly fails to distinguish noun and verb', whereas no 'other parts of speech' are 'imperatively required for the life of language'.[16]

3.37 Like the word, 'the sentence' 'has a psychological as well as a merely logical or abstracted existence' (SL 35) (cf. 12.7). Sapir ventures to assert that 'in all languages', 'the sentence is the outgrowth of historical and unreasoning psychological forces rather than of a logical synthesis of elements that have been clearly grasped in their individuality' (SL 90). 'The sentence is the logical counterpart of the complete thought only if it be felt as made up of the radical and grammatical elements that lurk in the recesses of its words' (SL 33).[17] Such passages invoking the failure of language to be 'logical' (also SL 89, 91, 97, 102, 119, 135, 156) call to mind the longstanding dispute among linguists over the use of logic as a model (cf. 12.17).

3.38 Sapir is more in tune with future trends of linguistics when he surmises that 'underlying the finished sentence is a living sentence type, of fixed formal characteristics' (SL 37) (cf. 7.95). A type can be recognized when 'we feel instinctively, without the slightest attempt at conscious analysis, that two sentences fit the same pattern, that they are really the same fundamental sentence' (SL 85) (cf. 4.68f; 5.40, 58; 7.51, 90f; 11.77). 'These fixed types or actual sentence-groundworks may be freely overlaid by such additional matter as the speaker or writer cares to put on, but they are themselves as rigidly "given" by tradition as are the radical and grammatical elements abstracted from the finished word' (SL 37). 'New sentences are being constantly created' 'in the same way' as 'new words may be consciously created from these fundamental elements' (cf. 7.44; 12.54). 'The enlarged sentence, however, allows as a rule of considerable freedom' of '"unessential" parts'. 'Such a sentence as "The mayor of New York is going to deliver a speech of welcome in French" is readily felt as a unified statement, incapable of reduction by the transfer of certain of its elements, in their given form, to the preceding or following sentences' (SL 36). But some 'contributory ideas', such as '"of New York"' or '"of welcome"', 'may be eliminated without hurting the idiomatic flow of the sentence' (cf. 7.51).

3.39 Still, this 'freedom' has its limits. 'Change any of the features of a sentence' like '"The farmer kills the duckling"', and it becomes modified, slightly or seriously, in some purely relational, non-material regard' (SL 85, 82). If the finite verb precedes both subject and object ('"kills the farmer the duckling?"'), we get 'an unusual but not unintelligible mode'; but if articles are omitted ('farmer kills duckling'), 'the sentence becomes impossible – it falls into no recognized pattern and the two subjects of discourse seem to hang in the void' (SL 87, 85). (As this judgment implies, 'newspaper headlines' 'are language only in a derived sense', SL 36n). Moreover, 'coordinate sentences' are disqualified on the opposite grounds of including too much: they 'may only doubtfully be considered as truly unified predications' (SL 36).

3.40 Alongside phonetic and grammatical structures, **'conceptual structure'** also 'shows the instinctive feeling of language for form' (SL 56) (cf. 3.16). 'The material of language reflects the world of concepts', and 'the essential fact of language' lies 'in the classification, in the formal patterning, and in the relating of concepts' (SL 38, 22). Moreover, 'the actual flow of speech may be interpreted as a record of the setting' of 'concepts into mutual relations' (SL 13). At least, 'the unconscious analysis into individual concepts' 'is never entirely absent from speech, however it may be complicated and overlaid with irrational factors' (SL 90). Reciprocally, a 'concept does not attain to individual and independent life until it has found a distinctive linguistic embodiment' (SL 17). 'As soon as the word is at hand', we feel 'that the concept is ours for the handling'.

3.41 Sapir proposes to look into 'the nature of the world of concepts' as 'reflected and systematized in linguistic structure' (SL 82). He raises the prospect of 'reviewing the purely formal processes used by all known languages to affect fundamental concepts – those embodied in unanalysable words or in the radical elements of words – by the modifying or formative influence of subsidiary concepts'. He tells 'the general reader' that 'language struggles toward two poles of linguistic expression – material content and relation – and that these poles are connected by a long series of transitional concepts' (SL 109). Particularly 'in exotic languages', we are not able 'to tell infallibly what is "material content" and what is "relation"' (SL 102).

3.42 'What then are the absolutely essential concepts in speech that must be expressed if language is to be a satisfactory means of communication?' (SL 93). 'We must have, first of all, a large stock of basic or radical concepts, the concrete wherewithal of speech'. 'We must have objects, actions, qualities to talk about', plus 'their corresponding symbols in independent words or in radical elements'. Sapir's 'tabular statement' of 'concepts' is divided on one side into **'concrete'**, which subsumes 'radical' and 'derivational'; and on the other side into **'relational'**, which subsumes 'reference', 'modality', 'personal relations' (i.e., subject and object), 'number', and 'time' (SL 88f). However, he warns that 'in the actual work of analysis difficult problems frequently arise' about 'how to group a given set of concepts' (SL 102) (cf. 12.59).

3.43 Besides, 'it would be impossible for any language to express every concrete idea by an independent word or radical element' (SL 84). Instead, it must 'throw countless concepts under the rubric of certain basic ones', using other 'ideas as functional mediators' (cf. 9.62–69). The latter 'ideas' may be called 'derivational' or 'qualifying' and may be 'expressed' by 'independent words, affixes, or modifications of the radical elements' (cf. 3.27f). '**Radical**' and '**derivational**' are thus 'two modes of expression' as well as 'two types of concepts and of linguistic elements'.

3.44 'In origin', however, 'all of the actual content of speech' is 'limited to the concrete; relations were originally not expressed in outward form but were merely implied and articulated with the help of order and rhythm' (SL 114) (cf. 3.35). 'No known language' 'succeeds in saying something without the use of symbols for concrete concepts' (SL 94). And 'no proposition, however abstract in its intent, is humanly possible without tying on' 'to the concrete world of sense' (SL 93). Accordingly, 'such relational concepts must be expressed as moor the concrete concepts to each other and construct a definite, fundamental form of proposition' allowing 'no doubt as to the nature of the relations'. 'Most languages' 'throw a bold bridge between' 'the concrete and the abstractly relational' (SL 95).

3.45 Sapir thus 'revises our first classification' (summarized in 3.43) and suggests another 'scheme' for the 'classification of concepts as expressed in language', proceeding through 'a gradual loss of the concrete' (SL 100, 103). He enumerates: 'I. *Basic Concrete Concepts*'; 'II. *Derivational Concepts*', 'less concrete'; 'III. *Concrete Relational Concepts*, still more abstract'; and 'IV. *Pure Relational Concepts*, purely abstract' (SL 101). Concepts in class I 'involve no relation' except what is 'implied in defining one concept against another'; concepts in II 'concern only the radical element, not the sentence'; concepts in III 'transcend the particular word'; and concepts in IV give 'the proposition' 'definite syntactic form'. Class I is 'normally expressed by independent words or radical elements', and the other classes by 'affixing non-radical elements to radical elements'. Sapir conjectures that 'concepts of class I' and IV are 'essential to all speech', whereas 'II and III are both common, but not essential' (SL 102).

3.46 Though he considers his classes 'logically' 'distinct', he concedes that 'the illogical, metaphorical genius of language' has 'set up a continuous gamut of concepts and forms that leads imperceptibly from the crudest of materialities' 'to the most subtle of relations' (SL 102) (cf. 3.37). The gamut runs parallel to 'a constant fading away of the feeling of sensible reality' (SL 103). In addition, 'impulses to definite form operate' 'regardless of the need' for 'giving consistent external shape to particular groups of concepts' (SL 61).

3.47 His scheme of concepts animates Sapir to propose an ambitious 'conceptual classification of languages' reflecting 'the translation of concepts into linguistic symbols' (SL 138). It would be ideal to have 'a simple, incisive, and absolutely inclusive method of classifying all known languages' (SL 136). But 'classifications', those 'neat constructions of the speculative mind, are slippery things' and 'have to be tested at every possible opportunity' (SL 144). 'Various classifications have been suggested' before, and 'none proves satisfactory' (SL 122) (cf. 4.62, 72). 'It is dangerous to generalize from a small number of selected languages'. Nor is the problem cured merely by throwing in 'a sprinkling of exotic types' to 'supplement the few languages nearer home that we are more immediately interested in'.

3.48 Since 'languages' 'are exceedingly complex historical structures', we should not 'pigeonhole' 'each language' but 'evolve a flexible method' to 'place it, from two or three independent standpoints, relatively to another language' (SL 140). 'We are too ill-informed as yet of the structural spirit of great numbers of languages to have the right to frame a classification that is other than flexible and experimental'. 'Like any human institution, speech is too variable, too elusive to be quite safely ticketed' (SL 121).

3.49 However, we must not rush to the other extreme and take the 'difficulty of classification' as a 'proof' of its 'uselessness' (SL 121). 'It would be too easy to relieve ourselves of the burden of constructive thinking' by asserting that 'each language has its unique history, therefore its unique structure'. We should rather proceed with caution, striving to resist the 'craving for a simple formula' – e.g., 'a triune formula' with 'two poles' and 'a "transitional type"' (SL 122f) (cf. 3.2).

3.50 Above all, linguists must beware of holding the 'grooves of expression' of their native language to be 'inevitable' (SL 89) (cf. 3.5; 12.42). 'The classification of language' remains 'fruitless' as long as one assumes that 'familiar languages' like 'Latin and Greek' 'represent the "highest development"', and that 'all other types were but steps on the way to this beloved "inflective" type' (SL 123) (cf. 3.53). Only 'when one has learned to feel what is fortuitous or illogical or unbalanced in the structure of one's own language' can one attain 'a sympathetic grasp of the expression of the various classes of concepts in alien types of speech' (SL 89). 'Not everything that is "outlandish" is intrinsically illogical and far-fetched. It is often precisely the familiar that a wider perspective reveals as the curiously exceptional'. 'If, therefore, we wish to understand language in its true inwardness we must disabuse our minds of preferred "values" and accustom ourselves to look upon English and Hottentot with the same cool, yet interested detachment' (SL 124). 'Any classification that starts with preconceived values or that works up to sentimental satisfactions is self-condemned as unscientific'.[18]

3.51 Outward appearances may be deceiving. 'The fact that two languages are similarly classified does not necessarily mean that they present a great similarity on the surface' (SL 141). 'We are here concerned with the most fundamental and generalized features of the spirit, the technique, and the elaboration of a given language'. Anyone who has felt 'the spirit of a foreign language' may suspect there must be a 'structural "genius"', 'a basic plan, a certain cut to each language' (SL 120) (cf. 3.7). The 'fundamental form intuitions' of 'diverse languages' may 'some day' be established well enough to reveal 'the great underlying ground plans' (SL 144). For the present, Sapir offers 'only a few schematic indications'; 'a separate volume would be needed to breathe life into the scheme' and disclose a full 'formal economy of strikingly divergent types' (SL 146n).

3.52 Sapir's scheme again has four classes of languages, related in diverse ways to his four classes of concepts summarized in 3.45. Two criteria are decisive: (1) whether the language 'keeps the syntactic relations pure' or 'expresses' them in forms 'mixed' with 'concrete significance'; and (2) whether the language 'possesses the power to modify the significance of radical elements by means of affixes or internal changes' (SL 137f). We thus get: A. *'simple pure-relational* languages' ('pure' 'relations', no 'modifying'); B. *'complex pure-relational* languages' ('pure' 'relations', 'modifying'); C. *'simple mixed-relational* languages' ('mixed' 'relations', no 'modifying'); and D. *'complex mixed-relational* languages' ('mixed relations', 'modifying').

3.53 Since this classification is still 'too sweeping and broad', a further 'subdivision' is added (SL 138).[19] *'Agglutinative'* languages apply a 'juxtaposing technique'; *'fusional'* languages apply a 'fusing technique'; *'symbolic'* languages use 'internal changes (reduplication; vocalic and consonantal change; changes in quantity, stress and pitch)'; and *'isolating'* languages use no 'affixes or modifications of the radical element' (SL 130, 126, 139) (cf. 4.62f). Though the 'fusing technique' is typical of 'inflective' languages, many are 'quite alien in spirit to the inflective type of Latin and Greek' (SL 130f). Moreover, a threefold subdivision is proposed between *'analytic'*, which 'does not combine concepts into single words at all' (e.g., Chinese) 'or does so economically' (e.g., English); *'synthetic'*, wherein 'concepts cluster more thickly' and 'words are more richly chambered' but within 'a moderate compass' (e.g., Latin); and *'polysynthetic'*, wherein 'the elaboration of the word is extreme' (e.g., Algonkin) (SL 129, 143). Sapir thus proffers a table of types wherein his original four groupings according to the two pairs 'simple/complex' and 'pure/mixed-relational' are broken down into classes, some rather elaborate: 'agglutinative–fusional–analytic' (e.g., Modern Tibetan), 'symbolic–fusional–synthetic' (e.g., Semitic), 'fusional–agglutinative–polysynthetic' (e.g., Chinook), and so on – twenty-one varieties in all (SL 142f).

3.54 This scheme is further complicated by the fact that 'languages are in a constant process of change', and their 'technical features' show 'little relative permanence' (SL 144f; cf. SL 171). 'The feeling' that 'our language is practically a fixed system' is 'fallacious' (SL 155). So 'there is no reason why a language should remain permanently true to its original form' (SL 144f). In 'the course of their development we frequently encounter a gradual change of morphological type' as well as 'changes' of 'grammatical classes' and word 'significances' (SL 144, 141). But 'languages' 'tend to preserve longest what is most fundamental in their structure' (SL 144). 'The degree of synthesis' 'seems to change most readily', 'the technique' 'far less readily', and 'conceptual type' 'persists the longest of all' (SL 145). 'Highly synthetic languages (Latin; Sanskrit) have frequently broken down into analytic forms (French; Bengali)'; 'agglutinative languages (Finnish)' have 'taken on inflective features'; and so on.

3.55 The causes of such changes are obscure (cf. 2.41f, 76). Sapir invokes 'some deep controlling impulse that dominates' the '**drift**' of 'languages' and 'linguistic features' (SL 122, 141, 144; cf. SL 150f, 161f, 167f, 172, 180f, 186, 200ff, 206, 218). 'A language changes not only gradually, but consistently', and 'moves unconsciously from one type toward another' (SL 121). Without 'gainsaying the individuality of all historical process', Sapir 'affirms that back of the face of the history are powerful drifts that move language, like other social products, to balanced patterns', 'to types' (SL 122). Yet 'why similar types should be formed, just what is the nature of the forces that make them and dissolve them – these questions are more easily asked than answered'. At present, we are 'very far from able to define' such 'fundamental form intuitions', and can only 'note their symptoms' (SL 144). 'Perhaps psychologists of the future will be able to give us the ultimate reasons' (SL 122) (cf. 3.12; 12.10).

3.56 Meanwhile, we 'must be careful not to be misled by structural features which are mere survivals of older stages, and which have no productive life and do not enter into the unconscious patterning of the language' (SL 140fn). We should be alert to 'the tendency for words that are psychologically disconnected from their etymological or formal group to preserve traces of phonetic laws' or of 'morphological processes that have lost their vitality' (SL 189). Also, 'the foreigner, who approaches a new language with a prying inquisitiveness', is 'most apt to see life in vestigial features which the native' 'feels merely as dead form' (SL 141n).

3.57 'The conception of "drift" in language' points to the problem of relating 'historical changes' to 'individual variations' (SL 154). 'What significant changes take place in language must exist, to begin with, as individual variations' (SL 155) (cf. 2.45; 3.64; 4.81). A 'new feature' 'may exist as a mere tendency in the speech of the few' until it 'becomes part and parcel of the common, accepted speech'. Due to this drift, 'language has a "slope"': 'the changes of the next few centuries are in a sense prefigured in certain obscure tendencies of the present'. 'Significant changes' 'begin' 'as individual variations' that are 'themselves random phenomena' until they acquire a 'special direction' through an 'unconscious selection on the part of the speakers'. This 'direction may be inferred' 'from the past history of the language'. For the future, though, 'our very uncertainty as to the impending details of change makes the eventual consistency of their direction all the more impressive'.

3.58 **Language change** is accordingly a major concern, since it introduces a leading parameter of **diversity** into language. Again like Saussure, Sapir likes to draw illustrations from 'gradual phonetic change', ranked as 'probably the most central problem in linguistic history' (SL 173; cf. CG 147; 2.76; 4.75). This domain supports the view that 'the drift of language is not properly concerned with changes in content', but 'with changes in formal expression' (SL 218) (cf. 11.66).

3.59 '"**Phonetic laws**" make up a large and fundamental share of the subject-matter of linguistics' (SL 173) (but cf. 2.13, 38; 3.18; 11.26f). Such 'laws' may 'participate' in a 'far-reaching' 'drift': 'not so much a movement toward a particular set of sounds as toward particular types of articulation' (SL 181). 'Phonetic changes' are none the less 'regular'; 'exceptions are more apparent than real', 'generally due to the disturbing influence of morphological groupings or to special psychological reasons which inhibit the normal progress of the phonetic drift' (SL 180). 'Phonetic laws' may be entirely 'regular' and 'sweeping', or may only 'operate under certain definable limiting conditions' (SL 178). These 'laws do not work with spontaneous automatism'; 'they are simply a formula for a consummated drift that sets in at a psychologically exposed point and gradually worms its way through the gamut' of 'analogous forms'.

3.60 We can also consider 'the general **morphological** drift of the language', as 'symptomized' by 'analogical adjustments' (SL 189). 'The general drift seizes upon those individual sound variations that help to preserve the morphological balance or to lead to the new balance that the language is striving for' (SL 186).[20] To describe this interactive process, Sapir 'suggests' that 'phonetic change is compacted of three basic strands': (1) a 'prevailingly dynamic' 'general drift in one direction'; '(2) a readjusting tendency to preserve or restore the fundamental phonetic pattern of the language; and (3) a preservative tendency which sets in when a too serious morphological unsettlement is threatened by the main drift'. Here, Sapir differs from the typical 'linguist' (including Saussure) who 'knows that phonetic change is frequently followed by morphological rearrangements' yet who 'assumes that morphology exercises little or no influence on the course of phonetic history' (SL 183) (cf. 2.54). 'A simple phonetic law' may 'colour or transform large reaches of the morphology of a language' (SL 191). 'If all phonetic changes' 'were allowed to stand', 'most languages' might 'present such irregularities of morphological contour as to lose touch with their formal ground-plan' (SL 187). However, presumably because 'phonetic pattern' and 'morphological type' 'hang together in a way we cannot at present quite understand', American linguistics did not always concur that the 'tendency to isolate phonetics and grammar as mutually irrelevant linguistic provinces is unfortunate' (SL 187, 184) (cf. 5.35; 7.46).

3.61 '**Analogy**' is a major force for 'regularizing irregularities that come in the wake of phonetic processes' (SL 189) (cf. 2.50–54). But it can also 'introduce disturbances'; indeed, 'analogical levelling' accounts for many of the 'remarkably' 'few exceptions' 'in linguistic history' (SL 189, 180; cf. SL 184) (cf. 2.51). Still, the effects work 'generally in favour of greater simplicity or regularity in a long established system of forms' (SL 189). 'A morphological feature that appears as the incidental consequence of a phonetic process may spread by analogy no less readily than old features that owe their existence to other than phonetic causes'.

3.62 As befits Sapir's mentalist orientation, he warns 'linguistic students' that 'sound change' is 'a strictly **psychological** phenomenon' (SL 183).[21] He believes 'the central unconscious regulator of the course and speed of sound changes' lies in 'the tendency to "correct" a disturbance by an elaborate chain of supplementary changes' (SL 182). 'The most important tendency in the history of speech sounds' is this 'shifting about without loss of pattern', e.g., when 'the unconscious Anglo-Saxon mind' deployed 'certain individual variations, until then automatically cancelled out', as a means for 'allowing the general phonetic drift to take its course without unsettling the morphological contours of the language' (SL 182, 185f). Or, 'phonetic changes' may 'be unconsciously encouraged in order to keep intact the psychological spaces between words and word forms' (SL 186). Or, an 'alternation' produced by 'an unconscious mechanical adjustment' might 'rise in consciousness' and become 'neatly distinct' and 'symbolic' (SL 174f).

3.63 Changes due to languages being in contact are explained as an interaction between the 'unconscious assimilation' to native 'habits' and the 'unconscious suggestive influence of foreign speech habits' (SL 197, 200). Here, too, 'as long as the main phonetic concern is the preservation of its sound pattern', a language may 'unconsciously assimilate foreign sounds that have succeeded in worming their way into the gamut of individual variations, provided' they 'are in the direction of the native drift' (SL 200). This account is plausible if we assume that each language indeed has 'innate formal tendencies' (SL 197), or its own 'genius' (cf. 3.7).

3.64 Diversity also appears at any single point in time. One parameter obtains among the **individual users** of a language. 'Two individuals of the same generation and locality, speaking precisely the same dialect and moving in the same social circles, are never absolutely at one in their speech habits' (SL 147). 'A minute investigation of the speech of each individual would reveal countless differences of detail – in choice of words, in sentence structure, in the relative frequency' of 'particular forms or combinations of words', and 'in all those features, such as speed, stress, and tone, that give life to spoken language'. But such 'individual variations are swamped in or absorbed by certain major agreements – say of pronunciation and vocabulary – which stand out very strongly when the language as a whole is contrasted' with another (SL 147f). Sapir concludes that 'something like an ideal linguistic entity dominates the speech habits of members of each group, and that the sense of unlimited freedom which each individual feels in the use of his language is held in leash by a tacitly directing norm'. 'The individual's variations' 'are silently "corrected" or cancelled by the consensus of usage'. 'All speakers' are subsumed in 'a very finely intergrading series clustered about a well-defined centre or norm'.

3.65 A second, and more problematic, parameter of diversity obtains among the **dialects** of a language. 'The explanation of primary dialectic differences is still to seek' (SL 149). 'Distinct localities' or 'social strata' need not 'naturally' produce 'dialects' (SL 149f; cf. CG 193, 210). If, as Sapir just contended, 'individual variations are being constantly levelled to the dialectic norm, why should we have dialectic variations at all?' The answer is strikingly like Saussure's: 'language is not merely spread out in space', but 'moves down time in a current of its own making' (cf. 2.43).

While 'each language' 'constantly moves away from any assignable norm, developing new features and transforming itself', 'local groups' 'drift independently' (SL 150f). 'No sooner are the old dialects ironed out' 'when a new crop of dialects arises to undo the levelling'. Sometimes, 'dialects develop into mutually unintelligible languages', and 'none but a linguistic student' 'would infer' 'a remote and common starting point' (SL 152f).[22] This inclination to explain language variety as the product of language change probably reflects Sapir's view that change is more tractable for study, a view Saussure both espoused and denied (cf. 2.42f).

3.66 From deliberations like these, Sapir concludes (here too like Saussure, CG 204) that ultimately, 'the terms dialect, language, branch, stock' 'are purely relative terms' (SL 153; cf. SL 204) (cf. 2.43; 4.74, 83; 12.59). 'A "linguistic stock"' may be revealed by 'our researches' as 'but a "dialect" of a larger group' (SL 153). 'All languages that are known to be genetically related' are judged to be 'divergent forms of a single prototype'. Indeed, Sapir's claim that 'language developed but once in the history of the race' (SL 154) suggests that all languages developed from a single one. The degree of development may produce a 'primitive' or a 'sophisticated language', a 'lowly' or a 'cultivated' speaker (SL 8, 22). Yet though 'the more abstract concepts are not nearly so plentifully represented in the language of the savage, nor is there the rich terminology and the finer definition of nuances', 'popular statements as to the poverty of expression to which primitive language are doomed are simply myths' (SL 22). 'Many "savage" languages' evince 'formal richness' and 'complexities' that 'eclipse anything known to the languages of modern civilization' (SL 124n, 22). 'When it comes to linguistic form, Plato walks with the Macedonian swineherd, Confucius with the head-hunting savage of Assam' (SL 219).

3.67 The features Sapir considers 'all but universal' (SL 65, 76) might be signs of this common origin. Elsewhere, however, he suggests that 'broadly similar morphologies must have been reached by unrelated languages, independently and frequently' (SL 122, 204). Or, 'parallels in unrelated languages' may be caused by 'borrowing', although 'fundamental features of structure' are more probably 'vestiges' of relatedness (SL 198, 205). He decides that the question of 'the single or multiple origin of speech' is not pressing, since 'such a theory constructed on "general principles" is of no real interest' 'to linguistic science' (SL 154) – just the contrary view to that held by Saussure, Pike, Hjelmslev, Chomsky, and Hartmann (cf. 2.8, 10f; 5.44; 6.10f; 7.19; 11.7, 37; 12.48, 62). 'What lies beyond the demonstrable must be left to the philosopher or the romancer' (cf. 12.16).

3.68 The final parameter of diversity treated by Sapir is a **stylistic** one. His book closes unconventionally with a disquisition on 'language and literature' – an interest shared by Pike, Firth, Halliday, van Dijk, and Hartmann, but not by Saussure, Bloomfield, Hjelmslev, or Chomsky (cf. 2.24; 4.40f; 5.56; 6.4; 8.83, 89; 9.104, 111; 10.47f, 57f; 11.99). This move befits his fondness for calling 'language' itself an 'art', e.g., 'a collective art of expression' (SL 220, 225, 231) (cf. 3.1, 3, 10).[23] 'Concealed' in each one are 'aesthetic factors – phonetic, rhythmic, symbolic, morphological – which it does not completely share with any other language' (SL 225; cf. SL 222). If the 'effects' due to 'the formal "genius"' of a 'language' or to 'the colour and texture of its matrix' 'cannot be carried over without loss or modification', we might imagine 'a work of literary art can never be translated' (SL 222). Yet 'a truly deep symbolism' 'does not depend on the verbal associations of a particular language', but 'on an intuitive basis that underlies all linguistic intuition' (SL 224).

3.69 'Insofar as style is a technical matter of the building and placing of words', however, 'the major characteristics of style' are 'inescapably' 'given by the language itself' (SL 226). 'These necessary fundamentals of style' 'point the way to those stylistic developments that most suit the natural bent of the language' – its 'phonetic groundwork', its 'morphological peculiarities', and so on. 'An artist must utilize the native aesthetic resources of his speech' (SL 225). For instance, 'the poet's rhythms can only be a more sensitive and stylized application of rhythmic tendencies that are character-istic of the daily speech of his people': 'the daily economy' or the 'unconscious dynamic habit of the language' (SL 161, 228ff). The question is then what the artist, 'deserving no special credit for felicities that are the language's own' (SL 225), can contribute.

3.70 Sapir defines 'literature' as an 'expression' of 'unusual significance', but 'does not exactly know' how to measure this (SL 221, n). 'Art is so personal an expression that we do not like to feel that it is bound to predetermined form of any sort'. 'The possibilities of individual expression are infinite' (cf. 3, 3.13; 12.43). 'Yet some limitation there must be to this freedom, some resistance of the medium'. 'In great art', despite 'the illusion of absolute freedom', 'the artist has intuitively surrendered to the inescapable tyranny of the material' and yet made the 'fullest utilization' of it. 'The material "disappears" precisely because there is nothing in the artist's conception to indicate that any other material exists' (SL 221f).[24] 'No sooner, however, does the artist transgress the law of his medium than we realize with a start that there is a medium to obey'.

3.71 'Literature' has 'two distinct kinds or levels of art': 'a generalized, non-linguistic art', and 'a specifically linguistic art' (SL 222f). 'The medium' 'intertwines' 'the latent content of language – our intuitive record of experience' – with 'the particular conformation of a given language – the specific "how" of our record of experience'. 'Artists whose spirit moves largely' 'in the generalized linguistic layer' have 'difficulty in getting themselves expressed in the rigidly set terms of their accepted idiom' (SL 224). Their 'expression is frequently strained', showing more 'greatness of their spirit than felicity of their art' (e.g., Whitman and Browning), or a 'technically "literary" art' 'too fragile for endurance' (e.g., Swinburne) (SL 224f) (cf. 8.52, 84, 8[39], 8[43]). 'The greatest – or shall we say the most satisfying – literary artists' 'subconsciously fit or trim the deeper intuition to the provincial accents of their daily speech' (SL 225) (e.g., Shakespeare).[25]

'Their personal "intuition" appears as a completed synthesis of the absolute art of intuition and the innate, specialized art of the linguistic medium'.

3.72 Sapir 'clarifies' his 'distinction' by 'comparing literature with science'. 'A scientific truth is impersonal, untinctured by the particular linguistic medium in which it finds expression' (cf. 4.22). 'The proper medium of scientific expression is therefore a generalized language that may be defined as a symbolic algebra of which all known languages are translations' (SL 223f) (cf. 2.82). 'One can adequately translate scientific' texts 'because the original scientific expression is itself a translation'. This quality matches the impression of 'art' that seems to be 'unconsciously striving for a generalized art language, a literary algebra that is related to the sum of all known languages as a perfect mathematical symbolism is related to all the reports of mathematical relations that normal speech is capable of conveying'.

3.73 If this comparison holds, Sapir might be expected to propose **algebra** as the general representation for language in linguistics, as Saussure, Hjelmslev, and Chomsky do (cf. 2.82; 6.8, 29, 51, 60; 7.41, 7^{18}; 12.15). He does 'understand why the mathematician and the symbolic logician are driven to discard the word' in favour of 'symbols which have, each of them, a rigidly unitary value' (SL 33) (cf. 3.31). Also, he puts some examples into 'formulas' for 'those who are mathematically inclined', and draws 'mathematical' analogies for relations between 'thought' and 'speech', or between 'spoken' and 'written language' (SL 132n, 25–32, 57, 15, 20) (cf. 5.40, 51f, 62; 7.48).[26] But he goes no further, presumably because he situates language closer to 'art' and 'experience' than to 'logical' 'symbols' (SL 33), whence his mistrust of 'the technical symbols of the linguistic academy' and of the 'craving' for 'formulas' (cf. 3.2, 50). Even the 'sentence' is described as an 'aesthetically satisfying' 'unit', and the word as 'a miniature bit of art' (SL 32, 35). 'Abstract form' is compared to 'the logical and aesthetic ordering of experience'; and a 'form pattern which is not filled out' is deemed 'unaesthetic' (SL 157n, 158).

3.74 In our retrospect shaped by decades of academic sobriety in linguistics, Sapir's exuberance is highly conspicuous. The range and diversity of his book has a monumental vitalism wholly unlike the abstraction and specialization we often take for granted. He was willing to turn in any direction that might reveal the 'fundamental' (SL vi, 25, 85, 93, 110, 116, 120, 144, 172, 226). He pursued the precept that 'adequate communication' depends on its 'context, that background of mutual understanding that is essential to the complete intelligibility of all speech' (SL 92). No doubt his palette of topics was too vast for any emerging science. His elaborate mentalism reached far beyond the scope of early twentieth-century psychology, and was soon to be repressed by 'physicalism' and 'mechanism' (cf. 4.8; 12.11).

3.75 All the same, Sapir's peculiar achievements continue to deserve recognition. He insisted on the equal status and interest of unfamiliar languages, notably Amerindian ones, so that the 'theoretical possibilities' would be 'abundantly illustrated from the descriptive facts of linguistic morphology' (SL 139). He explored the perilous problematics of form versus content, or thought versus expression, and made them a basis for an original, large-scale typology of languages. And he never tired of saluting the vast potential of language for developments as yet unrealized. He thus bequeathed to us the challenging conviction that any set of 'examples' will be 'far from exhausting the possibilities of linguistic structure' (SL 141).

Notes

1. Sapir's *Language* is cited as SL to distinguish it from Bloomfield's book of the same name (BL). It was Sapir's 'only full-length book for a general audience' (SL ii).
2. In practice, some of these 'relations' are not pursued very far. Sapir says 'it is easy to show that language and culture are not intrinsically associated'; and 'race' 'is supremely indifferent to the history of language and culture' (SL 213, 208; cf. CG 222f) (cf. 2.76; 3.7; 4.80). As for 'art', however, Sapir includes a chapter on 'literature' (cf. 3.3, 68–72).
3. Sapir suggests that 'the vocabulary of a language more or less faithfully reflects the culture whose purposes it serves'; but this is only 'a superficial parallelism' 'of no real interest to the linguist except in so far as the growth or borrowing of new words incidentally throws light on the formal trends of the language' (SL 219; cf. CG 225). Moreover, we should 'never make the mistake of identifying a language with its dictionary' (SL 219; but cf. 2.78). Nor is 'the actual size of a vocabulary' of 'real interest to the linguist, as all languages have the resources at their disposal for the creation of new words' (SL 124) (cf. 2.52; 6.23f).
4. This assertion leads to an opposition between 'the normal type of communication of ideas' versus 'involuntary expression of feeling' through 'instinctive cries' (SL 5). Even 'conventional interjections' 'are only superficially of an instinctive nature', rather more like 'art', and hence cannot have been the 'psychological foundations' of 'language' (SL 5ff) (cf. 2^{13}; 8.6)
5. Sapir's illustration is the fading of ' "whom" ' from common speech. But other cases still appear to him as 'grammatical blunders', 'un-English horrors', or 'insidious peculiarities' (SL 156, 166).
6. Benedetto Croce (1902, 1922) is saluted for having promulgated this 'insight' (SL v) (cf. 3.69). He is also lauded as 'one of the very few' 'contemporary writers of influence on liberal thought' 'who have gained an understanding of the fundamental significance of language' and 'pointed out its close relation to the problem of art'. Compare 3.68ff.
7. The parallel between 'silent speech' and 'normal thinking' (SL 18) enjoyed some vogue at the time (e.g., Watson 1920; Thorsen 1925), mainly to divert mentalistic conceptions over toward physicalist ones (cf. Beaugrande 1984a: 52ff). Compare 3.18, 3^{11}, 3^{31}; 4.9; 5.43; 8.22, 8^{17}; 13^{21}.
8. One change in word-forms, for instance, is said to involve 'unconscious desire' and 'unconscious hesitation' (SL 157, 163, 161).
9. Two causes are cited for this 'tendency': the 'inertia' of 'a system of forms from which all colour or life has vanished'; and 'the tendency to construct schemes of classification into which all the concepts of language must be fitted', using such absolute opposites as 'good or bad', 'black or white' (SL 98f). Sapir would mistrust the binary oppositions of later structuralism (cf. 2.70; 5.21, 49; 8.80).

10. Comparing this 'system' to a 'system' 'of symbolic atoms' (SL 56) again suggests a submerged sympathy for physicalism (cf. Note 7). Elsewhere, though, 'the laws of physics and chemistry' are declared an absurd foundation for 'explaining' 'languages' (SL 208f). Compare 12.11.

11. Like Saussure (cf. 2.83), Sapir is inconsistent in using 'mechanical concepts' (SL 161), especially to explain 'sound change' (SL 187, 174), while generally treating this aspect as irrelevant for linguistics (SL 11, 55, 62, 100, 121, 125).

12. The 'inspiratory sounds' of '"click"' languages like Hottentot are exceptions (SL 53n).

13. 'Quantitative processes like vocalic lengthening or shortening and consonantal doubling' 'may be looked upon as particular sub-types' of 'internal modification' (SL 61f).

14. 'Due to the bias that Latin grammar has given us', speakers of English 'generally think of time as a function that is appropriately expressed in a purely formal manner', even though English does not formally mark 'present' and 'future' (SL 69n; cf. SL 87).

15. An intriguing comparison is drawn: 'the radical and grammatical elements of the language, abstracted as they are from the realities of speech, respond to the conceptual world of science, abstracted as it is from the realities of experience'; 'the word, the existent unit of living speech, responds to the unit of actually apprehended experience, of history, of art' (SL 32f). For another view of science and art, see 3.72.

16. 'In Yana [of Northern California] the noun and the verb are well distinct', though they 'hold in common' some 'features' that 'draw them nearer to each other than we feel to be possible' (SL 199n). But the language has, 'strictly speaking, no other parts of speech'. 'The adjective', 'the numeral, the interrogative pronoun', and 'certain conjunctions and adverbs' are all 'verbs'.

17. In one demonstration, though, Sapir decides that 'the analysis' into 'radical' and 'derivational' 'elements' 'is practically irrelevant to a feeling for the structure of the sentence' (SL 84).

18. Sapir's distaste for 'sentimentalism', in which he himself indulges sometimes, is due to its abuse as a channel for cultural and racial chauvinism (SL 124n, 208f). Undue emphasis on 'feeling' is also rebuked (SL 39) (cf. 3.15).

19. Compare these categories with 'the still popular classification of languages into an "isolating" group, an "agglutinative" group, and an "inflective" group' (SL 123). Sapir suspects that his 'contrast of pure–relational and mixed–relational' is 'deeper, more far-reaching' than the older 'contrast', ostensibly because 'conceptual type' 'persists the longest of all' (SL 145f) (cf. 3.54).

20. For example, 'the English language' shows hardly 'one important morphological change that was not determined by the native drift', despite 'the suggestive influence of French norms' (SL 202). 'English was fast moving toward a more analytic structure long before the French influence set in' (SL 193n). Still, 'the language of a people that is looked upon as a centre of culture' is 'likely to exert an appreciable influence on other languages spoken in its vicinity' (SL 193) (cf. 4.40, 83; 8.7). 'Just five languages' had an 'overwhelming' impact of this kind: 'classical Chinese, Sanskrit, Arabic, Greek, and Latin' (SL 194). Sapir finds it 'disappointing' that the 'cultural influence of English has so far been all but negligible'. Today he would say otherwise (cf. 8.11, 13).

21. To 'think of sound change' as 'quasi-physiological' is a 'fatal error' 'many linguistic students have made' (SL 183). Compare Note 11.

22. This process of inferring relations was, as Saussure notes, 'a new and fruitful field' for linguistics in the nineteenth century, though it 'did not succeed in setting up a true science' (CG 3) (2.5). Sapir again separates the 'linguistic student' from the normal speaker (cf. 3.11; 12.49).

23. Compare the 'innate formal limitations' and the 'innate art of the language' (SL 222, 225). Sapir also uses the term 'inner form' (SL 109, 125, 197, 217), one made famous by Wilhelm von Humboldt in *Über die Verschiedenheit des menschlichen Sprachbaus* (1830–35) and covered in the chapter on Hartmann (cf. 11.18). Sapir's typology of languages also owes much to Humboldt, though without acknowledgement.

24. I would prefer to suppose, along with many theoreticians of art, that the work's main function is to foreground the otherness of its language (cf. Beaugrande 1986a, 1988a). The material disappears to the degree that the audience's schemas can incorporate it (cf. Gombrich 1960).

25. The stipulation that 'a truly great style' cannot 'seriously oppose itself to basic form patterns of the language' devalues the 'semi-Latin' of Milton and the 'Teutonic mannerism' of Carlyle (SL 227). 'It is strange how long it took the European literatures to learn that style is not an absolute', something 'to be imposed on the language from Greek and Latin models, but merely the language itself, running in its natural grooves.' Sapir's tastes are not entirely disinterested, since 'he published' 'some verse in periodicals' himself (SL ii).

26. 'The written word' is judged 'the most important of all visual speech symbolisms'; 'written language' 'is a point-to-point equivalence, to borrow a mathematic phrase, to its spoken counterpart' (SL 19f) (but cf. 12.33). 'The written forms are secondary symbols of the spoken ones – symbols of symbols – yet so close is the correspondence that they may', 'in certain types of thinking, be entirely substituted for the spoken ones'. People 'handle' 'visual symbols' like 'money', i.e., as a 'substitute for the goods and services of the fundamental auditory-motor symbols' (SL 21; cf. CG 115). Compare Note 10.

Chapter 4

Leonard Bloomfield[1]

4.1 Since the publication of Bloomfield's *Language* in 1933, according to Hockett's foreword, 'most American linguistic investigation, and a good deal of that done elsewhere, has borne the mark of Bloomfield's synthesis' (BL xiii). 'It towers above all earlier works of the sort and, to date, above all more recent ones' (BL ix). It 'is considered by many to be the most important general treatise on language ever written'. 'It drew together and unified' 'all three of the earlier traditions of language study': 'historical–comparative', 'philosophical–descriptive', and 'practical–descriptive' ('field research') (BL xiii, ixf).

4.2 Like our other theorists, Bloomfield declares his deference to language, saluting 'the strangeness, beauty, and import of human speech' (BL xv) (cf. 2.8, 32; 3.1, 3; 6.2; 12.22). 'Language plays a great part in our life', though 'because of its familiarity, we rarely observe it, taking it rather for granted, as we do breathing or walking' (BL 3) (cf. 3.1; 6.6; 11.9; 12.1). 'The effects of language are remarkable, and include much of what distinguishes man from the animals' (cf. 3.15; 7.35; 8.27; 12.12). Yet 'the study of language is only in its beginnings'.

4.3 Bloomfield also resembles our other theorists in criticizing previous approaches to language (cf. 12.4). He was intensely bent on establishing linguistics as a 'science' by dissociating it from all that fell short of his standards. His book fostered in American linguistics a spirit of confrontation not merely against rival approaches, but also against prevailing philosophy, pedagogy, language teaching, and the humanities at large (cf. 4.85ff).

4.4 Two groups are the main targets of Bloomfield's censure. One group is the '**philosophers**',[2] who indulged in 'speculations', as when they 'took it for granted that the structure of their language embodies the universal forms of human thought' or even 'of the cosmic order', and 'looked for truths about the universe in what are really nothing but formal features of one or another language' (BL 3, 5f) (cf. 12.16, 18). If they 'made grammatical observations', 'they confined these to one language and stated them in philosophic terms' (BL 5). In particular, they 'forced their description into the scheme of Latin grammar', holding Latin to be 'the logically normal form of human speech' and to 'embody universally valid canons of logic' (BL 8, 6) (cf. 2.5; 3.50; 5.24; 6.5; 8.5; 9.25; 11.20f). Bloomfield is far more impressed by early work on Sanskrit, notably because 'the Hindus' 'were excellent phoneticians' and 'worked out a systematic arrangement of grammar and lexicon' (BL 296, 11) (cf. 8.4, 54, 74; 11.20f).[3]

4.5 The other censured group is the '**grammarians**' of 'our school tradition', who followed suit by 'seeking to apply logical standards to language' (BL 6) (cf. 8.5, 17; 12.16). Their 'pseudo-grammatical doctrine' was to 'define categories of the English language as philosophical truths and in philosophical terms' (BL 500). They 'believed that the grammarian', 'fortified by his powers of reasoning, can ascertain the logical basis of language and prescribe how people ought to speak' (BL 7) (cf. 4.86; 8.4; 12.50). They thus felt free to 'ignore actual usage in favour of speculative notions' (cf. 7.4). They promulgated 'fanciful dogmas', 'doctrines', and 'rules', which 'still prevail in our schools', e.g., about ' "shall" versus "will" ' (BL 500, 496, 7f).

4.6 Bloomfield's indignation has not only social and political motives, but professional ones as well. He is annoyed that 'the knowledge' 'gained' by 'linguistics' 'has no place in our educational programme', which 'confines itself to handing on the traditional notions' (BL 3) (cf. 4.84). Despite their 'concentration on verbal discipline', 'the schools' remain 'utterly benighted in linguistic matters', as shown for instance by their 'crassest ignorance of elementary phonetics' and of 'the relation of writing to speech' (BL 499f). He also fears that authoritarian views may discourage or delude potential students of linguistics. 'The conventionally educated person discusses linguistic matters' by 'appealing to authority' or by applying 'a kind of philosophical reasoning' that 'derives, at no great distance, from the speculations of ancient and medieval philosophers' (BL 3). 'Many people have difficulty at the beginning of language study' 'in stripping off the preconceptions that are forced on us by our popular-scholastic doctrine' (BL 3f). Worse yet, 'informants' who think their own 'forms' are 'inferior' 'are ashamed to give them to the observer', who 'may thus record a language entirely unrelated to the one he is looking for' (BL 497) (cf. 4.19, 86; 12.49).

4.7 Bloomfield now pleads for a linguistics that genuinely qualifies as a '**science**', and, to drive his point home (he favours teaching by 'constant repetition', 4.86), he refers to it as such twenty-three times, especially when obstacles arise (cf. 4.15).[4] It is time to conduct 'careful and comprehensive observation', and to 'replace speculation with scientific induction', which provides 'the only useful generalizations about language' (BL 3, 16, 20) (cf. 4.67, 76; 5[28]; 6.16f; 7.6f; 11.8, 16, 95f; 12.45). At times, his faith in science seems extravagant: 'science progresses cumulatively and with acceleration'; 'as we preserve more and more records of more and more speech-reactions of highly gifted and highly specialized individuals, we approach, as an ideal limit, a condition where all the events in the universe, past, present, and future, are reduced (in a symbolic form to which any reader may react) to the dimensions of a large library' (BL 40) (cf. Weiss 1925). We may feel reminded here that it was Bloomfield (1949) who contributed the 'linguistics' portion of the positivist *Encylopedia of Unified Science*, a favourite collection for Pike as well (cf. 5[1]).

4.8 Bloomfield's ideal model is clear: 'the methods of linguistics, in spite of their modest scope, resemble those of a natural science, the domain in which science has been the most successful' (BL 509) (cf. 2.13; 4.18; 7.11; 9.112; 11.14, 49, 99; 12.11). To support this assessment, he contrasts 'two theories about human conduct, including speech' (BL 32). 'The **mentalist** theory, which is by far the older and still prevails both in the popular view and among men of science, supposes that the variability of human conduct is due to the interference of some non-physical' (later termed 'metaphysical') 'factor, a *spirit* or *will* or *mind*' that 'does not follow the patterns of succession (cause-and-effect sequences) of the material world' (BL 32f, 508). 'The **materialistic** or, better, **mechanistic** theory supposes that the variability of human conduct, including speech, is due only to the fact that the human body is a very complex system' (BL 33). Here, 'human actions' are construed to be 'part of cause-and-effect sequences exactly like those we may observe, say, in the study of physics and chemistry' (cf. 2.82; 3[10]; 4.10, 71; 5.28, 66; 7.16, 33, 36; 8.49; 12.11). Though he disavows a 'dependence' on 'any one psychological doctrine' because 'the findings of the linguist' should not be 'distorted by any prepossessions about **psychology**', Bloomfield ordains that 'mechanism is the necessary form of scientific discourse' (BL xv, 32). 'In all sciences like linguistics, which observe some specific type of human activity, the worker must proceed exactly as if he held the materialist view' (BL 38) (cf. 8.22, 24, 30, 8[21]). This insistence on 'observation' lands him in difficulties when he realizes the data he addresses either cannot be observed or will become explosively large if they are (cf. 4.17ff, 26, 29, 32, 50, 58, 61, 77f, 80; 5.80f; 12.45).

4.9 In such an ambience, ' "mental images", "feelings", "thoughts", "concepts" ', ' "ideas" ', or ' "volitions" ' 'are merely popular names for various bodily movements' (BL 142). These 'movements can be roughly divided into three types: (1) large-scale processes, which are much the same in different people and, having some social importance, are represented by conventional speech-forms, such as "I'm hungry" '; '(2) obscure and highly variable small-scale muscular contractions and glandular secretions, which differ from person to person' and therefore are not 'represented'; and '(3) soundless movements of the vocal organs, taking the place of speech movements' '("thinking")' (BL 142f). Significantly, 'thinking' is equated here with 'talking to oneself' and 'suppressing the sound-producing movements' in favour of 'inaudible ones' (BL 28) (cf. 3.10, 3[7]; 5.43; 8[17]).

4.10 Along similar lines, Bloomfield borrows from 'the sciences of **physiology** and **physics**' to suggest a model of how 'the gap between the bodies of the speaker and the hearer – the discontinuity of the two nervous systems – is bridged by the sound waves' (BL 25f, i.r.). He divides 'the speech-event' into 'three parts'. 'The speaker moves her vocal cords' to 'force the air into the form of sound waves'. These 'sound waves' 'set the surrounding air into a similar wave motion'. Finally, 'these sound waves' 'strike' the hearer's 'ear-drums and set them vibrating, with an effect' on the hearer's 'nerves'; 'this hearing acts as a stimulus'. This account makes 'speech' a set of '*substitute* stimuli' alongside '*practical* stimuli' 'such as hunger'. 'The mechanisms' for 'responding' to 'speech-sounds' 'are a phase of our general equipment for responding to stimuli' (BL 32). The lesson is: 'language enables one person to make a reaction when another person has the stimulus' (BL 24, i.r.). Bloomfield concludes: '*the division of labour, and with it, the whole working of human society, is due to language*' (cf. 3.1; 8.28; 9.7, 14; 12.22).

4.11 For demonstration, Bloomfield proposes to 'begin by observing an act of speech-utterance under very simple circumstances' (BL 22). He doesn't really observe anything, but fabricates a story of 'Jack and Jill walking down a lane'. 'Jill is hungry', 'sees an apple', and 'makes a noise with her larynx, tongue, and lips'. 'Jack vaults the fence, climbs the tree, takes the apple', and 'brings it to Jill', who 'eats' it. 'The act of speech' is thus shown between two sets of 'real or practical events' (BL 26f). 'The speech-event', 'worthless in itself', is 'a means to great ends' (i.r.). 'The normal human being is interested only in stimulus and response; though he uses speech and thrives by it, he pays no attention to it', because it is 'only a way of getting one's fellow-men to help'.[5]

4.12 Response and habit also figure in Bloomfield's account of language acquisition (cf. 7.30; 8.9, 21ff). Due to 'an inherited trait' and 'under various stimuli, the child utters and repeats vocal sounds' (BL 29). 'This results in a habit: whenever a similar sound strikes his ear', he makes 'mouth-movements' to 'imitate' it (BL 30). Since 'the mother' 'uses her words when the appropriate stimulus is present', 'the child forms a new habit' of saying the word for the object 'in sight'. Through 'further habits', 'the child' 'embarks upon *abstract* or *displaced* speech: he names a thing even when' it 'is not present'. This scheme requires no creativity: Bloomfield denies that 'children ever invent a word' (cf. 3³). Moreover, 'to the end of his life, the speaker keeps doing the very things which make up infantile language-learning' (BL 46).[6]

4.13 Such a mechanistic approach might foster a simple view of language, but Bloomfield tends in the opposite direction. 'The human body' and 'the mechanism which governs speech' are so 'complex' that 'we usually cannot predict whether' 'a speaker' 'will speak or what he will say' (BL 32f). 'The possibilities are almost infinite' (cf. 3.3; 5.25, 28; 8.42), and 'the chain of consequences' is 'very complicated'. Therefore, 'we do not understand the mechanism which makes people say certain things in certain situations' and 'makes them respond appropriately' (BL 31f). 'We could foretell a person's actions only if we knew the exact structures of his body at the moment', or 'the exact make-up of his organism at some early stage – say at birth or before – and then had a record of every change' and 'every stimulus that had ever affected' it (BL 33). We would also have to note the effects of 'private habits left over from the vicissitudes of education and other experience' (BL 143). Hence, 'the occurrence of speech and the practical events before and after it depend upon the entire life-history of the speaker and the hearer' (BL 23) (cf. 5.28).

4.14 Predictably, Bloomfield 'defines the **meaning** of a linguistic form' not as a 'mental event' but as 'the situation in which the speaker utters it and the response which it calls forth in the hearer' (BL 142, 139f; cf. BL 74, 143f, 151, 158). Since 'everyone' 'acts indifferently as a speaker and a hearer', the 'situation' and the 'response are closely co-ordinated' (BL 139). Still, because 'the speaker's situation' 'usually presents a simpler aspect', we can be content to 'discuss and define meanings in terms of a speaker's stimulus'. Once again, however, Bloomfield's relentless reasoning leads to a projection that is far from simple: 'the study of speakers' situations and hearers' responses' 'is equivalent to the sum total of all human knowledge' (BL 74). 'The situations which prompt people to utter speech include every object and happening in their universe' (BL 139) (cf. 5.80; 12.45). 'Almost anything in the whole world' may be involved, plus 'the momentary state of the nervous system' (BL 158). So 'to give a scientifically accurate definition of meaning for every form in the language, we should have to have a scientifically accurate knowledge of everything in the speaker's world' – far beyond 'the actual extent of human knowledge' (BL 139). Bloomfield apparently overlooks the empirical significance of the fact that ordinary speakers handle meaning with fairly modest stores of knowledge (cf. 11.60).

4.15 Bloomfield contends that 'the meaning of any given speech utterance' could be 'registered' only 'if we had an accurate knowledge of every speaker's situation and of every hearer's response', so the linguist would have to be 'omniscient' (BL 74). This argument spearheads the insistent warnings about the elusiveness of meaning – repeated twenty times in the book – with the lesson that 'meaning cannot be analysed within the scope of our science' (BL 161; cf. BL 93, 162, 167, 266, 268). Only 'if some science' 'other than linguistics' 'furnished us with definitions of the meanings' could 'the meaning of the utterance be fully analysed and defined' (BL 77, 168; cf. BL 140, 145). Meanwhile, 'the statement of meanings' is 'the weak point in language study, and will remain so until human knowledge advances far beyond its present state' (BL 140).

4.16 Bloomfield gives a further reason why 'the practical situations that make up the meaning of a speech-form are not strictly definable': 'since every practical situation is in reality unprecedented', 'every utterance of a speech-form' by 'a good speaker'[7] 'involves a minute semantic innovation' (BL 407, 443) (cf. 8.83; 12.39f). 'Almost any utterance of a form is prompted by a novel situation, and the degree of novelty is not subject to precise measurement' (BL 435). Moreover, 'every person uses speech-forms in a unique way' (BL 75).

4.17 This line of reasoning seems convincing enough, but creates severe problems for linguistic theorizing and entrains Bloomfield in contradictions. When he argues against performing 'observations' 'in the mass' or 'resorting to statistics', his reasoning is reversed. 'The linguist is in a fortunate position: in no other respect are the activities of a group as rigidly standardized as in the forms of language' (BL 37). 'Language is the simplest and most fundamental of our social' 'activities' (BL 38). 'Every speaker's language' 'is a composite of what he has heard other people say', and 'a complex of habits resulting from repeated situations in early life' (BL 42, 37, 32) (cf. 4.12; 8.21ff, 25, 53, 69). 'Large groups of people make up all their utterances out of the same stock of lexical forms and grammatical constructions' (BL 37). Moreover, to uphold the Saussurian notion of system, Bloomfield 'assumes that each linguistic form has a constant and definite meaning, different from the meaning of any other linguistic form in the same language' (BL 158) (cf. 2.26ff; 4.23, 26, 50). How such claims could be reconciled with universal innovation is nowhere explained.

4.18 Another perplexity is how '**observation**', for Bloomfield the very foundation of 'mechanism' and of the 'natural sciences' he says linguistics 'resembles' (cf. 4.8f), could proceed on the 'physiological' basis he envisions (cf. 4.8, 10f, 28f, 32, 50, 58, 61, 77f, 80; 5.28; 6.7, 12, 54; 7.71; 8.19f, 22). 'Mental processes or internal bodily processes of other people are known' 'only from speech-utterances and other observable actions' (BL 143). 'The working of the nervous system' is capable of 'delicate and variable adjustment', and 'is not accessible to observation from without', not even by one's own 'sense-organs' (BL 33f) (cf. 8.21). Also, 'the fluctuating and contradictory results of the search' for ' "speech centres" ' indicate that 'the points of the cortex are surely not correlated with specific socially significant features of speech, such as words or syntax' (BL 36) (cf. 7.31, 7[43]; 8[17]). And 'abnormal conditions in which speech is disturbed' – as in 'stuttering' or 'aphasia' – 'seem to reflect general maladjustments or lesions and to throw no light on the particular mechanisms of language' (BL 34f) (but cf. 8[20]; 9.1).

4.19 Denied such recourses, Bloomfield develops rather abstruse notions of 'observation'. At one point, he says that 'the speaker can observe better than anyone else' 'the processes' 'represented by conventional speech forms' (BL 143). But not even 'language enables a person to observe' 'the workings of his own nervous system' (BL 34). Besides, 'the normal speaker, who is not a linguist, does not describe his speech-habits, and if we are foolish enough to ask him, fails utterly to make a correct formulation' (BL 406) (cf. 4.54, 12.49). Nor can we trust 'educated persons, who have had training in school grammar' and the 'philosophical tradition' (cf. 4.4ff, 86; 12.16). 'The speaker, short of a specialized training', is incapable of 'describing his speech-habits' (BL 406). So 'all' 'statements in linguistics describe the action of the speaker' but 'do not imply that the speaker himself could give a similar description' (cf. 4.48; 12.49). Also ruled out are 'appeals' to 'common sense or to the structure of some other language or to psychological theory' (BL 38) (cf. 8.28; 9.7; 12.10f).

4.20 In effect, Bloomfield's scientific ambitions mix pessimism with optimism. The dilemmas of complexity and variation in human behaviour and communication are said to constitute 'an almost insuperable hindrance' (BL 407) so that he can justify a strategic withdrawal. Indeterminate and mutable phenomena, he argues, would resist or compromise a scientific analysis (but cf. 12.59). So he proposes to limit the scope of linguistics until such time as the sciences can fully determine meanings and hand them over in rigorously compiled forms. Meanwhile, we can 'act as though science had progressed far enough to identify all the situations and responses that make up the meaning of speech-forms' (BL 77).

4.21 In Bloomfield's eyes, the 'ideal use of language' is in '**mathematics**', 'where the denotations are very precise' (BL 29, 146) (cf. 2.82; 3.73; 5.86; 8.31; 11.33ff; 12.15). 'Mathematics' is a 'specially accurate form of speech', indeed, 'the best that language can do'; 'whole series of forms', 'in the way of selection, inclusion, exclusion, or numbering, elicit very uniform responses from different persons' (BL 147, 512). 'The use of numbers' is 'speech activity at its best' and 'the simplest and clearest case of the usefulness of talking to oneself' – the latter being, as we saw, Bloomfield's designation for 'thinking' (BL 29, 512) (cf. 4.9). His reverence for 'mathematics' jars somewhat, though, with his attack on 'grammarians' for using 'logic' (cf. 4.4f; 12.17).

4.22 Less ideal, but still a shining example, are '**scientific** terms', whose 'meanings' Bloomfield deems 'nearly free of connotative factors' (BL 152; cf. SL 32f, 223f) (cf. 3.72). He cites the 'terms of chemistry, mineralogy', 'botany', and 'zoology', and contemplates getting 'practical help' from a 'zoologist's definition' of 'meanings' (BL 139, 162). 'Although the linguist cannot define meanings, but must appeal for this to the students of other sciences', yet 'having obtained definitions for some forms, he can define the meanings of other forms in terms of these first ones' (BL 145f). 'Certain meanings, once they are defined, can be recognized as recurring in whole series of forms' (BL 147). This effect is 'plain' in 'mathematics', but 'appears also in many ordinary speech-forms' (BL 146). Still, Bloomfield admits that 'meaning' 'includes many things that have not been mastered by science'; and that 'the meanings of language do not agree' with 'scientific (that is, universally recognized and accurate) classification', witness 'the colour spectrum' (BL 75, 139f, 174, 280) (cf. 5.68; 6.54; 7.31, 71; 11.60). If nothing but the 'business-like denotations' of 'scientific discourse' were allowed, 'a great many forms in almost every language' would 'disappear' (BL 387). And 'mathematics' too retains a 'verbal character' (BL 507).

4.23 Alternatively, 'since we have no way of defining most meanings and of demonstrating their constancy, we have to take the specific and stable character of language as a presupposition of linguistic study, just as we presuppose it in our everyday dealings' (BL 144). 'We may state this presupposition as the *fundamental assumption of linguistics':* 'in certain communities', 'some speech-utterances are alike as to form and meaning'. This 'assumption' is claimed to 'imply that each linguistic form has a constant and specific meaning' (BL 145) (cf. 2.26; 4.17, 26, 50; 12.54). 'If the forms' are 'different, we suppose that their meanings are also different'. Bloomfield thus has to infer that 'there are no actual synonyms', but does admit 'homonyms', adding: 'our basic assumption is true only within limits, even though its general truth is presupposed not only in linguistic study, but by all our actual use of language'. Yet to argue that 'some' sameness lends 'each form' a 'constant meaning' is premature and collides with the thesis of continual innovation (cf. 4.16).

4.24 Consider 'the ordinary tie-up of phonetic form with dictionary meaning' (BL 148). 'Dictionary meanings' 'show instability' by having numerous 'variants', which Bloomfield places in two main classes: '*normal* (or *central*)' 'meanings' versus '*marginal (metaphoric or transferred)*'[8] 'meanings' (later also called '*deviant* meanings'); our 'assurance' and 'agreement' about which is which come from our knowledge of 'ideal situations' (BL 148f, 151, 431). 'We understand a form (that is, respond to it) in the central meaning unless some feature of the practical situation forces us to look to a transferred meaning' (BL 149, 431) (cf. 5.66). This link to the situation aids Bloomfield's stipulation that 'when the linguist tries to state meanings, he safely ignores displaced speech' (in the sense of 4.12), 'but does his best to register all cases of transferred meaning'. 'The practical situation' is also the guide for '*narrowed* meanings' (e.g., '"car"' for '"streetcar"') and '*widened* meanings' (e.g., '"fowl"' for 'any bird') (BL 151). 'Deviant meanings' are described as not 'natural' or 'inevitable', but specific to particular 'cultural traditions' (BL 150f); though I suspect *all* meaning arises from 'cultural traditions' (cf. 3.1; 9.6ff, 18; 10.8, 30, 56, 66).

4.25 Another 'way in which meanings show instability is the presence of supplementary values we call *connotations*' (BL 151) (cf. 4.72, 82; 6.52ff; 9.77; 11.19, 31). If 'the meaning of a form for any one speaker is nothing more than a result of the situations in which he had heard this form', Bloomfield must surmise that connotations come from 'hearing it under very unusual circumstances' (BL 151f) (cf. 4.82). He lists 'social standing', 'local provenience', and 'trade or craft'; connotative forms might be 'technical', 'learned', 'foreign', 'slang', 'improper', 'obscene', 'ominous', 'animated', 'infantile', or 'symbolic' (i.e., sound symbolism in words like '"snip-snap"') (BL 152–56) (cf. 8[37]). He imagines that 'the chief use of our dictionaries' is to 'combat such personal deviations', but concedes: 'the varieties of connotation are countless and indefinable' and 'cannot be clearly distinguished from denotative meaning' (BL 152, 155).

4.26 Despite all the problems he sees with meaning, Bloomfield declares that 'to study language' is 'to study' the 'coordination of sounds with meanings' (BL 27). 'A phonetic form which has a meaning is a *linguistic form*' (BL 138).[9] Here, too, he stipulates that 'in human speech, different sounds have different meanings' (BL 27) (cf. 4.17, 23, 50). On an 'ideal plane', 'linguistics' 'would consist of two main investigations: **phonetics**, in which we studied the speech-event without reference to its meaning'; and '**semantics**, in which we studied the relation' of the event to 'the features of meaning' (BL 74). In practice, this scheme won't work for two reasons. One reason we have already encountered (4.14f): 'our knowledge of the world' 'is so imperfect that we can rarely make accurate statements about the meaning of a speech-form'. The other reason is that 'purely phonetic observation' cannot 'recognize' the difference between distinctive and non-distinctive features of a language'; we can do that 'only when we know the meaning'. To escape this dilemma, Bloomfield counsels 'trusting to our everyday knowledge to tell us whether speech-forms are "the same" or "different"' (cf. 4.31; 5.14, 61, 65; 9.27).

4.27 Predictably, Bloomfield refers the issue to the 'distinctive' 'features which are common to all the situations that call forth the utterance of the linguistic form' (BL 141; cf. BL 74) (cf. 4.14). 'Hearing several utterances of some one linguistic form', 'we assume' that 'the situations of the several speakers contain some common features' (BL 158). 'The speech-sound is merely a means which enables us to respond to situations' 'more accurately' (BL 74) (cf. 4.11). Though the stimulus-response model is essentially causal (witness the Jack and Jill story, 4.11; cf. 5.15), Bloomfield follows the Saussurian idea that 'the connection between linguistic forms and their meanings is wholly **arbitrary**' and again illustrates it with words for the same thing ("horse") in different languages (BL 145, 274f) (cf. 2.28ff; 3.3; 9.13, 36; 10.86). Each 'combination' of 'signalling-units is *arbitrarily* assigned to some feature of the practical world' (a claim from which 'graphic symbols' are later excluded, however) (BL 162, 500). And he agrees with Saussure that 'form classes' seem less 'arbitrary' when 'languages' identify them by 'markers, e.g., particles in Tagalog', and grumbles about the 'arbitrary' 'form-classes' in languages that do not, like English (BL 270f, 165, 269, 280) (cf. 4.49; 12.27, 54).

4.28 'The phase of language study' in which 'we pay no attention to meaning' is called '**experimental** or **laboratory phonetics**' (BL 75). 'The phonetician can study either the sound-producing movements of the speaker in **physiological phonetics** or the resulting sound waves' in '**acoustic phonetics**; we have as yet', Bloomfield adds without detectable irony, 'no means for studying the action of the hearer's ear-drum'. Such devices as the 'mechanical record', the 'laryngoscope', and the 'kymograph' can be used (BL 85, 75f).[10] This approach, however, 'reveals only the gross acoustic features'; and 'identical acoustic effects' may be 'produced' by 'very different actions of the vocal organs' (BL 137, 108).

4.29 'In general', 'observations of the "basis of articulation" are bound to be vague', 'hazy, and inaccurate; we must wait for laboratory phonetics to give us precise, trustworthy statements' (BL 127f). Yet 'even a perfected knowledge of acoustics will not, by itself, give us the phonetic structure of a language' (BL 128) (cf. 2.68; 3.17; 4.29; 6.7). Viewed 'without regard to their use in communication', 'speech-sounds are infinitely complex and infinitely varied' (BL 76) (cf. 3.19). 'The phonetician finds that no two utterances are exactly alike'. 'The importance of a phoneme' therefore 'lies not in the actual configuration of its sound-waves, but merely in the difference' compared with 'all other phonemes of the same language' (BL 128) (cf. 2.69f; 4.33; 5^{12}; 11.89; 12.26). 'Each phoneme' must be 'a distinct unit', 'unmistakably different from all the others'; the rest of its 'acoustic character is irrelevant' (BL 128, 137).

4.30 Accordingly, Bloomfield decides that 'only the phonemes of a language are relevant to its structure' (BL 129) (cf. 2.69; 5.42f; 6.43; 8^{35}; 11.80; 12.26). 'Gross' or 'acoustic features' should not be 'confused' with 'distinctive' or 'phonemic features' (BL 77, 84) (cf. 3.20; 4.79; 5.42f). 'The study of *significant* speech-sounds is **phonology** or **practical phonetics**'[11]; both 'presuppose a knowledge of meanings' (BL 78, 137f). For Bloomfield, 'the description of a language begins with phonology' (BL 138) (cf. 2.17, 67, 70f; 3.18, 58f; 5.42, 44, 51; 7.46; 8.66f; 11.80, 82; 12.27). Here, 'the practical phonetician frankly accepts his everyday recognition of phonemic units' (BL 137) (cf. 4.26).

4.31 Economy is decisive: because 'a workable system of signals, such as a language, can contain only a small number of signalling units, whereas the things signalled about', i.e., 'the entire content of the practical world, may be infinitely varied' (cf. 3.3; 4.14ff; 5.25, 28; 8.42), 'linguistic study must always start from phonetic form and not from the meaning' (BL 162). Anyway, the use of meaning Bloomfield advocates is quite minimal: to identify 'phonemic distinctions' by telling 'which utterances are alike in meaning, and which ones are different' (BL 93, 128) (cf. 4.26). Some circularity may be entailed here in view of the theses that 'each linguistic form has a constant and definite meaning, different from the meaning of any other linguistic form in the same language'; and that 'if the forms' are 'different', 'their meanings are also different' (cf. 4.17, 23; 12.54). Such theses suggest that we need merely establish a difference in form, and can then take the difference in meaning for granted.

4.32 If the scheme of units 'lies entirely in the habits of speakers', its description entails a 'danger for linguistic work' (BL 77, 84). As a listener, 'the phonetician's equipment is personal and accidental'; he is trained to 'hear those acoustic features which are discriminated in the languages he has observed' (BL 84). Confronting 'a strange language', 'he has no way of knowing' which 'features are significant' (BL 93). So 'his first attempts at recording contain irrelevant distinctions' and omit 'essential ones'. Even 'the "exact" freehand notations of phonetic experts' might 'tell us little or nothing about the structure of a language' (BL 128) (cf. 2.69; 8.75). Such admissions point toward the central dilemma of linguists: only to the extent that they also *understand* the language can they make worthwhile 'observations' of it; and they must participate in creating the data (cf. 1.8f; 2.9; 12.1). Bloomfield may have considered this problem temporary until some future super-science explains all meanings exactly (cf. 4.21f), and 'refined physiological observation' becomes able to corroborate 'descriptions' 'made in terms of a speaker's movements' (BL 127). Meanwhile, 'the analysis and recording of languages will remain an art or practical skill' of 'little scientific value' (BL 93, 127, 137). 'The extent of observation is haphazard, its accuracy doubtful, and the terms in which it is reported are vague' (BL 127).

4.33 The linguist should proceed by 'making up a list or table of the phonemes of a language' (BL 90, 129). Bloomfield divides them into *'primary* phonemes', the basic stock, and *'secondary* phonemes', appearing 'only in combinations' – such as 'stress' and 'pitch' (BL 90ff). The phonemes are discovered by 'experimenting', namely by 'altering any one' of the 'parts of the word' (BL 78). Each 'replaceable part' must constitute a 'phoneme', i.e., 'a minimum unit of distinctive sound-feature' (BL 79, i.r.). For example, '"pin"' is contrasted with sets like '"sin"/"tin"/"fin"', '"pen"/ "pan"/"pun"' and '"pig"/"pill"/"pit"', to reveal exactly 'three phonemes' (BL 78f). Such contrasts impose 'a limit to the variability': 'each phoneme' is 'kept distinct from all other phonemes' (BL 81) (cf. 4.27, 29f). Thus, 'we speak the vowel of a word like "pen" in a great many ways, but not in any way that belongs to the vowel of "pin"' (an awkward example, since in the south-eastern US, the two words are homophones for many speakers).

4.34 Like Firth, Bloomfield says 'the throat and mouth' 'are not, in a physiological sense, "organs of speech"', 'for they serve biologically earlier uses' like 'breathing and eating', but derives his terms for phonemes from 'the shape of the oral cavity' and 'the movements of the tongue and lips' (BL 36, 93, 87) (8.6; but cf. 2.70; 3.11, 21; 12.26). The division between 'voiced and unvoiced speech-sounds' is aligned with one between 'musical sounds' and 'noises' (BL 94f, 98). 'The typical actions of the vocal organs' may be subjected to various 'modifications', affecting 'length of time', 'loudness', and 'musical pitch' (BL 109, 114) (as we just saw, creating 'secondary phonemes'). Also important is 'the manner in which the vocal organs pass' from 'inactivity' to 'the formation of a phoneme, or from the formation of one phoneme to that of the next' (BL 118).

4.35 Finally, Bloomfield proposes two more ways to treat phonemes. One is to 'count out the relative frequencies' (BL 136). The other is to 'describe the phonetic structure of a language' by 'stating' which 'phonemes appear in the three possible positions' inside the 'syllable': 'initial', 'medial', or 'final' (BL 131, i.r.). He devises an elaborate listing for English of what 'may be followed by' what, or 'occurs only before' it or 'never comes after' it', and so on (BL 131ff). With those criteria, 'we can easily show that no two' phonemes 'play exactly the same part' 'in the language' (BL 130, 134).

4.36 Bloomfield goes so far as to suggest that a 'language can be replaced' 'by any system of sharply distinct signals' (BL 128). **Gestures** might be an instance, but (like Sapir, cf. 3.10), he views them as a mere 'derivative of language' (BL 144).[12] 'Gesture accompanies all speech' and 'to a large extent it is governed by social convention' (BL 39). But 'all complicated or not immediately intelligible gestures are based on the conventions of ordinary speech' and have 'lost all traces of independent character'. And 'vocal gestures serve an inferior type of communication' (BL 147).

4.37   The strong focus on speech sounds puts '**writing**' too in the position of a 'mere derivative', arisen from 'gestures' of 'marking and drawing' (BL 144, 40) (cf. 4.44). Bloomfield's deprecation is much like Saussure's: 'writing is not language, but merely a way of recording language by means of visible marks' (BL 21) (cf. 2.21f; 6.50; 8.72–75; 9.42f; 11.83; 12.33). 'For the linguist, writing is merely an external device, like the use of a phonograph' (BL 282). We do not 'need to know something about' 'writing' 'in order to study' 'language'. Several arguments are deployed to marginalize writing, but Bloomfield repeatedly stumbles into inconsistencies or difficulties – just what we noticed with Saussure (cf. 2.21–24).

4.38   One argument is that 'the conventions of writing are a poor guide' for 'representing phonemes', ostensibly because 'alphabetic writing does not carry out' 'the principle of a symbol for each phoneme', though 'a few languages' are commended as exceptions: Spanish, Bohemian (i.e., Czech), Polish, and Finnish (BL 79, 85f, 89, 501) (cf. 2.22; 3.54; 6.50; 8.71). 'Philosophers' and 'amateurs' are chided for 'confusing' 'the sounds of speech', the 'phonemes', with the 'printed letters' of 'the alphabet' (BL 8, 137). But in another passage, 'alphabetic writing' is judged to work 'sufficiently well for practical purposes', and its 'help' is instrumental in 'listing' 'phonemes' (BL 128, 90), a view shared by Sapir (cf. 3.19) and Firth (cf. 8.71). Bloomfield suggests 'listing' 'phonemes' in 'alphabetical order' and does so (BL 162, 81), which by his own argument ought to be a category mistake. In language use, at least, he sees the influence going the other way: 'the writer utters the speech-form before or during the act of writing and the hearer utters it in the act of reading' (BL 285).[13] He seems annoyed at the 'alterations' inflicted on speech by 'orthography', and counsels us, on 'aesthetic grounds', to 'eliminate' 'ugly spelling-pronunciations' (BL 501) (cf. 2.21; 8.75).

4.39   In any event, Bloomfield avers that 'the effect of writing upon the forms and development of speech is very slight' (BL 13). 'In principle, a language is the same', whether 'written' or not (BL 282; cf. BL 501). And 'the conventions of writing develop independently of actual speech' (BL 486). Yet he also avers that 'the written record exerts a tremendous effect upon the standard language', at least 'in syntax and vocabulary' (BL 486). 'In German', in fact, 'the spoken standard' is 'largely derived from the written' (BL 487). A lesser contradiction appears when the 'conservatism' of 'writing' is claimed, and then this very claim is termed 'superficial' (BL 292, 488) (cf. 4.44).

4.40   Bloomfield's dim view of elitism in language (cf. 4.5, 87) is another factor. Because 'until the days of printing, literacy was confined to a very few people', 'writing' is suspected of being 'the property of a chosen few' and hence a tool for 'the discrimination of elegant or "correct" speech' (BL 13, 22). The 'native speakers' of 'the standard forms' are those 'born into homes of privilege' (BL 48). 'All our writing' 'is based on the standard forms' (BL 48) and on the 'literary standard' in particular (BL 48, 52). Yet how 'educational authorities and teachers' can enforce 'standard forms' is unclear if 'the schoolteacher, coming usually from a humbler class', is 'unfamiliar with the upper-class style' (BL 500, 487). Another stumbling block is Bloomfield's unqualified praise for the work of the 'Hindu grammarians' (cf. 4.4), who described only 'the upper-caste' 'official and literary language', a patently 'artificial medium for writing on learned' 'topics' (BL 11, 63).

4.41 Still, Bloomfield shows far less concern for literature than did Sapir (cf. 3.68–71). He sees it 'consisting of beautiful or otherwise noticeable utterances', in contrast to 'the language of all persons alike', which is the concern of 'the linguist' (BL 21f). His brittle conjecture that 'a beautiful poem' 'may make the hearer more sensitive to later stimuli' includes literature among the 'linguistic interaction' for 'refining and intensifying' 'human response' and promoting 'education or culture' (BL 41). Also, 'poetic metaphor' is depicted as 'an outgrowth of the transferred uses of ordinary speech'; 'language' is not ' "a book of faded metaphors" ', but 'poetry' is a 'blazoned book of language' (BL 443).

4.42 Another argument against writing is that 'all languages were spoken through nearly all of their history by people who did not read or write' (BL 21). 'To most of the languages' 'spoken today', 'writing' has been applied 'recently or not at all'. Yet if, as Bloomfield claims, 'writing and printing' are instrumental for 'the analysis of linguistic forms into words' and if 'words are the linguistic units that are first symbolized in writing' (BL 178, 285), the implication might be that unwritten languages lack the notion of the word, which seems implausible.[14]

4.43 Still another argument is that 'written records' are 'misleading', giving 'an imperfect and often distorted picture of past speech' and 'telling us little or nothing' about the issues of concern to the linguist (BL 481, 293, 69, 486). The use of such records is 'a handicap'; 'we should always prefer to have the audible word' (BL 21). Besides, they 'acquaint us with only an infinitesimal part of the speech-forms of the past' (BL 60, 441) (though I don't see how we can determine what proportion of speech-forms were not written down). Elsewhere, however, Bloomfield says that 'written records give direct information about the speech-habits of the past'; and we get such 'information' 'largely' from them (BL 282, 21). Also, his survey of 'languages of the world' (BL 57–73) continually refers us to 'written records', 'manuscripts', and 'inscriptions'.

4.44 So 'writing' needs to be 'studied' at least in regard to issues of 'history' (BL 21). Bloomfield starts from the idea of 'language' being 'our way of communicating the kind of things that do not lend themselves to drawing'; if meaning is defined as the speaker's situation (cf. 4.14), this idea implies that 'most situations contain features that do not lend themselves to picturing' (BL 284f). Although we 'can only guess at the steps' that came later, 'the origin' of 'systems of writing' was in 'conventional but realistic pictures, and many of them actually denoted the name of the object which they represented' (BL 283, 285). This 'resemblance' assumed 'secondary importance' as people developed the 'habit' of 'responding' to 'a uniform mark or set of marks' (BL 284). Then came 'the device of representing unpicturable words by phonetically similar picturable words' (BL 287). 'The symbols in this way' came to stand 'not for linguistic forms, but for phonetic forms'.[15] The 'syllabary' had a 'small number of symbols, each representative of some one syllable' (BL 288). Finally, 'alphabetic writing' used 'one symbol for each phoneme', though some 'actual systems' were 'inadequate' because of the 'conservatism of the people who write' like 'their predecessors' after 'the speech-forms have undergone linguistic change' (BL 291f).

4.45 In sum, writing is admitted as a domain for gathering evidence, but debarred from the theoretical conception, which rests on the more auspicious base of the system of sound-units (cf. 12.33). It's reassuring to envision 'every language consisting of a number of signals, linguistic forms', each of these being 'a fixed combination of signalling units, the phonemes' (BL 158). Bloomfield goes on to draw up a more elaborate taxonomy for 'the meaningful features of linguistic signalling' (BL 264) (Table 4.1).

TABLE 4.1

Unit	Lexical	Grammatical
1. Linguistic form	Lexical form	Grammatical form
Meaning: Linguistic meaning	Lexical meaning	Grammatical meaning
2. Phememe	Phoneme	Taxeme
Meaning: [None]	[None]	[None]
3. Glosseme	Morpheme	Tagmeme
Meaning: Noeme	Sememe	Episememe

'Meaningful units', whether 'simple or complex', are divided into 'lexical forms' (built from 'phonemes') and 'grammatical forms' (built from 'tagmemes', i.e., 'features of arrangement'). The 'smallest and meaningless units' are the *'phememes'*, comprising 'lexical *phonemes'* plus 'grammatical *taxemes'*. The 'smallest meaningful units' are the *'glossemes'*, whose 'meanings' are *'noemes'* and which comprise 'lexical *morphemes'*, whose 'meanings' are *'sememes'*, plus 'grammatical *tagmemes'*, whose 'meanings' are *'episememes'*. In most of the book, though, several of these terms (like 'phememes', glossemes', and 'noemes') are scarcely used or illustrated – a neglect even more pronounced in Hjelmslev's theorizing (cf. 6.4, 59).[16] Both linguists take it for granted that classifications should be based on the 'smallest' units, but neither gives any exhaustive analysis of real language samples to show how or where we find these units, and when we stop. Therefore, aside from the well-known 'phonemes', the units have an indeterminate quality; even the division between 'meaningless' and 'meaningful' would not be simple to maintain.

4.46 Bloomfield's two top categories, 'grammar' and 'lexicon', are complementary. 'If we knew the **lexicon** of a language', we would notice that 'every utterance contains some significant features that are not accounted for by the lexicon' (BL 162). This residual aspect, 'the meaningful arrangements of forms in a language, constitutes its **grammar**' (BL 163). Yet the two top categories are also connected in several ways. One connection is that the 'lexicon' is 'the total stock of **morphemes** in a language', and 'grammar' is 'the arrangement' of 'morphemes' 'in the complex form' (BL 162f). Another connection arises by grouping 'grammar' and 'lexicon' together as 'divisions' of '**semantics**', i.e., of 'the description' 'telling what meanings are attached' to 'phonetic forms' (BL 138, 513), though this scheme is not pursued very far.[17]

4.47 'Lexical form' is further 'connected in two directions with grammatical form': 'taken by itself in the abstract', it 'exhibits a meaningful grammatical **structure**'; and 'in any actual utterance', it has a 'grammatical **function**' defined by its 'privileges of occurrence', i.e., by 'the positions in which a form can appear' 'in any actual utterance' (BL 264f, 185) (cf. 7.63). 'The functions' 'appear as a very complex system', which Bloomfield traces back to a 'complex set of habits' (BL 265f) (cf. 4.12, 32). 'To describe the grammar of a language, we have to state the form-class of each lexical form, and to determine what characteristics make the speakers assign it to these form-classes' (BL 266).

4.48 Bloomfield strongly recommends that 'form-classes, like other linguistic phenomena', be 'defined' 'only in terms of linguistic (that is, lexical or grammatical) **features**' (BL 268) (cf. 7.69, 71–76). More specifically, 'the form-class of a lexical form is determined for the speakers, and consequently for the relevant description of a language, by the structure and constituents of the form', or by the 'inclusion of a special constituent' or 'marker, or by the identity of a form itself' (BL 268). 'Large form-classes that subdivide' the 'whole lexicon' or some major part of it 'into form-classes of approximately equal size are called **categories**' (BL 270). The 'petty form-classes' are more 'irregular'.

4.49 Though he claims 'every lexical form is used only in certain conventional functions', Bloomfield concedes that 'different functions may create overlapping form-classes'; and 'particular lexical forms may, by class-cleavage, exhibit unusual combinations of function' (BL 265, i.r.) (cf. 3.16, 22, 24, 33; 7.63; 8.25, 27; 11.25, 27; 12.54). Moreover, he allows for a class of 'lexical forms' that 'belong arbitrarily or irregularly to a form-class that is indicated neither by their structure nor by a marker'; these will have to be given as a 'list' of 'every form' in the 'lexicon' (BL 269) (cf. 4.52, 59). From here, he comes to perceive 'the lexicon' as 'an appendix of grammar' and 'a list of basic irregularities' (BL 274) (cf. 4.52, 59; 7.70f; 12.59).

4.50 Another problem is the prospect that although 'a morpheme can be described phonetically' 'as a set of one or more phonemes in a certain arrangement' (cf. 5.36, 45; 7.46, 61; 12.27), 'a proper analysis' is 'one which takes account of the meanings' (BL 161, 167) – just the aspect of language Bloomfield mistrusts the most. 'School grammar' is scolded for 'trying to define the form-classes by the class-meanings', which, 'like all other meanings, elude the linguist's power of definition' and 'do not coincide with the meanings of strictly defined technical terms' (BL 266). If 'the meaning of a morpheme' is a 'sememe' (4.45), Bloomfield, to be consistent, must 'assume that each sememe is a constant and definite unit of meaning' 'different from all others' 'in the language' (BL 162) (cf. 4.17, 23, 26, 31; 11.66). Consistent too is the idea that 'sememes could be analysed or systematically listed only by a well-nigh omniscient observer' (cf. 4.15). Besides, 'the meaning of each morpheme belongs to it by an arbitrary tradition' (BL 274f) (cf. 4.27). So 'no matter how refined our method, the elusive nature of meanings will always cause difficulties, especially when doubtful relations of meaning are accompanied by formal irregularities' (BL 208). For instance, some 'affixes' are 'vague in meaning', whereas for others, 'the meaning is more palpable' and 'concrete'; 'the roots' of words are 'relatively clear-cut as to denotation', being considerably more numerous' (BL 240f) (cf. 3.27).

4.51 These problems give Bloomfield one more occasion to voice his refrain: because 'we cannot gauge meanings accurately enough', 'the meaning of a morpheme' 'cannot be analysed within the scope of our science' (BL 227, 161) (cf. 4.15). 'To accept' 'makeshift' 'definitions of meaning' 'in place of' 'formal terms is to abandon scientific discourse' (BL 266). We are similarly cautioned against using 'philosophical terms', as was done in the 'traditional' 'parts-of-speech system' devised by the 'mistaken method' of 'school grammar' (BL 5, 196, 201, 268, 271) (cf. 4.4ff, 4.19, 38, 72, 4^2; 12.7). Due to such factors as 'overlap' and 'over-differentiation', a 'fully satisfactory' and 'consistent' 'system' 'cannot be set up' (BL 196, 269f).

4.52 How the discovery of morphemes might proceed in a formal way is an intricate question. They are designated the 'ultimate constituents' or 'components' of 'every complex form' (BL 160f, i.r.). Each 'morpheme' is 'a linguistic form which bears no partial phonetic–semantic resemblance to any other form' (befitting the idea of the 'lexicon' being 'a list of irregularities', (cf. 4.49, 59)). Therefore, we must look for 'partial resemblance of forms' larger than morphemes, e.g., in ' "John ran" ' versus ' "John fell" ' (BL 159) (cf. 5.46).

4.53 Morphemes come in two types: a **'free form'** can be 'spoken alone', whereas a **'bound form'** cannot (BL 160). So 'only free forms can be isolated in actual speech'; 'the speaker cannot isolate bound forms by speaking them alone' (BL 178, 208). Yet here too, methods of discovery are problematic. 'If we are lucky, we may hear someone utter the form' 'without any accompaniment', but we may also 'wait in vain for the isolated form' (BL 159f).

4.54 Bloomfield again has reservations about consulting native speakers (cf. 4.19; 12.49). Though he depicts 'the categories of language' 'which affect morphology' as being 'so pervasive that anyone who reflects upon language at all is sure to notice them', yet 'as a practical matter, observing languages in the field', 'it is unwise to elicit such forms' (BL 270, 160). 'One cannot look to the speakers for an answer, since they' are 'usually unable to describe the structure of words'; 'they do not practise morphological analysis', and would make 'false admissions' or 'give inconsistent or silly answers' (BL 208, 160) (cf. 5.46, 48; 9^{15}).

4.55 Bloomfield has no patent solutions either. Despite his own postulate of strict form–meaning correspondence (4.17, 23), he grants that 'defining' 'linguistic categories' 'in formal terms' will always leave a 'great difficulty in defining their meaning' (BL 271) (cf. 12.54). 'Class meanings are merely composites', or 'greatest common factors, of the grammatical meanings which accompany the forms' (BL 266f). Alternately, 'class-meanings' are 'only vague situational features, undefinable in terms of our science' (BL 268). 'Some linguistic categories' may 'agree with classes of real things', such as 'objects, actions', and 'relations', but 'other languages' may not 'recognize these classes in their part-of-speech system' (BL 271) (cf. 2.65; 3.23; 12.24). 'Number', 'gender', 'case', 'tense', and 'aspect' are cited as 'categories' that do not conform to 'the practical world' (BL 271f). Also, 'in every language', 'many complex forms carry specialized meanings which cannot figure in a purely linguistic description, but are practically of great importance' (BL 276). Some forms and features are so 'elusive' and variable that 'the definer' can only 'resort to a demonstration by examples' (BL 280) (cf. 8.82; 9.27). Others 'have no formal characteristic by which we could define them' and must be 'classified by purely practical features of meaning' (BL 215).

4.56 And so Bloomfield too proceeds in a makeshift fashion. He invokes such 'class-meanings' as ' "action" ', ' "strong stimulus" ',[18] and the ' "qualitative" ', ' "variable" ', or ' "identificational character of specimens" ' (BL 166, 267, 202f). 'The class meaning' of 'verbs' is said to be ' "action" ', and that of 'English finite verb expressions' to be ' "action performed by actor" '. Particularly obtuse is the suggestion that 'infinitive expressions', 'when spoken with exclamatory final pitch, have the meaning of a command' (BL 164ff, 172). Despite its different function, the imperative is called 'infinitive' because in English the two forms happen to coincide and not to require a subject (cf. 9.58, 91).

4.57 A 'set' of related 'inflected forms' is said to constitute a '**paradigm**' (BL 223) (cf. 5.74; 6.34; 7.75f; 8.57; 9.31, 9^{17}; 11.71; 12.27). Some are 'regular', whereas others are 'defective' (with missing forms) or 'over-differentiated' (with too many forms) (BL 223f). Yet in saying 'even a single over-differentiated paradigm' 'implies homonymy in the regular paradigms', Bloomfield hints that linguistic description should start from the most complex case, however isolated; if ' "be" ' has ' "was" ', ' "were" ', and ' "been" ', then a form like ' "played" ' would be actually three forms that happen to sound alike (BL 224). By that reasoning, the pronoun system (with 'I/me', 'he/him', etc.) might suggest that nouns have different 'cases' for 'subject' and 'object' which sound the same. Such conclusions hardly fit the 'aim' of 'getting, in the long run, the simplest possible set of statements that will describe the facts of English' (BL 213) (cf. 5.9, 38; 6.13, 21, 40; 7.36f, 50f).

4.58 What holds the 'paradigm' together is its *'derivational unity'* (BL 224). 'An English paradigm consists of an underlying word' 'and some secondary derivatives containing' it. In many other languages 'having a more complex morphology', 'none of the forms in a paradigm can conveniently be viewed as underlying the others' (BL 225). For such cases, Bloomfield postulates a 'kernel' or a 'theoretical underlying form' as a 'stem' (BL 225f, 267) (cf. 4.69; 7.95).

4.59 A morphological 'set of forms' is *'regular'* if it can be 'covered by a general statement' and its members can be 'formed by a speaker who has not heard them' (BL 213f).[19] This idea suggests each separate 'morpheme of a language' is 'an irregularity' in respect to the others, so that the '**lexicon**', i.e., the 'stock of morphemes', would again be 'a list of basic irregularities' (cf. 4.49, 52), the more so 'if meanings are taken into consideration' (BL 162, 274). Because in 'morphology', 'any inconsistency of procedure is likely to create confusion', 'the principle of **immediate constituents**' must be applied 'in all observation of word-structure' (BL 209, 221) (cf. 5.21, 50, 62; 7.37f, 63; 9.33; 12.26). 'Any complex form can be fully described (apart from its meaning) in terms of the immediate constituent forms and the grammatical features' whereby these 'are arranged' (BL 167).

4.60 Although a 'syllable' or 'phoneme' can be a 'linguistic form', the '**word**' constitutes 'the smallest unit' of 'free form', and 'for purposes of ordinary life', 'the smallest unit of speech' (BL 138, 183, 178) (cf. 12.29). 'The principle' that 'a word cannot be interrupted by other forms, holds good almost universally' (BL 180). 'In the few languages with no bound forms, the word' is also 'the smallest unit' of 'linguistic form in general' (BL 183) (a case that could confuse the taxonomy in 4.45). Bloomfield contrasts *'primary words'*, which do 'not contain a free form' (they either 'consist of a single free morpheme' or 'contain more than one bound form'), against *'secondary words'*, which do 'contain' one or more 'free forms' (BL 209, 240ff). This prospect of the word having 'immediate constituents' raises a familiar problem: 'it is impossible to distinguish consistently, on the one hand, between phrases and words and, on the other hand, between words and bound forms' (BL 209, 179) (cf. 2.55; 3.26, 34f; 5.51, 53f; 8.57; 9.75, 9[17]; 10.40; 11.75; 12.28). The distinction rests on 'grammatical features of selection', which are 'the commonest, but also the most varied and difficult to observe' (BL 229). 'Many words' 'lie on the border' (BL 180f). This 'border region' includes 'phrase-words (jack-in-the-pulpit)' and 'compound words (blackbird)' (BL 207, 180, 184, 234f, 276) (cf. 2.61; 5.32, 54; 9.93; 12.28).

4.61 In '**grammar**' (as in morphology), 'most speech forms are *regular* in the sense that the speaker who knows the constituents and the grammatical pattern can utter them without ever having heard them' by using 'analogies' and 'habits of substitution' (BL 275f).[20] Here, 'the observer cannot hope to list' all the forms, 'since the possibilities of combination are practically infinite', and many 'may never before have been uttered' (cf. 4.16; 7.95; 8.42; 12.26, 39f, 45). So although 'the number of words in any language is practically infinite', the real 'wealth of a language' lies in its 'morphemes', 'sentence-types, constructions, and substitutions' (BL 276f). 'The grammar lists only the kind of irregularities that are not present in all the morphemes of a language' (BL 274). 'Any form which a speaker can utter only after he has heard it from other speakers, is irregular'. Yet the criterion is not too reliable: 'when a speaker utters a complex form, we are in most cases unable to tell whether he has heard it before or created it' by 'analogy' (BL 276).

4.62 Bloomfield proposes to organize linguistic description for 'grammar' into 'two parts': '**morphology**' for 'the construction of words', and '**syntax**' for 'the construction of phrases' (BL 183f, 207) (cf. 2.55; 5.54; 6.49; 8.57; 9.31; 10.35). To support the division, Bloomfield reverses his position about borders (in 4.60): 'the constructions in which free forms appear in phrases differ very decidedly from the constructions in which free or bound forms appear in words' (BL 183).[21] '*Syntactic* constructions' are those 'in which none of the immediate constituents is a bound form' (BL 184). '*Morphological*' 'constructions' are those 'in which bound forms appear among the constituents' (BL 207). 'In general, morphological' ones are the 'more elaborate' (BL 207). 'The features of modification and modulation are more numerous and often irregular', i.e., 'confined to particular' cases rather than 'covered by a general statement' (BL 207, 213) (cf. 4.49). 'Features of selection' can be 'minute', 'arbitrary, and whimsical' (BL 207, 165). 'The order of the constituents is almost always rigidly fixed', though this 'criterion' may apply to some 'phrases' as well (BL 207, 229). Due to all these peculiarities, 'languages differ more in morphology than in syntax', and 'no simple scheme' can classify all languages (BL 207) (cf. 3.47; 4.72). Such 'schemes' as the one with 'analytic' versus 'synthetic', and the one with 'isolating, agglutinative, polysynthetic, and inflecting' are criticized because the classes were 'relative' and 'never clearly defined' (BL 207f) (cf. 3.54f).

4.63 Notwithstanding these guidelines, the border between syntax and morphology remains fuzzy, with the word caught in between. Bloomfield envisions a grey area of '*compounds*' ranging from 'syntactic' to 'semi-syntactic' to 'asyntactic' (BL 207, 233ff) (cf. 4.60). Moreover, its status as 'a free form' (BL 178, 181, 183) does not fully identify the word, because 'we do not mark off those segments of our speech which could be spoken alone' (BL 181). Bloomfield is forced to turn to writing: 'the analysis of linguistic forms into words is familiar to us because we have the custom of leaving spaces between words in our writing and printing' (BL 178) (cf. 4.38). Printed form must be the reason why he himself considers 'door-knob' to be 'English', but not 'door knob' (BL 233).

4.64 '**Grammar**' is assigned four kinds of 'meaningful arrangements': '(1) *order* is the succession' of 'constituents';[22] '(2) *modulation* is the use of secondary phonemes' like 'pitch' (cf. 4.33); '(3) *phonetic modification* is a change in the primary phonemes'; and '(4) *selection of forms*' is controlled by certain 'classes' (BL 163f) (cf. 3.25–30). Yet discovering 'arrangements', as Bloomfield admits, is not as easy as discovering 'phonemes, which we can pronounce or transcribe', and 'many students of language have been misled' (BL 168). A similar difficulty applies to the parallel whereby 'a taxeme', being 'a simple feature of grammatical arrangement', 'is in grammar what a phoneme is in the lexicon' – 'the smallest unit of form' (BL 167) (cf. 4.45; 5^{26}; 6.42). Bloomfield warns that 'taxemes' can be 'very complex' and 'elaborate', involving 'many peculiarities' (BL 266, 210). And his examples of 'taxemes' suggest as much, for instance, the 'selections' which 'delimit form-classes', 'assign certain finite verb expressions to certain nominative expressions', or make 'certain forms' become 'favourite sentence-forms' (BL 190, 166f, 171f). I see here nothing 'simple' or 'small'; 'taxeme' seems to be a name for any group of information the linguist needs to describe some aspect of an arrangement – witness Bloomfield's remark about one case: 'all these facts, taken together, may be viewed as a single taxeme' (BL 167f).

4.65 'Syntax' is said to 'consist largely' of 'taxemes of selection' 'stating' 'under what circumstances' 'various form-classes' 'appear in syntactic constructions' (BL 190). Every '*construction* shows us two (or sometimes more) free forms combined' in a '*resultant phrase*' (BL 194). Bloomfield's breakdown of 'constructions' hinges on a certain use of recursion: whether a 'phrase belongs' to the same 'form-class' as one or more of its 'immediate constituents'. If not, the 'construction' is '*exocentric*' (like '"John ran"'); if so, it is '*endocentric*' (like '"poor John"', where both the whole and '"John"' are 'proper-noun expressions' and have 'the same functions'). The 'endocentric' ones, which include 'most' of those 'in any language', 'are of two kinds': in '*coordinative* (or *serial*) ones (e.g., '"boys and girls"'), the 'phrase belongs' to the same 'form-class as two or more of the constituents' (e.g., nouns); in '*subordinative* (or *attributive*)' ones (e.g., '"very fresh milk"'), only 'one of the constituents' – 'the *head*' or '*centre*' (e.g., the noun) – meets this requirement (BL 195). This scheme has a vaguely transformational flavour in the sense that a part is construed as being, for syntactic purposes, of the same 'class' as the whole (cf. 12.54). But Bloomfield limits his ideas about 'kernels' or 'underlying forms' to morphology (cf. 4.59), where 'the structural order of constituents' 'may differ from their actual sequence', and 'the descriptive order of grammatical features is a fiction' serving 'our method of describing the forms' (BL 210, 213).

4.66 'The formation of a **phrase** is usually determined, at bottom, by the form-class of one or more of the included words' (BL 268). 'For this reason, the speaker (and the grammarian) need not deal separately with each phrase; the form-class of almost any phrase is known if we know the syntactic constructions and the form-classes of words' (cf. 7.95). Phrases are also held together by '*government*': a 'selection' stipulating 'the syntactic position' of one form with respect to another (BL 192) (cf. 6^{12}). '*Agreement*' is a 'narrower type'; 'the simplest kind' is *'concord* or *congruence'*, e.g., between 'actor' and 'action' (BL 191) (cf. 8.61; 9^{20}).

4.67 The '**sentence**' is defined as 'a linguistic form' occurring in *'absolute position'*, i.e., 'as an independent form not included in any larger' form (BL 170). This definition places the sentence at the end-point of recursion: it includes but cannot be included (but cf. 7.52). As a result, isolation – the *inability* to be in a structure – becomes a decisive aspect for describing structures. Even a word or two (like ' "John!" ' or ' "Poor John!" ') can be a 'sentence'; only the 'bound form' is 'never used' (BL 170, 177) (cf. 4.53, 61f; 5.58; 8.55; 11.77). Of course, 'a form which in one utterance figures as a sentence, may in another utterance appear in included position' (BL 170). Moreover, 'an utterance may consist of more than one sentence' if it 'contains several linguistic forms which are not' 'united' 'by any meaningful grammatical arrangement' (cf. 9.86). These cases collide with the criterion, mentioned later, that a sentence be 'spoken alone' (BL 179). The criterion wouldn't be decisive anyway: 'the linguist cannot wait indefinitely for the chance of hearing a given form used as a sentence', and 'inquiry or experiment may call forth very different responses'. Bloomfield remarks here that 'aside from' 'far-fetched situations, the general structure of language may make one classification more convenient than another for our purpose' (cf. 12.40, 43).

4.68 Bloomfield postulates 'various taxemes marking off the sentence' and 'distinguishing different types of sentences' 'in most, or possibly all languages' (BL 170) (cf. 12.28). 'Sentence-pitch' can mark the 'end of sentences' or their 'emphatic parts', or can 'unite' 'two forms' in 'parataxis', the latter including 'juxtaposition', 'parenthesis', and 'apposition' (BL 171). 'Taxemes of selection' 'distinguish' *'full'* from *'minor* sentences', or decide which are 'favourites' – in English, say, 'actor–action phrases' and 'commands' (BL 171f) (cf. 9.46). 'The meaning of the full sentence type' (its 'episememe', cf. 4.45) is expounded as 'complete and novel utterance' or 'full-sized' 'instruction' for 'altering the hearer's situation'; but we are warned again that 'it is a serious mistake to try to use this meaning (or any meanings)' 'as a starting point for linguistic discussion', because we cannot 'define' them 'exactly' (BL 172) (cf. 4.16; 5.65).

4.69 The '**predication**' is presented as a 'bipartite favourite sentence form' composed of '**subject**' and '**predicate**' (BL 173) – like the definition of the sentence used by school grammarians as well as linguists (cf. 3.36, 39; 5.55; 8.55; 11.78f). The 'interrogative' is identified by both 'special pitch' and 'selection'; it 'stimulates' 'the hearer to supply a speech-form' (BL 171, 248, 204) (cf. 9.58).[23] The 'minor' (i.e., not 'favourite') sentence-type is 'completive' ('supplements a situation', as in ' "Gladly, if I can" ') or 'exclamatory' ('occurs under a violent stimulus', as in ' "Damn it" ') (BL 176f). What a traditional grammar might call 'sentence fragments' are thereby subsumed under 'minor sentence types' (cf. 9.85).[24] In return, the structural status of the sentence is made almost as elusive as that of the word and depends on some indefinitely large and variegated set of 'taxemes' (cf. 4.64f).

4.70 Alongside 'constructions' and 'sentence-types', **'substitution'** is 'the third type of meaningful grammatical arrangement' (BL 247, i.r.) (cf. 5.32; 7.73; 9.92). 'A *substitute* is a linguistic form or grammatical feature which, under certain conventional circumstances, replaces one of a class of linguistic forms' in its *'domain'*. 'Substitutes' 'are often short words', 'atonic', and of 'irregular inflection and derivation'. They have great 'usefulness' and 'economy'; their 'meanings' are 'more inclusive', 'abstract', 'simple', and 'constant than the meanings of ordinary linguistic forms' (BL 250). Being 'one step farther removed from practical reality' and having 'grammatically definable' 'domains', 'substitutes' raise fewer 'practical questions of meaning' (BL 250, 247). They fit such 'simple' 'features of the situation' that they could be replaced by 'gestures' (BL 249f) (cf. 4.36). Bloomfield cites the 'closed system of personal–definite substitutes' (i.e., pronouns), which 'represent elementary circumstances' of 'the act of speech-utterance', such as 'the speaker–hearer relation' (BL 256, 248) (cf. 9.89).[25] For example, we may say ' "you" ' with 'no practical knowledge' of the 'hearer' (though this applies only to languages like English with a single pronoun of address). Also, Bloomfield is impressed by the forms for 'numerative and identificational relations' (like ' "all", "some", "any" ', etc.), because they remind him of 'the language of science' and 'mathematics' (BL 249) (cf. 4.21f).

4.71 Bloomfield's belief in the reality or universality of the descriptive concepts reviewed so far is signalled when he remarks: 'such features as phonemes, morphemes, words, sentences, constructions, and substitution-types appear in every language', because 'they are inherent in the nature of human speech' (BL 297) (cf. 2.10, 30; 7.45; 12.27). 'Other features, such as noun-like and verb-like form-classes', or 'categories of number, person, case, and tense, or grammatical positions of actor, verbal goal, and possessor, are not universal, but still so widespread that better knowledge will doubtless some day connect them with universal characters of languages' (but cf. 3.36). Such 'features' could 'exist' as 'realities either of physics or of human psychology' (BL 198f, 297) (cf. 5.68; 6.12; 13[16]).

4.72 Yet the danger always impends, even for 'linguists', of 'mistaking' the 'categories' of one's 'native language' 'for universal forms of speech or of human "thought", or of the universe itself' (BL 233, 270) (cf. 3.5, 50; 4.4; 8.14). 'A good deal of what passes for "logic" or "metaphysics" is merely an incompetent restating of the chief categories of the philosopher's language' (BL 270) (cf. 12.16). So 'linguistics of the future' will have 'to compare the categories of different languages and see which features are universal or at least widespread'. Meanwhile, we are told that at least in some areas like 'compound words', 'the differences are great enough to prevent our setting up any scheme that would fit all languages' (BL 233) (cf. 3.47; 4.62).

4.73 Of course, much comparing had already been done by earlier linguists (cf. 2.5, 10, 52, 63; 3.19f; 4.1; 11.90f). But although he extols philology as 'one of the most successful' 'enterprises' 'of European science in the nineteenth century', he has some reservations about 'comparative method' (BL 12). It 'shows us the ancestry of languages in the form of a family tree', yet 'the family tree diagram was merely a statement of the method' rather than of 'historical realities' (BL 311). 'Each branch' of the tree was assumed to 'bear independent witness to the forms of the parent language' (BL 310). 'Identities or correspondences', especially in 'the commonest constructions and form-classes', or in 'intimate basic vocabulary' of 'everyday speech', should 'reveal features of the parent speech' (BL 298, 310). 'Differences' which 'follow a system' might also indicate that 'forms are historically connected' (BL 300).

4.74 Yet appearances can be unreliable. 'Universals' may create deceptive 'resemblances' among 'wholly unrelated languages' (BL 297) (cf. 2.10; 7.20). Or, confusion may result from some 'accident' or 'borrowing of speech-forms' (BL 298f, 361f). Moreover, 'the comparative method' makes a risky assumption that the 'parent' language was 'completely uniform' until it got 'split suddenly and sharply into two or more' languages (BL 310, 318). Actually, the 'parent' might have been 'dialectally differentiated', and its offshoots might 'remain in communication'; 'clear-cut splitting' 'is not usual' (BL 321, 314). 'In actual observation, no speech-community is ever quite uniform' (BL 311) (cf. 2.43; 3.66; 4.17, 82; 7.12, 96).

4.75 Pursuing this train of thought with his usual relentlessness leads Bloomfield to acknowledge the problems in determining what constitutes or belongs to a language. 'The language of any speech-community appears to an observer', 'at any one moment', 'as a stable structure of lexical and grammatical habits' (BL 281). 'This, however, is an illusion: every language is undergoing, at all times', a 'process of **linguistic change**' (cf. 2.44–54; 3.58–63). 'At any one stage of a language, certain features are relatively stable and others relatively unstable' (BL 409). 'The systematic study' of how 'speech-forms change' may offer 'the key to most linguistic problems' (BL 5) (cf. 3.58). Whereas Bloomfield had previously said that 'in order to describe a language one needs no historical knowledge whatever', he now says that 'change' 'offers the only possibility of explaining the phenomena of language' (BL 19, 281). After all, 'our speech depends entirely on the speech of the past' (BL 47). 'Speakers acquire their habits from earlier speakers' (BL 281). Thus, 'the explanation of our present-day habit' 'consists' in 'the existence' of 'the earlier habit' plus any 'intervening change' (BL 282). Bloomfield surmises that 'linguistic change is far more rapid than biological change, but probably slower than the changes in other human institutions'. 'Every speaker is constantly adapting his speech-habits to interlocutors; he gives up forms', 'adopts new ones' or 'changes the frequency' (BL 327f) (cf. 12.39).

4.76 Bloomfield is pleased to report how, in the later nineteenth century,[26] studies of 'language change' 'replaced the speculation of earlier times with scientific induction' (BL 16) (cf. 4.7, 73, 79; 12.4). 'When no one had the key', 'the results of linguistic change' seemed 'chaotic' (BL 346). But now 'we have a method which brings order into the confusion of linguistic resemblances' (BL 346). 'The observed facts' 'resisted all comprehension until our method came upon the scene' (BL 347).

4.77 What these 'observed facts' tell us is less clear than Bloomfield's confident tone suggests (cf. 4.8, 17ff). 'The process of linguistic change has never been directly observed'; 'observation, with our present facilities, is inconceivable' (BL 347). Even 'mass-observation' made by 'recording every form' we 'can find' 'can tell us nothing about the changes'; we would need a 'genuinely statistical observation through a considerable period of time' (BL 38) (cf. 2.45).[27] Bloomfield also sees 'observed facts' in 'the results of linguistic change as they show themselves in etymologies', i.e., in 'the history' of 'speech-forms' (BL 347, 15). Yet if 'every word has its own history' (BL 328, 335, i.r.),[28] language change would be a diffuse amalgamation of minute trends, and observation could scarcely claim generality anyway.

4.78 In the section on '**semantic change**', 'the student' is counselled to 'observe very closely the meanings of the form in all older occurrences' and to find 'the context in which the new meaning first appears' (BL 440). Evidence includes 'contexts and phrasal combinations', 'comparisons of related languages', and 'the structural analysis of forms' (BL 425). Though he seems uneasy about the attempts of 'earlier students' to describe 'classes' of 'logical relations that connect successive meanings' – 'narrowing', 'widening', 'metaphor', 'metonymy', and so on (BL 426f) – Bloomfield offers no scheme of his own. Nor does he explain how genuine semantic change differs from the 'semantic innovation' he attributes to 'every utterance of a speech-form' by 'a good speaker' (cf. 4.16). He predictably suggests that 'a change in meaning' 'is merely the result of change in use' (BL 426) (cf. 8.47; 11.42, 66). An 'expansion of a form into new meanings' entails a 'special' 'rise in frequency'; but for 'fluctuations in the frequency of forms to be accurately observed', we would need 'a record of every utterance that was made in a speech-community' in a given 'period of time' (BL 435, 394) (cf. 4.14, 16f). And ritual warnings are sounded again: any 'fluctuation depending on meaning' 'escapes a purely linguistic investigation'; in 'the spread of linguistic features', 'the factor' of 'meaning (including connotation)' 'cuts off our hope' for 'a scientifically usable analysis' (BL 399, 345).

4.79 Again like Saussure, Bloomfield prefers to focus on '**phonetic change**' and declares it 'independent of non-phonetic factors, such as the meaning' (BL 353f) (cf. 2.74). 'The beginning of our science was made by a procedure which implied the regularity of phonetic change' and thereby 'enabled linguists to find order in the factual data' (BL 355, 364) (cf. 8.67; 12.27). Saussurian too is the reluctance to see such change following 'laws' (BL 348, 354) (cf. 2.14f, 38). At most, the change of 'phonemes' was fairly 'regular', although the 'actual data' may be extremely 'irregular' and may include 'deviant' or 'residual' (or 'relic') 'forms' (BL 351, 352f, 360ff, 331). 'Phonetic change' could be 'observed only by means of an enormous mass of mechanical records' 'through several generations' (BL 365; cf. BL 38). Moreover, 'changing' 'phonemes' would have to be carefully filtered out from 'the non-distinctive acoustic features of a language', which 'are at all times highly variable' (BL 365).

4.80 'Since a sound-change is a historical happening', 'its cause cannot be found in universal considerations or by observing speakers at other times and places' or 'in a laboratory'; 'we have no guarantee of its happening again' (BL 388f, 368). Like Saussure and Sapir once more, Bloomfield is sceptical about seeing the 'cause' of 'sound-change' in ' "race", climate, topographic conditions, diet, occupation, and general mode of life' (BL 386) (cf. 2.76; 3^2). He is also unconvinced by appeals to 'rapidity of speech', 'culture and general intelligence', or 'imperfections in children's learning', and above all by elitist contentions that 'changes are due to ignorance and carelessness' and 'corruptions of the vulgar' (BL 490, 8; cf. BL 469, 476) (cf. 2.46, 49). 'Psychological explanations' are also ruled out, on the grounds that they 'merely paraphrase the outcome of the change' (BL 435) (cf. 3.62; 12.14). The effects of a 'substratum' language formerly spoken in an occupied territory are discounted too, as well as the notion that 'forms of weak meaning' are 'slurred in pronunciation' and 'lost' (BL 386ff, 469) (cf. 3.63).

4.81 Bloomfield believes 'the general processes of change are the same in all languages', but 'no permanent factor' 'can account for specific changes' (BL 20, 386). Instead, he attributes 'the change of language' partly to 'linguistically definable characteristics', such as 'shortness' of words, avoidance of 'homonymy', 'patterning of recurrent phonemes', 'simplification of sound clusters', 'dissimilation' of sounds, or preservation of 'semantically important features'; and partly to 'historical change in human affairs' or 'shifts in the practical world', including the mechanism of receiving a 'strong stimulus' or making 'a good response' to a 'situation' (BL 509, 395f, 372, 390, 363, 435, 389, 399, 426, 396, 440, 401). Some 'new forms' may be 'individual creations' of 'one speaker' that were congenial to the 'general formal patterns' and 'habits of the community'; but usually 'it is useless to ask what person' made the start (BL 421, 424, 443, 480) (cf. 2.45; 3.57, 64; 4^6).

4.82 Though we may 'ignore the lack of uniformity' 'when we describe a language' 'by confining ourselves to some arbitrarily chosen type of speech', 'we cannot do this' when 'studying linguistic change', 'because all changes are sure to appear at first in the shape of variant features' (BL 311f; cf. BL 365, 480). We need to probe the 'social conditions' for 'the spread of features' in space as well as in time (BL 345) (cf. 2.43; 3.65). 'The most important kind of social group' is the **speech community**', because 'society', i.e., 'the close adjustment among individuals', 'is based on language' (BL 42) (cf. 3.1; 4.10, 74f; 7.12; 8.13). 'Every person belongs to more than one minor speech-group' and acts as 'a mediator between groups', 'as an imitator and a model', responding to 'the density of communication and the relative prestige of different social groups' (BL 476f, 345) (cf. 8.77). 'Rival forms' 'differ in connotation', according to the 'circumstances' where 'a speaker' 'has heard them' (BL 394) (cf. 4.25).

4.83 'Dialect' is a complex notion in this regard, since 'there is no absolute distinction between dialect and language boundaries, or between dialect borrowing' and 'cultural borrowing' (BL 444f, i.r.) (cf. 3.66; 4.74). 'Dialects' are 'for the most part mutually intelligible', whereas languages are not; yet 'there are all kinds of gradations between understanding and failing to understand' (BL 57, 44, 52f). Also, 'dialect geography' reveals 'no sharp lines of linguistic demarcation' between 'dialect areas', but only more 'gradations' (BL 51, i.r.). 'In sum', we see that 'the term "speech community" has only a relative value' (BL 54). Still, 'dialect study' is useful in making 'atlases' and 'maps of distribution' for 'lexical or grammatical differences' (BL 323f).[29] This work refuted earlier doctrines that 'the literary and upper-class standard language was older and more true to reason than the local speech-forms, which were due to the ignorance and carelessness of the common people' (BL 321) (cf. 2.24; 3.69; 4.40). 'The standard language' may 'arise' 'from local dialects', or these may 'preserve' some 'ancient feature' lost in 'the standard'.

4.84 Of course, we can still try to 'distinguish between the *upper* or *dominant* language' of the 'more privileged group, and the *lower* language' of 'the subject people' (BL 461). 'In all cases, it is the lower language which borrows from the upper'; each 'speech-group' 'imitates' people of 'highest "social" standing' (BL 464, 476).[30] Bloomfield's 'upper' side includes 'conquerors', 'masters', 'officials', 'merchants', 'lecturers', and 'educated persons'; his 'lower' side includes 'working men', 'rustics', 'proletarians', 'peasants', 'poorest people', 'street-sweepers', 'tramps', 'law-breakers', 'criminals', 'Gipsies', 'Negro slaves'[31] and – 'in the United States' – 'humble immigrants' (BL 461, 474, 330, 47, 441, 50).

4.85 Bloomfield's concern for social differences in language is most urgently reflected in his insistent connection between language and **educational policy**: 'society deals with linguistic matters through the school system' (BL 499) (cf. 4.5f; 8.7; 9.17; 12.60, 64). 'A few generations ago', 'practical matters' seemed simple enough for the child to 'learn without the help of the school, which needed to train him only in the three Rs' (reading, 'riting, 'rithmetic). 'Schools have clung to this pattern' and 'concentrated on verbal discipline'. 'The chief aim' 'is literacy', but the 'ignorance' and 'confusion' of 'educators' lead to 'primers and first reading books' that 'present the graphic forms in a mere hodgepodge, with no rational progression' (BL 500) (cf. 9.16). Compared with the 'European' system, 'our eight years of grammar school represents a waste of something like four years of every child's time' (BL 504). 'To get a general education', the 'American' 'must still go through a four-years' college course. In all respects except formal education, he is too mature' for 'general and elementary studies' and 'turns instead to the snobberies and imbecilities which make a by-word of the American college'. 'Selection' is made not 'by the pupil's aptitude', but 'by his parents' economic means, combined with chance or whim'.

4.86 The 'delay' of 'professional study' 'works most adversely upon the effectiveness of foreign-language study' (BL 504). 'The work' in 'high schools and colleges' is 'an appalling waste of effort: not one pupil in a hundred learns to speak and understand, or even to read, a foreign language' (BL 503). Bloomfield blames the prevalence of 'analysis' and 'puzzle-solving translation', and 'incompetent teachers who talk about the foreign language instead of using it' (BL 505). He recommends 'constant repetition' as the only way to 'master' the 'thousands of morphemes and tagmemes of the foreign language' – an idea that later became the backbone of the audio-lingual method, due in part to Bloomfield's (1942) own design of instructional methods for strategic languages during World War II. Since 'the meaning of foreign forms is hard to convey', instruction should focus on 'practical objects and situations – say, of the classroom or of pictures'. 'The content' should have 'practical bearing' by 'showing the life and history of the foreign nation' (BL 506). 'Grammatical doctrine should be accepted only where it passes a test of usefulness' and has been 're-shaped to suit the actual need'. 'The memorizing of paradigms' 'bears so little relation to actual speech as to be nearly worthless' (cf. 9^{11}).

4.87   Bloomfield assails the schools even more fiercely for their 'authoritarian' 'attitude' about 'speech', whereby 'the non-standard speaker' is 'injured' 'in childhood' by 'the unequal distribution of privilege' (BL 499f) (cf. 4.5). Grammarians pretend that 'one way of speaking' 'is inherently right, the other inherently wrong' (BL 3) (cf. 2.5f, 32; 3.4; 4.40; 8.26). Labelling 'undesirable variants as "incorrect" or "bad English" or even "not English"' makes 'the speaker grow diffident' and 'ready to suspect almost any speech-form of "incorrectness"' (BL 496, 48). 'It would not have been possible for "grammarians" to bluff a large part of our speech community' 'if the public had not been ready for the deception': worrying about whose 'type of language has a higher prestige' makes people 'easy prey to the authoritarian' (BL 497). They struggle to 'revise' their 'speech' to fit 'the model of printed books' or the 'minor variations' and 'snobbery' of 'modish cliques' or of a 'small minority of over-literate persons' (BL 497, 502). The result is 'unnatural speech', a mix of 'non-current forms' and 'outlandish hyperforms' (BL 497f). 'The non-standard speaker' should 'rather take pride in simplicity of speech and view it as an advantage'; and should 'substitute' 'without embarrassment' 'standard forms' for 'non-standard' (BL 499).

4.88   And so Bloomfield's classic book concludes with an appeal for a linguistics able to ameliorate social and educational policy through enlightenment about language. Although 'lexical and grammatical analysis' are not powerful enough to 'reveal the truth or falsity of a doctrine', 'linguistics can' 'make us critical of verbal response habits' and 'injurious practices' 'rationalized' by 'appeal to a higher sanction' (BL 507f, i.r.) (cf. 8^7). Ultimately, the 'investigation' of 'the languages of the world' may provide the basis for a 'sound knowledge of communal forms of human behaviour'. 'It is only a prospect, but not hopelessly remote, that the study of language may help us toward the understanding and control of human events' (BL 509).

Notes

1. The key for Bloomfield citations is BL: *Language* (Bloomfield 1933). An earlier (1914) edition was much smaller and based 'on the psychological system of Wilhelm Wundt', which Bloomfield now abjures in favour of 'mechanism' (cf. 4.8). As of the 1984 reprint, the reverent editors have still not ventured to make corrections in the 1933 version (see Hockett's foreword, BL xiiif).
2. The whole 'logic and dialectic of ancient and medieval times' is designated 'a mistaken effort' (BL 507), though Bloomfield borrows from it, for instance, for defining the 'predication' (cf. 4.69; 12.17f). Hockett's belief that Bloomfield had integrated the 'philosophical–descriptive tradition' (cf. 4.1) apparently refers to the latter's reliance on common-sense examples and his own intuitive judgments about them. Compare 4.19, 38, 51, 72; 7.9ff; 12.1.
3. Thanks to 'the grammar of Pāṇini', 'no other language, to this day, has been so perfectly described' as Sanskrit (BL 11) (cf. 7.3; 8.5). Perhaps to accentuate his turn against school grammar, Bloomfield expropriates from the terminology of 'the ancient Hindu grammarians': 'sandhi', 'samprasarana', 'karmadharaya', 'davanda', 'tatpurshana', 'amredita', 'bahuvrihi', 'dvigu' and 'avyayibhava', accrediting them as 'technical terms of linguistics' (BL 186, 384, 235, 237). He also commends 'the Hindus' for 'the apparently artificial but eminently serviceable device' of the 'zero element', which he equates with 'nothing at all' (BL 209); but surely the difference between zero and nothing is precisely the point – that we can view 'absence as a positive characteristic' (BL 264f) (cf. 2^{26}; 5.21, 5^{12}; 6^{16}; 12.28).
4. The passages are found in BL xv, 3, 12, 16, 21, 32, 38, 45, 77, 140, 145, 161f, 167, 347, 355 and 508f. The usual obstacle to 'science' is 'meaning' (BL 93, 139, 161f, 167f, 174, 266), whose elucidation is consigned to some 'other science' (BL 77, 140, 145, 508). Compare 4.15.
5. Fellow-*men*, indeed. As if the story weren't sexist enough, Bloomfield remarks: 'the lone Jill is in much the same position as the speechless animal'; if she 'gets the food', she 'has far better chances of surviving and populating the earth' (BL 24). The traditional 'pail of water' was apparently dropped because it was a mentally conceived goal for 'going up the hill', rather than a chance reaction to the countryside.
6. Yet, we are told, 'any speaker is free to invent nonsense-forms' with 'vague' or 'no denotation at all'; 'in fact, any form he invents is a nonsense-form, unless he succeeds in the almost hopeless task of getting fellow-speakers to accept it as a signal for some meaning' (BL 157) (cf. 2.45; 3.57; 4.81). But advertisers succeed rather often.
7. This referral to 'good' (or 'gifted', cf. 4.7) speakers is a bit awkward, since Bloomfield champions 'simplicity of speech' and suspects that the drive to use 'apt and agreeable forms' may foster 'stilted', 'unnatural speech' (BL 498f).
8. 'The structure of the language recognizes the transferred meaning' if the latter is 'linguistically determined by an accompanying form' (BL 150). This condition fits Bloomfield's stipulation that 'language can convey only such meanings as are attached to some formal feature' (BL 168) (cf. 12.54). But metaphor is a strong counter-example (cf. 5.66f; 9.97ff; 10.86; 11.11, 31, 33, 83).
9. This definition covers 'any English sentence, phrase', 'word', 'meaningful

syllable', or 'phoneme', though the 'phoneme' is later called a 'meaningless unit' (BL 138, 264, 354) (cf. 6.43).

10. The 'laryngoscope' is 'a mirror device' for 'seeing another person's (or his own) vocal cords'; the 'kymograph' 'transforms the movement' of the 'vocal organs' into an ink line on a 'strip of paper' (BL 75). Such devices often 'interfere with normal speech and can serve only for very limited phases of observation'. Compare 8^{33}.

11. These two diverge in that 'phonology pays no heed to the acoustic nature of the phonemes' (BL 137). Compare Saussure's assessment in 2.70.

12. But surely gestures differ from language in the nature of, and constraints upon, their arbitrariness, as in 'pointing back over one's shoulder to indicate past time' (BL 39).

13. Current research is divided about whether readers recode words into a phonological representation (cf. 4^{15} and 10^{35}; 12.34).

14. Bloomfield says: 'people who have not learned to read and write have some difficulty' when 'called upon to make word-divisions' (BL 178). But Sapir's 'experiences' with 'native speakers' he was teaching to write found them 'determining the words' 'with complete and spontaneous accuracy' (SL 34n) (cf. 3.31).

15. 'Real writing' is said to require 'the association of the characters with linguistic forms' (BL 284). Bloomfield, of course, rebukes 'the metaphysical doctrine' that 'connects the graphic symbols directly with "thoughts" or "ideas"' (BL 500) (cf. 4.9). That rebuke might be aimed at Sapir, who said: 'the written forms are secondary symbols of the spoken ones', 'yet so close is the correspondence that they may', 'in certain types of thinking, be entirely substituted for the spoken ones' (SL 20).

16. Hjelmslev doesn't give even one example of 'glossemes', the 'minimal forms' and 'irreducible invariants' of 'glossematics' and 'the highest-degree invariants within a semiotic' (PT 99f, 80; RT 100) (cf. 6.42). To demonstrate that 'the glossemes of different languages differ in practical value', Bloomfield contrasts not 'smallest units', but whole words (BL 278f). He also oddly imagines 'pupils' 'learning the arbitrary glossemes of a foreign language' (BL 503).

17. However, the tendency of American linguists to treat 'semantic' as the converse of 'formal' is foreshadowed by Bloomfield (BL 395, 399) (cf. 12.54).

18. 'Strong stimulus' is also given as the 'episememe' of 'the tagmeme of exclamatory final-pitch' (BL 166) – a picturesque admixture of behaviourism with grammar.

19. Compare the sketch of 'innovation' (BL 408) (4.16). Earlier, however, Bloomfield's account of language acquisition suggested that 'every speaker's language' is 'a composite of what he has heard other people say' (BL 46; 4.12). And distaste is expressed for adopting written forms 'one has not heard' (BL 498).

20. Bloomfield compares this act to 'the solving of a proportional equation with an indefinitely large set of ratios on the left-hand side' (BL 276). He likes using 'formulas' to 'embody' our 'observations' (cf. 2.85; 3.2, 49, 59, 73; 5.40, 51f, 62; 7.48), because with them, 'our inability to define meanings need give us no pause' (BL 302f, 408). He waves aside the 'objections' of 'psychologists' to a 'formula' – 'that the speaker is not capable of the reasoning' – on the grounds that 'the normal speaker' is also 'incapable of describing his speech-habits' in any other way (BL 406) (cf. 4.19, 54; 12.49).

21. 'Debate as to the usefulness of the division' is deflected with the argument that 'the meanings' 'are definable in terms of syntax' rather than of 'practical life' (BL 184). The hope that 'semantic difference' might be 'defined in terms

of syntactic construction' would also pervade American linguistic research (cf. 7.59, 95).

22. Another standard tactic is introduced here: showing 'the significance of order' with an ungrammatical example ('"✳Bill John hit"'), pressing into service the 'asterisk' normally reserved for 'speech forms' of the 'past' 'known to us only by inference' (BL 163, 299). English is contrasted against Latin, where 'the words appear in all possible orders' 'with differences only of emphasis and liveliness' (BL 197) (cf. 3.53). Understandably, its more rigid word order made English the foredestined model language for the later trend toward formal syntactic theories (cf. 7.5, 18, 41, 61, 66, 79, 81, 7^{39}; 9.25; 12.7).

23. This account is vague; most utterances 'stimulate' the hearer to produce 'speech forms'. Equally obtuse is the idea that a 'negative' like '"nobody"' 'excludes the possibility of a speech-form' (BL 248f). More helpful is the statement that an 'interrogative' 'prompts the hearer to supply' 'the identification of the individual' (BL 260).

24. Even the 'dialogue "Is? – No; was"' is judged to consist of 'sentences', because 'forms' are 'spoken alone' (BL 179). Further on, however, a phrase starting with a 'relative substitute' like '"which"' or '"that"' is judged to be 'marked' 'as not constituting a full sentence' (BL 263).

25. Here, Bloomfield proposes for once to 'leave the ground of linguistics and to examine the problems' in 'sociology and psychology', in order to 'return' 'bolder' (BL 248, 250). His discussion is more commonsensical than technical, however.

26. The work of Whitney (1867, 1874) and Paul (1880) is cited, but the latter's book is scolded for such 'faults' as 'the neglect of descriptive language study' and the 'insistence upon "psychological" interpretation' (cf. Note 1) – plus being 'not so well written' and having a 'very dry style' (BL 16f) (look who's talking!).

27. Though 'fluctuation in the frequency of a speech-form' 'can be observed', its 'disappearance cannot', because 'we can have no assurance that it will not be used again' (BL 393). 'The doctrine of our grammarians' is of course judged ineffective in 'banishing or establishing specific speech-forms' (BL 498) (cf. 2.44; 8.26).

28. Yet Bloomfield decries the search for 'the motives of change in the individual word' (BL 420). He emphasizes diversity in space as well as time when he 'demands a statement of the topographic extent of each feature' of a 'dialect', charted on 'as many maps as possible' (BL 323f) (cf. 2.43; 3.65; 4.82).

29. However, Bloomfield is displeased that samples were often 'written down' by 'schoolmasters and other linguistically untrained persons' (BL 324) (cf. 4.5, 84ff).

30. To this overstatement add the ones maintaining that 'different economic classes' 'differ in speech', which is hardly true of the US today; and that 'a form used by a less privileged class' 'often strikes us as coarse, ugly, and vulgar' (BL 49, 152). Bloomfield knows after all that 'slang' is favoured not merely by 'vagrants', and 'criminals', but by 'young persons' and by 'most other speakers in their relaxed, unpretentious moods' (BL 154; cf. BL 49, 147, 394). And the speech of 'native servants' and 'slaves' did 'influence the language of the masters' in 'South Africa' (BL 474).

31. Bloomfield disparages 'creolized language' as 'an inferior dialect of the masters' speech', and a 'desperate attempt' greeted by 'the English speaker's contemptuous imitation' (BL 473f).

Chapter 5

Kenneth Pike[1]

5.1 Kenneth Lee Pike's weighty volume (762 pages) *Language in Relation to a Unified Theory of the Structure of Human Behaviour* (hereafter LB) documents his 'ambitious' 'attempt' to 'revise the conceptual framework of language study' and to foster 'extensive deep-seated changes in language theory' (LB 5f). Though published as a whole in 1967, its chapters had been composed (and some published) between 1945 and 1964. Pike made no 'full revision' to enhance 'consistency', but left the parts largely intact, even 'sections' that seem to 'come out of another age, so fast have battle grounds shifted' (LB 85n, 424n, 389n, 6, 8). 'The reader is warned in footnotes' that 'points of view in the text have been modified' or expressly 'withdrawn' in Pike's later thinking, and 'changes' have been made 'in terms', or new 'views' 'adopted, but not integrated into the early chapters' (LB 10, 424, 232nf). Sections with newer references were inserted next to older ones. Though at odds with the book's title, the disunified quality allows us to follow a gradual evolution spurred by steady 'confrontation with a wide variety of natural-language data' (cf. LB 9).

5.2 Pike's 'total work arose from a struggle to describe empirical data (especially the Mixtec and Mazatec languages of Mexico') in the absence of 'a satisfactory basis' in 'the current literature' (LB 5, 34). With a team of students and colleagues, including his wife Evelyn and his sister Eunice, he developed 'principles' for 'the analysis of scores of languages', chiefly under the auspices of the Summer Institute of Linguistics, which by 1964 had studied 'more than 350' languages (LB 9) (cf. 5.89; 12.56). Pike himself often 'took the first steps in the analysis of various languages of Asia, Africa, Australia, New Guinea, Europe, and North America' (LB 29f). Through such uses, the 'approach' began to 'meet many requirements' on 'theory and method' and to 'provide the theoretical basis' for notions previously 'postulated on empirical grounds' (LB 555n, 398) (cf. 12.43).

5.3 Pike's 'tagmemic' approach differed from mainstream American linguistics in many ways (cf. 5.6, 30, 35, 54ff, 61f), but most of all in its sheer elaboration and complexity. The organization of language was to be treated in: (a) 'variable depths of focus' determining which data or aspects merited attention (5.16); (b) a dyad of 'approaches' (etic, emic) to units seen either outside or inside a system (5.22); (c) a triad of 'views' (particle, wave, field) on the interrelatedness of units (discrete, continuous, arrayed) (5.31f); (d) a matching triad of 'modes' (feature, manifestation, distribution) (5.33); (e) a triad of 'hierarchies' (phonological, lexical, grammatical) (5.36f, 39f); (f) a structure of indefinitely many 'levels' (morpheme, word, phrase, etc.), arranged chiefly according to unit size (5.34f); (g) a miscellany of 'styles' related to social and geographical dialects, social roles, individual personalities, emotions, or voice quality (5.82); and so on. Although Pike gives sporadic examples from many languages, he nowhere fully analyses a discourse in terms of all or even most of these constructs. Their justification rests mainly on theoretical arguments that are sometimes intricate and provisional, as can be expected for so complicated an approach.

5.4   This profusion is partly offset by the absence of familiar schemes and dichotomies. The 'parts of speech' are not reconstructed (cf. 5.73). Mainly to facilitate data-gathering, the division into 'langue' and 'parole' is expressly discarded, and language is not separated from non-language, nor verbal from non-verbal (cf. 5.7f, 25, 32, 48). The observer is included in the observation, and the analyst in the analysis (cf. 5.9, 11, 16, 22f, 36, 44, 71). Form and meaning are handled not in opposition but as two sides of a 'composite' (cf. 5.48, 64, 76). And above all, language is 'unified' with 'human behaviour', as the book's title portends.

5.5   Pike's 'tagmemic' approach seeks an 'oscillation between theory and method rather than a one-way priority' on either side (LB 509) (cf. 12.42ff). On the method side, the 'principles' are intended 'as sign-posts' for 'structures to be discovered' and as 'exploratory tools for further work' (LB 518; cf. LB 70). A 'multiple-stage and multiple-level approach' should 'reflect' 'the practical working procedure of every practising descriptive linguist, even of those who most vigorously attempt to eliminate' or 'reduce to a minimum' 'cultural references' in 'linguistic analysis' (LB 215, 59). Pike doesn't 'object to an "as-if" procedure' of 'temporarily or deliberately ignoring data', but only to 'forgetting' that one's 'description' 'is limited in validity by the initial selection' and 'insisting' that the 'selection' is 'the only' 'scientific one' (LB 59) (cf. 5.35, 57). In 'practical fieldwork', even the 'methodologically helpful' tactic of 'working with "cleaned-up text"' and 'sentences' 'separated' or 'dictated' 'by the informant' can be 'fatal' for 'theory' (LB 571) (cf. 5.12f).

5.6   A '**theory** may be viewed rather broadly as a statement purporting to describe, or to explain, or to help one to understand a phenomenon', not merely to 'present a claim of truth, or assert relationships between phenomena, or predict the occurrence of phenomena' (LB 68) (cf. 11.84–98). This goal requires 'a unified theory', 'set of terms', and 'methodology' for 'analysing' 'any kind of complex human activity' 'without sharp theoretical or methodological discontinuities' (LB 26). In contrast to 'American writers' who 'place priority on dichotomous constructions', Pike expects 'theoretical advances' from an 'emphasis upon unity' (LB 358) (cf. 5.35f, 38, 54, 63).

5.7 'As more and more materials in speech begin to appear structured, the traditional view that "language" as a structure differs from "speech" as activity is threatened' (LB 536). So Pike 'abandons the distinction between "**langue**" and "**parole**" proposed by de Saussure' (cf. 2.20; 6.33, 46; 7.12; 8.30; 9.5; 11.12, 26, 47, 55, 67; 12.36). He extols 'the strength' of 'a theory of linguistics' 'which has a few theoretical constructs applying to the whole system of human behaviour' and which can 'portray adequately the universe as a system in which units can interact' (LB 547; cf. 5.38f, 89). He braves 'the dangers of leaving one's own discipline' in search of 'analogies between linguistic structure and the structure of society' (5.84), and advocates 'unity' among 'linguists, archaeologists, ethnologists', 'anthropologists, sociologists, and students of personality' (LB 6, 641) (cf. 12.35).[2] Though one might 'come from the opposite direction', e.g., from 'ethnological theory' into 'linguistics', 'recent formal studies in the linguistic area' offer 'a base which at the moment is easier to build on' (LB 6f) (cf. 2.7; 4.88; 6.10, 32, 51; 8.6, 12, 33; 10.5; 12.21).

5.8 'For best results, linguists' should 'raise their focus' to 'a high level of abstraction' and 'generalization' by 'treating language data within a single hierarchical structure along with non-verbal activity' (LB 111; cf. LB 26, 6, 120) (cf. 5.37, 60, 78f; 8.43; 9.42, 49; 10.7, 9, 86). We should 'give for the total event, as a unit, a unified description' which 'would simultaneously analyse and describe non-linguistic behaviour as well as the smallest and most intricate elements of linguistic structure' (LB 26). Motives for this demand include: 'language and non-language behaviour are fused in single events'; 'verbal and non-verbal elements' may be 'interchangeable' or 'substitute structurally for one another'; the respective 'structures' are 'partly alike'; and 'language behaviour' 'obtains its structuring *only* in reference to' the 'larger behavioural field' (LB 26, 30, 32, 35, 68; cf. LB 26, 134f, 120). Ultimately, a full 'description' might 'allow an outsider' 'to act as would a native member of the culture' (LB 121n).

5.9 Pike 'insists that an **observer** component enters into all ability to discover, understand', 'report on, or act as a member of a community', and forms 'part of any equation where perception is involved' (LB 58, 659). The main tactic of the 'analyst' is therefore to 'observe regularities of sequence in events' (LB 156). 'The study of observables' transcends any 'solipsistic' confinement to 'the study of one's own speech' and fosters a 'belief in the possibility of empathy with other persons' (LB 289). 'The scholar's observation and understanding of his own behaviour' can then enhance the 'fruitfulness', 'elegance, and simplicity' of the 'approach' (LB 663). Admittedly, 'one cannot guarantee uniformity of judgment in natural language' when 'observer intuitive components must enter analytical procedure'; though not 'unique', 'solutions' may be at least 'alternative, simple, and mechanically convertible' into each other (LB 259n, 289) (cf. 8.35; 10.90; 11.55; 12.3).

5.10 Since 'language' cannot be 'analysed or described without reference to its function in eliciting responses', we should consult 'the normal expected response of the community' (LB 40, 27). Pike 'insists' that 'explicit observable reactions' constitute 'data' and 'objective evidence' (LB 352, 63, 67, i.r.) (cf. 5.15, 70; 8.25, 41, 91; 10.16). Citing the concern of 'psycholinguistics' for ' "publicly observable indices of subjective events" ' (Carroll 1953: 72), he discounts demurrals that ' "the linguistic processes of the 'mind' as such are quite simply unobservable" ' (Twaddell 1935: 9), and that ' "the native speaker's feeling" ' ' "is inaccessible to investigation by the techniques of linguistic science" ' (Bloch and Trager 1942: 40) (LB 351f, 66f) (cf. 4.8f; 7.9ff; 8.24; 11.38).

5.11 Problems do persist, because, as Pike concedes, 'observable' 'clues' are 'a usable' but not a 'precise criterion' (LB 81) (cf. 4.8; 5.11, 13, 16, 18, 27f, 30, 43). 'Responses' may be not 'immediate', but 'delayed for a much longer time', or may not be 'uniform', or may be either 'conscious or unconscious' (LB 43, 66, 83). A 'relativity of phenomena' can arise when 'equally true' 'observations come from different standpoints' and 'observers' (LB 659). 'Observers' may 'differ' in 'ability', 'training', 'hearing', 'memory span', 'attention', or 'interest' (LB 46f). One's own 'cultural background' may foster a 'bias' toward 'familiar' 'events' or make one 'notice' 'alien' things 'native participants do not' (LB 45f) (cf. 3.50; 4.4, 72; 5.24, 78; 8.14; 12.1).[3]

5.12 Pike's own methods stemmed from using a '**monolingual approach**': working 'without written or translated documents and without an interpreter', and relying heavily on 'gesture' (LB 29f, 34f, 40, 61, 225, 601). There, 'the interdependence of language and non-language behaviour' is 'striking' and must be reflected in 'the analysis' and 'description' (LB 29). 'Working through' the 'interlacing problems' of 'data' helps 'make concrete' the 'principles of linguistic structure' (LB 215). The 'student' who 'views data from many viewpoints' can 'treat the problem as a whole', and 'dive into the structure' (cf. 5.23, 25, 89).

5.13 Even using a monolingual approach, it is hard to 'avoid encroaching on the innate linguistic naivity of the **informant**' (as 'recommended by Bloomfield' [1942]) (LB 62) (cf. 4.6; 12.47). 'Verbal' 'data' in 'normal cultural settings' may become 'abnormal' 'due to the intrusion of the linguist' (LB 68). 'Too rigorous a direct attempt to observe persons' or 'test' them may 'change their reactions' by making them 'self-conscious' and 'forcing' 'items' into 'awareness' – a 'tool for a psychoanalyst' perhaps, but a 'detriment' for a 'linguist' (LB 191, 238, 159, 657; Zipf 1935:12). When asked for 'the meaning of words' by a 'language analyst', 'informants' may be 'unable to express' the 'meanings', or 'misinformed', or even 'deliberately deceptive' for the sake of 'psychological comfort' (LB 90, 156) (cf. 12.49). Their 'observational and analytic ability may be poor'; or their 'variation of purposes' may render their 'reports confused or conflicting' (LB 156).[4]

5.14 The modest tactic of asking informants 'whether elements are the "same" or "different" ' (cf. 4.26, 31; 5.61, 65) already entails 'difficulties' because 'the reaction' is 'an exceedingly complex process', not a 'simple' '"yes" or "no"' (LB 61f, 223f). Here too, the 'questioning' adds a new 'context' and may 'change the structure we were investigating' or 'destroy the naivity' of the 'informants' by making them 'quasi-analysts' (LB 159, 224, i.r.). 'An elaborate gestural situation' or 'specific linguistic training' may 'help the informant identify the level on which the linguist is working', but may also 'destroy the apparent simplicity of the procedure' (LB 62). Do the 'units' 'differ by their distribution' in 'larger units', 'by their structural function within the total system', or by their 'purpose or meaning' (LB 160)?

5.15 Various solutions are aired for these dilemmas with informants. Pike mistrusts the 'elaborate distributional substitute for this procedure' proposed by Harris and others (LB 613), because of the unacknowledged steps involved (cf. 5.61). A better tactic is to 'check' one's 'conclusions' 'against fresh data unbiased by such questioning', e.g., to 'gather comments when' 'the actor' 'is "off guard"', or to examine 'a body of textual materials' obtained from 'recorded conversation' among 'other speakers' (LB 159, 656). Even 'more objective' is to 'study the kinds of slots in which activity occurs' and to look for relations between an 'activity' (as a 'cause') and a 'response or sequel' (as an 'effect') (LB 90f, 663) (cf. 4.8; 5.10, 47, 49ff).

5.16 Observation vitally depends on '**focus**', i.e., what a person attends to. 'Observer status affects the focal hierarchy', and any 'change in focus is necessarily accompanied by a sharp change in observer attitude or participant type', especially when acting as 'analyst' (LB 107, 111). 'Individual differences' imply an 'indeterminacy of focus' (LB 80). Depending on their 'attention', 'interest', or 'concentration', 'participants' may raise focus to the 'whole' or 'lower' it to 'a shorter sequence' (LB 110, 79f). 'We can never be certain' what is 'essential', 'since any particular person may be acting analytically rather than participating', 'and this difference of purpose' affects the recognition of 'units' (LB 80). Whereas an 'ordinary participant' does not 'normally go' beyond certain 'lower limits', 'an analyst' might do so, e.g., as 'a linguist' 'quoting' 'items', or as an 'observer' 'noticing' only some 'grammatical infelicity or non-current pronunciation' (LB 80, 155; cf. LB 129) (cf. 5.36, 46). 'Teaching situations' also 'change the focus' and 'thresholds of attention' by 'focusing attention on details which later must drop below the threshold' (LB 292f, 154f).

5.17 Pike applies the term '**hypostasis**' when, 'in order to give it separate analytic attention', 'any unit of activity is abstracted' from the 'purposive activity sequence expected by regular participants' (LB 107) (cf. 5.36, 76; 6.16; 8.71). We can 'try to pick a predominant focus unit' inferred from 'cultural evidence', or 'start at some arbitrary but convenient' 'threshold' (LB 106, 153, 293). 'In a systematic hypostasis', 'scientists' may 'arbitrarily set upper and lower limits' and 'concentrate on a smaller body of data' – whence 'the difference between disciplines' (LB 111) (cf. 9.3–9). But 'normal' and 'hypostatic verbal systems may be' only 'partially congruent' (LB 107, 155).

5.18 Accordingly, a 'complete theory' 'must include the theorizing of the theorist' and distinguish between 'analytical and non-analytical' 'activity' (LB 222) (cf. 5.13f, 16, 20, 36, 46; 12.36). 'The analysis of words or sentences outside of normal behavioural contexts' 'itself constitutes an activity' meriting 'analysis' 'in structural terms' by 'students of human behaviour' (LB 134) (cf. 5.54). 'In some situations', 'the activity of bringing an item into focus' can be 'partly observed' as a 'physical act' (e.g., 'turning' one's 'head or eyes'), but not when 'inward concentration' or the 'use of memory' is involved (LB 112f). So 'the objective study of concrete verbal utterances' of 'participants' must be accompanied by 'tests to determine the accuracy of one's powers of discriminating' (cf. 12.36). After 'the intuitive steps' whereby 'a system is arrived at' through 'guess and check' 'procedures', 'description' should not 'present' only 'the formal part' of 'the data'; instead, we should 'attempt to understand and systematize this heuristic' of 'intuitive' 'steps' as a 'possibility of knowledge' (LB 225n, 317n) (cf. 7.9ff). This project would be 'profitable' provided 'its results and procedures are not allowed to vitiate the results of an analysis of normal participant activity' (LB 134).

5.19 One key problem of focus and analysis is to decide ' "the proper *size*" ' of the ' *"unit"* ' and to 'differentiate' 'units of size' (LB 96, 42; cf. Zipf 1935: 12) (cf. 12.29). In a 'unified theory', 'large and small units' should be 'mutually defining': 'minimum' 'units' 'can be defined only as relative points in the larger units and systems'; and 'one must start with some knowledge' 'of large units before studying smaller' ones (LB 150, 120; cf. LB 72, 142) (cf. 10.32; 12.57). The lower limit can be set by consulting 'meaning or purpose', 'cultural' 'relevance', and 'observable native reactions', rather than relying on a 'structural regress from the point of view of a physiologist or biophysicist' (LB 130, 83, 304, 306, 409) (cf. 2.31, 68; 3.9; 4.18, 32; 5.15, 28, 42; 6.7, 54). For the 'top limit' on 'maximum' units, Pike can 'find no evidence' for 'setting up theoretical limits' (LB 130) (cf. 5.51).

5.20 An equally 'difficult' 'theoretical problem' with units is 'the balance' between 'giving priority to *relationships*' or to the '*items*' they relate, e.g., to 'oppositions' or their 'poles' (LB 179, 358). A 'theory will look very different' depending on which receives 'emphasis' (LB 358). Pike's basic tendency is to 'place attention on units': 'elements viewed' as 'whole entities set apart' (LB 9) (5.32). In his opinion, 'we perceive a structure being made of units' as 'parts of a system', just as ' "the speaker acts as if he were using units which start and stop" ' (LB 271f; Longacre 1964: 14) (cf. 5.26). ' "Purely relational units" ', in contrast, might ' "have nothing to relate" ' (LB 357; Vachek 1936: 38). These arguments oppose the 'glossematic' claim that 'to the scientific view, the world' 'consists' 'only of functions' (LB 271, 282; cf. Vidall 1957) (cf. 6.25, 28; 11.25). Yet Pike doesn't mean to 'imply that units exist *apart from* their occurrence in any relationship'; 'the present theory' merely 'interprets' 'relationships' as 'conceptualized hypostatic constructs' of 'the analyst' (LB 282).

5.21 Pike's 'interest' thus lies in 'a system of *units*', not 'of *oppositions*' – a point of conflict between 'American' and 'European' work, respectively

(LB 345, 358) (cf. 2.57f, 70, vs 4.45). He questions the idea of '"*binary oppositions*"' being the only '"distinctive"' kind, or 'the "most advantageous way of coding any verbal behaviour', or the '"child's first logical opposition"' (LB 359; Jakobson 1949, 1962; Jakobson and Lotz 1949; Jakobson and Halle 1956). He foresees 'confusion' when 'binary oppositions as wholes' get 'treated as distinctive features', or when '*absence*' as 'one pole of an opposition' 'is treated as essentially *present*' (LB 348, 358) (cf. 4^3; 5^{12}). 'Binary emphasis' also makes 'immediate constituent analysis', which seems 'intuitively' 'valid',[5] 'extremely difficult to handle empirically' (LB 477) (cf. 4.60ff, 5.50, 62; 7.36f; 9.33). In Pike's 'theory', 'immediate constituents' are not 'the point of initial attack' as in 'current linguistics', but 'the end product of analysis'; and 'binary' 'end products' are a just 'special instance' among all kinds of 'series' (LB 477, 444, 244; cf. Pike 1958). 'Starting from unity' is better than the 'traditional' 'starting' by 'looking for "cuts" in the string of materials' (LB 478) (cf. 5.6).

5.22   To reform and refine linguistic analysis, Pike found it 'convenient – though partially arbitrary – to describe behaviour from two different standpoints', whose 'results' 'shade into one another' (LB 37). 'The **etic** viewpoint' is 'an essential initial approach' that 'studies behaviour as from outside of a particular system'; it 'treats all cultures or languages, or a selected group of them, at one time'.[6] 'The **emic** viewpoint' 'studies behaviour as from inside the system', sees 'every unit' as 'functioning within a larger structural unit or setting in a hierarchy', and 'treats' 'only one language at one time' (LB 37f). 'Etic units' can be 'created by the analyst' or can come from 'broad samplings, surveys' or 'training courses', and may thus be 'available in advance' of the 'analysis' (LB 37f, 55). 'Emic units' 'must be determined during the analysis of the language; they must be discovered, not predicted'.

5.23   Of course, we have to 'assume a philosophy of science' 'granting that in the universe some structures occur other than in the mind of the analyst' (LB 38).[7] 'Structure really exists in language' '"as much as any scientific structure really obtains in the data which it describes"' (LB 56; Harris 1954: 149). 'This viewpoint' 'does not rule out alternate descriptions'.[8] If '"the constructs were in the metalanguage"' only, it would not be sensible to '"look for behavioural correlates or psychological reality"' (LB 72; Saporta 1958: 328) (cf. 5.23; 10.42, 10^{32}; 12.57). Moreover, if 'the linguist' 'denies structure', 'his own statements, descriptions or rules' must be 'without publicly available structure or ordering; linguistic statement comprises a subvariety of language utterance, and hence can have no structure if language has no structure' (LB 38) (cf. 12.48).

5.24   'An **etic** system may be set up by criteria or a "logical plan" whose relevance is external to the system' or comes from 'partial information' (LB 38). '**Emic**' 'criteria' must be 'relevant to the internal functioning of the system' and hence 'require a knowledge of the total system'. So 'etic data' are 'tentative' and 'preliminary', whereas 'emic data' are 'refined' and 'final' (LB 38f). Still, 'etic and emic' may often be 'the same data from two points of view' (LB 41). Many 'etic units turn out to be emic'; or, when 'emic units' are 'compared' from one language to another, they 'change into etic' by being 'viewed as generalized instances of abstract stereotypes, rather than as living parts' (LB 41f, 75).[9] Moreover, the 'ultimate' 'replacement' of an 'etic description' by a 'totally emic' one, though foreseen 'in principle', 'probably never' occurs 'in practice' (LB 39). Still, 'emic procedures' help to 'eliminate' 'etic' 'distortion' or a 'margin of error' in the 'preliminary recording and analysis' due to a bias toward or against 'Indo-European languages' like 'Latin', or to 'over-recording' 'more elements than can be relevant' for 'the whole system' (LB 182, 142; cf. LB 72, 213, 141, 173) (cf. 3.5, 50; 4.4, 72; 5.11, 60, 78, 92; 8.24).

5.25 Some units are 'etically' 'similar but emically different' (LB 43, 47, 105).[10] Far more are just the opposite, because 'etically, each repetition' of 'any unit' is 'distinct' in respect to 'absolute physical differences' (LB 44) (cf. 5.19, 28f; 7.91; 12.45). 'Delicate measuring instruments' show it's 'impossible to repeat any movement' *'exactly'*, and 'every movement' 'differs etically according to the sequences' wherein 'it occurs' (LB 316, 44ff, 164). 'Variations' may also happen 'below the threshold of perception' (LB 45, 87f). So we could have 'an infinite number of etic differences', while 'the emic unit is a composite of all' (LB 87) (cf. 3.3; 4.13; 8.42). 'The investigator' should thus assume every 'form of purposive activity' to be 'a variant of an emic unit' (or a 'part' or a 'sequence of units'); what seems 'random' is 'not structureless' but is 'emically unanalysed', or shows 'a greater range of variation' than other forms, or 'does not forward the purpose of the activity' 'in focus' (LB 518, 115). In this spirit, 'the linguist' should try to 'use *any* observable data' to 'discover the emic units of a language', including 'extralinguistic' 'actions' 'eliciting' or 'resulting in speech' (LB 68).

5.26 The special 'value' of 'the etic approach' is to 'give to the beginning student' an overview of 'the kinds of behaviour occurring around the world' and to enable a 'faster handling of the data of an unfamiliar language' (LB 40, 182). Pike envisions an 'etic "lens"' making 'tacit reference to a perspective oriented to all comparable events' 'of all peoples, of all parts of the earth'; but a more modest hope is that 'sufficient uniformity throughout the world' will enable 'the analyst' 'to make early guesses' (LB 41, 176) (cf. 5.84; 9.18; 12.38). The special 'value' of 'emic study', on the other hand, is to show 'a language or culture' 'as a working whole' and to 'help one understand the individual actors in such a life drama – their attitudes, motives, interests, responses, conflicts, and personality' (LB 40f). We might strive toward a 'predictive science of behaviour'; 'even statistical' 'studies' require that 'homogeneity in behaviour' be 'emically defined'.

5.27 A particularly compelling motive for the 'etic' viewpoint is Pike's loyalty to **physicalism** (cf. 4.8; 6.26; 7.15; 8[14]). In fact, 'physical' can appear instead of (or with) 'etic' as the counterpart to 'emic' (e.g., LB 43f, 87, 89, 99, 105, 120, 151, 164, 168, 677). By using an 'etic physical description', 'emic structural units' can be 'presented' 'not only as algebraic points' in 'a structural system, but also as elements physically described' (LB 39, 120).[11] Indeed, 'we never' 'completely "abstract"' a behavioural emic unit' 'away from the actual physical action' (LB 89, 187, 645). This loyalty explains the preoccupation with 'the physical setting of society' and 'language'; witness such insistent locutions as 'physical dwellings', 'physical clothing', 'physical bodies', etc. (LB 121, 128, 169, 645, 658) (cf. 5.82). Language entities are also said to have a 'physical order', 'position', or 'place in the uttereme' (LB 209, 281, 246, 253, 511, 251, 457, 196) (cf. 12.33). Pike admits 'all "facts", all "things" reach' human beings 'only through perceptual psychological filters' for 'the physical data we observe' (LB 645), but such data seem to make him feel most comfortable (cf. 5.84).[12]

5.28 If 'each overt or covert type of physical movement must ultimately enter into the analysis of activity' (LB 112f), we might end up considering events down through 'muscles' to 'molecules' and 'atoms' (cf. LB 90, 106, 111, 118, 130, 292f, 306, 365n, 393n, 516, 590, 660, 662f) (cf. 12.45). Pike recognizes an 'insoluble' 'difficulty' for 'science' here if the search for 'minimum units' enters such 'an infinite regress' (LB 303fn). It would be a *'reductio ad absurdum'* to 'treat the movement' of a 'molecule' in a 'nerve fibre' in a 'muscle' of 'the vocal organs' as a unit (LB 130). And 'the study of the movement of muscles' is 'more complex than' 'the anthropologist's' 'techniques of observation can handle' (LB 304). Anyway, 'describing' something as 'a concatenation of molecules', as a 'physicist or chemist' might, still entails 'the emic structuring of a person – the scientist' and his whole 'cultural history' upon which his '"understanding"' depends (cf. 4.13); so 'the observer is not bypassed by going to the microscopic level' (LB 660). We should be content to 'treat subperceptual variants' only 'in special studies' of 'a small amount of data', e.g., a 'microscopic and physiological analysis' of 'movements even down to submolecular size' (LB 88, 292). But when 'analysing behaviour *as the actors themselves react to it*', such minuscule actions 'appear non-contrastive' (LB 292f, 297).

5.29 'The **emic** analytic process' also has its 'problems' (LB 95). It 'must deal simultaneously with emic units as discrete parts' both 'of a system' and 'of sequences' within 'complex events'. 'Models of the emic unit' as 'a mere sum' of 'separate parts' 'must be rejected' (LB 513) (cf. 2.29). In line with his devotion to observed behaviour, Pike says 'the basic problem' for 'linguistics' and for 'epistemology and theory of perception' is to find 'a theory and procedure for analytically breaking up the physical etic continuum into a sequence of discrete emic units' (LB 94).[13] 'Sharp points of change' inside a 'continuum' or 'fusion' may be 'impossible' to 'set up in theory or practice' (LB 95) (cf. 5.47, 77). 'No absolute physical criterion' or 'simple measurement' can apply when 'physical variants overlap' (LB 94). Moreover, 'a complete description of the manifestation modes of an emic unit' could include an 'infinite number' of 'actual and potential variants' (LB 88) (cf. 5.25).

5.30 Such factors render Pike uneasy about the American trend whereby 'the approach through item and process was largely replaced' with one through 'items and their arrangements' (LB 502, 556) (cf. 7.75). 'In this respect, linguistics' 'was moving counter to the general stream of the philosophy of science', which was '"thinking more in terms of process"' than '"of things"' (LB 557; Sinclair 1951: 80). Carried too far, either 'approach' 'leads to serious problems' and 'distortions' (LB 550, 547). The 'item-and-arrangement approach' entails 'arbitrariness' in 'requiring sharp-cut segmentation', even if this tactic has 'advantages' for 'dealing' with 'actual utterances, not constructs', and is 'effective' for 'listing morphemes separately, as in a dictionary' (LB 551, 553, 558; cf. Lounsbury 1953: 12, 15). 'The resulting discrete localizations of meaning' 'may be highly unrealistic' (LB 558) (cf. 5.65; 6.47f; 12.51). And 'the approach may be forced to list laboriously every stem' 'as if no regularity could be observed' (LB 551). 'The item-and-process approach', on the other hand, entails the 'distortion' of 'setting up' '"norms"' as 'convenient theoretical starting points' which 'are at times arbitrarily chosen' or even 'imply' an 'irrelevant normative judgment' (LB 553) (cf. 12.27). The 'approach' also 'implies' that 'forms' '"first" come together in sequence and "then" are modified'; this 'pseudo-history' overlooks the prospect that the 'unmodified forms', though 'present in the description', 'may never have occurred in sequence in the observed data' (LB 552) (cf. 5.87; 7.48, 51; 12.54).[14]

5.31 To incorporate item, process, and arrangement, Pike finds it 'highly attractive' to combine 'three separate technologies' or 'theoretical concept sets': a *'static* view' of 'a sequence of units' as 'discrete segments' or '**particles**'; a *'dynamic* view' of 'a sequence of units' 'treated as **waves** flowing into one another'; and a *'functional'* view of a '**field**' of 'complex but unanalysable units' 'with unpredictable unitary characteristics' (LB 468, 511n, 545f, 563, 553). 'The particle view' can use 'psycholinguistic data on segmentation', 'the wave view' can use 'physical data on continuous articulatory movements or sound waves', and 'the field view' can use 'a theory of classes and systems of phonemes, morphemes, and tagmemes' (LB 513).

5.32 In the 1954–60 sections of the book, Pike 'gave special attention to particles' and 'less' to 'waves'; later he turned to 'fields', e.g., in his 'matrix studies' (LB 512n).[15] He extols the 'field' view for 'helping explain' how 'some high-level units' 'are semantically relevant as a whole' (e.g., 'compounds' and 'phrasal idioms') (LB 554) (cf. 2.61; 4.60; 5.54). The 'field' view also stresses the role of 'reacting to a pattern' within 'the theory of learning': 'the child' can 'learn complex expressions as wholes' before being able to 'manipulate substitutable items' (LB 554; cf. LB 547) (cf. 9.11). 'In practical language learning it is often simpler' 'to memorize a few "exceptions" than to learn complex analytical descriptions' not vital to the 'recurrent pattern in the language'. However, the field view will need some new 'techniques' in 'theory and method' to handle 'non-segmentable' 'junctions', 'mixtures', 'diverse' 'inventories', 'disparate' 'fusions', 'concentrations of energy', and so on (LB 555). And we must not 'adopt the field approach' exclusively, lest we 'no longer find' 'language' 'in our data'. As we will see, most of the book is in fact dominated by the particle view.

5.33   Pike matches his triad of views with a triad of 'modes', defined as 'distinct' 'simultaneous structurings' of 'activity' (LB 86, 93, 513).[16] The three 'modes are not parts nor pieces of the whole: they each comprise the entire substance' or 'physical data' (LB 93, 86). The 'modes' are also not 'merely points of view', but 'reside in the behavioural data' (LB 514). The **feature** mode' shows units *statically'* as 'discrete particles or segments of activity'; 'the **manifestation** mode' shows them *'dynamically'* in 'continuous waves' (as 'simple vs complex', 'free' vs 'conditioned', or 'fused vs clearly segmented'); and 'the **distribution** mode' shows them *'functionally'* in a 'total field' (LB 511, 463f). The three modes cover (a) *'contrast* or *identification'*, (b) *'complementation* or *free variation'*, and (c) *'distribution* or *'class membership'*, respectively (LB 85f, 426, 510f).

5.34   Pike also distinguishes 'levels',[17] each one 'representing some phase of structuring in the material examined' (LB 480). As units on respective 'levels' he mentions (in descending order or size) 'conversation', 'topic', 'monologue', 'utterance-response', 'utterance', 'sentence', 'clause', 'phrase', 'word', 'morpheme', 'stem', and 'phoneme' (LB 441ff, 437f, 517, 362). These 'levels' 'are quasi-absolutes' 'in that etic criteria' can 'differentiate them' (LB 437).[18] Yet 'the levels' are 'still somewhat relative' in 'specific details of the available criteria', and in the 'numbers which are structurally relevant to any one language'. The 'crucial' 'requirements' are that 'unit types on one level' must 'control the occurrence and relative (fixed or free) order of included constituents, and be structurally organized' 'sharply in contrast' to the 'next higher or lower' level, despite some 'indeterminacy' of levels' reflecting 'built-in indeterminacies in the system' (LB 482) (cf. 5.37, 39, 45, 53; 12.27, 57).

5.35   So despite all 'contrastive' 'criteria', 'levels' cannot be studied in the 'complete separation' some American linguists demanded in the belief that 'rigid, water-tight compartments or levels are aesthetically satisfying and provide the only valid scientific conclusions' (LB 443, 59f, 66; cf. Hockett 1942, 1955; Moulton 1947; Trager and Smith 1951) (cf. 3.60; 7.46; 12.27). They excoriated the practice of 'level mixing' as a 'sin', a 'dragon' to be 'slain', or a 'ghost' to be 'exorcised' (LB 410, 362; cf. Martin 1956; Joos 1957). They condemned '"the Pike heresy – introducing morphological considerations into phonemic analysis"' (Voegelin 1949: 78) (LB 362) (cf. 5.45; 8.68). 'Grammar' might be used at most 'heuristically' in 'search', but not in 'presentation'. For Pike, however, 'to insist on a rigid separation of levels' is 'to fail to report the empirical data' in its 'integration' (LB 591, 406). 'Compartmentalization' fosters a 'fragmentation' he cannot judge 'elegant' or 'rigorous in scientific description' (LB 406; but see LB 555). Moreover, 'a rigid separation of levels' relegates 'meaning' to a level 'beyond the sentence', 'gives priority' to 'phoneme' over 'morpheme', and 'leaves no room for the tagmeme' (LB 586) (cf. 5.50f).

5.36   To re-integrate the levels, Pike undertakes to portray 'human activity' within a 'pyramided **hierarchy**' (LB 194, 226, 245, 409, 479, 586). Here, the 'traditional' scheme with 'phonemes combining to make morphemes, morphemes to make words, words to make sentences, etc.' is 'rejected' in favour of 'three hierarchies with partial overlap': 'phonological', 'lexical', and 'grammatical' (LB 409; cf. LB 586) (cf. 4.50; 5.45; 7.56; 12.27).[19] Thus, several levels of 'hierarchical structure' can 'occur pyramided' 'within a unit' (LB 434, 109).[20] Our perspective can vary according to (a) *'height'*, i.e., 'the hierarchical element cut out for attention from a sequence', or the 'place' of 'a unit' 'in a hierarchy'; (b) *'depth'*, i.e., 'simultaneous attention on both the high and low' 'units of one or more hierarchies'; and (c) *'breadth'*, i.e., 'the composite range' of 'hierarchies' under 'attention' (LB 177). But *size* still seems to be the chief factor, e.g., when 'high' is opposed to 'small', or 'depths' are labelled 'large' or 'small' (just the terms often used for 'segments' or 'parts') (LB 109ff, 75, 79, 83, 79, 135). 'Limits to the lowest level of focus are set by the purpose of the participant or observer' (5.16f), but with some 'indeterminacy'; for example, 'focus' on 'a single word or syllable' is 'best treated as' a 'hypostasis in which the hearer becomes analyst' before ' "shifting gears" ' back into normal communication' (LB 111) (cf. 5.17, 20). 'The upper limit fluctuates greatly' with 'permanent or temporary purpose and interest' and is 'less rigid culturally' 'than the lower limit' (LB 111) (cf. 5.19, 46, 59).

5.37 A total event (like a 'football game) is composed' of an 'enormously complex network' of 'interwoven hierarchies of activity' (LB 117f) (cf. 5.78ff). 'The classes of units' in each 'included hierarchy constitute a simultaneous componential system', 'the most important and obvious' being the 'verbal and the non-verbal'; beyond that, 'linguists differ' about 'how large' or 'how small a part of language is best called a "system"', 'according to their area of attention' (LB 132; 584f) (cf. 12.43). 'The hierarchies' are 'relatively or partially independent' and 'interpenetrate' with a 'margin' of 'indeterminacy' (LB 132) (cf. 5.39, 45, 53). Pike contrasts this approach to one based on 'a simple linear sequence', which 'conceals the hierarchical structuring of the data' by 'squeezing data' and 'mashing a hierarchy' 'into a linear sequence' (LB 406, 589). Chomsky, Halle, and Lukoff (1956: 79), for instance, propose to ' "simplify linguistic theory by restricting it to the consideration of linear systems" ' (LB 417f) (cf. 9.109).

5.38 Pike judges his 'behaviouremic theory elegant and fruitful' because it 'describes' the 'enormous complexity of interlocking systems, levels, and units' in terms of 'a few simple components', rather than seeking 'simplicity' 'by a rigid separation of levels' (LB 586f) (cf. 5.3, 6, 35; 12.45). All things in a 'system' 'are mutually defining'; indeed, 'all the terms in any system, in our view', are 'in part circular' (LB 555, 440) (cf. 8.40; 9.29; 12.48). 'Neither unit types, nor subsystems, nor levels of structure' can 'be discovered or adequately described' without regard for others 'which are diverse from those momentarily under' 'attention' (LB 555f). 'High-level material must be anticipated' sometimes when 'presenting' 'low-level' and vice versa in order 'to make the empirical situation clear' (LB 577) (cf. 5.19, 34; cf. 12.43).

5.39 If 'no language system can occur' without 'interlocking', 'tagmemic theory' must 'stand or fall by demonstrating' how 'hierarchies interlock' (LB 565f) (cf. 9.34). The 'details' of this 'interlocking' 'must be discovered through empirical research for any particular language' (LB 581). The 'interlocking' may be 'lateral' among 'units' on one level (e.g., 'fusion of units at their borders'), or else 'vertical' among 'units' on 'low' and 'high' levels' (e.g., 'inclusion of smaller units within larger units') (LB 565, 582; cf. LB 474). 'Structure' itself is 'in part a function of the interlocking' of 'levels'; and 'fusion', 'double functions, and indeterminacies' enhance the 'integration' and 'dynamics of a system' (LB 566, 582) (cf. 5.34, 36f, 58f; 12.59).

5.40 'Hierarchies' are mutually 'relevant' if at *some* 'points or regions' their 'units' are 'co-terminous or co-nuclear', but not *all* (or we would have 'merely a single structure') (LB 566, 581). Although 'parallels' may be 'aesthetically satisfying', the 'nonconformity' of 'borders' was what originally 'started' Pike 'on the quest for a new' 'theory' to supplant 'theory' which uses 'artificially selected data' to 'eliminate empirical areas where multiple hierarchies must be postulated' (LB 570ff) (cf. 5.48, 89; 9.46, 55, 75, 109; 12.50). The vital question is how 'grammatical', 'phonological', and 'lexical hierarchies' exert 'mutual control' on 'patterns' and 'borders' (LB 573). For example, 'the units of the lexical' and 'phonological hierarchies often have borders in common', though not 'every word' is a 'phonological' 'unit' (LB 567) (cf. 5.52). Or, the 'presence' of a 'morpheme' can 'signal the presence' of a 'lexical unit', a 'lexical class', and a 'grammatical unit' (LB 576) (cf. 4.53; 5.46, 53). Still, 'the lexical and grammatical hierarchies' are 'distinct' in several ways: 'in two utterances', 'the same 'lexical unit' may have 'different grammatical functions'; two 'sentences' can be 'lexically different' but 'grammatically the same', whence the distinction between 'sentence and sentence type'; 'lexical units' can be 'expressed' in 'phonemes' but 'grammatical' 'structures' only in 'formulas'; and so on (LB 577f).

5.41 When one unit or 'sequence' 'manifests' 'two or more levels simultaneously', Pike 'postulates **portmanteau levels**' (LB 440, 452, 483, 548n) (cf. 5.52ff, 59, 5^{16}, 5^{27}). On the middle levels, 'portmanteau' relations are found among 'word', 'phrase', 'clause', and 'sentence' (LB 441f, 455, 459) (cf. 2.55; 3.26; 4.61; 5.51, 54; 8.55; 10.40, 79; 11.75, 93). On the low levels, 'portmanteaus' may combine the 'phone', 'syllable', and the 'stem' (LB 317, 548, 330, 443).[21] On the high levels, the 'sentence' may be 'portmanteau' with a 'monologue' or even a 'total discourse', and the 'utterance-response' may be 'portmanteau' with a 'conversation' (LB 442, 466) (cf. 5.59). To prevent portmanteaus from unduly clouding his hierarchy, Pike stipulates that a level counts as 'higher in the hierarchical scale' when '*some*' of its 'units' 'are larger than the longest units in the next lower' level (LB 364, 404f) (cf. 12.29). This manoeuvre allows him to retain size and length as organizing criteria even when they don't happen to differ, and thus to make his hierarchy quantitative as well as qualitative.

5.42 The **phonemic** level is the lowest, and the most basic to Pike's approach. The 'phoneme' is 'probably the one unit which can be demonstrated to exist both linguistically and psychologically' (LB 352; cf. Saporta in Osgood and Sebeok [eds] 1954: 62). Its 'threshold criteria' relate to 'articulatory movements' (LB 432, 78, 25) (cf. 2.70f; 3.14, 18, 21; 4.29, 34; 8.66, 70; 12.26). So it is a 'threshold unit' of 'behaviour', not of 'acoustics'; its 'locus' is not 'the sound wave', but the 'actor and his actions' (LB 306, 309). 'The essential physical substance' of its 'manifestation' is 'the physiological movement of the body parts' during its 'production' (LB 306) (cf. 12.26). These 'movements' are not 'absolutes or constants', but 'relative' to the 'identificational–contrastive features of the phoneme'.

5.43 If we 'focus' 'on the speaker', we face a 'difficulty': 'how can a listener "hear" a phoneme?' (LB 309f) (cf. 2.71). Maybe the hearer 'reacts' 'by empathy' 'to the physiological movements', such that 'spoken and heard phonemes' function within 'congruent systems' sharing 'neurological movements' (LB 310). Even 'the phonemes in a thought sequence' could be 'neurologically' 'congruent' (or entail 'suppressed articulatory movements'), though this 'activity' can be 'observed' 'only through gross patterns of electric activity', and 'the person thinking' has 'no proprioceptive sense' of it (LB 311) (cf. 3.10; 4.9).

5.44 At all events, Pike devotes his most massive efforts to describing 'the phonological hierarchy' in terms of movement. He meticulously labours upward through 'the phoneme', 'the hyperphoneme', 'the syllable', 'the rhythm group', 'the stress group', 'the pause group', and 'the breath group', frequently referring to movements of the 'chest' and 'abdomen' (LB 290–423) (cf. 8.22). He invokes 'the chest pulse' to 'differentiate the syllable from the phoneme'; 'the abdominal pulse' to 'differentiate' 'the rhythm group from the syllable'; and so on (LB 432).[22] The degree of detail and the physical grounding encourage Pike to see in 'phonological movement' the 'clearest' model to 'be generalized to other linguistic levels' (LB 547) (cf. 12.27). His 'tagmemics' 'looks forward to a universal etics of grammatical types' 'analogous' to 'phonological types' (LB 470n). He started out by coining his main terms 'etic and emic' (5.19) 'from phonetic and phonemic' and seeking '"cultural equivalents of phonemes"' (Kroeber and Kluckhohn 1952: 124), such as 'the behavioureme' (LB 37, 33, 121) (cf. 5.60).[23]

5.45 The **morphemic** level is also treated in detail, though less so than the phonemic. Here, 'a language' is 'constituted' by the 'set of all systems of morphemes which are congruent and/or simultaneous', plus 'all other verbal elements congruent with them' (LB 178) (cf. 4.46). A 'system of morphemes' is a 'class of distribution classes'; a 'large system' may 'include' 'smaller' ones, e.g., for 'segmental' and 'intonational morphemes'.[24] 'The internal structure of the morpheme' has 'a sequence of actions' 'resulting in some typical sequence of sounds' (LB 175). 'Morphemes' can thus be 'characterized' 'by a transcription of a series of single phonemes, linearly'; the fact that 'phonemic features' can also have 'morphemic status' indicates a 'fuzzy' or 'indeterminate threshold', as with 'many classificatory boundaries in the theory' (LB 305) (cf. 4.50; 5.36; 12.27, 59).

5.46 'Ordinarily, a morpheme' 'is below the threshold of participant awareness and shorter than a unit' of 'focus' (LB 175) (cf. 4.54; 5.13, 48; 9^{15}; 12.49). It goes unnoticed unless it 'happens to manifest a complete uttereme under conscious attention' (e.g., '"Boy!"') 'or is under the immediate scrutiny of the analyst' (e.g., in a 'dictionary listing'). Consequently, the methods for discovering morphemes can be complex. Pike advises us to start with an etic 'procedure for identifying **morphs**' by 'finding the least common denominator' in 'two utterances' 'partly alike in form and meaning', or an 'element' whereby 'the two differ' (LB 179) (cf. 4.52). 'Once a morph is identified', we should decide if it is a 'free or conditioned variant' of a 'morpheme', or a 'part' of a 'complex variant', or 'a sequence' of 'variants', or 'a fused composite' – or just 'an error' to be 'eliminated' or 'corrected by later comparison with other occurrences' (LB 182, 179).[25] 'No technique' 'can lower to zero the margin of error' in a 'guess', but 'errors' can 'in principle' 'be corrected' by 'more adequate data' (LB 222).

5.47 An 'important' 'characteristic' of both 'morph' and 'morpheme' is the potential to be '*active* (or live, productive)', 'entering regular analogies'; but 'serious practical difficulties' can arise in telling which ones qualify (LB 169ff, 190) (cf. 2.52f; 7.76; 8.58). Pike suggests a battery of 'tests for activeness': if the morph or morpheme is 'one of a large number' that can 'occur' in 'a slot' or 'larger unit'; if it 'can occur in a wide variety of different kinds of functional slots'; if it is used 'in new combinations' created 'in recent times'; if its 'meaning' is 'easy to determine' and 'contributes in a regular fashion to the total meaning' of the 'sequence'; if a 'native speaker, upon questioning, can describe', 'discuss', or 'define' it; if an 'investigator' can 'easily segment' it 'out of a continuum'; and so on (LB 170f). These tests too leave some 'indeterminacy', so that between 'active' and 'inactive (or passive, dead')' we may find 'semi-active' ones, or several 'degrees' within 'a progressive gradation' (LB 170ff, 174, 191). 'Indeterminacy' also enters when morphemes 'fuse' or their 'boundaries blur' (LB 177) (cf. 5.39, 45, 53, 77, 87; 9.29; 12.59).

5.48 'The morpheme' is a '*form-meaning composite*' (LB 163) (cf. 5.64, 76). Although the 'relationship' is not 'one-to-one' ('biunique'), the 'formal component' is not 'separable' from 'the meaning', and 'neither may be abstracted as a unit for normal participants' in 'non-hypostatic behaviour' (LB 162f; 187, 189) (cf. 12.54). To be sure, when a 'morpheme' is 'below the threshold of focus of non-analytic members of a culture, they will be unable to report, on questioning, any meaning' (LB 157f). Only 'lexical' or 'dictionary meaning' is 'sometimes above the awareness threshold of the untrained native speaker' (LB 160). Besides, 'the meaning of a morpheme can be so greatly weakened in certain contexts' (e.g., '"terrible"' vs '"terribly good"') that its 'variants' 'have little meaning in common'. No meaning at all 'can be detected' for 'an empty' 'morpheme', which is 'identified only as a residue' after analysing out the 'meaningful elements' (e.g., '"does"' in '"does he go to the school?"' (LB 160f, 199). Still, the 'majority of those sequences of sounds' that 'appear meaningless' 'early' on can later prove to be 'meaningful' ones, or else 'mistakenly segmented parts of a larger morpheme' (LB 161). 'Communicative' functions' 'could not be served by a language' with too many 'meaningless elements'; and 'few' 'are in fact found'.

5.49 Although the 'morpheme' makes a fairly tidy 'correlate of the phoneme', Pike's method was crucially shaped by his conviction that 'grammar' might contain 'some other correlate' (LB 5, 9). Just 'as the phoneme was reflected in practical orthographic work for millenia before being "found" by the scientists', so some 'unknown unit of grammar' might have remained hidden from 'current theory of linguistic structure' (LB 5, 287). Here also, his reasoning was steered by the idea that the 'inclusive analytical principle' is to 'treat items in slots on a higher level' (LB 477) (cf. 5.47). 'The most basic relationship is between a unit and its slot-occurrence', rather than a 'binary' link 'between units of equal rank or of the same level' (LB 282) (cf. 5.21; 12.29). At 'each level of focus', 'classes of segments occur and are determined by the slots they fill' (LB 83). In return, 'each kind of slot' has 'a class of appropriate segments', though 'appropriateness' can be 'indeterminate' (LB 83f). 'This slot-class potential' for 'occurring' engenders 'positive and negative predictions' about what might happen or be said, even if 'slots' in 'lower-level focus' 'need not be filled in every manifestation' within the 'activity' (LB 86, 88). 'The 'probability' or 'prediction' applies to 'structural components', not to 'particular' 'words' (LB 605) (cf. 7.90f; 9.93; 10.16, 56).

5.50 To designate this key 'correlation' between a 'slot' and a 'class', Pike selected the '**tagmeme**', a term of Bloomfield's now given a new meaning[26] and declared 'more basic than' 'immediate constituents' (LB 194f, 490, 282). The tagmeme embodies the theses that the 'function in the slot of a higher structure' 'is always immediately relevant to the nature of a unit'; and that 'a unit cannot be defined' as 'discoverable or describable in itself', but only within 'a larger unit of behaviour' (LB 451, 195) (cf. 5.8, 14f, 19, 22, 39, 47). Because 'the total' of a 'class' 'cannot all occur at one time as an event', 'the tagmeme seems' 'much less concrete than the morpheme', yet is claimed to be 'an objective emic unit' in 'normal participant behaviour, not a mere conceptual construction of the linguist' (LB 203). Predictably, Pike rests this claim on the 'physical basis' in a 'manifestation' (cf. 5.24, 28, 31, 39).

5.51 More encompassing than the tagmeme is the '**hypertagmeme**' for the 'high-level' 'members of the grammatical hierarchy', such as the 'conversation', 'monologue, utterance', and so on (LB 432, 517) (cf. 5.59). Pike is uncertain whether 'hypertagmemes' and their 'levels' should be 'absolute' or 'relativistic' (LB 443, 446f), i.e., whether they could be 'listed' independently of 'focus', using a fairly 'mechanical' 'methodology' (LB 443, 445ff). A 'relativistic' outlook enables 'a unit to simultaneously represent a low level and a higher one' (e.g., 'word' and 'clause level'); and we can 'abbreviate complex formulas into simple high-level forms in a less arbitrary' and more 'consistent' way (LB 443f). Yet 'disadvantages' 'result' as well (LB 445). The 'tagmeme' comes to depend on 'the temporary focus of attention', their 'number' 'fluctuates', and 'levels' 'proliferate' (e.g., 'within the word stem'). The 'minimum' 'tagmeme' is not 'as directly seen' as are 'phoneme' and 'morpheme'. 'Threshold criteria' are needed 'for determining when one has passed from one level to another', and 'the total coherence of the theory' is affected (LB 445f). 'In *some* sense' then, 'terms need to be made absolutistic'. To resolve the problem, however, 'a major change is required in the theoretical framework' (LB 450).[27]

5.52 A closely related quandary is whether the 'hypertagmeme' should be *'obligatorily complex'*, i.e., 'composed of two or more' units or sequences (LB 432f). At first, this standard seemed 'useful' because it was 'simple', 'sharp-cut', and 'easy to state', 'understand', and 'apply'; and it allowed a 'simple discovery procedure', 'hierarchical results', a 'quick recognition' of 'minimum formulas', and 'immediate work' 'without determining' 'the point of word boundaries' (LB 435). Moreover, 'data' could be 'structured' 'in an elegant, concise fashion' 'easily transferable to pedagogical treatment for language learning'. Yet because a 'hypertagmeme' may sometimes have 'a single emic slot', the standard raised problems in 'field studies', until it 'collapsed' and was 'withdrawn' (LB 447, 433ff, 439). 'Just as a morpheme' 'could be simultaneously a word and a phoneme' (cf. 5.50, 58f), a 'tagmeme could also be a hypertagmeme' – another 'portmanteau' (LB 449) (cf. 5.40). 'The theory' becomes 'more coherent' when 'one point of view' includes 'reference to minimal units, to portmanteau levels, to division subclasses, and to hypermorpheme classes' (LB 452).

5.53 Moving upward from morphemes brings us to 'the **word** level'[28], for which 'general etic criteria are available', but may not always 'apply' nor 'lead to the same results' (LB 437f) (cf. 2.18; 3.31; 4.54; 6.23; 12.29). To count as 'words', units must be 'isolatable', 'interruptible', 'versatile of occurrence', and 'rigid in order' of 'parts' (cf. 3.62, 4.53, 60; Nida 1949). Further factors are 'special relationships', 'junctures', or 'sequences' within the 'unit', as well as 'phonological markers' like 'pause' and 'rhythm', and so on. Yet Pike admits that the 'word level' may not be 'structurally relevant and useful' for every 'language', e.g., not in 'the Mayan family' (LB 481f). And the 'indeterminacy between the levels' is acute when 'border-line instances occur between word and bound form, and between word and phrase' (LB 438) (cf. 12.28). High 'frequency' can convert a 'sequence of morphemes' into a 'fixed' 'idiomatic unit' (LB 605). Or, a 'single word' may 'constitute an entire' 'phrase', 'clause', or even a 'sentence' (more cases of 'portmanteau') (LB 439f, 483) (cf. 2.55; 3.34; 4.67; 5.51; 6.45; 8.56f; 12.28).

5.54 The next higher level is that of the '**phrase**': 'a unit' 'filling an emic slot in a clause or sentence structure' and 'composed' of 'two words' or 'one word which is optionally expandable in that same slot' (LB 439) (cf. 12.54). Here again, Pike departs from 'Bloomfield' and 'the American scene', for whom 'the phrase' is 'a free form' made of 'two or more lesser free forms' (LB 486) (cf. 4.42, 65f). Pike wants to allow for 'a single word' being 'portmanteau' with 'a phrase', and rejects 'obligatory complexity' (cf. 2.55; 3.26, 34f; 4.60; 5.51; 8.56; 9.75; 10.40; 11.75). Indeed, he warns that the 'dichotomy between morphology and syntax' should not be made 'too early' or 'rigid'; it is not 'sharp' for some languages (e.g., Mixtec, Chinese) and creates problems with 'phrase-words' (e.g., '"the king of England's hat"') or 'stereotyped phrases' (e.g. 'rack and ruin') (LB 580, 479, 481, 162) (cf. 2.61; 4.60; 5.32; 12.28). Still, in 'English' at least, the 'phrase has a much greater expansion potential than the word' and more 'freedom' to 'vary' 'the order' of its parts, and 'is more likely to be interruptible by parenthetical forms or phonological junctures' (LB 440f).[29]

5.55 Next comes the 'level' of 'the **clause**', which had previously been 'undefined', 'due to the great influence of Bloomfield', for whom it was 'never an integral part of his description' (LB 486) (hence no mention of it in Ch. 4). Following Longacre (1964), Pike accords 'the clause level, though definable separately for each language', 'a place in the grammatical hierarchy between phrase and sentence, as the syllable is between phoneme and rhythm group' (LB 441). 'Clause' is an 'especially useful' 'term' for '*subject* and *predicate*',[30] since the 'typical' 'overall structural meaning' is 'predication', 'equation', 'query, or command' (LB 425, 441) (cf. 3.36; 4.69; 8.55; 11.78f).

5.56 Next comes the level of the **sentence**, described as 'a minimum utterance', 'isolatable in its own right' (LB 442). 'Some but not all are clauses', while others are 'non-clause phrases or words' (cf. 4.67; 9.82). And whereas a 'clause' can add 'tagmemes of time, manner location', etc., 'the sentence' can add 'further clauses in coordinate, subordinate, and paratactic relations'. In 'its broader setting', the sentence entails 'the deep problem of identity of unit against ground' and 'remains' 'immune from attack' only if 'it is taken, in a regularized form, as an axiomatic starting point' (LB 8n) (cf. 12.54). That 'the sentence is "the unit of language, not the word"' was asserted by Sweet, Cassirer, Humboldt, and Firth, though Sweet (1913: 5) too hedged by terming the word '"an ultimate or indecomposable sentence"' (LB 482, 146) (cf. 8.56; 12.54). In America, 'linguistics in the past' had 'made its most striking progress by dealing with units no larger than the sentence' (LB 145). Yet ultimately, Bloomfield's definition of 'the sentence' as 'an independent linguistic form' (4.67) imposed a 'limitation which has prevented, in this country, the development of linguistics' (LB 146, 484). 'Large language units' were 'left to students of literature' (more 'written' than 'spoken'), 'metrics', 'public address', and 'speeches' (LB 146). Among the 'few linguists' to address such units, Jakobson and his co-workers 'studied verse patterns', while Harris proposed a '"discourse analysis"' which Pike finds 'atomistic', based on 'assumed, not procedurally identified sentences in juxtaposition' rather than in 'integration' (cf. Jakobson 1960; Harris 1952) (cf. 10.2).

5.57 For dealing with 'the total language event in a total cultural setting', 'the sentence is a totally inadequate starting' or 'ending point' (LB 484, 147, 484). 'Sentences must not be studied outside of total concrete behavioural contexts'; 'conclusions' about 'isolated hypostatic data' (in the sense of 5.17) may not be 'valid for the description of units of normal contextual speech' (LB 155) (cf. 10.3; 12.55). 'The abstracting out of sentences for study' is 'legitimate and useful', but must be recognized to be an '"as-if" procedure' and 'a deliberate distortion' for 'handling data' (LB 484) (cf. 5.5; 12.39). 'Many important characteristics of sentence structure can be adequately handled' 'only in reference to discourse structure', e.g., to tell whether or not a structure is 'independent' or 'complete' (LB 485f, 148).

5.58 In Pike's classification *'full'* 'sentence types' include 'sentence–word', 'question', 'actor–action', 'instrument–action', 'equational', 'narrative', 'emphatic', 'surprise', and 'disappointment'; *'minor* sentence types' include 'interjection', 'completive', 'exclamatory', and 'aphoristic' (LB 139; compare BL 171–77). By taking discourse into account, Pike can identify types by quite diverse criteria, ranging across 'form', 'elements', 'constituents', 'order', and 'pitch', plus 'meanings as determined by their occurrence in the cultural setting' (LB 139). Still, the examples from Menomini given by both Pike (LB 139) and Bloomfield (BL 175f) suggest that a sentence type (e.g., 'disappointment sentence', BL 176) can be set up whenever *some* language marks it *formally* (cf. 4.68; 12.54).

5.59 The even 'higher levels' – '**monologue**' for 'the connected discourse of a single speaker' (e.g., 'lecture, soliloquy'), '**utterance-response**' for an 'exchange between two speakers', and whole '**conversation**' – are barely described aside from the relative size, the number of speakers, and the flow ('merging', 'diverging', 'overlapping', 'interrupted', etc.) (LB 442, 125). Perhaps Pike supposes that portmanteau relations and level-independent concepts like 'tagmeme' and 'hypertagmeme' provide a channel for transposing up to these higher levels the results for the lower levels he explores in much greater detail. For instance, he suggests that the '**topic**' as a 'unit in between the utterance-response unit and extended conversation' might be 'treated somewhat like the meaning of a morpheme' (LB 442, 136) (but cf. 10.63–69).[31]

5.60 Pike devotes more concern to the '**behavioureme**': the 'emic unit of top-focus behaviour' 'related to its cultural setting in such a way that cultural documentation may be found for its beginning, ending, and purposive elements' 'within the verbal or non-verbal behaviour of the domestic participants or observers' (LB 121; cf. LB 128ff, 140, 153f). 'The size of behavioduremes' and their 'closure' help to indicate 'when one's analysis is complete' rather than 'arbitrarily' 'ended' (LB 129f) (cf. 5.51). 'An **acteme**' is the 'minimum segment or component of human activity' in a 'behaviour-eme' (a 'verbal acteme being a phoneme' and a 'non-verbal' one a 'kineme') (LB 291).[32] 'A verbal behavioureme is an **uttereme**' – a 'unit which receives participant focus in non-hypostatic situations' – 'large' 'types' being 'hyperutteremes' and 'small' ones 'minimum utteremes' such as the 'single sentence' (LB 157, 121, 133). 'In the analysis of language', 'uttertics' would be a 'classification' of 'utterance types around the world' (LB 133, 135) (cf. 5.23).

5.61 It can been seen that Pike provides no special 'level' for '**meaning**' nor a separate hierarchy for '**semantics**'. At first, we might be reminded of the deliberate exclusion proposed by other American linguists (cf. Morris 1946; Chomsky 1957; Lamb 1962) (cf. LB 148f, 279, 474f, 497, 500, 617, 620; 4.15, 26). Lacking an 'algorithm for the discovery of semantic components', some 'analysts' adopted a 'formalistic approach' using strictly 'distributional criteria' and 'eliminating' even 'structural meaning' both from 'definitions' and from 'procedures of analysis' (e.g., Harris 1951) (LB 620, 277). ' "Meaning" ' got set aside as a ' "metalinguistic" ' aspect of ' "the material" ', or postponed ' "until the linguistic system has been completely described" ' – ' "phonology" ', ' "morphology" ', and ' "syntax" ' (LB 61, 278; Smith 1952: 59; Trager and Smith 1951: 68). At most, 'meaning' was to be 'the linguist's and the layman's shortcut to a distributional' result, a source of 'quick clues', or an aid for deciding 'whether elements are the same or different' (LB 60f, 180; Harris 1951; Fries 1952) (cf. 5.14, 65; 4.26, 31). ' "Grammatical meanings" ' might be admitted if they are ' "definite and sharp, essential features of every utterance" ' (Fries 1962: 99) (LB 279).

5.62 Pike also started out in 1948 seeking 'formulas' for the 'immediate constituents of any utterance' 'without reference to meaning', but 'later' gave up and 'abandoned an algorithm for analysis' (LB 286fn) (cf. 5.86; 9.110; 10.14; 12.50). 'Bloomfield overstated his case' in arguing that 'since meanings cannot be known exactly, they cannot be utilized' (LB 148) (cf. 4.14ff, 26, 51, 68). So Pike's pique is now added to the 'protest' against ' "the stultifying exclusion" ' or ' "delay" ' of meaning (e.g., Pulgram 1961; Haas 1960) (LB 188). In his opinion, 'the use of no meaning' 'implies that the linguist' 'is not interested in language as it functions as a communicating device, and cannot analyse the communication process' (cf. 11.32) and its 'content'; and one 'attempts to reject the implications of one's own procedures' (LB 60ff). 'Semantic components' are essential for the 'presentation' of 'language as a communicative system'; we need to know what a 'structure' 'means, not merely that it is well formed', and to 'generate sentences which are meaningful and usable by the speaker' (LB 225n, 280). To exclude 'meaning or purpose' is 'to abandon the most useful structural threshold between the reciting of a poem and the minutiae of atomic structure' (LB 304) (cf. 5.28). Linguists can only 'bypass the mention of meaning', not 'the use of meaning' (LB 61).

5.63 On the other hand, Pike 'rejects with Fries and Harris an analysis by meaning *alone*' just as much as one by 'form alone' (LB 278, 181). He also 'rejects the dualism of Hjelmslev' with a 'functional dichotomy of expression and content' (cf. 6.25ff) for 'leading to a theory in which "signs", "symbols", and "semiotics" ' are 'too widely divorced' from 'human behaviour', and for implying 'emes of meaning' as 'abstracted relationships' with no 'physical manifestation' (LB 187) (cf. 6.50–56). He joins Firth in 'rejecting the theory of signs of de Saussure and Hjelmslev', who imply that 'a "sign" ' ' "is the bearer of a meaning" ' (LB 63) (cf. 6.23; 8.20). Pike predictably likens 'form' and 'meaning' to 'physical' and 'functional' 'characteristics' (LB 55).

5.64 Thus, meaning is for Pike not a level or a hierarchy, but an omnipresent aspect of all levels and hierarchies. 'Every step in linguistic analysis' must deal with 'a form-meaning composite', in which 'form and meaning do not have to be in a one-to-one relationship' (LB 278, 63n, 55, 63, 149, 162, 472, 516) (cf. 5.48, 76). 'Meaning has its locus not in the individual bits and pieces', but 'within the language structure as a whole' or within 'verbal behaviour' in a 'frame', i.e., in an 'identified context' (LB 609, 134). For example, 'each **morpheme** ultimately obtains its meaning only in relation' to others in 'the total system' and in 'particular sequences' (LB 605) (cf. 5.67). So by 'defining the morpheme only in relation' to a 'total structure', we can resolve 'difficulties' when morphemes seem 'lexically meaningless' or 'lack' an 'unchanging core of meaning' (LB 184, 186, 598f; cf. Bazell 1949; Bolinger 1950; Hockett 1947; Nida 1948, 1951) (cf. 5.48). Or, we can handle 'semantic variants' by asking how they are 'conditioned by the universe of discourse', 'the style', the 'physical matrix', or 'the neighbouring morpheme' (LB 599) (cf. 5.84f).

5.65 'The sharp-cut segmentation of meanings' 'is therefore in principle impossible' (LB 609) (cf. 5.27; 12.59). 'The meaning of one unit in part constitutes' and 'is constituted of the meaning of a neighbouring unit'. 'Meaning' is a 'contrastive component of the entire complex' and 'occurs only as a function of a total behavioural event in a total social matrix' (LB 148f, 609).[33] So we must foreground 'the social components of language meaning' by focusing on 'the activity of the communicating individuals', both 'overt' ('verbalization', 'physical activity') and 'covert' ('intention', 'understanding') (LB 598). 'Perhaps the answer will lie' in 'finding a statistically' measurable 'set of common contexts', or in 'testing for native reaction' (e.g., '"same or different" tests'), or in consulting 'the common' 'cultural effect' of 'physical events' or 'behaviour' (LB 600) (cf. 5.10, 26, 70).

5.66 Pike suggests that 'meaning in verbal behaviour' has as its 'analogue' 'cause and effect in physical matters' (LB 663) (cf. 4.8, 80; 6.62; 7.33; 8.41; 12.11).[34] 'Units of physical motion' 'underlie all the physically manifested units of purpose and meaning' (LB 290) (cf. 5.27). This outlook leads him to imagine a metaphoric 'orbit' of 'meaning' (LB 603). 'The *central* meaning' applies when 'words occur' in 'descriptions' 'close to the physical situation which they name directly', and gets 'more difficult' to state when no 'reference' is made to 'physical objects', 'actions, or qualities' (the case with 'small distribution classes, such as "if", "an", "who", "the", "to"') (LB 602f) (cf. 4.24). Or, the 'central meaning' may have 'greater frequency' among 'the community' than 'marginal meanings', except for 'special universes of discourse' (LB 601). Or, 'the central meaning' may relate to 'the physical context in which the words were first learned by a child' (LB 603f, 600f).[35] 'As the speaker grows older', 'the central meaning' may become 'relative to the universe of discourse' (LB 601). Pike even envisions 'a hierarchy of universes of discourse with progressive degrees of centrality' (LB 602).

5.67 Pike's scheme has 'no specific number of distributional orbits, or degree of remoteness from the central' (LB 604). 'The outer' 'orbits carry the greater communication energy' for 'hearer impact', e.g. in 'poetry', 'puns', and 'slang'. Major examples of the outer 'dependent or derived meanings' are the *'idiomatic'* meaning not 'predictable' from 'the meanings of its parts', and the *'metaphorical* meaning' (LB 601ff) (cf. 9.97ff). 'Nonsense' 'results if one attempts to carry back the "meaning"' of a 'metaphor' ' "to the primary physical context" ' (Urban 1939: 639f) (LB 632). 'Metaphor', and 'poetry' in particular,[36] are domains for 'going beyond verbal responses to physical stimuli' and 'discussing non-physical problems' (LB 615). But a 'metaphoric meaning', which starts out being 'less frequent for the community as a whole', can 'spiral down into the central orbit', 'gradually becoming the only linguistic item' to 'label' an 'object or situation' (LB 604).

5.68 This orbit scheme befits a physicalist approach. Also fitting is the 'behaviourist' notion of ' "non-linguistic reality serving as a guide" ' (LB 635) (cf. 12.24). But Pike approves Malinowski's (1935: 64f) warning against the 'dangerous assumption that language mirrors reality'; and Cassirer's (1946: 9) tenet that the ' "mutual limitation and supplementation" ' among 'symbolic forms' is a more ' "basic philosophical question" ' than ' "their relation to an absolute reality" ' (LB 625f) (cf. 4.71; 6.12; 10.10). For Cassirer (1946: 8), these 'forms' are 'not imitations, but *organs* of reality' whereby ' "anything real becomes an object for intellectual apprehension" ', e.g., 'codable colours' are 'recognized' 'more often' (cf. 4.22; 6.54; 7.31, 71); 'the grasp of reality' must be 'mediated' by 'concepts', even 'mass and force'. For Pike, to know 'the ultimate truth, the ultimate structure of physical reality' would require 'the emic perception of God', whereas that of 'individual men' is a 'component of the total reality available to His observation' (LB 659). Since 'His views' 'are not available to us', they don't figure in 'our discussion'.

5.69 Of course, Pike is less willing to identify language with thoughts and concepts than was his teacher Sapir (cf. 3.10f) (to whose memory the book is dedicated, LB 3). ' "Units of thought and speech do not coincide" ', ' "showing unity but not identity" '; 'thought is "there simultaneously, but in speech it has to be developed successively" ' (Vygotsky 1939) (LB 640) (cf. 10.15). Also, 'a person may attain a concept' 'without verbalizing it', or may have the 'ability to think' despite 'incapacities for speech' (e.g., in 'expressive aphasia') (LB 634, 544, 639; cf. Goldstein 1948; Miller 1951). Even so, Pike concurs with Cassirer that ' "the chaos of immediate impressions takes on order and clarity" ' only by means of ' "linguistic thought and expression" '; and he 'closes the volume' by quoting George Herbert Mead that 'the perception of objects as enduring is not possible without language' (LB 639, 678) (cf. 2.17, 27, 32; 3.10ff, 17, 32, 35, 40; 6.2, 6f, 26, 30f; 7.3, 44; 8.24f; 11.17f, 22, 60f).

5.70 From a more behaviourist standpoint, 'concepts' are said to ' "tie together" ' ' "sensory experiences" ', organize ' "data" ', and provide ' "hypo-

theses about the way one should react to one's environment"' (LB 633, 635;
cf. Vinacke 1951: 1ff; Postman 1951: 267f).[37] 'Meaning' and 'purpose' form
'the bridge by which' 'a physical behaviour pattern enters into the
structuring of society or of the individual', and allow 'similar or identical
events' to 'function differently' (LB 660, 42). We can 'determine the
presence and nature of meaning and purpose' from the 'elicitation of
response' – a domain whose 'data' are open to 'objective study' and
'evaluation' (LB 156, 158) (cf. 4.14, 27; 5.10, 15; 7.10; 8.23; 10.92; cf. Fries
1954: 65). 'Purpose' is strategically placed here alongside 'meaning' because
it is 'frequently obvious' and 'easily' 'detected' in an 'observable larger
sequence of events' as a 'regular association of units in activity' toward 'a
goal' and as 'a response' or 'impact on the hearer' caused by an 'utterance'
(LB 42, 116, 598). We can 'assume that human activity is purposive if it
regularly elicits either (a) a positive response activity' 'or (b) a deliberately
verbalized or non-verbalized resistance' or 'rejection' (LB 156). 'To study
behaviour *as it actually functions*', we must 'assume that the analyst can
detect' such data (despite 'a margin of indeterminacy and error') by
'studying the formal components of the physical activity' (LB 158, 156).
Even 'epistemological attitudes, belief systems' ('conscious or unconscious,
vague or organized'), and 'character' can be discovered by 'examining overt
behaviour' (LB 533).

5.71 Since 'participants in human behaviour' 'affirm an awareness of
meaning or purpose', the 'analyst' can also combine 'technical' and 'lay
analysis' by consulting 'the popular hypostatic reaction to meaning', e.g.,
when participants 'discuss' 'meaning and purpose' (LB 156f). Or, we can
study the 'deliberate conscious choice' among 'alternative purposes' or
'meanings' when '"hunting for the right word"' (LB 197).[38] There,
'attention is likely to be focused' on 'higher levels' and 'purposes', in
contrast to the 'intricate unconscious selection' of 'internal elements'. When
the latter do become 'conscious' during 'disputes', 'challenges', or 'new
situations', we have 'a different kind of behavigoureme' from a 'routine' one
(cf. 5.11, 46). Pike raises but skirts 'the metaphysical problem' of 'free will'
versus 'biological and cultural determinism' by remarking that 'people talk'
and 'act' '*as if* they thought they had free will, purpose, and choice'.

5.72 Instead of addressing 'the general nature of a theory of meaning',
Pike only shows how 'a hierarchical view of language illuminates a few
special problems' in the 'general study of meanings' (LB 598). One problem
is '*class meaning*', which may be 'detectable within many members of the
class' and 'separable from the structural meaning' of 'the slot'; or may be 'in
part observable' through 'the statistical probability' of any 'member' having
a certain 'lexical meaning' or 'semantic component' (LB 253; 198, 227, i.a.).
A 'strong class meaning' may even 'clash' with, 'modify', 'eliminate', or
reverse the meaning' expected in a context (LB 199, 226). But 'class
meaning' may also be 'vague' or 'derived from only some members of the
class' (LB 606). 'Function words' form 'a marginal group of lexical items in
which tagmemic, morphemic', and 'class meaning become fused or
indeterminate' – evidence for Sweet (1900: 74) that '"there is no absolute"'

'"demarcation"' between '"the grammar and the dictionary"' (LB 274). So 'making class meaning a basic starting criterion for determining the classes is fatal to any structural analysis' (LB 201).

5.73 Glaring mistakes of this kind were made in 'the study of **parts of speech**', e.g., the 'incomplete' and 'inaccurate' 'definition' of the 'noun' as '"the name of a person, place, or thing"' (LB 488, 181) (cf. 2.65; 3.23; 4.55; 6.49; 9^{13}; 12.7). But '"it is easier"' '"to muckrake the parts of speech than to replace them with word-categories valid for every language"' (LB 285; Sheffield 1912: 20). For Henry Sweet (1913: 16, 18), '"the real difficulty of determining the meaning of the parts of speech lies in the fact, which logicians and grammarians obstinately ignore, that they often have no meaning at all"' – 'so that the "definition of a part of speech must be a purely formal one"' (LB 273) (cf. 12.54). For Fries (1952: 73), '"a part of speech is a functioning pattern"' and '"cannot be defined by means of a simple statement; there is no single characteristic that all examples of one part of speech must have in the utterances of English"' (LB 272).[39]

5.74 Pike hopes his own 'tagmemic model approximates our traditional feeling as to the relevance of certain components of language structure', but he doesn't try to resolve the 'difficulties in determining membership in parts of speech' (LB 444, 488; cf. Paul 1889: 403ff; Jespersen 1940–49: 2). To 'set up' 'a part of speech' or to 'preserve' 'the groupings of traditional grammar' would 'require criteria' of considerable 'complexity': 'identity of stem across the paradigm, comparability of kinds of relations between stem and affix, mutual exclusivity' among 'stems', and so on (LB 489). Pike's own examples of 'class meaning' mix grammatical aspects (e.g., 'person, tense, aspect') with conceptual ones (e.g., 'action', 'quality', 'substance') (LB 198f, 253; cf. LB 180, 284f).

5.75 Another problem is *'segmental meanings'*, which are 'components of structurally segmented verbal material' (LB 611). They can 'frequently' be 'abstracted by speakers', '"put into words"', and 'discussed overtly' with 'some assurance of accuracy', however 'naive' from the standpoint of 'scientists' (cf. 4.22). 'Linguists or dictionary makers' also set up 'segmental meanings', by giving them 'explicit verbalized attention' (LB 612). 'Subsegmental meanings' in contrast, tend to be 'vague', supplied by 'a "hunch" or "feeling"'; Pike likens them to 'subsegmental phonological features' in that both are 'covert backgrounds' (LB 611, 615).

5.76 Yet another problem is the *'sememes'*, defined as 'minimum structural units of meaning' by Bloomfield (LB 187, 620f; cf. 4.45, 50, 68; 6.47; Nida 1951; Joos 1958; Lamb 1962) (LB 187). For Pike, these are 'units of functional or analytical conceptualized hypostasis' and cannot be 'on an entirely different plane of behaviour' from 'morphemes', which are 'form-meaning composites' (LB 187, 162) (cf. 5.48). Yet 'the entire semantic system is in a fluid state': 'human communication' requires the 'possibility of change in meanings' (LB 623).[40] 'Language' 'functions' by 'extending the meanings of words to a variety of contexts which are only vaguely related'

(LB 600) (cf. 4.16). A 'theory' of 'semantic markers' (e.g., Katz and Fodor 1963) is unrealistic in 'omitting' a speaker's 'knowledge "about the nature of their world and about momentary situational, motivational and linguistic contexts"' (LB 628; Osgood 1963: 738) (cf. 7.67, 77; 12.59).

5.77 A final problem is *'hypermeaning'*, appearing when 'participants' identify 'two or more utterances' 'as having the same meaning' 'even though the morpheme sequences' are 'different' (LB 612f). This direct appeal to 'informant reaction' allows for 'hypermeanings' differing among various 'native speakers', e.g., 'scientists' and 'poets', or showing 'indeterminacy at the borders' (LB 613f) (cf. 5.39, 45, 47, 53, 87). 'Hypermeanings' can 'enter into a hierarchy of meanings' formed by 'inclusion' and 'subtype', and 'come into play' in 'translation' (LB 615f; cf. Nida 1955). They 'may be considered as conceptual quanta' that aid 'useful and rapid reaction to one's environment', but 'may lead to stereotyping' (LB 614).

5.78 To provide major demonstrations of his 'unified theory of verbal and non-verbal behaviour' Pike 'discusses' 'large units of activity' (LB 72; cf. LB 142), such as a football game, a church service, and a family breakfast. Having been present himself as participant and observer, he could collate his recorded data with his own impressions. We thus are not shown how an alien fieldworker could extract form, meaning, and purpose by observing such events. Being inside the culture, Pike attends the 'homecoming' game at 'dear old Michigan' (LB 100) without using observation to decide why people gather to witness a violent struggle (seldom played with the foot) for an odd-shaped ball that hardly even rolls or bounces.[41] He can tell the 'fans' are animated by 'nostalgia' and 'sentimentality', the university by 'public relations', and the teams by 'the purposes of playing the game according to the written rules' (in 'contrast' to those of 'baseball, tennis, hockey, or warfare'), gaining 'the Conference lead', and qualifying for 'the Rose Bowl' (LB 100f, 649). His insider knowledge also filters out 'irrelevant' or 'unofficial related activities' and focuses on those governed by 'official' 'rules and unwritten customs' or announced in a document calling itself '"Official Programme"' (LB 81, 99, 104, 649, 100).

5.79 Nor does Pike use the other techniques he recommends for discovery and fieldwork, such as consulting informants, making phonetic transcriptions, deliberately eliciting grammatical forms, or communicating by gesture as a substitute for language. So we do not get to see him at his best, analysing, say, a complete Mazatec 'planting or harvest' ceremony (LB 27). In addition, he fails to take his own advice by 'including the theorist' in the 'theory' (cf. 5.18). This failure is serious if 'each person to some extent constitutes a separate subculture'; 'a common experience', whether 'verbal or non-verbal', 'never occurs for any two people' (LB 51). He does not explicate his own sense of the occasions as typical ceremonies of the white middle class of the 1950s, where meals like 'breakfast' have an 'official opening' ('saying grace') and 'closing', where children must arrive at the same time (after being awakened by a 'symphony on the phonograph') and ask to be 'excused', and 'have been taught to take turns' 'to talk' or to ask for 'the floor' (LB 122–25, 193). A deep irony of some such ceremonies (like the church service) is that children's behaviour, other than sitting silent and motionless (i.e., non-behaviour), is seen as 'misbehaviour' (LB 84).[42]

5.80 Another problem with the demonstrations is the staggering explosion of data implied, even though Pike wants to show not so much 'the details of any complex behavioural pattern' as the 'structure' of 'wheels within wheels' (LB 78f). For the church service, he considers time ('a few minutes later', 'simultaneously', 'immediately'; 'day', 'week', 'year'), space ('auditorium', 'pew', 'aisle'), and (of course) the 'continuum of physical activity', 'divided into significant major chunks' 'during which the purpose' is 'vigorously forwarded', but also including 'noise' and 'non-emic' or 'non-directed activity' (LB 73f, 77f). The 'behaviour sequence' contains 'pulsations of activity'; 'segments end' or 'begin' with every 'appreciable change of activity' ('stand up', 'sit down', 'look up', 'sing'), 'actor' ('organist', 'song leader', 'usher'), or 'motion' of a 'body' 'part' ('arms', 'eyes', 'legs', 'lips', 'tongue', 'vocal cords') (LB 75f). For the football game, Pike distinguishes (a) 'human activity'; (b) 'products of human behaviour' which either are 'relevant' ('stadium, field, goalposts, whistle, horn') or are not ('coats, hats, cigarettes');[43] and (c) 'behaviour of non-human elements which are not products' ('dogs', 'sun', 'winds', 'molecules') (LB 118). The breakfast includes not merely 'conversation' with 'slots for give and take, i.e., utterance and response', either 'integrated' with 'eating' ('refusal of bananas') or 'unrelated' to it ('husky warning'), but also the 'physical setting' ('house', 'dining room' 'table', 'pots and pans') with its 'contrasts' ('between bowl and plate, or dining room and kitchen') and 'variants' ('heat of the stove', 'cloudiness of the sky') (LB 125, 128). '"Adults eating a bowl of cereal" is an emic motif' with its 'purpose-meaning of sustenance' and its 'physical components' ('filling the spoon', 'swallowing') (LB 151). 'A toast-eating motif' gets special focus for 'a young child' learning the 'emic motif of buttering toast' (LB 151, 292f) (an emetic buttereme?).

5.81 Pike concedes that 'if all components of the spectacle were to be treated on a par, the data would be unmanageable and a description hopelessly unwieldy and unintelligible' (LB 114f) (cf. 12.45). He hopes to 'avoid this chaotic result' by postulating 'sub-assemblies of component hierarchies' of 'structurally related' 'items' within the 'activity' (cf. 5.17, 36–40). But the data would still be enormous if we are resolved to describe a 'total system, 'event', or 'structure' (cf. 5.8, 14, 24, 37, 57, 64f).

5.82 Or, a 'congruent system' of 'permitted' 'types' might be set up under the term **'style'** (LB 132, 208, 599; cf. LB 463–67) (cf. 3.69; 4.40; 5.3, 64; 6.52, 54; 8.23, 70, 77, 83; 9.102f; 10.57, 86). Pike's behavioural outlook would focus on 'the style of speaker at that particular moment' (LB 152). The 'style' may be 'careful' or 'uncareful', 'slow' or 'rapid', 'normal' or 'lively', 'trite' or 'literary' (LB 316f, 412, 320, 343, 462, 550, 236, 605). 'Informal' or 'colloquial' contrasts with 'formal style', where 'formal' has the everyday sense of 'rigid' or 'ceremonial', e.g., in 'public address' (LB 72, 89,

155, 169, 208, 316, 343, 427).[44] 'Style' can also vary with 'voice quality', e.g., 'high-pitched', 'harsh', or 'emphatic', or used in 'whisper, song, shout', or 'chanting' (LB 311, 397, 400, 343, 378, 395, 582). 'Dialects' may also differ 'somewhat as styles' do; any one 'style or dialect' may 'contain coexistent systems or fragments of systems' (LB 582, 643).

5.83 'Style' acts as a 'systemic conditioning' for 'variants' that 'help to signal its presence' and to make a 'text' 'a uniform document' (LB 168f, 208). Variants include 'nouns', 'verbs', 'slots', 'lexical sets', 'morphemes', 'tagmemes', 'pauses', and 'vocabulary' (LB 208, 235f, 169, 238, 466f). Pike recognizes the perplexing 'implication that the system of morphemes must be determined separately for each' 'style', even though we might later 'find' 'many or most morphemes in common' (LB 169). He reassures us that 'styles share most of their units' despite 'different physical manifestations' (LB 132). And 'variants' of 'phonemes' 'are structurally the same in a topological sense': 'the two total patterns are identifiable point by point' (LB 312).

5.84 Pike closes his book with an ambitious sketch of 'analogies of society with language' (LB 642).[45] Both sides have a 'structure comprising a set of relationships within a network'; this 'structure' 'can be detected only by observing individuals in action', yet is 'relatively stable, outlasting the lives' of 'members' or 'speakers' (LB 643). 'A society constitutes a system of individuals' 'just as a language has a network of sounds', 'syllables', 'words, and sentences' (LB 644). 'Groups of individuals' resemble 'phonemes, syllables, and stress groups' in having 'identifying criteria' that (a) are 'physical,[46] essential, universal or nearly universal in all societies', (b) 'cut across the entire population', and (c) are 'functioning units in the society' (LB 646). 'The formal features of society' 'identify and contrast it with other societies' and include 'language as part of a communication system' integrated with 'habitual shared patterns of behaviour essential for coherence in self-awareness, for maintenance of life', and for 'carrying out tasks' related to 'economic, normative, political, or educational' 'goals' (LB 644).

5.85 If 'anthropologists' find 'this approach' 'merely formal' and 'lacking in insight' into 'deeper problems', 'the same difficulties may be seen in linguistic analysis', whose devotion to 'phonemes and morphemes' over-shadows 'the ultimate goal of the study of communication' (LB 642). 'Nevertheless', 'formal studies have been very stimulating to understanding the "mechanics" of language activity'. But those studies have succeeded only through drastic limitations on the data; they would explode if applied to a whole 'hierarchy' of 'personal activities and history' and to each person's 'total personal or social participation', including 'movements', 'facial expressions', 'utterances', 'restless activity', and so on (LB 646, 115ff) (cf. 12.45). 'The individual is at least as complex in his internal structure as the language he speaks' (LB 655). 'Something within his structure' may be 'responsible for the structuring of his language', though Pike is 'not prepared for' 'seeking' 'analogous materials in detail'.

5.86   And after all, the wide scope of 'tagmemics' is precisely what sets it apart from formal studies. Pike has little use for 'formal algebraic systems' or 'mathematical networks of abstracted relationships', such as the 'algorithmic view of the theory of grammar', 'automata', and 'machines' (LB 501, 645, 69; Bar-Hillel and Shamir 1960: 156) (cf. 2.70, 82; 3.72f; 6.8; 7.40, 7^{18}; 9.110; 10.14; 12.17, 50). A 'theory influenced by logic sets up axiomatic affirmations', 'presents a mechanical device' like 'a known mathematics' 'to predict some' 'phenomena of the real world, and tests' 'this prediction' against 'a few observed data' (LB 68f). But a 'theoretical system' can have fully 'axiomatic form' only when it remains 'uninterpreted' and is hence not 'applied to facts of nature' – 'a "mere calculus"' 'floating in the air' and 'constructed' 'from the top' rather than 'anchored at the solid ground of the observable facts' (Hempel 1952: 33, 53f; Carnap 1955: 210, 207) (cf. 6.56, 64). Also, 'mathematical notation' makes no 'reference to meaning or purpose' (LB 663).

5.87   Distinctly non-formalist also is Pike's thematic recognition of 'indeterminacy' in both theory and data (e.g., LB 64, 159f, 192, 230, 232f, 237, 251, 356, 546, 552f, 594; cf. 5.16, 34, 36f, 39, 45, 47, 49, 53, 70, 72, 77) (cf. Bazell 1952, 1953). For 'fidelity of description', 'the indeterminacy in the theory' should 'reflect' that 'in the activity of the community'; an 'arbitrary attempt' at a ' "clear-cut" theory' might 'conceal' 'the facts' and 'do violence to the structure' (LB 129, 159) (cf. 12.27). 'Indeterminacy' might 'never be resolved' or might even 'increase as one attempts to resolve' it 'more vigorously' (LB 222, 158; cf. LB 248, 356) (cf. 12.52). Pike's preoccupation with units and segments (a particle view) is thus attenuated by his attention to the 'indeterminacy' of their 'borders' or 'boundaries' (LB 45, 79, 95, 113, 116, 132, 180, 342, 381f, 468, 552f, 585, 645f) (a wave view) (cf. 12.59).[47] '*Well-described units*' need not be '*well-defined units*' (LB 121n).

5.88   As I remarked at the outset, Pike's book shows us work in progress, a continuing effort to develop a complex theory based on a limited set of notions for a wide domain. To satisfy the scientific climate of the times, he tries to remain loyal to a conception of objective observation whose last recourse is always the physical domain (cf. 5.18, 25, 27ff, 31, 33, 42, 44, 50, 63f, 65–68, 70, 80, 83f). The complexity of language had to be reconstructed by multiplying levels or hierarchies and justifying them by the (at least partially) different borders of the respective units (cf. 5.36ff, 41). Pike tends to proceed as if he felt the reality of units and constructs were somehow *in* the material itself. Yet he acknowledges that the analyst is more likely than the ordinary native speaker to be aware of them (cf. 5.11, 13f, 16, 18, 22, 46, 48, 71; 12.49). If language 'causes' a 'hearer' or a 'community' to react (5.15, 66), linguistic analysis is a special reaction, and Pike gets himself into his sights when he confronts technical factors (e.g., discovering the 'tagmeme') but not raw data (e.g., attending a church service). He does not, therefore, seriously question whether his 'unified theory' can genuinely be achieved by reconstructing the organization of discourse in terms of slots and fillers. That view may appear plausible to the analyst after the fact, when suitable end-results and protocols are made available, but hardly plausible to the participants during the event, when the discourse is in progress.

5.89 Still, Pike's method fostered the incontestable accomplishments of describing hundreds of previously little-studied languages and widening the scope of linguistics (cf. 5.2). He strove not 'solely to catalogue units, or provide expanded paraphrases', but to provide a 'description' that is 'useful for productive' 'purposes in the community setting', such as 'learning to speak' or 'read' (LB 121n, 493, 388; cf. LB 43, 51f, 65, 68, 352) (cf. 12.61).[48] Moreover, 'the human observer' he presents 'resists being dissected into logical parts' or 'forced into a single logical–coherent Procrustian view or set of one-dimensional rules', and 'demands the right of multiple perspective' as he 'reacts to criss-crossing, intersecting vectors of experience, mental tools, values, and psychological presets' (LB 10). By insisting that 'the structure of language shares' many 'characteristics with the structure of society', Pike 'hopes to demonstrate' 'more pervasive' 'structural traits' of 'man' 'than have previously been suspected' (LB 641). 'Behaviouremic theory' may 'bring into coherent, organized relationship many facts' 'which before this were isolated, ignored, buried in footnotes, or treated in an offhand manner'; or may 'lead to an observation of new relationships in old trouble spots of theory' and 'stimulate the creation of new hypotheses' (LB 519f). At the end of the quest may lie 'a theory, a set of terms, and an analytical procedure' to make 'intelligible' 'all human overt and covert activity', 'all psychological processes', all 'responses to sensations, all of thinking and feeling' (LB 32).

Notes

1. The key for Pike citations is LB: *Language in Relation to a Unified Theory of the Structure of Human Behaviour* (1967 [1945–64]). The title may be intended to echo the *Encyclopedia of Unified Science*, of which Pike cites the volumes by Carnap, Hempel, and Morris (cf. 4.7).
2. Actually, disciplines like 'psychology', 'psychiatry', and 'personality theory' (with its familiar triad of ' "id, ego, and superego" ') appear only sporadically; 'anthropology' is more prominent, due to its interest in a 'universal cultural pattern' (Wissler 1935), and 'standardized' 'behaviour' (Nadel 1951) (LB 537, 674f, 144f; cf. LB 71, 183, 444, 641).
3. Pike 'remembers the surprise' of learning that 'the two "p" sounds in "paper" were not the same', and he needed 'two years before he heard the difference easily' (LB 45f).
4. According to Opler (1948: 116), 'culture is what the investigation of its carriers by the anthropologist proves it to be, not what informants think it is'; their 'rationalization, idealism, self-righteousness, and hope' are 'part of the culture', but 'not a definition' of it (LB 157).
5. Yngve (1960: 445) proffers the 'immediate constituent framework' as 'a model for sentence production' with the 'rules' 'unordered' 'in the memory' (LB 479) (cf. 7.54, 10.33, 10[18]).
6. 'The etic approach' 'might well be called comparative' if that term did not suggest an approach for 'reconstructing parent forms' (LB 37) (cf. 2.5, 10, 53,

63; 3.19f; 4.1, 73; 11.90f). Yet the etic method is mostly applied in Pike's book to one culture at a time (cf. 5.78ff). And for linguists like Hjelmslev and Chomsky, a systematics for 'all languages' would be emic (cf. 6.11, 35; 7.20).

7. Quine's (1953: 14) claim – "'logicism holds that classes are discovered, while intuitionism holds that they are invented"' (LB 58) – seems backwards to me. Surely logic invents classes, and intuition is a domain where real classes of things are rarely questioned. Quine hedges by siding logic with 'realism' and yet making it 'epistemologically' rather than 'physically fundamental'.

8. 'The emic system', however, counsels against 'accepting too readily' alternative 'analyses which appear to be equally valid but contradictory' (LB 56). The 'etic criteria' were revised, at the 'suggestion of Longacre' (1964), to eliminate 'alternates' being 'theoretically correct even when one' 'was empirically undesirable' (LB 471).

9. Or, one could expect the emic to be 'generalized' and 'abstract', and the etic to include 'living parts of an actual sequence of behaviour events' (cf. LB 41).

10. Examples include 'homophones', 'mimicry', 'irony', and 'a lie' – outward sameness, but different intentions (LB 43, 132f). Pike describes a 'lie' differing from a 'parallel normal sentence' by 'breaking the normal connection between' 'sentences and reality' (LB 602) (cf. 5.66, 76f) – but surely many hypothetical or counterfactual statements do so. Elsewhere, 'deliberate deception' is more appropriately described as a case of a 'hidden purpose' or an 'inappropriate response' (LB 42f, 105, 115).

11. An 'etic approach' might 'ignore meaning or purpose', apply 'absolute' 'criteria', and rely on 'instrumental measurements' (LB 44, 38, 46). Or, it might use only 'differential purpose and meaning', but not 'the full systems' (LB 44) (cf. 4.26, 31; 5.14). These provisions suggest that some American linguists were working only etically (cf. 5.61).

12. And such data resist the notion of 'zero', whose 'overuse' seems 'fatal' (LB 561) (cf. 2^{26}; 4^3; 5.46; 7.75, 90; 11.42; 12.28). Pike calls it a 'pseudosegment' and a 'distortion' in 'an item-and-arrangement approach' in which no 'element' can 'contain two morphemes' without being 'segmentable' (LB 562). He stipulates that 'zero must contrast with overt forms "in some of its environments"'; we 'must not contrast the presence' and 'absence of zero', lest we 'multiply zero constructs out of all proportion' to 'behaviour' (LB 562, 297, 558) (cf. 5.21). 'Zeros' are particularly 'awkward' in 'phonological material, which above all others' 'in the language' is 'essentially concrete' (LB 407) (cf. 12.27).

13. He compares the duality of 'discrete' versus 'continuous' with that of 'analogue' versus 'digital computer' (LB 94). He cites von Neumann (in von Foerster [ed.] 1951: 27) that 'in almost all parts of physics the underlying reality is analogical', whereas 'the digital procedure is a human artifact for the sake of description'. Sapir (1949) makes a similar contrast between 'music' and 'mathematics'.

14. If these comments call to mind Chomsky's methods, his concern for 'rules' is in fact cited as part of the return to the 'approach through process' (LB 558).

15. The 'field' view led Pike to see 'units' and 'items' as 'cells in matrices', where 'matrix' 'means an array of intersecting dimensions representing some type of system or subsystem of behaviour' (LB 511n, 641n). In the book, the 'matrix' pops up mostly in footnotes. It is presented as an 'emic' 'unit of field'; its 'intersecting contrastive vectors' 'lead to field relationships' and provide 'contrastive categories' for 'differentiating and recognizing units' (LB 179n, 282n, 443n, 297n). 'Interlocking hierarchies' can be treated as 'intersects in matrices' (LB 565n). The 'largest', the 'matrix of matrices', is 'the behaviour-emic matrix of human activity as a whole', including the 'total language matrix'

(LB 298n, 584f). Pike hopes this newer construct will help represent 'dimensional', not just 'linear' 'order': 'no one kind of order' can capture 'the multiple dimensionality of observation' and 'complementary human experiences' (LB 641n, 512n) (cf. 5.89).

16. In a footnote, he suggests changing names: 'feature' to 'contrast', and 'manifestation' to 'variation'; but the earlier names better fit his preoccupation with observed behaviour. The modes are advocated also on the grounds that they project units of different size and borders (LB 513ff). Pike uses 'simultaneous' sometimes for concurrent events in real time (e.g., LB 74, 90; cf. 5.82), and denies 'emic status' to some 'divisions' that are not of this type, such as 'past, present, and future' or 'introduction, body, and end' (LB 515). But more often the term applies to (a) correlated levels or components in a system or hierarchy outside real time (e.g., LB 93, 132, 178, 305; cf. 5.48, 59) (like Saussure's 'synchronic', cf. 2.35ff, 55); or (b) a unit identifiable on more than one such level (LB 118, 153, 162, 440, 443, 449, 483; cf. 5.44f, 51) (a 'portmanteau' relation, cf. 5.41, 52ff, 59); or (c) analytic attention to more than one aspect (LB 8, 26, 47, 95, 110, 177; cf. 5.8, 29, 36). Compare the uses of the term in 9.34, 48, 103; 10.15; 11.43, 47.

17. Pike interchanges the term 'level' with 'layer' (e.g., LB 100, 109, 437, 566, 577, 579, 586, 589). Since I see no gain from this inconsistency and the hint of spatial fixity (cf. the 'layer cake' metaphor, LB 93), I use 'level' throughout. Though 'phoneme' is sometimes counted a level, the 'phonological hierarchy' actually has several levels (cf. 5.44).

18. Whereas emic units have matching names (ending in '-eme'), etic units do not, e.g., 'phone', 'morph', 'tagma', 'etic utterance', and so on (LB 343, 151, 195, 142, 513). 'Phrase', 'clause', and 'sentence' are sometimes treated as 'emic' units (e.g., LB 40, 424, 439f, 459, 486) (as they would have to be to match the 'morpheme' in 'portmanteau' cases, cf. 5.52ff), but Pike never spells out their etic counterparts. The 'sentence' is termed 'a specific occurrence or manifestation of an uttereme'' and a 'variation of a minimal uttereme', whereas an 'uttereme' is a 'sentence syntagmeme' and an 'utterance' 'represents a sentence' (LB 425, 133, 499) (cf. Note 25).

19. When criticizing transformational theory (which rated grammar over lexicon), Pike says that if 'tagmemic theory' 'were forced' to 'give priority to one of the three hierarchies', 'the lexical one' would be chosen (LB 476). But the book is heavily devoted to phonological and grammatical matters, whereas 'work' on the 'lexical hierarchy' was 'not ready for publication' (LB 521n) (cf. Note 28). In his table of 'kinds of modification or restriction', a fourth category of 'stylistic' is shown parallel to the three (LB 463f) (cf. 5.82f).

20. The 'sentence syntagmeme', for example, is broken down according to (a) 'specific clause', 'phrase', 'word', 'cluster', and 'morpheme'; (b) 'breath group, pause group, stress group, syllable', and 'phoneme'; and (c) 'clause type, phrase type, word type, tagmeme cluster', and 'tagmeme' (LB 515) (cf. 5.40f, 53–58).

21. And a delicate distinction is drawn between 'the tagmemic portmanteau' having 'only one morpheme' with 'two semantic components', versus 'the morphemic portmanteau' having 'two morphemes in a phonologically fused form' (LB 550).

22. He even coins the 'abdomineme', which, along with the 'roleme' (an unexplained minimum 'behavioureme'), counts among his most '"fanciful-emes"' (LB 313, 385, 392ff, 194; cf. LB 271, 506).

23. Pike's favourite examples of 'waves' with 'peaks', 'ripples', and 'troughs' are in 'motion' or 'physical activity', including 'articulation' (LB 76, 79, 116, 308f, 319, 347, 519f). He points to 'new tools' like the 'spectrograph', 'electromyo-

graph', 'photoelectric cell', and 'high-speed X-rays' for detecting 'vocal cord vibration', 'electrical discharge of the muscles', and so on (LB 347) (cf. 4.28; 8.23). But these tools wouldn't help for 'grammatical waves', and still less for a 'meaning cluster' as a 'wave' (cf. LB 468f, 505, 603n).

24. After coping with tone languages like Mixtec, Pike hoped his 'frame techniques' for 'tonal analysis could be generalized for all kinds of phonemes', or even be 'a model for determining all linguistic units' (LB 5, 376, 522). These 'techniques' could 'handle units which differed not by absolute quality but only by degree'. The 'tone phoneme' would be 'one of the simplest', having 'a single pure abstract characteristic relatively determined'. But it would be 'awkward, though not necessarily impossible' to 'set up *all* contrastive components, such as voicing', 'as phonemes' (LB 523). 'Tone phonemes' must be 'different' from 'segmental' ones, the latter being 'more concrete', 'observable', and 'chunk-like' and thus 'the obvious starting point' in regard to 'the manifestation mode of units' (LB 523f). There might also be both 'morpheme hierarchies of intonation', but 'the present volume' omits the issue (LB 528).

25. These same 'principles' are offered for relating 'phones' to 'phonemes', 'tagmas' to tagmemes', 'hypertagmas' to 'hypertagmemes', and 'etic utterances' to 'emic utterances' (LB 344, 255, 471, 142) (cf. 5[18]). Note that it may be 'indeterminate' whether 'a "difference in meaning" suffices to recognize' 'distinct morphemes' rather than 'two morphs' of 'a single morpheme' (LB 599).

26. Pike first used 'grammeme' to 'imply "unit of grammar"' and then 'abandoned' it 'on etymological grounds' (LB 5, 490; cf. Pike 1958). 'Tagmeme' is an uneasy choice in that 'Bloomfield lacked a clear concept of a slot-plus-class correlation' and used the term for '*any* grammatical characteristic', so that it 'overlapped' with the 'taxeme' (LB 490, 286) (cf. 4.45, 64f, 68f, 86). Pike's own 'tagmeme' shares some 'indeterminacy of meaning' with 'morpheme' (LB 274, 455) (cf. Note 27).

27. It might be strategic to postulate that all 'tagmemes are distributed' 'not directly' 'into a hypertagmeme', but 'into a hypermorpheme class' ('as a set of instances') or into a 'syntagmeme' ('as a structure') (LB 450f, i.r.). But 'the implications of this change have not been fully worked out'. 'The new hypertagmeme' would call for 'portmanteau levels', and 'word–phrase–clause–sentence levels' as 'classes of hypermorphemes' (LB 459) (cf. 5.53f, 5[12], 5[21]).

28. 'The term **lexeme** is useful' when a 'cluster of words' acts as a 'single semantic unit' (LB 431), but does not have its own level. A whole 'lexical hierarchy' is proposed as the 'usual' place for 'discussing meanings', such as those of 'idioms, words, phrases, or novels' (LB 598f) (cf. 3.14, 32, 41–48), but sketchily handled (cf. 5.47; Note 19). Within it, 'the problem' of 'meaning is closely related to concept formation' (LB 633). 'Dynamic thought' during 'deductive and inventive concept formations' need not fit 'formal logic, especially where "the premises are not well established"' – '"in actual living"' (LB 639, 637; Leeper 1951: 754f) (cf. 12.17). Some 'concepts' are defined not by '"the common features"' of '"exemplars"', but by '"what the category is *not*"' (LB 634; Bruner *et al.* 1956: 159).

29. One listing of 'phrase types' (Pickett 1960) has '9 major and 53 minor' ones, e.g., in 'location, time, manner, or purpose slot' (LB 471) (cf. 9.65f; 12.28). Their 'meanings (sometimes identical with the meaning of the slot)' are as diverse as those for Pike's sentence types (cf. 5.58): 'possession, modification, apposition', 'aspect, speed', 'exclamation, vocative, and so on'.

30. The 'actor-as-subject tagmeme', with 'subject-as-actor' being the 'functional' or 'slot meaning', illustrates how both 'form and structural meaning help to identify' the 'tagmeme' (LB 247, 198, 448, 607, 647) (cf. 5.36). In a later phase

of theory, Pike introduced 'dramatis personae' and 'action' to clarify 'grammatical versus situational role' (LB 607n, 576nf, 246n, 424n). 'Situational roles' need not 'change' along with 'grammatical' ones, or vice-versa (LB 246n). 'In the change from active to passive', for example, 'the grammatical subject position is invariant', 'but the dramatis personae shift'; 'the "logical subject"' 'becomes agent', 'whereas the "subject" slot is filled with the "logical object"' (cf. 7.63; 9.46).

31. 'Studies in preparation' were trying to define the 'paragraph' by 'sentence–sequence restrictions', 'topic', or 'focused attention' (LB 442n, 485). 'Topic' in the different sense of counterpart to 'comment' is episodically mentioned, e.g., as alternative to 'actor and action' (LB 276, 279), but not elaborated or integrated into Pike's scheme.

32. 'In the non-verbal sphere', Pike sees 'greater difficulty in locating a minimum' 'unit' (LB 270). He counsels 'starting in the middle' and not 'waiting to find maximum and/or minimum units' (LB 271).

33. Pike draws an obscure 'analogy' between meanings and 'morphemic shapes' with 'fusions' and unclear 'boundaries' (LB 609) (cf. 5.45, 47, 87).

34. On '"language as causative"' for 'holding certain attitudes', Sinclair (1951: 120f, 172, 204) is cited. Morris (1938) would replace 'the idea' with 'disposition to response', and all '"mental entities"' with 'terms' 'for things and properties' in 'functional relations' (LB 638) (cf. 4.9; 12.34).

35. 'The adult linguist, who cannot recapitulate the child's experience', might detect 'central meaning' by 'studying' the 'monolingual' 'learning processes of children in the culture' (LB 601) (but cf. 7.87; 9.10ff, 14f). Pike doesn't relate his 'central meanings' to 'denotational meanings', which people often take to be 'the "real" meaning of the word' (LB 611) (cf. 4.21f; 11.19).

36. Pike uses poems as examples and enjoys comparing 'poets' to 'linguists' (a Sapirian touch) (LB LB 87n, 304, 390f, 427, 431, 494, 512n, 528–32, 604, 611ff). He views 'a poem format' as 'a special subsystem of language', and illustrates 'componential systems' with three readings of a poem, by a 'graduate student' (in linguistics?), a 'poet', and a 'literary critic' (LB 528–32). See also 5.64, 91.

37. The claim that 'systems of hypotheses' can guide 'active reconstruction' during 'the "process of remembering"' (LB 635) anticipates van Dijk and Kintsch (cf. 10.71ff, 77).

38. For Bloomfield (1930: 554), the term 'choice' 'reflected "the primeval drug of animism"' and was 'replaced by the word "selection"' in his 1933 book (LB 281). Actually, most of the 'selections' in Bloomfield's description are in terms of forms and features, not behavioural options (cf. 4.21, 60, 64ff, 68).

39. Fries (1952) tried to 'avoid traditional labels' and 'define new terms (numbers) by their occurrence in frames' (LB 489) (cf. 7[36]). But his son Peter Fries tells me the attempt failed because people simply used the numbers as new names for the old parts of speech, e.g., 'Class 1' as 'nouns'.

40. If so, Pike seems unfair to see 'a distortion of human experience' in any 'denial of the emic unity' of 'meanings', and to blame '"General Semantics"', which 'focuses attention on variants of meaning' and warns against 'primitive, "over-emotional" generalization' (LB 623; cf. Korzybski 1933).

41. He invokes, but doesn't state, the 'meaning' of 'the football' for 'an American', and never raises the issue of violence as public spectacle. Instead, he regales us with the ball's 'formal contrastive features', e.g., 'lacings, seams, bladder, and pressure of air' (LB 660). Compare Notes 45, 47.

42. Pike seems aware that his young son 'S___' (Stephen) can find little purpose or

meaning in the church service (except to get it over with), but counts him a 'participant' anyway (cf. LB 79, 81).

43. For Pike, 'many products of behaviour may themselves have behaviour', as in 'automatic factories' and 'machines with feedback operations', provided that 'human observers' are involved (LB 661). He also compares 'linguistics' to 'an automatic factory' whose 'components' form 'a feedback system' (LB 591) (cf. 8^3). But his theorizing is fairly free of the 'mechanistic' metaphors common among physicalists, perhaps to keep his distance from the formalists and logicians (e.g., Bar-Hillel and Shamir 1960) who advertised their 'grammars' as '"automata"' and '"machines"' (LB 69) (cf. 5.86; 7.38; compare Chomsky's 'device', 7.92ff).

44. At one point, 'formal ceremony' is said to be 'without content' and contrasted with 'genuine' 'activity' (LB 91) – a jarring note in view of Pike's use of ceremonial occasions (cf. 5.79).

45. As a hopeful but facile gesture, Pike creates terms for 'society' by tacking an 'S-' on to names of linguistic entities, e.g., 'a particular society' is 'called an S-language' (LB 642f). In the football game, a 'quarterback' is an 'S-tagmeme', a 'team on field' is an 'S-sentence', a 'pair of such teams in combat' is 'an S-utterance-response unit', the 'Big Ten' 'league' is an 'S-paragraph', and 'the national collegiate league' is 'an S-conversation' (LB 650ff). Movements in a 'football game' are likened to 'phonemes', and 'light waves reflected from the players' to 'sound waves'. The 'alphabetical' 'listing' of 'personnel for a game' 'on a programme' is compared to 'a dictionary labelling entries as nouns', etc. (LB 649f). 'At each substitution of a player, a new S-sentence is formed'.

46. Stressing a 'physical component' in 'the grouping of individuals organized' seems to bypass the social aspect, even for 'the grouping of all individuals into kinship elements' (LB 645f). Elsewhere, Pike suggests instead that groups formed 'for special purposes' are 'analogous to lexical units' (cf. Note 47).

47. Some cases are picturesque: in 'geography', 'emigrants retaining nationality abroad'; in the 'family', 'half-siblings' by 'remarriage'; in the 'individual', 'Siamese twins'; and in the 'physical setting', the 'atmosphere penetrating the skin of the football' full of 'air' (LB 646, 654, 657, 660). Pike also finds 'indeterminacy' between 'verbal' and 'non-verbal', 'same and different', 'grammatical' and 'lexical', 'simple' and 'complex' 'morphemes' or 'active' and 'passive' ones, 'loan words' and 'assimilated' ones, and so on (LB 251, 159, 248f, 497, 233, 170ff, 583). 'Indeterminacy' can pertain as well to 'meaning' 'modes', 'classes' and 'class membership', 'level of focus' 'participant type', 'dialects', and data from 'informants' (LB 43, 158, 166, 92, 84, 185, 80, 111, 129, 585, 171, 238).

48. Pike's book actually says little about written language, perhaps because 'the printed word' conveys the 'feeling that language stands apart' from 'behaviour' (LB 27). Compare 12.33.

Chapter 6

Louis Hjelmslev[1]

6.1 Hjelmslev purports to offer neither a general survey of language and its types (like Sapir's and Bloomfield's) nor a general theory of linguistics (like Saussure's and Hartmann's), but a preparatory 'prologue' to the formulation of any 'theory of language'. The *Prolegomena* (PT), his central book, published in Danish in 1943 and in English in 1953, proposes to stipulate in the broadest terms the conceptual layout for any such theory. His *Résumé* (RT), circulated in a few typed copies in 1941–43 and eventually published in 1975, is a technical compilation of terms, symbols, definitions, rules, and notes. His ideas often build on Saussure's, but are, in an ambivalent way, more radical, digging for the roots while trying not to get dirty.

6.2 Like our other theorists, Hjelmslev declares his profound respect for language as a human faculty (cf. 2.8, 32; 3.1, 3; 4.2, 10, 82; 5.69; 12.22). 'Language – human speech[2] – is an inexhaustible abundance of manifold treasures' and 'the distinctive mark of the personality', of 'home, and of nation' (PT 3). 'Language is the instrument' whereby man 'forms thought and feeling, mood, aspiration, will and act'. It 'is inseparable from man' and 'all his works', 'from the simplest activities' to the 'most sublime and intimate moments' during which the 'warmth and strength for our daily life' flows from 'the hold of memory that language itself gives us'. 'Language' is thus 'a wealth of memories inherited by the individual and the tribe, a vigilant conscience that reminds and warns'. It is 'the ultimate and deepest foundation of human society', but also 'the ultimate, indispensable sustainer of the human individual, his refuge in hours of loneliness, when the mind wrestles with existence and the conflict is resolved in the monologue of the poet and the thinker'. 'Before the awakening of our consciousness language was echoing about us, ready to close around our first tender seed of thought' (cf. 3.3). Such praises might portend a mentalistic, phenomenological, or humanistic approach, but Hjelmslev offers nothing of the kind.

6.3 Again like our other theorists, Hjelmslev is stringently critical of 'conventional linguistics' (PT 4, 5, 44, 65, 73, 79, 99) (cf. 12.4).[3] He asserts that 'the history of linguistic theory cannot be written', being rendered 'too discontinuous' by 'superficial trends of fashion' (PT 7) (a view I hope to refute with this volume). In his opinion, 'linguistics' was 'frequently misused as the name for an unsuccessful study of language proceeding from transcendent and irrelevant points of view' (PT 80, i.r.). 'Attempts to form a linguistic theory have been discredited' 'as empty philosophizing and dilettantism, characterized by apriorism' and 'subjective speculation' (PT 7). 'Until now, linguistic science' has 'remained vague and subjective, metaphysical and aestheticizing', and relied on 'a completely anecdotal form of presentation' (PT 10). In this state of affairs, we might do well to 'forget the past' and 'start from the beginning' (PT 7). Instead, Hjelmslev elects to work 'in contrast to previous linguistic science and in conscious reaction against it', seeking 'an unambiguous terminology' 'in linguistic theory' (PT 37) (cf. 5.33; 8.40; 12.7, 15, 48).

6.4   Past failings are attributed to several obstacles. One obstacle was the 'humanistic tradition which, in various dress, has till now predominated in linguistic science' (PT 8) (cf. 8.36; 11.49). This 'humanism' 'rejects the idea of system', and 'denies a priori the existence' of any 'integrating constancy' and 'the legitimacy of seeking it' (PT 10, 8). Hence, 'the humanities' 'have neglected their most important task': 'establishing' their 'studies' as 'a systematic, exact, and generalizing science' (PT 9). The 'most' 'humanistic' 'disciplines', i.e., 'the study of literature' and 'art', have been 'historically descriptive rather than systematizing'. They offer the justification that 'humanistic phenomena are non-recurrent', and thus 'cannot, like natural phenomena, be subjected to exact and generalizing treatment'; and that 'we cannot subject to scientific analysis man's spiritual life' 'without killing' it (PT 8, 10). Their only method is either 'a discursive form of presentation, in which the phenomena pass by, one by one, without being interpreted through a system'; or a 'mere description', 'nearer to poetry than to exact science' (PT 8f) (cf. 11.38).

6.5   Another obstacle was the 'transcendent aim' and 'objective' of many researchers, including 'philologists' (PT 6, 10). In this work, 'the theory of language' was often 'confused with the philosophy of language', including some modern 'offshoots of medieval philosophy' (PT 6, 77).[4] Researchers would seek a 'universal' 'system', a set of 'generally valid' 'types', an 'eternal scheme of ideas', or a 'construction of grammar on speculative ontological systems' (PT 76f) (cf. 12.16ff). Or, they would try to 'construct' one 'grammar on the grammar of another language', e.g., 'blindly transferring the Latin categories' 'into modern European languages' (PT 75f; cf. EL1 125) (cf. 2.5; 3.50; 4.4; 5.24; 8.5; 9.25; 11.20f). 'Such projects are necessarily foredoomed to miscarry', lacking any 'possible contact with linguistic reality' (PT 76f).

6.6   A further and related obstacle was the tendency to treat 'language, even when it is the object of scientific investigation', not as 'an end in itself, but a means' 'to a knowledge whose main object lies outside language' (PT 4) (cf. 11.23). Here, too, 'language is a means to a transcendent knowledge', 'not the goal of an immanent knowledge'. For example, 'language' 'was expected to provide the key to the system of human thought, to the nature of the human psyche' (cf. 3.10ff; 5.69; 6.2; 7.10; 8.24; 11.17ff, 22; 12.10, 14). Or, 'it was to contribute to a characterization of the nation', to an 'understanding of social conditions, and to a reconstruction of prehistorical relations among peoples and nations' (PT 4f) (cf. 11.19, 91). 'The main content of conventional linguistics – linguistic history and the genetic comparison of languages' – was a 'knowledge of social conditions and contacts among peoples'. Such research fails to 'grasp the totality of language', and incurs 'the danger' of 'overlooking' 'language itself' (cf. 2.5f). To be sure, 'it is in the nature of language to be overlooked, to be a means and not an end'; 'only by artifice' can we direct a 'searchlight' on it (cf. 3.1; 4.2; 11.9; 12.1). 'This is true' both 'in daily life, where language normally does not come to consciousness', and 'in scientific research'.

6.7   More recently, 'science has been led to see in language a series of sounds and expressive gestures, amenable to exact physical and physiological description, and ordered as signs for the phenomenon of consciousness' (PT 3f) (cf. 4.28, 32; 5.44; 6.54; 8.20, 22). Here, science is restricted to 'the physical and physiological description of speech sounds', which 'easily degenerates into pure physics and pure physiology' (PT 4). Or, science 'has sought in language, through psychological and logical interpretations, the fluctuation of the human psyche and the constancy of human thought – the former in the capricious life and change of language, the latter in its signs'. Here, 'words and sentences' are held to be 'the palpable symbols of concept and judgment respectively' (cf. 3.32, 36); and 'the psychological and logical description of signs (words and sentences)' leads to 'pure psychology, logic, and ontology'. Either way, 'the linguistic point of departure is lost from view'. 'Physical, physiological, psychological, and logical phenomena per se are not language itself, but only disconnected, external facets of it' (PT 4f) (cf. 12.5).

6.8   To offset all these misconceptions, Hjelmslev offers his 'prolegomena' to 'a linguistic theory that will discover and formulate the premises' of 'a real and rational genetic linguistics', 'establish its methods, and indicate its paths' (PT 6). 'A true linguistics' 'cannot be a mere ancillary or derivative science' (PT 5) (cf. 8.17; 12.9–20). It 'must attempt to grasp language, not as a conglomerate of non-linguistic' 'phenomena, but as a self-sufficient totality, a structure of its own kind' (PT 5f) (cf. 12.22). 'Only in this way can language in itself be subjected to scientific treatment'. Hjelmslev sees 'an immanent **algebra** of language' as the 'main task' of 'linguistics' 'whose solution has been almost completely neglected in all study of language', apart from 'a beginning in certain limited areas' (PT 79f) (cf. 2.82; 5.86; 6.29; 7.40, 7[18]; 12.15).[5] 'To mark its difference from previous kinds of linguistics', he proposes to call this 'algebra' by the 'special name' of '**glossematics** (from "glossa", "a language")' (PT 80).

6.9   By centring linguistics firmly on language and 'removing' the 'provincialism in the formation of concepts' (PT 6), Hjelmslev expects far-reaching benefits for science at large (cf. 12.21f). Because 'it is impossible to elaborate a theory of a particular science without an active collaboration with epistemology', 'the significance of such a linguistics' can be 'measured by its contributions to general epistemology' (PT 15, 6). Just as Hjelmslev's own 'presentation' is 'forced' 'into a more general epistemological setting', 'every theory is faced with a methodological requirement whose purport will have to be investigated by epistemology' (PT 102, 11). Yet 'such an investigation may, we think, be omitted here'. And the 'terminological reckoning' 'to be made with epistemology' is postponed for 'later', though he hopes that 'the formal foundation of terms and concepts given here should make possible a bridge to the established usage of epistemology' (PT 11, 31f). Besides, 'the science of categories presupposes such a comprehensive and closely coherent apparatus of terms and definitions that its details cannot be described without its being presented completely', so it cannot 'be treated in the prolegomena of the theory' (PT 101).

6.10 Hjelmslev feels 'led to regard all science as centred around linguistics' (PT 78) – a popular aspiration (cf. 2.7f; 5.7, 84; 6.41, 53; 7.8; 8.16, 29; 11.6, 9, 12, 33, 64; 12.21, 59). He 'supposes that several of the general principles we are led to set up in the initial stages of linguistic theory are valid' 'for all science' (PT 80). His 'basic premises' 'are all of so general a nature that none would seem to be specific to linguistic theory' (PT 15). He hopes for a 'universal applicability to sign systems' or to 'any structure whose form is analogous to that of a "natural" language' (PT 102; cf. 6.48–55). 'Precisely when we restrict ourselves to the pure consideration of "natural" language', 'further perspectives' 'obtrude themselves with inevitable logical consequence' (PT 101, i.r.). 'If the linguist wishes to make clear to himself the object of his own science', he gets 'forced into spheres which according to the traditional view are not his' (PT 101f). For example, 'the systematics of the study of literature and of general science find their natural place within the framework of linguistic theory', as do 'general philosophy of science and formal logic' (PT 98, 102) (cf. 6.54). This grand vision leads to an interesting tension in Hjelmslev's work. On the one hand, he is anxious to demarcate the borders and independence of linguistics and to centre it on language in an 'immanent' fashion (PT 19, 108, 127), assigning related issues to 'the non-linguistic sciences' (PT 78ff). On the other hand, his ambition to make linguistics the model science keeps him at some distance from language and entrains him in the transcendent theorizing he criticizes.

6.11 The scope is set as wide as possible: 'a theory' 'must enable us to know all conceivable objects of the same premised nature', and to 'meet' 'any eventuality' (PT 16). The 'main task is to determine by definition the structural principle of language, from which can be deduced a general calculus' (PT 106) (cf. 7.18). Such 'a general and exhaustive calculus of the possible combinations' would provide the foundation for 'a systematic, exact, and generalizing science, in the theory of which all events (possible combinations of elements) are foreseen and the conditions for their realization established' (PT 9) (cf. 6.11, 30, 33, 36, 38, 50, 63). 'The linguistic theoretician must' even 'foresee all conceivable possibilities' 'he

himself has not experienced or seen realized', i.e., 'those that are virtual in
the world of experience, or remain without a "natural" or "actual"
manifestation' (PT 17, 106) (cf. 6.18f, 35; 9.8; 11.55f).

6.12 'Linguistic theory' must also 'seek a constancy which is not
anchored in some "reality" outside language', but which 'makes a language
a language' and makes it 'identical with itself in all its various manifestations'
(PT 8, i.r.) (cf. 4.71; 8.33; 12.57). 'This constancy' 'may then be projected
on the "reality" outside language' – 'physical, physiological, psychological,
logical, ontological – so that even in the consideration of that "reality"',
language as the central point of reference remains the chief object – and not
as a conglomerate, but as an organized totality with linguistic structure as
the dominating principle' (cf. 6.20, 38; 12.24ff, 57). The essential strategy
would be to 'search for the specific structure of language through an
exclusively formal system of premises' (cf. 12.54). And this search is just
what Hjelmslev pursues.

6.13 In such a project, the notion of '**empiricism**' is given a peculiar
interpretation, one whereby Hjelmslev's 'theory is at once clearly distinguishable from all previous undertakings of linguistic philosophy' (PT 11)
(cf. 7.85). On the one hand, 'a theory must be capable of yielding, in all its
applications, results that agree with so-called (actual or presumed) empirical
data'. On the other hand, his '**empirical principle**' makes no mention of
data, stating only that 'the description shall be free of contradiction (self-
consistent), exhaustive, and as simple as possible' – 'freedom from
contradiction taking precedence over' 'exhaustive description', and the latter
over 'simplicity'. 'Linguistic theory' 'can be judged only' by these criteria: 'a
theory, in our sense', 'says nothing at all about the possibility of its
application and relation to empirical data' (PT 18, 14). 'It includes no
existence postulates', 'replacing' them with 'theorems in the form of
conditions' (PT 14, 21). Hjelmslev thereby resolves to make 'linguistic
theory' 'as unmetaphysical as possible'; it should shun 'implicit premises'
and should not try to 'reflect the "nature" of the object' or rely on the
'concept' of '"substance" in an ontological sense' (PT 20, 22, 81) (cf. 6.28;
12.26).

6.14 It seems odd to find the existence of objects, the traditional
recourse of realism, reckoned under 'metaphysics', a term usually applied to
the 'transcendent', 'supersensible', or 'supernatural' (*Webster's Dictionary*).
But this move abets Hjelmslev's plan to design theories in purely formal
terms. He praises 'the special advantage' of avoiding any 'recourse to
sociological presuppositions which the "real" definition' of 'terms would
necessarily involve' and which would 'at best' 'complicate' 'the apparatus'
and 'at worst' 'involve metaphysical premises' (PT 20, 89) (cf. 12.16f). For
Hjelmslev, the 'concept of sociological norm' 'proves to be dispensable
throughout linguistic theory' (PT 89), though I can't see how such a thing
could be 'proven' at so preliminary a stage.

6.15 In place of 'the **real** definitions for which linguistics has hitherto striven insofar as it has striven for definitions at all', Hjelmslev recommends 'giving a strictly **formal**' and 'explicit character to definitions' and 'replacing postulates partly by definitions and partly by conditional propositions' (PT 21). A 'theory' 'consisting of a calculation from the fewest and most general possible premises' 'permits the prediction of possibilities, but says nothing about their realization' (PT 15). A reciprocity is proposed whereby 'the object determines' 'the theory' and 'vice-versa': 'by virtue of its arbitrary nature the theory is *arealistic*' and '*calculative*'; 'by virtue of its appropriateness, it is *realistic*' and '*empirical*' (PT 15, 17). '**Arbitrariness**' means here that 'the theory is independent of any experience'[6] and only a means for 'computing the possibilities that follow from its premises' (PT 14). '**Appropriateness**', on the other hand, means that 'the theory introduces certain premises concerning which the theoretician knows from preceding experience that they fulfil the conditions for application to certain empirical data' (cf. 7.10, 7[7]). Hjelmslev goes on to argue that 'empirical data can never strengthen or weaken the theory itself, but only its applicability'.

6.16 Hjelmslev stresses that his 'empirical principle' is 'not the same' as '**inductivism**', which, in 'linguistics', 'inevitably leads to the abstraction of concepts which are then hypostatized as real' (PT 11f) (cf. 4.67, 76; 5.17; 7.6f; 8.71; 11.8, 16, 95f; 12.57).[7] In the 'inductive' 'procedure, linguistics ascends' from 'particular to general', from 'more limited' to 'less', or 'from component to class', e.g., from 'sounds' to 'phonemes'. 'Induction' is thus 'a continued synthesis', 'a generalizing, not a specifying method', and cannot 'satisfy the empirical principle with its requirement of an exhaustive description' (PT 31, 12). 'Induction leads' 'not to constancy but to accident', and to 'class concepts' that are not 'susceptible of general definition' (PT 12) (cf. 7.25, 30; 12.44f).

6.17 In order to 'clarify our position as opposed to that of previous linguistics', Hjelmslev asserts: 'linguistic theory' is 'necessarily **deductive**'; it is 'a purely deductive system' used only 'to compute the possibilities that follow from its premises', which 'are of the greatest possible generality' and thus 'apply to a large number of empirical data' (PT 11f, 13f) (cf. 6.17f, 33, 36f, 45, 49, 51f, 62; 11.8; 12.44f). The proper 'procedure' is 'a continued analysis' 'progressing from class to components' in an 'analytic and specifying, not a synthetic and generalizing movement' (PT 13, 30) (cf. 6.36ff). The 'object' of 'treatment should not be an inductively discovered class', 'but a deductively discovered linguistic localized variety of the highest degree' (PT 84).

6.18 Hjelmslev is optimistic that 'it is both possible and desirable for linguistic theory to progress by providing new concrete developments that yield an ever closer approximation' to 'the ideal set up and formulated in the "empirical principle"' (PT 19) (cf. 6.13). On that basis, when we 'imagine several linguistic theories', 'one of these must necessarily be the definitive one' (but cf. 12.3). Yet his standards for deriving and evaluating theories are peculiarly abstract. 'From certain experiences', which 'should be as varied as possible, the linguistic theoretician sets up a calculation of all the conceivable possibilities within certain frames' (PT 17) (cf. 6.11). 'These frames he constructs arbitrarily: he discovers certain properties present in all the objects that people agree to call languages, in order then to generalize those properties and establish them by definition' (PT 17f). 'From that moment the linguistic theoretician has – arbitrarily, but appropriately – decreed to which objects his theory can and cannot be applied'. 'He then sets up, for all objects of the nature premised in the definition, a general calculus, in which all conceivable cases are foreseen' (cf. 6.11). 'This calculus', 'deduced from the established definition independently of all experience, provides the tools for describing or comprehending a given text' or 'language'. 'Linguistic theory, then, sovereignly defines its object by an arbitrary and appropriate strategy of premises; the theory consists of a calculation from the fewest and most general possible premises, of which none that is specific to the theory seems to be of axiomatic nature' (PT 15) (cf. 5.86; 6.15, 22, 44).

6.19 The startling upshot is that 'linguistic theory cannot be verified (confirmed or invalidated) by reference to any existing texts and languages' (PT 18) (cf. 12.25). 'Propositions' and 'theorems' 'will be true or false depending on the definitions chosen for the concepts' (PT 24). 'A theorem', which 'must have the form of an implication (in the logical sense) or must be susceptible of transposition into such a conditional form', 'asserts only that if a condition is fulfilled, the truth of a given proposition follows' (PT 14). Yet 'on the basis of a theory and its theorems we may construct hypotheses (including the so-called laws), the fate of which, contrary to that of the theory itself, depends exclusively on verification'. 'No mention' is made of 'axioms or postulates; we leave it to epistemology to decide whether the basic premises explicitly introduced by our linguistic theory need any further axiomatic foundation', and Hjelmslev hopes 'the number of axioms' might be 'reduced' 'to zero' (PT 15, 21) (cf. 6.22, 44).

6.20 When 'seeking an immanent understanding of language as a self-subsistent, specific structure', 'linguistic theory begins by circumscribing the scope of its object', but without any 'reduction of the field of vision' or any 'elimination of essential factors in the global totality which language is' (PT 19) (cf. 11.2). 'It involves only a division of difficulties and a progress of thought from simple to complex, in conformity with Descartes' rules'. 'The circumscription' is 'justified if it later permits an exhaustive and self-consistent broadening of perspective through a projection of the discovered structure on the phenomena surrounding it, so that they are satisfactorily explained', i.e., 'if after analysis, the global totality – language in life and actuality – may again be viewed synthetically as a whole', 'organized around a leading principle' (PT 19f) (cf. 12.43). 'Linguistic theory' is 'successful' only when it has done all this, thereby 'satisfying the empirical principle in its requirement of an exhaustive description; the test may be made by drawing all possible general consequences from the chosen structural principle' (cf. 6.11).

6.21 A choice among 'several possible methods' should also follow 'the

simplicity principle': pick the method that yields 'the simplest possible description' via 'the simplest procedure' (PT 18) (cf. 6.13). 'Only by reference' to 'this principle' can we 'judge linguistic theory and its applications' or 'assert that one solution is correct and another incorrect' (but cf. 12.57). Again, immanence is emphasized: 'a theory will attain its simplest form by building on no other premises than those necessarily required by its object' (PT 10).

6.22   The 'main task' of 'linguistic theory' 'is to make explicit the specific premises of linguistics as far back as possible' by 'setting up' 'a system of definitions' that in turn 'rest on defined concepts' (PT 20). As we saw (cf. 6.14f), Hjelmslev recommends 'strictly **formal**' 'definitions' rather than '**real**' ones, and 'hopes to guard against any postulates about the essence of an object' (PT 20f, 32). Here, 'it is not a question of trying to exhaust the intensional nature of the objects or even of delimiting them extensionally on all sides, but only of anchoring them relatively in respect to other objects' (PT 21) (cf. 6.25). 'In addition to the formal definitions', Hjelmslev would admit '**operative** definitions, whose role is only temporary'; 'later', they 'may be transformed into formal definitions', or else their 'definienda do not enter into the system of formal definitions' (PT 21; for examples, see PT 46, 48, 81, 118). 'This extensive defining' should help keep 'linguistic theory' free both 'from specific axioms' and from 'implicit premises' or 'postulates' – perhaps a suitable 'strategy' for 'any science' (PT 21, cf. PT 15, 21) (cf. 6.18f).

6.23   Like Saussure, Hjelmslev grants the 'evident and fundamental proposition' 'that a language is a system of signs' (PT 43) (cf. 2.8, 21, 25ff, 69; 5.63; 8.54; 11.9ff, 42f, 54, 62–67). 'Linguistic theory must be able to tell us what meaning can be attributed to this proposition and especially to the word **sign**'. According to 'the vague concept bequeathed by tradition', 'a "sign"' is 'a sign *for* something', and 'the bearer of a meaning' (cf. 5.63; 6.47). Such a usage might fit 'the entities commonly referred to as sentences, clauses and words' (PT 43f) (cf. 11.69f, 75f, 78). But problems arise if we 'try to carry out the analysis as far as possible, in order to test for an exhaustive and maximally simple description'. '**Words** are not the ultimate, irreducible signs', despite 'the centring of conventional linguistics around the word' (but cf. 2.17, 55; 3.31–38, 73; 4.42, 60, 63, 4^{14}; 5.18, 36, 41, 49, 51–54, 56, 58; 7.70, 7^{34}; 8.47f, 53; 9.75; 11.66, 69; 12.29). 'Words can be analysed into parts', such as 'roots' or 'derivational' and 'inflectional elements', that are also 'bearers of meaning' (cf. 2.55, 57, 62ff; 3.26, 32, 34, 41ff, 53; 4.50, 59f, 62). So Hjelmslev postulates a further system of 'minimal' 'invariants' he calls by the 'purely operative term' '**figurae**', which are 'non-signs' (PT 65, 46). 'Through ever new arrangements' of 'a handful' of these 'figurae', 'a legion of signs can be constructed'; otherwise, a 'language' 'would be a tool unusable for its purpose' (PT 46) (cf. 2.52; 3^3). Hence, a 'language' is by its 'external functions' a 'sign system', but by its 'internal structure' a 'system of figurae' (PT 47). In this sense, 'the definition of language as a sign system' proves 'on closer analysis to be unsatisfactory'.

6.24   This view suspends the problem of determining the size of the set of signs. Since 'a language' 'must always be ready to form new signs', their 'number' must be 'unrestricted' in the 'economy' of 'inventory lists', whereas the 'number' of usable 'non-signs' 'is restricted' (PT 46). 'To understand the structure of a language', 'this principle' of 'analysis' 'must be extended so as to be valid for all invariants of the language', 'irrespective' of 'their place in the system' (PT 65). So far, though, 'conventional linguistics' has focused only on 'figurae of the expression plane',[8] whereas 'an analysis into content-figurae has never been' 'even attempted' (PT 65, 67) (cf. 6.26, 30). 'This inconsistency has had the most catastrophic consequences', making 'the analysis of content' seem 'an insoluble problem' (PT 67). Thanks to 'the solidarity between the form of the expression and the form of the content', 'the content plane' can also 'be resolved' 'into components with mutual relations that are smaller than the minimal-sign-contents' (PT 65, 67) (cf. 6.41, 47f; 12.30). Indeed, the two 'terms' 'are quite arbitrary': 'their functional definition provides no justification for calling one, and not the other, of these entities *expression*' or '*content*' (PT 60) (cf. 11.31).

6.25   This same solidarity indicates why the 'popular conception' of 'a sign *for* something' is 'untenable' in view of 'recent linguistic thinking' (PT 47). The 'sign' is not 'an *expression* that points to a *content* outside the sign itself', but, according to Weisgerber (1929) and of course Saussure, 'an entity generated by the connection between an expression and a content' (cf. 2.25; 11.19). For this connection, Hjelmslev selects the term '**sign function**'; '**expression** and **content**' are 'the functives that contract this function', where '**functive**' means the 'terminal of a function' it 'contracts' (PT 33, 48, i.r.). The concept of 'function', 'adopted' 'in a sense that lies midway between the logico-mathematical and the etymological sense' (PT 33),[9] occupies the central role in Hjelmslev's 'theory', in which 'only the functions have scientific existence', and 'objects' are purely 'functives' (PT 85, 81, 33) (cf. 5.20; 6.28). 'A 'function' can also be a 'functive' in some higher 'function'; and 'a functive that is not a function' is 'called an **entity**' (PT 33). A '**constant**' is 'a functive whose presence is a necessary condition for the presence' of its other terminal; a '**variable**' is 'a functive whose presence is not necessary' (PT 35). Hjelmslev introduces a profusion of specific 'functions' and 'functives', many with colourful names like 'heteroplane' and 'homoplane' or 'plerematic' and 'cenematic' (RT 5f, 99, 136), but since he never gives examples, their usefulness is hard to judge (cf. 6.59).

6.26   For every 'sign', Hjelmslev emphasizes the 'solidarity between the sign function and its two functives, expression and content'; these two 'necessarily presuppose each other' (PT 48). 'We understand nothing of the structure of a language if we do not constantly take into first consideration the interplay between the planes' (PT 75). 'Except by artificial isolation, there can be no content without expression', nor 'an expression without a content' (PT 49). 'If we think without speaking, the thought is not a linguistic content'; 'if we speak without thinking, and in the form of series of sounds to which no content can be attached', 'such speech is an abracadabra, not a linguistic expression'. 'Saussure's "Gedankenexperiment"' of 'trying to consider expression and content each alone' was therefore pointless (PT 49f). A 'content' might appear 'meaningless' from the standpoint of 'normative logic or physicalism', 'but it is a content' (cf. 8^7; 8^{14}).

6.27 None the less, 'a description in accordance with our principles must analyse content and expression separately' into 'entities which are not necessarily susceptible of one-to-one matching with entities in the opposite plane' (PT 46) (cf. 3.22; 5.48, 64; 9.39; 12.55). Though the 'grammatical method' of 'recent times' 'starts' from 'the expression' and 'goes from there to the content', one could 'with the same right' 'proceed from the content to the expression' (PT 75). Hjelmslev proposes 'two disciplines', each for the 'study' of one plane; yet they must be 'interdependent', since they cannot 'be isolated from each other without serious harm'. If we consider 'two or more signs in mutual correlation, we shall always find that there is a relation between a correlation of expression and a correlation of content' (PT 65f). 'If such a relation is not present', then we have 'not two different signs, but only two different variants of the same sign'.

6.28 As we can see, Hjelmslev's vision of a sign system follows from Saussure's but is elaborated and revised. One major revision concerns 'Saussure's distinction between **form** and **substance**' (PT 123) (cf. 2.16f). 'If we maintain Saussure's terminology', 'it becomes precisely clear that the substance depends on the form to such a degree' that it 'can in no sense be said to have independent existence' (PT 50). 'What from one point of view is "substance" is from another point of view "form"', this being connected with the fact that functives denote only' 'points of intersection for functions, and that only the functional net of dependences has knowability and scientific existence, while "substance", in an ontological sense, remains a metaphysical concept' (PT 81; cf. PT 23) (cf. 5.20; 6.13, 25, 44, 6^{15}; 11^{15}).

6.29 Still, Saussure was 'correct in distinguishing form and substance', and in 'asserting that a language is a form, not a substance' (PT 54, 23; EL1 30) (cf. 2.16), and Hjelmslev too carefully separates substance from the concerns of his projected science. He hopes to cover 'language in a far broader sense' 'precisely because the theory is so constructed that linguistic form is viewed without regard for "the substance"' (PT 102). '"Substance" cannot in itself be a definiens of a language' (PT 103, i.r.). So 'linguistics must be assigned the special task of describing the linguistic form, in order thereby to make possible a projection of it upon the non-linguistic entities' which 'provide the substance' (PT 78f) (cf. 12.54). Hjelmslev's 'science would be an algebra of language' whose 'arbitrarily named entities' 'have no natural designation' and 'receive a motivated designation only on being confronted with the substance' (cf. 6.8; 12.15). Concurring with his already cited detachment of theory from reality (cf. 6.12, 15), Hjelmslev argues that in his 'calculus, there is no question of whether the individual structural types are manifested, but only whether they are manifestable' 'in any substance whatsoever' (PT 106). 'Substance is not a necessary presupposition for linguistic form', but the 'form' is 'necessary' 'for substance'. In any 'manifestation', 'the language form is the constant and the substance the variable'. 'The substance of both planes can be viewed both as physical entities (sounds in the expression plane, things in the content plane) and as the conception of these entities held by users of the language' (PT 78).

6.30 Form and substance are then deployed as categories for subdividing the two planes of content and expression. On the side of form, 'the **content-form** and the **expression-form**' are the 'two functives' of 'the sign function' (PT 57). On the side of substance, the '**expression-substance**' is 'the sound sequence' and 'is ordered to an expression-form'; the '**content-substance**' is the 'thing' or 'thought' and 'through the sign, is ordered to a content-form and arranged under it together with various other entities of content-form' (PT 57f, 78, 50). This account is intended to supplant the old notion that 'a sign is a sign for something' 'outside the sign itself' (PT 57) (cf. 6.23).

6.31 Hjelmslev's elaborated four-part scheme is clouded somewhat by an added notion called 'mening' in Danish and translated into English as '**purport**' (cf. PT 135). In several passages, the term is associated with 'substance', and 'content-purport' appears where we might expect 'content-substance' (PT 76f, 78f, 102f, 111). For instance, 'purport' is said to 'have no possible existence except through being substance' for a 'form': 'the content-form' 'is independent of, and stands in arbitrary relation to, the purport, and forms it into a content-substance' (PT 54, 52) (cf. 6.15; 12.24). 'Linguistic form' 'lays arbitrary boundaries on a purport-continuum' that 'depends exclusively on this structure' (PT 74). Otherwise, the 'purport' 'exists provisionally as' 'an unanalysed entity'; 'subjected to many different analyses', it 'would appear as so many different objects' (PT 50f). To make his point, Hjelmslev uses metaphors, which are otherwise conspicuously absent in his theory books. 'Purport' is an 'amorphous "thought-mass"' 'formed in quite different patterns', like a 'handful of sand' or a 'cloud in the heavens'; 'form is projected on to the purport, just as an open net casts its shadow down on an undivided surface' (PT 52, 57) (cf. 2.32; 3.3; 6.2, 57).

6.32 Who is to study 'purport' and how is even less clear. At one point, we read that 'purport is inaccessible to knowledge', because 'knowledge' presupposes 'an analysis' (PT 76). Yet elsewhere, the 'description' of 'purport' is allotted 'partly to the sphere of physics and partly to that of (social) anthropology'; 'logical', 'psychological', and 'phenomenological descriptions' are suggested as well (PT 51, 77f). Later, a 'science of linguistic content-purport' is envisioned as a project for 'a great number of special sciences outside linguistics', and ultimately for 'a collaboration of all the non-linguistic sciences', because 'they all, without exception, deal with a linguistic content' (PT 103, 77f) (cf. 6.54; 12.21). These 'non-linguistic sciences' 'must undertake an analysis of the linguistic purport without considering the linguistic form', whereas 'linguistics' 'must undertake an analysis of the linguistic form without considering the purport' (PT 78) (cf. 12.54). And 'since the linguistic formation of purport is arbitrary', 'these two descriptions – the linguistic and the non-linguistic – must be undertaken independently' (PT 77; cf. PT 103). Yet this division of labour is redundant if 'the non-linguistic analysis of the purport' 'by the non-linguistic sciences' will lead 'to a recognition of a "form" essentially of the same sort as the "linguistic form"'; or else unworkable if 'purport can be known only through some formation' and 'has no scientific existence apart from it' (PT 80, 76).

6.33 Instead of distinguishing '**langue**' and '**parole**', Hjelmslev draws an analogous division between '**schema**' and '**usage**' (PT 81; EL1 72) (cf. 2.20; 12.36).[10] The 'schema' is 'the linguistic hierarchy discovered' by 'deduction' and is 'the *constant*', whereas the 'usage' is the 'non-linguistic hierarchy' discovered by the 'analysis of purport' and is 'the *variable*' (PT 81, 106). While Saussure's 'langue' was 'static' (CG 81), Hjelmslev's 'schema' is not even 'subjected to the law of life'; if the 'language dies out', 'the schema' remains an 'ever-present realizable possibility' that happens to be 'latent' rather than 'manifested'; only the 'usage' can 'come into being' and 'die out' (EL2 116). This assertion too reflects Hjelmslev's demand that linguistic theory cover 'all conceivable possibilities' (cf. 6.11, 18, 20, 36, 38, 50, 63).

6.34 A similar division, one Hjelmslev develops in more detail (though without comparing it to Saussure's), falls between '**system**' and '**process**' – 'concepts' of 'great generality' or even 'universal character' (PT 39, 102) (cf. 9.41). 'For every process there is a corresponding system, by which the process can be analysed and described' (PT 9). 'A process and a system' 'together contract a function' 'in which the system is the constant' (PT 39). Hjelmslev aligns the pair 'process' versus 'system' with the pair '**text**' versus '**language**' and also with the pair '**syntagmatic**' versus '**paradigmatic**' (PT 39, 85, 109, 135), though this latter pair again is not developed in detail (cf. 6.39ff; 12.27).

6.35 'The process is the more immediately accessible for observation' and 'more "concrete"', 'while the system must be' '"discovered" behind it by means of a procedure and so is only mediately knowable' (PT 39). But we must not assume that 'the process can exist without a system'. On the contrary, 'the existence of a system is a necessary premise for the existence of a process'; 'the system' is 'present behind it', 'governing and determining it in its possible development'.[11] Conversely (befitting his detachment of theory from reality, 6.12), however, Hjelmslev claims that the 'existence' of 'a system' 'does not presuppose the existence of a process'. He 'imagines' 'a language without a text constructed in that language', and requires 'linguistic theory' to 'foresee' such a language 'as a possible system' (PT 39f). Its 'textual process is *virtual*' rather than '*realized*' (cf. 6.11, 42, 63; 12.39).

6.36 To 'test the thesis that a process has an underlying system', the 'process can be analysed' into 'a limited number of elements recurring in various combinations' (PT 9f). Hence, 'linguistic theory prescribes a **textual analysis**, which leads us to recognize a linguistic form behind the "substance" immediately accessible to observation by the senses, and behind the text a language (system) consisting of **categories** from whose definitions can be deduced the possible **units** of the language' (PT 96). This analysis is a 'purely formal procedure' for treating the 'units of a language' in terms of 'figurae' for which 'rules of transformation hold' (cf. 6.23). The 'basis' is in the 'definitions', 'made precise and supplemented' by 'rules of a more technical sort'. The *Résumé* presents no less than 201 such rules, which predictably state that 'one must operate with the lowest possible number of variants'; that 'in free articulation, all conceivable configurations are to be anticipated'; and so on (RT 20, 40).

6.37 'If the linguistic investigator is given anything (we put this in conditional form for epistemological reasons), it is the as yet unanalysed **text** in its undivided and absolute integrity' (PT 12) (cf. 2.88; 3.31; 5.5, 15; 8.35, 44; 9.1, 3, 8, 16, 41f, 107, 9[19]; 10.1f; 12.31). So 'linguistic theory starts from the text as its datum' and 'object of interest', and attempts to produce 'a self-consistent and exhaustive description through an analysis' (PT 21, 16). 'To order a system to the process of that text', 'the text is regarded as a class analysed into components, then these components as classes analysed into components, and so on until the analysis is exhausted' (PT 12f) (cf. 6.39). 'This method of procedure' is a '**deduction**', and to 'provide' it is 'the aim of linguistic theory' (PT 13, 16) (cf. 6.17, 33; 11.8; 12.44f).

6.38 The 'theory' must also 'indicate how any other text of the same premised nature can be understood in the same way' by 'furnishing us with tools that can be used on any text' (PT 16). 'Obviously, it would be humanly impossible to work through all existing texts', and 'futile' as well 'since the theory must also cover texts as yet unrealized' (PT 17). But though it 'must be content' with a 'selection', 'linguistic theory' may draw enough 'information' to 'describe and predict' 'any conceivable or theoretically possible texts' 'in any language whatsoever' (PT 16f) (cf. 6.11). 'This principle of analysis' must be 'treated' by 'the deepest strata of its definition system' (PT 21). Such a broad demand is contrasted with 'the restricted practical and technical attitude' which 'demands' that 'linguistic theory' be 'a sure method for describing a given limited text' (PT 125) (but cf. 6.61; 7.7; 8.44; 9.1f, 109ff; 12.43). Hjelmslev proposes instead 'an ever broader scientific' and 'humanistic attitude, until the idea finally comes to rest in a totality-concept that can scarcely be imagined more absolute' (PT 125f).

6.39 'The whole textual analysis' 'consists of a continued **partition**', 'each operation' being 'a single minimal partition' until all 'partitions' are 'exhausted' (PT 30). At each 'partition', we 'make an **inventory**' of the entities that have the same relations, i.e., that can occupy the same position in a chain', e.g., 'all primary' or 'secondary clauses', 'all words, all syllables, and all parts of syllables' (PT 41f). For 'exhaustive description', 'we must not omit any stage of analysis that might be expected to give functional return' (PT 42, 97). 'The analysis must move from the invariants' with 'the greatest extension conceivable' to those with 'the least' and 'traverse' 'as many derivative degrees' 'as possible' in between (PT 97). This 'analysis differs essentially' from that in 'conventional linguistics', which 'is very far from having carried the analysis to the end' (PT 97, 99). A 'traditional' analysis 'is concerned neither with' 'very great' nor 'very small extension' (PT 97). 'The linguist' would 'begin with dividing sentences into clauses' and would 'refer the treatment of larger parts of the text' 'to other sciences – principally logic and psychology' (PT 97f). Researchers didn't ask whether any 'logico-psychological analysis of the larger parts' 'had been undertaken', or whether it had been 'satisfactory from the linguist's point of view' (cf. 12.17).

6.40 The 'size' of 'the inventories' is expected to 'decrease as the procedure goes on': 'unrestricted inventories' yield to 'restricted', which in turn 'decrease in size' 'until all inventories have been restricted' 'as much as possible' (PT 42, 71). Since 'we cannot know beforehand whether any given stage is the last', every 'inventory' 'must satisfy our empirical principle' by being 'exhaustive and as simple as possible' (PT 60) (cf. 6.13). 'This requirement' applies most of all to 'the concluding stage', where we 'recognize the ultimate entities of which all others' are 'constructed'; keeping their 'number' 'as low as possible' is vital 'for the simplicity of the solution as a whole' (cf. 12.26). Here, Hjelmslev invokes 'the principle of **economy**', calling for a 'procedure' that gives 'the simplest possible' 'result' and is 'suspended if it does not lead to further simplification'; and 'the principle of **reduction**', requiring 'each operation' to be 'continued or repeated until the description is exhausted' and to 'register the lowest possible number of objects' 'at each stage' (PT 61).

6.41 The 'partitioning' of a 'linguistic text' 'defines' 'parts' according to 'mutual selection, solidarity, or combination' (PT 98).[12] The first 'partition' is 'into **content line** and **expression line**, which are **solidary**' (i.e., 'interdependent in a process') (PT 98, 24) (cf. 2.27; 4.17; 6.26, 47). We can then 'analyse the content line' into such classes as 'literary genres' or 'sciences' (PT 98) (cf. 6.10). 'At a more advanced stage', 'the larger textual parts must be further partitioned into the productions of single authors, works, chapters, paragraphs', and then 'into sentences and clauses' (PT 98f).[13] 'At this point', 'syllogisms will be analysed into premises and conclusions – obviously a stage' where 'formal logic must place an important part of its problems' (cf. 12.18). 'In all this is seen a significant broadening of the perspectives, frames, and capacities of linguistic theory, and a basis for a motivated and organized collaboration' with 'other disciplines which till now, obviously more or less wrongly, have usually been considered as lying outside the sphere of linguistic science' (cf. 6.49; 12.9–21).

6.42 'In the final operations', the 'partition descends to entities of a smaller extension than those' traditionally 'viewed as the irreducible invariants' (PT 99). Both 'the content plane' and 'the expression plane' are now to be 'analysed' into 'an inventory of **taxemes**' (cf. 4.45, 64; 5[26]). These are 'virtual elements' that may (but need not) be 'manifested by phonemes' in 'the expression plane', but how they are manifested in the content plane is a major mystery in Hjelmslev's outlook (cf. 6.47; 12.30). Finally, 'the end points of the analysis' are reached by partitioning 'the taxemes' into '**glossemes**', 'the minimal forms' and 'irreducible invariants' of 'glossematics'

(PT 99f, 80) (cf. 4.45; 6.8). Hjelmslev mentions here 'parts of phonemes', but not a single example of an actual 'glosseme' appears in PT or RT, though the latter defines many types of 'glossemes', such as 'median' and 'peripheral', 'centrifugal' and 'centripetal', 'primary' and 'secondary', 'principal' and 'accessory', and so on (RT 100, 179f, 184, 187, 192) (cf. 6.52). These definitions merely refer the term back to 'taxemes' (e.g., 'a median glosseme is a glosseme that enters into a median taxeme') (RT 179) (cf. 6.59). Thus, although 'glossemes' are the 'highest-degree invariants within a semiotic' (RT 100), we find no reliable way to tell their particular nature or status. Nor are they anywhere situated in respect to the 'figurae' said to compose signs (cf. 6.23, 36).

6.43 The 'method' must 'allow us, under precisely fixed conditions, to identify two entities with each other' (PT 61).[14] This 'requirement' is needed because in each 'inventory', we shall 'observe that in many places in the text we have "one and the same"' entity (PT 61f). 'These specimens' are the '**variants**, and the entities of which they are specimens' are '**invariants**' – a distinction 'valid for functives in general'. A prime example 'in modern linguistics' is 'the so-called phonemes' as the 'highest-degree invariants of the expression-plane' (cf. 2.69; 4.29f, 33; 5.42f; 8[35]; 11.80; 12.26). But neither 'the London school' (e.g., Daniel Jones) nor 'the Prague Circle' (e.g., N.S. Trubetzkoy) 'recognized that the prerequisite for an inventory is a textual analysis made on the basis of functions' (cf. 8.69). Instead, they used a 'vague "real" definition' with 'no useful objective criteria in doubtful cases', e.g., when they 'defined' 'vowel and consonant' by 'physiological or physical premises' (PT 62f) (cf. 12.26). The London group used 'position' to define the 'phoneme' and made no 'appeal to the content', whereas the Prague group insisted on the '**distinctive** function' that allowed 'differentiations of intellectual meaning' (PT 63ff) (cf. 2.70; 7[27]; 12.26f). Hjelmslev judges the 'distinctive criterion' of 'the Prague Circle' 'undoubtedly right', though he adds gruffly that 'on all other points strong reservations must be made' about their 'theory and practice' in 'phonology'.

6.44 The criterion of '**appropriateness**' stated for 'the empirical principle' (cf. 6.13, 15) suggests that the 'basis of analysis may differ for different texts' (PT 22). Still, 'the principle of analysis' is 'universal'. 'Naive realism' might 'suppose that analysis consisted merely in dividing a given object into parts', 'then those again into parts', 'and so on'. But to 'choose between several possible ways of dividing', the 'adequate' 'analysis' is the one 'conducted' 'so that it conforms to the mutual dependences between parts'.[15] Hence, 'the principle of analysis' is centred on the 'conclusion' that 'the object' 'and its parts have existence only by virtue of these dependences' (PT 22f) (cf. 6.25, 28). 'The objects of naive realism' are found to be 'nothing but intersections of bundles of such dependences' and can be 'defined and grasped scientifically only in this way'. 'The recognition' 'that a totality does not consist of things but of relationships, and that not substance but only its internal and external relationships have scientific existence' 'may be new in linguistic science' and shows 'the exclusive relevance of functions for analysis' (PT 23, 80f) (cf. 5.20; 6.25; 11.25). 'The postulation of objects' 'is a superfluous axiom' and 'a metaphysical hypothesis from which linguistic science will have to be freed' (PT 23; cf. PT 81) (cf. 6.13ff, 25).

6.45 This line of argument is intended to strengthen the thesis that 'the principle of analysis must be a recognition' of '**dependences**' (PT 28). We may 'conceive of the parts to which the analysis shall lead as nothing but bundles of lines of dependence'. 'The basis of analysis' must therefore 'be chosen according to what lines of dependence are relevant' and proper for 'making the description exhaustive'. 'The analysis' proceeds by 'registering certain dependences between terminals' 'we may call parts of the text', these too 'having existence precisely by virtue of the dependences'. Both 'the dependence between the whole' '(the text)' 'and the parts', and the one between 'the so-called parts' are 'characterized' by '**uniformity**' (PT 28f). For example, we shall 'always find the same dependence between a primary clause and a secondary clause', or 'between stem and derivational element or between the central and marginal parts of a syllable'. In sum, 'we can define' '**analysis**' 'formally as description of an object by the uniform dependences of other objects on it and on each other'; 'the object' is 'a *class*' and the others are its '*components*' (cf. 6.17, 33). To fit his concept of 'a **deduction**', Hjelmslev requires that 'each operation will premise the preceding operations' (PT 30f). He advocates 'a special rule of transference' to 'prevent a given entity from being analysed at a too early stage' and to 'ensure that certain entities under given conditions are transferred unanalysed from stage to stage' (PT 41). Examples include 'a sentence' of 'one clause, and a clause of only one word' (cf. 5.51, 53). 'The Latin imperative "*ī*" ("go")', for instance, can be 'at the same time a sentence, a clause, and a word' (and a morpheme and a phoneme too).

6.46 Since 'the registration of certain functions' 'cannot be reached by a mere mechanical observation of entities that enter into actual texts', we may have to 'interpolate certain functives which would in no other way be accessible to knowledge' (PT 93).[16] This method is called '**catalysis**' (PT 94). Hjelmslev points here to the 'incalculable accidents' and 'disturbances' 'in the exercise of language' (in 'parole'), such as when a text is 'interrupted or incomplete', and he says that 'in general' they could be 'eliminated' (cf. 7.12). Yet 'an exhaustive description' should 'register' 'the outward relations which the actually observed entities have', including 'aposiopesis and abbreviation', which form 'a constant and essential part' in 'the economy of linguistic usage'. This proviso may seem unexpected for such an abstract approach, and Hjelmslev warns us to 'take care not to supply more in the text than what there is clear evidence for' (PT 95).

6.47 But 'clear evidence' and 'outward relations' might be hard to find for the '**content plane**'. He stresses the 'solidarity' of 'content with expression' (cf. 6.26, 41) presumably because he hopes, like many linguists, to analyse content with the methods available for analysing expression, i.e., form (cf. 12.54). He hails the 'far-reaching' 'discovery' that 'the two sides (planes) of a language have completely analogous categorical structure', even though the 'analysis into content-figurae has never been made' (PT 101,

67) (cf. 6.24). He 'predicts with certainty that such an analysis can be carried out' for both 'planes' 'according to a common principle', and considers it an 'inevitable logical consequence' that the same 'tests can be applied to the content plane' and 'enable us to register the figurae that compose the sign-contents' (PT 66f, 70). 'Experience shows that in all hitherto observed languages, there comes a stage in the analysis of the expression when the entities' 'no longer' appear as 'bearers of meaning and thus are no longer sign-expressions' (PT 45) (cf. 6.23). But to decide whether something 'bears meaning' (in the sense that changing it also changes the meaning, cf. PT 66, 68f, 70), or what that meaning is, may not be easy. He gives one list of 'entities of content', including ' "man", "woman", "boy", "girl" ' (PT 70), but these are also words, and he doesn't analyse them further. His 1957 paper on 'structural semantics' (EL1 96–112) (the earliest proposal I know of for that field) also lacks lengthy or detailed analysis, and offers as 'elements of content' ' "be" + "1st person" + "singular" + "present" + "indicative" ' (EL1 111); but these are more notions of grammar than of meaning per se.

6.48 At one point, Hjelmslev remarks that 'the "meaning" ' which any 'minimal entity can be said to bear' is 'a purely *contextual* meaning' (PT 44f). In 'the continued analysis' of a text, 'there exist no other perceivable meanings than contextual meanings'; 'any entity' or 'sign is defined relatively, not absolutely, and only by its place in the context'. Nor do 'dictionaries' 'yield definitions that can be immediately taken over by a consistently performed analysis' (PT 71f). 'So-called lexical meanings in certain signs are nothing but artificially isolated contextual meanings or paraphrases of them' (PT 45). This argument implies that analysts might have to generate or design, on each new occasion, the units of content they propose to discover; and the results might not apply to other texts or even to other analyses of the same text. Also, determining what the entities of meaning are should get steadily harder as the partitioning proceeds, and would seldom come to a 'self-consistent, exhaustive, and simple' conclusion (cf. 6.13, 37, 54). The most restricted inventories (cf. 6.40) would be very general meanings like the 'small closed classes' ' "large"::"small" ' or ' "long"::"short" ' (EL1 110), which don't match the content of the most restricted inventories of expression like phonemes or letters. The inverse might hold: the most general meanings might reflect the largest segments of text (cf. 10.19, 32, 49, 65).

6.49 Nevertheless, Hjelmslev remains confident that the 'method of procedure' during 'the whole analysis' 'proves to result in great clarity and simplification, and it also casts light on the whole mechanism of language in a fashion hitherto unknown' (PT 59). Now 'it will be easy to organize the subsidiary disciplines of linguistics according to a well-founded plan and to escape at last from the old, halting division of linguistics into phonetics, morphology, syntax, lexicography, and semantics'. 'Logically', 'process dependences' could be 'registered only in syntax', 'i.e., between the words of a sentence but not within the individual word or its parts; hence the preoccupation with grammatical government' (PT 26f). But 'the description of a language on the basis of the empirical principle does not contain the possibility of a syntax or a science of parts of speech' (PT 101) (cf. 12.7). 'The entities' of 'ancient grammar' 'will be rediscovered in refined form in far different places within the hierarchy of the units'; and 'the entities' of 'conventional syntax', such as 'primary' and 'secondary clauses' or 'subject and predicate', 'are reduced to mere variants' (PT 101, 84, 73) (cf. 2.6; 6.43; 7.4; 8.38; 11.41, 88; 12.7). So 'the distribution of functives into' 'invariants and variants' 'eliminates the conventional bifurcation of linguistics into morphology and syntax', (for once) 'in agreement with several modern schools' (PT 73, 26) (cf. 2.55; 5.54; 8.57; 9.31; 10.35; 12.28). In addition, 'we must not expect any semantics or phonetics', because they are not 'deductive' and 'formal' enough to handle 'non-linguistic "substance"' (PT 96) (cf. 6.13, 28ff). Against 'linguistics', which has 'neglected' its 'main task' (stated in 6.8), Hjelmslev calls for 'a description of the categories of expression on a non-phonetic basis' (PT 79n) (cf. 12.26, 32).

6.50 Although he thus rejects the 'conventional' domains, Hjelmslev proposes in return a **'semiotic'** of such expansive scope that 'semiotic structure is revealed as a stand from which all scientific objects may be viewed' (PT 127). This inclusion will end 'the belief' fostered by 'conventional phonetics' that 'the expression-substance' 'must consist exclusively of sounds' (PT 103) (cf. 3.18; 4.28ff). Hjelmslev wants to include as well 'gesture', 'sign-language', and 'writing', the latter being 'a graphic "substance" which is addressed exclusively to the eye and which need not be transposed into a phonetic "substance" in order to be understood' (PT 103f) (but cf. 2.21f; 6.50; 4.37ff; 8.72; 9.42f; 11.83; 12.33). The best illustration is 'a phonetic or phonemic notation', or a 'phonetic orthography' like 'the Finnish' (cf. 2.69; 3.54; 4.38; 6.50; 8.75). The written mode is welcomed as evidence that 'different systems of expression can correspond to one and the same system of content', and as another reason why 'the linguistic theoretician' must not merely 'describe' the 'present' 'system', but must 'calculate what expression systems in general are possible' (PT 105) (cf. 6.11). Moreover, 'the invention of the alphabet' is a model for 'linguistic theory' of an 'analysis that leads to entities of the least possible extension and the lowest possible number' (PT 42f) (cf. 8.75). Hjelmslev dismisses the objection that 'all these "substances"' are '"derived"' from sound and '"artificial"' rather than '"natural"'; this 'opinion is irrelevant' because, even if '"derived"', the substance is still 'a manifestation', and because we cannot be sure that 'the discovery of alphabetic writing', 'hidden in pre-history', 'rests on a phonetic analysis' – a 'diachronic hypothesis' anyway, and in 'modern linguistics, diachronic considerations are irrelevant for synchronic description' (PT 104f) (cf. 2.36ff).

6.51 The framework of Hjelmslev's 'semiotics' would be a hierarchy of 'orders'. The minimal requirement for a 'semiotic' is 'two *planes*' that do not 'have the same structure throughout', i.e., are not '*conformal*' (PT 112) (cf. 6.26). A 'test' could be used 'for deducing whether or not a given object is a semiotic'. But Hjelmslev 'leaves it to the experts to decide' if the 'symbolic systems of mathematics and logic', or 'art' and 'music' 'are to be defined as semiotics'; they may not be 'biplanar', such that we could not 'encatalyze [i.e., supply from outside] a content-form' (PT 113) (cf. 6.10, 41). 'Games', on the other hand – including 'chess', Saussure's favourite model (cf. 2.80) – 'lie close to' or 'on the boundary' 'between semiotic and non-semiotic' (PT 110). Whereas 'the logical side' sees 'a game' as 'a transformation system of essentially the same structure as a semiotic', 'the linguistic side' sees 'a game' as 'a system of values analogous to economic values'. Still, to the extent that 'there exist for the calculus of linguistic theory not interpreted, but only interpretable systems' (to 'interpret' here being to 'order' a 'content-purport'), 'there is no difference between' 'chess' or 'pure algebra' and 'a language' (PT 111f).

6.52 'To establish a simple model situation', Hjelmslev had 'proceeded on the tacit assumption that the datum is a text composed in one definite semiotic, not in a mixture of two or more' (PT 115). Yet 'any text' 'not of so small extension that it fails to yield a sufficient basis for deducing a system generalizable to other texts, usually contains derivates that rest on different systems', among which he names 'styles', 'media', 'tones', 'idioms', 'vernaculars', and 'physiognamies' (individual speaking styles), alongside 'national' and 'regional languages' (PT 115f). As types of 'style' he enumerates 'belletristic', 'slang', 'jargon', 'colloquial', 'lecture', 'pulpit', 'chancery', and so on. The 'members' of these classes and their 'combinations' are called '*connotators*'. A 'connotator', Hjelmslev explains, is 'an indicator which is found, under certain conditions, in both planes of the semiotic' and thus can 'never' 'be referred unambiguously to one definite plane' (PT 118). He 'views the connotators as content for which the **denotative semiotics** are expression'; this pair of 'content' and 'expression' therefore constitute 'a **connotative semiotic**' (PT 119).

6.53 Hjelmslev thus places a 'denotative semiotic', that is, an ordinary semiotic 'none of whose planes is a semiotic', alongside a 'connotative semiotic', that is, 'a non-scientific semiotic one or more of whose planes' is 'a semiotic' (PT 137f).[17] The next higher order is a '**metasemiotic**', that is, 'a scientific semiotic one or more of whose planes' is a 'semiotic'.[18] Next comes a '**semiology**', being a 'metasemiotic with a non-scientific' (i.e., 'connotative') 'semiotic as an object'; and a '**metasemiology**' as a 'meta-scientific semiotics' with at least one 'semiology' for 'an object'. Within this multi-order apparatus, 'all those entities' 'provisionally eliminated as non-semiotic elements are reintroduced as necessary components into semiotic structures of a higher order' (PT 127). Ultimately, 'we find no non-semiotics that are not components of semiotics, and in the final instance, no object that is not illuminated from the key position of linguistic theory' (cf. 2.8; 6.9f, 22, 32, 41; 11.9; 12.21).

6.54 'The metasemiology of denotative semiotics' will 'treat the objects of phonetics and semantics in a reinterpreted form' (PT 125). 'The metasemiotic of connotative semiotics' will treat 'sociological linguistics and Saussurean external linguistics', including 'geographical', 'historical, political', 'social, sacral', and 'psychological content-purports that are attached to nation', 'region', 'style', 'personality', 'mood, etc.'. 'Many special sciences', notably 'sociology, ethnology, and psychology', are invited to 'make their contribution here' (provided they don't mind working within 'non-scientific semiotics'). Moreover, 'metasemiology' can provide the 'description of substance' excluded from linguistic theory – by 'undertaking a self-consistent, exhaustive, and simplest possible analysis of the things' of 'content' and of 'the sounds' of 'expression' (PT 124, i.r.) (cf. 6.29f; 12.24). Sounding unexpectedly like Pike, Hjelmslev says this can be done 'on a completely physical basis' (cf. 5.27). Perhaps 'the analysable continuum' of 'zones' in the 'phonetico-physiological sphere of movement' could be studied with 'a sufficiently sensitive experimental–phonetic registration' (PT 54, 82) (cf. 4.28, 4^{10}; 7.20; 8^{33}). But how 'the continuum' of 'zones of purport' for 'the system of content' can be studied on a 'physical basis' is hard to conceive; the 'colour spectrum' Hjelmslev uses as an example (PT 52f) is too orderly to be representative (cf. 4.22; 5.68; 7.31, 71).

6.55 'Usually, a metasemiotic' is 'wholly or partly identical with its object semiotic' (PT 121). 'Thus the linguist who describes a language' 'uses that language in the description'; the same holds for the 'semiologist who describes a semiotic' (cf. 12.48). 'It follows that metasemiology' 'must in very great part repeat the proper results of semiology', a prospect in conflict with 'the simplicity principle'. So 'metasemiology' should be restricted to dealing not with 'the language', but with the 'modifications' or 'additions' entailed in the 'terminology' and 'special jargon' of 'semiology' (PT 121). 'The task of metasemiology' is 'to subject the minimal signs of semiology, whose content is identical with the ultimate content- and expression-variants of the object semiotic (language), to a relational analysis' through 'the same procedure' as 'textual analysis' (PT 123). The 'terms for' 'glosseme-variations' would be a major concern here (PT 122) (but cf. 6.42).

6.56 During his discussion of semiotics, Hjemslev pays tribute to some predecessors who evidently influenced his thinking quite profoundly. Alongside 'a semiotic whose **expression plane** is a semiotic', he places 'the logistic' of 'the Polish logicians' like Alfred Tarski (1935) as a 'metalanguage' or 'metasemiotic' whose '**content plane**' would be 'a semiotic'; and declares that 'linguistics itself must be' just 'such a metasemiotic' (PT 119f, 109). 'The logical theory of signs' is derived from 'the metamathematics of [David] Hilbert [1928a, 1928b], whose idea was to consider the system of mathematical symbols as a system of expression-figurae with complete disregard for their content, and to describe its transformation rules' 'without considering possible interpretations'. 'This method is carried over by the Polish logicians into their "metalogic" and is brought to its conclusion by [Rudolf] Carnap [1934, 1937] in a sign theory where, in principle, any semiotic is considered as a mere expression system without regard for its content' (PT 110f) (cf. Jørgensen 1937) (cf. 6.60, 64; 11.36; 12.17).

6.57 Another expansion of scope follows from the thesis that 'the object of the linguist' is not 'the individual language alone', 'but the whole class of languages', which 'explain and cast light on each other'. So Hjelmslev calls for a 'typology whose categories are individual languages, or rather, the individual language types' (PT 106) (cf. 2.20; 3.47–54; 4.62; 7.19f). 'It is impossible to draw a boundary between the study of the individual linguistic type and the general typology of languages' (PT 126). 'The individual type is a special case within that typology', and 'exists only by virtue of the function that connects it with others' (cf. 6.25, 44). This proviso supports the thesis that 'in the calculative typology of linguistic theory all linguistic schemata are foreseen; they constitute a system with correlations between the individual members' (cf. 6.33). We can explore 'differences between languages' due to 'different realizations' not of 'substance' but of 'a principle of formation' applied to 'an identical but amorphous purport' (PT 77; cf. PT 56f) (cf. 6.31). 'On the basis of the arbitrary relation between form and substance', the 'same entity of linguistic form may be manifested by quite different substance-forms as one passes from one language to another' (PT 97, 103) (cf. 2.28ff). Or, we may look into 'contacts between languages': either 'loan-contacts' or 'genetic linguistic relationships' which 'produce linguistic families' (PT 126) (cf. 2.42, 76; 4.73; 5^{47}).

6.58 An appealing prospect for so broad a framework is to apply it to science itself, and Hjelmslev foresees this opportunity (cf. 11.12f; 12.48). 'Under the analysis of the sciences linguistic theory must come to contain within itself its own definition' (PT 98) (cf. 12.36). So the terms applied to the language could be turned back on the theory as well (cf. 8.33; 9.27). For instance, 'the distinction between process' versus 'system' (6.34) might be pictured as that between the 'both–and' or 'conjunction' 'in the process or text', versus the 'either–or' or 'disjunction' 'in the system' (PT 36). Or, 'the concept of syncretism' 'reached from internal linguistic premises' might help us 'attach a scientific meaning to the word *concept*' itself, and might 'cast light' on 'the general problem of the relation between class and component' (PT 92f). Or again, 'an analysis of logical conclusion' as a 'linguistic operation' could treat it as 'a premised proposition' wherein the 'syncretism which appears as an implication' is 'resolved' (cf. 6.10, 41, 49).

6.59 I hope my survey has conveyed some of the breadth and variety of Hjelmslev's theoretical concerns. In a lecture where he identifies himself as a 'linguistic theoretician', he remarks that such persons have 'very abstract aims' and 'overwhelm their audience with definitions and with terminology' (EL2 103) (cf. 7.89). The remark was certainly apt; in RT, he presents formal definitions of no less than 454 terms, only a small fraction of which I have mentioned. Many are brittle neologisms scarcely found elsewhere in linguistics, such as 'ambifundamental exponent' or 'heterosubtagmatic sum' (RT 177, 198) (cf. 6.42). Even the most familiar terms receive unwonted definitions. A 'word' is a 'sign of the lowest power, defined by the permutation of the glossematies' ('extrinsic units') 'entering into it'; a 'noun' is 'a plerematic syntagmateme'; a 'verb' is 'a nexus-conjunction'; an 'adjective' is 'a syntagmateme whose characteristic is a greatest-conglomerate of intense characters' (sounds to me like a linguistics department); an 'adverb' is 'a pseudotheme that is not a connective and that does not include converted taxemes or converted varieties of ambifundamental taxemes'; and so on (RT 202, 99, 206f, 209) (cf. 12.7). Significantly, 'phrase', 'clause', and 'sentence' are not defined at all, nor are 'meaning', 'reference', and the like.

6.60 Managing so vast an apparatus would be a considerable task. The definitions interlock and cross-refer in such meticulous ways that we would have to either memorize them all or keep looking them up. Nearly every one is accompanied by a formal symbol, but almost none by an example (cf. 6.25, 42). We are again reminded how 'the naming' of 'the "algebraic" entities' 'is **arbitrary**' in that they 'do not at all involve the manifestation' (PT 97) (cf. 6.15, 18, 29). But the motto that 'all terminology is arbitrary' (PT 58) would certainly need qualifying as soon as we confront a manifestation and try to assign it to one category rather than another (cf. 12.27). To the extent that Hjelmslev's 'algebra' of terms and symbols is indeed free of all manifestation, it comes close to being no 'semiotic' at all – since the step of 'encatalyzing a content' is always deferred – but 'a *symbolic system*' like those propounded in 'metamathematics' and 'logic' (PT 110, 113) (cf. 6.56). And although Hjelmslev wants to 'reckon with the possibility of certain sciences not being semiotics' 'but symbolic systems' (PT 120n), it is hard to imagine linguistics being such a one.

6.61 He claims that the 'names' of the 'entities' are also '**appropriate**' because they help us to 'order the information concerning the manifestation in the simplest possible way' (PT 97). But the claim is premature until we have a reasonable corpus of demonstrations, and his network of terms and rules could hardly be applied in any simple way. He himself is plainly reluctant to venture beyond the preparatory stage. A paragraph was 'added to the *Prolegomena*' in 1960 'as a warning' 'not to confuse the theory' with any 'application' or 'practical method (procedure)' (RT xiii; PT 17). Yet the fact that 'no practical "discovery procedure"' is 'set forth' does not impair Hjelmslev's confidence that his 'theory will lead to a procedure' (PT 17) (cf. 7.7). Nowhere in his two volumes on theory nor in his two volumes of essays does he actually analyse or describe a text in any detail. Aside from isolated words and phrases, he brings up only a handful of sentences or utterances ('*énoncés*') (PT 50f, 56, 94; EL1 66, 156, 158ff, 172, 177, 199, 247; EL2 249), and none of these is treated in any remotely exhaustive manner.

6.62 Hjelmslev seeks 'the object of science' in 'the registration of cohesions'; 'science always seeks to comprehend objects as consequences of a reason or as effects of a cause' (PT 83f) (cf. 12.11). Only when 'the analysis is exhausted' must 'clarification by reasons and causes' 'give way to a purely statistical description' (PT 125). He believes this to be 'the final situation' of 'deductive phonetics' and 'physics', the latter perhaps being the non-causal quantum theory prominently developed at his own university in Copenhagen (cf. 11.59). But his own apparatus of rules and definitions makes no provision I can see for assigning reasons or causes to entities. The indeterminacy of quantum phenomena might well be analogous to that of the content plane in general (cf. Beaugrande 1989a; Yates and Beaugrande 1990).

6.63 Still, no one could fail to be impressed by the range and rigour of Hjelmslev's thought within the bounds he sets. His proposals are put forth only in the anticipation of a beginning and their abstractness and difficulty helps make us appreciate the vast domains to be covered. His 'test' for the 'success' of a 'linguistic theory', namely to 'draw all possible consequences from the chosen structural principle' (PT 20) (cf. 6.11, 18, 20, 33, 36, 38), promises to keep researchers busy for a long time. Equally vast is the utopian prospect of the 'unrestricted text' 'capable of being prolonged through constant addition of further parts', the grandest instance being an entire 'living language taken as text' (PT 42; cf. PT 45, 83) – whereupon the dualism of 'process' and 'system' (cf. 6.34) would yield to total unity. Finally, 'the general typology' for 'the whole class of languages', including even 'virtual' ones (PT 126, 106) (cf. 6.11, 35, 57) is another imposing challenge.

6.64 In a 1948 lecture, Hjelmslev quotes a letter from Bally, 'the successor of Saussure', saying: 'You pursue with constancy the ideal formulated by F. de Saussure in the final sentence of his *Cours*', namely that 'the true and unique object of linguistics is language studied in and for itself' (EL1 31; CG 232) (2.9). Also cited with warm approval is Carnap's motto that 'all scientific statements must be' 'about relations without involving a knowledge or a description of the relata themselves' (EL1 32) (cf. 6.44; 6.56). Within this constellation of allegiances, Hjelmslev was certainly consistent and, in his way, quite radical in 'seeking an immanent understanding of language as a self-subsistent, specific structure' and 'seeking a constancy inside language, not outside it' (PT 19) (cf. 12.25). 'A temporary restriction' is needed to 'elicit from language itself its secret' (PT 127). Ultimately, however, 'immanence and transcendence are joined in higher unity'. Then, 'linguistic theory' can 'reach its prescribed goal' by 'recognizing not merely the linguistic system in its schema and its usage, in its totality and its individuality, but also man and human society behind language, and all man's sphere of knowledge through language'.

Notes

1. The key for Hjelmslev citations is: EL1: *Essais linguistiques* (1970); EL2: *Essais linguistiques II* (1973); PT: *Prolegomena to a Theory of Language* (1969 [1943]); and RT: *Résumé of a Theory of Language* (1975 [1941–42]). Most of this material was translated from the Danish by Francis J. Whitfield. French sources are cited in my own translation.
2. Though usually in agreement with Saussure, Hjelmslev does not distinguish between 'speech' and 'language' (cf. 2.20). But he makes two analogous distinctions: between 'usage' and 'schema', and between 'process' and 'system' (6.33f).
3. Hjelmslev's censure includes even the phonology of the schools in London (Daniel Jones) and Prague (N.S. Trubetzkoy), who were neither humanistic nor philosophical (cf. 6.43).
4. Even Bloomfield (1926) and Bühler (1933, 1934) are included for having proposed a 'system of axioms' for 'transcendent kinds of linguistics' (PT 6, 6n).

In fact, however, Bloomfield rebuked the 'philosophical' trends in language study (cf. 4.4ff, 19, 38, 51, 72; 6.13; 12.16).

5. Contributors to this 'beginning' are named: Saussure (1879), Sechehaye (1908), Bloomfield (1933), Trager (1939), Vogt (1942), Bjerrum (1944), and Kuryłowicz (1949), along with Hjelmslev himself and his collaborators Uldall (1936) and Togeby (1951) (PT 79nf). Hjelmslev gives several statements of 'the main task' (compare 6.11, 22).

6. Hjelmslev stipulates that 'there is no experience before one has described the object by application of the chosen method'; 'only after the method has been thoroughly tested can experience be obtained' (EL2 103). But how could 'experience' and 'theory' then be 'independent'? And how can we invent a method *before* having any experience of the 'object' to be described (cf. 7.28)?

7. Hjelmslev warns that he is using 'induction' in 'a quite different meaning' from 'logical argument', but is using 'deduction' in the usual 'sense of "logical conclusion"' (PT 32).

8. Hjelmslev thinks the 'invention of alphabetic writing' was an early result of an 'analysis into expression-figurae' (PT 67) (cf. 6.48; 8.71).

9. The 'etymological meaning of the word "function" is its "real" definition', but Hjelmslev 'avoids' 'introducing it into the definition system, because it is based on more premises than the given formal definition and turns out to be reducible to it' (PT 34). Elsewhere, logic is criticized for 'neglecting' 'the results of the linguistic approach to language' and thus attaining a 'sign concept' 'unmistakably inferior to that of Saussure' by not understanding that 'the linguistic sign is two-sided' (EL1 33).

10. In another paper, Hjelmslev proposes to divide the **'langue'** side into three: 'schema' ('pure language form'), 'norm' ('material language form'), and 'usage' ('the ensemble of habits') (EL1 72). He says the **'parole'** side is 'as complex as that of the langue', but he declines to 'conduct an analogous analysis' (EL1 79).

11. 'Determine' is an action performed by a 'variable' on a 'constant' (PT 35). Since Hjelmslev says 'the system is the constant', his statement that 'the process determines the system' (PT 39, i.r.) makes more sense than this one here.

12. These three terms are part of a scheme created because in 'some cases' 'the difference between process and system is only a difference in point of view' (PT 25). 'Interdependence between terms in a process' is *'solidarity'*, and one 'in a system' is *'complementarity'* (e.g., between 'vowel and consonant') (PT 24ff, 24n, 41). 'Determination' 'in a process' is *'selection'* (some 'have long been known under the name of *government*', cf. 4.66) and 'in a system' *'specification'*. 'Constellations in a process' are *'combinations'* and 'in a system' *'autonomies'*.

13. This passage seems to count 'clauses' and 'sentences' as units of 'content', quite unlike the usual explicit practice in linguistics.

14. Instead of stating these 'precisely fixed conditions', Hjelmslev says 'the problem of identity' can 'be dismissed' 'as an unnecessary complication' (PT 61n). He refers us to Saussure, who raised the problem (e.g., CG 43, 91, 107f, 161, 181, 186) but certainly didn't solve it.

15. This conclusion is said to hold even when 'the analysis' is seen 'from the point of view of a metaphysical theory of knowledge', though elsewhere, the 'metaphysical' view is claimed to rely on 'substance' and ignore 'the functional net of dependences' (PT 22, 81).

16. To limit the book-keeping to interpolations of less than a whole sign, Hjelmslev juggles his idea of 'function': if 'the encatalyzed entity' is of 'content', it 'has the expression zero, and if it is' 'of expression', it 'has the content zero' (PT 96). The silent ' "-d" ' in French *"grand"'*, which becomes audible in ' *"grand*

homme" ', is used as evidence that 'latency is an overlapping with zero' (PT 93) (cf. 2^{26}; 4^3; 5^{12}).

17. 'Non-scientific' means here that the 'semiotic' 'is not an operation', an 'operation' being 'a description' 'in agreement with the empirical principle' (PT 120, 131, 31, 138; RT 14). Even so, it is hardly a tactful term.

18. Elsewhere, though, the 'metasemiotic' is allowed to have only a 'content plane' as its 'semiotic' (PT 114, 119). 'The Polish logicians' are cited for having prepared the way to such a construction (PT 119) (cf. 6.56).

Chapter 7

Noam Chomsky[1]

7.1 Both inside and outside the discipline, Chomsky's work has funda-mentally affected views of what of linguistics is or should be, and reopened issues many linguists had long thought were settled. On the jacket of *Aspects of the Theory of Syntax* (hereafter AT), a reviewer calls the 'approach' 'truly fresh and revolutionary'; and Chomsky often stresses how it is different from, and better than, various alternatives. Yet many of his ideas are conservative in that they derive from traditional philosophy, grammar, and logic. The most 'revolutionary' aspect lies in his claims about how these ideas apply to language and linguistics (cf. 7.78, 95).

   7.2 A skilful public debater, Chomsky intensifies the forensic and polemical aspects of the discipline by using theoretical arguments about 'the nature of language' to fortify his positions against competitors (cf. 9.3; 12[2]). He foregrounds points of contention even where he implicitly agrees with or borrows from his adversaries, and uses a highly confident rhetoric for his 'tentative' views and proposals (cf. 7.85, 94).[2] His argumentation oscillates from intuitive reasoning and philosophical speculations on 'the mind', over to technical points drawn from formal language theory and from such sciences as biology and neurology. Due in part to this diversity of sources, his terminology and notation take on a strategic plurality of meanings (cf. 7.15, 28, 78, 83ff).

   7.3 Chomsky turns away from 'modern linguistics' (cf. 7.5, 19, 30, 62, 75) and cites far earlier sources: Pāṇini, Plato, and both rationalist and romantic **philosophers**, such as René Descartes (1647), Claude Fauré Vaugelas (1647), César Chesneau DuMarsais (1729), Denis Diderot (1751), James Beattie (1788), and Wilhelm von Humboldt (1836) (AT v, 4f, 49, 198f, 233f).[3] He sees 'the conception of linguistic structure that marked the origins of modern syntactic theory' in the *Grammaire générale et raisonnée* (Lancelot and Arnauld 1660), which claimed that 'aside from figurative speech' the '"natural order of thoughts"' is 'mirrored by the order of words'[4] – an idea Chomsky rejects as a 'naive view of language structure' blocking 'a precise statement of regular processes of sentence formation', though his notion of 'deep structure' being 'interpreted' via 'semantic universals' has a similar cast (AT 6, 117f, 137) (cf. 7.20, 71f; 10.84). Such allegiances brought 'Cartesian linguistics' into fashion (cf. Chomsky 1966) in a discipline that had been rather hostile to philosophy (cf. 4.4ff, 19, 38, 51, 72; 6.3, 5, 13; 8.5, 17, 60, 8^{14}; 9.3ff, 31; 12.16).

7.4 Another chief source is '**traditional grammars**', staunchly defended for having 'exhibited' 'linguistic processes', 'however informally', and 'given a wealth of information concerning the structural descriptions of sentences' (AT 5). For Chomsky, this 'information is 'without question substantially correct, and is essential to any account of how the language is used or acquired' (cf. 2.6; 6.49; 11.41, 88; 12.7); that such 'grammars' 'have been "long condemned by professional linguists"' is deemed 'irrelevant' (AT 63f, 194; cf. Dixon 1963). Admittedly, these 'grammars were deficient in that they left unexpressed many of the basic regularities of language', and never went 'beyond the classification of particular examples to the stage of formulation of generative rules on any significant scale'; but this 'defect' is also found in 'structuralist grammars' (AT 5). Chomsky's grammatical terms in works like AT are not attributed to any source; language philosophers are cited only in theoretical arguments.

7.5 A source Chomsky roundly repudiates is '**structural linguistics**', his chief competitor. His 'discussion' of work in this discipline leads the agenda of *Syntactic Structures* (hereafter SS) and is cited in AT as 'unanswerable' or at least 'for the moment, not challenged', whereupon he presumes that 'the inadequacy' of 'structuralist grammars' 'for natural languages' 'has been established beyond any reasonable doubt' (AT 54, 67). He simply ignores the merits of such grammars for describing a host of previously unrecorded languages (cf. 7.87; 12.56). He sees only their theoretical flaws and 'no compensating advantage for the modern descriptivist reanalysis', and even vows that 'knowledge of grammatical structure cannot arise' from the 'operations' used in that kind of 'linguistics' (AT 174, 57) (cf. 7.7, 24, 29, 33, 76, 96). Also, descriptivist fieldwork conflicts with his own plan to focus on English and to discount the formal diversity of languages as a 'surface' issue (cf. 7.18f, 41, 55, 62; 12.71).

7.6 Chomsky charges that 'descriptivists' rely unduly on **induction**: the 'limitation-in-principle to classification and organization of data, to "extracting patterns" from a corpus of observed speech' (AT 15) (cf. 4.7; 12.45). 'Structural linguistics' makes an 'extremely strong demand' on 'discovery' by 'assuming that the techniques for discovering the correct hypotheses (grammar) must be based on procedures of segmentation and classification of items in a corpus' (AT 202f) (cf. 12.30). Thus, 'general linguistic theory' seems to 'consist only of a body of procedures' which 'determine' the 'restrictions on possible grammars' and otherwise leave 'the form of language unspecified' (AT 52). 'Proposals' 'attempt to state methods of analysis that an investigator might actually use' 'to construct a grammar of language directly from the raw data' (e.g., Wells 1947; Bloch 1948; Harris 1951, 1955; Hockett 1952; Chomsky 1953) (SS 52). 'This goal' can 'lead into a maze' of 'complex analytic procedures' unsuited to answer 'many important questions about the nature of linguistic structure' (SS 53).

7.7 In SS, Chomsky does 'not deny the usefulness' of 'discovery procedures' in 'providing valuable hints to the practising linguist', but only admonishes that 'linguistic theory' is not 'a manual' of 'procedures' (SS 55n, 59, 106) (cf. 6.38, 61; 8^3; 11.33). In AT, however, he pointedly devalues the discovery of data, saying that 'no adequate formalizable techniques are known for obtaining reliable information concerning the facts of linguistic structure'; and that 'there is no reason to expect that reliable operational criteria for the deeper and more important notions of linguistic theory' 'will ever be forthcoming' (AT 19). 'Knowledge of the language, like most facts of interest and importance, is neither presented for direct observation nor extractable from data by inductive procedures of any known sort' (AT 18). 'Allusions' to '"procedures of elicitation" or "objective methods"' simply obscure the actual situation in which linguistic work' must 'proceed' (AT 19) (cf. 5.10). So 'theoretical' 'investigation of the knowledge of the native speaker can proceed perfectly well' without 'operational procedures'. 'The critical problem is not a paucity of evidence but rather the inadequacy of present theories of language to account for masses of evidence' 'hardly open to serious question' (AT 19f). These arguments lead to a saving of labour: 'once we have disclaimed practical discovery procedures', 'certain problems' likely to stir up 'intense methodological controversy simply do not arise' (SS 56). Indeed.

7.8 'The relation between the general theory and the particular grammars' is where Chomsky's 'approach' 'diverges sharply from many theories' (SS 50). In his view, 'a **discovery procedure**' whereby 'the theory' 'provides a practical and mechanical method for actually constructing the grammar, given a corpus of utterances', is an unduly 'strong requirement' (SS 50f). 'A weaker requirement' is 'a **decision procedure**' whereby the 'method' 'determines whether or not a grammar is' 'the best grammar' for the 'corpus', without asking 'how this grammar was constructed'. 'Even weaker' is 'an **evaluation procedure**' for telling which of 'two proposed grammars' (or 'small sets of grammars') is 'better'. He thinks 'it is unreasonable to demand of linguistic theory' 'more than a practical evaluation procedure' (SS 52f). Having one would 'guarantee significance' for linguistics as one of the 'few areas of science' seeking a 'practical mechanical method for choosing among several theories, each compatible' with 'the data'.

7.9 So a 'theory may not tell us in any practical way' how to 'construct the grammar, but it must tell us how to evaluate' and 'choose' (SS 54). Chomsky again saves labour by 'never considering the question of how one might have arrived at the grammar', and declaring 'such questions' 'not relevant to the programme of research' (SS 56) (cf. 12.38). 'One may arrive at a grammar by intuition, guesswork', 'partial methodological hints', 'past experience', etc.'. We might 'give an organized account of useful procedures of analysis', but these cannot be 'formulated rigorously, exhaustively, and simply enough' to ensure valid 'discovery'. Instead, his 'ultimate aim is to provide an objective, non-intuitive way to evaluate a grammar once presented'.

7.10   As Chomsky sets the task, 'the grammarian must construct a description, and, where possible, an explanation, for the enormous mass of unquestionable data concerning the linguistic **intuition** of the **native speaker**, often himself' (AT 20) (cf. 6.15). Against much of earlier American linguistics, Chomsky vows that 'linguistic theory is **mentalistic**', 'concerned with discovering a mental reality underlying actual behaviour' (AT 4) (cf. 4.8; 12.57). He decries 'behaviourism' for consulting only 'data' and 'expressing a lack of interest in theory and explanation', due to 'certain ideas' (like 'operationalism' and 'verificationism') 'in positivist philosophy of science' (AT 193f). Instead, 'linguistic theory' should 'contribute to the study of human mental processes and intellectual capacity' (AT 46) (cf. 3.10ff; 5.69; 6.6; 7.10; 11.17ff, 22; 12.22). 'Observed use of language or hypothesized dispositions to respond, habits, and so on, may provide evidence' about the 'mental reality, but surely cannot constitute the subject-matter of linguistics' as 'a serious discipline' (AT 4).

7.11   'Introspective judgments of the informant' cannot be 'disregarded' 'on grounds of methodological purity' without 'condemning the study of language to utter sterility' (AT 194). In SS, however, Chomsky had warned against 'asking the informant to do the linguists' work' by eliciting a 'judgment about his behaviour'; such 'opinions may be based on all sorts of irrelevant factors' (SS 97n) (cf. 12.49). SS also announced that 'the major goal of grammatical theory is to replace' the 'obscure reliance on intuition by some rigorous and objective approach' (SS 94; cf. SS 5, 56).[5] But in AT, the prospect that 'giving such priority to introspective evidence' and 'intuition' might 'exclude' 'linguistics' from 'science' is downplayed as a 'terminological question' with 'no bearing at all on any serious issue' (AT 20). Though 'the successful sciences' are 'concerned' with 'objectivity', the latter ideal can, as 'the social and behavioural sciences' show, 'be pursued with little gain in insight and understanding'. Chomsky's preferred model is 'the natural sciences', which 'have sought objectivity as a tool for gaining insight, for providing phenomena' to 'suggest or test deeper explanatory hypotheses', rather than 'as a goal in itself' (cf. 2.13; 4.8, 18; 7.16; 9.112; 11.14, 49, 99; 12.11, 18). Regarding whether 'a wider range and more exact description of phenomena is relevant', Chomsky asserts that 'in linguistics', 'sharpening the data by objective test' is 'of small importance' for a 'new and deeper understanding of linguistic structure' (AT 20f). 'Many questions' 'today' 'do *not* demand evidence' 'unattainable without significant improvements in objectivity of experimental technique' (i.a.).

7.12   Chomsky makes the declaration, soon to be famous, that 'linguistic theory is concerned primarily with an **ideal speaker-hearer** in a completely homogeneous speech community, who knows its language perfectly, and is unaffected by such grammatically irrelevant conditions as memory limitations, distractions, shifts of attention and interest, and errors (random or characteristic) in applying his knowledge of the language in actual performance' (AT 3) (cf. 7.96; 9.5; 10.69; 11.44; 12.14, 18, 36, 13^2). Chomsky thus draws an influential 'distinction between **competence**, the speaker-hearer's knowledge of his language, and **performance**, the actual use of language in concrete situations' (AT 4) (cf. 9.6; 12.39). 'Only under the idealization' of the 'speaker-hearer' 'is performance a direct reflection of competence', but not 'in actual fact'. 'A record of natural speech will show numerous false starts, deviations from rules, changes of plan in mid-course, and so on'. Chomsky's 'distinction' 'is related to the **langue–parole** distinction of Saussure' (cf. 2.20), but 'rejects his concept of language as merely a systematic inventory of items, and returns to the Humboldtian conception of underlying competence as a system of generative processes'.

7.13 Chomsky subscribes to the 'view' 'that the investigation of performance will proceed only so far as the understanding of underlying competence permits' (AT 10). 'The only concrete results' and 'clear suggestions' so far for 'a theory of performance' have come from 'models that incorporate generative grammars' by making 'assumptions about underlying competence'; and he finds it 'difficult to imagine any other basis' (AT 10, 15). Only within such models will 'actual data of linguistic performance' provide 'evidence for determining the correctness of hypotheses about underlying structure, along with introspective reports by the native speaker or the linguist who has learned the language' – this being 'the position universally adopted in practice' (AT 18). He cites 'observations concerning limitations on performance imposed by organization' and 'bounds of memory', or 'concerning exploitations of grammatical devices to form deviant sentences' (AT 10) (cf. 7.41).

7.14 Chomsky stipulates that 'a theory of linguistic intuition', a 'grammatical description', or 'an operational procedure' 'must be tested for adequacy' 'by measuring it against' 'the **tacit knowledge**' it tries to 'describe' (AT 19ff) (cf. 7.24, 29, 91). But even if it is 'the ultimate standard' of 'accuracy' and 'significance' for both 'grammars' and 'tests', this 'tacit knowledge may very well not be immediately available to the user of the language' (cf. 12.49). Precisely due to the 'elusiveness of the speaker's tacit knowledge', the linguist is needed to 'guide and draw it out' in 'subtle ways' (AT 24). By 'adducing' examples, we can 'arrange matters' so that people's 'linguistic intuition, previously obscured, becomes evident to them'. Chomsky's favoured tactic is to show that an isolated 'sentence' (like '"flying planes can be dangerous"') can be 'assigned' more than one 'interpretation' 'by the grammar', although 'in an appropriate' 'context, the listener will interpret it immediately in a unique way' and 'may reject the second interpretation', if 'pointed out to him, as forced or unnatural' (AT 21) (cf. 7.53, 61, 79, 82; 12.39).

7.15 Along similar lines, Chomsky finds it 'obvious' that 'every speaker of a language has mastered and internalized a generative grammar that expresses his knowledge of his language' (AT 8). Indeed, Chomsky 'uses the term "**grammar**" with a systematic ambiguity' both for 'the native speaker's internally represented "theory of his language"' and for 'the linguist's account of this' (AT 25) (cf. 7.28, 78; 12.45). Yet people may not be 'aware of the rules', or even able to 'become aware', nor are their 'statements about their intuitive knowledge' 'necessarily accurate' (AT 8) (cf. 12.49). 'Any interesting generative grammar will be dealing, for the most part, with mental processes' 'far beyond the level of actual or even potential consciousness' (AT 8; cf. AT 59) (cf. 2^{16}; 12.49). Since 'the speaker's reports and viewpoints about his behaviour and competence may be in error', a 'grammar attempts to specify what the speaker knows, not what he may report'. Chomsky sees a 'similarity' here to 'a theory of visual perception' trying to 'account for what persons actually see and the mechanisms that determine this rather than for their statements about what they see and why, though these statements may provide useful, in fact compelling evidence' (AT 8f) (cf. 7.35, 89). However, seeing objects or scenes differs from 'seeing' language, if in 'linguistics' 'the viewpoint' 'creates the object', as Saussure asserted (cf. 2.9; 12.58).

7.16 Further analogies with other sciences are strategically drawn. Using a 'grammar' to 'reconstruct formal relations among utterances in terms' of 'structure' and to 'generate all grammatically "possible" utterances' is 'analogous' to using 'chemical theory' to 'generate all physically possible compounds' (SS 48) (cf. 2.82; 4.8; 5.28; 12.18). A 'chemical theory' 'serves as a theoretical basis for techniques of qualitative analysis and synthesis of specific compounds, just as a grammar' supports 'the investigation' of the 'analysis and synthesis of particular utterances'. Or in physics, 'any scientific theory is based on a finite number of observations', which it 'relates' and 'predicts' 'by constructing general laws in terms of such hypothetical constructs as' '"mass and electron"' (SS 49) (cf. 4.8, 71; 5.66; 7.36; 6.62; 8.49; 12.43). 'Similarly, a grammar of English is based on a finite corpus of utterances (observations)', 'contains grammatical rules (laws) stated in terms of phonemes, phrases, etc.' '(hypothetical constructs)' and 'expresses structural relations among sentences of the corpus and the indefinite number of sentences generated by the grammar' ('predictions'). Such 'physical' analogies stand out in a mentalist approach, especially one whose main 'metaphor' seems to be mathematics (cf. 7.93; 12.10, 15, 18).

7.17 Chomsky proposes to 'construct a formalized general theory of linguistic structure and to explore' its 'foundations', hoping to 'fix in advance for all grammars' the way they are 'related to a corpus of sentences' (SS 5, 14). 'We can attempt to formulate as precisely as possible both the general theory and the set of associated grammars' (SS 50).[6] His 'motivation' is not just a 'mere concern for logical niceties or desire to purify well-established methods of linguistic analysis' (SS 5). 'Precisely constructed models' 'can play an important role, both negative and positive, in the process of discovery' (cf. 7.98). 'By pushing a precise but inadequate formulation to an unacceptable conclusion' and 'exposing the source', we can 'gain a deeper understanding of the linguistic data'. Or, 'positively, a formalized theory may automatically provide solutions for problems' for which it wasn't 'originally designed'. To 'determine the fundamental underlying properties

of successful grammars', 'linguists' should 'recognize the productive
potential' of 'rigorously stating a proposed theory and applying it strictly to
linguistic material' without 'ad hoc adjustments or loose formulations'
(SS 11, 5). In any event, 'neither the general theory nor the particular
grammars are fixed for all time' (SS 50). 'Progress and revision may come'
from 'new facts' or 'purely theoretical insights', i.e., 'new models for
linguistic structure'.

7.18 In fine, Chomsky's priorities sound like Hjelmslev's:[7] 'a theory of
language must state the principles interrelating theoretical terms' and
'ultimately must relate this system to potential empirical phenomena, to
primary linguistic data' (AT 208).[8] We should 'describe the form of
grammars (equivalently, the nature of linguistic structure)' and 'the
empirical consequences of adopting a certain model' (SS 56). 'The ultimate
outcome' 'should be a theory of linguistic structure in which the descriptive
devices utilized in particular grammars are presented and studied abstractly',
without 'reference to particular languages' (SS 11, 50) (cf. 6.11). Having
'data' from 'relatively few languages' 'is not particularly disturbing', because
the 'conditions' of 'a single language may provide significant support' for
'some formal property' belonging to 'general linguistic theory' (AT 209).
Chomsky sees 'an important advance in the theory of language' when an
apparent 'peculiarity of English' is made 'explicable' by 'a general and deep
empirical assumption about the nature of language', which can be 'refuted if
false' by 'grammars of other languages' (AT 36). This step fits the hope of
'replacing' 'assertions about particular languages' with ones about 'language
in general', so that 'features of grammars in individual languages can be
deduced' (AT 46). Conversely, 'the difficulty or impossibility of formulating
certain conditions within' a 'theory of grammar' may signal that they are
'general' for 'the applicability of grammatical rules rather than aspects of the
particular language' (AT 209).

7.19 So against 'modern linguistics', Chomsky calls for 'the grammar of
a particular language' 'to be supplemented by a **universal grammar**'
'expressing deep-seated regularities' (AT 6) (cf. 2.10; 3.67; 4.4, 71f, 74;
5.44; 6.5, 10, 34; 7.22, 29, 33f, 45, 55, 62, 65, 71, 78f, 91, 93, 7^{10}, 7^{32}, 7^{39};
8.19, 60, 86; 9.3, 25, 60; 11.94; 12.18). Indeed, 'the main task of linguistic
theory must be to develop an account of linguistic universals' (AT 28). He
contests the 'commonly held' view that 'modern linguistic and anthropological investigations have conclusively refuted the doctrines' of 'universal
grammar' (AT 118) (cf. 7.55, 62). 'Linguistic theory' may yet 'develop an
account of linguistic universals' that reveals 'the properties of any generative
grammar' and is 'not falsified by the diversity of languages' (AT 27f). An
important (and labour-saving) corollary is that 'universal' 'regularities' 'need
not be stated in the grammar' of a 'language' but 'only in general linguistic
theory as part of the definition of the notion "human language"' (AT 6,
117; cf. AT 35f, 112, 144, 168, 225) (cf. 7.65, 72).

7.20 'Universals' fall into two kinds. The '**substantive**' ones, a 'traditional
concern of general linguistic theory', involve 'the vocabulary for the

description of language' and state that 'items of a particular kind in any language must be drawn from a fixed class' (AT 28). The best case comes from phonology, the old standby of linguists, namely the 'theory of distinctive features', 'each of which has a substantive acoustic–articulatory characterization independent of any particular language' (cf. 2.70; 5.42f; 6.54; 7.71, 7^{10}; 8^{36}; 12.26). Another case is the assumption of 'traditional universal grammar' that 'fixed syntactic categories (Noun, Verb, etc.) can be found in the syntactic representations of the sentences of any language' and 'provide the general underlying syntactic structures of each language'. 'More abstract' and 'recently' studied are the '**formal** linguistic universals' stating 'formal conditions' such as 'the character of the rules' in 'grammar' and 'the ways' they are 'interconnected' (AT 29). Such 'deep-seated formal universals' 'imply that all languages are cut to the same pattern', though without any 'point-by-point correspondence' (AT 30).[9] These 'formal constraints' 'may severely limit the choice' 'of a descriptive grammar'. Not surprisingly, Chomsky's favoured candidate here is that 'the syntactic component of a grammar must contain transformational rules'; and that even 'the phonological component' 'consists of a sequence of rules, a subset of which' is 'a transformational cycle' (AT 29). This move, too, saves labour: if 'the transformational cycle is a universal feature of the phonological component, it is unnecessary, in grammar of English, to describe' the 'functioning of phonological rules that involve syntactic structure' (AT 35).[10] A new rationale for separating levels?

7.21 Therefore, 'our problem is to develop and clarify the criteria for selecting the correct grammar for each language, that is, the correct theory of this language' (SS 49). 'A linguistic theory is **descriptively adequate**' and 'empirically significant' if it 'makes available for each language' a 'grammar' (or 'a class of grammars'), 'correctly' 'states the facts', 'describes the intrinsic competence of the idealized native speaker' for 'understanding arbitrary sentences', and 'accounts for the basis of that achievement' (AT 24, 27, 34, 40). '*External* conditions of adequacy', hinging on whether 'the sentences generated' are 'acceptable to the native speaker', apply to a 'merely descriptive' 'theory' (SS 49f, 13, 54). '*Internal* grounds' constitute a 'much deeper' and more 'principled' 'level' of adequacy (SS 13; AT 41, 27). For the moment, however, Chomsky simply 'tests the adequacy' of an 'apparatus' by 'applying it directly to the description of English sentences' (SS 34) (cf. 7.80). In fact, he makes do with the 'weak test' of 'a certain number of clear cases'; a 'strong test' would require these to 'be handled properly for each language by grammars all' 'constructed by same method' (SS 14) (cf. 7.42; 12.40).

7.22 'The structural descriptions assigned to sentences by the grammar' and its 'distinctions between well-formed and deviant' 'must correspond to the intuition' of the 'speaker, whether or not he' is 'aware' of it (AT 24) (cf. 7.11; 12.50). Yet a 'descriptively adequate' theory may 'provide such a wide range of potential grammars' that 'no formal property distinguishes' them, or may 'leave unexpressed' 'the defining properties of natural languages' that 'distinguish' them 'from arbitrary symbol systems' (AT 35f).

So 'the major endeavour of the linguist must be' to 'enrich the theory of linguistic form' and 'restrict the range of possible hypotheses by adding structure', 'constraints, and conditions' to 'the notion "generative grammar"' and 'to reduce the class of attainable grammars' until 'a formal evaluation measure' can be applied (AT 35, 46, 41). 'This requires a precise and narrow delimitation of the notion "generative grammar" – a restrictive and rich hypothesis' about 'universal properties that determine the form of language' (AT 35). 'Given a variety of descriptively adequate grammars' we need to discover if they are 'unique' or share 'deep underlying similarities attributable to the form of language as such'. Only the latter discovery yields 'real progress in linguistics'.

7.23 Hence, Chomsky deems it 'crucial for the development of linguistic theory' to 'pursue' 'much higher goals' than 'descriptive adequacy', even 'utopian' ones (AT 24f). He envisions **'explanatory adequacy'** when 'a linguistic theory succeeds in selecting a descriptively adequate grammar on the basis of primary linguistic data' and in relating 'an explanation of the intuition of the native speaker' to 'an empirical hypothesis about the innate predisposition of the child' (AT 25ff) (cf. 7.27f). Instead of 'gross coverage of a large mass of data', which is not 'an achievement of any theoretical interest or importance' (cf. 7.6f, 10f), 'linguistics' should 'discover a complex of data that differentiates between conflicting conceptions of linguistic structure' by showing which ones 'can explain' the 'data' via 'some empirical assumption about the form of language' (AT 26). Even for 'descriptive adequacy', an 'explanatory theory of the form of grammar' provides a 'main tool', because 'the choice' is 'always underdetermined by data' and because 'relevant data' from 'successful grammars for other languages' can be collated (AT 41) (cf. 12.43). Though both 'unrealized goals', 'descriptive' and 'explanatory adequacy' are 'crucial at every stage of understanding linguistic structure' (AT 36, 46).

7.24 Since 'all concrete attempts to formulate an empirically adequate linguistic theory' leave 'room for mutually inconsistent grammars', an 'evaluation measure' might be drawn from **'language acquisition'** (AT 37). For Chomsky, 'a theory of language' can in fact 'be regarded as a hypothesis' about the '"language-forming capacity" of humans' and 'language learning' (AT 30). We can thus 'formulate' 'problems of linguistic theory' and 'language learning' 'as questions about the construction of a hypothetical language acquisition device' or 'model' (AT 47, 25). The 'child' or 'device' 'constructs a theory' that 'specifies its tacit competence, its knowledge of the language', by 'devising a hypothesis compatible with presented data' of 'performance' (AT 32, 36, 4). To outflank descriptive linguists, who never claimed to proceed like a language-learning child, Chomsky draws a handy parallel (cf. 7.87f). Just as 'the theorist' is 'given an empirical pairing of collections of primary linguistic data with certain grammars' 'in fact constructed by people', so does the child confront 'primary linguistic data consisting of signals, classified as sentences and non-sentences', that are 'paired with structural descriptions' (AT 38, 47, 32). For this purpose, 'the child has developed and internally represented a generative grammar': 'a theory' and 'a system of rules that determine how sentences are to be formed, used, and understood' (AT 25).

7.25 'In part, such data determine' which 'possible language' 'the learner is being exposed' to (AT 33). But the child's 'internalized grammar goes far beyond the presented primary linguistic data', 'and is in no sense an "inductive generalization"' (AT 33, 25) (cf. 7.5ff, 30, 34, 93). Because, apart from occasional 'corrections of learners' attempts' by 'the linguistic community', 'no special care is taken to teach' 'children', the latter 'must have the ability to "invent" a generative grammar that defines well-formedness and assigns interpretations to sentences even though linguistic data' are 'deficient' (AT 31, 201). Indeed, Chomsky's idealizations imply that data in 'actual speech' are not merely 'finite', 'scattered', and 'restricted in scope', but also 'degenerate in quality', replete with 'non-sentences', 'fragments, and deviant expressions' (AT 43f, 31, 58, 201, 25) (cf. 7.12; 9.4f). He compares this factor with the 'traditional view' that '"the pains"' of '"conversation" lie in '"extricating"' '"the thought from the signs or words which often agree not with it" (Cordemoy 1668a, b)' (AT 201), but his own concept of well-formedness is unrelated to the deviousness or over-elaboration Cordemoy probably had in mind.

7.26 The child again parallels a Chomskyan linguist if 'as a precondition for language learning, he must possess a linguistic theory that specifies the form of the grammar of a possible human language' plus 'a strategy for selecting a grammar' 'compatible' with the 'data' (AT 25). Chomsky envisions the 'child' applying 'a class of possible hypotheses about language structure' and 'determining what each' 'implies for each sentence' so as to 'select one of the presumably infinitely many hypotheses' 'compatible with the given data' (AT 30, 45). Perhaps 'an acquisition model' entails a 'strategy for finding hypotheses' by 'considering only grammars' above 'a certain value' before 'language learning can take place' (AT 203).[11] Or, 'it is logically possible that the data' are so 'rich' and 'the class of potential grammars' so 'limited' that only a 'single permitted grammar will be compatible with the available data' (AT 28). Or, even 'a system not learnable by a language acquisition device', which 'is only one component of the total system of intellectual structures' applied to 'problem-solving and concept formation', might be 'mastered by a human some other way'; but Chomsky 'expects' 'a qualitative difference' in how 'an organism' 'approaches' 'languagelike' 'systems' (AT 56).

7.27 As 'the most interesting and important reason for studying descriptively adequate grammars' and for 'formulating and justifying a general linguistic theory', Chomsky states this 'issue': that 'the general features of language structure reflect not so much the course of one's experience' as the 'capacity to acquire knowledge' by '**innate** ideas' and 'principles' (AT 59, 27, 78). Invoking 'the traditional belief that "the principles of grammar form an important part of the philosophy of the human mind"' (Beattie 1788) (AT 59), he postulates a 'structure' that 'pertains to the form of language in general' and 'reflects what the mind

brings to the task of language acquisition, not what it discovers or invents'
during 'the task' (AT 59, 117). He hopes 'linguistic theory' can thereby
'contribute to the study of human mental processes and intellectual capacity'
via 'the abilities that make language learning possible under empirically
given limitations of time and data' (AT 46f, 31) (cf. 7.10; 12.22).

7.28   So 'a long-range task for general linguistics' is an 'account of this
innate linguistic theory' forming 'the basis for language learning', although
Chomsky short-circuits this task with another 'systematic ambiguity': using
'"theory of language"' for 'both the child's innate predisposition' and for
'the linguist's account' (AT 25) (cf. 7.15, 78). A 'hypothesis concerning the
innate predisposition of the child' can help 'explain the intuition of the
native speaker' and can be 'falsified' when 'it fails to provide' a 'grammar'
for 'data from some other language' (AT 25f). An 'extremely strong' 'claim'
is involved here 'about the innate capacity' or 'predisposition' 'of the child'
(AT 32) (cf. 7.93). It is 'maintained' 'that the child has an innate theory of
potential structural descriptions' 'rich and fully developed' enough to
'determine from a real situation' 'which structural descriptions may be
appropriate to a signal' that 'occurs'; and that this can be done 'in advance
of any assumption as to the linguistic structure of this signal' (AT 32f)
(cf. 6⁶).

7.29   'A theory of language' along these lines 'should concern itself' with
'linguistic universals', a 'theory' or 'tacit knowledge' of which is 'attributed'
'to the child' (or to the 'language acquisition device') (AT 30, 27, 55f)
(cf. 7.23, 89). 'The child approaches the data with the presumption that they
are drawn from a language' of an 'antecedently well-defined type', and
'determines which of the humanly possible languages is that of the
community' (AT 27). A 'theory' with 'universals' 'implies that only certain
kinds of symbolic systems can be acquired and used as languages', whereas
'others are beyond it' (AT 55). We thus arrive at 'the question: what are the
initial assumptions' about 'the nature of language that the child brings' and
how 'specific is the innate schema (the general definition of "grammar") that
gradually becomes more explicit and differentiated as the child learns the
language?' (AT 27).

7.30   'Acquisition of language' offers 'a special and informative case' for
'a more general' 'discussion' of 'two lines of approach to the acquisition of
knowledge' (AT 47). '**Empiricism**' (spurred by 'eighteenth-century struggles
for scientific naturalism') 'assumes that the structure of the acquisition
device is limited to certain elementary "peripheral processing mechanisms"',
e.g., 'an innate "quality space"', or to a set of primitive unconditioned
reflexes' or (for 'language') a set of '"aurally distinguishable components"',
plus 'elementary' 'analytical data-processing mechanisms or inductive
principles', e.g., 'weak principles of generalization' or (for language)
'principles of segmentation and classification' like those of 'modern
linguistics' (AT 47, 51, 58f, 207) (cf. 7.5ff, 25, 33, 96; 12.26, 30). 'A
preliminary analysis of experience is provided' by those 'mechanisms' as
'concepts and knowledge are acquired' through 'inductive principles'

(AT 48). Such claims are said to portray 'language' as 'an adventitious construct' (AT 51). Moreover, Chomsky complains that 'empiricist views have generally been formulated in such an indefinite way' as to be 'next to impossible to interpret', 'analyse, or evaluate' (AT 204). Skinner's (1957) account (reviewed in Chomsky 1959) is 'grossly, obviously counter to fact' if 'terms like "stimulus", "reinforcement", "conditioning", etc.' are used 'as in experimental psychology'; if they are just 'metaphoric extensions', we get only 'a mentalist account differing from traditional ones' by 'the poverty of the terminology' and not by any 'scientific' quality.[12]

7.31 '**Rationalism**' is a 'different approach' to the 'acquisition of knowledge' and holds that 'innate ideas and principles', 'fixed in advance as a disposition of mind', 'determine the form of acquired knowledge' in a 'restricted and highly organized way' (AT 48, 51). A main inspiration is 'seventeenth-century rationalist philosophy' (AT 49). Descartes (1647) said that '"innate ideas"' about '"movements and figures"', '"pain, colour, sound"', etc. – as well as 'such notions as that things equal to same thing are equal to each other' – arise from '"our faculty of thinking"', not '"from external objects"' (AT 48). 'The Port-Royal *Logic* (Arnauld [and Nicole] 1662)' made 'the same point': 'no idea' 'in our minds has taken its rise from sense', because 'ideas' have 'rarely any resemblance to what takes place in the sense and in the brain', and 'some have no connection with any bodily image' (AT 49f). 'Lord [Edward] Herbert [of Cherbury] (1624) maintained that' without 'innate ideas and principles', '"we should have no experience"' or '"observations"', nor ever '"distinguish between things or grasp any general nature"' (AT 49). Leibniz (1873 [1702–03]) declared 'the senses' 'necessary' but 'not sufficient' for 'actual knowledge', furnishing only 'examples, i.e., particular' 'truths', whereas 'the truths of numbers', i.e., 'all arithmetic and geometry, are in us virtually' to 'set in order what we already have in the mind' (AT 50). 'Necessary truths must have principles whose proof does not depend on examples nor consequently' on 'the senses', and which 'form the soul' of 'our thoughts', 'as necessary thereto as the muscles' for 'walking'.

7.32 Descartes' claim that 'corporeal movements' 'reach our mind' 'from external objects' and 'cause' it to 'envisage these ideas' (AT 48) matches Chomsky's stipulation that 'innate mechanisms' must be 'activated' by 'appropriate stimulation' and are then 'available for interpretation of the data of sense' (AT 48, 51). 'The rationalist view' implies that 'one cannot really teach language, but can only present the conditions under which it will develop spontaneously in the mind' (cf. Humboldt 1836) (but cf. 11.17, 11[11]). 'Thus the form of a language, the schema for its grammar, is to a large extent given', though it must be 'set into operation' by 'experience' (AT 51).

7.33 'Empiricism' is surprisingly accused of being not '"scientific"' but more 'dogmatic and aprioristic' than 'rationalism' in saying that 'arbitrarily selected data-processing mechanisms' 'are the only ones available' (AT 207). 'Rationalism', to which Chomsky finds it 'difficult to see' 'an alternative', is praised for holding 'no preconceptions' about 'the internal structure' of the 'input-output device', and only 'studying uniformities in the output', i.e., 'universals' (AT 48, 207) (but cf. 7.93). If 'rationalism' does 'not show how internal structure arises', neither does 'empiricism' (AT 206). The rival is further outflanked by putting physics and biology, of all things, on the innatist side: we cannot 'take seriously a position that attributes a complex human achievement to months or at most years of experience rather than to millions of years of evolution or to principles of neural organization' 'even more deeply grounded in physical law' (AT 59).

7.34 Thus, even though 'the empiricist notion' is 'the prevailing modern view', Chomsky avers that 'a hypothesis about initial structure' able to 'account for acquisition of language' cannot fit 'preconceptions' from 'centuries of empiricist doctrine' – 'implausible to begin with', 'without factual support', and 'hardly consistent' with how 'animals or humans construct a theory of the external world' (AT 51, 58). He raises the prospect of 'testing' the two sets of 'principles' against 'those we in fact discover' in 'real languages', or gauging the 'feasibility' for 'producing grammars within the given constraints of time and access' and the 'observed uniformity of output' (AT 53f). But his own verdict is already decided: 'empiricist theories about language acquisition are refutable wherever they are clear', or else 'empty', just as 'evidence' about 'language acquisition' 'shows clearly that taxonomic views' are 'inadequate' because 'knowledge of grammatical structure cannot arise' by 'inductive operations' 'developed in linguistics, psychology, or philosophy' (AT 54, 57) (cf. 7.5ff, 24, 96; 12.45). In contrast, 'the rationalist approach exemplified' by 'transformational grammar seems to have proven productive' and 'fully in accord with what is known about language', and to offer the 'hope of providing a hypothesis about the intrinsic structure of a language acquisition system' (AT 54). Chomsky thereby preserves the hope that his 'theory' with its 'linguistic universals' may grow 'rich and explicit enough to account for the rapidity and uniformity of language learning, and the remarkable complexity and range of generative grammars that are the product', whereas 'taxonomic linguistics' can make no such 'empirical claim' (AT 28, 52f).

7.35 'The problem of mapping the intrinsic cognitive capacities of an organism and identifying the systems of belief and the organization of behaviour that it can readily attain should be central to experimental psychology' (AT 56f). But due to 'the atomistic and unstructured framework' of 'empiricist thinking', 'learning theory' has instead 'concentrated' on the 'marginal topic' of 'species-independent regularities in acquisition' of 'a "behavioural repertoire" under experimentally manipulable conditions' (AT 205, 57). 'Attention' has focused on 'tasks' 'extrinsic to cognitive structure' 'that must be approached in a devious, indirect, and piecemeal fashion' (AT 57) (cf. 10.92). Chomsky is a bit inconsistent here. To discredit 'empiricism', he dismisses 'comparisons with species other than man' because 'every species has highly specialized cognitive capacities' and 'language' is 'a human creation' 'reflecting intrinsic human capacity' (AT 206, 59) (cf. 3.15; 4.28; 8.27; 11.10; 12.12, 18). The 'analysis of stimuli' 'provided' by 'peripheral processing in the receptor systems or in lower cortical centres' is 'specific to the animal's life-space' and 'behaviour patterns' (AT 205). Yet to discredit the 'view that all knowledge is derived solely by the senses' via 'association and "generalization"', Chomsky denies that 'man is' 'unique among animals'; and to make a point about 'situational context' (cf. 7.88), he turns to 'animal learning' (e.g., 'depth perception in lambs' 'facilitated by mother-neonate contact' upon which 'the nature of the lamb's "theory of visual space"' does not 'depend') (AT 59, 34) (cf. 7.15).

7.36 All these arguments about mind, thought, and learning were absent from Chomsky's advocacy in SS. There, his 'basic requirement' for 'any conception of linguistic structure' was merely that 'the grammar of English become' 'more simple and orderly' and yet be able to 'generate exactly the grammatical sentences' (SS 68, 54n). The claim that his own approach can '**simplify**' both 'theory' and 'grammar' has remained a major theme (SS 37, 41, 47, 55, 58, 65, 72, 106; AT 17, 87, 134, 136, 144, 202, 224) (cf. 7.39f, 42f, 47f, 50f, 54). He also stresses the 'simplicity' of very specific areas or tactics (usually 'transformations'), and judges what is 'simpler' or the 'simplest' (SS 18, 84, 80; AT 62; SS 14, 56f, 74f, 85, 107, AT 55). Indeed, SS said Chomsky's '*sole* concern' was 'to decrease the complexity of the grammar' 'of English' and make it 'simpler than any proposed alternative' (SS 83f, i.a.). Admittedly, 'the notion of "simplicity"' 'was left unanalysed'; Chomsky foresaw it being 'defined within linguistic theory', and he compared 'choosing' it to 'determining the value of a physical constant' as a 'matter with empirical consequences' (SS 103; AT 37f) (cf. 7.16). Instead of 'simplifying one part' and 'complicating others', 'the right track' lies where 'simplifying one part leads to' 'simplifying others' (SS 56). But SS proposed to 'simplify the grammar' 'by formulating rules of a more complex type' 'than immediate constituent analysis';[13] and AT supports its arguments about 'language learning' by pointing to 'the remarkable complexity' of 'generative grammars' (SS 41; AT 28) (cf. 7.50).

7.37 Simplicity was also a key point in Chomsky's original 'contention that the conceptions of phrase structure are fundamentally inadequate and that the theory of linguistic structure must be elaborated' through 'transformational analysis' (SS 69). Though not using 'the strongest proof of the inadequacy of a linguistic theory' ('that it literally cannot apply to natural language'), Chomsky did apply the 'weaker' one that it 'can apply only clumsily, in complex, ad hoc, unrevealing' ways, and that 'fundamental formal properties of natural language cannot be utilized to simplify grammars' (SS 34). His plan was to compare 'three models for linguistic structure' and 'their limitations': a 'communication theoretic model', an '"immediate constituent"' or 'phrase structure' model, and a 'transformational model', and to show that the first two 'leave gaps in linguistic theory' and 'cannot properly serve the purposes of grammatical description', unless they are made 'so hopelessly complex that they will be without interest' (SS 6, 23, 41, 44, 18–49) (cf. 7.94).

7.38 The '**communication theoretic** model', outlined by Shannon and Weaver (1949), implies only 'a minimal linguistic theory' (SS 18f, 34).

'A machine' 'can be in any one of a finite number of different internal states', and 'switches' among them 'by producing a certain symbol', e.g., 'an English word' (SS 18f). The 'sequence' from 'an initial' to 'a final state' is 'a "sentence"' (i.r.). A 'language produced in this way' is 'a finite state language' and the 'machine itself a finite-state grammar' or a '"Markov process"' (SS 19ff). 'To complete' the 'model', 'we assign a probability to each transition from state to state', 'calculate the uncertainty', and thus 'the "information content"' (cf. 7.90; 9^{23}). Plainly, 'English is not a finite-state language'. Its 'symbols' may be not 'consecutive', but 'embedded'; and 'Markov process models' cannot 'account for the ability of a speaker of English to produce and understand new utterances' (SS 21ff). Imposing 'arbitrary limitations', e.g., that 'sentences' must be 'less than a million words', won't help, because in 'English' some 'processes have no finite limit'.

7.39 A 'description in terms of **phrase structure**' is 'more powerful' than a 'finite state' one (SS 30f). Chomsky fits this second model to the 'conception of linguistic structure' of the last 'half a century', namely 'the "taxonomic" view' he wants to supplant (AT 88). He 'does not know' if 'English itself is literally outside the range of analysis' by 'phrase structure', but finds such grammars 'certainly inadequate in the weaker sense', e.g., in failing to 'handle' 'discontinuous elements' (SS 34, 38, 41, 75) (cf. 8.61; 12.28). Still, such 'grammars' are 'quite adequate for a small part of the language', while 'the rest' 'can be derived by repeated application of a rather simple set of transformations to the strings given by the phrase structure grammar' (SS 41fn) (cf. 7.62). In contrast, if we merely 'extended phrase structure to cover the entire language directly, we would lose the simplicity of limited' versions (SS 42).

7.40 We can thus attain 'an entirely new conception of linguistic structure' and 'develop a certain fairly complex but reasonably natural algebra of transformations having properties we apparently require for grammatical description' (SS 44) (cf. 2.82; 3.72f; 5.27, 86; 6.8, 29, 51, 60; 7.40, 7^{18}). This '**transformational** model' is still 'more powerful', applying to 'languages beyond the bounds of phrase structure' and 'accounting' for 'relations between sentences' 'in a natural way' (SS 6, 47, 75). Here, 'apparently arbitrary distinctions' are shown to 'have a clear structural origin' and to belong to a 'higher-level regularity' (SS 75, 107). 'A wide variety of apparently distinct phenomena all fall into place'; 'linguistic behaviour that seems unmotivated and inexplicable in terms of phrase structure appears simple and systematic' from a 'transformational point of view' (SS 68, 75). Now, 'apparently irregular behaviour' and 'glaring and distinct exceptions' 'result automatically from the simplest grammar' and from 'our rules' for 'regular cases', and emerge as 'instances of a deeper underlying regularity' (SS 63f, 66f, 68, 85, 88f; AT 190). This is a 'remarkable indication of the fundamental character of this analysis' (SS 66f).

7.41 The transformational model must be 'a **generative grammar**': 'a system of rules that in some explicit and well-defined way assigns structural descriptions to sentences' (AT 8). Here, 'the linguist's task' is 'to produce a device of some sort (called a grammar)' for 'generating all grammatical sequences' and no 'ungrammatical ones' (SS 85, 11, 13). Hence, 'the fundamental aim in the linguistic analysis of language is to separate' these two sets and 'to study the structure of the grammatical sequences' (SS 13f). The 'task' may 'explicate' the 'intuitive concept' not just of '"grammatical in English"' but of '"grammatical"' in 'general' (SS 13). To simplify the task, a distinction is drawn between **'grammaticalness'** in 'competence' versus **'acceptability'** in 'performance' (AT 11) (cf. 7.12). Sentences may be 'high' on one 'scale' and 'low' on the other. 'Grammaticalness is only one of many factors' that 'determine acceptability', along with 'memory limitations, intonational and stylistic factors, "iconic" elements of discourse, and so on' (AT 10f) (cf. 7.13, 56).[14] These limits may be probed with 'operational tests' of 'rapidity, correctness, and uniformity of recall and recognition, or normalcy of intonation', whereas 'the much more abstract' and 'important notions of grammaticalness' may not. It may in fact be 'quite impossible to characterize' 'unacceptable sentences in grammatical terms', e.g., by 'formulating rules' 'to exclude them' or by 'limiting the number of reapplications of grammatical rules' (AT 11f). For Chomsky's 'purposes', '"acceptable" refers to utterances that are perfectly natural and immediately comprehensible without paper-and-pencil analysis, and in no way bizarre or outlandish' (AT 10).

7.42 Chomsky's reasoning leaves it unclear just how 'a study of performance' might 'investigate the acceptability' of 'sentences' or how a grammar could test its claims about 'speakers' 'rejecting' 'sequences as not belonging to the language' (cf. AT 12; SS 23). He postpones the problem by relying on 'clear cases' (preferably 'violating purely syntactic rules' rather than 'semantic or "pragmatic"' ones), by not 'appealing' to 'far-fetched contexts', and by promising that for 'intermediate cases' we can 'let the grammar itself decide' once it is 'set up in the simplest way' to 'include clear sentences and exclude clear non-sentences' (SS 14, 16; AT 76, 208) (cf. 4.67; 7.21; 12.40). But such a stage presupposes that 'linguistic theory' has 'stated the relation between the set of observed sentences and the set of grammatical sentences' (SS 14n, 55), which has proven far harder than Chomsky implies here. He expects 'a systematic account of how application of the devices and methods appropriate to unequivocal cases can be extended and deepened' for others (AT 77f). Meanwhile, he follows his own judgment in adducing sentences that 'we do not have', or that 'many would question the grammaticalness of', or that are 'much less natural' (SS 73, 35n).[15] Or, he proposes 'degrees of grammaticalness', depending on how 'completely we violate constituent structure', and hopes this 'can be developed in purely formal terms' (SS 36n, 43nf) (cf. 7.72, 93; 12.40). Doubtful cases would be 'interpreted' 'by analogies to non-deviant sentences', at least by 'an ideal listener' (AT 76, 78, 149). The snappiest evasion of all, which Chomsky admits leaves 'a serious gap in theory', is to 'assume that the set of sentences is somehow given in advance' (SS 103, 85, 11, 18, 54).

7.43 These issues bear on how a 'theory' might 'provide a general method for selecting a grammar, given a corpus of sentences' (SS 11). Noting that the whole 'set of sentences' a language allows for 'cannot be identified with any partial corpus obtained by the linguist in his fieldwork', which is necessarily 'finite and somewhat accidental' (cf. 12.43), Chomsky defines a '**language**' as an 'infinite set of sentences,[16] each finite in length and constructed out of a finite set of elements' (SS 15, 13). 'All natural languages in their spoken or written form are languages in this sense, since each' 'has a finite number of phonemes or letters', and 'each sentence is representable as a finite sequence' of these (even a 'formal system of mathematics' qualifies) (SS 13) (cf. 6.51, 56, 60). 'The assumption that languages are infinite' can 'simplify the description' by allowing the 'grammar' to have 'recursive devices' for 'producing infinitely many sentences' (SS 23f). 'Hence, a generative grammar must be a system of rules that can iterate to generate an indefinitely large number of structures' (AT 16).

7.44 Specifically, 'the infinite generative capacity of the grammar arises from a formal property' of 'rules': 'inserting' basic structures 'into others', 'this process being iterable without limit' (AT 142). 'In this respect, a grammar mirrors the behaviour of the speaker who' 'can produce and understand an infinite number of new sentences', and 'knowledge of a language involves this implicit ability' (SS 15; AT 15). This notion is said to capture the '**creative** aspect' 'all languages have': they 'provide the means for expressing indefinitely many thoughts and for reacting appropriately to an indefinite range of new situations' (AT v, 5) (cf. 3.38; 7.67, 83; 8.18, 28, 43, 83; 11.56, 58). The 'technical devices for expressing a system of recursive processes', as developed in 'mathematics', not only account for 'sequences' 'longer than any ever before produced', but offer 'an explicit formulation of creative processes' (AT 8; SS 17n). Yet saying a language (or a grammar) is 'creative' because it has no longest sentence is like saying mathematics is creative because it has no highest number. Iteration and recursion are the exact opposite of creative: they just churn out the same thing at fixed increments. The real creativity of language, as shown, say, in poetry, would fall in a trouble zone of Chomsky's theory, namely on the borders of the 'grammatical', and unsettle his constructs ('rules', 'restrictions', etc.) for stating what can or cannot be 'generated' (cf. 12.40f).

7.45 Because 'the grammar of a language is a complex system with many and varied interconnections between its parts', 'the linguist's task' should be 'to describe language' by 'a universal system of **levels of representation**' (cf. Chomsky 1955) (SS 60, 85, 11; AT 222) (cf. 4.71; 5.34f; 8.51f; 9.30; 10.16f, 35, 56; 11.82; 12.27). Indeed, SS saw ' "linguistic level" ' as 'the central notion in linguistic theory', a 'level' consisting of 'descriptive devices' 'for the construction of grammars' (SS 11). Borrowing (without acknowledgement) from structuralism, Chomsky proposes to 'rebuild the vast complexity of the actual language more elegantly and systematically by extracting the contribution' of 'several linguistic levels, each' 'simple in itself', although the higher 'levels' must attain 'more powerful modes of linguistic description' by 'increasing complexity' (SS 42n, 11).[17] Perhaps 'we can determine the adequacy of a linguistic theory by developing rigorously and precisely the form of grammar corresponding to a set of levels' and applying them to 'natural languages' (SS 11). 'Each level' is in turn 'a system' having a 'set' (or 'alphabet') of 'minimal elements' ('"primes"'), plus 'relations', 'mappings' to other 'levels', and 'operations of concatenation which form strings' of 'arbitrary finite length' (AT 222; SS 109).[18]

7.46 'A hierarchy of linguistic levels' in 'a satisfactory grammar of English' might subsume 'phonetic, phonological, word, morphological, phrase structure', and 'transformational structure' (AT 223, SS 11f, 18, 85).[19] Chomsky dislikes 'the idea that higher levels are literally constructed out of lower level elements', though he still depicts a 'sentence' as a 'sequence' of 'phonemes, morphemes, or words' (SS 58f, 106, 18, 32f). Against earlier American linguists, he sees 'no objection to mixing levels' (SS 57, 59, 106) (cf. 5.35; 12.27). The 'interdependence of levels' – for instance, 'if morphemes are defined in terms of phonemes' and 'morphological considerations' are 'relevant to phonemic analysis' – does not entrain 'linguistic theory' in any 'real circularity'; the 'compatibility' of 'phonemes and morphemes' helps 'lead to the simplest grammar' (SS 57) (cf. 4.50; 5.36, 45; 12.27). This insight, however, 'does not tell how to *find* the phonemes and morphemes in a direct, mechanical way', but then 'no other' 'theory' does 'either, and there is little reason to believe' any can. This argument is meant to refute the 'commonly held view' that 'syntactic theory is premature' when 'problems' 'on the lower levels' are 'unsolved' – 'a faulty analogy between the order of development of linguistic theory and the presumed order of operations in discovery' (SS 59f). 'Developing one part of grammar' is rather aided by a 'picture' of 'a completed system' (cf. 5.28; 12.43); and working down from 'higher levels' can bypass 'absurd' and 'futile tasks' like 'stating principles of sentence construction in terms of phonemes and morphemes' (cf. 7[33]).

7.47 On 'the level of **phrase structure**', 'each sentence is represented by a *set* of strings, not by a single string' or 'sequence' as 'on the level of phonemes, morphemes, or words' (SS 32f, 47). This factor makes 'phrase structure' a 'level' of 'different and non-trivial characteristics', not able to be 'subdivided' into some 'set of levels' 'ordered from higher to lower' (SS 32f, 47). 'The break between' 'phrase structure and the lower levels' is 'not arbitrary', because 'similarities' and 'dissimilarities' of 'representation', such as 'rules with different formal properties', 'prove' its 'existence' (SS 33, 47, 87).

7.48 In SS, Chomsky resolves the levels into 'a picture of grammars' with 'a natural tripartite arrangement', each part having its own set of 'rules': 'phrase structure', 'transformational structure', and 'morphophonemics' (SS 45f, 114).[20] A 'grammar' provides 'rules' for 'reconstructing' 'phrase structure' and for 'converting strings of morphemes into strings of phonemes'; these two rule sets are 'connected' by 'a sequence of transformational rules' for 'carrying strings with phrase structure into new strings to which morphophonemic rules can apply' (SS 107). 'Phrase structure' is created by means of 'instruction formulas' called '**rewriting rules**' (SS 26, 29, 110; AT 66). For example, 'X → Y is interpreted: rewrite X as Y', or 'A → Z/X ____ Y' as 'category A is realized as the string Z' 'in the environment' 'of X to the left and Y to the right'; in '**context-free** rules', 'X and Y are null, so that the rules apply independently of context' (SS 26, 110; AT 66) (cf. 7.73f; 12.39).[21] These 'rules' apply to 'only a single element' and proceed in a 'sequence' from an 'initial symbol' to 'a terminal string', where 'no further rewriting is possible' (SS 29f, 26f; AT 66f).[22] The sequence of strings is termed a '**derivation**', and each sentence has a 'history of derivation' (SS 37, 107) (cf. 7.52). A 'system of rewriting rules' can 'present' 'grammatical information' 'in the most natural way', state 'grammatical functions', and 'provide a simple method for assigning a unique and appropriate phrase marker to a terminal string, given its derivation' (AT 72, 66f).

7.49 For Chomsky, 'the most obvious formal property of utterances is their bracketing into **constituents**' (AT 12) (cf. 3.22; 4.59; 5.21, 50, 62; 7.63; 9.33; 12.26). Hence, 'constituent analysis' by '**parsing**' is 'customary' for 'linguistic description on the syntactic level' (SS 26) (cf. 10.3, 14, 16, 33f, 77, 79, 94). As a better means for 'assigning' or 'imposing constituent structure' and obtaining 'valuable, even compelling evidence' about it, Chomsky proposes '**transformations**' (SS 83, 73, 81). 'A grammatical transformation' is 'a rule' that 'applies to a string with a particular structural description' (AT 89). So 'a transformation is defined by the structural analysis of the strings' it 'applies' to and by 'the change it effects' on them (SS 111, 61, 91). Reciprocally, 'the representation of a string on the level of transformations is given by the terminal string' and the 'transformations by which it is derived' (SS 91).

7.50 A 'transformational treatment', as we saw, is claimed to enhance '**simplicity**' (SS 62, 72, 81) (cf. 7.36ff). As a 'general principle' stressed in SS, 'if we have a transformation that simplifies the grammar and leads from sentences to sentences in a large number of cases', we can 'simplify the grammar even further' by 'assigning constituent structure to sentences in such a way that this transformation always leads to grammatical sentences' (SS 83). And we can gain still more by using 'the same underlying transformational pattern' for several constructions, e.g., 'negatives and interrogatives' (SS 64ff). But in AT, Chomsky says these 'operations' need no 'a priori justification' by being 'the most simple or "elementary" ones' (AT 55). '"Elementary operations"' are often not 'transformations at all', while those that are may be 'far from elementary'. 'Transformations' 'manipulate substrings only in terms of their assignment to categories', 'independently' of the 'length or internal complexity of strings belonging to these categories'. Evidently, Chomsky's hopes for simplicity were waning (cf. 7.36).

7.51 In SS, however, he had proposed to 'simplify the description of English and gain new insight' by 'limiting the direct description in terms of phrase structure to a **kernel** of basic sentences: simple, declarative active with no complex verb or noun phrases' (SS 106f, 47f, 61) (cf. 4.58, 65). 'All other sentences can be described more simply as **transforms**', i.e. 'strings' 'derived' by 'simply statable transformations' (SS 80, 48). Chomsky promised 'clear and easily generalizable considerations of simplicity' for 'determining which set of sentences belongs to the kernel, and what sorts of transformations' can 'account for the non-kernel sentences' (SS 77). We thus establish 'the transformational level'[23] where 'an utterance is represented' 'abstractly' via 'a sequence of transformations by which it is derived, ultimately from kernel sentences' (SS 47). The 'kernel of the language' can be 'defined' 'as the set of sentences produced by obligatory transformations' (SS 45f, 61, 91), i.e., those needed to make a sentence at all. All others pass through a 'transformational history', which might be a concept for 'determining sentence types' in 'general' (SS 71, 89, 91f; AT 130) (cf. 7.48; 12.28).

7.52 Neither SS nor AT remotely attempts to give a comprehensive list of transformations. A handful are cited for demonstration, such as those for 'negations', 'questions', 'emphatic affirmatives', 'nominalizations', and 'comparatives' (SS 61f, 64, 66, 72, 111–14; AT 178). When 'adjective modifiers' are derived from whole sentences ('converting "the boy is tall" into "the tall boy"') or 'relative clauses' (i.e., ' "the boy who is tall" ') (SS 72; AT 217), we see simpler constructions being derived from more complex ones, not the other way around (cf. 12.54). And these very cases are adduced as 'independent support' and 'syntactic justification' for a transformational analysis' (SS 73; AT 189).

7.53 A 'paradigmatic instance' is 'the **passive** transformation' (SS 77). Having 'both actives and passives in the kernel' would make 'the grammar' 'much more complex' 'than if passives are deleted and reintroduced by a transformation' for 'inverting subject and object', and, where needed, 'deleting the unspecified agent' (SS 77, 72, 79; AT 128) (cf. 9.70). ' "Quantificational" sentences such as ' "everyone in the room knows at least two languages" ' versus ' "at least two languages are known by everyone in the room" ' lead to the overstatement that 'not even the weakest semantic relation (factual equivalence) holds in general between active and passive', whose 'relations' would 'not have come to light' in terms of 'synonymy' – a warning against 'vague semantic clues' (SS 100f).[24] But the relation, I think, is semantic similarity plus difference in focus: in each sentence, focus goes to the identity and size of the set named in subject position (just which persons versus just which languages), while the set named via direct object or prepositional agent is not in focus (any two languages versus anyone in the room).

7.54 In SS Chomsky felt that despite possible 'difficulties and complications', 'the *order*' must be defined among the 'rules' and 'transformations' (SS 32, 111, 114, 66, 44, 35). But in AT he sees 'no way' to decide 'a priori' whether 'the rules' should be 'ordered' or 'unordered', e.g., in terms of 'simplicity' or 'elegance' (AT 39). And 'the theory of transformation markers permits a great deal of latitude' in 'the ordering of transformations'

(AT 133).[25] Yet Chomsky evokes 'strong reasons' for 'assigning an internal organization and an inherent order of derivation' (AT 125).[26] He uses the term 'sequential derivations' for those 'preserving ordering' and considers them central to 'empirical studies of transformational grammar' (AT 67, 211).

7.55   Chomsky limits his 'theory of transformations' by not covering 'the full range of possibilities for **stylistic** inversion' and 'reordering' (AT 126f, 227f). 'Richly inflected languages' (e.g., Russian, Mohawk) 'tolerate' much 'reordering' unless it 'leads to ambiguity' – maybe a 'universal' constraint (AT 126f) (cf. 3.27). Again saving labour while advancing his cause, Chomsky insists that 'the rules of stylistic reordering are very different from grammatical transformations', the latter being 'much more deeply embedded in the grammatical system' and using 'markers drawn from a fixed, universal language-independent set', while 'stylistic' ones are 'peripheral', apply to 'performance', and 'have no apparent bearing' 'on the theory of grammatical structure' (AT 127, 222f).

7.56   In contrast to SS, AT presents 'grammar' with a different group of three parts: 'a **syntactic**', 'a **semantic**', and 'a **phonological component**' (AT 141, 16) (cf. 7.48; 9.30). Morphemics fades, and semantics finally enters the picture. The exact 'relation between syntax and semantics' is a question Chomsky often raises and fails to resolve, regarding it as 'a side issue' and a 'dangerous ground' fraught with 'difficulties', 'confusion', and 'speculation' (SS 93, 101n; AT 75, 148). But he devotes explicit sections to it in both SS (92–105) and AT (14–163). In SS, he follows structuralists like his teacher Harris (1951) by asserting 'the independence of grammar' from 'semantics' and 'concluding that only a purely formal basis can provide a firm and productive foundation for construction of grammatical theory' (SS 13, 106, 100) (cf. 5.61; 12.54). His own 'theory' is 'completely formal and non-semantic', 'meaning' being no more relevant for 'constructing a grammar' than 'the hair colour of speakers' (SS 93). The idea that 'one can construct a grammar with appeal to meaning' is 'widely accepted' (cf. 3.40) but 'totally unsupported', and obscures 'important generalizations about linguistic structure' (SS 93, 101; AT 32, 78).

7.57   So SS proffers 'a purely negative discussion of the possibility of finding semantic foundations for syntactic theory', leading to the 'conclusion that grammar is autonomous and independent of meaning' (SS 93, 17). Chomsky denies having 'acquaintance with any detailed attempt to develop a theory of grammatical structure in partially semantic terms' (though the traditional grammars he praises in AT were this, cf. 4.50, 8.5, 11.41) nor any 'rigorous proposal for using semantic information in constructing or evaluating grammars' (SS 93). He turns the tables, placing 'the burden of proof' 'completely on linguists who claim' to 'develop some grammatical notion in semantic terms' (SS 94)[27] – a bold move, since the burden of proof should rest on the challenger of 'widely accepted' views. Or, he advocates postponement, because 'a decision as to the boundary separating syntax and semantics' 'is not a prerequisite for theoretical and descriptive study'

(AT 160). 'Correspondences' and 'relations between semantics and syntax can only be studied after the syntactic structure has been determined on independent grounds' and within 'some more general theory' (SS 17n, 102, 108). Semantics can wait, but syntax can't (cf. 7.46).

7.58 Moreover, 'despite the undeniable interest and importance of semantic' 'studies of language', 'semantic notions' like 'reference, significance, and synonymity' 'have no direct relevance' for 'characterizing the set of grammatical utterances', which is the true 'problem of syntactic research' (SS 17, 102f).[28] His demonstration that ' "grammatical" cannot be identified with "meaningful" or "significant" ' hinges on the now-famous sentence ' "colourless green ideas sleep furiously" ' (SS 15; AT 149). This example reminds me of the grammatical but nonsensical examples adduced by structuralists to show the self-sufficiency of 'grammatical categories', like Chomsky's own ' "Pirots karulize etalically" '; but he finds their 'notion of "structural meaning" ' 'quite suspect' and doubts 'that the grammatical devices' are 'used consistently enough so that meaning can be assigned to them' (SS 104, 108; cf. SS 103n, 104f) (cf. 5.61).[29]

7.59 Chomsky favours moving in the reverse direction: 'linguists with a serious interest in semantics' should 'deepen and extend syntactic analysis' to supplant 'unanalysed semantic intuition' (AT 75) (cf. 7[5]). A 'purely formal investigation' of 'syntactic structure' 'isolated and exhibited by the grammar' is 'rated more highly' when it 'provides' 'insight into problems of meaning and understanding' and 'supports semantic description' (SS 93, 102, 12). He believes his own 'requirement' of a 'completely formal discipline is perfectly compatible' for making 'significant interconnections with a parallel semantic theory' (SS 103). However 'imperfect' and 'inexact', the 'striking correspondences' between 'syntactic structures' 'in formal grammatical analysis and specific semantic functions' at least indicate that 'syntactic devices' are 'used fairly systematically' (SS 104, 101f, 108).

7.60 Such arguments help us to appreciate why AT adds a '**semantic component**' and states that 'a descriptively adequate grammar' is also 'a theory of **sentence interpretation**' (AT 76). Yet Chomsky hedges his bets by requiring 'that all information utilized in semantic interpretation must be presented in the **syntactic component**' (AT 75). At one point, he unexpectedly says he sees 'no way to decide' 'a priori' 'whether the burden of presentation should fall on the syntactic or semantic component'; 'in fact, it should not be taken for granted that syntactic and semantic considerations can be sharply distinguished' (AT 77f). But this indecision applies specifically to an issue he is reluctant to face anyway, namely '*deviant* sentences'. 'The syntactic component' could treat them only via 'structural similarities to perfectly well-formed' ones, while the 'semantic' one could provide 'lexical items' to 'specify' 'rules' for 'determining the incongruity' (cf. 7.72). Chomsky proposes 'selectional rules' that 'impose a hierarchy of deviation from grammaticalness' on 'sentences' 'generated by relaxing' 'constraints while keeping the grammar unchanged' (AT 152). These rules could be 'dropped from the syntax' and put in 'the semantic component' with 'little violence to structure of the grammar' (AT 153, 158).

7.61 In practice, the role of meaning is marginalized by sticking close to the literal wording of sentences or by replacing words with symbols, and suggesting thereby that the relations between 'transforms' depend on the identities of written words or symbols rather than on similarities of meaning (cf. 12.33). Emblematic here is Chomsky's use of 'ambiguity and similarity of understanding' as 'a motivation for' the 'levels' of 'phrase structures' and 'transformations', e.g., to clear up constructions like ' "the shooting of the hunters" ' or ' "flying planes can be dangerous" ' (SS 86ff; AT 21). 'Transformational grammar' offers a way to make 'ambiguity' 'analysable in syntactic terms' by treating it as 'constructional homonymity' (SS 28, 33, 86fn, 107). An 'ambiguity' signalled by some 'intuitive similarity of utterances' points to 'dual representations on some level', while 'synonymity' points to a 'similar or identical representation' (SS 107). A very simple case is 'a phoneme sequence' that can be 'ambiguously understood' in terms of 'morphemes' (e.g., /ǝneym/ as ' "a name" or "an aim" ') (SS 85) (a prominent trait of English).

7.62 But the most elaborate and explicit means for absorbing semantics and meaning into 'the syntactic component' is by adding the conception of a '**deep structure**' that '**underlies**' the 'actual sentence' and 'determines its **semantic interpretation**' (AT 16, 23, 135, 138). This 'deep structure' 'expresses' 'grammatical relations' and gets 'mapped' by 'transformational rules' into '**surface structure**' (AT 99, 16f, 123, 99, 135). Chomsky complains that the 'syntactic theories' in 'modern structural (taxonomic) linguistics' 'assume that deep and surface structures are actually the same' (AT 16) (cf. 7.80). Making the two 'distinct' is now 'the central idea of transformational grammar', with 'surface structure determined by repeated application of formal operations called "grammatical transformations" ' to objects of a more elementary sort' (AT 16f) (which are also more abstract than 'kernels' and look less like sentences). Against 'immediate constituent analysis', which 'may be adequate' for the 'surface', Chomsky's concern is 'primarily with deep structure' as the site of 'the significant grammatical relations of an actual sentence', while he finds 'surface structure' 'unrevealing' and 'irrelevant' (AT 17, 220, 24) (cf. 7.84, 82; 12.47). He warns how 'surface similarities hide underlying distinctions' which 'no English grammar has pointed out', nor are they 'clear to the speaker' (AT 24, 22) (cf. 12.49). '**Universality** is claimed' only for 'deep structures', whereas 'surface structures' need have no 'uniformity', as 'modern linguistics' has indeed 'found'; this argument keeps their 'findings' from conflicting with 'the hypotheses of universal grammarians' (AT 118) (cf. 7.18f, 55).[30] Also, 'a very general, and perhaps universal way' for 'defining the system of grammatical relations' is ascribed to the '**categorial component**', which 'determines the ordering of elements in deep structures' (AT 122f).

7.63 This new design enables '**grammatical functions**', which are 'relational' and sometimes have 'traditional' 'names' like ' "Subject" ' and

"Object"', to be 'sharply distinguished from '**grammatical categories**' like '"Noun Phrase"' and '"Verb Phrase"' (AT 68f, 104) (cf. 4.69; 5.55, 5^{30}; 6.49; 9.46, 70; 10.34; 11.70, 79).^{31} 'The so-called "grammatical Subject" belongs to 'surface structure', while 'functional notions' like '"logical Subject"' belong to 'deep structure'; thus, a '"grammatical Subject" may be a '"logical Object"' (AT 70, 23, 68, 163, 230). This 'difference' 'provides the primary motivation and empirical justification for the theory of transformational grammar' (AT 70) (cf. 7.79). 'A sentence' is assumed to have 'a basis' whose 'phrase markers' 'directly represent' 'semantically relevant information concerning grammatical function' (AT 70, 117, 230). Yet 'the extension to surface structure of such functional notions' is not 'entirely straightforward', and 'different definitions are needed' (AT 220f). For example, 'Topic–Comment' might be 'the basic grammatical relation of surface structure corresponding (roughly) to the fundamental Subject–Predicate relation of deep structure'; 'often' 'Topic and Subject coincide'. Disregarding communicative functions, Chomsky 'defines the Topic' 'as the leftmost NP immediately dominated by S [Sentence] in surface structure and the Comment' as 'the rest of the string' (but cf. 9.57, 9^{27}; 10.45, 64). Also, 'case' is attributed to 'the position of the Noun in surface structure rather than deep' (AT 221f), an idea 'case grammar' was later to dispute (cf. 10.28, 41).

7.64   The home of 'underlying' or 'deep structure' is 'the **base** of the syntactic component' (AT 17). This is 'a system of rules that generate a highly restricted (perhaps finite) set of *basic strings*, each with an associated structural description called a *base Phrase marker*' – the 'elementary unit' of 'deep structure' (AT 17, 135). 'The *basis* of the sentence', namely its 'underlying' 'sequence of base Phrase markers', gets 'mapped into the sentence by the transformational rules', which 'automatically assign to the sentence a derived Phrase marker, ultimately, a surface structure' (AT 17, 128, 135). To 'simplify the exposition', Chomsky assumes that 'no ambiguities are introduced by rules of the base' (AT 17). The '"kernel sentences"' of SS are briefly mentioned as having 'a single Phrase marker' and 'involving a minimum of transformational apparatus'; but they have a merely 'intuitive significance' (AT 18) (cf. 7.51, 53, 82).

7.65   Being associated with 'deep structure' and 'the categorial component', 'much of the structure of the base' 'is common to all languages' (AT 123, 117) (cf. 7.62). Chomsky finds it 'natural to suppose that formal properties of the base will provide the framework for the characterization of **universal** categories': either the 'rules' themselves, or 'constraints' on the choice' of 'rules' and 'elementary structures', or 'a fixed' 'alphabet' of 'category symbols' (AT 117, 141f). And 'the form of the categorial component' may be 'determined by universal conditions that define "human language"' (AT 120f). This 'traditional view' dates back 'at least to the *Grammaire générale et raisonnée*' and in light of 'relevant evidence' remains 'true' 'today' – and convenient, too: 'aspects of base structure' 'not specific to a particular language' 'need not be stated in the grammar' (AT 117) (cf. 7.19f, 72).

7.66 Therefore, 'the account of the base rules' 'may not belong to the grammar of English any more than the definition' 'of "transformation"' (AT 117f). 'Not all phrase markers generated by the base will underlie actual sentences and thus qualify as deep structures' (AT 138). But 'the transformational rules provide' a 'very simple' 'test', namely whether the 'rules can generate' a proper 'surface structure' from a 'deep' one. This 'filtering function' of the 'rules' was 'true of the earlier version' (in SS) as well, though 'never discussed' (AT 191, 139), since 'deep structure' hadn't been proposed then. Transformations which didn't filter would be useless, since they wouldn't supply the restrictions the formalism requires.

7.67 'The **syntactic component**' is the 'sole "**creative**" part' of the 'grammar', while the other 'two are purely **interpretive**' and 'play no part' in 'generating sentence structures' (AT 135f, 141, 16) (cf. 7.44; 12.32). 'The deep structure of a sentence is submitted to the semantic component for semantic interpretation, and its surface structure enters the phonological component' for 'phonetic interpretation' (AT 135, 141, 16, 138, 99).[32] 'The final effect of a grammar, then, is to relate a semantic interpretation to a phonetic' one – 'that is, to state how a sentence is interpreted' (AT 136). 'When we define deep structures' as ' "generated by the base" ', we 'assume that the semantic interpretation of a sentence depends only on its lexical items and the grammatical functions and relations represented in the underlying structures'. 'This is the basic idea that has motivated the theory of transformational grammar since its inception', though not 'clearly formulated' until Katz and Fodor (1963) (cf. 5.76; 7.71).[33]

7.68 Though they are 'not our concern' and have not been 'worked out', Chomsky thinks his two 'interpretive components function in parallel ways' (AT 143). 'Phonological rules' 'apply' 'first to minimal elements (formatives), then to the constituents of which they are parts', 'and so on, until the maximal domain of phonological processes is reached'. 'In this way a phonetic representation of the entire sentence is formed' via 'the intrinsic abstract' 'properties of its formatives' and 'categories' 'in the surface structure', and 'related' to a 'signal' (AT 143f, 16). 'Similarly, the projection rules of the semantic component operate on the deep structure' and 'assign' 'a "reading" to each constituent on the basis' of those 'assigned to its parts', all the way down to 'the intrinsic semantic properties of the formatives and categories' 'in the deep structure' (AT 144) (cf. 7.82; 12.59).

7.69 Chomsky's 'syntactic component', centred between the other two, is naturally the one AT is 'concerned with' (AT 3), and is assigned a whole range of diverse and complex duties. It provides 'rules that specify the well-formed strings of minimal syntactically functioning units ("formatives") and assigns structural information to these strings and strings which deviate from well-formedness'. It 'specifies the infinite set of abstract formal objects, each of which incorporates all the information relevant to a single interpretation of a particular sentence' (AT 16). It 'contains a **lexicon**', with each 'item specified' by its 'intrinsic' 'features', such as 'Animate' and 'Human' (AT 78, 82f, 85f, 150f, 153, 226) (cf. 4.69; 7.72, 74).[34] Though they are evidently borrowed over from reality, Chomsky insists these features belong to 'purely syntactic rules' and to the 'syntactic component, no matter how narrowly syntax is conceived' (AT 150f). Maybe their absence in traditional grammar worries him.

7.70 The 'lexicon' is designed to be not just a list of 'dictionary definitions' (AT 37), but an enormously diverse and complex complement for the grammar (cf. 12.52). It contains not words as such, but '**formatives**': 'minimal syntactically functioning units', including both 'lexical items ("sincerity, boy") and grammatical items ("Perfect, Possessive")' (AT 87, 3, 65) (cf. 12.30). Since 'a careful grammar' 'reveals that many formatives have unique or almost unique grammatical characteristics', 'substantial simplification' is gained (and labour saved) by putting all these 'properties' into 'the lexicon', 'where they most naturally belong', and 'excluding' them 'from the rewriting rules' (AT 86f) (cf. 12.59). We thus have the 'advantage' of making 'the lexical entries' absorb all 'idiosyncrasies' and 'irregularities of the language' (AT 86f, 216, 142, 214; cf. Sweet 1913: 31) (cf. 4.49, 52; 12.59).

7.71 The 'entries' in 'the lexicon' 'each consist of a descriptive feature matrix and a complex symbol' (AT 164, 222). The '**features**' are 'phonological', 'syntactic', and, in the 'definition', 'purely semantic' (AT 214). (cf. Katz and Fodor 1963) (AT 214). The 'semantic features' are 'distinct but related' to the 'syntactic' ones and 'constitute a well-defined set in a given grammar: a feature belongs' here if 'it is not referred to by any rule of the phonological or syntactic component' (AT 88, 120, 142). Lest he imply that 'the system of dictionary definitions' is without 'intrinsic structure' and hence 'atomistic', Chomsky invokes 'relations of meaning (rather than relations of fact)' that 'cannot in any natural way be described within' 'independent lexical entries' (AT 160). Examples include the '"field properties"' studied in 'componential analysis', or the 'referential domains' of terms that are 'mutually exclusive', e.g., 'colour words' (AT 229, 160f, 229) (cf. 4.22; 5.68; 7.32). Moreover, Chomsky foresees 'universal language-independent constraints on semantic features' – 'in traditional terms, the system of possible concepts' (AT 160) – presumably innate rather than extracted from reality (but cf. 7.69; 12.24). This hope again rests on a parallel to 'the theory of phonetic distinctive features', which gives 'a language-independent significance to the choice of symbol' for 'lexical formatives' (cf. 7.20; 12.26); Chomsky 'assumes' that 'the grammatical formatives and the category symbols' in the lexicon 'too are selected from a fixed universal vocabulary, although this assumption' has no 'effect' on his 'descriptive material' (AT 65f, 160). Only 'our ignorance of the relevant psychological and physiological facts' hides the 'a priori structure' in 'the system of "attainable concepts"' (AT 160).

7.72 The 'lexical entry' gets the tough jobs of supplying 'information' for 'the phonological and semantic components' and for 'the transformational part of the syntactic component', and of 'determining the proper placement' 'in sentences, and hence by implication degree and manner of deviation of strings' not 'generated' (again relieving the 'rules') (AT 87ff). Some 'features' are '**inherent**' to a 'formative', being 'part of the complex symbol of the lexical entry', while others are '**contextual**', being 'introduced by grammatical rules' when the 'item' is 'inserted into a phrase marker' (AT 171, 122, 176f). 'This analysis of a formative as a pair of sets of features' is 'tentatively proposed' 'as a linguistic universal' on 'slender evidence', but with the (labour-saving) corollary that the 'features need not actually be mentioned' 'in the rules of the grammar' (AT 181, 141f) (cf. 7.19, 65). Also, a possible explosion of features in the lexicon is to be counteracted by 'redundancy rules' for ' predictable' 'feature specifications' – another carry-over from the 'phonological' domain to the 'syntactic' and a prompt new candidate for 'universal notation' (e.g., '[+ Human]' again) (AT 168f, 222, 166).

7.73 'A lexical entry is substituted' in 'positions' where 'its contextual features match those of the symbol' (AT 121). Since the 'rules' can 'assign' 'contextual features' also to the 'frames in which a symbol appears', we have '**context-sensitive** rules' in the lexicon instead of '**context-free**', and thereby get them too out of 'the grammar' (AT 121f) (cf. 7.48; 12.52). In exchange, the 'features determined by context' are 'non-inherent' and, being 'unspecified in underlying structures' and 'added' by 'redundancy rules', can make 'no contribution to sentence interpretation' (AT 182) (cf. 7.82). Or, 'determining the restrictions' via 'feature specifications' might be 'preferable, since it does not affect the structure of the lexicon', leaving it 'simply a list of entries' (AT 188). Chomsky wonders whether to 'list in the lexicon only the features' for 'frames in which the item' '*cannot* appear'; or to list those in which it '*can* appear' and to assume it is 'automatically' 'specified negatively' for 'every contextual feature not mentioned' (AT 110f, 166, 230). Or, a 'distinct subpart of the base of the syntactic component' could contain 'lexical rules' derived by a 'general analysis of lexical items' and empowered to 'introduce lexical formatives' (AT 68, 190, 74).

7.74 Beyond 'the lexicon', Chomsky's 'base' has a '**categorial component**', 'defined' as a 'system of rewriting rules' (AT 123, 120) (cf. 7.48). 'Among the rewriting rules' 'we can distinguish **branching** rules', which 'analyse a category symbol' 'into a string of (one or more) symbols', either 'terminal' or 'non-terminal'; versus '**subcategorization** rules', which 'introduce syntactic features and thus form or extend a complex symbol' (AT 112). Again, these two types of 'rule may be context-free', 'introducing inherent features' (like '[Human]'); or 'context-sensitive', 'introducing contextual features' (like '[Transitive]') by 'environment' (AT 112, 120, 90, i.r.).[35] In 'theory', 'a grammar is obviously more highly valued if subcategorization is determined by a set of contexts that is syntactically definable' (AT 97f). But midway through AT, Chomsky decides it would be less 'restrictive' and more 'flexible' to change 'the base component' in his 'earlier proposal' by discarding 'subcategorization rules' as 'rewriting rules and 'assigning' them too 'to the lexicon', thus leaving only 'branching rules', 'all context-free' (like in a 'simple phrase structure grammar'), inside 'the categorial component' (AT 123, 120, 128, 122). Now, 'strict subcategorial and selectional restrictions' get 'listed in lexical entries' and 'defined by transformational rules' (AT 139).

7.75 The place of **morphology** in the tripartite AT model, lacking the older 'morphophonemic level' (cf. 7.48), is merely sketched. Chomsky 'compares' 'the traditional method of **paradigms**' whose 'dimensions' are 'inflectional categories of gender, number, case, and declensional type', against 'the descriptivist method of morphemic analysis', which Chomsky (after Hockett) classes as an '"item-and-arrangement" grammar' (AT 170, 172, 232) (cf. 4.57; 5.50, 74, 5^{12}; 6.34; 7.75f; 8.57; 9.31, 9^{11}; 11.71). The older 'paradigmatic description' can be 'restated' or 'incorporated directly' in 'the theory of syntactic features', using 'not + and − but integers' 'associated with traditional designations' (AT 171f).[36] The concept of 'morphemes' in 'modern linguistics', in contrast, is 'clumsy' and 'inelegant' to 'represent' by 'a grammar based on rewriting rules or transformations', and is 'in fact designed' 'to exclude' 'all but the most elementary general rules' (AT 173, 323). 'The order of morphemes is quite arbitrary, whereas this arbitrariness is avoided in paradigmatic treatment, the features being unordered' (AT 174). Also, 'many morphemes are not phonetically realized' and so are treated, 'in particular contexts, as zero elements', such that 'each case' needs 'a specific context-sensitive rule'; Chomsky finds these rules 'superfluous', and his 'feature analysis simply gives no rule' (AT 173). So he judges 'the modern descriptivist reanalysis' 'in terms of morpheme sequences' 'an ill-advised theoretical innovation' (AT 174) (cf. 7.5).

7.76 But he doesn't quite throw it out: 'within our framework, either paradigmatic analysis' by 'features or sequential morphemic analysis is available, whichever permits the optimal and most general statement' (AT 174).[37] He foresees no 'difficulty in extending the theory of transformations' to 'formalize traditional rules' for 'inflectional systems' (AT 175f). Yet he admits that morphemic 'derivation processes' are a bigger 'problem' for 'generative' grammar because 'they are typically sporadic and only quasi-productive', even when 'the meaning' is 'to some extent predictable' from 'inherent semantic properties of the morphemes' (AT 184, 186). Still, 'all presently known theories of language fail' here, so 'quasi-productive processes' need not 'support an alternative theory of grammar' (AT 235f) (argued by Bolinger 1961).

7.77 Though I have had to pass over some technical details about 'rules', 'features', and so on, the major 'aspects' of Chomsky's 'theory of syntax' should now be evident. The two books I have summarized are far from being the whole story. He and his associates produced a flood of additional books and papers revising numerous aspects of the model or refuting objections to it; in fact, the grammar got more and more 'transformational' because it kept getting transformed, even to the point where many 'transformations' themselves were dropped, along with 'deep structure' (Chomsky 1977). But AT and SS were and still are by far the most widely read of his works, and Chomsky himself later (1971 [1968]: 184f) called AT 'the standard theory'. I have treated the two books mainly as two advocacies of one overall project, while pointing out the important innovations and greater development of AT over SS. The vacuum left by not acknowledging his debt to 'modern' linguistics (cf. 7.5, 19, 29, 57, 76) is filled in AT by garnering sources among philosophers of previous centuries (cf. 7.3) and by citing himself as a main source. AT contains 113 references to eighteen works he had by that time authored or co-authored,[38] and relies heavily on works of his associates and followers (e.g., Halle, Miller, Katz, Fodor, Postal, Lees, Bever).

7.78   Above all, AT reveals a marked change in Chomsky's estimation of the project. He now presents the approach not merely as a way to make English grammar 'simpler', more 'adequate', and so on, but as a leading candidate in the investigation of 'linguistic competence', 'innate language capacity', 'language acquisition, 'language universals', and 'philosophy of mind'. To retain much of the conceptions and terminology originally designed for 'grammatical description', he makes them 'systematically ambiguous', even though the correspondence between a speaker's or a child's knowledge and 'the linguist's account' is precisely what linguistics has to demonstrate (cf. 7.15, 28; 12.45). He thus lends a more exalted significance to the rather traditional centrepiece of his project: analysing, describing, and comparing phrases or sentences in terms of grammatical structure (cf. 7.88).

7.79   Since many grammatical relations and distinctions are not formally marked in English, Chomsky promises to offset the lack by postulating 'underlying structures', 'markers', and 'features'. He stresses superficial similarity with underlying difference, and underlying similarity with superficial difference (cf. 7.14, 53, 61, 82; 12.7, 30, 43, 54). We are justified in 'transforming' linguistic data to put such cases into clearer forms, which competing 'grammars' fail to do. He nourishes the prospect that, on the 'underlying' ('deep', 'base', etc.) level, structure is far more precise, distinct, orderly, and general than everyday utterances indicate. Down there, categories are 'universal' ('determined by the nature of language as such'), relationships are crystal-clear, constraints on what may or may not be constructed are exactly stated, meanings are rigorously decomposed, and ambiguities are fully resolved. Such demanding goals force Chomsky to be evasive about his deep level, or to advance peculiar claims. To limit 'functional' 'issues' to 'surface structure', he says 'order' 'plays no role in determining grammatical relations in deep structures', even though he has already said 'the categorial component determines the ordering of elements in deep structures' (AT 220f, 122ff). To keep his 'deep structure' simple, he says 'features determined by context', being 'unspecified in underlying structure', can make 'no contribution to sentence interpretation' (AT 182) (cf. 7.72); but what can 'context' be if not an influence on how people interpret?

7.80   Chomsky's evasions are predictably clustered at points of contact between his technical, underlying apparatus and the facts or patterns it purports to 'account for' or 'explain'. One evasion, already in SS, is to insist

that 'the transformational part of grammar applies' 'properly' to 'the forms'
('the terminal strings' or 'phrase markers') that 'underlie' sentences, yet to
show them applying to the sentences themselves (SS 45, 47f, 66, 71, 73, 88f,
91, 107 vs SS 35f, 42f, 74f, 78f, 80ff). In AT, too, he may make 'no careful
distinction' 'between the basic string and sentence itself' and proceed on the
'simplifying and contrary to fact assumption that the underlying basic string
is the sentence', and the 'base phrase marker is the surface structure as well
as the deep structure' (AT 18). This matter is by no means trivial if making
the two levels 'distinct' is 'the central idea of transformational grammar'
(AT 16f) (cf. 7.62). Surely more precision could be attained, especially if
Chomsky is 'concerned' 'primarily' with 'extremely simple sentences', e.g.,
those 'with a single element in the basis' (AT 63, 18). He condemns 'modern
structural (taxonomic) linguistics' for 'assuming that deep and surface
structures are actually the same', yet says his 'grammar does not, in itself,
provide any sensible procedure for finding a deep structure of a given
sentence' (AT 16, 141) (cf. 6.38, 61; 7.7). The pathway between surface and
deep is further obscured by Chomsky's habit of 'leaving out quite a few
transformations', 'refinements', qualifications', or 'details of formalization'
he says aren't 'relevant' (AT 131, 92, 81f, 222).

7.81   Also, he makes use of scant data from English, and far less from
other languages. Most examples are merely quoted, or are listed without
further analysis as 'grammatical' or 'deviant'. Only twenty-eight invented
sentences in SS and twenty-four in AT are analysed, i.e., broken into
constituents, formalized, paraphrased or 'transformed'. One sentence
('"sincerity may frighten the boy"') and its alterations gets analysed and
discussed over twenty-six pages in the two books (SS 42f, 78; AT 63ff, 68f,
71, 73, 75f, 85f, 107, 111, 119, 149, 152f, 157, 165, 211, 228, 230) – a lot of
work for it (Humpty Dumpty would have paid it royally). 'Diagramming' a
'"**tree structure**"', in which 'a sequence of words is a constituent' if it is
'traced' 'back to a single point' (SS 27f; AT 12), is done for one sentence in
SS and six in AT. The trees are called '(base) phrase markers' (AT 65,
69, 71, 86, 108f, 128, 130f, 171, 184), but one is called a 'deep structure'
(AT 178) (compare the much simpler 'deep structure' of 'Noun phrase –
Verb – Noun phrase – Sentence' on AT 23).[39] Chomsky calmly remarks that
'the interpretation of such a diagram is transparent', and that 'the procedure
for constructing a phrase marker' from a 'derivation' is a 'minor matter of
appropriate formalization and involves nothing of principle' (AT 164, 107)
(cf. 7.86).

7.82   Yet another evasion regards the role of underlying entities in the
process of language understanding. Chomsky proposes to 'judge formal
theories' by 'their ability to explain' and 'clarify' 'facts' about how 'sentences
are used and understood (SS 102). In SS, he stipulates that 'understanding a
sentence' requires 'knowing the kernel sentences from which it originates
(more precisely the terminal strings underlying these)', and raises the hope
that 'the general problem of analysing the process of "understanding"'
might be 'reduced' to 'explaining how kernel sentences are understood'
(SS 87, 92, 104n, 107f). In AT, he announces (with no mention of his earlier

statement) that 'kernel sentences' 'play no distinctive role' in the 'interpretation of sentences' (AT 18). In return, 'phrase markers' are now presented as 'the elementary content elements from which semantic interpretations of actual sentences are constructed' – an 'insight as old as syntactic theory itself' (AT 117, 221) (though he didn't know it in 1957). 'The manner of combination provided by the surface' 'structure is in general almost totally irrelevant to semantic interpretation, whereas the grammatical relations expressed in deep structure are in many cases just those that determine the meaning of the sentence' (AT 162; cf. AT 135) (cf. 7.84; 10.100; 12.47). This 'determining' requires that 'the meaning of a sentence be based on the meaning of its elementary parts and manner of their combination' (AT 162f) (but cf. 2.29; 5.67, 75f; 10.36; 11.93; 12.59). The requirement is congenial for an approach based on analysing and assembling structures, but is violated even by his own hand-picked samples. His interpretation of ' "I had a book stolen" ' depends not on the parts and their combination, but on 'elaborations of the sentence' to supply contexts (like ' "I had a book stolen from his library by a professional thief who I hired" ') – just the recourse to 'entirely different constructions' he later calls 'irrelevant' (AT 21f, 161).

7.83 A similar evasion pertains to the production of sentences. In SS, Chomsky cautions against a 'misunderstanding' that 'grammars' 'described' as 'devices for generating sentences' are 'concerned with the process of producing utterances rather than' 'analysing and reconstructing' their 'structure' (SS 48). The 'synthesis and analysis' 'speaker and hearer must perform' 'are both outside the scope of the grammars' he proposes, and (he adds without evidence) 'are essentially the same' – a reason why such 'grammars' 'are quite neutral as between speaker and hearer' (but cf. 10.81, 85; 11.47). A 'grammar is simply a description' of the 'set of utterances' 'which it generates', and his 'schema for grammatical description' does 'not permit us to state the actual processes at work' (SS 48; AT 92). These are issues for a 'theory' or 'performance model' of 'language use', which 'must incorporate a grammar' but must not be 'confused' with it (AT 141, 9). Yet Chomsky himself is the one who pictures the 'grammar' *'producing* language' or 'strings' or 'sentences', who refers to 'the *process* of generating sentences', and who equates 'generating' with *'creating'* (SS 11ff, 18, 30f, 38, 45f, 103, 35, AT 135f, i.a.) (cf. 12^{13}).

7.84 In AT, he again laments the 'continuing misunderstanding' of 'generative grammar' being 'a model for a speaker or a hearer', or for the 'production and perception' of 'speech' (AT 9). He is 'attempting to characterize in the most neutral possible terms the knowledge of the language that provides the basis for the actual use of language by a speaker-hearer'; he 'says nothing about how' they 'might proceed, in some practical or efficient way'. To 'speak of a grammar as generating a sentence' 'means simply' that it 'assigns this structural description to the sentence'. This 'persistent' 'confusion' might 'suggest a terminological change', but Chomsky 'sees no reason for a revision', noting that 'the term "generate" is familiar' in this sense 'in logic' (e.g., 'the theory of combinatorial systems'). But what better reason for 'revision' could there be than to clear up a 'continuing misunderstanding'? Probably, the terms are retained because the conflation between theory and reality, between technical and common-sense terms, between grammar and real processes, forms a vital bridge to human language after competence gets detached from performance (which is 'degenerate') and deep structure from surface structure (which is 'unrevealing' and 'irrelevant') (cf. 7.25, 62, 82; 12.47).

7.85 For the same reason, Chomsky, like Hjelmslev, has to use '**empirical**' in a special technical sense, the more so after his harsh appraisal of 'empiricism' (cf. 6.15–18; 7.18, 21, 23f, 27, 34, 36, 54, 63). And he has good reason to invoke 'the highly *tentative* character of any attempt to justify an empirical claim about linguistic structure', and to say a 'theory of language' '*ultimately* relates' 'a system' of 'theoretical terms' 'to *potential empirical* phenomena' (AT v, 26, 208, i.a.) (cf. 7.94).[40] Yet a lack of 'strong empirical motivation' is often adduced as grounds *not* to alter his model (AT 73, 116, 188, 44). Although he says it's 'important to see' how far 'the freedom to use' 'transformational rules' 'is actually empirically motivated', he is already sure that 'the central role of grammatical transformations in any empirically adequate generative grammar' is 'established quite firmly'; and that 'generative grammars will provide the only empirical data critical for evaluating a theory of the form of language' (AT 99, 34, vi, 209).

7.86 'Empirical claims' are also associated with '**notational** conventions', like the 'parentheses, brackets, etc.' 'adopted in explicit (that is generative) grammars' (AT 42) (cf. 9.33; 10[32]; 12.25, 49, 51). He likes to think that 'a person learning a language will attempt to formulate generalizations that can easily be expressed' 'with few symbols' in the 'notation' of 'the theory' (AT 45). One 'notational convention' (for 'tenses') is held to 'embody a factual claim about the structure of natural language and the predisposition of the child' (AT 43f). A 'full set of notational conventions' might even 'constitute an evaluation procedure'. So the notation can be as systematically ambiguous as the terminology and provide the same kind of bridge.

7.87 Similarly problematic is Chomsky's move of 'interpreting taxonomic linguistics as making an empirical claim' that 'grammars result from applying postulated processes to a sufficiently rich selection of data' (SS 52). He even says their 'procedures constitute a hypothesis about an innate language-acquisition system'; he admits 'it is not at all clear' if this is 'fair', but he blames the lack of clarity on 'structural linguistics' for 'giving little attention to the normal use of language' (SS 52; AT 205), actually just what his own theory devalues. In fact, however, the structuralists never contemplated advancing such 'hypotheses' or 'claims'. They emphasized that their methods demand specialized techniques and procedures that must be consciously acquired and developed well beyond ordinary language awareness (cf. 2.33, 3.5, 11, 19, 59; 4.19, 54; 5.11, 13f, 44, 48, 88; 8.5, 27, 42, 57; 12.49). Pike (who studied many more languages than Chomsky) stipulated that 'the adult linguist' 'cannot recapitulate the child's experience' but at most study the 'learning processes of children in the culture' (LB 601;

5^{35}), a recourse rejected by Chomsky's *Aspects*. Moreover, the assertion that 'the methods' of 'taxonomic linguistics are intrinsically incapable of yielding systems of grammatical knowledge that must be attributed to the speaker of a language' (AT 54) is (empirically) wrong: by 1964, those methods had done so for 'over 350 languages' (cf. 5.2; 12.56).

7.88 Chomsky's assertion hinges on his own wilful move to short-circuit linguistic method onto language learning and 'linguistic theory' onto 'acquisition' (7.24ff), thus allegorizing the activity of 'constructing grammars'. He vows 'language learning would be impossible unless' 'the child approached the data' expecting 'a language of a certain antecedently well-defined type' (AT 27). We are told to 'distinguish carefully between' 'two functions of external data': 'initiating and facilitating the operation of innate mechanisms' versus 'determining' the 'direction' of 'learning' (AT 34). This distinction is designed to justify the argument that 'semantic reference' only 'facilitates' 'syntax learning' without 'affecting the *manner* in which the acquisition of syntax proceeds' nor 'determining which hypotheses are selected by the learner' (AT 33). 'It would not be at all surprising' if 'normal language learning requires use of language in real-life situations', but Chomsky doubts that such 'information' 'plays any role in how language is acquired, once the mechanism is put to work'. For good measure, the 'acquiring' of 'grammar' is declared 'independent of intelligence, motivation, and emotional state' (AT 58).

7.89 The low feasibility of acquiring a language without constant reliance on meaning, reference, and situation has to be compensated by strong claims about an 'innate device' preprogrammed to operate primarily on just the data Chomsky's approach emphasizes. How this could work is passed over when Chomsky, who had vowed never to 'consider the question of how one might have arrived at the grammar' (7.9), follows suit by adopting an 'idealized "instantaneous" model' where 'successful language acquisition' happens in one 'moment' (SS 56; AT 36) (cf. 12.38). He wants to 'consider' (though he has left little to say about it) only this 'moment of acquisition of the correct grammar', and not the 'order and manner' in which 'linguistic data' 'are presented', nor the 'series of successively more detailed and structured schemata corresponding to maturational stages' (AT 202).[41] He can thus dispense with examining 'the gradual development of an appropriate hypothesis' and 'the continual accretion of linguistic skill and knowledge'. And 'no evaluation procedure will be necessary as a part linguistic theory' 'in this case' (AT 36). None the less, he refers us to 'the best information now available' (which he doesn't cite) as proof 'that a child cannot help constructing' a 'transformational grammar' 'any more than he can control his perception of solid objects or his attention to line and angle' (AT 59) (cf. 7.15; 12.38). The (Saussurian) idea is aired here that 'the individual has no conscious control' and 'society' has 'little choice or freedom' concerning 'the structure of particular languages' (cf. 2.35, 44, 52, 59; 3.4, 11, 58). Yet the process whereby 'the child discovers' a 'deep and abstract theory (a generative grammar)' 'only remotely related to experience by long and intricate chains of unconscious quasi-inferential steps', and makes no 'conscious' 'formulation and expression of rules' (AT 58) can hardly be parallel to the process whereby a linguist does all that deliberately.

7.90 Another empirical problem is the **'acceptability'** of 'sentences' (AT 12) (cf. 7.41f). At one point, 'probabilistic models for the use of language' are deemed 'rewarding' (SS 17n). But elsewhere, the idea that 'more acceptable sentences are 'more likely to be produced' is rejected as 'vague' and 'obscure'; '"likely"' or '"probable"' is 'objective' only if 'based on' 'relative frequency' (AT 11f, 195). Chomsky dismisses this 'useless notion' because 'almost all highly acceptable sentences' 'have probabilities empirically equal to zero', as do 'the sentence types' they 'belong to' (AT 195). He wants to show why 'probabilistic models give no particular insight into the basic problems of syntactic structure', and why 'grammatical' must not be defined as having a '"high order of statistical approximation to English"' (SS 16f).[42] He offers examples with varying degrees of oddness (e.g., '"colourless green ideas sleep furiously"' versus '"furiously sleep ideas green colourless"') and conjectures that none of 'the sentences nor any part of them have ever occurred in any English discourse' or in 'the linguistic experience of a speaker', so 'statistically' they are all 'equally remote'.

7.91 This argument, though often quoted, simply does not hold, and if it held, it would undermine Chomsky's project just as thoroughly as those he wields it against. All of linguistic theory, including his own notions of 'grammar', 'grammaticalness', 'competence', 'intuition', 'rules', 'kernels', and (above all) 'universals', depends crucially on the assumption that some structures are much more probable and predictable than others. The structuralists expressly presented their schemes of 'levels' and '-emic' units as a means to discover what is common to many utterances, though each one is unique in physical and phonetic detail, and (as Bloomfield stressed) in semantic and situational detail as well (cf. 4.14, 16, 31, 75, 78; 5.25; 12.40); we could disregard '"likelihood relative to a given situation"' only as long as situations are specified in terms of observable physical properties' (cf. AT 195). Chomsky's argument collapses the frequency or likelihood of the *sentence or utterance as such* with that of its *type or underlying organization* – just the move he cannot require, since his enterprise hinges on the distinction. He was too anxious to fend off the prospect that his own 'grammar' of 'rules' must be probabilistic, witness the continuing failure to find precise boundaries for 'grammaticalness'. Given a reliable method for relating real sentences or utterances to underlying types, representative frequencies could be obtained from the large corpuses of data Chomsky disdains to collect (cf. 7.7, 93). In the process, the 'intuitions' he rates so highly could be examined and made explicit, rather than merely 'tacit'. Until then, I see no evidence that 'a generative grammar does not rely on intelligence of an understanding reader, but provides an explicit analysis of his contribution' (cf. AT 4).

7.92 Chomsky resembles an inventor who has designed a new 'device', which he equates with both a 'grammar' and a 'theory' (SS 11, 13, 18, 48, 85, 52), but, instead of actually building it, puts only the design on the market with confident or technical reassurances that the device will function and save labour (cf. 7.9, 19f, 56, 70, 72). It will 'produce' or 'generate sentences', 'interpret' them, and 'utilize primary linguistic data as an empirical basis for language learning' (SS 11, 13, 18, 48, 85; AT 32). It will take 'data' (or 'signals') as 'input' and give 'grammar' as '"output"' (SS 52; AT 47, 30, 38, 206, 207). It will help things get 'automatically' done or accounted for (SS 5, 67f, 85, 89, 104, 107; AT 100, 104, 110f, 128, 166f, 234) (cf. 7.17, 40, 64, 73). But the directions for assembly are so busy telling the prospective user how superior and 'powerful' the device is that crucial steps in the construction get simplified, blurred, or left out.

7.93 The notion of a 'device' injects a mechanistic aspect into an avowedly 'mentalistic' model (cf. 7.10). Perhaps the reason why Chomsky dismisses Bloomfield's 'dualism' (of 4.8) as 'irrelevant' (AT 193) is that his own outlook straddles both sides. 'Rationalism' is lauded for holding 'no preconceptions' about 'the internal structure of this device' and only 'studying uniformities in the output' (AT 206) (cf. 7.33). Even a very 'specialized input–output relation' need not 'presuppose a complex and highly structured device'. Chomsky pleads too 'little knowledge about the brain' or 'engineering insight into plausible physical systems' to decide whether the 'mind' 'contains the schema for transformational grammar' or 'a mechanism for making arbitrary associations' and 'carrying out' 'inductive and taxonomic operations' (AT 206f).[43] But he has by this time dismissed 'inductive and taxonomic operations' (cf. 7.7, 25, 30, 34); and his handling of 'universals' (which are not '*in* the output' at all, but ascribed to some deeper level) and 'innateness' entails, as he says himself, an 'extremely strong' 'claim about the innate capacity' or 'predisposition' 'of the child' (cf. 7.28), if not the most extensive 'preconceptions about a language acquisition device' ever articulated by a major linguist.

7.94 Chomsky concedes that 'only some of the possibilities permitted by this general theory have been realized convincingly with actual linguistic material' (AT 133) (cf. 6.11). 'A vast range of linguistic phenomena' have 'resisted insightful formulation in any terms' (AT vi). 'Few grammars' have 'attempted to give an explicit characterization of the range of sentences and structural descriptions', 'even in a partial sketch' (AT 116). He offers his own 'discussions' as 'partial', 'inconclusive', 'informal', 'superficial', and 'oversimplified' (AT 116, 163, 230, 3, 164, 235), and his views as 'tentative' (SS v, vi, 26; AT 37, 55, 128, 159, 163, 164, 181, 219) (cf. 7.2, 72, 85). Yet he expects that 'as explicit grammatical descriptions' 'accumulate, it will no doubt be possible to give empirical justification for various refinements and revisions of such loosely sketched proposals as these' (AT 116). He foresees 'no problem in principle in sharpening or generalizing' his 'definitions' so as to encompass 'many formal features of the grammar'. He feels confident that the 'analysis', 'description', 'definition', 'explication', 'terminology', 'grammar', 'notation', or 'rule' he favours is *natural* (SS 68, 75, 85; AT 10f, 14, 29, 66f, 97, 113ff, 152f, 160, 176, 182, 227), whatever that may signify.

He never seems to suspect that his approach might add to the 'many mysteries' and 'obscurities' he sees (AT 63, 184); or that the constructions needed to coordinate his theory with real data (or 'deep' with 'surface structure', or 'syntax' with 'semantics', etc.) might prove as 'hopelessly complex' as the rival grammars he repudiated in SS (cf. 7.37).

7.95 And, in the last analysis, Chomsky's proposals, despite his 'revolutionary' rhetoric, are not so different from those of other theorists. His greatest debt was to Zellig Harris, from whom he 'incorporated' 'so many ideas' in SS that he doesn't 'attempt to indicate them' (SS 6; cf. AT 221, 119). No acknowledgement is made to Sapir, who suggested that 'underlying the finished sentence' there is a 'sentence type of fixed formal characteristics', whereby 'new sentences are being constantly created'; and who foretold 'great underlying ground plans' for the 'fundamental form intuitions' of 'diverse languages' (SL 37, 144) (cf. 3.38, 51). And only a single attribution is made to Bloomfield for having postulated a 'kernel' or a 'theoretical underlying form' (BL 225f, 267; SS 108n), but not for having remarked that 'the speaker who knows the constituents and the grammatical pattern' can 'utter' 'speech forms without ever having heard them', that 'the possibilities of combination are practically infinite', that 'the form-class of almost any phrase is known if we know the syntactic constructions and the form-classes of words', and that 'semantic difference' might be 'defined in terms of syntactic construction' (cf. 4.58, 61, 66, 4[21] vs 7.51, 43f, 59). Bloomfield also likened this combining to 'the solving of a proportional equation with an indefinitely large set of ratios on the left-hand side', and introduced the 'asterisk' for ungrammatical examples (BL 276, 302, 184, 163) (cf. 4[20], 4[22]).

7.96 Chomsky's clearest tribute to his predecessors is a bit inaccurate, namely when his 'idealization' of 'linguistic theory being primarily concerned with an ideal speaker-hearer in a completely homogeneous speech community' is depicted as 'the position of the founders of modern general linguistics' (AT 3f). Perhaps Hjelmslev is meant, who contemplated 'eliminating' 'accidents' and 'disturbances' 'in the exercise of language' (in 'parole') (PT 94) (6.46), but he had no 'speaker' or 'hearer' at all. Otherwise, the modern founders I have reviewed were, on the contrary, much concerned with the issues of variety and change in language communities (cf. 2.12, 37, 41–45; 3.28, 54–66; 4.26, 30, 74–84; 5.1, 16).

7.97 Chomsky proposes to 'study language as an instrument or tool' and 'describe its structure with no explicit reference' to how it is 'put to use', because 'no other basis' 'will yield a rigorous, effective, and "revealing" theory of linguistic structure' (SS 103). He promises for later a 'more general theory of language that will include a theory of linguistic form and a theory of the use of language'; then, the 'formal study of the structure of language' will 'provide insight into the actual use of language' (SS 102f). So far, transformational generative grammar has provided no such theory, and steadily fewer linguists seem to believe that it will.

7.98 Back at the start of SS, we recall, Chomsky praised 'precisely constructed models' for 'both negative and positive' 'roles' (SS 5) (cf. 7.17). On the 'negative' side was the 'deeper understanding of linguistic data' gained 'by pushing a precise but inadequate formulation to an unacceptable conclusion'. Though Chomsky evinced no awareness of doing this himself, the consensus in the discipline seems to be that he was. We can now look on the 'positive' side, and reconsider whether and how 'a formalized theory' can 'provide solutions for problems' for which it wasn't 'originally designed', and what benefits can be had from 'rigorously stating a proposed theory and applying it strictly to linguistic material' (cf. SS 11, 5). Computer programming seems the safest bet, though even AT, written with 'support' from the MIT 'Research Laboratory of Electronics' (AT iv), doesn't say so. Apart from that, only the extensive empirical and experimental labour SS and AT proposed to save or postpone can decide what aspects of language can or should be formalized.

Notes

1. The key for Chomsky citations is AT: *Aspects of the Theory of Syntax* (1965); and SS: *Syntactic Structures* (1957). On the motive for selecting these two works, see 7.77. A sketch of post-*Aspects* theorizing up to the elimination of the transformations themselves was provided in the Winograd chapter, which unfortunately had to be removed (cf. 1.14).
2. And he is quite assertive about other people's 'confusions' or about what issues are 'vacuous' and 'empty' or have 'no bearing' (AT 40, 204, 54, 20, 41, 53, 126f) (cf. 7.11, 33f, 55f).
3. DuMarsais (1729) argued that 'observations' in 'general grammar' 'fit all languages' (AT 4f, m.t.) (cf. 7.18ff). 'The idea that language is based on a system of rules' for 'infinitely many sentences' is referred to Humboldt's remark that 'a language "makes infinite use of finite means"' (AT v), although 'infinite' possibilities were often invoked by Sapir and Bloomfield as well (cf. 3.3, 6, 70; 4.13, 29, 31, 61; 12.34). 'Deep' and 'surface structure' are aligned with the 'Humboldtian notions' of '"inner" and "outer form"', and 'generate' with his '"*erzeugen*"' (AT 198f, 9) (cf. 11.18f, 22, 11[11]).
4. Diderot (1751) quaintly asserted that French ranked above all other languages in this regard. So 'French is made to instruct, clarify, and convince; Greek, Latin, and English to persuade, move, and deceive' (AT 7, m.t.).
5. And '"intuitions about meaning"', condemned as 'vague and undesirable' in SS (94), are still decried as 'unanalysed' and not 'useful' in AT (75) (cf. 7.59).
6. He denies any 'circularity in this conception', or in his use of 'transformations' both as means and results of 'phrase structure analysis' (SS 50, 83).
7. Compare also 6.16, 46, and 61. Hjelmslev is among the few modern linguists Chomsky cites with no hint of attack: his '"appropriateness" and "arbitrariness"' are aligned with Chomsky's 'adequacy' and 'generality' (SS 50n) (cf. 6.15, 18, 44). Further similarities include: a vision of linguistics as a centre of theory (6.10 vs 7.8); a demand for a general typology of languages (6.11, 57 vs 7.18) and for an 'algebra' of representation (6.8 vs 7.40); a peculiar notion of 'empirical' (6.13 vs 7.85); a dislike of 'inductive' methods (6.16 vs 7.6f); a disinterest in 'discovery procedures' (6.61 vs 7.7, 81); and a hope of putting old 'grammar' to new uses (6.49 vs 7.4).
8. The term 'primary data' is not defined in AT. 'Non-primary' or 'secondary'

data are never mentioned, but the argument examined in 7.88 suggests it might be 'semantic' and 'situational' data (and cf. AT 202f). The idea that 'primary' 'data constitute a small sample' (AT 25) is fortified by seeing a language as 'an infinite set of sentences' (cf. 7.43).

9. Chomsky here denies any 'reasonable procedure for translating between languages' without 'an "encyclopedia"' of 'extralinguistic information' (AT 30, 201f).

10. Chomsky demands that 'a theory of linguistic structure' 'must contain a universal phonetic theory that defines the notion "possible sentence"' (AT 31) (cf. 2.70; 7.20). Yet a sentence is surely not a *phonetic* unit, and Chomsky himself says it is 'futile' to 'state principles of sentence construction in terms of phonemes' (SS 59f) (but cf. 7.46).

11. For 'easy' 'choice', 'competing hypotheses should be "scattered" in value' – 'a major empirical constraint on a theory'; Chomsky even considers 'specifying' 'integers' for 'the value' of 'a grammar' (AT 61f, 44, 31). He suggests that 'a numerical measure of valuation' could come from 'the degree of linguistically significant generalizations', i.e., 'a set of rules' being 'replaced by a single rule', or from 'length', i.e. 'number of symbols' (AT 42, SS 53f). But AT makes no attempt to demonstrate this.

12. Chomsky unexpectedly questions whether 'behaviourist tendencies' belong to 'empiricism at all' (AT 206) – a move either for dividing the enemy or for leaving room to mend his 'empirical' fences while denouncing behaviourism. The 'vacuity of Skinner's scheme' lies partly in his notion of 'reinforcement'; 'he does not enumerate rewards' and the 'reinforcing stimulus' can be merely 'hoped for or imagined' (AT 204f) (cf. Chomsky 1959: 37f).

13. Compare also: 'even this very simple sentence' ('"sincerity may frighten John"') 'is the result of a transformational development from a complex basis' (AT 186).

14. I cannot quite see how 'placing the logical subject and object early' in a sentence counts as 'iconic' (AT 11), at least not as the term is used in semiotics. See 9.56 and 9.81 for different accounts.

15. He also suggests that people use 'special phonemic features' of 'stress and intonation' when 'reading non-grammatical strings' (SS 35nf), though stress and intonation are usually counted as prosodic, not phonemic features.

16. This phrase became standard in linguistics, but 'indefinite', which Chomsky uses at times (SS 49; AT 6, 15f), might be a better term for language sets of all kinds (cf. 2.32, 65; 3.6; 4.69; 7.16, 96; 9.18, 24, 62). A grammar in which the number of options and the length of sentences are indeed infinite will explode (cf. Woods 1970; 10.79).

17. The 'simple linear method' of 'generating' a 'level from left to right' is 'rejected' on the grounds of 'complexity' of other kinds (SS 24nf).

18. These 'terms and notations are all borrowed from concatenation algebras' (cf. Rosenbloom 1950) (AT 222). Why they should apply to language is suggested in Note 26.

19. Of these, the idea of a 'word level' is not pursued, probably because words are replaced by the more abstract and less richly associative 'lexical formatives' (cf. 7.70f, 73; 12.29). Morphology is left in limbo (cf. 7.46, 75, 7[20]). Phonetics and phonology are conflated (see Notes 27 and 32).

20. 'Morphophonemics' (the topic of Chomsky's 1951 master's thesis on Hebrew) 'states the phonemic structure of morphemes' (SS 32; cf. SS 57, 109). The three-part AT model (syntax, semantics, phonetics, cf. 7.56) leaves no place for this level.

21. But the demand is relaxed for 'morphophonemic rules' (SS 32f). In my own

discussion, I omit Chomsky's letters (like 'X', 'Y', 'Σ' for a 'string', 'grammar', etc.), which, though they also started a fashion in linguistics, don't add anything substantive.

22. 'Only a single element can be rewritten' in a 'rule' if we are to 'recover properly the phrase structure of derived sentences'; compare the restriction to 'only recoverable deletions' (SS 29; AT 138). 'Only' 'grammars with terminal strings' 'describe some language' (versus an 'empty language containing no sentences') (SS 30) (cf. 6.35). In AT, intermediate 'strings' of 'grammatical formatives and complex symbols are' 'preterminal strings'; 'terminal' ones are 'formed' by the 'sequence of transformations' and by the 'insertion of lexical formatives' via 'lexical rules' (AT 84, SS 91, i.r.) (cf. 7.74, 80, 82).

23. Chomsky needs 'a very general definition of linguistic level' to give one to his 'transformations' (SS 47). Later, he assigns them a 'component' within the 'syntactic component' (cf. 7.76).

24. AT says, however, that the 'passive marker' 'has no independent semantic interpretation' once the 'passive transformation' is made 'obligatory' and hence 'non-stylistic' (AT 223) (cf. 7.55).

25. In 'a transformational derivation', 'rules' apply '"bottom up"' by doing the 'embedded phrase markers' before those in which they're embedded (AT 143; cf. SS 37). But Chomsky finds 'no known cases of ordering among generalized embedding transformations' or of 'singulary transformations that must apply to a matrix sentence before a sentence transform is embedded in it' (AT 133).

26. 'Proponents of *set-systems*', claiming these to be 'more "abstract" than concatenation systems', want to 'study grammatical relations' 'independently of order' and treat the latter as only 'a phenomenon' in 'surface structure' (AT 124). But Chomsky says (without citing any) that there is 'empirical' 'evidence' 'in favour of concatenation systems' (AT 125) (cf. Note 18).

27. Even for 'phonemic distinctness', 'in practice every linguist uses' 'simple' 'non-semantic devices' (SS 96) (cf. 2.70; 4.26, 28; 6.43; 8.46). In any case, the AT model puts 'phonetic' and 'semantic' at opposite ends.

28. In passing, Chomsky hopes that 'the meaning of words can be at least in part reduced' to 'reference of expressions' (cf. Goodman 1949, 1953) (SS 102fn). Yet 'semantic reference' appears in AT only as a factor which 'facilitates syntax-learning but does not affect the manner', and as a factor of 'sameness' in 'reflexivization' (AT 33, 226).

29. The nonsense elements (or blanks) in such demonstrations signal the 'productivity or "open-endedness"' of the categories' they stand for, and not 'any presumed feature of meaning' (SS 105).

30. 'Surface structures' can at most 'reveal 'statistical tendencies' (cf. Greenberg 1963) (AT 118), which Chomsky mistrusts (SS 17, n) (cf. 7.38, 90; 7^{42}).

31. But he wants the 'functional notions' 'analysed as purely formal' ones in 'the theory of grammar', e.g., 'defined' by 'rewriting rules' (SS 104) (cf. 7.48).

32. Demanding a *'phonetic'* reading from a *'phonological'* component and thus blurring a distinction made by earlier linguists (cf. 2.68; 4.30; 6.43; 8.70; 11.80) may be intended to get close to the 'surface' and to tie in with the claimed 'universality' of the 'phonetic feature' system (7.20; 7^{10}; cf. 2.70; 12.26). But the 'rules' Chomsky shows could specify only phonological features, not the motor programmes for performing articulation or audition (cf. MacNeilage 1970, 1980).

33. And their proposal is 'further simplified' here, since making the semantic level 'non-generative' means it needs no 'transformations' or '"projection rules"' (AT 136).

34. The 'lexicon' will also enter such fixed 'phrases as "take for granted"' as 'single

lexical items', although 'morphology' mixes here with issues 'beyond the word level' (AT 190). Many such phrases admit of 'applying familiar transformational rules', and Chomsky 'sees no way, for the present, to give a thoroughly satisfactory treatment'. On the issues of morphology versus syntax, see also 2.55, 61; 3.34f; 4.61ff; 5.53f; 6.49; 8.57; 9.31; 10.35; 11.77; 12.28.

35. Following 'a distinction' that is 'formally well defined' and yet 'correlates' with 'language use', 'the 'context-sensitive subcategorization rules' are further divided into 'strict subcategorization rules' and 'selectional rules'; these classify 'a lexical category' either by its 'frame of category symbols', or by 'syntactic features' in 'specified positions in the sentence', respectively (AT 113). For example, a 'rule' might put an 'auxiliary' between 'the verb' and 'the immediately preceding noun' (AT 113, 107). Or, 'the rule that introduces Nouns into the grammar' – 'NP → (Det) N(S')' – yields 'the categories' of 'Common Nouns' (with a 'Determiner'), 'Proper Nouns' (without one), and 'Nouns with sentential Complements' (AT 100). Thus, 'selectional restrictions determine grammatical relations' and 'seem more natural', 'avoiding' 'problems' like the 'pseudorelation Subject–Object' (AT 113f, 73f; cf. SS 79, 104; AT 97, 118, 123).

36. C.C. Fries (1951), whom SS and AT utterly ignore, had the same idea of designating word classes with numbers, but the discipline wouldn't go along (5[39]).

37. If 'the paradigmatic solution' is 'correct', 'we must allow the transformational component to contain rules that alter or expand a matrix of features' for 'a lexical item', e.g., for 'agreement', instead of just 'introducing' 'non-lexical formatives' (AT 174f).

38. Chomsky conceals this tactic somewhat by omitting his own name from the index. In SS, he acted as his own source by constantly referring us to his 'mimeographed' dissertation for refinements: 'a more careful formulation' of 'the theory of grammar', 'a detailed analysis' of 'order among the rules', 'a workable notion of degree of grammaticalness' 'in purely formal terms', 'methods of evaluating grammars in terms of formal properties of simplicity', 'a very natural general definition of linguistic level', and so on (SS 39n, 35n, 43n, 55n 47n). But mimeographs were hard to get in 1957, and the work wasn't published until 1975, which hardly speaks for its urgency and value.

39. Despite claims for the 'universality' of base categories, English-based entities like 'determiner', 'Article', or 'definite' turn up in these diagrammed 'phrase markers' (e.g., AT 107ff). Since they vary widely or are completely absent in many languages, such as Chinese, articles should be an obvious 'surface' category (cf. 7.19; 10.44).

40. The term 'ultimate(ly)' quite often turns up in similar issues bearing on theory versus data (SS 11, 47, 56, 62, 110; AT 21, 117, 128, 208) (cf. 7.9, 18, 51, 64, 85).

41. Chomsky speculates that 'the language acquisition system may be fully functional only during a critical period of mental development' (AT 206). Bloomfield, in contrast, conjectured that 'to the end of his life, the speaker keeps doing the very things which make up infantile language-learning' (BL 46) (cf. 4.12).

42. Further motives include discrediting 'statistical' 'Markov' models of English, justifying Chomsky's distaste for 'statistics of usage', and supporting the tenet that 'grammar is autonomous and independent of meaning' (SS 106; AT 212; SS 17) (cf. 7.38, 57).

43. He is at least circumspect enough not to 'imply that the functions of language acquisition are carried out by entirely separate components' of 'the physical brain' (AT 207) (cf. 3.9; 8[17], 8[20]).

Chapter 8

J.R. Firth[1]

8.1 Although John Rupert Firth helped to found linguistics in Great Britain, he published no major theoretical book. He wrote two short popular books early in his career, intended to arouse general interest in language study – *Speech* (1930) and *Tongues of Men* (1937) – but otherwise only assorted occasional papers eventually collected in two volumes, one posthumous. According to Frank Palmer, who edited the second, Firth was rumoured to be 'preparing a book entitled *Principles of Linguistics*', but 'among the papers he left at his death was not one sheet' of it (P2 2). So I will essay to reconstruct Firth's theory and method from the four extant volumes, whose materials were designed for a variety of general or specific purposes and audiences. Despite vacillations and contradictions,[2] Firth's position remained fairly consistent during the three decades summarized here. The popular books, according to Peter Strevens (editor of their 1964 re-issue), already contained 'the seeds of a great many concepts' used in Firth's 'subsequent academic works on linguistics' (TMS viii).

8.2 In Palmer's estimate, Firth 'alone pioneered' 'linguistics' 'in Britain', developing 'his own original brand' and many 'exciting new ideas' (P2 1). Firth held 'the first chair in general linguistics' in England, which 'was established in the University of London in 1944 at the School of Oriental and African Studies' (P1 v; P2 96). He remained, Strevens says, largely 'unknown to linguistics in the American tradition' (TMS vii), aside from Pike (cf. Kachru 1981);[3] in the US, 'British ideas' were deemed 'a variant of Bloomfieldian linguistics' or even 'a deviant consequence of having misunderstood American linguistics' (TMS ix; cf. P2 2). Firth did espouse some ideas also encountered in Bloomfield,[4] but this was mainly due to 'the intellectual climate' and 'the context of science' in the Anglo-Saxon world at the time (cf. P1 169). Sometimes Firth showed solidarity with American linguists, but at other times depicted their work as narrow or misguided and fundamentally different from his own.[5]

8.3 Unlike our other theorists (even pious Pike), Firth salutes 'the importance of **religion**' 'in the history of Western linguistics' alongside 'science', notably Christian missions like the 'Sacra Congregatio de

"Propaganda Fide"' and the 'Summer Institute of Linguistics' that 'trains missionaries' (TMS 11, 136, 138, 55f, 59, 107; P1 164; P2 162) (cf. 5.2). At 'the Third International Congress of Linguists' in 1933, the Pope 'said that the whole redemption was the work of the "Word"', and Firth alludes to legends and holy books portraying language as the invention of a god (TMS 13, 3–6, 15f). But he recognizes 'religious and linguistic expansion' as a 'supplement' to 'more material interests' (TMS 59). After all, 'world languages' are 'built on blood, money, sinews, and suffering in the pursuit of power' and made by 'men of action': 'statesmen, soldiers, sailors', not just 'missionaries' (TMS 71). Firth is thus sceptical about 'universal languages' invented by 'amateur **grammarians**' and 'linguists trying to undermine Babel', the 'most successful' being Esperanto (TMS 70, 11, 49, 66, 68) (cf. 8.6). He wants to reserve the role for English (cf. 8.12).

8.4 Being an Orientalist, Firth also salutes the dawn of language study in India and 'the discovery of Sanskrit by the West' (TMS 147; P1 111; P2 114, 1168) (cf. 2.5; 4.4, 4^3; 8.74).[6] Admittedly, 'the ancient Hindu grammarians, and later the Arabs, were not interested in vernacular' but in 'preserving the purity of sacred languages from vulgar mutilation and defilement' (TMS 147) (cf. 4.40). Much 'word-craft' has similarly been 'transmitted by privileged elites: elders, priests, clerks, sheiks, mandarins, bureaucrats'; some 'men of "letters"' even 'became rulers' (TMS 48, 146). Their descendants are 'all those who believe in arbitrary linguistic standards' and 'purity', and adopt a 'static, mainly prescriptive or normative' 'point of view' from which 'linguistic evolution' gets 'evaluated' as 'decay', 'degeneration', or 'corruption' (TMS 147f) (cf. 2.49).

8.5 Still, Firth thinks 'the great languages of older civilizations' were 'well served by grammarians', e.g., 'Pāṇini for Sanskrit', 'Dionysius for Greek', 'Priscian for Latin', or 'Al Khalil for Arabic' (P1 216) (cf. Robins 1951) (cf. 8.19, 58, 88). The trouble arose later when 'Latin grammar was misapplied to an ever-increasing number of languages', along with 'Greek logic and metaphysics' (P1 216) (cf. 2.5; 3.50; 4.4; 5.24; 6.5; 9.25; 11.20f; 12.7, 16). Today, the 'modern technician' 'finds traditional grammatical categories logically and philosophically pretentious, and a nuisance in practice' – a 'medieval scholastic instrument' 'out of harmony with general scientific theory' (TMS 87, 136). They 'deal with' 'form and meaning' 'in the vaguest of logico-philosophical terms', and even 'some linguists follow' this 'method' (TMS 136; P2 12) (cf. 2.5; 3.4; 4.4f; 8.16; 11.7, 38, 64). Yet 'traditional logic' 'shows no connection with or understanding of language', or 'rational use of words and sentences in everyday life' (TMS 104) (cf. 12.17).[7]

8.6 Firth also mistrusts 'comparative, historical' '**philology**' with its affinities to 'evolutionism', 'Darwinian' 'ideas', 'biological analogies' and 'the Romantic Reaction' (TMS 147f; P1 16f; cf. P1 139) (cf. 2.5f, 13; 4.73f; 6.5; 8.15, 40; 11.20; 12.13). Like Sweet and Malinowski, he prefers the 'analysis' of 'living languages', at least until 'descriptive linguistics' and 'functionalism' enable a 'reformulation of problems in comparative and historical work' (P2 144f; P1 120, 218) (cf. 11.99). He also sees the 'quest' for the 'origins' of language as 'largely futile', citing the 1866 'Statutes' of the 'Société de Linguistique' against 'accepting any communication concerning the origin of language or the creation of a universal language' (TMS 144) (cf. 8.3, 18; 2.47; 3.67; 11.17f). Instead of 'going back' and getting 'further and further away from the habits we know and can observe', we should 'look for the origins of language in the way we learn and use it' in 'our everyday social life' (TMS 189, 26) (cf. 9.12). Using quaint 'reduplicative nicknames' ('bow-wow', 'pooh-pooh', 'ding-dong', 'yo-he-ho', 'ta-ta'), he glides over some 'theories of the origin of speech' from activities in the natural environment (TMS 25f, 141ff). Yet an account he favours is biological and Darwinian too: 'the larynx' first ' "subserved the functions of locomotion, prehension, olifaction, and deglutition" ' and the 'voice' was then developed for its 'survival value' in 'leaving the hands and eyes free, travelling well', and 'conveying identity' (TMS 145; cf. Negus 1949) (cf. 4.34).

8.7   In modern times, Firth sees another grave flaw in language study. Though 'the distinction between "educated" and "uneducated" English dates' from the 'seventeenth century' and its 'grammarians', 'the Education Act of 1870' was decisive, leading to 'execrable' 'grammars for the young' and to 'much prejudice and difficulty of intercourse', e.g., when the 'schoolmaster's "educated" speech made children ashamed of the speech of their parents' (TMS 195; P1 160) (cf. 4.40). In 'traditional school grammars, the rules' are 'based on value judgments usually deprecatory' and on 'puritan' 'taboos', e.g., against 'using a preposition to end a sentence with' (P2 120, 23) (cf. 4.5).[8] In America, the 'Pure-English crusade' greets 'the living language' with ' "sneers and prohibitions" '; 'according to most writers on the subject, the speech habits of about 90 per cent of the English-speaking world are bad' (TMS 200). In return, the 'artificiality' of ' "good English" ' prevents ' "schools and colleges from turning out pupils who can put their ideas into words with simplicity and intelligibility" ' (TMS 201; cf. Mencken 1919) (cf. 4.85ff).

8.8   This grim situation provides the backdrop to Firth's 'appeal for more disciplined modern linguistic studies', including 'grammar', 'in the English schools of the universities' to accompany the 'switch-over to science and technology just ahead of us' (P2 117) (cf. 4.6). 'The problem of establishing a grammar of the main languages of life' must 'be dealt with at the level of science', 'by general or theoretical linguistics' (P2 115). 'In the journals of the future Institute of Language, competent technicians will give routine indications of any common or influential linguistic phenomena which are "definitely bogus" ' (e.g., 'the British transmogrification of the ablative absolute, and all the rest of the "bogus" grammar which teachers of classics impose' on 'vernacular languages'); 'grammars' and 'language books will be "X-rayed" and the results stated with as little feeling as possible' (TMS 105; cf. TMS 87).

8.9   'Clearing the litter' of 'generations of pedagogical mediocrities' should provide 'more wholesome surroundings' for 'children' to do 'linguistic exercises' (TMS 105). 'In schools', 'children should be shown how interesting it can be to talk in an orderly way' 'about their language as a vital part of their experience' (P2 179, 120). Also, research can explore 'the language of social control' in 'education' and 'apprenticeship'; 'properly trained observers in nursery schools and all children's institutions' can study 'speech habits in formation' (P2 179; TMS 151). And finally, we can 'encourage open and natural use of local forms of speech' and 'literature', not just the 'Received English' of 'the elite of the public school class' or a 'purely negative' English 'free from unusual features' – a 'strained form of speech' that 'masks social and local origin' (TMS 200, 196f, 18, 200).

8.10 Meanwhile, Firth is 'shocked to realize that we English, largely responsible for the future of the only real world language' and 'representatives of the civilization of all Europe in the four quarters of the globe, have up to the present made no adequate provision for the study of practical linguistic problems' (TMS 211). 'Some national provision should be made for more modern linguistic sciences on a scale commensurate with the wealth and position of Britain and America' (TMS 138). By showing that 'linguistics' is a 'more important social science', we may 'secure an endowment' for an 'Institute of Linguistic Research' to address 'educational, administrative, and social problems throughout the Empire' (TMS 151, 211; cf. P1 172) (cf. 12.14).

8.11 Firth patriotically advocates language study because of 'the vastness of our Empire' with 'so many religions, faiths and tongues' (P2 144; TMS 138). 'Great voyages of discovery' led to 'the widening of the linguistic horizon', 'the study of exotic alphabets', and 'World English' (TMS 54; P1 103f). Even now, Firth sees 'our young men and women' 'coming back from their voyages', and predicts 'another revival of learning' (P1 103, 119, 141) – a wistful hope for us in the 1990s, when British education has been brutally cut back by Conservative politicians. But we can still keenly appreciate the academic and political policy behind Firth's vision of 'a new awareness everywhere of the powers and problems of speech and language' (P1 141).

8.12 Firth hints that linguistics might reward investment by helping to unify the British Empire through language, and to ensure the worldwide pre-eminence of English. He proclaims that 'the use of the English language today is the greatest social force in the whole world, and we in England should lead the way in training young people', including 'all foreigners who wish to join this active world fellowship', 'towards a critical understanding of language behaviour' (TMS 137f). Otto Jespersen 'found modern English the most advanced language in the history of mankind'; this 'world language' spoken by 'the successful English and American peoples' and vital to 'the spread of European civilization and the culture of the white race',[9] should be 'praised and used' by 'men of learning as well as men of affairs' (TMS 209, 148). 'For the sake of mankind it is to be hoped that English will drown the others; let all men of goodwill do their utmost to strengthen its service of mankind' (TMS 54).

8.13 In contrast to the 'older order of things', when 'knowledge and culture were the privilege of a small international elite using one international language of learning' while 'the vast masses were left in the dark', Firth sees 'the days of self-determination and popular culture' dawning, when 'every member of any considerable speech community should have the opportunity of cultivating' the 'mind' 'in his mother tongue' (TMS 209f; cf. TMS 148f, P2 132) (cf. 8.4). But he finds the 'social and cultural value' of a language with fewer than 100,000 speakers 'extremely doubtful'; 'below 10,000 it almost ceases to be of any value outside the most primitive forms of group action' (TMS 208). In contrast, English is said to be 'spoken by 150 million people now [i.e. 1930]' (swelling to '180 million' two pages later) and is 'the official language of 540 million', a figure including all India so as to surpass Chinese with '430 million' (TMS 205, 207).[10] These numbers fuel Firth's belief that 'English is the only practicable world language' and can be 'taught in a normalized form' ('described by competent authorities') 'the world over as a second language', being 'easier to learn than French or German and much more useful' (TMS 136, 200).[11]

8.14 By 'regarding language from a world point of view', we can 'carry out useful language work' by 'declassicalizing in both East and West' and discarding the 'distinction' 'between primitive and civilized' 'languages' (P1 171; P2 135; cf. TMS 141). 'To deal with the theory of language, the Western scholar must de-Europeanize himself', and 'the Englishman must de-Anglicize himself' (P2 96) (cf. 2.32; 3.5, 50; 12.42). Firth thus thinks it 'all to the good' to have the 'chair of General Linguistics' placed 'at the School of Oriental and African Studies', and hails the 'enormous scope in the application of general linguistics' 'for the development of the free countries of Asia and Africa' following 'their rise' (from colonialism!) (P1 171; P2 135). In 'under-developed countries', 'nationalism leads to a longing for linguistic equality', and 'the leaders are quick to realize the value of linguistics' 'for their national aims' (P2 131f, 135f).[12] Here, the 'general linguist' must 'offer help and guidance', though 'the fields of research' 'cannot be fully exploited, even if all the linguists of the world were to unite' (P2 135f).

8.15 Firth's national pride is conspicuous also in his attention to the work of past centuries. He lauds the 'weighty contributions' of 'English linguists', grammarians, rhetoricians, phoneticians, and orthographers (including shorthand inventors), since the time of Elizabeth I or indeed since 'Ælfric's Latin Grammar' 'in English' (P1 103, 100f). He cites such 'pioneers' as Thomas More, Thomas Wilson (1553), John Cheke, Thomas Smith (1568), John Hart (1569), Roger Ascham, William Bullokar (1580a, b), Timothe Bright (1588), Alexander Hume, Charles Butler (1634), Cave Beck (1657), William Holder (1669), John Wilkins (1688), John Wallis, George Dalgarno, Elisha Coles (1692), Thomas Gurney, John Byrom, William Blanchard, Isaac Pitman, William Jones, Walter Haddon, Richard Temple (1899a, b), Joseph Wright, the Bell family, and above all his idol Henry Sweet (our 'pioneer leader' and 'greatest philologist', 'one of the cleverest thinkers on language', etc.), to whom Firth 'loved to be compared' (Palmer) (P1 103, 100f, 110; P2 54, 137; cf. P1 168, 92–120, 166f; TMS 12,

63–66).[13] Then, too, Firth outdoes American theorists in citing early American linguists before Whitney: Samuel Haldeman, John Pickering, Peter Stephen DuPonceau, James Smithson, Alexander Bryan Johnson, and so on, plus grammarians and language planners like Benjamin Franklin, Noah Webster, and Lindley Murray; and he is quick to point out if they came from, or moved to, Great Britain (cf. P1 7, 157–166, 116–119).

8.16 Though his geographical and historical scope is expansive, Firth is uncertain about how broad his discipline should be. On the one hand, he feels 'the linguistic sciences' should seek 'alliance' with 'the biological and social sciences' and 'develop proper semantic relationships' with all 'sciences of man' (P1 143, 139) (cf. 9.7; 12.14). As 'a social science', 'linguistics' 'is ahead of the others in theoretical formulation and technique of statement'; its 'findings' 'are basic and must be carefully studied' (P2 159, 189) (cf. 8.33; 12.21). Remarking that 'electronics has become a key subject', and 'mathematics and physics have always ruled us',[14] he sees 'linguistics of the future becoming their opposite number'; 'universities will encourage its study as one of the more austere disciplines fit to be ancillary' to 'sciences which promise us miraculous machines' (P2 95). Besides, linguists 'share' an 'interest in the meaning of meaning' with 'sociologists', 'biologically oriented psychologists', and 'philosophers' in the 'empiricist tradition' of Locke, Hume, Moore, Russell, and Wittgenstein (P2 96) (cf. 11.97). Indeed, 'during the next fifty years general linguistics may supplant a great deal of philosophy; the process has begun', e.g., in Hjelmslev's *Prolegomena* (P1 168, P2 44) (cf. 12.16). In addition, it should be 'easier' for 'linguists' to 'acquire sufficient psychology and sociology' than for 'a psychologist or sociologist to acquire the necessary linguistic technique' (P1 28) (cf. 12[15]).

8.17 On the other hand, Firth is gratified that 'linguistics in Europe' has 'recently' undergone 'a revolution in status' and 'become an autonomous discipline', not having its 'point of departure in another science' (P2 130; P1 177, 181, 190) (cf. 12.9–20).[15] We incur a 'great handicap' by 'depending' on 'prior disciplines', such as 'logic, rhetoric, philosophy', 'psychology, sociology', 'biology', 'pedagogy', 'metaphysics', or 'literary criticism' (P2 130; P1 181, 191). Nor should 'linguists' 'play second fiddle to cybernetics, communication theory, digital computers, speech machines, or telecommunications engineering' (P2 130). And 'our studies of speech and language', as well as our 'educational methodology, have been dominated far too much by psychology and logic'; 'individual psychology' 'emphasizes' 'incommunicable' 'experience', and 'logic has given us bad grammar and taken the heart out of language' (P1 186; cf. TMS 175) (cf. 4.5; 8.5, 7). So despite 'some serious misapprehensions among linguists about modern logic', it cannot 'form an integral part of linguistics of any school' (P1 217) (cf. 2.5, 35, 84; 3.23; 5.7, 10, 41, 49, 54, 56; 8.36; 12.17). Besides, 'philosophers are still unaware of the developments in linguistics during the last thirty years', and their 'analyses' of 'language' and 'meaning' are 'not linguistic' (P2 70, 85) (cf. 3.62; 4.4f, 51; 5.3, 5, 10, 13; 10.40; 12.16).

8.18 Such assertions cloud Firth's avowal that the 'branches of linguistics

cannot be seen in proper proportions and perspective' without a 'fundamental **philosophy** of language' (TMS 3). Little can be made of playful,
offhand remarks like 'for his philosophy, the linguist need go no further
than the second chapter of Genesis', i.e., the 'naming' of 'creation' by the
'magic power of the voice', the more so as Firth elsewhere chides 'the
confusion of speech and life, race and language dating back to the book of
Genesis' (P1 35; TMS 76). Firth's allusions to the 'magic' of 'language' –
projecting from 'linguistic' 'studies of the magical word' to the thesis that
'language can be regarded as magic in the most general sense', with
'miraculous' 'creative functions' (TMS 23, 32, 46, 113, 135; P1 185; P2 155)
– chiefly reflect his reaching for popular effect and his perplexity (sharpened
by his anti-mentalism, cf. 8.24, 41) about how the processing of language
works.

8.19 A further check to philosophy arises if 'it is not the task of
linguistics to say what language is' (P1 177) (cf. 9.1; 11.16, 39). 'The
techniques of linguistics have not been developed to deal with language in
general human terms' – a limitation Firth relates to Saussure's 'opinion that
"le langage"' is ' "inconnaissable"' (P1 190nf; cf. P2 110) (cf. 2.19). Firth
can envision at most a 'general physiology of utterance', 'perception',
'urges, and drives in our human nature' (P1 191, 186), areas favoured for
their generality and their amenability to behaviourism (cf. 8.22f, 25ff). We
need 'a general linguistic theory applicable to particular linguistic descriptions' and 'language problems', 'not a theory of universals for general
linguistic description' (P2 202, 190, 130f, P1 xii) (cf. 7.19f; 8.60; 12.18).

8.20 Another peril Firth vehemently denounces is the 'duality' or
'dualism' between 'mind and body', ' "signifiant et signifié"', expression and
content', 'language and thought', 'thought' and 'expression', 'thought and
word', 'idea and word', etc., dating from Descartes and upheld by 'Swiss,
French, and Scandinavian linguists' (TMS 20, 150; P1 19, 192, 227; P2 84,
90, 128, 203) (cf. 2.25f; 12.10). Instead, Firth wants 'general linguistics' to
adopt a 'psychosomatic' 'approach' to 'mind and body taken together and
acting in specific living conditions' (P2 207). We must look to 'the whole
man thinking and acting as a whole, in association with his fellows' (P1 19,
189, 225). Just as 'the study of the whole man by biologists, anatomists,
physiologists', 'neurologists, and pathologists is a commonplace of science',
'the linguist' 'must assume that normal linguistic behaviour as a whole is a
meaningful effort' for 'maintaining appropriate patterns of life' (P1 225)
(cf. 8.25ff, 47, 74; 12.13).

8.21 Firth thus insists that 'the human body' is 'the primary field of
human experience' and 'expression', yet 'continuous with the rest of the
world' (P2 199, 91) (cf. 4.8, 10, 13; 5.27, 42, 80; 10.12). Both 'the body' and
'the world' are 'a set of structures and systems' we can expect to discover in
'the whole of our linguistic behaviour' viewed as 'a network of relations
between people, things, and events' (P2 90; cf. P1 143). Yet to say (with
Whitehead) that 'voice-produced sound is organically rooted in living
beings' or (with Russell) that 'meaning can only be understood if we treat

language as a bodily habit', raises problems if 'most' 'organic processes' are 'intimate and secret' (P2 206, 90, 199; TMS 150). 'We need to know a good deal more of the action of the body from within, and especially of the nervous and endocrine systems', if 'human knowledge' is 'a function of that action' (P1 143; cf. P1 142, 188) (cf. 4.18f; 12.12).

8.22 All the same, Firth 'views speech' as 'a bodily habit having a physical basis' within 'the central machinery for the control and coordination of behaviour' (TMS 152f) (cf. 8.53, 69). As an 'act', 'speaking' points not only to 'the functioning of the brain', but to 'localized speech centres with all their connected processes', plus 'movements of the face, head, arms, hands', 'legs', 'diaphragm' and 'abdomen', and 'general bodily gesture' (TMS 152, 154) (cf. 5.44).[16] Some 'influential schools of modern physiology and psychology' hope for 'a purely mechanical or materialistic explanation of all thought' in terms of its 'motor accompaniment' (TMS 178). John B. Watson (1925) vowed 'there is no such thing as thinking', 'only "inner speech" or the incipient activity of laryngeal and other speech processes' (TMS 150, 179; P2 171) (cf. 3.10; 4.9; 5.39; 12.12, 12[21]).[17]

8.23 However, Firth stops short of 'Professor Pavlov of Leningrad' by arguing that whereas 'instinctive' 'habits' 'require no learning', being 'controlled by innate settings of the nervous system', 'all characteristically human habits', including 'speech', 'involve learning by experience', 'adjustment', 'experimental attunement, retention' 'recognition', and 'adaptability' (TMS 180f) (cf. 7.30). Following the mood of the times, Firth may portray 'words' as 'stimulus-response acts', and 'spoken sentences' as 'successions of directive stimuli' to 'evoke a suitable habitual response' (TMS 175) (cf. 4.10–14; 5.67). But he stipulates that 'habits' 'are based on' 'flexibility of response, substitutions, replacements', and 'variations', whereby 'intelligent behaviour' can 'adjust' 'to our environment'; 'if intelligibility depended on a narrow reflex connection between speaking and hearing, we should all speak exactly alike and be no better than poultry' (TMS 181, 23).[18] Besides, 'no two people pronounce exactly alike, and most' 'use more than one style'; 'familiar sounds are constantly being made' in 'partly new contexts' (TMS 181f) (cf. 4.16; 5.38, 47; 8.77).

8.24 Firth's strong concern for 'the bodily system, personality, and language through life' (P1 188) leads him to capsule off the mental side, creating a fresh dualism. He applauds 'Malinowski's warning': '"all mental states" "postulated as occurrences within the private consciousness of man" are "outside the realm of science"'; and '"there is nothing more dangerous than to imagine that language is a process running parallel and exactly corresponding to mental process" and that it "duplicates the mental reality"' (P2 158, 156) (cf. 5.10; 12.11). Hence, 'general linguistics' must not study 'language as an instrument of thought' or 'an organ of the mind' (P2 206; cf. P2 97ff) (but cf. 3.10ff; 5.69; 6.6; 7.10; 11.17ff, 22; 12.10, 14). Firth says 'we do not deny the concept of mind, but we have no methodology or technique for studying it' and 'no technical language for mentalistic treatment'; nor should we 'embrace materialism to avoid a foolish bogey of mentalism', as Bloomfield did (P2 207; P1 192, 167; P2 175) (cf. 4.8; 7.93). Nevertheless, Firth's horror of 'taking refuge in mentalistic psychology' (TMS 90) and his aversion to meanings apart from language – he calls them 'naked ideas', as if their exposure were indecent (P2 75f, 78f, 81f, 85, 197) – create important blind spots (cf. 8.50, 81ff).

8.25 He is even reluctant to 'regard language as expressive or communicative', lest he 'imply it is an instrument of inner mental states', 'thoughts', or 'ideas', which are 'mysterious' because 'not observable' (TMS 173, 135; P2 169f, 187). 'Rather than as a countersign of thought', Firth (with Malinowski and against Sweet, Whitney, and Hermann Paul) wants to 'regard language as a mode of **action**' (P2 148; TMS 150). 'Language' is thus 'a way of doing things and getting things done', of 'behaving and making others behave' 'in relation to' 'surroundings and situations' (P1 35, 31, 28f) (cf. 4.88; 5.7ff, 12, 26f, 50; 8.20ff, 27, 46; 9.7ff; 10.5f, 11f). 'By regarding words as acts, events, habits, we limit our inquiry to what is objective and observable in the group life' (TMS 173) (cf. 12.12, 14, 45).

8.26 'A normal complete act of speech is a pattern of group behaviour', 'of common verbalizations' of the 'situational' and 'experiential contexts of the participants' (TMS 173; cf. P1 35; TMS 135, 152). Admittedly, the 'pattern' is 'without clearly defined boundaries'; 'it is difficult to isolate and describe individual speech behaviour'. Yet there are 'fine distinctions in speech behaviour determined by typical recurrent social situations', wherein 'locutions' are 'organs or functions' (P1 75) (cf. 9.8, 40). Due to 'contextual elimination', 'what you say raises the threshold against most of the language of your companion and leaves only a limited opening' for a 'likely range of responses' (P1 32; cf. TMS 94). 'Conversation in our everyday life' is 'narrowly conditioned' by 'culture' and by 'small speech groups, such as the family, caste, or class'; its 'ritualistic give-and-take' entails 'grave social risks' for 'unexpected and highly individual' 'behaviour' that seems 'unusual', 'misdirected', 'tactless', or 'eccentric' (P1 31, 75, TMS 181; cf. TMS 93). Moreover, 'social requirements' call for 'clarity, decency, uniformity, and correctness of utterance' (TMS 22). Indeed, 'good manners require' that 'everyday speech' be 'full of banalities and cliches'; and for many 'situations' in 'churches, law courts, or offices', 'conventionally fixed' 'words' 'bind people to a line of action' (TMS 113; P1 30) (cf. 10.97).

8.27 Firth thus sees 'the most universal forms of language behaviour' in 'routine service' and 'social ritual', not in the 'freedom' of the 'individual soul'; 'even in literature', 'extreme' 'nonconformity is rare' (TMS 94, 113; P1 28, 31) (cf. 3.38f, 64, 70). He proposes the term '**tact**' for a 'complex of manners which determines the use of fitting forms of language as functional elements of a social situation'; and the term '**set**' for a 'general pattern of behaviour' 'belonging to a social group' or 'type', including 'instincts' ('sex, hunger, fear, anger'), 'urges, sentiments, interests, abilities', 'feelings', and 'curiosity', plus a 'sense of order and system', 'fellowship', 'superiority, inferiority, snobbery', 'obligation', 'licence', 'submission', and 'domination'

(TMS 17, 89f, 95, 100) (cf. 8.19). The 'language behaviour' 'observed in the actual context of situation' 'may be regarded' as a 'manifestation' of the 'sets', which 'tune themselves automatically' to 'link selected input with appropriate output' (TMS 93). Still, the 'sense of order' – you may 'call it' 'reason, thought, intelligence, logic, genius, insight, inspiration, or just craftsmanship' – 'is always in peril of being overruled' by 'primitive feelings' 'we share with the animals' (TMS 100, 95).

8.28 If both 'language and personality are built into the body', and 'the organization of personality' 'depends on the built-in potentialities of language', then 'linguistics' must address 'the key notion' of **'personality'**, whose 'basic principles' are its 'unity, identity, and continuity' within 'the social process' and 'the creative effort and effect of speech' (P1 143, 184, 141; P2 13f) (cf. 3.70ff; 5.7, 26; 6.2, 54; 8.40, 43, 81; 9.14, 71; 10.18, 66; 11.58). Moving 'a long way from Saussure's mechanical structuralism', in which 'the speech' of 'the underdog speaking subject' 'was not the "integral and concrete object of linguistics"', Firth stresses 'the study of persons, personality and language' as 'vectors of the continuity of repetitions in the social process and the persistence of personal forces' (P1 183) (cf. 2.20; 3.1; 4.10; 9.7). Due to the 'close association between personality and social structure', he favours 'sociology' over 'individual psychology' (P1 185f) (cf. 9.7; 12.14). 'Linguistics' 'is mainly interested in persons and personalities as active participators in the creation and maintenance of cultural values', rather than as 'separate natural entities in their psycho-biological characters'. Hence, 'the study of spoken language' should 'stress the study of specific persons' over 'the collection of haphazard and colloquial oddments' from 'speakers at random' (P2 32).[19]

8.29 'The human being' is therefore to be regarded not 'as an individual', but as a 'person' 'acting in his many **social roles**', whose 'interaction' is 'a conservative force in personality' and 'society' (P2 207; P1 28f). 'The relevant forms of language' are 'the lines of the leading roles', which 'interlock' without 'conflict or serious disharmony' in 'an integrated personality', favouring 'social responsibility and stability' (P2 207; cf. P1 186). Firth chooses the terms **'idiolect'** for 'a form of language used between two personalities chiefly in one of their personal roles' versus **'monolect'** for a form limited to one person, e.g., by 'language disorder' (P2 209). Hence, he 'recommends that more attention be given to linguistics by psychoanalysts and psychiatrists', just as 'general linguistics' should 'place more emphasis on our activities, drives, needs, desires, and tendencies of the body than on mechanisms and reflexes', although it 'recognizes' them 'indirectly' (P2 209; P1 143, 225) (cf. 8.19).[20]

8.30 The breadth of concerns outlined so far should indicate why 'for any given language' 'no coherent system' 'can handle and state all the facts', and 'linguistics must be polysystemic' (P2 24; P1 121; P2 43, 200) (cf. 9.19). Firth therefore repudiates 'the monosystemic principle' 'stated by Meillet ("Chaque langue forme un système où tout se tient"') as a pretext for 'static structural formalism' and 'mechanical materialism in linguistics'; and rejects Saussure's division between ' "langue" and "parole" ' (P1 180f, 121, 144; P2 28, 41, 127, 139f) (cf.2.20; 5.7; 6.33, 46; 7.12; 8.30; 9.5; 11.12, 26, 47, 55, 67; 12.36).[21] Firth hopes for a 'synthesis of contemporary theories': 'we are *all* right', not merely 'dogmatic interpretations of Saussure' (P2 24, i.a.). 'Polysystemic' 'hypotheses' may not render 'problems easier' than 'the monosystemic analysis based on a paradigmatic technique of opposition', but may render 'the highly complex patterns of language clearer' within 'the plurality of systems' that are 'not necessarily linear' nor related to 'successive fractions or segments of the time-track of instances of speech' (P1 137; cf. P1 147) (cf. 12.35).

8.31 In this connection, Firth takes pains to deny being 'a "structuralist" ', a school he traces back to Baudouin de Courtenay, Saussure, and Meillet (P2 145, 41). '*Structuralist*' work 'forms only one part' of '*structural* linguistics' that from his 'point of view' 'aims at employing all technical resources systematically for multiple statements of meaning in the appropriate linguistic terms' (P2 145, 44, 50, 3) (cf. 8.45, 48f). In contrast, 'structuralism' 'emphasizes segmentation and phonemics' and 'excludes meaning' (P2 47; cf. P2 44, 48, 129) (cf. 4.14ff; 5.61; 7.56ff; 12.27). Originally 'an established technique for reducing languages to writing' 'in ethnographic studies of the American Indian', 'phonemics for its own sake' became 'a theoretical discipline' – a trend 'like generalizing pure mathematics from practical arithmetic' (P2 129). Moreover, structuralism seeks 'a linguistic mathematics or a completely axiomatized science', which in Firth's estimate 'will not be found workable as a truly empirical science' but will 'become a dead technical language' (P2 47; cf. P2 43) (cf. 12.15).[22] Nor is he deeply impressed by the 'use of logical and statistical theories', or with displays of 'postulates and axioms' to announce 'a more scientific methodology akin to mathematics' (P2 129, 43) (cf. 8.17, 55; 12.17).

8.32 As a 'first principle', Firth recommends 'distinguishing between **structure** and **system**' (P2 186). 'Structure' is '**syntagmatic**' and 'horizontal', whereas 'system' is '**paradigmatic**' and 'vertical' (P2 186, 200) (cf. 2.30, 56, 65; 6.34; 9.3; 11.71). 'Since systems furnish values for elements of structure and since the ordering of systems depends on structure', 'the exponents of elements of structure and of terms in systems are always consistent', though not of the same 'order' – 'the term **exponent**' referring here to the actual 'shape of words or parts of words' (P2 183f) (cf. 8.53, 59, 68f; 11.86).[23] Against the Americans, Firth rejects any account in terms of 'segments in any sense'; 'elements of structure' 'share a mutual expectancy in an *order* which is not merely a *sequence*' (P2 186, 200f) (cf. 8.52, 60, 64, 69). He further postulates such an 'expectancy not only between' 'elements of discourse', but also between 'words and the surrounding living space' (P2 206). The fact that expectancy is a mentalistic notion does not disturb him, since he usually assigns it not to people but to language 'elements' like 'words and sentences' (P1 195; P2 69, 181, 186, 200, 206) (cf. 8.64).

8.33 As we might expect, Firth 'ventures to think linguistics is a group of related techniques for handling **language events**' (P1 181, 190). For 'systematic empirical analysis', 'descriptive linguistics must be practical'; 'its abstractions, fictions, inventions' must be 'designed to handle *instances* of speech, spoken or written' (P1 173) (cf. 9.4; 12.36). 'A theory derives its usefulness and validity from the aggregate of experience to which it must continually refer' (P2 168). Yet just as 'theories are inventions' or 'constructions', 'four-fifths of linguistics, including even experimental phonetics, is invention rather than discovery' (P2 124; P1 173) (cf. Panconcelli-Calzia 1947). 'Systematics' are 'ordered schematic constructs, frames of reference' or 'scaffolding' intended to 'cover' a 'field of phenomena'; they 'have no ontological status', 'being, or existence'; 'they are neither immanent nor transcendent, but just language turned back on itself' (P1 181, 190, 121, 147; P2 124) (cf. 8.23; 9.27; 12.48). 'The descriptive linguist does not work in the universe of discourse concerned with "reality"', nor ask 'whether his isolates can be said to "have an existence"' (P2 155f; cf. P2 154) (cf. 8.44; 5.12f, 28f; 6.12; 12.57). At best, such 'fictions' as 'speech, language', 'tact', 'set, and context of situation' 'have a certain practical value' (TMS 135).

8.34   Since 'we are all participants in those activities which linguistics sets out to study', and 'all linguists rely on common human experience' to 'make abstractions', 'linguistics is reflexive and introvert' (P2 169, 8; P1 121, 147) (cf. 1.8f; 11.12; 12.48). 'Each scholar makes his own selection and grouping of facts determined by his attitudes', 'theories', and 'experience of reality', and his 'statements' must 'be referred to personal and social conditions' (P2 29) (cf. 12.1, 36). So we should be 'constantly mindful of the different levels of abstraction' (P1 173). Reciprocally, Firth insists that 'there are no scientific facts until they are stated' 'in technical language' within 'a system of related statements all arising from a theory and application' (P2 30, 43, 154, 199) (cf. 12.48). He suggests we 'regard' 'facts' as 'myths' 'we believe' and 'live with', and quotes Goethe's epigram: '"the highest state would be to grasp that all facticity is already theory"' (P2 156, 146, m.t.).

8.35   For clarification, Firth distinguishes three 'methods of stating linguistic facts': (1) 'language under description' ('exemplified by texts'), (2) 'language of description' ('technical terms', 'notation', etc.), and (3) 'language of translation' (P2 49, 87, 98, 112, 149, 158, 202). We shall survey them in turn. The **language of description** is essential because linguistics can contribute to 'the progressive standardization of the universal languages of science' and the 'internationalizing of terms' (TMS 67, 121, 210). 'Sciences' try to 'frame international languages to serve their special needs', and Firth thinks it 'desirable' 'that an international technical language be developed in English for the use of linguists all over the world', even if he does 'not believe very much in conferences on standard terminology', nor in 'the internationality and universality' of 'linguistics' as 'common united knowledge in a variety of languages' (TMS 71; P1 140; P2 28ff; cf. TMS 106). 'Scholars' in some fields may 'agree that a number of alternative theories can be regarded as special cases' of one 'comprehensive theory', but 'linguistics' is 'far from' 'this happy state' (P2 29) (cf. 5.9; 12.3).

Instead, 'linguists' 'have always disagreed most about terminology and nomenclature' in their own 'technical' language (TMS 71; P2 83).

8.36 This state of affairs is aggravating, because 'linguists should be the first to control, direct, and specialize almost every word they write in linguistic analysis' and should remain 'language-conscious at all levels' (P2 34). 'Scientific terminology is in no sense self-explanatory', but 'relative and functional' (P2 120) (cf. 12.48). 'We must have orderly language to discuss language, which is obviously based on ordered relations' (P2 120). 'The accurate formal description' of 'the constituents of a language' 'demands a highly specialized technique' (TMS 87). 'The more we take humanism out of linguistics the more we must' 'examine' 'our languages and techniques of statement' to see if they are 'proper' 'for a science' (P2 34). In 'such a science', we should 'state our results not only for one another but for all who may need them' (cf. 2.88; 3.2; 12.62).

8.37 Firth himself can't decide between new terms and old ones.[24] Hjelmslev is lauded for his (probably 'unsuccessful') 'attempt' to create a 'terminology' within 'a system of thought' and 'a rigid framework in which to test a special language for linguistic analysis', so as to 'emancipate' us 'from the handicap of the common-sense idiom and "self-explanatory" nomenclature' (P2 46) (cf. 6.3, 55, 59). But work 'bristling with neologisms' brings 'discredit' to 'modern linguistics' (P1 140). The Americans are scolded both for creating 'a set of unattractive new terms' and for using 'a large number of traditional terms' like ' "possessive case" ' 'without definition' (P2 119). 'The further we go with modern studies', 'the more ridiculous our traditional grammatical apparatus will become', 'due to its naiveté and obvious incompleteness and inadequacy both in formal description and in dealing with meaning' (TMS 87; P2 188) (cf. 7.4; 8.5, 7, 58; 12.5, 7).

8.38 Although it would be 'foolish to abandon' it, the 'nomenclature' of the last 'two thousand years' should be 'checked and sorted out', and 'fitted into an entirely serviceable technical apparatus for linguistic analysis and statement in keeping with the advances of linguistic theory' (P2 189) (cf. 2.6; 6.49; 7.4, 75; 11.41, 88; 12.7). 'Most of the older definitions' of ' "system" ', for instance, including Saussure's, 'need overhauling in the light of contemporary science' (P1 143) (cf. 2.26f, 36; 6.34ff; 8.30, 32, 53). For the future, Firth calls for 'a systematic study of the languages of linguistics' by 'applying the techniques of semantics, both historical and descriptive, to the language used about language' and to 'the conceptual framework and systems of ideas' wherein 'our own technical terms' 'function' as 'focal or pivotal' 'key words' (P1 139, 141; P2 98) (cf. 12.36). Also, we should 'welcome new systems of linguistic thought with their terminology' as a 'radical criticism' of ours (P1 141).

8.39 We should bear in mind too that the 'technical restricted languages' in which 'the empirical data of such sciences as linguistics are usually stated' 'involve indeterminacy', since the 'terms' can also appear in 'common usage in general language' (P2 46) (cf. 12.69). 'Linguistics which does not fully recognize this' cannot be 'applied to the study of language in society'. Although 'the general national language' imposes some 'epistemological conditions of scholarship' on 'modern linguistics', 'the meaning of a technical term' 'cannot be derived or guessed at from the meaning of the word in ordinary language' (P2 27, 169).

8.40 For 'the new approach' Firth envisions, a compromise is proffered: 'many of the traditional terms survive, but their meanings are determined by the new contexts in which they are used' (P2 119) (cf. 9.29; 12.48).The 'pivotal terms' 'are given their "meaning" by the restricted language of the theory' and its 'applications' (P2 169). In a chapter whose abstract announces 'a rectification of terms', terse explications are offered for 'language', 'speech event', 'nature', 'nurture', 'system', 'phoneme', and 'feature' (P1 139, 142–46). But other terms like 'philology' and 'personality' are critiqued by consulting Dr Johnson and the *Oxford English Dictionary* (P1 141f, 183f) – hardly 'new' or 'radical' sources.

8.41 Ultimately, 'abstract linguistics' gets its 'justification' when 'the linguist' 'finally proves his theory by a renewal of connection with the processes and patterns of life' and 'experience' (P2 19; cf. P1 xii; P2 17, 19, 24, 129, 154, 168, 175, 184f, 190ff) (cf. 12.57). Firth presents his own 'monistic approach' as the means whereby those 'processes and patterns' 'can be generalized in **contexts of situation**' (P1 226, P2 24, 90, 169).[25] Because 'a speech-event' is an 'expression of the language system from which it arises and to which it is referred', 'we can only arrive at some understanding of how' 'language' 'works' if we 'take our facts from speech sequences' 'operating in contexts of situation which are typical, recurrent, and repeatedly observable' (P1 144, 35) (cf. 5.10). To avoid invoking 'mental processes', Firth suggests that any 'memory context or causal context' must be 'linked up with the observable situation' (P1 19) (cf. 8.24). 'A stated series of contexts of situation' may thus contribute to 'a theory of reciprocal comprehension, level by level, stage by stage' (P2 200) (cf. 5.65; 8.48).

8.42 To 'make sure of the sociological component', each 'context' should in turn 'be placed in categories' 'within the wider context of **culture**' (P1 182, 35) (cf. 8.48; 12.62). Though 'situations are infinitely various' and cannot be 'strictly classed' within 'hard and fast lines' (cf. 4.13, 31, 61; 5.25, 28; 12.26, 40), Firth sees 'great possibilities for research and experiment': 'contexts can be grouped into types of usage' and 'social categories' like 'common, colloquial, slang, literary, technical, scientific', and so on, applying 'the principle of relative frequency' (P1 28; P2 177). Or, we can 'refer contexts to a variety of known frameworks of a more general character': 'economic, religious and other social structures'; 'types of linguistic discourse such as monologue, choric', 'narrative, recitation, explanation, exposition'; 'personal interchanges', varying with 'the number, age, and sex of the participants'; 'speech functions' such as 'address', 'greetings', 'direction', 'control', 'drills', 'orders', 'flattery, blessing, cursing, praise, blame, concealment', 'deception, social pressure and constraint', and 'verbal contracts of all kinds' (P2 178f; TMS 111; P1 30f) (cf. 9.71).

8.43 'A **situation** is a patterned process conceived as a' 'dynamic and creative' 'complex activity with internal relations between its various factors (TMS 110f) (cf. 4.16; 9.11). The 'relations' in a 'situation' may be among the 'participants' (as 'persons' and 'personalities'), their 'verbal' and 'non-verbal actions', and the 'effects' of these, plus 'relevant objects' and 'events' (P2 108, 148, 155, 173, 177, P1 182). 'The text' 'is seen in relation to the non-verbal constituents and the total effective or creative result' (P1 18n). Firth thus shares Pike's concern for 'relations' 'between elements of linguistic structure and non-verbal constituents of the situation' (P2 203, 148, 173, 177) (cf. 5.8; 10.7, 9, 86). Indeed, 'references to the nonverbal constituents' may be 'essential' for describing 'formal linguistic characteristics stated as criteria for setting up parts of speech or word classes', e.g., 'nominal and verbal categories' (P2 187) (cf. 9.2; 12.40).

8.44 All the same, Firth leaves no doubt that 'in contexts of situation', 'the **text** is the main concern of the linguist' (P2 24, 90, 173) (cf. 12.39). 'All texts' 'in modern spoken languages' are 'considered to carry the implication of utterance' and are 'referred to typical participants in some generalized context of situation' (P2 201, 13, 98, 123; P1 220, 226; cf. P2 30f, 175) (cf. 8.72). We should thus give 'due attention to the form of discourse' and 'the style and tempo of utterance' (P2 32) (cf. 8.65, 69). The 'attested language text' should be 'duly recorded' and 'abstracted from the matrix of experience', which Firth likes to call, after Whitehead, 'the mush of general goings on' (P2 199f, 99; P1 187) (hardly suggesting order or structure). 'The linguist' then retains the 'selected features or elements of the cultural matrix of the texts' needed to 'set up' 'formal contexts of situation' (P2 200). Although 'it may not be 'possible or desirable to present the whole of the materials collected during the observation period', some '"corpus"' is 'essential' (P2 32). This emphasis on 'texts' (see also P1 xi, 75, 145, 192; P2 13, 18f, 69, 85, 97, 108, 121, 140, 145, 169, 177, 181, 187, 190, 196) is shared by Pike, Hjelmslev, Halliday, van Dijk and Kintsch, and Hartmann (cf. 5.5, 15; 6.37; 9.1, 3, 8, 16, 41f, 107, 9[19]; 10.1f; 12.39).

8.45 Less widely shared is Firth's demand for a 'situational approach' derived by 'general theoretical abstraction with no trace of "realism"' (P2 154) (cf. 6.12; 8.33; 12.57).[26] 'The context of situation' would be a 'schematic construct to be applied to language events' as 'technical abstractions from utterances and occurrences' (P2 154, 175f; P1 144, 182; cf. P2 200). 'Since science deals with large average effects' via 'observation', we should 'generalize typical texts or pieces of speech in generalized contexts of situation' (P2 13). 'We study the flux of experience and suppress most of the environmental coordination', looking for 'instances of the general categories of the schematic constructs' (P2 16). The 'elements of the situation, including the text, are abstractions from experience and are not' 'embedded in it, except perhaps in an applied scientific sense' (P2 154). Again repudiating mentalism, Firth excludes from 'the concern of linguistic science' 'the intention of a particular person in a particular instance of speech' (P2 16) (as Saussure excluded 'the will of speakers', cf. 2.20, 44).

8.46 Despite his behavioural outlook, however, Firth is adamant that 'descriptive' or 'structural linguistics' 'deals with **meaning** throughout the whole range of the discipline' and 'at all levels of analysis'; 'meaning *must* be included as a fundamental assumption' and 'main concern' (P2 50, 160; P1 190; cf. P1 xi; P2 145; TMS 86). 'Linguistics' can attain 'no unity' or 'synthesis' 'unless we all turn' to 'the "second front"' of 'linguistic meaning' (Jakobson's term) (P2 48, 50, 74, 159f). The warning that 'linguistics without meaning is sterile' is addressed to American linguists like Bloch, Trager, and Harris, who claimed to 'exclude meaning' (P2 160, 47f, 85, 117; P1 227) (cf. 5.61; 7.56; 12.27). Yet Daniel Jones, whom Firth esteems, also avowed that 'meanings' don't 'enter into the definition of a phoneme' (P2 48) (cf. 2.70; 4.26, 28; 6.43; 7[27]). And, Firth himself is 'convinced of the desirability of separating semantics' 'from grammar of the technical and formal kind' (P1 6, 16) (cf. 8.62; 12.54). But without more illustration, I can't tell what he expects from 'a strictly formal study of meaning' 'in strictly linguistic terms' (P2 160, 169, 81, 97, 176; P1 x).

8.47 Predictably, Firth's idea of a proper ' "semantics"' is a 'situational and experiential study' of 'contexts of situation' 'along sociological lines', in which 'linguistics accepts' 'language texts as related' to 'the "meaning" of life' (P1 27, 16; P2 169; TMS 113, 184; cf. P2 82, 206) (cf. 8.41; 12.14).[27] 'Meaning is best regarded' 'as a complex of relations between component terms of a context of situation' (TMS 110f, 174; cf. P1 183). Only a 'contextual theory of meaning employs abstractions which enable us to handle language in the interrelated processes of personal and social life' (P2 14). Against the 'logician' who 'treats words and sentences as if they could somehow have meanings in and by themselves', Firth agrees with Wittgenstein that 'words' 'mean what they do' and 'the meaning' 'lies in their use' (TMS 110; P2 138, 162) (cf. 4.78; 11.42, 66; 12.36). Seeing 'meaning' 'deeply embedded in the living processes of persons maintaining themselves in society' defies 'intellectuals' who emphasize 'only the symbolic use of words' over ' "evocative" or "affective" language' (P2 13; TMS 176) (cf. 9.15). For Firth, most 'abstract words are based on other words integrated in ordinary social behaviour'; the truly 'primary words' are those 'standardized' by 'convergence of action in some social group' (TMS 176) (cf. 3.45; 4.24; 5.66). He wonders if 'the promotion' and 'maintenance of communion of feeling is perhaps four-fifths of all talk' – even at 'conferences and congresses' in 'science' (TMS 112; cf. TMS 110, 175).

8.48 Because 'the statement of meaning' for 'whole texts' is a 'vast subject', we must 'split up the problem' (P2 108; cf. P1 10, 18f). One recourse Firth airs but rejects is to distinguish 'denotation' as 'primary meaning (except perhaps' 'as highest-frequency meaning') in opposition to 'connotation' as 'secondary meaning' (P1 10f) (cf. 4.21f, 25; 6.52ff; 11.19). He especially rejects the idea, put forth by Trench (1832) and Skeat (1887), that the 'primary' or 'true meaning' is the 'original' or 'etymological' meaning (P1 8, 10f; P2 85, 121, 149). Such an idea emerges only when 'scholars' 'study change' of meaning and look for a 'seminal meaning' as the 'ultimate origin' (P1 19, 9). Firth places his own hopes on 'generalization' as a means to 'avoid the appalling consequences of the continuous change of content in all expressions of a living language and of the belief that meaning can only be real in individual instances of human invention' (P2 118) (cf. 4.16; 8.19; 11.67f). With Stöcklein (1898) and Sperber (1923), Firth demurs also that 'a change of meaning is not' 'in the single word', but in a 'functioning context' (P1 13).

8.49 Instead of these recourses, Firth's 'central proposal' 'is to split up meaning' 'into a series of component **functions**' (P2 173; P1 19). The 'phonetic' is 'a minor function', whereas 'lexical, morphological, syntactic' and 'situational' are 'major functions' (P1 20, 24, 33, 35, 37, 40f, 48f; P2 174).[28] To ensure an 'analysis in terms of linguistics, we first accept language events as integral in experience', 'whole', 'repetitive and interconnected', and then 'apply theoretical schemata' and make 'statements' in terms of '**structures** and **systems** at a number of **levels of analysis**' (P2 176, 97). For this purpose, he envisions a 'spectrum of linguistic analysis whereby' 'the total meaning of a text in situation' is 'dispersed at a series of levels' (P2 92, 33, 81f, 97, 108, 110, 112, 118, 124, 174, 200f; P1 xi, 19, 24, 183, 192, 195, 220) (cf. 8.52, 61f, 84). This '"spectrum" analysis makes sure of the social reality of the data' 'before breaking down the total meaningful intention' (P1 170f).

8.50 'Meaning' thus becomes a term 'for the whole complex of functions which a linguistic form may have' (P1 33; P2 174; cf. P1 7) (cf. 8.64). 'Semantic study' becomes the place where 'the work' of 'the phonetician, grammarian, and lexicographer' is 'integrated' (P1 27). Hence, 'semantics' can proceed only if 'phonetics', 'morphology' and 'syntax' 'are sound' (P2 197, 33; P1 18f, 23, 28, 75) (cf. 7.57). This rationale allows his discussions of meaning to keep turning to those other levels. One paper title, 'Further Studies in Semantics', got changed into 'Sounds and Prosodies' (P1 123). In another paper called 'The Techniques of Semantics' (P1 7–33), the only treatment of semantics in the usual sense is an attack on approaches Firth dislikes (e.g., Ogden and Richards, who appeal to 'relations in the mind'); otherwise, the paper deals with past mentions of the term 'semantics' (e.g., in 'the Society's Dictionary'), historical principles, morphology, and phonetics. Finally, the 'context of situation' gets referred to 'sociological' issues like 'social roles' and 'customs', or 'cultural heritage'. Such papers are emblematic: Firth keeps heralding a new 'semantics' for making 'statements of meaning', yet instead of making such statements, he 'disperses meaning' to other levels. He never really proves that 'the accumulation of results at various levels adds up to a considerable sum of partial meanings in terms of linguistics without recourse to any underlying ideas'; or that if 'linguistic analysis' 'states the **structures** it finds both in the text and in the context', these 'statements' 'then contribute to the statements of meaning' (P2 197, 17).

8.51 Nor is Firth's overall scheme of **levels** terribly clear. Although 'level' is not a term in the early books, the two later ones mention some twenty-four 'levels' in various listings.[29] Most frequently named are: 'phonetics', 'phonology', 'grammar', 'morphology' (or 'morphematics'), 'syntax' (or 'syntagmatics'), 'stylistics', 'situation' (or 'context of situation'), and 'collocation'; only occasional reference is made to 'pronunciation', 'phonaesthetic', 'semantic', 'lexical', 'vocabulary', 'word formation', and 'colligation'; and 'prosodic', 'graphematic', 'spelling', 'sociological', 'phrase formation', 'word description', 'word isolate', 'etymology', and 'glossaries' are termed 'levels' only once each (P1 xi, 24f, 171, 192, 197, 206; P2 16, 18, 30, 40, 91f, 97, 99, 106, 110f, 113, 118, 124, 127, 147, 149, 154, 175f, 181ff, 188, 195, 200ff, 208). Sometimes, too, 'modes' is used in a very similar sense (P1 192, 198f; P2 33, 82, 110). If 'the levels of analysis' are 'constantly increasing in number and specialization' (P2 82), Firth's work is a good foretaste.

8.52 Comments on the 'series of levels' indicate that the '*higher* levels' are closer to 'culture', 'context', and 'situation', and the '*lower*' to 'phonology' and 'phonetics' (P1 201f; P2 33, 175f). Firth may say that analysis can go either way; or that 'the descending procedure is the right one', 'the total complex' of 'the higher levels' being 'a first postulate'; or he may 'adopt' the ascendant one to avoid or postpone dealing with 'ideas', 'concepts', or 'thoughts, and may not get to the higher ones at all, as in his treatment of Swinburne (P1 192; P2 175; P1 171, 198ff, 202f) (cf. 8.83). In favour of his 'prosodic approach' (cf. 8.64ff), he argues that 'a theory of analysis dispersed at a series of levels must require synthesis' and 'congruence of levels', and (against Pike) that 'all levels are mutually requisite'; yet elsewhere that the 'analytic dispersion does *not* imply that any level constitutes a formal prerequisite of any other': 'the levels' 'are only connected in that the resulting statements relate to the same language text'; and 'the levels' must be 'congruent and complementary in synthesis on renewal of connection with experience' (P2 202, 111, 30, 192, 176f) (cf. 8.40, 54).

8.53 Some of this perplexity reflects the difficulties of 'determining what are the units of speech' (TMS 182). 'General opinion' points to '**words**', which, particularly in 'literate societies', are often 'institutionalized' (TMS 182f; P2 155; P1 122, xi). Also, 'word analysis is as ancient as writing' and has produced 'the alphabet' (P1 122; TMS 33) (cf. 4.42, 63; 6.50; 8.73). Thus, for certain 'purposes', 'words' can be viewed as the 'principal isolates' within 'texts' (P1 122, xi). An 'emphasis on the word as a unit is a useful corrective' for 'over-segmentation and fragmentation' (P2 40, i.r.) (cf. 8.31f). Sometimes, Firth imagines 'words staring you in the face from the text' (inspired maybe by Wittgenstein's idea that 'a word in company' has a 'physiognomy') (P1 xii; P2 179, 186). At other times, he regards 'words' as 'bodily' or 'habitual acts', 'events, habits' (TMS 173, 149, 181) (cf. 8.6, 21ff, 25). In that mood, he pictures 'families of linked words' arising from 'related habits'; a word with 'fewer derivatives and analogues' has a 'weaker background of bodily habit' (TMS 183).

8.54 Yet Firth sees little prospect of an 'acceptable definition of the word' 'in general human terms' (P1 191n) (cf. 2.18; 3.31; 4.54, 60; 5.53; 6.23; 8.54; 12.29). He appears to have three motives for this reservation. First, words are not *sufficiently theoretical* entities. In grammar and syntax, units and structures involve 'categories', 'relations', or 'abstractions' rather than 'words' (P1 180; P2 112f, 121f, 152, 181, 186, 203) (cf. 8.79). Here at least Firth agrees with the 'strict Saussurian doctrine' of 'structural formalism': 'language' is 'a system of signs placed in categories', i.e., of 'differential values, not of concrete and positive terms' (P1 180) (cf. 2.26). Second, words usually appear within *larger units*. Already for 'the Ancient Hindus', ' "a word had no existence detached from a sentence" ', and ' "resolving a sentence into parts" ' was ' "a fanciful procedure" ' (TMS 15) (cf. 9^{13}). Moreover, 'since in many languages the exponents of the grammatical categories may not be words', 'syntactical analysis must generalize beyond the level of the word isolate'; in fact, 'some scholars' believe there are 'wordless languages' (P2 182, 122).[30] Third, words are not satisfactory for dealing with *meaning*. Firth deplores 'the naive approach' which regards 'the meanings of words' as 'immanent essences or detachable ideas' (P2 15; cf. P2 12, 16) (cf. 8.24). A 'word' 'by itself can have meaning only at the level of spelling' or 'pronunciation' (P2 91).

8.55 For these three motives, he falls back on an intermediary unit he terms a ' "**piece**" ', i.e., a 'combination of words' (P1 122; cf. P1 146, 192) (cf. Halliday's 'group', 9.75). His 'main purpose is to guide' not just 'the descriptive analysis of languages', but also 'the synthesis for dealing with longer pieces of language' (P2 202, 130) (cf. 8.43, 64, 88). Such a 'longer piece' is a 'meaningful complex' to be 'described as a relational network of structures and systems at clearly distinguished but congruent levels, converging again in renewal of connection with experience' (P2 192; cf. P2 102, 122) (cf. 8.40). This recourse permits him to remain undecided about the 'commonplace of linguistics': that 'the **sentence** and not the word is its main concern' and 'primary datum' (P2 156; P1 170) (cf. 9^{13}). He doesn't 'define the sentence', but does say what he thinks it is *not*. For him, 'the sentence' is neither 'the lowest unit of language' nor 'a "self-contained or self-sufficient unit" ' (P2 156); and his mention of 'one-word sentences' and 'verbless sentences' (P2 102) seems to depart from traditional or generativist definitions (cf. 4.67; 5.56, 58; 12.54). Nor will he accept a 'definition of the sentence' as a ' "unit of predication" ', a 'judgment', or a 'proposition', since he wants to 'abandon' 'all this logical or psychological analysis' (P1 170f; P2 102) (cf. 3.35f, 39; 4.69; 5.55; 8.17, 31; 9.14, 72; 10.39ff; 11.78f; 12.14).

8.56 Notwithstanding, he finds it 'natural' that 'the sentence and syntactical analysis find a central place' in a 'general theory' (P2 148). 'When we speak', we 'use a whole sentence', so 'the unit of actual speech is the holophrase' (TMS 83). Therefore, 'the technique of syntax is concerned with the word process in the sentence' (P1 183). He even approves Wegener's (1885) speculation that 'all language elements are originally sentences', such that 'sentences' might contain 'the origins of all speech', both 'biographically' and 'historically' (P2 148) (cf. 12.54). Yet this view conflicts with his usual search for origins in habits and social organization (cf. 8.6), and seems unrelated to such notions as the generativist 'history of derivation' (cf. 7.48), which is neither 'biographical' nor 'historical'.

8.57 The indecision between word and sentence naturally carries over to Firth's views on organizing the levels of **morphology** and **syntax** (cf. 2.55, 61; 3.34f; 4.61ff; 5.53f; 6.49; 7^{34}; 9.31; 10.35; 11.77). At one point, he says they 'have quite distinct sets of categories', but later that 'the distinction between morphology and syntax is perhaps no longer useful in descriptive linguistics' (P1 6; P2 183) (cf. 2.55; 3.34; 4.61; 7.58; 8.77; 12.28). In line with the second view, 'morphological categories are to be treated syntagmatically and only appear in paradigms as terms or units related to elements of structure' – whence 'the need for prosodic analysis' (P2 183) (cf. 8.64). 'The study of syntactical categories' should consider how 'subordinate constituents are expressed and integrated', and how 'the utterance analyses or synthesizes the aspects of a complex situation' in 'the social conditions of employment' (P1 223, 226; cf. TMS 190) (cf. 8.42).

8.58 Indecision also appears in his attempts to state how 'the categories of morphology' and 'the parts of speech' 'arise from the formal conditions of the language' (P1 24). He cautiously suggests 'using fourteen parts of speech in a common grammar of careful polite English that can be written in orthography' (P2 12), but doesn't tell us what they are, or how many might be needed, say, for careless rude English that durst not be written. He admits (with Richard Temple) that since 'the functions a word fulfils in any particular sentence can be indicated by its position with or without variation of form', a 'word' can 'belong to as many classes as there are functions which it can fulfil' (P2 142) (cf. 3.16, 22, 24, 33; 4.47, 49; 7.63; 11.25, 27). An imposing task for description looms here, the more so if 'classes' are to 'include as complete a list as possible of examples' as well as 'indications of productivity' (P1 223).[31]

8.59 In addition, the 'verbal characteristics in the sentence' 'are rarely in parallel with' the 'verbal paradigms' and 'tabulated conjugations in the grammar books' (P2 103f) (cf. 9^{11}; 12.27). In dealing with 'operators' (cf. 8.64), for instance, 'tabulated paradigms' like that of 'the English verb' 'will get you nowhere' (P2 121). He contemplates 'putting aside' 'the paradigmatic approach to the morphology of separate words', e.g., in 'hyphenated lists of orthographic forms of individual words', lest we 'obscure the analysis of elements of structure in the syntagmatic interrelations of grammatical categories' (P2 189, 203) (cf. 7.75f). Still, he allows that 'systems' of 'units or parts of speech' constitute 'paradigms' wherein 'values' are 'given' by 'relations' (P2 112, 173). He terms a 'paradigm' a 'formal scatter', 'involving all the morphology of word-bases, stems, affixes, and compounds' (P1 25, 15; P2 103, 122) (cf. 4.57f). These 'scatters' 'can be arrived at' 'by recollecting, or by asking the native speaker, or by collecting verbal contexts' (P1 25).

8.60 Unlike Hjelmslev and Chomsky, Firth denounces 'general or universal grammar', on the grounds that 'grammatical meanings are determined by their interrelations in systems set up for that language' and that 'grammatical forms of a language are never in a strict sense parallel in another' (P1 191n; P2 191, 65, 123) (cf. 6.10; 7.19f; 8.19, 86; 12.18). 'The use of traditional grammatical terms' for 'a wide variety of languages' entails 'the dangers and pitfalls' of 'personifying categories as universal entities' and practising 'bogus philosophizing in linguistics' (P2 190) (cf. 4.72; 8.5). 'Every analysis of a particular "language" must determine the values of the ad hoc categories to which traditional names are given'.

8.61 Firth's own plan for 'a new approach to grammar' to match his 'new approach to meaning' turns out to be another 'dispersal' of 'inquiry' and 'statement at a series of levels' (P2 114, 117) (cf. 8.49f, 52, 84). Accordingly, 'the description of grammatical systems' entails 'graphematic, phonological, morphological, and syntactic' 'criteria' or 'functions' (P1 222f, 24; P2 118, 174). Instead of 'grammatical analysis which deals with relations of the individual words', our study should 'look for verbal characteristics in the sentence as a whole'; after all, 'the categories of grammar are abstractions from texts, from pieces or stretches of discourse' (P2 188, 113, 121; cf. P2 183) (cf. 8.54; 11.71; 12.39). Regarding 'criteria' for 'nominal and verbal categories', for example, we 'usually find that verbal features are distributed over a good deal of the sentence' (P2 187). A favoured example is: '"he kept popping in and out of the office"', which is 'grammatically close knit as a verbal piece'; it's hard to say 'where's the verb' (P2 103f, 121, 188). Similarly, 'such categories as voice, mood', 'tense, aspect, gender, number, person, and case, if found applicable' to 'any given language', should be 'abstracted from, and referred back to, the sentence as a whole' (P2 190). We would then not be perplexed when the 'exponents' are not 'words or even affixes', or are 'discontinuous and cumulate', as in 'Latin', 'Swahili', and 'Modern Hindi' (what 'is traditionally referred to as "concord" or "agreement"' (P2 182, 190) (cf. 4.67; 9^{20}).

8.62 Despite the diversity implied, the 'dispersal' of 'grammatical description' is given a major restriction running throughout linguistics: it should 'recognize only those linguistic distinctions which are *formally expressed*' (P1 222) (cf. 12.54). By implication, meanings not distinguishable by form would get left out rather than 'dispersed' to other levels, and Firth is evasive on this point. He attacks Bloomfield's suggestion that 'the study of meaning is the study of grammar', yet says later that 'grammar' is 'a study of meaning in generalized terms' (P1 15; P2 118) (cf. 4.45ff, 50, 64). Similarly, the 'grammatical' 'level' is named in some lists of the 'levels' at which 'statements of meaning' are to be 'dispersed' (P1 19; P2 82, 92, 112, 124), but in others 'morphological and syntactic' appear instead (P1 192; P2 33, 118, 200f).

8.63 For Firth, the converse of 'formal' 'criteria' is '*notional*' ones (P2 223). He wants to 'put aside all notional explanations' as a 'manifest disadvantage' fostering a 'confusion of grammatical and semantic thinking' which 'clouds the precise statement of fact' in 'linguistic analysis' (P2 189,

204, 152). They should therefore be 'rigidly excluded' from 'grammatical or phonological' 'levels' (P2 177). But some evasion occurs here, too. 'Notional elements' might be 'unavoidable' for 'classifying contexts of situation and describing' them 'as wholes'; here, 'notional terms are permissible', provided they do not 'involve the description of mental processes or meaning in the thoughts of participants', nor of 'intention, purport, or purpose' (P2 177f, 200) (cf. 8.24, 45).

8.64 In between formal and notional, Firth introduces the term **'colligation'** for a 'syntagmatic relation' and 'mutual expectancy' among 'elements' of 'grammatical' 'structure' (P2 186, 111, 183). For instance, 'contemporary English' has a category of 'syntactical operators' (like ' "was, were, have, has" ', ' "do, does" ', etc.) which 'function in negation' and 'interrogation'; 'all negative finite verbs are colligated with one of the operators' (P2 182) (cf. 5.48; 9.79). Here again, 'syntactic analysis must generalize beyond the level of the word isolate' (cf. 8.54). And since the 'relations of the grammatical categories in colligation' do not 'necessarily have phonological shape', we are once more discouraged from 'segmental analysis of the phonemic type' (P2 182f) (cf. 8.31f, 53, 65, 70).

8.65 'The investigation of words, pieces, and longer stretches of text leads to the **prosodic** approach', which 'emphasizes synthesis' and 'refers' 'features' 'to the structure taken as a whole' (as 'Sweet foresaw') (P1 xi, 138; P2 100, 193). Firth hopes this approach can deal with a range of issues, including 'syllable structure',[32] 'stress', 'intonation', 'quantity', and 'grammatical correlations', in 'the piece, phrase, clause, and sentence' (P2 193, 122, 100, 102; P1 130, 134). The approach is also 'more comprehensive than traditional' 'word studies', fits the 'view that syntax is the dominant discipline in grammar', and may be 'useful grammatically' and 'practically in teaching pronunciation', as well as relevant to 'fieldwork on unwritten languages', 'the study of literature', 'literary criticism', and 'stylistics', maybe even to 'historic linguistics' (e.g., for issues like 'Ablaut' and 'laryngeals') (P2 126; P1 137f; P2 101, 195) (cf. 8.6, 81, 83f). Moreover, by 'regarding the elements of structure as prosodically interdependent and mutually determined', this 'approach' is a clear alternative to 'the American procedure by segmentation or succession' of 'units', and can treat items which are 'prosodically one' (e.g., contractions like ' "won't" ') or 'holophrastic' (e.g., 'verbal pieces') (P2 102, 104f, 193) (cf. 8.56).

8.66 To 'state' 'prosodic features' and 'isolate prosodic groups', Firth particularly commends 'the technical resources of **phonetics**, both descriptive and instrumental', plus those of '**phonological** analysis' (P2 193, 100) (cf. 8.70). His reasoning is that 'the systematic study of sounds' is far more advanced 'in modern linguistics' than that of 'prosodies' (P1 123). In exchange, 'phonological' 'analysis', such as for the 'features' of 'positions and junctions,' can 'more profitably proceed' via 'prosodies' of 'words, pieces, or sentences' (P1 xi, 123; P2 100). By this route, Firth joins the other theorists who based their conceptions on the domain of sounds and articulation (cf. 2.17, 67, 70f; 3.14, 18; 4.29, 34; 5.42, 5^{12}; 12.26). He too finds the physical base reassuring: 'the sounds and prosodies of speech are deeply embedded in organic processes in the human body' (P2 90).[33] A patriotic motive is involved as well: 'the English have excelled in phonetics' (P2 137, 60; P1 120, 92) (cf. 8.15).

8.67 And so Firth salutes the study of sounds. 'Every important advance during the last century' was made by 'attacking the problem from the phonetic side' (P1 74) (cf. 4.79). His hero Sweet is called to witness that 'phonetics', 'useless by itself', is 'the foundation of all study of language, whether theoretical or practical' (P1 119). And 'phonetic analysis has made possible a grammar of spoken language', 'in the face of' which 'classical grammar recedes into obsolescence' (P1 23; TMS 136) (cf. 9.24; 12.33). In sum, 'phonetics is one of the most practical of the social sciences', providing 'techniques for the study of utterance', 'systemic analysis', 'statement of linguistic facts', and 'establishment of valid texts' (TMS 203; P1 145). So 'morphology', 'syntax', 'descriptive grammar', and 'descriptive semantics' must all 'rest on reliable phonetic and intonational forms' (P1 18, 3). Moreover, Firth's group has 'developed general linguistic theory in close application to particular descriptions' which 'have in the main been phonological' (P2 126). He feels that 'adequacy in the higher levels of linguistic analysis' demands 'the same rigorous control of formal categories' as 'in all phonological analysis'; and that 'phonemic description should serve primarily as a basis for the statement of grammatical and lexical facts' (P2 191; P1 222) (but cf. 7.46). It therefore seems harsh to fault 'American structural linguistics' for creating 'a surfeit of phonemics', and for 'attempting' to 'directly develop' 'the analysis of discourse – of the paragraph and the sentence' – 'from phonemic procedures' or 'by analogy to such procedures' (P2 160, 191) (cf. 5.44; 8.31, 60).

8.68 By association, the multi-level scope of prosody naturally carries over into sound study. 'Phonology states the phonematic and prosodic processes within word and sentence' and 'the phonetician links all this with the processes and features of utterance' (P1 183; P2 175).[34] The 'differential values' 'represented' in 'phonetic notation' 'may have 'morphological, syntactical, or lexical function'; and 'the identification and contextualization of the phonemes' is 'important' for 'studying' 'forms in morphology and syntax' (P1 3f) (cf. 4.34f, 40; 5.35, 45; 11.81). 'Grammatical classification limits and groups the data in parallel with phonological analysis': 'the exponents of some phonological categories may serve also for syntactical categories', and those of 'grammatical categories' may 'require' 'phonetic description' or 'notation' (P2 192, 184; P1 3). 'The interrelations of the grammatical categories stated as colligations form the unifying framework, and the phonological categories are limited by the grammatical status of the structures' (P2 193).

8.69 If 'phonological statements' can profit from knowing 'the grammatical **meaning** of the materials', Firth must oppose Daniel Jones (praised for 'carrying' the work of 'the English school of phonetics' 'to all parts of the world') by maintaining that 'phonetics and phonology must be linked with

studies of meaning' (P2 192; P1 166; P2 72; cf. P2 48, 86, 192, 14; P1 226n)
(cf. 6.43). With the usual Firthian twist, he says 'sounds direct and control',
but 'do not hold or convey meaning'; 'in the normal contexts of everyday
life, the sounds of speech are a function of social situations', from which
'meaning is largely gathered by' applying an 'assumed common background
of bodily habits' (TMS 171) (cf. 8.21f).

8.70 For further 'clarity of statement' in sound study, Firth presents
three 'separate' 'terms: phonic, phonetic, and phonological' (P2 99) (cf. 2.68;
4.30; 6.43; 8.70; 11.80).[35] 'The **phonic** material' comes from 'the raw
material of experience' 'in all its fullness'. A 'description' is then made 'in
the technical' 'language of **phonetics**'; 'beyond this again', 'the **phonological**
analysis' 'selectively' works at 'a different level of abstraction', though its
'categories, features, or units will have exponents describable in the
phonetic language of description' (P2 99; cf. P1 3f). So 'phonetics and
phonology', though 'differing in scientific levels' and 'systems of discourse',
'must work in harness' (P1 145). 'Phonetics' is 'the most specialized
linguistic technique', tending to be 'narrower and more abstract', while
'phonology' might be called 'systemic phonetics', 'giving each sound a place
in the whole phonetic structure of system' (P1 34f). To prove he is 'not a
phonemicist and does not set up unit segments' each 'occupied by a
phoneme', Firth postulates whole 'systems applicable' to 'elements of
structure' (P2 99).[36] Due to 'the "context" of the whole' 'system', 'in actual
speech situations the elements' reflect 'general attributes or correlation of
articulation, such as length, tone, stress, tensity, voice', as well as 'styles'
('rapid, colloquial', 'familiar', etc.) (P1 21, 42) (cf. 8.44).

8.71 The question is then how to find a 'scientific notation' for the
'transcription' of 'sounds' (P1 109–13; TMS 150). 'Alphabetic transcription
of speech' is 'a highly abstract proceeding' and cannot produce 'an exact
record of every detail of sound, stress, or intonation' (P1 53, 3) (cf. 9.52).
'The units of a phonetic transcription are at best abstractions from
utterances' and may call for 'terms and notations not based on orthography'
or 'any scheme of segmental letters' (P1 149f; P2 190). Indeed, 'letters' may
'lead phonetics astray' by not 'corresponding with the facts of speech' or by
hiding 'the overlapping and mutual interpenetration' of 'sounds, and the
integration of movement for the whole word or phrase' (P1 148; TMS 29,
39). 'Separate letters' can also foster the 'hypostatization of the symbols and
their successive arrangement' in the 'theories' of both 'historical and
descriptive linguistics', witness 'the apotheosis of the sound-letter in the
phoneme' (P1 147, 125f, 123; cf. P1 21f, 71ff, 165) (cf. 2.69; 4.38, 45; 6[8];
12.26). 'Similarity of sound being no safe guide to functional identity', Firth
'abandons' 'the principle of "one symbol, one sound"', but all he can
propose is 'a store of good letters' in 'different founts of type' (P1 51, 4f,
148, 146).

8.72 Despite all this concern for sounds, Firth asserts that 'scientific
priority cannot be given to **spoken** language as against **written** language'
(P2 30) (cf. 2.21; 4.37ff; 6.50; 9.42f; 11.83; 12.33). As Trench (1855)

remarked, 'a word exists as truly for the eye as the ear' (P2 90; P1 9n). Just as 'all forms of written language' have 'the implication of utterance', 'all forms of speech have also the implication of writing for linguistic statement' (P2 30f) (cf. 8.44). 'In a sense, written words are more real than speech' in being 'portable, tangible', 'material, permanent, and universal' (TMS 40, 146). Though 'written language' does entail 'an abstraction from insistent surroundings' and its 'context is entirely verbal', it is still 'immersed in the immediacy of social intercourse' and 'largely "affective"', and 'refers to an assumed common background of experience' (P2 14; TMS 174f) (cf. 8.47). In any 'symbol' like a 'written form', 'the general and particular meet', and 'a high standard of literacy is the foundation of modern civilized society' (TMS 30, 40, 135).

8.73 So 'the actual forms of writing or spelling are a near concern for the linguist in dealing with his material' (P2 31). 'Orthography' can 'transcend the vagaries of individual utterance', being 'grammatically and semantically representative' as well as 'phonetically' (TMS 48). 'Grammar must concern itself with letters and marks', because 'spelling and writing' present 'the first level of structural analysis in sorting out the grammatical meanings of texts' (P2 116) (cf. 8.53). Also, 'explorations in sociological linguistics' use 'the pedestrian techniques of the ABC as the principal means of linguistic description' (P1 75). But Firth admits 'the linguistic "economies" of speech are not those of writing', and 'it is impossible to represent fully to the eye what is meant for the ear' (TMS 174, 146). 'For the masses of people, too, the written language shows very little correlation with speech behaviour' (TMS 116) (cf. 2.22).[37] 'Spoken and written languages are two distinct sets of habits': 'ear language is intimate, social, local', 'eye language is general and nowadays everybody's property' (TMS 198). Thus, 'unwritten languages have a freedom of progressive economy' (TMS 174f).

8.74 Special 'study' should be devoted to 'world systems of writing', such as 'Roman', 'Arabic', 'Indian' and 'Chinese' (P2 31). Sometimes Firth favours 'the Roman alphabet', calling it 'the best' 'of all ABCs', and urging its 'universal adoption' (TMS 136; P1 75).[38] It has 'worked well from the days of a greater Rome to the present', when 'Western civilization is become world civilization' (P1 68). It also has 'merits as the framework for scientific linguistic notation'; it 'lends itself to analysis and synthesis', 'produces easily recognized differentiated word-forms', and 'uses a comparatively small number of signs' that can 'suit the phonology and morphology of almost any language' (P1 69). Yet at other times, he says our 'alphabetic notation' 'does not rest mainly on modern acoustic and physiological categories, but on fictions' 'set up by grammatical theory' (P1 148). And he contemplates 'how much was lost' by imposing 'a theory of the Roman alphabet' on languages in India, whose 'syllabaries' for 'Sanskritic dialects' are 'models of phonetic and phonological excellence' (P1 124f).

8.75 Moreover, 'English' 'spelling', though it may have 'the longest literary tradition in Western Europe', is a 'handicap', 'preposterous' and 'disgraceful' (P2 137; TMS 136; P1 112, 125). It 'should be reformed' 'in the interests of the whole world' (TMS 136, 48; P1 73), but Firth can't decide how. He is shy about adding 'new letters' or 'written signs' for fear of 'swamping the characteristics of the alphabet' or creating a 'pepperbox spelling' with ' "accents" ' and the like (P1 70, 124). 'Purely phonetic spelling' 'is out of the question', because 'removing phonetic ambiguity' 'creates other functional (grammatical and semantic) ambiguities' (P1 5; TMS 47f; P1 25) (cf. 2.69). And he shows no sympathy for 'spelling pronunciations', though they are 'increasingly common' (TMS 198f) (cf. 2.21; 4.38).

8.76 Firth's diffuse schemes for a **'language of description'**, which I have essayed to review so far (cf. 8.35–75), come into sharper perspective in his advice about the **'language under description'** (cf. 8.35). He vows that 'descriptive linguistics' 'is at its best when applied to a **restricted language'**, which he defines as 'serving a circumscribed field of experience or action' and having 'its own grammar and dictionary' (or 'a micro-grammar and a micro-glossary') (P2 124, 87, 98, 105f, 112, i.r.). Such a domain is easier than 'when the linguist' must draw 'abstractions' from 'a whole linguistic universe' comprising 'many specialized languages' and 'different styles' (P2 30, 97, 118). 'The material is clearly defined: the linguist knows what is on his agenda' and can 'set up ad hoc structures and systems' for 'the field of application' (P2 106, 116) (cf. 8.32). Once 'the statement of structures and systems provides' 'the anatomy and physiology of the texts', it is 'unnecessary' 'to attempt a structural and systemic account of a language as a whole' (P2 200).

8.77 'Linguistics' can regard each 'person' 'as being in command of a constellation of restricted languages, satellite languages', 'governed' by 'the general language of the community' (P2 207f). As domains of 'restricted languages', Firth looks to 'science, technology, politics, commerce', 'industry', 'sport', 'mathematics', and 'meteorology', or to 'a particular form or genre', or to a 'type of work associated with a single author or a type of speech function with its appropriate style' or 'tempo' (P2 106, 98, 112, 118f) (cf. 9.106, 9[48]).[39] By 'promoting such restricted languages', we may 'advance international European cooperation' and 'unity', e.g., among 'teachers' and 'colleagues in various professions' (P2 106). Ironically, Firth's own 'successful application' of 'operational linguistics' was not for unity, but for 'air-war Japanese' 'during the Second World War', when he assisted 'the Royal Air Force' (P2 29; P1 95, 125, 182) – a motive perhaps in setting up the London chair (and one Mrs Thatcher would have saluted) (cf. 8.1).[40]

8.78 The 'restricted language' is a prime domain for discovering **'collocations'**: for 'studying key words, pivotal words, leading words, by presenting them in the company they usually keep' (P2 106ff, 113, 182) (cf. 9.93). This 'study' 'may be classified into general or usual collocations and more restricted technical or personal' ones, or into 'normal' and 'idiosyncratic' ones (P1 195; P2 18). 'Characteristic distributions in collocability' can constitute 'a level of meaning in describing the English' of a 'social group or even one person' (P2 195). Ominously, Firth's favourite demonstration word seems to be '"ass"', said of a person ('collocation' with '"silly", "obstinate"', etc.) (P1 195; P2 108, 113, 150, 179). (Perhaps he should have lived to see the Thatcher government after all.)

8.79 'The collocations presented should usually be complete sentences', or, in 'conversation', 'extended to the utterances of preceding and following speakers' (P2 107).[41] Unlike '**colligations**', 'collocations' obtain 'between words as such', not between 'categories' (P2 181, 69) (cf. 8.64). Nor is 'a colligation' to be 'interpreted as an abstraction in parallel with a collocation of exemplifying words in a text' (P2 182f). But 'the study of the collocation' can be 'completed by a statement of the interrelations of the syntactical categories within' it (P2 23; cf. P1 xi).

8.80 'The study of the usual collocations' 'ensures that the isolate word or piece' 'is attested in established texts', and provides 'a precisely stated contribution' to 'the spectrum of descriptive linguistics' by 'circumscribing the field for further research', e.g., by 'indicating problems in grammar' or aiding 'descriptive lexicography' with 'citations' for 'dictionary definitions' (P2 195, 180f, 196) (cf. 8.43, 48). We should state 'first the structure of appropriate contexts of situation', 'then the syntactical structure of the texts', and then 'the criteria of distribution and collocation' (P2 19). For example, 'grammatical collocation and distribution provide differentiating criteria' that 'establish' 'the categories of noun substantive and verb', or 'guarantee the binary opposition of singular and plural'.

8.81 Firth recommends making 'an exhaustive collection of collocations' in 'a restricted language for which there are restricted texts' (P2 181). His own most ambitious attempt is far from exhaustive, however. He examines 'English letters [i.e., epistles] of the eighteenth and early nineteenth centuries' to contrast 'collocations' 'recognized as current for at least two hundred years' against those which 'seem glaringly obsolete' or 'dated' (P1 204f). This contrast is to be made by 'applying the categories of context of situation and of meaning', but his 'outline sketch' merely 'suggests by hints' how 'a linguist' might proceed 'at a series of levels' (P1 204, 214). For vocabulary, he turns to a dictionary of 'Synonymes' from 1824; for grammar, he focuses on the '"-ing" participle', mainly 'with preceding genitive' (e.g., '"your trying it"') (P1 205, 207–13). A handful of passages accompany the recommendation for a study of Dr Johnson's 'English in all his prose styles examined objectively and statistically', plus 'a biographical study of his personality', to 'give us a statement of stylistics in a social setting' (P1 206).

8.82 Firth claims that he has 'illustrated as many modes of meaning as possible from the language forms themselves', and that 'the name of a collocation is the hearing, reading, or saying of it' (P1 214; P2 181). These claims suggest we need merely present the data to speak for itself (cf. 4.55). And such is clearly the method for his 1937 'revue' of texts (from management, 'technology', 'politics', 'business', 'advertising', 'religion', etc.) (TMS 118–134). We are asked to 'imagine' the 'response they would evoke' in people past and present, including 'feelings, social attitudes, prejudices, fears, fantasies, ambitions' (TMS 117f), but Firth tells us little about his own response. Perhaps he feels he could not produce an analysis meeting his own demands for stringency, especially for complex and subtle materials.

8.83 Similar limitations beset Firth's sallies into '**stylistics**', which he also claims as a 'level of linguistic analysis' (P2 106) (cf. 8.50, 64). Deriding '"discourse analysis"' 'in America', he wants a 'much more systematic' and 'disciplined approach to the study of language' and 'literature', stating 'features or elements' 'in linguistic terms' and 'avoiding value judgment' and 'aesthetic appreciation' (P2 106, 125; cf. P1 190, 202). 'Style' results from 'fusing' 'elements of habit, custom, tradition,' and 'innovation' within 'verbal creation' (P1 184) (cf. 3.69; 5.82; 6.52; 9.102; 10.57). Even if 'whenever a man speaks', it is 'in some sense as a poet', 'poetry' stands apart as 'any piece of prose for which another' 'cannot be adequately substituted' ('attributed to Paul Valéry') (P1 193; P2 18, 25). 'The poet so shapes his composition' that 'a great deal of its meaning is the form he gives it' (P1 214) (cf. 3.69).

8.84 Not surprisingly, Firth disperses 'stylistic analysis' to a number of 'levels' and favours the 'lower' ones: 'phonetic, phonological, prosodic, and grammatical' (P2 195; P1 198, 200) (cf. 8.51; 9.103). In his treatment of Swinburne, he recommends, but does not demonstrate, 'starting' from 'the contextual study of the whole poem' 'by the methods of linguistics' (P1 201). 'Criticism at higher levels' would attend not just to 'the culture context', including 'biography and history', but also to 'word-formation or descriptive etymology', 'syntax', and 'phrasal stylistics', e.g., 'the association of synonyms, antonyms, contraries, and complementary couples', 'reversed and crossed antitheses', or 'patterns of opposition' (P1 199–202). Since, however, 'a detailed study of the words and pieces' 'would be laborious', 'scholars might be satisfied' to 'guess the probable result', and Firth is content to do 'without reference to the higher levels' (P1 201, 203). He proffers the alibi that Swinburne is 'the most "phonetic" of all English poets' (P1 197; TMS 188).[42]

8.85 Having covered the first two 'methods of stating linguistic facts' ('language of description' and 'language under description'), we now come to the '**language of translation**' (P2 49, 87, 98, 112, 149, 158, 202) (cf. 8.35). In its usual sense, 'translation' is a 'science and art' offering 'a world-wide range for experiment' and 'inter-cultural cooperation' (P2 135). 'The fact of translation' is both 'a necessity' on 'general human grounds' and 'a main challenge' to 'linguistic theory' to apply its 'technical' 'description' (P2 77, 66, 82; cf. P2 83, 197). But 'in the widest terms', 'we are really translating' 'whenever we enter into the speech of someone else or our own past speech', so we must account for '"translation" within the same language' (P2 77f, 198).

8.86 'No translation is ever final or complete' or 'really equivalent'

(P2 79, 197, 76, 112). 'One can never expect the modes of meaning' to be 'parallel or equivalent' between 'languages', especially the 'phonetic and phonaesthetic' (i.e., sound symbolism),[43] and 'universal grammar' is of course rejected (P2 92, 196, 82) (cf. 8.19, 60). But 'translation problems' can be solved 'in the mutual assimilation of the languages in similar contexts of situation' and in 'common human experience' (P2 87, 76, 82).

8.87 While 'the basis for any total translation' 'must be found in linguistic analysis', 'the reverse process of using a translation as a basis for linguistic analysis at any level' is an 'error' (P2 76, 157). Firth scolds 'linguists who constantly make use of translation in linguistic analysis' 'without a systematic statement of the nature and function of the translation methods used' (P2 83). Again, he singles out 'Americans': 'ethnographic linguists' (e.g., Voegelin, Yegerlehner and Robinett 1954) who 'confuse' 'translation with grammatical and collocational statements'; and 'structural-ists' (e.g., Harris 1951) in whose work the 'loose, impressionistic', 'casual', 'slipshod, and uncritical' 'use of translation vitiates linguistic analysis' (P2 165, 197, 49, 204nf).[44]

8.88 Firth prefers 'statement of meaning by various forms of translation and definition' (P2 198) (cf. Malinowski 1935). As possible forms, Firth lists 'bit-for-bit translation', 'interlinear word-for-word translation (sometimes described as "literal" or "verbal" translation'), and 'free' (or 'running' or 'idiomatic') translation' (P2 149, 198).[45] A '"comparison"' of these can make 'the text become quite clear', aided by '"the contextual specification of meaning"' and 'detailed commentary', e.g., 'phonetic and grammatical notes' (P2 165, 149). 'Translation' serves here merely to furnish 'identification names for language isolates', i.e., 'reference labels' (P2 197, 158, 33).

8.89 In tribute to his own spirit, I shall end my survey on a bright note. (I would be happy if I have covered just a fourth of Firth.) 'Again and again, linguistic scholarship has served the formal education of its time' (P2 130), and he hopes it will again (cf. 12.64). 'Linguistic methods' can 'help the study of the Mother tongue', combat 'speech defects', or develop 'orthographies for Oriental and African languages' (P1 93). Closely related tasks include 'translating into Asian and African languages for education' and 'specialized occupations', plus 'collecting and collating traditional oral literature and other creative compositions' (P2 135). And if 'every cultured man needs a second and perhaps a third foreign language', linguistic methods can 'help learners' to 'acquire good pronunciation' or to learn 'a foreign language for reading only' (TMS 211; P1 93; TMS 136) (cf. 4.86; 9.1).[46]

8.90 Firth sees 'the tasks' of 'linguistics' 'increasing in responsibility' (P2 132). At such a time, 'the greatest need of linguistic scholarship' is 'a new outlook over a much wider field of life', and 'new values' (P1 32, 29f). We should 'try other theories', 'overhaul our descriptive instruments' and 'languages of description', and seek 'more accurately determined linguistic categories for principal types' of 'usage in various social roles' (P2 189;

P1 28). 'Vast research' also awaits in 'the biographical study of speech' and in 'sociological linguistics' (P1 29, 27).

8.91   Above all, 'general linguistic theory' should be made useful in 'describing particular languages and in dealing with specific language problems' (P2 130). It should 'guide' 'analyses' and 'provide principles' for 'synthesizing' 'the useful results of linguistic studies of the past' (P2 130) (cf. 1.6f; 12.64). It should undertake 'a serial contextualization of our facts, context within context, each one a function' 'of a bigger context, and all contexts finding a place' in 'the context of culture' (P1 32) (cf. 8.26, 42, 44; 9.22f; 12.62). And it should also 'produce the main structural framework for the bridges between different languages and cultures' (P2 130, 202). To meet such tasks, Firth calls for a 'linguistically centred social analysis'; 'a description of speech and language functions with reference to effective observable results'; and a 'study of conversation' to seek 'the key to understanding what language really is and how it works' (P2 177, 112; P1 32). Much remains to be achieved in the 'study' of 'language', 'and we are still far from understanding how it functions' (TMS 147).

Notes

1. The key to Firth citations is: P1: *Papers in Linguistics 1934–1951*; P2: *Selected Papers of J.R. Firth 1952–1959*; and TMS: *Tongues of Men and Speech* (London, Oxford, 1964 [1937 and 1930]). The works often repeat passages or overlap.
2. Strevens notes that Firth's early work differs from later in views about 'grammar', 'spelling', and 'experimental phonetics' (TMS viiif). Further indecisions or contradictions involve: whether linguistics should be a separate discipline (8.16f); whether to use old or new terms (8.37); whether levels are mutually prerequisite (8.51); whether grammar should be stated in terms of meaning (8.45, 62); whether the sentence is the basic unit (8.54f); whether morphology and syntax should be merged (8.56); whether the roman alphabet is good or needs reform (8.74f); and whether collocations concern syntactic form (8.78f). To smoothe the lines of argument, I consign some contradictory statements to footnotes (cf. Notes 7, 10, 18, 26, 30, 33, 39, 43).
3. Pike's quotes of Firth are: 'schematic constructs have no ontological status' (LB 56; P1 181); 'each fact finds its place in a system of related statements, all arising from theory' (LB 56; P2 43); and 'even in mathematics the possibilities of complete axiomatization have been overestimated' (LB 56; P2 44). Pike finds Firth's 'place and order' similar to 'etic slot', though the emphasis on categories over words (cf. 8.53) suggests an 'emic' view; and he identifies Firth's 'prosody' with 'phonemics', which Firth denies (LB 420; P2 27f). In return, Firth mentions Pike's differentiating the 'etic' from the 'emic', and his 'grammatical prerequisites of phonemic analysis', but protests that 'all levels are mutually requisite' (cf. 8.51); and he sees Pike's 'procedural approach' as 'an assembly line for the production of "linguisticians"' – an ambition Firth seems to share (P2 130, 30; P1 164; P2 44) (cf. 5.26; 8.11f). Another similarity is the concern for situations, including the participants and non-verbal events and objects (e.g., furniture, TMS 110 and LB 128) (cf. 8.26, 34).
4. Resemblances include: a stimulus-response model for language (4.10–14; 8.23); a distaste for mentalism and traditional grammar (4.8, 5; 8.24, 5, 7); a

reverence for Sanskrit grammarians (4.4; 8.4f); and a strong interest in language sound studied in contexts (4.35, 8.65–70) or with the aid of machines (4.28, 4^{10}; 8^{33}).

5. Though the negative moments are more noticeable (cf. 8.32, 37, 46, 62, 65, 67, 83, 87, 8^{29}), some positive moments are quite emphatic (cf. Note 26). Firth expansively coins the term 'Atlantic linguistics' with 'Western Europe' plus America as 'the home base', and 'English' as 'the main vehicle of communication around' this 'common pool' (P1 156) (cf. 8.12). Yet he cannily includes 'Russian or Slav or other Central European scholars', since they had influence in America or emigrated there (P1 169, 156).

6. Personal credit goes to Sir William Jones for having, in Calcutta in 1786, devoted 'an epoch-making paragraph' of his speech before the 'Asiatic Society of Bengal' to 'comparing' 'the languages of India, Iran, and Europe' within 'one great linguistic family' (TMS 75f; P1 17, 55, 177f) (cf. W. Jones 1824). But at first scholars mistook Sanskrit itself for the 'original' 'parent language' (TMS 76; P1 178) (cf. 2.5).

7. In an utterly different mood, Firth lauds the 'special' 'logico-experimental languages' 'linked with direct experience for purposes of science' and 'writing in parallel with facts' (TMS 101) (cf. Note 14). He denies that the 'languages of 'reason' and 'logic' are ' "unreal" '; 'the more' our 'habits' are 'influenced' by 'such reasonable languages' – 'exact and definite', 'as free as possible from sentiment, wishful thinking', 'the mythical, magical, and fantastic – the better the world will be' (TMS 102). He uses the term 'sense' (following '[Rudolf] Carnap, [Otto] Neurath and others') for 'statements' which are 'verifiable in the space-time world' and 'refer to immediate experience', and vows 'that all the technical achievements of contemporary civilization' 'are the result of sense' (TMS 104, 117, 108). 'Exercising our ability to distinguish' 'sense and nonsense' would aid 'a critical use of language' and 'an understanding' of 'how language is used for and against us every day' in 'speeches', 'books, and papers', e.g., in 'propaganda for morons and cretinous advertising' (TMS 137, 107) (cf. 4.88). Even 'at the expense of all the pretty talks about books', 'let us have more sense and less nonsense in linguistic education' – intriguing advice in view of 'the regular use of nonsense in phonology' and 'grammar' (e.g., by Sapir, Nida, Jespersen, and Gardiner) (TMS 108; P1 24, 170). However, Wittgenstein is also quoted admitting 'a good deal of his own writings was nonsense': once we 'recognize them as senseless' we 'surmount' them and 'see the world right' (TMS 108).

8. The censure reflects 'the custom of labelling each word' as 'one part of speech' and forbidding 'a preposition' to 'be used as an adverb' (P2 121).

9. Firth is embarrassingly sure that 'ours is the cultural supremacy without the shadow of a doubt' (TMS 205) (cf. 8.74). 'Let no one forget, whatever his race, that Europeans by their will to make the most of what the whole earth has to give have made the world one' (TMS 53) – and let no one remember how often they did so by exploiting, subjugating, or exterminating others.

10. Though he finds 'appalling' Lord Macaulay's decision that the British should 'press our ABC' and 'literary arcana on our Indian fellow subjects', Firth remains impressed by this 'biggest Imperial language and culture undertaking the world has ever seen', and claims 'English continues to serve the best interests of India as an Indian language' (P1 55). As for Chinese, contrast Firth's claim that 'the Mandarin, or Pekin [Beijing] dialect, is spoken by a comparatively small number' (TMS 207) with Li and Thompson's current (1981:1) estimate of 'over a billion people' due to the 1955 'proclamation' of 'a common language for the nation'.

11. Yet scant regard is shown for C.K. Ogden's 'Basic English', whose ancestry
     Firth sees in 'the English Rationalists of the seventeenth century' (P1 169). It
     fails to select 'truly international words' and is too general to suit the concept of
     a 'restricted language' (TMS 67; P2 111) (cf. 8.76ff) Also, Firth raises the 'fear
     of murdering a living language': 'by limiting' people to 'a small number of
     words and sentence patterns', you may 'make things more difficult' (TMS 70).
12. Firth's scenario slyly touches on the cold war: the nations 'turn to the United
     States' with its 'books', 'men' and 'money', 'to Russia' with its 'gospel and
     creed, and also to England – I hesitate to summarize what we have got
     nowadays, but we may have a little of something the others haven't' (P2 136).
13. Further presumed sources are given in my References: Ascham (1570), Hume
     (1610), Dalgarno (1680), Wallis (1727), Gurney (1752), Blanchard (1787),
     Byrom (1834) and Wright (1905); Wilkins and Dalgarno are also acknowledged
     by Pike in regard to an 'etics of meaning' (LB 193). Among the American
     works, Murray (1795) and Haldeman (1856) are featured (cf. Edgerton 1942);
     see also Pickering (1815, 1820), Johnson (1832), DuPonceau (1838), and
     Haldemann (1877). The itinerant Bells, Alexander (1790–1865), Alexander
     Melville (1819–1905), and Alexander Graham (1847–1922), are 'the best
     symbol of Atlantic phonetics, since they linked up Scotland, England, Ireland,
     Canada, and the United States by their own work, and eventually the entire
     world by telephone' (P1 166) (cf. A.M. Bell 1867, 1897).
14. In a rush of positivist and rationalist orthodoxy, Firth quotes Hume's advice to
     ' "commit to the flames" ' any ' "volume" ' that does not contain ' "abstract
     reasoning concerning quantity and number" ' or ' "experimental reasoning
     concerning matter of fact and existence" '; and hails 'the *unity of science*' by
     quoting Carnap, a 'leading exponent of physicalism', who assigns the 'greatest
     importance' to 'physical language' about 'physical things' as 'the basic language
     of all science' and the most 'universal, comprehending the contents of all other
     scientific languages', and who abjures any 'philosophy of nature', 'mind',
     'history', or 'society' (TMS 105f) (cf. 4.9; 8[7]).
15. This has occurred 'during the last forty years' (i.e., 1917–57), an intriguing
     timetable if (as Whitehead remarked) 'the span of useful life' for a 'scientific
     theory is about thirty years' (P2 124, 24; cf. P1 216). But when noting the
     continued disregard for meaning, Firth admits 'there has been no revolution in
     linguistics' (P2 72). Together, these statements suggest that the real revolution
     must be to open 'the second front' and study meaning in earnest (cf. 8.46).
16. Firth keeps referring to speaking as 'disturbing the air' (P1 19, 75; TMS 21f; P2
     170, 172), or as 'molecular' or 'acoustic disturbances' accompanying those 'in
     the bodies of speakers and listeners' (P2 13). He also remarks that 'speech'
     depends on 'continuous active control' of the 'outgoing column of air'; that
     'babbling is the basis of all speech'; that 'chiming and rhyming are the two
     fundamental principles' of 'all language'; and that 'personal identity' is related
     to 'the behaviour' of 'the larynx and the pharynx' (TMS 153f, 22, 33, 36f, 31).
17. Still, 'a man can think when without a larynx or when he is deaf and dumb',
     thanks to 'a widespread network of processes' in 'the brain', 'the respiratory
     tract, the abdomen, and so on' (TMS 179; cf. TMS 152). Compare also: 'in
     1879 Bain and Ribot' claimed that 'in reading or recalling a sentence we feel the
     twitter of the organs' (cf. Bain 1873; Ribot 1874); but 'a few years ago' 'an
     experimental investigation' found that 'movements of the tongue in internal
     speech or "verbal thought" ' 'corresponded to overt speech only in 4.4 per cent
     of the cases' (TMS 177f) (cf. 3[7]). 'Talking' or 'conversing with oneself' is
     related not to the ' "internal speech" ' of 'neurologists', but to 'babbling' (P2 25,
     13f, 206; P1 186) (cf. Note 16).

18. But compare: 'a phonetic habit is an attunement, a setting of the central nervous system touched off by appropriate phonetic stimulus' (TMS 181). Or: 'a spoken sentence is a series of phonetic conditions progressively completed'; 'any similarly conditioned listener would be able to complete the pattern'.

19. One whole chapter (P1 76–91) written with B.B. Rogers is devoted to 'a systematic analysis' of 'the Chinese monosyllable' based on data from 'Mr K.H. Hu of Changsha' (P1 76f).

20. 'Morbid linguistics', dealing with 'speech disorders' like 'aphasia', would be a domain 'for joint research' with 'the medical profession' (P1 188; P2 208; cf. P2 25; TMS 149) (cf. 9.1). 'Brain injuries can destroy phonetic', 'syntactical, and semantic habits' (TMS 153). 'Verbal aphasia means the loss of the active powers of speech'; 'nominal aphasia disturbs the active association of the right word with the right object'. 'These results' are enlisted to 'support' Firth's 'view of speech' as 'a bodily habit having a physical basis' (cf. 8.22).

21. Firth acknowledges as 'fair' and 'important' the Soviet 'criticism' (Nikolai Marr, Ivan I. Meshchaninov, Nikolai S. Chemodanov) that 'dialectical materialism' was neglected in favour of 'mechanical', wherein 'the structure' is 'treated as a thing', and of 'fossilized formalism without the sociological component' (P1 169f, 181, 170, 178; P2 129). He hopes his '"spectrum" analysis' meets these objections by 'making sure of the social reality of the data at the sociological level' (P1 170f) (cf. 8.41, 48).

22. He quotes André Martinet's (1954: 125) grim jest that 'in descriptive linguistics', 'the rigour after which some of us are striving too often resembles rigor mortis' (P2 47).

23. 'The introduction of exponents brings results together and ensures renewal of connection in experience with the language', yet 'keeps the levels of analysis separate' and enables a 'direct and positive phonetic approach' that 'avoids a false realism' (P2 185).

24. For Richard Temple, it was '"all one"' whether we '"put new definitions on old words or have new words"' (letter, 1907) (P1 140; P2 120, 142). Since '"there is no universally acknowledged set of definitions"' or '"views about linguistic categories"', everyone must '"use his own discretion and coin his own terminology"' (P2 142).

25. Firth adopted the '"context of situation"' from Malinowski (1923, 1935) and Wegener (1885) (P2 4, 108, 138f, 146ff, 153, 162f, 203; P1 181f; TMS 150) (cf. Halliday and Hasan 1985: 6f). To 'give native words the full cultural context of ethnographic description' and to 'give an outline of a semantic theory useful in the work on primitive linguistics', Malinowski explored 'situations' like 'trading, fishing, gardening', or 'hunting', but didn't attain 'a technique of analysis satisfying the demands of linguistic science' (P2 138, 147, 149; P1 30). Wegener was more mentalistic, classifying 'situations' in terms of 'perception' ('Anschauung'), 'memory' ('Erinnerung'), and 'consciousness' ('Bewusstsein'), which disturbs Firth (TMS 150; P2 147).

26. But here, too, Firth is not fully consistent. When declining to 'propose an a priori system of general categories', he says 'science should not impose systems on languages', but 'look for systems in speech activity' and 'state the facts' (P1 144). And he sees the 'English' 'joining our American colleagues in the movement for an objective and realist science of language' (TMS 88).

27. To avert confusion, Firth cautions that 'the term "general semantics" of Alfred Korzybski' designates a 'linguistic therapy quite unrelated to technical linguistics' (P1 191n) (cf. 5[40]). The movement is also judged less 'sophisticated and stimulating' than Malinowski's analyses of 'systems of words' (P2 156).

28. These terms are also used for levels (cf. 8.50). The 'major' functions are those

whereby 'functional discrepancies widen' and 'engulf' a 'superficial similarity' 'between sounds' (P1 41). Later, 'phonaesthetic' gets added to the 'major' list and 'substitution' to the 'minor' (P1 37, 48) (cf. 8.71).

29. Firth notes that his 'use of the term "levels"' 'is not to be confused' with Bloomfield's in *Language* (P2 175), where it applies only to language 'levels' of social strata (BL 49) (cf. 4.25, 84) Also, Firth spurns the American level of 'morphophonemics' as 'uneven and inadequate', unhelpful for 'syntactical analysis', 'without value in the learning of English' or 'machine translation', and 'tearing stylistics to shreds' (P2 119; cf. P2 74, 187f, 201) (cf. 7.48, 7^{21}).

30. When explaining why 'sequence and arrangement' are 'important' for 'recognizing' 'recurrences of known words', Firth says (in a rare moment of mentalism) that 'the patterns of language in the "unconscious" background are just as important as the patterns of speech we make and hear' (TMS 183). For the sound level, the goal is to 'record' 'specific components of speech acts' so as to 'represent' 'the way the native uses his 'sounds' – not so much what he 'says, but what he thinks he says' (P1 47, 3).

31. 'Numeration' is too neat an instance of 'sets of grammatical categories falling into systems and correlating with social conditions of use' (P1 223, 228) to be typical (cf. 4.21f, 70). Firth cites 'the system' 'in Fijian, which formally distinguishes singular, dual, "little" plural, and "big" plural' (P1 227). 'The application of the word "meaning" to the function of an element' in a 'specific system' of a 'language' is claimed to illustrate 'the mathematical method', such as demanded by Martin Joos: '"we must make our 'linguistics' a kind of mathematics within which inconsistency is by definition impossible"' (P1 227, 219) (cf. 3.15). Can this be a hint of Firth's 'strictly formal statement of meaning in linguistic terms' (cf. 8.45; 12.54)?

32. Because 'the syllable structure of any word or piece' is 'prosodic', 'no general definition of the syllable' is 'possible'; the 'structure must be studied in particular language systems' (P2 193; P1 131; P2 101, 201) (cf. 8.58). Among 'the prosodic features of a word', Firth lists the 'number', 'nature' ('open or closed'), 'quantity', 'sequence', and 'quality' ('dark or clear') of 'syllables', plus 'vowel harmony' among syllables (P1 130).

33. However, Firth tells 'writers of theses' to 'please note' William Jones's motto: 'it is superfluous to discourse on the organs of speech' (P1 112). But then, too, Haldeman's complaint is cited over 'grave errors' among 'linguists' about 'speech organs that can be seen and felt' (P1 115). Such 'machines' as the 'kymograph', 'the palatograph', 'X-ray', or 'gramophone' offer resources for more exact study (P1 148–55, 173–76; TMS 151, 159) (cf. 4.28, 4^{10}).

34. Firth 'distinguishes prosodic systems from phonematic' in that only the former 'analyse' in terms of 'words and pieces'; but 'the exponents' of the two types of 'units need not be mutually exclusive' and 'a phonematic constituent in one' 'language' 'may be a prosody in another' (P1 122, 184; P2 137).

35. According to Jan Baudouin de Courtenay, it was Mikołaj Kruszewski, working 'among the linguists at Kazan', who 'proposed to employ the term "phoneme"' as different from "phone"' 'in an essay' on 'vowel alternances' (P1 1) (cf. Kruszewski 1879; Baudouin de Courtenay 1882). 'The terms' attained 'widespread currency' through 'other schools' (cf. 2.69; 4.29f, 33; 5.42f; 11.80), especially the English School and the Prague School (cf. 6.43). And '"the phoneme idea"' 'was implicit in the work of all phoneticians and orthographists who have employed broad transcription' (P1 2).

36. 'Position' is one aspect of such systems, e.g., 'vowel systems' have 'in final unstressed position' 'fewer terms than in stressed' (P2 99) (cf. 4.35). Firth opposes 'universal definitions' and 'cardinalizations' of 'vowels and consonant'

as proposed by Sweet and Daniel Jones, because such elements 'must be determined' for each 'particular language' (P1 131, 146; cf. P1 124, 165; P2 99) (cf. 7.20, 7¹⁰; 8.66).

37. Firth remarks on the 'time lag' 'among literary elites' (cf. 8.4; 4.40) and cites T.S. Eliot as 'a "fade-out" voice of a disappearing world' (TMS 116).

38. Firth points to the 'League of Nations' 'report' of 1934 advising 'universal adoption', and to the 'advantages' of 'the alphabetic revolution in Turkey'; and glosses Lenin's vision of 'latinization' as 'the great revolution of the east' (P1 68f, 75, m.t.). Yet Firth says that the act of 'reducing a language to writing' can be 'a reduction indeed', and he seems sceptical about Melville Bell's 'Visible Speech' (1867), announced as a 'Science of Universal Alphabetics or Self-Interpreting Physiological Letters for the Writing of All Languages' (P2 31f; P1 118). Still, 'phonemics' has become 'an established technique, notably in the ethnographic studies of the American Indian' (P2 129; P1 164; cf. P1 172) (cf. 8.31).

39. However, in a mood of abstraction, Firth says that 'the term "restricted language"' designates 'a scientific fiction required by linguistic analysis', not 'an actual institutionalized form of language easily recognized by the average man' – such as 'the language of babies, or boys, girls, and adolescents of different classes and regions', or of 'specialized situations determined by manners and customs and recognized institutions' (P2 207). But I don't see anything fictional about the groups of texts he cites (e.g., 'Swinburnese lyrics, modern Arabic headlines') or even 'a single text' (e.g., the 'unique thirteenth-century Chinese text' studied in Halliday's [1955] thesis) (P2 29, 34, 98, 106, 116).

40. At least, it seems significant that the chair was finally granted in 1944 after Firth had been recommending it for over a decade. Also, Firth published nothing from 1937 to 1946, the only hiatus of such length in his career; maybe his project materials were classified.

41. Without more demonstration, I cannot follow the precept that although it 'may be supported by reference to context of situation', 'meaning by collocation is not at all the same thing as contextual meaning, which is the functional relation of the sentence to the processes of a context of situation in the context of culture' (P1 xi, 195; P2 180). Nor is 'meaning by collocation' to 'involve the definition of word meaning by means of further sentences', nor to be 'directly concerned' with 'concepts', 'ideas', or 'essential meaning' (P1 196; P2 20) (cf. 8.24f).

42. Compare Sapir's similar estimate but lower valuation (cf. 3.71). Firth warns that 'the philosophy of Swinburne's poetry forms no part of a linguist's technique language', and that anyway 'Swinburne had nothing to say as a philosopher' (P1 201f). But a statement is attempted: 'holism supported by pan-humanism and worship of "the earth-soul Freedom"' in a 'strange world in which contrast and concord are one and contraries divine' (P1 201f).

43. Firth decries the 'misleading' or 'fallacious' notions of 'sound symbolism' or 'onomatopoeia' (TMS 187; P1 45, 191f, 194; cf. CG 69) (cf. 4.25; 11.92). He substitutes his 'invented' term 'phonaesthetic', included (unlike 'phonetic') among the 'major functions' or 'modes' (P1 194, 39, 37, 41, 44, 197ff, 201) (cf. 8.48). This 'function can be shown' with 'obvious correlations between alliterative words' and 'experience', e.g., '"str-"' words ('"strap"', "string", "streak" etc.) having a "long, thin, straight, narrow, stretched out" correlation' (P1 44). The cause is not an '"impression on the ear resembling the effect of the object on the mind"' (Humboldt), but a 'habitual similar phoneticizing of similar contexts of experience', or an 'association' of 'phonological features' with 'social and personal attitude' (TMS 187f; P1 44, 194). Yet his evidence

comes not from ordinary experience, but from 'nonsense verse', and from 'experiments' in matching a 'round bellying shape' and a 'sharp' 'zigzag' one with words like '"kikeriki" and "oombooloo"' (P1 193f). Puzzling too is his claim of 'interlingual' generality for 'functions' like 'the "plosivity" of plosives', and his invocation of 'phonaesthetic habits' shared among languages, e.g., 'European', 'Romance', or 'Germanic' ('Gothonic'), plus his cryptic aphorism that 'it is part of the meaning of an American' or 'a Frenchman' (or 'a German word) to sound like one' (P1 41; TMS 191, 193; P1 192, 226; P2 110).

44. To illustrate some 'absurdities and futilities of interlinear word for word translation', Firth picks from I.A. Richards (1932): 'With-not-bear-others-of-mind, carrying-out not-bear-others-of-government, rule the world can (be) turned around palm-on' (P2 78; cf. TMS 82).

45. Along other lines, Firth lists 'creative translation', mainly for 'literature'; 'official translation', used in 'institutionalized' 'languages'; 'descriptive' 'translation', used by 'linguists' for 'illustrative texts'; and 'mechanical translation' by machines (P2 86f; cf. P2 67ff, 93f, 119, 196).

46. But 'learning another language from books' can lead to 'a service of words that is not speech', lacking 'the habitual economy of the native in social situations', and encouraging 'sentences' that are 'much too long', 'complete', and 'grammatical' (TMS 176).

Chapter 9

M.A.K. Halliday[1]

9.1 Michael Alexander Kirkwood Halliday was a pupil of Firth's, and, with greater elaboration, has pursued similar precepts, above all that 'linguistics' should 'deal with meaning' 'at all levels of analysis' and should study 'texts' 'in contexts of situation' (cf. 8.46f vs. 9.8, 22f, 38, 49, 107). Halliday finds 'the question "what is language?"' unduly 'diffuse' and 'disingenuous', because 'no one account of language will be appropriate for all purposes' (IF xxix; EF 9) (cf. 12.22). 'A theory being a means of action', we must consider what 'action' we 'want to take' 'involving' 'language', so we know what is 'relevant' and 'interesting' for 'the investigation or the task at hand' – 'the nature and functions of language', its 'formal properties', its 'role' 'in the community and the individual', its 'relation' to 'culture', and so on (EF 9; IF xixf) (cf. 9.111; 10.6; 12.58). We may inquire 'what all languages have in common' or how they 'differ', and how they 'vary according to user' and 'function' or 'evolve through time'; or 'how a child develops language, and how language may have evolved in human species'. Or, we may explore 'the quality of texts' such as 'written and spoken' or 'literary and poetic' (IF xxx). Or, we may seek ways to 'help' people 'learning their mother tongue' or a 'foreign language', or 'training translators and interpreters', or composing 'reference works (dictionaries, grammars)' or 'computer software' to 'produce and understand' 'text' and 'speech'. Or, we may focus on 'language and the brain' to help in 'the diagnosis and treatment of language pathologies' ('tumours', 'autism', 'Down's syndrome'), or in the 'design of appliances' for 'the hard of hearing'.

9.2 Halliday compares two 'depths of focus' in 'linguistics': 'the more immediate' *'intrinsic'* aim to 'explain the nature of language', 'implying an *"autonomous"* view'; versus 'the further, *extrinsic* aim to explain features of the social structure' through 'language', 'implying an *instrumental*' view (EF 69). He 'stresses the instrumentality of linguistics' (EF 96), but the two views are not really separable. 'Autonomy' can be only 'conditional and temporary' along the way to a 'general account of language' (EF 53). The 'linguist' who 'insists on autonomy' studies 'grammar and phonology' as 'the "inner" strata of the linguistic system, the core of language', but these are 'contingent upon other systems' depending on 'extra-linguistic phenomena' (EF 96; cf. EF 105) (cf. 12.40). 'Grammatical phenomena' are 'related' 'to features of a culture' in 'extremely complex and abstract' ways; 'linguists' who 'avoid the language/culture issue' blot out 'an important area of research' (IF xxxi).[2] Moreover, 'criteria' of 'well-formedness' are 'not easy to find' 'within language'; 'in "autonomous" linguistics', 'orthography', 'a codified form of idealization', 'usually' 'decides' (EF 68) (cf. 9.43, 82, 9[41]). But in 'a theory' of 'social structure', 'what is well-formed' is 'interpretable as a possible selection within a set of options based on some motivated hypothesis about language behaviour' (EF 69).

9.3 Halliday draws a different 'basic opposition in grammars of the second half of the twentieth century' than the one featured in 'the public debates of the 1960s' between ' "structuralist" ' and ' "generative" ' approaches (IF xxviii). On one side he places '**paradigmatic**' or ' "choice" grammars' – 'the **functional** ones, with their roots in rhetoric and ethnography' – 'interpreting language as a network of relations with structures' that 'realize[3] these relationships', 'emphasizing variables among different languages', and 'taking semantics as foundation; hence grammar is natural and organized around the text or discourse' (IF xxviii, xiii, xix). On the other side he places '**syntagmatic**' or ' "chain" grammars'– 'the **formal** ones with their roots in logic and philosophy' – 'interpreting language as a list of structures' connected by 'regular relations' (shown as 'transformations'), 'emphasizing universal features of language, and taking grammar (which they call "syntax") as the foundation of language; hence the grammar is arbitrary' and 'organized around the sentence'. Despite some 'cross currents' and 'borrowing' of 'insights', the two sides have found it 'difficult to maintain a dialogue' or 'exchange ideas' (IF xviii).

9.4 Chomsky 'called his own syntagmatic formal grammar "generative" ' to 'distinguish' it from the ' "structuralists" ', on whom he was 'building' despite his 'polemics', and to suggest that his was 'written in a way which did not depend on unconscious assumptions of the reader' but 'operated as a formal system' (IF xxviii) (cf. 7.91). In return, 'the language has to be so idealized that it bears little relation to what people actually write, and still less to what they actually say'. The so-called 'Chomskyan revolution' was more 'a shift of emphasis' 'from the anthropological to the philosophical standpoint' (cf. 7.1ff). 'The return' to 'discourse in the 1970s', however, 'restored the balance' and reinstated 'the ethnographic tradition' (Malinowski, Whorf, Pike), of which 'Chomsky seems to have been unaware' (IF xxviiif).

9.5 In its 'extreme form', 'the philosopher's approach to language' encourages 'linguistics' to 'idealize out *all* natural language as irrelevant and unsystematic, and to treat only constructed logical languages' (EF 53) (cf. 12.50). 'A lesser extreme' 'reduces' 'all sentences of natural language' 'to a "deep structure" ' of 'logical relations' (7.62–66). Chomsky's 'idealization', by 'reducing them to the same level as stutterings, false starts, clearings of the throat', 'irons out' 'behaviourally significant variations in language', e.g., 'features of assertion and doubt' (cf. 7.12; 9.51f). 'In a sociological context', 'the image of language having a "pure" form ("langue") that becomes contaminated in the process of being translated into speech ("parole") is of little value' (EF 67) (cf. 12.47). So Halliday discards the 'boundary between language and speech', '"langue" and "parole", or competence and performance' (cf. 2.20; 5.7; 6.33, 46; 7.12; 8.30; 10.69; 11.12, 26, 47, 55, 67; 12.36).

9.6 Against 'the Chomskyan notion of competence', Halliday's notion of 'meaning potential' 'is defined' 'in terms of culture', not 'mind': 'what speakers can do' and 'can mean', not what they 'know' (EF 52f, 25, 55, 57, 72, 110). We 'force a distinction between meaning and function' if we 'characterize language subjectively as the ability or competence of the speaker, instead of objectively as a potential or set of alternatives' (EF 25) (cf. 11.45). '"Can do"' is 'related' to '"does"' 'as potential to actual', whereas 'the relation' between '"knows"' and '"does"' 'is complex and oblique' (EF 52f) (cf. 9.12; 12.39). 'A hypothesis about what the speaker can do in a social context' 'makes sense of what he does', which might otherwise 'appear merely as a random selection' (EF 67). We must 'pay attention to what is said' and 'relate it systematically to what might have been said but was not' (cf. 9.21; 12.43).

9.7 'Language is the primary means of cultural transmission' whereby 'behavioural options' are 'typically realized', 'social groups are integrated, and the individual is identified and reinforced' (EF 45, 107, 8, 48, 69f) (cf. 3.1; 4.10; 8.28). Therefore, Halliday concurs with Firth (who 'introduced the term "sociological linguistics"' 'in 1935' [in 'The Techniques of Semantics', P1 27]) that 'language as social behaviour' is 'an acknowledged concern of modern linguistics' (EF 48f; cf. Halliday and Hasan 1985: 8) (cf. 8.50). His own 'orientation is to language as social rather than individual' and is 'aligned' with 'sociological rather than psychological' 'research' (IF xxx; EF 53f) (cf. 8.17, 28; 9^{47}; 12.15).[4] Studying 'social man' 'shifts the emphasis from the physical to the human environment' (EF 48) (cf. 8.23). 'The individual is seen as the focus of a complex of human relations which collectively define the content of his social' and 'linguistic' 'behaviour' (EF 48, 52).

9.8 Whereas the '"context of culture"' 'defines' 'the **potential**', i.e., 'the range of possibilities', the '"context of situation"' determines 'the **actual**', i.e., the 'choice' that 'takes place' (EF 49) (cf. 6.11; 11.55f). Firth's 'interest' was 'in the actual, the text and its relation to its surroundings' – not, however, 'in the accidental but the typical': 'repetitive, significant, and systematizable patterns of social behaviour' (EF 49, 26, 40, 43) (cf. 8.26f). Hence, the 'actual' is not 'unique' or a 'chance product of random observation'; and 'the analysis of language comes within the range of a social theory' and leads toward 'an account of semantic options deriving from the social structure' (EF 49ff, 64; cf. EF 62) (cf. 12.14).

9.9 Research therefore demands a 'theory of social meanings' – a 'socio-semantics', a 'meeting ground of two ideologies, the social and the linguistic'

(EF 44, 56, 64). Moreover, 'a behavioural semantics' is needed to map out the 'intermediate levels' which 'relate behavioural options' 'to the grammar' (EF 55, 83). In this view, 'the meaning potential' of 'language' 'realizes behaviour potential' and is 'in turn realized in the language system as lexicogrammatical[5] potential' ('what the speaker "can say"') (EF 51, 55, 69). 'Meaning is a form of behaving', and '"to mean" is a verb of the "doing" class' (EF 55) (cf. 9.15).

9.10 'The connection between' 'the social functions of language and the linguistic system' is 'clearest in the case of the language of the very young **child**' (EF 34, 31). Those 'functions' 'determine both the options the child creates for himself and their realizations in structure' (EF 44, 33, 29). 'Language development' is thus 'the mastery of linguistic functions': learning 'the meaning potential associated' with 'the uses of language', i.e., 'learning how to mean' (EF 24, 7) (cf. Halliday 1975). 'Insights into how language is learned' ought to shed light on 'the internal organization of language' (IF 45) (cf. 7.24). We already have 'important work' in the 'theory of social meanings' based on 'the socialization of the child', e.g., that of Basil Bernstein (EF 44f, 63; cf. EF 8, 18f, 48, 52, 64, 68ff, 73).[6]

9.11 In 'learning his mother tongue, a child' 'is, in effect, learning new modes and conditions of being' (EF 7). He 'first tends to use language in just one function at a time'; 'structure' and 'internal form reflect' a given 'function' 'rather directly', and 'the utterance has just one structure' (EF 7f, 34, 27, 97, 44) (cf. 5.32; 11[16]). The 'two-level system with meanings coded directly into expressions (sounds and gestures)' gets 'replaced, in the second year of life, by a three-level system' with a 'grammar', whereby 'meanings are first coded into wordings and these then recoded into expressions' (IF xviif) (cf. 9.36f). 'This step' 'opens up' 'the potential for dialogue, the dynamic exchange of meanings with other people', and 'for combining different kinds of meaning in one utterance – using language to think with and to act with at the same time'. 'Later' 'in the evolution' 'of the system', the 'child' 'learns the principle of "grammatical metaphor"', 'whereby meanings may be cross-coded, and phenomena represented by categories other than those evolved to represent them' (cf. 9.97ff). Eventually, in 'adult language', 'utterances are functionally complex': almost 'every linguistic act' 'serves several functions' that 'interact' in 'subtle and complex' ways (EF 34, 8) (cf. 9.14, 25).

9.12 Following Malinowski in aligning 'ontogeny' with 'phylogeny', Halliday speculates that 'the developing language system of the child traverses, or at least provides an analogy for, the stages through which language itself has evolved', and thus 'opens up' 'a discussion about the nature and social origins of language' (EF 34; IF xviii) (cf. 12.38). Having 'no living specimens of its ancestral types', we can gather 'evidence' 'from studying the language and how it is learnt by a child' (EF 23f) (cf. 5[35]; 7.24ff, 87). 'To judge from children's "protolanguage"', 'language evolved in the human species' from 'an early stage' 'without any grammar', the 'meanings' being 'expressed through rather simple structures whose elements derive directly from the functions' (IF xvii; EF 97) (cf. 9.39, 72).

9.13 By this line of argument, 'the lexicogrammar is a **natural** symbolic system' (IF xviii) (cf. 9.3, 32). 'Both the general kinds of grammatical pattern that have evolved in language and the specific manifestations of each' 'bear a natural relation to the meanings they have evolved to express' (IF xvii). The early stage has a 'relatively small range of meanings for which natural symbols can be devised' (IF xviii). 'In the later protolinguistic stage', the 'interface' between 'meaning' and 'sound' 'develops' a 'frontier of **arbitrariness**' to make 'communication' less 'restricted'; but the 'interface' between 'meaning and wording' 'should not' 'become arbitrary', since 'such a system, by the time it got rich enough to be useful, would also have become impossible to learn' (cf. 12.27). This account goes against 'the psycholinguistic movement of the 1960s', 'concerned primarily with the mechanism of language rather than with its meaning and function', and focused on 'the acquisition[7] of sounds' ('articulation', 'phonology') or of 'linguistic forms' ('vocabulary', 'grammar') (EF 24). Research measured 'the size of the child's vocabulary', 'the relative frequency of different parts of speech', plus 'the control of sentence syntax in the written medium'. Later, work centred on 'the acquisition of linguistic structures' according to 'the "nativist" view' (cf. 7.22–28, 31f).

9.14 For 'our conception of language' to be 'exhaustive, it must incorporate all the child's own "**models**"' (EF 17, 10). In 'the *instrumental* model', 'language' is 'a means of getting things done', and in 'the *regulatory* model', a means for 'exercising control over others' and 'their behaviour' (EF 11f, 31). In 'the *interactional* model', 'language' serves 'the interaction between the self and others' in 'complex and rapidly changing' 'patterns', and 'defines and consolidates the group' (EF 13). In 'the *personal* model', 'the child' becomes 'aware of language as a form of individuality' and of its 'role' in 'the development of personality' (EF 14). In 'the *heuristic* model', 'language' serves 'to explore his environment' and 'investigate reality', and in 'the *imaginative* model', 'to create his own environment' (EF 14f). 'Finally', in 'the *representational* model', 'language is' 'a means of communicating about something, expressing propositions', and 'conveying a message' with 'specific reference to processes, persons, objects, abstractions, qualities, states, and relations of the real world' (EF 16) (cf. 12.24). 'The *ritual* model', with 'language' as 'a means for showing how well one was brought up', comes much later and 'plays no part in the child's experience' (EF 16f).

9.15 With all these facets, the child's total '"model" of language is highly complex' (EF 11) 'Most adult notions of language', in contrast, even if 'externalized and consciously formulated', are 'much too simple', implying that 'language' is only for 'transmission of content' and that 'the representational function' is 'dominant' (EF 11, 16) (cf. 3.15; 8.47; 12.24). 'We tend to underestimate the total extent and functional diversity of the part played by language in the life of the child' (EF 11). Because, 'for the child', 'language' 'has meaning in a very broad sense' and 'a range of functions which the adult does not normally think of as meaningful', we have here a 'vital' domain for 'redefining our notion of meaning' to include 'all functions of language' as 'purposive, non-random, conceptualized activity' (EF 18). 'The young child' 'can be internalizing language while listening and talking', and can 'constantly ask questions' to get 'not merely facts', but 'generalizations about reality that language makes it possible to explore' (EF 14f) (cf. 11.60). Also, 'language in its imaginative function is not necessarily "about" anything', not even 'a make-believe copy of the world'; it may be for 'pure sound' and 'linguistic play' (EF 15f).

9.16 For effectual **'language teaching'**, 'the teacher's own model of language' should 'encompass all that the child knows language to be' and 'take account of the child's own linguistic experience' in its 'richest potential' (EF 10, 19) (cf. 8.7). The model should also be 'relevant' to 'later experiences' and 'to the linguistic demands of society' – where we are 'surrounded' not by 'grammars and dictionaries or randomly chosen words and sentences' but by ' "text" or language in use' in a 'situation' (EF 20) (cf. 10.86, 91; 12.31). 'If the teacher's own "received" conception of language' is 'less rich' and 'diversified, it will be irrelevant to the educational task', witness the 'unhappy experience' caused by 'the view of language as primarily good manners' (EF 10f, 19) (cf. 8.7). 'In school', 'the child' 'is required to accept a stereotype of language contrary to insights' from 'his own experience', as in 'the traditional first "reading and writing" tasks' (EF 11). 'The old "see Spot run"' 'reader' 'bore little' 'relation to any use of language' (EF 12) (cf. 4.85).

9.17 Such issues are urgent because 'educational failure is often' 'language failure', due to 'a fundamental mismatch between the child's linguistic capabilities and the demands' being 'made upon them' (EF 18f; cf. Bernstein 1971–72) (cf. 4.85; 8.7). The problem lies not in 'dialect or accent', nor in 'lack of words (vocabulary' is 'learnt very easily' through 'opportunity' and 'motivation'), nor in 'an impoverishment of grammar' or a 'narrower range of syntactic options' (EF 18).[8] Instead, 'the child' 'suffers some limitation' in 'linguistic models' and some 'restriction on the range of uses of language'; the 'functions' 'have developed one-sidedly', perhaps at the expense of 'the personal function and the heuristic', which do 'not follow automatically from the acquisition of the grammar and vocabulary' (EF 18f).

9.18 Halliday's concern for language development and pedagogy lends urgency to his broad social vision of language. He holds it to be 'a universal of culture that all languages are called upon to fulfil a small set of distinct though related demands' which, though 'indefinitely many and varied', are 'derived ultimately from a small number of general headings' (NT 3/207, EF 104f) (cf. 5.26, 84, 5^2; 8.27). And it is 'the nature of language' to 'have all these functions built into its total capacity' such that 'the social functioning of language' is 'reflected in' 'the internal organization of language as a system' (cf. Malinowski 1923) (EF 23).[9] Thus, 'functional theories of language' seek to 'explain the nature' and 'organization' of the 'language system' by asking which 'functions it has evolved to serve' 'in the life of social man' and how these are 'achieved' 'through speaking and listening, reading and writing' (EF 66, 42ff, 7).

9.19 Halliday now proposes a **'functional grammar'** that can reveal how 'the form of language' is 'determined by the functions', and the 'grammatical patterns' by 'configurations of functions' (EF 7; IF x) (but cf. 3.16, 22, 24, 33; 4.47, 49; 7.63; 8.58; 9.28, 33; 11.25, 27, 50, 53–58). 'Each element in a language is explained by reference to its function in the total linguistic system'; and most 'linguistic items are multi-functional' (IF xiii, 32, xxi) (9.25; cf. 12.43). Among the 'many grammars that are functional in orientation' is **'systemic grammar'** (IF x).[10] 'Systemic theory' 'interprets' 'meaning as choice' and 'a language' or 'semiotic system' 'as networks of interlocking options', in line with 'Firth's category of the "system"' ' as 'a functional paradigm'[11] and with his 'polysystemic principle' (IF xiv, xxvii; EF 55) (cf. 8.30, 32). 'A **system** is a set of features one' 'of which must be selected if the **entry condition** is satisfied' (NT 1/37; EF 55). 'Such a "selection expression" is then realized as a **structure**, the structural representation being fully derived from the systemic; each element of the structure is a point of entry into a further systemic network' (NT 1/37). 'Whatever is chosen in one system' leads to 'a set of choices in another' as we move from 'the most general features step by step' to the 'specific' (IF xiv).

9.20 But the *Introduction* does not 'present' 'the **systemic** portion' of 'networks and realization statements', which 'is currently stored in a computer' (IF x, xv) (cf. Mann and Matthiesen 1984). I would have liked to know more about the 'semantic network', for which extensive claims have been made. For language, it was to be 'a statement of potential at that stratum'; 'a representation' of 'paradigmatic relations'; 'the input to the grammar'; and 'a description of each meaning selection and an account of its relationship to all the others' (EF 76, 79, 83). For human action, it was 'the linguistic realization of patterns of behaviour'; 'the bridge between behaviour patterns and linguistic forms'; and an 'account of how social meanings are expressed in language' (EF 79, 83, 65).

9.21 Instead, the *Introduction* presents 'the **structural** portion', 'showing how the options are realized' – seeking 'breadth before depth' and not 'making explicit all the steps' (IF xv, x) (cf. 9.111). Though it 'presents structures which are the output of networks', the 'grammar' is not ' "structural" ' (nor ' "structuralist" ' 'in the American sense'), i.e., **'syntagmatic'** (IF xvii) (cf. 8.31). 'A systemic grammar is **paradigmatic'**; 'describing something consists in relating it to everything else' (cf. 9.7). The resulting 'theory'[12] is 'not parsimonious', but 'extravagant', with 'a wealth of apparatus' (IF xix) (cf. 9.109f). The 'grammar' has 'a round of choices and operations (a "system-structure cycle") at each rank'; and 'higher rank choices' are 'essentially choices in meaning without the grammar thereby losing contact with the ground'.

9.22 The *Introduction* propounds a 'comprehensive view of grammar' for 'interpreting a text in its context of culture' (IF xxxii, xvii) (cf. 8.91; 12.63). Every 'interpretation of texts, of the system, and of elements of linguistic structure' is based on 'how the language is *used*'; 'the uses' 'have shaped the system' and must be studied, not just the 'properties of the system as such' (IF xxi; NT 3/207) (cf. 8.47; 12.36). But 'whatever the final purpose' or 'direction', the analysis must have 'a grammar at the base' (IF xvi) (cf. 12.54). 'The study of discourse ("text linguistics") cannot properly be separated from the study of the grammar' (IF 345). Although 'the text is a semantic unit, not a grammatical one', 'meanings are realized through **wordings**' (i.e., through 'sequences' or 'syntagms' of 'lexical' and 'grammatical items'), and only a 'grammar' as 'a theory of wordings' allows one to 'make explicit one's interpretation of the meaning of a text' (IF xvii, xix, xxxivf, 19f) (cf. 9.37f).

9.23 So '**discourse analysis**' 'provides a context within which grammar has a central place, and points the way to the kind of grammar required': 'functional and semantic', able not just to 'characterize text in explicit formal terms', but to 'relate it to the non-linguistic universe of its situational and cultural environment' (IF xvii) (cf. 9.109; 10.35). 'The wheel has come full circle: when the mainstream of linguistics' was in its 'syntactic age', Halliday 'argued against grammar' being 'the beginning and ending of all things'; 'now he insists on the importance of grammar' lest 'discourse analysis or text linguistics' 'be carried on without grammar' (IF xvif). 'A discourse analysis' 'not based on grammar is not an analysis at all, but simply a running commentary on a text', appealing to 'non-linguistic conventions' or 'trivial' 'linguistic' 'features' 'like the number of words per sentence', whose 'objectivity' 'is often illusory'.

9.24 Halliday himself proffers only 'a thumbnail sketch', 'a minute fragment of an account of English grammar' (IF 339, 286, 88, xiii). He grants that 'many aspects of English' should be 'much more fundamentally re-examined'; 'twentieth-century linguistics' 'has tended to wrap old descriptions' inside 'new theories', whereas we really need 'new descriptions', e.g., 'grammars for spoken language' (IF xxxiv; cf. EF 57) (cf. 8.38, 67; 9.43; 12.8). Of course, no 'account' could be ' "complete" ' 'because a language is inexhaustible' (IF xiii) (cf. 12.22). We have 'a finite body of text, written or spoken', but 'the language itself, the system' 'behind the text, is of indefinite extent' (cf. 7^{16}; 9.18; 12.43). Besides, 'distinctions' can be pursued only up to a certain 'degree of fineness or "delicacy" ' (IF xiii, 124; cf. IF xxvii, 286; EF 55, 58, 61, 75f, 94; IG 9).

9.25 Halliday also leaves it undecided if his 'introduction to functional grammar' is just for 'English', or if it's a 'general' one 'using English as the language of illustration' (IF xxxiv; cf. NT 3/209). He admits the 'danger' of 'ethnocentrism': now that 'more has been written about English than any other language', 'modern linguistics' 'tends to foist the English code on others' as if they were 'imperfect copies', as once was done with 'Latin' (IF xxxiii, xxxi) (cf. 2.5; 3.50; 4.4; 5.24; 6.5; 7.79; 8.5, 14; 11.20f; 12.53).

For his own part, 'those features' 'explicitly claimed as universal are built into the theory', notably his 'hypothesis' that three '"metafunctions"' 'organize' 'the content systems' 'in all languages' (IF xxxiv) (cf. 9.47f). 'But the descriptive categories are treated as particular'; 'it is far from clear just how similar a pair of features in different languages should be in order to justify calling them by the same name'.

9.26 To 'attempt' 'a "grammar" of English', we need to 'treat the system as a whole' (IF 372) (cf. 12.46). If 'grammar is not specialized according to language use' but applies to 'all texts', we could 'cover all functional varieties of the language' (cf. 9.40). 'The components of the grammatical system' thus 'represent the functions of language in their most generalized form, as these underlie all the more specific contexts of language use' (EF 67). 'Grammar' enables us to 'mean more than one thing at once', 'combines' 'functionally distinct meaning selections' 'into integrated structures', and thus 'turns meanings into text' (IF xxxv; EF 67, 42, 92f, 100).

9.27 Such a broad outlook raises substantial 'problems for a grammatical theory' when we 'write about language' and 'turn' it 'back on itself' (IF xxv, xxxiiif) (cf. 8.33; 12.48). First, 'the whole grammatical system hangs together, and it is difficult to break in without presupposing' 'what is still to come'; 'the discussion of any one system' or 'component' may 'require frequent reference to others' (IF xxxiiif; NT 2/215, 3/180). Second, to determine 'what is systematic and what is irrelevant in language', we need to 'decide what are different' entities and what are 'instances of the same'; and this 'question' 'is not determined by the system', but 'by the underlying social theory' (EF 53, 49f) (cf. 4.26, 31; 5.15, 61, 65). Third, 'categories of grammar' are hard to 'gloss in exactly equivalent wordings', because 'they have evolved to say something that cannot be said any other way' and are on 'a purely abstract level of coding with no direct input–output link with the outside world' (IF xxvi, xxxv) (cf. 3.23). 'The best one can do is display them at work, in paradigmatic contexts, so as to highlight the semantic distinctions they enshrine' (IF xxvi) (cf. 4.55; 8.82). Fourth, 'until linguistics begins to meddle', 'spontaneous speech' has an 'unconscious nature', 'performed without thinking' (IF xxivf) (cf. 2^{16}; 12.49). Our 'generalizations' are 'statements about what actually happens subconsciously in natural speech' (IF xxvi, 272). Also, the 'unconscious' 'slices of meaning' which 'the categories of our language represent' may not 'correspond to our conscious structuring of the world' (e.g., 'the gender system in English') (IF xxv) (cf. 3.23; 12.24). And 'a category only existing in the unconscious semantic system' is hard to 'define succinctly or even discursively' – it may even be 'threatening' to bring it to 'consciousness' (IF xxvi). Like '"tone deaf"', people may be '"grammar deaf"' and 'fail to recognize' 'subtle semantic distinctions' or 'even deny that they are possible'.

9.28 Accordingly, grammar entails 'severe' 'problems' in selecting '**labels**', which 'become reified' when we 'forget how we arrived at them' (IF xxxiif). The 'two significant ways to label a linguistic unit' are to 'assign it to a **class**' (e.g., 'adjective and noun'), or to 'assign a **function** to it' (e.g.,

'Modifier and Head') (IF 27). 'If all the members of a class always had' 'only one function, it would not matter which sets of labels we used'. But 'class labels' are 'part of of the dictionary' and 'indicate potential'; 'functional labels are an interpretation of the text' and 'indicate the part' actually 'played' in a 'particular structure' as well as the 'relation to the system of language as a whole' (IF 29, 31f, i.r.) (cf. 9.6, 8f; 12.39).[13] Here, 'description and analysis should not be distinct and unrelated operations', but should 'proceed side by side', revealing each 'structure' as a 'meaningful' and 'viable configuration of functions' (IF 32, 37).

9.29 For his own labels, Halliday undertakes to deploy 'familiar categories' and 'terms in general use', 'redefined, in part, to fit in with the total picture' (IF xxxiv, 28) (cf. 8.40; 12.48). 'Most of the labels' he uses are 'functional', signalled by 'beginning with a capital letter'.[14] He does 'refer to classes' 'in the discussion', but notes that many 'are defined' on 'mixed' 'criteria'; he offers 'generalized glosses designed to suggest the core meaning of the category' – 'basic semantic motifs' rather than 'definitions' (IF 27, 31, 202). We must acknowledge the 'high degree of indeterminacy' pervading 'language in its categories', 'relations', 'classes', 'types', and 'tokens' (EF 108, IF 31) (cf. 9.19, 35, 9^{32}, 38; 12.59). 'There rarely are any sharp lines in language, since it is an evolved system, not a designed one', witness the many 'fuzzy lines' and 'borderline cases' in the book (IF xix, 318, 171; EF 33; cf. IF 163f, 186, 209, 219, 267, 327; EF 32, 112; NT 2/223, 3/196) (cf. 5.47; 9.73; 10.22).

9.30 Halliday also reconsiders the 'traditional linguistic' 'terms used for the **levels** or "strata" of a language – the stages in the coding process from meaning to expression' – such as 'phonology', 'semantics', and 'grammar' (IF xiv) (cf. 4.71; 5.34f; 7.45; 8.51f; 10.16f, 35, 56; 11.82; 12.29). Though 'phonological' is named alongside 'grammatical' and 'semantic' as a 'level' of 'options in natural language' (cf. 7.56), Halliday's main 'concern' is 'with grammar'; and as a 'general principle', 'only those distinctions' shown to be 'meaningful' in 'the grammatical description' 'are represented in the phonological analysis' (EF 55; IF 17f; IG 47) (cf. 9.39f, 53). As we'd expect, he views 'phonological structures, such as syllable and foot', as 'configurations of functions', but the 'options' are seldom 'directly' specifiable as 'output' for 'options in the grammar' (EF 94f). So aside from a gloss on the 'phonometric structures' of 'spoken verse' (IF 10–16) (cf. Note 15), IF is concerned only with tone and key, which are crucial for signalling prominence in clauses and clause complexes (cf. 9.53). Hence, Halliday's model is among the few that did not treat phonology as the basic system and work from the smallest units (phonemes) on upward to grammar, stressing structure and constituency over function and meaning (cf. 12.27).

9.31 'Formal linguistics' 'replaces "grammar"' with ' "syntax"', following 'the philosophy of language, where syntax is opposed to semantics' and 'pragmatics' is 'a third term'; but in '**functional** linguistics', 'grammar consists of syntax and vocabulary', plus 'morphology' 'in languages which have word paradigms' (IF xiv, EF 93) (cf. 9.4, 6f; 9^6, 9^{14}; 2.55; 12.28).

Within the 'direction' in 'Western linguistics' since 'ancient Greece', the term '"syntax"'' 'suggests' that 'language is interpreted as a system of forms to which meanings are then attached' (IF xiv) (cf. 12.54). 'In functional grammar', 'the direction is reversed: a language is interpreted as a system of meanings accompanied by forms through which the meanings are realized'. 'The forms' are a 'means to an end', not 'an end in themselves'; we ask not 'what do these forms mean?' but 'how are these meanings expressed?' (IF xiv, 320).

9.32 Even so, Halliday says 'grammar is the level of formal organization in language' – a 'purely internal level' and 'the main defining characteristic of language' (EF 98) (cf. 12.54). Yet 'it is not **arbitrary**'; it is '**natural**', having 'evolved as "content form"'' on 'a functional basis' (cf. 2.28ff; 6.30; 9.3, 13, 35f; 12.27). As the 'complexity' of both 'linguistic function' and 'language' increased, 'the stratal form of organization' 'emerged', 'with a purely formal level of coding at its core' to 'integrate' 'complex meaning selections' into 'structures' by 'sorting specific uses of language into a small number of highly general functions' (cf. 9.11ff, 37).

9.33 Halliday rejects '**immediate constituent analysis**' by 'maximal bracketing', which 'never allows more than two elements in a bracket', in favour of '**ranked constituent analysis**' by 'minimal bracketing', which takes as 'constituents only those sequences that actually function as structural units in the item' (NT 37; IF 22, 24, 26, 30) (cf. 4.59; 5.21, 50, 62; 7.37f, 63, 86; 12.26). In 'trying to explain as much of grammar as possible in terms of constituent structure', the 'maximal' way suggests an 'order in which elements of a string are combined', with some being 'more closely bonded'; 'it says nothing about the function' of 'any of the pieces' (IF 30, 25, 22, 26f). 'Function' must be shown by 'labelling parts' and 'nodes' (in 'the tree metaphor') to 'indicate' the 'configuration' and 'explain the value in relation to the whole' (IF 27).

9.34 'A scale of **rank** for grammar' can be 'defined' by 'adopting' 'sentence, clause, group, word, and morpheme as a strict hierarchy of constituents' (IF 25) (cf. 12.29).[15] But 'language' 'embodies a multiplicity of constituent hierarchies, coexisting in different parts of the system' (IF 18) (cf. 5.36f, 39f).[16] 'Units of different rank tend to carry patterns of different kinds'; and 'the functional specification of units of different functions is of fundamental significance in determining grammatical structure'. Almost every 'constituent enters into more than one structural configuration' 'at a number of levels simultaneously', and 'has more than one function at a time' (IF 32, 271; EF 44) (9.19, 59; cf. 12.57). 'The choice of a word may express one type of meaning, its morphology another, and its position' yet another (EF 42) (cf. 9.37; 11.43, 72). The upshot is 'infinite possibilities of matching them up in meaningful ways' (IF 18) (cf. 9.18, 24).

9.35 Moreover, 'since the relation of grammar to semantics' is 'natural, not arbitrary, and both are purely abstract systems of coding', 'there is no clear line between' them; 'functional grammar' is 'pushed in the direction of semantics' (IF xix, xvii). 'In principle, a grammatical system is as abstract (is as "semantic") as possible given only that it can generate integrated structures', i.e., 'its output can be expressed in terms of functions mapped directly on to others' to yield 'a single structural "shape"' that is 'multiply labelled' (EF 95) (cf. 9.44). In this manner, 'the combination of system and structure with rank leads' to a 'grammar' whose 'abstractness' ('"depth" in the Chomskyan sense') we can 'specify fairly accurately in theoretical terms'.

9.36 Although we cannot 'spell out all the steps from meaning to wording', we should recognize the 'principle' 'that all categories employed must be clearly "there" in the grammar of the language', 'not set up simply to label differences in meaning' (IF xx) (cf. 9.62). Without some 'lexicogrammatical reflex', such 'differences' are not 'systemically distinct in the grammar'. However firmly 'based on meaning', 'a functional grammar' is 'an interpretation of linguistic forms': 'every distinction' – 'every set of options, or "system"' – must 'make some contribution to the form of the wording' (IF xx, xvii) (cf. 9.22; 12.54). So 'grammar' is 'a theory of wordings', which 'are purely abstract pieces of code' to be 'recoded in sound or writing' before you can 'see or hear them' (IF xx, xvii, xix). This 'recoding', and not 'the relation between the meaning and the wording', is the domain of 'arbitrariness' (IF xviif).[17]

9.37 In the 'grammar', 'meanings are accepted from different metafunctional inputs and spliced together to form integrated outputs or wordings' (IF xxxivf) (cf. 9.32, 35). 'The wording "realizes" or encodes the meaning' and is 'in turn "realized by" sound or writing' (IF xx). We needn't ask 'which determines which' or what 'each symbol as an isolate' 'means'; 'the meaning is encoded in the wording as an integrated whole'. 'The choice' of an 'item', its 'place in the syntagm', 'its combination' with another, and its 'internal organization' may each have a 'meaning'; 'the grammar' 'sorts out these possible variables and assigns them to their specific semantic functions' (cf. 9.34).

9.38 Therefore, 'a language' 'is a system for making meanings: a semantic system with other systems for encoding the meanings it produces' (IF xvii) (cf. 8.46f). Halliday warns that 'everyday terminology' and '"meaning" in its lay use' may 'imply' that many 'areas of syntactic choice are not meaningful'; and he discards the term 'content' because it 'calls to mind' the 'irrelevant' 'form/content opposition' (NT 3/209).[18] '"Semantics" does not simply refer to the meanings of words' but to 'the entire system of meanings' 'expressed by grammar' and 'vocabulary' (IF xvii). And 'semantics' is 'a stratum' 'intermediate between the social system' ('wholly outside language') and 'the grammatical system' ('wholly inside language') (EF 96). He expansively looks 'beyond' 'existing human languages' to 'possible languages that do not exist but could'; such an 'imaginative exploration could throw' 'light' on 'our own unconscious semantics' (IF xxxv) (cf. 6.11, 38; 7.18). 'At the present state of our knowledge', though, we cannot give 'a general account of English semantics', but only for 'a particular register' or 'body of text' (IF 372, xx) (cf. 9.105; 12.31).

9.39 'Semantic systems' 'relate' to 'grammatical systems' through the 'pre-selection' of 'options' (EF 98). Due to 'indeterminacy between the strata', we usually find not 'one-to-one correspondences' between 'grammar', 'semantics' and 'phonology', but rather 'neutralization and diversification' – 'many-to-many' (cf. Lamb 1970) (EF 82, 93, 56f) (cf. 3.32; 5.48, 64; 12.54). 'In some instances', however, we can go from 'semantics' 'directly to the "formal items": to the actual words, phrases, and clauses of the language', with 'no need' for 'grammatical systems and structures' (EF 83ff) (cf. 9.11f). True, this 'happens only' with 'a closed set of options in a clearly circumscribed social context', e.g., 'a greeting system in middle-class British English' or in a 'closed transaction such as buying a train or bus ticket' (EF 83f). In such cases, 'the formal items' 'are rather like non-linguistic semiotic systems', e.g., 'traffic signs and care labels on clothing, where the meanings are directly encoded into patterns in the visual medium, with a minimum of stratal organization'. In genuine 'language, such systems are marginal', 'a small fraction of the total phenomena' among 'much more open' and 'general settings'.

9.40 For similar reasons, it is not clear how far 'grammatical and lexical properties of sentences used by the speaker in the speech situation' 'can be "predicted" from a semantics of behaviour based on social context' (EF 90) (cf. 12.40). We will 'find' 'a direct link' between 'features of the social structure' and 'forms of the language' only 'in odd cases', e.g., 'phonological variables' of 'dialect' and ' "accent" ' (EF 65; cf. Labov 1968). We can 'specify' 'general' or 'principal grammatical features' and 'narrow down' the 'lexical set' by 'exploring areas of behaviour where the meanings are expressed through very general features' 'involved in nearly all uses of language' (EF 91, 84) (cf. 9.26). But we might 'not go very far in delicacy', and might have to use 'favourable instances' and 'restricted types of situation', not 'the whole of an individual's language behaviour' (EF 92, 62). We would cover 'only a small proportion' 'of the total' 'speech by educated adults in a complex society' (EF 92).

9.41 Along another dimension of language versus context, 'grammar is at once both' 'of the **system**' and 'of the **text**' (IF xxii) (cf. 6.34; 12.39). Halliday follows Saussure's view of 'the relationship between the system of language and its instantiation in acts of speaking', but not his implied 'conclusion' that 'the texts can be dispensed with' after 'being used as evidence for the system' (cf. 2.19f; 12.36). 'This mistake' 'haunted linguistics for much of the twentieth century', 'obsessed with system at the expense of text', up to 'the present swing' 'in the opposite direction' (cf. 9.4).[19] 'An elegant theory of the system' has 'little use' 'if it cannot account for how the system engenders text'. So 'discourse analysis must be founded on the study of the system', which in turn 'throws light on discourse' and shows 'the text' 'as process'.

9.42 'The 'experience' of a 'process' with 'a continuous flow, without clear segments or boundaries' – 'as **text** (mass noun) rather than as *a text/texts* (count noun)' – is best found in '**speech**' (IF xxiii). 'Speech' is 'important' not just because 'it comes first in the history of the race and the individual', but because in it 'the potential of the system is more richly developed' and 'fully revealed', 'its semantic frontiers are expanded, and its potential for meaning is enhanced' (IF xxiiif, 201) (cf. 12.33). 'Speech' 'responds continually' to 'subtle changes in the environment, both verbal and non-verbal', and 'exhibits a rich pattern of semantic' and 'grammatical variation' not 'explored in writing' (IF xxiv). 'Spoken language' can '"choreograph" very long and intricate patterns of semantic movement while maintaining a continuous flow of discourse that is coherent without being constructional' (IF 201f). These 'systems that vary the form of the message' get 'neglected in grammars of English' 'because they are much less richly exploited in written language'. What 'writing' 'achieves' by 'packing together lexical content' in a 'static and dense' way, 'speech' 'achieves' through 'grammatical frames' in a 'mobile and intricate' way. That 'spoken language is disorganized and featureless' is a 'folk belief', sustained by 'transcriptions' in which 'speech' 'looks silly' 'written down', due to 'the disorder and fragmentation' in 'the way it is transcribed' without 'intonation or rhythm or variation in tempo and loudness' (IF xxiv).

9.43 Besides, 'it being much harder to represent a process than' 'a product', 'the text' is easily viewed as a 'perceptible' 'object', made most tangible 'as a piece of writing' (IF xxiif, 290) (cf. 9.2). And 'traditionally, grammar' has been 'product grammar' for 'written language' (IF xxiii). 'In its earliest origins, classical Greek grammar', 'tied to rhetoric', was for 'speech'; 'but Aristotle took grammar' 'into logic', and focus shifted to 'written discourse' through 'medieval and renaissance syntax' up to the 'received "traditional grammar"' of 'today' (cf. 8.17; 12.33). The latter is 'unsuited to spoken language, which needs a more dynamic and less constructional form of representation' (cf. 9.24). Yet 'constructing' a new 'grammar for speech' 'from the beginning' might 'force an artificial polarization of speech versus writing', deny 'mixed categories' (like 'dramatic dialogue'), and make it 'difficult to compare spoken and written texts'.

9.44 So Halliday calls for 'a much more dynamic model of grammar' he does not 'offer here', but hopes his treatment of 'the **clause complex**' may go 'a little way in that direction' (IF xxiii). He designates the 'clause' 'the most significant grammatical unit' and 'the best example' of 'linguistic structure' as 'a means for the integrated expression of all the functionally distinct components of meaning in language' (IF 101; EF 42) (cf. 5.55; 9.46ff, 50f). 'The grammar of the clause' 'expresses' 'the semantic system of the language', which in turn 'sorts out' the '"goings-on"' of 'reality' (IF 101) (cf. 12.24).

9.45 This process involves variations in '**markedness**'. 'Within a systematic framework' of 'options', the 'typical form' is '**unmarked** "with respect to" some other option' (EF 58f, 79). Though 'usually less frequent than an unmarked one', 'a **marked** option' need not be 'rare'; its 'effectiveness' comes from 'contrasting with unmarked', which is 'less motivated than others in the same system and therefore selected unless there is specification to the contrary' (NT 2/219, 213) (cf. 12.43). Halliday 'invokes the "good reason" principle': 'the "unmarked" one' 'is chosen unless there is good reason to choose otherwise' (EF 57; IF 45, 287).

9.46   We can get some flavour of his approach from his treatment of the '**Subject**', which so far lacks 'a definitive account' despite being a 'basic' 'concept' 'in the Western tradition of grammatical analysis' (IF 32f) (cf. 4.69; 5.55; 6.49; 7.63; 9.70; 10.34; 11.70, 79).[20] He sees 'three broad definitions' of 'Subject': 'the concern of message', 'the doer of the action', and 'that of which something is predicated' (IF 33f, 102). Though these 'definitions are obviously not synonymous', they were usually treated as 'aspects of one and the same general notion' by sticking to 'idealized clause patterns' wherein they 'coincide' – namely, in 'the typical unmarked form' of 'the English declarative (statement-type) clause' (IF 33f, 36, 77; NT 2/213) (cf. 4.68; 9.75, 109; 10.68; 12.50). But a full 'account of natural living language' requires that they be 'interpreted' as 'three' 'distinct functions', 'subtly but significantly different in meaning', which Halliday calls 'Theme', 'Actor', and 'Subject', respectively (IF 35f).

9.47   This trinity brings us to the centrepiece of Halliday's approach. He sees 'the basis of the grammatical system', and a 'universal' 'feature' of 'language', in a triad of '**metafunctions**' – 'tendencies worked out differently in every language but clearly discernible in all' (EF 66; IF xxxiv, 169; NT 2/243) (cf. 9.25). These contribute 'three distinct principles of organization in the structure of grammatical units' ('as described by' 'the Prague school', e.g., Daneš 1964) 'expressing three rather distinct and independent sets of underlying options' (EF 66, IF 158). 'Intersecting' in 'the clause', these sets express 'experiential meaning, speech function, and discourse organization' (NT 2/243). Halliday's 'grammar' is extensively organized around this triad and the threes related to it (cf. IF xiii, xviif, 33, 35, 37f, 53, 78, 101, 128, 158ff, 321; NT 2/199, 243; EF 66, 99, 105f) (and a photo of Henry Moore's sculpture of 'Three Points' appears on the cover of IF). Indeed, he expressly warns us when some aspect or structure is *not* seen these three ways (IF 158, 169, 176) (cf. 9.74, 78).

9.48   The three 'metafunctions' are 'the **textual**', 'the **ideational**' and 'the **interpersonal**' (EF 66, 99, 101, 105ff; IF xiii, xxxiv, 53, 158; NT 3/209).[21] Through them, 'three distinct structures are mapped on to one another to produce a single wording', such that 'the clause' is 'the simultaneous realization' of three 'meanings': a 'message' ('meaning' as 'relevance to the context'), a 'representation' ('meaning in the sense of "content"'), and an 'exchange' ('meaning as a form of action') (EF 42; IF 36f, 158, 53, xiii). The three aspects are not 'discrete' 'components' 'expressed' by 'segments' 'we can point to' (EF 42). They tend to be 'embodied' or 'scattered' throughout an 'entire structure', wherein they are 'mapped on to one another' in a 'simultaneous' 'complex of structural roles'; a certain 'alignment of roles' may 'represent a favourite clause type' (IF 169f, 365; NT 2/215f, 243, 224).[22] In terms of 'the triad first proposed by Pike' (cf. 5.31ff), Halliday envisions 'textual meaning' as 'a wave-like pattern of periodicity', with 'peaks of prominence and boundary markers'; 'experiential' (i.e., ideational) 'meaning' as a 'particle-like' pattern of 'building blocks'; and 'interpersonal meaning' as a 'field-like' 'prosodic' 'pattern' (IF 169).

9.49 'The **textual**' metafunction enables 'language' to be 'operationally relevant' and 'have texture in real contexts of situation' (EF 42) (cf. 8.41). Here, 'language becomes text, is related to itself and to its contexts of use', including 'the preceding and following text, and the context of situation' (EF 44, IF 53). One division under the 'textual' heading is '**information**': 'a process of interaction between what is already known or predictable and what is new or unpredictable' (IF 274f).[23] 'The information unit is a structure made up of two functions, the **New** and the **Given**.' The ' "New" ' is either 'not previously mentioned' or is 'presented' by 'the speaker' as 'not being recoverable from the preceding discourse' and thus as 'textually and situationally non-derivable'; the ' "Given" ' is 'what is not "New" ' (NT 2/204f, 211; IF 277). 'The idealized form' of the 'information unit' has 'a Given' and 'a New element', but does not apply when 'a discourse' 'starts' nor when 'the Given' 'refers to something already present in the verbal or non-verbal context' (IF 275). So only the 'New element' is 'obligatory', while the 'Given' is 'optional' (IF 275; NT 2/204).

9.50 'The structure of the information unit contributes in large measure to the organization of discourse', and 'frequently defines' 'the domain of constituents' more than does their 'status in sentence structure' (NT 2/210f). 'The distribution of information specifies a distinct constituent structure' on one 'plane', which is 'then mapped on to the constituent structure' of 'clauses' (NT 2/200, 242). This 'distribution' 'determines' the number of 'points of information **focus**' and 'represents the speaker's blocking out of the message into quanta of information, or message blocks', and deciding 'where the main burden of the message lies' (NT 2/202, 204). A 'discourse' with 'much factually new material' tends to have many 'short information units, each with its focus' (NT 2/205).

9.51 'Within each' 'unit', 'elements' are selected as 'points of prominence': 'one primary point of information focus', and possibly a 'secondary' one for 'dependent', 'incomplete, contingent, or confirmatory' 'information' (NT 2/203, 209). The 'structure' is 'realized' in a ' "natural" (non-arbitrary)' way, with 'the New marked by prominence' and 'typically' placed after 'the Given' (IF 275) (cf. 10.85). In 'the unmarked or default condition', 'the information unit' 'corresponds to a clause', but may be 'more' or 'less' in 'marked' cases (NT 2/201, 203; IF 59, 274, 287, 315, IG 19f).[24] Any 'unit' 'less' or 'more' than this is 'marked'; 'in continuous informal discourse', 'the average number of information units per clause lies between 1 and 2' (NT 2/201).

9.52 'In any utterance in English, three distinct meaningful choices' are made, which 'usually are subsumed under' ' "**intonation**" ': ' "tonality", "tonicity", and "tone" ' (IG 18, 30, 38). Such options suggest that a 'notation' is needed for 'showing intonational and rhythmic structure' which 'has to be accounted for in a functional grammar' (IF 286) (cf. 8.71; 9.42). 'Discourse consists of a linear succession' of 'information units, realized by **tonality**, that is, as a sequence of **tone groups**' (NT 2/211; IG 30; cf. IF 8, 59, 271, 273f). Within 'each information unit', the 'choice' of 'focus' is 'realized by **tonicity**, the structuring of the tone group into a tonic' (for 'the general meaning') 'optionally preceded by a pretonic' (for 'more delicate distinctions') but with 'no separate post-tonic' (NT 2/211, 205, 243; IF 283; IG 12f, 30).

9.53 '**Tone**' concerns 'phonological prominence' allotted by 'pitch movement' and to a lesser degree by 'duration' and 'intensity' (NT 2/203; IG 14). In each 'tone group', 'prominence', and thus 'information focus', is given to 'the element' that 'carries the main pitch movement: the main fall, or rise, or change of direction' (IF 275). 'The English tone system is based on an opposition' between 'falling' and 'rising pitch', and 'the choice of tone' yields the 'semantic values of **key**' (IF 281; IG 16f, 30).[25] This 'opposition' is so 'fundamental' that it 'probably plays a part in the system of every language' (IF 281). In English, 'falling pitch' means 'certain', while 'rising pitch' means 'uncertain' (IF 281f). Correspondingly, 'falling–rising means "seems certain, but turns out not to be" '; and 'rising–falling means "seems uncertain, but turns out to be certain" '. The 'neutralized' 'level tone' means ' "not (yet) decided whether known or unknown" '. 'In normal conversational English', 'falling tone' 'is most frequent', followed by 'falling–rising'. 'Rising tone' is 'more common in dialogue than in narrative'; 'in formal speech and loud-reading' 'level tone' 'increases'; and 'rising–falling tone' is 'characteristic of children's speech'.

9.54 As might be expected, 'the unmarked realization of a statement' 'in a declarative clause' 'is falling tone' (IF 281, 284; IG 25). The 'other tones convey a statement' with 'additional' 'features', e.g., 'rising tone' for 'contradiction or protest', 'falling–rising' for 'reservation', and 'rising–falling' for 'strong assertion' (IF 284, 281). A 'falling tone' is used for a 'WH–question' (in the sense of 9.58), and a 'rising' one for a 'yes–no question' (IF 281, 284). The 'imperative' has 'two unmarked tones': 'falling' 'for command', and 'level' 'for invitation' (IF 284). 'Minor clauses' (in the sense of 9.74) 'have varied tones depending on their function', especially 'calls (vocatives)' (IF 285).

9.55 '**Theme**' – the other aspect of textual meaning alongside 'information structure' – is concerned with 'the status of elements' as 'components of a message' (NT 2/199; IF 36, 38f).[26] 'The interplay of thematic and information structure carries the rhetorical gist' (IF 280). Yet whereas 'information' and the 'Given–New' 'dimension' 'determine the organization' of 'a text' 'into discourse units', and whereas 'information options' are not 'clause systems', 'theme' affects the 'organization' and 'sequence of elements of the clause in sentence structure' (IF 287, NT 2/200, 223). 'The choice of information focus' 'expresses the main point' 'of the discourse'; in contrast, 'the choice of theme, clause by clause', 'carries forward the development of the text as a whole' (IF 315). Whereas 'information focus' 'favours the more "peripheral" elements, especially circumstances', 'thematic prominence' favours 'the more "central" among the clause elements (the participants' in 'the most active roles in transitivity', cf. 9.60) (NT 2/214). Also, 'information structure' is 'listener-oriented' ('"what I am asking you to attend to"'), whereas 'thematic structure' is 'speaker-oriented' ('"what I am talking about"') (IF 278, 316, 368). For all these reasons, 'information' and 'theme' are 'independently variable': being 'combinable in only one way' would 'curtail the potential of these two systems' and remove an occasion for 'meaningful choice' (NT 2/205, 211f, IF 287) (cf. 12.50).[27]

9.56   As shown by 'the linguists of the Prague tradition', who 'explored' 'functional sentence perspective' (cf. Vachek 1964; Firbas and Golková 1976), 'the sequence of elements in the clause tends to represent thematic ordering' rather than 'actor–action–goal' (NT 2/205; IF 315; EF 107) (cf. 4.68; 7[14]; 9.46, 67). 'Thematization' 'assigns to the clause a structure in terms of the functions "**Theme**" and "**Rheme**"' (NT 212). 'If a clause is structured as two information units, the boundary' 'nearly always coincides with that between Theme and Rheme' – 'a strong piece of evidence for construing the Theme' this way (IF 40, 56). Since 'Theme always precedes Rheme', 'the unmarked case' 'associates' 'the Theme with the Given' and places 'the focus of information' (and 'the New') 'within the Rheme', though not always 'extending over the whole of it' (NT 2/205, 212; IF 60, 278). The 'Theme', 'usually marked off as a tone group', may 'consist of just one element' or of 'two or more forming a single complex element' (IF 40f).

9.57   'Typically' 'in a *declarative* clause', 'the Theme is conflated with the **Subject**' – a 'mapping' yielding 'the *unmarked Theme*' (IF 44f, 60) (cf. 9.46; 10.68). 'In everyday conversation, the item most often' used as such is 'the first person pronoun "I"'; 'next' 'come the other' 'pronouns', and then 'nominal groups' (with 'common' or 'proper noun as Head) and nominalizations' (IF 45). In contrast, 'a Theme' 'other than the Subject in a declarative clause' is '*marked*', 'usually an adverbial group' or a 'prepositional phrase' 'functioning as *adjunct* in the clause'. 'Thematic status' makes 'adjuncts' of 'time/place', 'cause, manner, etc.' into 'sentence adjuncts'; 'their domain may extend over various levels of sentence structure' (NT 2/220). Such cases show how 'theme plays a part in the bracketing function of information structure'; if a 'marked thematic element' 'occurs as a separate information unit', its 'domain extends over the whole of the next following information unit', but if not 'separate', over only the 'unit in which it occurs' (NT 2/219f) (cf. 9.24). Also, 'adjuncts' 'occurring *obligatorily* in initial position' because they have 'floated to the front of the clause' during 'the evolution of the language', 'do not take up the whole' position of 'theme'; the next element functioning as 'Subject, Complement, or Adjunct' is included too (IF 51, 53, i.r.).

9.58   '*Interrogative* clauses' 'embody the theme principle in their structural make-up': the 'theme' 'element' 'comes first' because of 'the thematic significance attached to the first position in the English clause' (IF 47f). In a 'polar' ('yes–no') 'question' that 'element' is 'the finite verb', but in a 'non-polar' or 'content' ('WH–') 'question' (with ' "who", "what", "when", "how", etc.') it is 'the element that requests' 'a missing piece of information' (IF 47, 44, 85; NT 212f) (cf. 4.69). 'The preference for the "inverted" interrogative structure in English' confirms the 'importance of thematic organization by sequence in the syntax of the English clause'; 'interrogatives have a built-in unmarked theme' (NT 2/214). 'In the declarative the thematic pressure on the subject is much less strong, and marked themes are frequent in all registers' to 'foreground the speaker's point of departure' (NT 2/215). The 'imperative', however, 'commonly' 'with no subject or finite verb', has 'no explicit theme'; 'the basic message is realized simply by the form of the clause', which 'consists of rheme only' (IF 49) (cf. 9.52, 72, 96; 4.56).

9.59 'The **ideational**'[28] metafunction has a 'vast and complex' 'meaning potential' (EF 39). In Halliday's earlier scheme, it was two 'separate' metafunctions ('components'), 'the **experiential**' and 'the **logical**' (NT 3/209; EF 106). Maybe he merged them because he likes threes (cf. 9.47), but his concern remains for the 'basic **logical** relations' in 'natural language', such as 'in a **univariate** structure' with a 'recurrence of the same function' and in a '**multivariate** structure' with a 'constellation' of distinct functions' (EF 66; IF 193, 172) (cf. 9.75, 80, 82f). Since these 'relations' form 'part of the semantics of a language', they do not 'fit exactly into non-linguistic logical categories' (understatement) – 'although since the latter derive from natural language in the first place there will obviously be a close resemblance' (overstatement) (IF 202). However, Halliday frequently criticizes the reliance on 'logic' by linguists or grammarians, as when he warns against 'problems' 'arising in linguistic analysis' by 'attempting to make the logical structure do duty for the other components', or opines that 'the logical element in the description of the clause appears to be, in English, entirely dispensable' (NT 3/211f) (cf. 9.3, 5, 48; 8.5, 17; 12.17f).

9.60 The '**experiential**' aspect covers 'the interpretation and expression in language of different types of **process** of the external world, including material, mental, and abstract processes of every kind', plus those 'of our own consciousness' (EF 39; IF 66). 'A process' can have 'three components: the process itself, the participants', i.e., all things that 'can become a Subject', and the 'circumstances' (IF 101, 54, 114). 'This tripartite interpretation' of 'how phenomena of the real world are represented as linguistic structures' 'lies behind the grammatical distinction of word classes into verbs, nouns, and the rest' – a 'probably universal' 'pattern' 'among human languages' (IF 102) (cf. 12.18). In 'the preferred' ('unmarked') 'clause type', 'the initiating' 'element in the message' is the 'most closely associated with the process; and the culminating, information-carrying element' is the 'most remote' (NT 3/214f).

9.61 'The grammar of the clause' as 'a structural unit' for 'expressing a particular range of ideational meanings' is called **'transitivity'** (EF 39). This domain is 'the cornerstone of the semantic organization of experience'; it subsumes 'all participant functions' and 'all experiential functions relevant to the syntax of the clause' (EF 134; NT 3/182). 'Endless variation is possible' and 'meaningful'; 'the textual component provides' 'the means for distributing the experiential functions in every possible way over the functions Theme–Rheme and Given–New' (NT 3/215) (cf. 12.43). The term thus denotes not the familiar 'opposition' between 'transitive and intransitive verbs in English', but 'a set of clause types embodying a full range of possible transitivity distinctions' (EF 39; NT 3/181f, 1/52; IF 103). 'The potential distinction' 'between verbs which are inherently goal-directed or not is less useful as a generalization than the actual distinction between clauses' which either have or lack 'a feature of goal-directedness' (NT 3/182) (cf. 9.67).

9.62 Halliday's way of classifying 'processes' instructively shows his balancing the plausible with the technical as well as the semantic with the grammatical (IF 131) (Table 9.1).

TABLE 9.1

Process type	Category meaning	Participants
Material	'doing'	Actor, Goal
action	'doing'	
event	'happening'	
Mental	'sensing'	Senser, Phenomenon
perception	'seeing'	
affection	'feeling'	
cognition	'thinking'	
Relational	'being'	Token, Value
attribution	'attributing'	Carrier, Attribute
identification	'identifying'	Identified, Identifier
Behavioural	'behaving'	Behaver
Verbal	'saying'	Sayer, Target
Existential	'existing'	Existent

Since 'there are indefinitely many ways of drawing lines on purely semantic grounds', we must inquire which 'have systematic repercussions in the grammar' (IF 108) (cf. 9.36; 12.54). We see a good illustration in the 'criteria' to show why **'mental'** (i.e., 'sensing') and **'material'** (i.e., 'doing') 'processes' 'constitute distinct grammatical categories' (IF 108, 102, 106). 'Mental process' is 'distinct' from 'material process' in: (a) having as 'participants' a 'human Senser' 'endowed with consciousness' and a 'Phenomenon' (as in ' "I like the quiet" '), which 'cannot be equated with

Actor and Goal in a material process' (as in '"the lion caught the tourist"');
(b) being 'representable' 'as two-way' or 'bi-directional' (as in '"Mary liked
the gift"' versus '"the gift pleased Mary"'); (c) 'that which is felt, thought
or perceived' being 'a "Fact"' ('a representation' 'ready packaged', as in
'"Jane saw that the stars had come out"') as well as 'a Thing' ('a phenomenon of our experience', as in '"Jane saw the stars"'); and (d) having as
'unmarked' 'tense' 'the simple present' (as in '"I see the stars"'), whereas
the 'material process' has 'present in present' (as in '"they are building a
house"') (IF 108–11, 136, 227f, 243).[29]

9.63 'Mental processes' have the 'principal subtypes' of *perception*
("seeing, hearing", etc.), *affection* ("liking, fearing", etc.), and *cognition*
("thinking, knowing, understanding", etc.)' (IF 111). 'Material processes',
in contrast, are divided into *disposative* ('"doing to"') and *creative*
('"bringing about"'), each of which may be either 'concrete' or 'abstract'
(IF 103ff). Halliday recognizes as a third type '**relational** processes of being'
(IF 112). 'Every language accommodates in its grammar a number of
distinct ways of being'; 'English' has *intensive* (i.e., 'a relation of
sameness') (as in '"Tom is the leader"'), *circumstantial* (as in '"the fair is
on a Tuesday"'), and *possessive* (as in '"Peter has a piano"') (IF 112,
114). Each of these three 'comes in two modes: *attributive*' has the
'functions' 'Attribute and Carrier' (as in '"Sarah is wise"'), whereas
identifying has 'Identified and Identifier' (as in '"tomorrow is the tenth"')
(IF 113). Only 'identifying clauses are reversible' and have a 'passive' (as in
'"Tom plays the leader"' and '"the leader is played by Tom"');
'attributives' do not (as in '"the fair lasts all day"' but not '"all day is lasted
by the fair"'), because an 'Attribute is not a participant' and so cannot
'become a Subject' (IF 114, 119f) (cf. 9.60).

9.64 Beyond these 'three principal types of process found in the English
clause', Halliday sets up 'three other subsidiary types' (IF 128). '**Behavioural**
processes', both 'physical and psychological' (e.g., '"breathing, dreaming"'),
are 'intermediate between material and mental', are usually 'conscious', and
have the structure of 'Behaver' and 'Process' (as in '"the Mock Turtle
sighed deeply"') (IF 128f). '**Verbal** processes' (e.g., 'saying') are 'unlike
mental processes' in 'not requiring a conscious participant', and in having
the structure of 'Sayer', 'Receiver', and 'Verbiage' (the 'proposition' or
'proposal') (as in '"he told me it was Tuesday"') (IF 129f). '**Existential**
processes' (e.g., 'existing', 'happening') have the structure of 'Existent',
'Process', and optionally 'Circumstance' (as in '"there was an old woman
tossed up in a basket"') (IF 130f).

9.65 Even the six 'process types' cover only 'participant functions'
'directly involved in the process'; 'grammatically these are the elements that
typically relate directly to the verb, without a preposition' (IF 131). The
'other participant functions' for the 'oblique or "indirect" participants' that
are more 'optional' than 'inherent' 'in the process'[30] are 'grouped' under
Beneficiary', including the 'Recipient' of 'goods' and the 'Client' of
'services' (e.g., '"John"' in '"I gave John a parcel"' or '"I painted John a

picture"''); and *'Range'*, i.e., the 'scope of the process' (e.g., '"croquet"' in '"do you play croquet with the Queen today?"'') (IF 132ff).

9.66 Besides 'participants', Halliday has *'circumstantial elements'*, 'the principal types' of which, 'in English', are: *'Extent* and *Location* in time and space (including abstract space)' (as in '"stay for two hours"'', '"walk for seven miles"''); *'Manner* (means, quality and comparison)' (as in '"beat with a stick"''); *'Cause* (reason, purpose, and behalf)' (as in '"for want of a nail the shoe was lost"''); *'Accompaniment'* ('comitative', i.e., 'what with', as in '"Fred came with Tom"'', and 'additive', i.e., 'what else', as in '"Fred came as well as Tom"''); *Matter* (i.e., 'what about', as in '"I worry about her health"''); and *Role* (i.e., 'what as', as in '"I come here as a friend"'') (IF 137–42). This classification is drawn four ways: by meaning, by presupposed questions, by prepositions, and by illustrations (cf. Table on IF 148). Some interesting comparisons emerge. 'Extent and Location' show up the 'close parallels between temporal and spatial expressions': having 'standard units', being 'either definite or indefinite', and being either 'absolute or relative' (IF 138). In return, 'time is unidimensional' and 'moving' whereas 'space is three-dimensional and static'; and only 'time' appears 'in the tense system of the verb' (IF 138f).

9.67 'From one point of view', each 'type of process' 'has a grammar of its own' (IF 144f). Yet 'from another point of view they are all alike' and share 'just one generalized representational structure', based on one **'ergative'** 'variable' of 'causation': 'is the process brought about from within or from outside?' (IF 145, 147, NT 3/182). 'The majority of verbs of high frequency in the language yield' only 'pairs' of this kind (IF 145). Halliday attributes this 'predominance' in 'modern English' to 'a far-reaching complex process of semantic change' in the 'language over the past five hundred years or more' (IF 146). 'The changes' tend to 'emphasize the textual function in the organization of English discourse' over the 'experiential function', and within the latter function, 'the cause-and-effect aspect' over 'the deed-and-extension' or 'actor–action–goal' aspect (IF 146; EF 127; cf. IF 10f) (cf. 9.56). The 'waves of change' indicate that 'the transitivity system is particularly unstable in contemporary language', due to 'great pressure' 'for the language to adapt to a rapidly changing environment' (IF 146) (cf. 11.59).

9.68 Halliday accordingly proposes 'another interpretation' of 'the semantics of English' vis-à-vis 'the real world', and of 'the clause in its experiential function' for 'making generalizations about processes in the real world' (IF 144–47). 'Every *Process'* has the 'obligatory' 'participant' or 'element' called 'the *Medium'*, 'through which the process is actualized' (e.g., '"boat"' in '"the boat sailed"'') (IF 146).[31] 'The Process and the Medium together form the nucleus of an English clause' that 'determines the range of options' for 'the rest of the clause' (IF 147). 'The most general' 'option', 'turning up in all process types', is the *'ergative* one': 'the participant functioning as an external cause', such that 'the process' is 'represented as engendered from outside' (e.g., '"Mary"' in '"Mary sailed the boat" "). We might need to 'restructure our thinking' to move from the 'linear interpretation' in terms of 'transitive', 'emphasizing the distinction between participants' and 'circumstances', to the 'nuclear' 'interpretation' in terms of 'ergative', allowing 'a whole cluster of participant-like functions in the clause' (IF 145, 149). These functions subsume further types of 'causative agent' – '*initiator*' (as in ' "the police exploded the bomb" '), '*inducer*' (as in ' "the report convinced Mary" '), and '*attributor*' (as in ' "the sun ripened the bananas" ') – which 'in the transitive analysis' would be 'assigned different structural configurations' ('doing' versus 'making do') (IF 152f).

9.69 'Probably all transitivity systems, in all languages, are some blend of these two semantic models of processes, the transitive and the ergative' (IF 149). 'Semantically, therefore, Agent, Beneficiary, and Range have some features of participants and some of circumstances'; 'grammatically, also, they are mixed' and may 'enter' 'directly as nominal groups or indirectly in prepositional phrases'. The 'choice' to use a 'preposition' is thus not 'random variation', but 'serves a textual function'; 'a participant other than the Medium' and having 'prominence in the message' – i.e., 'occurring either earlier' ('as marked theme') 'or later' ('as "late news" ') 'than expected in the clause' – 'tends to take a preposition'.[32]

9.70 A related drift 'away from a purely transitive type of symbol organization can be seen in the system of **voice**', another major 'resource of transitivity' (IF 150; NT 3/203). Instead of labelling just 'verbs' as '*active*' and '*passive*', we might use 'ergative terms' and sort whole 'clauses' into '*effective*' (with a 'feature of agency', as in ' "the cat broke the glass" ') and '*middle*' (without it, as in ' "the glass broke" '). 'The choice between active and passive' is open only for an 'effective' 'clause', and 'the reasons for choosing passive' are: 'to get the Medium as subject' and thus as 'unmarked theme', or 'to make the Agent either "late news" by putting it last' in the slot for 'unmarked' 'information focus', or else 'implicit by leaving it out' (IF 151, 118; NT 3/205, 2/215, 217).[33] 'In spoken English the great majority of passive clauses are, in fact, Agent-less' (IF 151f) (cf. 7.53).

9.71 'The **interpersonal**' metafunction concerns 'forms of interaction' and 'embodies all use of language to express social and personal relations', 'personalities, and personal feelings', as well as 'the speaker's intrusion into speech situation and speech act' (EF 41, 66, 106; NT 3/210). This 'function' 'extends beyond' the 'rhetorical' by 'expressing both the inner and the outer surfaces of the individual', and is thus 'personal in the broadest sense' (EF 107). 'The speaker' ('a cover term for both speaker and writer') 'expresses his comments, attitudes, evaluations', 'adopts' a 'speech role', and 'assigns the listener a complementary role', 'the most fundamental' being 'giving' and 'demanding' (IF 68; EF 106; NT 3/210). But 'we can recognize an unlimited number' of 'specific' 'socio-personal' 'uses of language': 'ask and answer', 'approve and disapprove', 'greet, chat up, take leave', 'express belief, opinion, doubt', and 'feelings', 'include in' or 'exclude from the social group', and so on (EF 41) (cf. 8.42). 'The act of speaking' might well 'be called an "interact"' (IF 68).

9.72   The 'interpersonal function of the clause is that of exchanging roles in rhetorical interaction' (IF 53). 'Goods-&-services' are also 'exchanged' via 'offers and commands', wherein 'language functions simply as means' toward 'non-linguistic ends'; these uses have 'priority in the ontogenetic development of language' and 'serve as a point of entry to a great variety of different rhetorical functions' (IF 68, 70f) (cf. 9.14). 'Information'[34] is 'exchanged' via 'statements and questions', wherein 'language is the end' and 'the means', and 'the clause takes on the form of a **proposition**' 'that can be affirmed or denied, qualified', 'regretted, and so on' (cf. 3.36, 44f; 8.55; 9[24]; 10.39–50). 'Propositions' are 'useful to look at' because they 'have a clearly defined grammar' with more 'special resources' (IF 70).

9.73   '**Mood** represents the organization of participants in speech situations' and 'speaker roles', such as 'informing', 'confirming', 'contra-dicting', etc. (NT 2/199). In 'the clause as domain', if 'theme is the grammar of discourse' and 'transitivity is the grammar of experience', then 'mood is the grammar of speech function'. The 'choice' of an 'element' 'as theme' may 'depend on the choice of mood'; and 'some options are on the borderline of theme and mood' (IF 44; NT 2/243n). 'Any thematic element' not 'derived from the mood of the clause' must be 'a "marked Theme"' (NT 2/223). Yet 'unlike the Theme', which 'carries forward the development of the text as a whole', 'the Mood element has little significance beyond the immediate sequence of clauses' (IF 98).

9.74   In the grammar, 'the Mood' is the 'constituent' formed by '**Subject** and **Finite**' 'closely linked together', 'the remainder of the clause' being 'the **Residue**' (IF 73f). Every 'major clause', 'whether independent or not', 'selects for mood'; 'those which do not' are 'minor clauses' (e.g., in 'calls, greetings, and exclamations') (IF 44; 61, 63) (cf. 9.54). The 'independent major clause', in which 'the constituent specified by the mood systems' 'is obligatory' and which 'exhibits the options of theme in its full interpretation', is either '*indicative* or *imperative* in mood' (IF 44, NT 2/213, 221). As a 'general principle', 'the indicative' is 'used to exchange information', either by 'statement' in 'the *declarative*' (with 'Subject before Finite'), or by 'question' in 'the *interrogative*' (with 'Finite before Subject', unless a 'WH–element is the Subject') (IF 74). Another 'subcategory' of 'declarative clause' is 'the *exclamative*' with a 'WH–element as theme' (e.g., in '"what tremendously easy questions you ask!"') (IF 47).

9.75   '*Below* the clause' is 'the grammar of the **group**', 'interpreted as a word complex' with 'Head' and 'modifying element' (IF 158f, 192) (compare Firth's 'piece', 8.55). 'In the Western grammatical tradition, it was not recognized as a distinct structural unit; instead, simple sentences' '(clauses in our terms) were analysed directly into words' (IF 158f). 'Such an analysis' requires 'confining our attention' to the 'idealized isolated sentences that grammarians have usually dealt with' (e.g., '"John threw the ball"') and 'ignoring several important aspects of the meanings'; 'and in the analysis of real-life discourse it leads to impossible complexity' – like 'describing a house' as 'bricks' without 'intermediate structural units' such as 'walls and rooms'. So 'the group' should be 'recognized' 'as a distinct rank in grammar' with its own 'multivariate constituent structure', even if it 'no doubt evolved by expansion outwards from the word' just as the 'sentence' did from the 'clause' (IF 192, 159) (cf. 9.82; 12.54). This factor divides the group from the 'phrase', which has 'roughly the same status on the rank scale' but 'is a contraction of a clause'.

9.76 In 'the group', 'the three' metafunctions are 'represented' not as 'separate whole structures, but rather as partial contributions to a single structural line' (IF 158). This 'difference between clause and group', though 'only one of degree', allows us to 'analyse the group in one operation, not three' (IF 158, 169, 176) (cf. 9.46ff, 80). However, Halliday does 'split the ideational' back into **'experiential'** and **'logical'**[35], the latter showing 'the group' as 'a *word complex*': 'a combination of words built up on the basis' of 'generalized logical–semantic relations' 'encoded in natural language' (IF 158f, 170) (cf. 9.57).

9.77 The 'main classes of group' are 'nominal', 'verbal', and 'adverbial' (IF 159). **'Interpersonal** meanings' in 'the **nominal** group' are 'embodied in (a) the person system', (b) 'the attitudinal' 'Epithets' (like ' "splendid!" '), (c) 'the connotative meanings of lexical items', and (d) 'prosodic features such as swear-words and voice quality' (IF 169f). 'The **experiential** structure of the nominal group' includes 'the functional elements Deictic, Numerative, Epithet, Classifier, and Thing' (IF 160, 164). 'The *Deictic*' 'indicates whether or not some subset' of 'a class of things' is 'intended' (e.g., ' "all" ', ' "some" '), and, used 'demonstratively', can stipulate 'proximity to the speaker' (e.g., ' "this" ') or 'possession' (e.g., ' "your" '). The '*Numerative*' 'indicates some numerical feature of the subset' and can be 'quantifying' (e.g., ' "two" ') or 'ordering' (e.g., ' "second" '), matching the familiar classes of 'cardinal' and 'ordinal numerals', plus 'inexact number' (e.g., ' "many" '). 'The *Epithet* indicates some quality of the subset', with 'no hard and fast line' between 'objective property of the thing' ('experiential in function') (e.g., ' "old" ') versus 'the speaker's subjective attitude' ('interpersonal' in function) (e.g., ' "silly" ') (IF 163) (cf. 12.24).[36] The '*Classifier* indicates a particular subclass of things' in terms of 'material', 'scale', 'origin', and so on (e.g., ' "wooden" ') (IF 164). Finally, the '*Thing*' is 'a phenomenon of our experience' and 'the semantic core of the group', usually 'realized' as a 'noun' (e.g., ' "nose" ') (IF 108, 167, 164). We could thus have the sequence ' "your two silly old wooden noses" '.

9.78 The '*ordering*' of 'the nominal group' is thereby 'interpreted' in terms of an 'experiential pattern' (IF 165). 'The progression' goes from 'greatest specifying potential to' 'the least' (IF 166). 'The Deictic' 'starts by relating to the speaker in the context of the speech event', and then come 'elements with successively less identifying potential' and more concern for 'permanent attributes'. Hence, we 'begin with the immediate context' and 'go on to quantitative features' ('order and number'), then 'qualitative features', and 'finally' 'class membership' (IF 165f). 'We should beware, however, of assuming that the taxonomic order of modification always corresponds to something in the extra-linguistic universe' (IF 171) (cf. 12.24).

9.79 'The **verbal** group' has the 'structure' of '*Finite*' plus '*Event*' (with an optional Auxiliary' if 'the Finite' is not 'fused with the Event', as in 'one-word verbal groups such as "ate"') (IF 175) (cf. 9.74).[37] 'Finiteness' is 'expressed by means of a verbal operator which is either temporal or modal' (IF 75) (cf. 8.59, 64). This 'finite element' gives 'the proposition' 'a point of reference in the here and now', 'relates' it 'to its context in the speech event', and 'refers' either 'to the time of speaking' (via 'primary tense': 'past, present, or future') or 'to the judgment of the speaker' (via 'modality': 'probabilities', 'obligations', 'desires') (IF 75f, 86).[38]

9.80 Beyond this '**experiential**' aspect, 'the verbal group' (like the nominal) needs no 'separate analysis' for the other two metafunctions (IF 176) (cf. 9.76). 'Textual meaning is embodied in the ordering of the elements'; 'interpersonal meaning resides in the deictic feature associated with finiteness (primary tense or modality)' and in 'attitudinal colouring' of 'the lexical verb'. However, 'the **logical** structure' carries 'most of the semantic load', and in a way having 'no parallel in the nominal group', where the main issue is 'the recursive aspect of the modifying relation' for 'generating long strings' 'in univariate' and 'multivariate structures' (IF 175, 172) (cf. 9.59). In 'the verbal group', in contrast, the 'logical' issue is 'the recursive **tense** system' (IF 176f). 'The primary tense' is 'relative to speech event' ('past, present, future'), and 'the secondary tenses' are 'relative to time selected in previous tense'. Though a 'recursive' 'system' has 'no longest possible tense', 'in practice, the total set' of 'finite tenses' is 'limited' to 'thirty-six' by '"stop rules"': 'future' and 'present occur only once' and 'the same tense does not occur twice consecutively' (IF 179).[39] Also, 'the system varies for different speakers' and 'is tending to expand all the time, although it has probably just about reached its limits' (IF 184).

9.81 Albeit only 'the elements of verbal group are purely grammatical' in that 'the options they represent are closed' rather than 'open-ended', Halliday sees a major 'parallelism' between 'the verbal group as the expansion of a verb' and 'the nominal group as the expansion of a noun' (IF 175, 178). Both 'Finite' and 'Deictic' 'relate' 'to the "speaker-now"' (IF 176, 160). 'The Event' 'is the verbal equivalent of the Thing' in that 'both represent the core of the lexical meaning', although since 'Things are more highly organized than Events', the 'nominal' has 'additional lexical elements' (IF 176, 184n).[40] In sum, 'both verbal and nominal groups begin with the element that "fixes" the group in relation to the speech exchange; and both end with the element that specifies the representational content' (IF 176). This makes sense: 'initial position is thematic', the 'natural theme' being the 'relation to the here-and-now', whereas 'final position is informative', the natural place for 'the newsworthy' (cf. 9.51f; 7[14]). 'So the structure of groups recapitulates, in the *fixed* ordering of their elements, the meaning' 'incorporated as *choice* in the message structure of the clause' (IF 176, 166).

9.82 'One step *above* the clause' is 'the **clause complex**', which has 'the typical sequence' of 'Head (dominant) clause plus Modifying (dependent) clause' or, for 'thematic' 'motives', 'the reverse order' (IF 57, 192). The 'clause complex corresponds closely to a **sentence** of written English' and has in fact 'led to the evolution of the sentence in the writing system' while 'the sentence' 'evolved' 'over the centuries' by 'expansion outward from the clause' (IF 288, 192f) (cf. 9.75; 12.54). Yet 'the sentence' does not qualify 'as a multivariate constituent structure with its own range of functional configurations' (IF 192). It does not have 'elements that are distinct in function, realized by distinct classes, and more or less fixed in sequence'. Instead, 'the tendency is' 'for any clause to have the potential for functioning with any value in a multi-clausal complex'. Halliday accordingly makes 'the "clause complex"' 'the only grammatical unit above the clause' and 'assumes' it 'enables us to account in full for the functional organization of the sentence' (IF 193). 'The sentence' will be not 'a distinct grammatical category' but 'an orthographic unit' 'between full stops' – 'a constituent of writing, while a clause complex' is one of 'grammar'.[41]

9.83 'The relations between clauses' are again referred to 'the **logical** component' (IF 193) (cf. 9.59). In one 'system', '*expansion*' makes 'the secondary clause' (the later one) relate to 'the primary clause' (the earlier one) by 'elaborating' (as in '"John didn't wait; he ran away"'), 'extending' (as in '"John ran away and Fred stayed behind"'), or 'enhancing' it (as in '"John was scared, so he ran away"'), whereas '*projection*' makes the 'primary clause' 'instate' 'the secondary clause' as a 'locution' ('a construction of wording', as in '"John said, 'I'm running away'"') or 'an idea' ('a construction of meaning', as in '"John thought he would run away"') (IF 195ff). 'Expansion and projection form the basis of the English clause complex', and 'generally' 'recur throughout the semantic system' and 'the lexicogrammar' (IF 378). In another 'system', '*parataxis*' links 'two elements of equal status' in 'sequence', 'one initiating and the other continuing' but both 'free' (i.e., able to 'stand as a functioning whole'), whereas '*hypotaxis*' links two of 'unequal status' in 'dependence', the 'dominant' one being 'free' but the 'dependent' one not free (IF 193, 195) (cf. 4.68; 5.53). 'Parataxis and hypotaxis' are 'the two basic forms of logical relations in natural language' and can 'define' 'univariate structures' in 'complexes of any rank' – 'word, group, phrase, and clause alike' (IF 198, 193) (cf. 9.59). In 'the tone system', for example, they appear as 'tone concord' ('two or more instances of same tone') and 'tone sequence' (different tones), respectively (IF 285).

9.84 A familiar type of hypotaxis is '**relative clauses**', which Halliday again divides in two groups. '*Defining*' ones 'define subsets' (as in '"the only plan which might have succeeded"'), whereas '*non-defining*' ones '(also called "non-restrictive", "descriptive")' 'add a further characterization of something' 'taken to be already fully specific' (as in '"inflation, which was necessary for the system, became also lethal"') (IF 204, 167, 379; NT 2/209). This division is 'clearly signalled in both speech and writing' (IF 205). In 'speech', the 'defining' relation is marked by 'tone concord', whereas 'the non-defining relative forms a separate tone group'. In writing, only the 'non-defining' 'is marked off by punctuation, usually commas but sometimes' 'a dash'. Halliday sees 'an analogy' between 'identifying process' and 'defining relative' on the one hand, and between 'attributive process' and 'non-defining relative' on the other (IF 379) (cf. 9.63).

9.85 'In the clause complex', 'dependent clauses may be finite or non-finite' (IF 199, 204ff). The '*finite*' kind is well known, though Halliday's conception of 'finiteness' is unusually elaborate (cf. 9.58, 74, 79f). What he calls the '*non-finite clause*', however (e.g., '"selling office equipment"', IF 206), has often not been counted a clause at all, but a participial modifier (cf. 4.69). He admits it may 'occur' without a 'marker' or 'indication of its logical–semantic function' or its 'category' (IF 217f). 'The best solution here is to find the nearest finite form' and classify that. But 'in most instances the Subject is left implicit, to be presupposed from the primary clause'; it can be 'difficult to identify' because 'the non-finite' 'makes it unnecessary to decide' (IF 207). Or, we could suspend the problem by not postulating a clause at all, and assuming the presupposed material to be semantic (agent), not grammatical (subject), but that would violate the principle that all categories be 'there in the grammar' (cf. 9.36).

9.86 Beyond the clause complex lies the domain of '**cohesion**', based on 'additional relations within the text' which 'hold across' 'gaps of any distance' and 'link items of any size' 'from single words to lengthy passages' (IF 288f; cf. Hasan 1968; Halliday and Hasan 1976) (cf. 10^{15}). 'Typically any clause complex in connected discourse will have from one up to half a dozen cohesive ties with what has gone before it', plus 'some purely internal ones' (IF 290). These ties are termed 'non-structural forms of organization' on the grounds that 'the clause complex' sets 'the upper limits of grammatical structure', and that not 'words and structures' but 'ongoing semantic relationships' 'make text' (IF xxi, 288, 318, 291; cf. IF 380f; NT 2/206) (cf. 4.67; 9.3, 22, 91f, 95). Yet since the whole grammar is to some degree text-based and semantic, this division is troublesome, as we shall see (cf. 9.95).

9.87 'English' has 'four ways by which cohesion is created': 'conjunction', 'reference, ellipsis', and 'lexical organization' (IF 288, 313). '**Conjunction**' covers a 'cohesive bond', 'expressed' by a 'conjunction' (like '"but"') or a 'conjunctive adjunct' (like '"however"') between two 'typically contiguous elements', ranging from 'clauses' up to 'paragraphs or their equivalent in spoken language' (IF 303f, 289) (cf. 10.48). The 'semantic relations' 'are basically of the same kind' as 'between clauses' in a 'clause complex': 'elaboration, extension, enhancement' (IF 289, 303f) (cf. 9.81). But Halliday now breaks them down further into 'categories' of 'apposition', 'clarification, addition', 'variation', 'temporal', and 'causal-conditional'; these are further subdivided, yielding around thirty final categories, some with erudite names like 'adversative addition' ('"however"'), 'verifactive clarification'

('"actually"'), and 'punctiliar temporal conjunction' ('"at this moment"')
(IF 303–08). The 'categories' are mainly commonsensical (but not all, e.g.,
'distractive' and 'dismissive' are listed as 'clarifying') and 'may be found
useful in the interpretation of texts' (IF 303f, 308f).

9.88 'Conjunction' is 'a way' of 'achieving texture' by 'setting up
logical–semantic relations' 'between messages' 'in the absence of structural
relationships' (IF 308, 301, 289, 317). Such relations are obviously 'cohesive'
when 'expressed' by 'words' (e.g., '"consequently"' expressing 'cause');
'implicit conjunction' applies where 'the semantic relationship is clearly felt
to be present but unexpressed' (IF 301f, 308). We could 'recognize' these
cases 'by the possibility of inserting a conjunction without changing the
logical–semantic relation'; or we could 'treat them as semantically unrelated'
because 'if the speaker had wanted to relate' them 'he could have done so'
(IF 217). 'Including' these 'relations' 'in the analysis leads to a great deal of
indeterminacy' about whether they are 'present' and which kind 'hold
between pairs of adjacent sentences, or between each sentence and anything
that precedes it' (IF 308f). So we should be 'cautious in assigning implicit
conjunction' by 'noticing' where it is 'recognized', yet 'characterizing the
text without it: to see how much we still feel is being left unaccounted for'.
'The presence or absence of explicit conjunction' is a 'principled variable in
English discourse' and should not be 'obscured'. We should look also to
'other forms of cohesion' to assist 'our intuition' about the 'pattern of
conjunctive relationships'.

9.89 'Reference', usually termed '**co-reference**' in text linguistics,[42] is 'a
relation between things or facts', 'usually' 'single elements that have a
function within the clause – processes, participants, circumstances' (IF 289).
Probably, 'reference first evolved' as '*exophoric* reference': 'linking
"outwards" to some person or object in the environment' (IF 290) (cf. 12.24).
'We may postulate an imaginary stage in the evolution of language when the
basic referential category of person was deictic', 'referring to the situation
here and now' (IF 291) (cf. 9.77f, 80f). 'First and second person' pronouns
'retain this deictic sense' (cf. 4.70), as do the 'demonstratives "this/that"';
but 'third person' pronouns are 'more often than not *anaphoric*', i.e.,
'pointing' 'to the preceding text', or, more rarely, '*cataphoric*', pointing to
'the following text' (IF 291ff). Whenever 'the listener has to look
elsewhere', the 'effect' is 'cohesive', 'linking the two passages into a
coherent unity'. 'If the pronoun and referent are in the same clause
complex', we have 'already one text by virtue of the structural relationship
between the clauses'. If not, 'cohesion' is 'the sole linking feature and hence
critical to the creation of text'. So 'the cohesive relationship' 'carries a
greater load' beyond the 'clause complex'.[43]

9.90 '**Ellipsis**' occurs when 'a clause, or a part of a clause' or 'of a verbal
or nominal group' is 'presupposed at a subsequent place' via 'positive
omission' – 'saying nothing where something is required to make up the
sense' (IF 288). Again, what is missing depends upon one's grammatical
expectations, and here Halliday takes a rather extreme view. In 'clausal

ellipsis', as is 'typical in a dialogue sequence', 'everything is omitted' 'in a response turn' 'except the information-bearing element', so that 'the listener' must 'supply the missing words' 'from what has gone before' (IF 300). 'It is always possible to "reconstitute" the ellipsed item' and make it 'fully explicit' (more overstatement); 'the exact wording' is 'taken over', aside from 'reversal of speaker–listener deixis' and 'change of mood where appropriate'. In a 'question–answer sequence', mere ' "yes" ' and ' "no" ' are taken to be 'elliptical' for 'the whole clause', as are ' "Why?" ' and ' "Who?" ' in responses to statements (IF 297).

9.91 Ellipsis doesn't fully match the other means of cohesion. It is a relation not between two actual passages in a text, but between an actual passage and a virtual or theoretical complete version. Also, though it 'contributes' to 'the semantic structure', it 'sets up a relationship that is not semantic but lexicogrammatical' – 'in wording', not 'meaning' (IF 296, 300). For instance, since 'every independent clause in English requires a Subject', 'the listener will understand the Subject' removed by 'ellipsis' – e.g., ' "I" ' 'in a giving clause (offer or statement)' (e.g., ' "carry your bag?" '), or ' "you" ' 'in a demanding clause (question or command)' (e.g., ' "play us a tune" ') (IF 90f). In this view, despite 'most accounts of English grammar, the imperative' is not 'a special case' but 'an instance of this general principle by which a Subject is understood' (cf. 4.56).

9.92 'A **substitute** serves as a place-holding device, showing where something has been omitted and what its grammatical function would be' (IF 297; cf. NT 2/239ff). ' "Do" ' is a 'verbal substitute', and ' "one" ' 'a nominal substitute', both 'derived by extension from an item in the full, non-elliptical group' (IF 300f). Although differing by 'environments', 'ellipsis and substitution are variants of the same type of cohesive relation', in that 'the missing words' listeners presumably 'retrieve' 'must be grammatically appropriate' for being 'inserted in place' (IF 297, 301f). 'This is not the case with reference', where 'the relationship' is 'semantic' and has 'no grammatical constraint: the class of the reference item need not match that of what it presupposes, and one cannot normally insert the presupposed element' (IF 302). For that 'reason', 'reference' 'can reach back a long way, whereas ellipsis–substitution is largely' 'confined to closely contiguous passages', e.g., ' "adjacency pairs" in dialogue' (IF 302, 289, 317). In return, 'reference' usually 'refers to the same thing' while 'ellipsis–substitution' need not (IF 302).[44]

9.93 'Lexical cohesion' 'selects items' 'related in some way to previous ones' and creates whole 'referential chains' whose 'interaction' 'gives the text its coherence' and 'dynamic flow' (IF 316, 310, 289) (cf. 10.30, 45). Subtypes include 'repetition', where a repeated item is the same word or some 'inflectional' or 'derivational variant' (e.g., ' "dine – dinner" '); and 'synonymy' (e.g., ' "sound – noise" '), along with its 'variants': 'hyponymy' of 'general' and 'specific' (e.g., ' "vegetation – grass" '), 'meronymy' of 'whole' and 'part' (e.g., ' "bottle – stopper" '), and 'antonymy' of 'opposites' (e.g., ' "fell asleep – woke" ') (IF 310ff). Also, Firth's 'collocation' is included as a '"co-occurrence tendency"' having a 'semantic basis' and a 'considerably greater probability' than is implied by 'their overall frequency in the language' (IF 312f) (cf. 8.78ff). The 'cohesive effect' of 'synonymy' actually 'depends more on collocation', which affects 'our expectations of what is to come next' in 'strong' though 'localized' ways (IF 313, 317). However, 'fixed phrases and cliches' (like '"stretch of the imagination"') 'contribute little', since they 'behave almost like single lexical items' (IF 313) (cf. 2.61; 4.60; 5.32, 54; 7³⁴; 12.28).

9.94 One 'way to see how these resources work is to deconstruct a text, destroying its textual patterns one by one', 'removing the cohesion' and 'selecting options at random' (IF 314f). For a piece of a dialogue about 'the art of selling silver', the original passage '"if they come in they're usually people who love beautiful things"' gets turned into '"the people who love beautiful things are usually people if people come in"' (IF 283, 315; cf. IF 346–59). But this is a patently 'artificial exercise': 'in real life the different "metafunctions" are so closely interwoven' that one can hardly be 'disturbed while the others remain unaffected', aside from 'aphasia' (IF 315). Surely a functional grammar should address the relation among *genuine* alternatives, all cohesive but differing in effect and impact.

9.95 An inconsistency arises when Halliday argues cohesion is needed because 'the organization of text is semantic rather than formal', 'much looser than that of grammatical units' (IF 290) (cf. 9.3, 22, 32, 36, 91f, 86; 12²⁴). Since 'text' is 'an ongoing process of meaning', we should 'think of' 'cohesion as an aspect of this process, whereby the flow of meaning is channelled along the speaker's purposive courses instead of spilling out in every possible direction'. However, since '"text"' is usually taken as referring to the product' (cf. 9.43), it seems 'natural to talk about cohesion as a relation between entities, in the same way we talk about grammatical structure' in 'the clause'. 'In the last resort, a clause (or any other linguistic unit) is also a happening; but since a clause has a tight formal structure, we do not seriously misrepresent it' as 'a static configuration' (cf. 11.55). And Halliday is content to 'represent cohesive relations simply by additions to the structural notation'.

9.96 Moreover, the devices Halliday presents are not really what prevents the 'flow of meaning' from 'spilling out aimlessly'. 'For a text to be coherent', 'it must be cohesive, but must be more besides' (IF 318). It must not merely 'have structure', but must also 'be semantically appropriate, with lexicogrammatical realizations to match (must make sense)'. Yet Halliday is inconsistent here again. On the one hand, he declares that 'structure is not the appropriate concept for interpreting the semantic domain', and he views cohesion as 'non-structural forms of organization' (IF 188 xxi, 288, 318) (cf. 9.86). Also, 'semantic structures' 'need by no means have the same shape as structures at any other level' (EF 94f). On the other hand, he grants that 'a text has' 'semantic structure' 'above the clause complex', and that 'the concept of structure is the same' as in 'grammatical structure', albeit 'the level at which it is coded is different' (IF 318). Also, 'structure'

should be 'defined as any viable' or 'meaningful' 'configuration of functions',
and this 'definition' is 'abstract enough to cover semantic structure' (IF 32,
37; EF 95). The 'concept of semantic structure' might even 'handle more
complex areas of behaviour', e.g., 'in the study of institutional communication networks', and might render 'complex decision-making strategies'
'accessible to linguistic observation' (EF 95f). But these prospects are 'a
matter of speculation' because 'sociological semantics' is at an 'elementary
stage', still 'investigating' 'closely circumscribed' 'contexts', describable by
'direct pre-selection between semantic and grammatical systems' (cf. 9.11f, 39).

9.97 The range of the approach is further increased by introducing a
broad 'lexicogrammatical' conception of '**metaphor**' for any 'aspect of the
structural configuration of the clause' that 'differs from that which would be
arrived at' by 'the most straightforward coding of the meanings' (IF 345).
Each 'metaphorical expression corresponds' to one or more '**congruent**'
('"literal"') ones for the same 'semantic configuration' that are attainable
by 'a natural sequence of steps' (IF 321). 'The congruent' version need not
be 'better', 'more frequent', or 'maximally simple', nor 'function as norm';
as 'the history of every language' shows, the 'metaphorical' one can 'become
the norm' by 'a natural process of linguistic change' (IF 321f, 327, 329).[45]
'We do not know' if 'language evolved' from 'congruent modes of
representation' being 'gradually elaborated', or if 'metaphor has been
inherent' 'from the very beginning' (IF 322), although the argument based
on child development suggests the former (cf. 9.11), as do physicalist
notions of meaning (cf. 4.24; 5.66f). 'In most types of discourse', 'we
operate in between' 'two extremes': 'the totally congruent', which 'sounds
flat', and 'the totally incongruent', which sounds 'artificial and contrived'
(IF 324).

9.98 As with 'logic' at the other end of normalcy (cf. 9.59), Halliday airs
some problems with metaphor, but remains undismayed. He says 'it is not
always possible to say exactly what is' 'metaphorical' (understatement), and
yet 'it is always possible to analyse such clauses in non-metaphorical terms'
(overstatement) (IF 334, 157; cf. IF 327, 343). 'We are able to recognize
congruent forms', because 'knowing a language' includes 'knowing what is
the most typical "unmarked" way of saying a thing' (IF 322) – true in
general, but not for all specific locutions. Also, two alternate versions will
not be 'totally synonymous', since the 'metaphorical' one 'adds' 'semantic
features'; yet the two 'will be systematically related in meaning, and
therefore synonymous in certain respects' (IF 321, 58). And, the 'concept of
grammatical metaphor' is itself 'a metaphorical extension of the term from
its rhetorical sense as a figure of speech' (IF 345).

9.99 These various qualifiers suggest Halliday's own uneasiness about a
possibly huge inflation beyond the 'pointedly metaphorical' usage he 'largely
avoids' (IF 157). We see this trend in his 'ideational' 'metaphors of
transitivity' (IF 321). It seems reasonable to include ' "the fifth day saw them
at the summit" ' versus ' "they arrived at the summit on the fifth day" ':
'time' 'has been dressed up' as 'participant', making ' "a day" ' a 'conscious

being' (IF 322–25). But including '"she has brown eyes"' and '"he writes good books"' by contrast with '"her eyes are brown"' and '"he writes books, which are good"' seems to reserve 'congruence' for syntactically simple (kernel-like) clauses (cf. 7.52), even where, as here, the 'metaphorical' version is 'part of the system of English' and 'the unmarked choice' (IF 327f).

9.100   The same inflation impends for the 'interpersonal' 'metaphors of mood and modality' (IF 321, 342). 'The explicitly subjective and objective forms of modality are all strictly speaking metaphorical' in 'representing the modality as being the substantive proposition' rather than the 'adjunct' required for a 'congruent form' (IF 340). So all statements depending on 'projecting clauses' like '"I think that"' or '"I'm certain that"' get counted as 'metaphorical' counterparts to 'congruent realizations' with 'a modal element' like '"probably"' or '"certainly"' 'within the clause' (IF 332f). Halliday remarks here that in 'the "games people play" in the daily round of interpersonal skirmishing', we 'give prominence to our own point of view' by 'dressing it up' as 'the assertion' and 'making it appear' 'objective' by 'claiming' 'certainty' (IF 340; cf. IF 333). Indeed, 'the entire system' of 'the grammar of interpersonal exchanges' 'rests' on a 'paradox': 'we only say we are certain when we are not' (IF 340, 358).

9.101   Lending 'metaphor' so wide a sense raises the question: 'how far does one go in this direction in the course of textual analysis?' (IF 331).[46] 'A general guide would be: unscramble as far as is needed', e.g., for 'explaining the impact' of a 'text' (IF 332, 345; cf. IF 329). Even if we can 'establish a chain of metaphorical interpretations' leading from the clause under scrutiny' to a 'congruent form' via 'a series of intermediate steps', we have no '"history"' of the clause' as 'the process whereby speaker or writer has arrived at' it (IF 328, 345) (cf. 7.48, 51; 12.54). Still, if we can 'suggest how an instance in text may be referred to the system of the language as a whole', we can gain 'an important link in the total chain of explanations whereby we relate text to system' (IF 345).

9.102   Halliday takes an equally wide view of **style**, declaring that 'there are no regions of language in which style does not reside' (EF 112) (cf. 3.69; 5.82; 6.52; 8.83; 10.57). Here, too, the 'central problem in the study of style' is '*relevance*': 'determining whether any particular instance of linguistic prominence' 'is significant' and 'motivated (EF 103, 112). A 'prominent' 'feature', which 'stands out in some way', is 'foregrounded only if it relates to the meaning of the text as whole' (EF 112f).[47] It may be seen either as 'a departure from a norm' or as 'an attainment or establishment of a norm'. 'The use of ungrammatical forms has received a great deal of attention' because it supports 'a deterministic concept' of 'deviation' ('forms prohibited by rules'), which is however 'of very limited interest in stylistics' (EF 114) (cf. 12.40). 'Prominence' can be 'probabilistic', based on 'departures from some expected pattern of frequency' (EF 115, 113). Or, '"the impact of entire work may be enormous"' without showing anything '"unusual or arresting in grammar or in vocabulary"' (EF 115; cf. McIntosh 1965: 19).

9.103   As befits his broad approach, Halliday looks beyond ' "effects" in grammar and vocabulary', in the sense of 'syntactic or lexical patterns', to the 'subject-matter' and the 'vision of things' (EF 118, 120). 'In stylistics we are concerned with language in relation to all the levels of meaning a work may have' (EF 120) (cf. 8.84). 'Language, by the multiplicity of its functions, possesses a fugue-like quality in which a number of themes unfold simultaneously' (EF 121). 'Powerful impact' results when 'the subject-matter is motivated by deeper meaning, and the transitivity patterns realize both' (EF 120).

9.104   In a Sapirian manner, Halliday turns to literature: 'the relation' of 'the language system' 'to the meanings of a literary work' (EF 133) (cf. 3.68ff). In William Golding's *The Inheritors*, 'the literal use' of 'syntactic patterns provides a context for their metaphorical use' (EF 121). To invoke a 'Neanderthal' 'tribe's point of view', 'the language conveys' a 'picture in which people act, but do not act on things' (EF 123). 'Such normally transitive verbs as "grab" occur intransitively'. Often 'the Subjects are not people', but 'parts of body or inanimate objects'. The effect is 'an atmosphere of ineffectual activity' and 'helplessness', and a 'reluctance to envisage the "whole man" ' 'participating in a process' (EF 123, 125). In sum, 'transitivity' is 'the theme of the entire novel: man's interpretation of his experience' (EF 134). In some such way, 'every work achieves a unique balance among the types and components of meaning, and embodies the writer's individual exploration of the functional diversity of language' (EF 135).

9.105   Kindred to style but with a broader range is the concept of **'register'**, such as 'narrative, transactional, expository', and so on (IF 318).[48] 'Elements', 'configurations', and 'collocations' 'vary from one register to another', as does 'the patterning of clause themes throughout a text' (IF 318, 313, 315). But in IF Halliday decides not to 'go into questions of register structure', which 'we are only beginning to be able to characterize' (IF 290, xxxv). He merely assumes that 'a speaker of the language "knows" ' 'how likely a particular word or group or phrase is' 'in any given register'; but the 'treatment of probabilities', albeit 'an important part of the grammar', is also 'outside the scope' (IF xxii; cf. EF 114). We thus cannot evaluate his claim that 'registers select and foreground different options, but do not normally have a special grammar'; yet 'some registers do', such as 'newspaper headlines' (IF 372; cf. IF 373–77).[49]

9.106   More 'specialized' than registers are the ' **"restricted languages"** ' that make up 'much of the speech' of 'daily life' in 'contexts where the options are limited and the meaning potential' 'closely specifiable' and 'explainable' (EF 25ff) (cf. 8.76ff). Exploring them might 'throw light on certain features in the internal organization of language' (EF 27). Halliday lists 'games', 'greetings', 'musical scores', 'weather reports', 'recipes', 'cabled messages', and so on, along with 'routines of the working day' like 'buying and selling' (EF 25f, 63).[50] In such domains, 'the language is not restricted as a whole' and 'the transactional meanings are not closed', but 'definable patterns' and 'options' do 'come into play', e.g., for 'beginning and ending' a 'conversation on the telephone' (EF 26).

9.107 By now we can appreciate the scope and motives in Halliday's plea to 'construct a grammar' for the 'analysis' and 'interpretation of texts of a broad variety of registers in modern English' (IF x, xv, xx). This 'analysis' 'has two aims' or 'levels' (IF 371, xv). The 'lower level' – 'always attainable' if we 'relate the text to general features of the language' – is 'to show why the text means what it does'. The 'higher level' is 'to show why it is valued as it is' – as 'effective or not' 'in relation to its purpose'. 'This goal' is 'more difficult' and presupposes the first: 'evaluation rests on interpretation' of the '"context of situation" and "context of culture"' (cf. 8.91; 9.1, 8, 18; 22f; 12.62). Moreover, we must ask 'how the linguistic features of a text relate systematically to the features of its environment, including the intentions of those involved in its production' (IF xvif). Like 'any systematic inquiry', 'the study of language in a social context' 'involves' 'some idealization', because 'the object' of 'linguistic study' is never an 'unprocessed language event' but a '"**text**", that is, language in a context', 'an operational unit' – and 'the text, whether invented, elicited, or recorded, is an idealized construction' (EF 68, 107) (cf. 5.5). But in communication, 'success does not depend' on whether a text is 'consciously' 'planned and polished'; a 'spontaneous' one is not 'formless and unstructured' (IF 371). 'Most discourse falls in between the rhetorical ideal and the total flop.'

9.108 The problems and inconsistencies I have pointed out are due largely to the friction between the intent to construct a fully general grammar and the drive to fit it closely to a wide range of realistic data. 'Ideally, every example should be a whole text', but 'increasing the length and picking' out a given 'feature' can be difficult (IF xxxiii). An 'example' may 'illustrate a category' 'clearly and unambiguously', but 'discourse' 'in real life' has 'vastly greater scope and variation' (IF xxxiii, 92). In fact as 'a general principle in language', 'the easier a thing is to recognize, the more trivial it is', whereas 'a semantically significant category is usually not simple or clear-cut' (IF xxxiii). Halliday prefers to analyse 'a brief extract' 'understandable out of its context', or 'a passage from a well-known text' – *Alice in Wonderland* being his standby (also in Hasan 1968) – though, for purposes of publicity, he uses some excerpts by linguists like Saussure, Firth, Hjelmslev, and Whorf (IF xxxiii, 45, 40f). He 'invents' examples 'as a last resort' or 'to keep illustration down to manageable size' (IF xxxiii). He does lean heavily on one 'hypothetical example': a mother's response to a naughty boy who has been 'playing' 'on a building site' – will she 'smack him', or will she use 'moral' 'disapproval', 'threat of punishment', or 'emotional blackmail' (EF 61, 58ff, 73–78, 85–91, 94)?

9.109 Traditional grammar and much of linguistics have analysed 'grammar' within a single system or account by carefully selecting examples wherein the multiple systems correspond fairly well (cf. 5.37; 9.46, 55, 75; 12.50). Halliday's comprehensive functional grammar pries these interacting systems apart in order to explore the rich variety of ways for mapping from system to system (cf. 9.48, 50, 57). Predictably, the foray plunges him into a multitude of decisions and perplexities about how to identify and label things and how to interrelate them. Whereas Chomsky's grammar and its successors herald an analysis in which rigour and uniformity steadily increase as we move away from the 'surface' data, Halliday's grammar enables an analysis in which richness and multiplicity steadily increase (cf. 9.21). We therefore produce not some tidy artifact, logical formula, or 'deep' tree structure, but a still open-ended exegesis of yet farther-reaching issues. The text is not transformed into a vast feature matrix or configuration of minimal units, but rewoven into a complex pattern of vectors that gives a renewed sense of intricacy.

9.110 And herein lies the realism. Halliday wants to emphasize, not downplay, the prospect that the 'text' may not be 'homogeneous, univocal, or "flat"' but replete with 'multiple meanings, alternatives, ambiguities, metaphors, and so on' (IF 318, xv). 'Discourse is a multidimensional process; "a text"' 'is the product of that process' and 'embodies the same' 'polyphonic structuring as is found in the grammar'. Yet 'the text' is also 'functioning at a higher level of the code, as the realization of semiotic orders "above" the language', and 'may contain' 'all the inconsistencies, contradictions, and conflicts that can exist within and between such semiotic systems' (IF 318). When we analyse 'a text' as 'a highly complex phenomenon', we may move 'further away from the language into more abstract semiotic realms, with different modes of discourse reinterpreting, complementing, and contradicting each other as the intricacies are progressively brought to light' (IF xvi) (cf. 9.92, 104). This 'exegetical work' cannot be 'turned into an algorithm' by 'specifying a series of steps or operations' leading to 'an objective account of the text, still less of the culture' (cf. 5.62, 86; 10.14; 12.50).

9.111 For Halliday, 'the test of a theory' is: 'does it facilitate the task at hand?' (IF xxx) (cf. 9.1). He sees a 'trade-off' between 'depth' and 'breadth', i.e., between 'highly specialized machines' for 'just one job' and 'less specialized' ones for 'a broad range of jobs' (cf. 9.21). His 'account' 'is biased toward breadth' and has already served 'a variety' of 'practical' and 'theoretical' 'purposes' (IF xv, xxx). These involve 'the relation between language' and 'culture'; the 'analysis of text, spoken and written', notably 'spontaneous conversation'; 'computational' and 'developmental linguistics'; the 'study of socialization' and 'functional variation'; the 'comparison of registers, or functional varieties of English'; and the 'stylistic analysis of poems and short stories'. 'Educational applications' include 'teacher education'; 'analysis' of 'textbooks', 'teacher–pupil communication', and 'children's writing'; 'language in secondary education'; 'error analysis'; and 'the teaching of literature' and 'foreign language'. Halliday's 'approach' is thus more 'applied' than 'pure', more 'functional' than 'formal', more 'actual' than 'ideal', more 'rhetorical' than 'logical', and addresses 'the text rather than the sentence' (IF xviii).

9.112 Such tasks and applications form the framework of his search for a 'concept of linguistic function' that would allow us to 'understand language in educational, developmental, social, and aesthetic aspects' (EF 8). We also need to seek 'criteria' 'at the interfaces between language and non-language', notably 'the socio-semantic interface' (EF 68f). We must explore the respective role of 'language' 'in humanities, social science, natural science, medicine, and engineering' (IF xxix) (cf. 12.63). The prospect is imposing, and most of the work still lies in the future. But Halliday has already covered much ground to make us aware that 'a text is not a mere reflection of what lies beyond' but 'an active partner in the reality-making and reality-changing process' (IF 318).

Notes

1. The key to Halliday references is: EF: *Explorations in the Function of Language* (1973); IF: *An Introduction to Functional Linguistics* (1985); IG: *Intonation and Grammar in British English* (1967a); and NT: 'Notes on transitivity and theme in English' (1967–68). NT has three parts, cited as NT 1, NT 2, and NT 3. IG and EF consist (like Firth's later books) chiefly of 'previously published papers' (IG 7; cf. EF 20, 45, 70, 101, 139). IF is a fairly organic whole, 'grown out of' 'class notes prepared for students' of 'discourse analysis' (IF ix). It only partly fulfils the promise of 'a monograph with revisions' to be made from the 'Notes' of 1967–68 (IF ix; NT 1/215n), because it does not 'spell out all the arguments' (letter to me, 16 November 1988) – a reason why IF was entitled *A Short Introduction* until the publishers objected. I faced special problems for this chapter: treating Halliday's work apart from Ruqaiya Hasan's; condensing his 'spontaneous' 'style' (IF 371); and having for IF no 'index', judged 'superfluous' because 'the table of contents' 'makes the structure of the book immediately clear' (IF xii) (of course it does, but that's not what *indexes* are for!).

2. Whorf (1956) 'pointed out' the 'naiveté' of picking out 'isolated' instances, such as large numbers of 'Eskimo words for "snow" or Arabic words for "camel"', as measures of 'importance' in the 'culture' (IF xxxi). 'Chinese has a single word for "rice"', being 'a language' 'that favours general nouns'.

3. Halliday (1988: viii) distinguishes '**realization**', as 'the relationship among the levels of the system', from '**instantiation**' between 'instance and 'system', and says Saussure 'confused' the two (cf. 9.27, 39; 12.39).

4. Still, his 'theory' 'has been used in a general cognitive framework' and allied with 'neurolinguistics', 'learning theory', and artificial intelligence (IF xxxi; cf. IF xxix; IG 10n).

5. Being 'cumbersome', 'lexicogrammar' is often replaced by 'grammar', but we should remember 'that syntax and vocabulary are part of the same level in the code' (IF xiv) (cf. 12.28).

6. And a lot on Halliday's own son Nigel (IF 94–98, EF 27–33, 37), who, Halliday told me in October 1989, is the only child he directly studied. A thick manuscript collection of data on Nigel lies unpublished in Halliday's desk. One wonders how representative a child can be whose parents are both famous linguists, but recent casework confirming Halliday's view of acquisition is provided by Painter (1984).

7. Halliday complains that '"acquisition"' is a 'misleading metaphor, suggesting that language' is 'property to be owned' (EF 24). Probably, the psycholinguists used the term to dissociate their work from behaviourist research on learning (e.g., word-list experiments, cf. 10.70, 93).

8. Actually, Bernstein's concept of the 'restricted code' (first proposed in 1961) was widely interpreted in just the sense Halliday disputes here: as a 'lack of words', 'grammar', and 'syntactic options' (EF 18). A reinterpretation in terms of 'functions' would be highly significant and helpful for educational programmes.

9. 'Classifications of functions', such as Bühler's (1934) 'representational, expressive, and conative', or Malinowski's (1923) 'pragmatic and magical', are cited as 'alternatives to the undifferentiated notion of language as the expression of thought' (NT 3/207; cf. EF 104, 107) (cf. 3.10ff; 5.69; 6.6; 7.10; 8.24f; 11.17ff, 22; 12.10). Unlike Malinowski, Bühler 'was concerned with the functions of language from the standpoint not so much of the culture but of the individual' (Halliday and Hasan 1985: 15) (cf. 12.14).

10. 'Systemic theory follows in the European functional tradition': 'Firth's system-structure theory', Hjelmslev's 'principles', and 'Prague school' 'ideas' (IF xxvi) (cf. 9.47, 56, 9^{19}). Halliday's 'publishers' said he 'should not be renaming "his" grammar functional instead of systemic'; he 'found that difficult to accept', the more so as he associates the 'systemic part' with 'networks', which are omitted from IF (IF x, xv) (cf. 9.20; 9^{12}).

11. Like Firth, Halliday would extend 'paradigms' from the 'word to larger units' (IF xxxii) (cf. 8.57; 9.27). The traditional sense entails a 'contradiction': when we display 'things that do not go together' 'by definition', they get 'turned into syntagms' (cf. 2.66; 8.59; 12.27). Besides, 'paradigms have a role' less 'in language learning' than 'in learning linguistics and in carrying out linguistic research' (IF xxxiif) (cf. 4.86).

12. He says 'the theoretical component' was omitted, namely 'the system networks and realization statements' (IF x). How these notations count as 'theory' needs explaining (cf. 12.25); and plenty of theoretical groundwork remains in the book.

13. 'In the European linguistic tradition, classes were originally derived from an analysis of sentences into parts; the term "**parts of speech**" is a mistranslation', though I don't see why Halliday's 'parts of a sentence' is necessarily more accurate for 'meroi logou' and 'partes orationis' (IF 30) (cf. 8.54, 61). Still, 'the scheme of word classes' based on the 'inflectional potential' of 'words in classical Greek' (hence 'case, gender', etc.) (IF 30) is clearly removed from both 'speech' and 'sentence'. 'English' calls for 'other principles'.

14. For consistency, I use capitals for these terms also when citing earlier works before Halliday used the device. When he puts whole terms in small capitals for emphasis, I make my best guess whether to capitalize them in the citation.

15. Of these ranks, the 'morpheme' gets scant coverage, figuring briefly as 'a creation of modern linguistics' 'for the smallest unit', although 'words' may 'consist of only one morpheme' (IF 25, 20) (cf. 4.53, 60; 12.28). Because 'in speaking English we are not normally aware of the internal structure of words', 'constituent morphemes have never come to be marked off' 'in writing' (IF 20) (cf. 4.54; 5.46, 48). We are 'more aware of how words combine into larger units', such as 'group' and 'clause' (IF 20f), and these ranks are covered in detail (cf. 12.29).

16. For an easy start, Halliday presents 'orthographic constituents' with neatly 'layered part-whole relationships among units of a written text, each unit consisting of *one or more* of the next smaller' (cf. 5.41) – all 'without reference to the grammatical structure' (IF 2f; cf. IF 22, 271). Then follows 'constituent structure in verse': 'stanzas', 'lines', 'feet', and 'syllables' – admittedly not 'the most fundamental' 'form of organization in language' but 'the most readily observable' (IF 4, 18). Noting that 'all the elements of verse structure have

their basis in the spoken language', he proposes a 'phonometric interpretation' to replace the 'classic metric' one from 'Latin and Greek' (IF 8, 10, 12, 14). This gives 'a more accurate account of verse as spoken aloud', 'correctly predicts the relative length of syllables within the foot' and 'allows for silence' 'wherever it would occur in a natural rendering' (i.e., 'a silent beat' or 'foot' to fill out 'odd numbers' 'because all phonometric structures in English are binary') (IF 14, 12, 273). 'The foot' is also treated as 'a unit of ordinary everyday speech, with no definite number of syllables' (IF 13, 271; cf. IG 12f).

17. Like Saussure's and Bloomfield's, Halliday's examples are words in different languages for the same thing ('"rain"'), showing 'there is nothing natural about the relation of the sounds' to the 'phenomenon beyond the code' (cf. 2.28; 4.27).

18. He offers terms for three 'different aspects' of a 'combined function': '"semantic" suggests its place in the total linguistic system; "representational" emphasizes its relation to extra-linguistic factors'; and '"logical" implies an underlying structure' 'independent of syntax' and 'opposed' to '"grammatical" as "meaning" to "form"' (NT 3/209; cf. Sweet 1891). In IF, the term 'logical–semantic' (or 'logico-semantic') seems to collapse this division (cf. 9.74, 84f, 99).

19. Even so, 'the European functional "schools"' in Prague, France, London, and Copenhagen 'all regarded the text as the object of linguistics' (IF xxii) (though to me, Hjelmslev's is a prime case of 'an elegant theory' with no attempt to 'account for how the system engenders text'). '"Systemic" description' seems to be a British product, however: the earliest references are 'mimeographs' by Halliday, Alick Henrici, and Rodney Huddleston, dating from 1964–66 (NT 1/37, 81) and produced within a research project on scientific English. These papers were finally published in Halliday and Martin (eds) (1981).

20. Halliday's notion 'corresponds to the "surface subject" in transformational grammar'; a '"deep subject" is unnecessary' and 'self-contradictory', since the relations it would account for are handled 'systemically' by 'a transitivity function' (NT 1/39n, 2/213) (cf. 7.63). To 'identify' 'the subject' 'in a text', we can treat it as 'the nominal group' 'picked up by the pronoun' in a 'tag question'; for '"that teapot your aunt got from the duke"' the tag would be "didn't she?"', not '"didn't he?"' or "wasn't it?"'' (IF 73). The results 'accord with the classical conception of the subject' based on 'concord with the verb' – hardly a helpful basis 'in Modern English' with its scant 'manifestation of person and number'. And we 'bring in things not traditionally regarded as subject, like "it" in "it's raining"' expressing an 'unanalysed' 'process' with no 'participants' (IF 102; NT 3/193, 195). Halliday often uses 'tag questions' to reveal or differentiate grammatical categories (IF 59, 69, 72, 85, 91, 119, 169, 333, 389; NT 3/213; EF 55). Compare Note 29.

21. For clarity, I use the term 'metafunctions' throughout, though Halliday may call them 'functions', 'elements', 'components', or 'meanings'. I also unify variations in the names, e.g., 'discoursal' for 'textual', and 'speech-functional' for 'interpersonal' (cf. NT 3/209f); on the merger of 'experiential' and 'logical' into 'ideational', see 9.59.

22. One case is the 'cleft' form, as in '"What we want is Watney's"' (NT 2/223f; cf. IF 43, 59, 280f). In his own writing, Halliday favours it to the verge of cleftomania; pressed for space, I removed dozens of cleft constructions in my quotes.

23. Halliday finds his 'term' 'different from the mathematical concept of information'; but 'transitional probabilities' and 'statistic concepts' are elsewhere related to 'prominence' (IF 275; EF 115) (cf. 7.38).

24. 'More specifically, it is one non-embedded clause with all the clauses embedded in it' (NT 2/201). An 'embedded' 'item' was 'earlier' called 'rankshifted' or 'downranked', because it has an 'equivalent or higher rank' in respect to the item in which it is a 'constituent' (IF 166f, 129, 219; NT 2/243n, IG 20f). Perhaps because Halliday sees 'no direct relationship between an embedded clause and the clause within which it is embedded', or at least 'not a structural one', he tends to 'ignore embedded clauses'; 'they do not function as propositions or proposals' and 'play no part in the structure of the interaction' (IF 219, 225, 98) (but cf. 10.67).

25. Also, 'tone realizes modal options' whereas 'tonality and tonicity' 'realize thematic options' (NT 2/243n). IG has a more elaborate scheme: besides the five 'tones' in the 'primary system' treated here (I use the names of tones instead of Halliday's numbering from 1 to 5), some eighteen 'tones' across eight 'secondary systems' (IG 16f). 'Strictly speaking, "key" is outside the scope' of IF, being 'not expressed structurally but prosodically' (IF 281).

26. In NT, Halliday had listed 'six distinct but related sets of options' 'within the theme system': 'information, thematization, and identification for the clause as a whole', and 'predication, substitution, and reference' for a 'single element in the clause structure' (NT 2/200, 236–41). These are redistributed in IF across various domains, including 'cohesion' (cf. 9.46, 89, 92, 9[37]).

27. Halliday 'avoids' the terms 'topic and comment' because they are 'used in ways which conflate' these 'distinct functions' (NT 2/200, 205). For him, 'topic' is 'only one' 'kind of theme', namely 'the first element in the clause that has some function in the ideational structure' (IF 39, 56; cf. IF 54, 61, 67n) (cf. 7.63).

28. 'The term "cognitive"' for 'ideational' is 'misleading', since it could apply to 'all linguistic functions' (EF 105f; NT 3/209); but the term does get used (NT 2/236ff) (cf. Note 37).

29. Also, 'mental processes' are not 'probed or substituted by the verb "do"'; 'we cannot say "What John did was know the answer"' (IF 108–111).

30. 'In earlier stages of the language', '"indirect" participants' 'required an oblique case and/or a preposition' (IF 132). 'In modern English, the distinction between direct and indirect participants has largely disappeared': they 'all' 'can take on the function of subject; there are no cases'; and the use of 'a preposition is determined on other grounds' (cf. 9.65, 69, 9[32]).

31. 'Except' for the 'middle' or 'mediopassive voice' in 'a clause with no feature of "agency"', as in '"the light turned on"' (IF 146, 150, 152; NT 3/183–88) (cf. 9.68).

32. Some 'indeterminacy' remains: 'participants can sometimes occur with a preposition' (as in '"play a tune for me"' vs '"play me a tune"'), and 'circumstances' can occur 'without one' (as in '"they stayed two days"' vs '"they stayed for two days"') (IF 150, 133). Furthermore, 'a complement' can be made 'subject' with the 'preposition' put at the end (as in '"the bed had not been slept in"') (IF 150; cf. IF 48).

33. Halliday points out the 'systematic distinction between "which am I?" ("which part do I play?") and "which is me?" ("which one depicts me?")' (IF 117). It has to be '"me"' because 'all complements in English are in the oblique case'. '"Which is I?"' (like '"it is I"'), though 'beloved of English teachers', is '"bad grammar"', i.e., not 'consistent with the rest of the grammar'.

34. Like several terms appearing on different levels in Halliday's scheme, this informal use of 'information' is inconsistent with the 'informational metafunction': content, not 'news value', is being 'affirmed'. Compare the inconsistent uses of 'transitive' (mutually implying), 'marked' (signalled by word, tone, punctuation, etc.), and 'theme' (main idea or concern) (IF 198f, 216; EF 120, 133).

35. Fired I suppose by the aura of 'logic', Halliday dresses his exposition of 'nominal' and 'verbal group' (and later of 'parataxis and hypotaxis') in Greek letters and mathematical symbols (IF 170–84, 197–201), which he seldom uses.

36. Still, only the 'experiential' ones are 'potentially defining' (IF 163). As 'participles', 'verbs' may also 'function as Epithet' (as in ' "knowing smile" ') and 'Classifier' (as in ' "spoken language" ') (IF 164).

37. The 'Predicator' is introduced here as 'the verbal group' minus 'the Finite', or 'the verb function' 'in the mood structure' (IF 175, 78, 80, 49). However, the term 'predication' also survives in IF (33, 280) from NT, where it was a whole system for featuring 'cognitive themes' in cleft constructions (NT 2/236–39; cf. NT 1/64, 2/221) (cf. Note 26).

38. A 'further semantic feature' of 'finiteness' is *polarity*: 'positive or negative' (IF 75, 85). Yet this dimension is not really polar: 'intermediate degrees' allow for 'indeterminacy' 'between yes and no', and 'collectively' constitute 'modality' for 'information' ('probability', 'frequency') and 'modulation' for 'goods-&-services' ('inclination', 'obligation') (IF 86, 88). Yet Halliday says that 'since the finite element is inherently positive or negative, its polarity does not figure as a separate constituent', so that ' "not" ' fits 'in the structure of verbal group, not' 'of the clause' (IF 86).

39. Some ponderous constructions are allowed, though. Halliday accepts ' "couldn't have been going to be being eaten" ', ' "has been going to have known" ', and ' "will have been going to have been taking" ' (IF 175, 179, 181), none of which I could imagine using.

40. 'Nominalization' is indeed prized for 'freedom and flexibility'; it is a 'resource for achieving maximum thematic variation, since it allows any set of elements – processes, participants and circumstances – to be grouped together as a constituent and thus to be mapped on to any function in the discourse structure' (NT 3/215; IF 376; cf. NT 3/180; IF 42, 135, 172) (cf. 12.27). 'Such flexibility is not mere decoration, but is a prerequisite to the functioning of language as a meaningful system' (NT 3/215).

41. Yet 'with a spoken text, we will be able to use the grammar to define and delimit clause complexes in a way that keeps them as close as possible to sentences of written English' (IF 193) – the idealizing Halliday elsewhere disdains (cf. 9.2, 46, 75).

42. 'Reference' is an unwise term because of all its philosophical uses, which Halliday partly echoes in his 'exophoric' type. 'Co-reference' makes it clearer that at least two expressions refer to the same thing (cf. citations in Beaugrande and Dressler 1981). Also, 'pro-verb' is usually grouped with 'pronouns' and other 'proforms', whereas Halliday puts it under 'substitutes' because only for the latter can 'the presupposed element' be 'inserted in place' of it (cf. 9.92). I don't see why this can't be done with pronouns.

43. Yet Halliday and Hasan (1976: 8f) find 'irrelevant' 'the question whether the two fall in the sentence' (i.e., clause complex). Strange, too, is the claim that 'there is no structural relation between the reference item and its referent' (IF 295). Structure in Halliday's sense is certainly involved in selecting and placing a 'reference item'.

44. In the dialogue ' "where's your hat?" – "I can't find it" – "take this one" ', the ' "it" ' refers to the same hat, and the ' "one" ' to a 'different' hat (IF 302).

45. For instance, 'technical language becomes more complex if one "simplifies" it by removing the metaphors' (IF 329), especially when one's notion of 'metaphor' is so broad.

46. When Halliday says ' "you sell it with beauty" ' is 'not really metaphorical', but only 'vague' (IF 369), I suppose it's because he can't decide on a congruent

form. Many locutions widely counted as metaphors would entail just this problem, witness the endless disputes of critics over poetry.

47. Like formalist (or 'New') literary critics, Halliday says his 'concern' 'is not with psychological problems of response to literature but with the linguistic options selected by the writer and their relation to the total meaning of the work' (EF 116). That relation is of course viewed in terms of his own response.

48. According to Halliday (1978: 110), 'the term "register" was first used' for 'text variety by [Thomas Bertram] Reid (1956); the concept was taken up and developed by Jean Ure (Ure and Ellis 1972)', and by Halliday, McIntosh and Strevens (1964). See now Halliday (1988).

49. Here Halliday goes against Firth, who argued that 'a restricted language' has 'its own grammar and dictionary'; but then Firth, unlike Halliday, did not 'attempt a structural and systemic account of a language as a whole' (P2 200) (cf. 8.76; 9.26, 40).

50. Halliday points to the *language* used in 'games' as a sample system (EF 25, 63, 80ff, 98) and, figuratively, to 'the games people play' (IF 279, 340) (cf. 9.100, 106). Saussure pointed to the *rules* of games, notably chess, for his system of abstract 'values' (cf. 2.80f).

Chapter 10

Teun van Dijk and Walter Kintsch[1]

10.1 The volume *Strategies of Discourse Comprehension* (1983) (hereafter SD), co-authored by a linguist and a psychologist, marks a new 'surge' since 'around 1970' (SD ix, 1). 'The study of discourse' arose from the decision that 'actual language use in social contexts', rather than 'abstract or ideal language systems', 'should be the empirical object of linguistic theories' (SD 1f, ix) (cf. 3.1; 4.17; 5.65; 8.50, 9.6f; 12.14, 36). The study requires an 'interdisciplinary background' and 'diverse' 'scientific approaches': 'linguistic analysis', 'psychological laboratory experiments', 'sociological field studies', 'computer understanding of text' and so on (SD 19, ix) (cf. 12.22f). We can also look to 'historical sources': 'classical poetics and rhetoric', 'Russian Formalism', 'Czech Structuralism', and 'literary scholarship' (SD 1). More recent work comes from 'sociolinguistics', examining 'forms' and 'variations of language use' like 'verbal duelling and storytelling'; and from 'anthropology' and 'ethnography', moving from 'verbal art' in 'myths, folktales, riddles', etc. to 'a broader analysis of communicative events in various cultures', notably in 'conversational interaction' (SD 2). Today, 'we witness a major 'integration of theoretical proposals' in 'the wide new field of cognitive science' (SD 4) (cf. 10.5, 102; 12.64).

10.2 'Until the 1970s, modern **linguistics** in America rarely looked beyond the **sentence** boundary', aside from '**tagmemics**' with its 'fieldwork on indigenous languages' (SD 2) (cf. 5.56). 'The prevailing **generative transformational paradigm** focused on phonological, morphological, syntactic, and later also semantic structures of isolated, context- and text-independent sentences, ignoring' the 'call for discourse analysis by Harris' (1952) (cf. 5.56; 7.73, 79). So 'interest' in 'discourse' was 'restricted' to 'European linguistics', which was 'closer to the structuralist tradition and had less respect for the boundaries of linguistics' and 'of the sentence unit', as revealed in 'studies' 'at the boundaries of **grammar**, **stylistics**, and **poetics**'. Also in Europe, attempts to 'account for the systematic syntactic structures of whole texts' led to 'text grammar', which however 'remained in a programmatic stage, still too close to the generative paradigm' (e.g., van Dijk 1972).

10.3 Influenced too by the 'generative transformational trend', '**psycho-linguistics**' focused not on 'discourse' in 'language processing' but on 'the syntax' and 'semantics of isolated sentences' (SD 3). Since then, we have realized that 'models of sentence recognition' based on 'transformational grammar should be discarded' (SD 74) (cf. 10.14ff, 34, 81; 12.19). 'Through analysis by analysis or analysis by synthesis', such 'models' 'try to match an input string of lexical items to structures generated by grammatical rules'; yet 'even for a moderately complex sentence, the number of possible structural descriptions (trees) is astronomic', precluding 'effective search' (cf. Woods 1970). Many 'models less close to the grammar' (e.g., of Fodor, Bever and Garrett 1974, Chomsky's one-time associates) also foresee a 'sentence recognition device' for 'syntactic analysis' 'trying to discover clauses' as 'surface representations of underlying sentoids'[2] without using 'other kinds of information', such as 'semantic, contextual, or epistemic' (SD 74f) (cf. 7.73, 82). This 'information', so often neglected by 'philosophers, psychologists', and 'linguists' (with their tidy ' "lexicon" '), is just what the 'language user' deploys to derive 'powerful expectations about the meaning of a sentence, and therefore also about the correct surface analysis' (SD 305, 75) (cf. 5.57; 12.55). 'Moreover, morphophonemic surface signals for syntactic structures' may be 'few' and 'difficult to perceive in natural speech' (SD 75) (cf. 10.36, 41f, 44, 56, 81; 7.48). 'Hence, a semantically and pragmatically based system' is 'more effective', able to 'select among alternative parses' or 'even to circumvent syntactic analysis altogether' (Clark and Clark 1977: 72) (cf. 10.34; 12.53).

10.4 '**Psychology**' also saw 'a breach in the paradigm' in the 1970s and a revival of 'work on discourse in the gestalt tradition' (with its 'notion of schema') (e.g., Bartlett 1932; Cofer 1941) (SD 3) (cf. 10.23–28). 'Discourse materials' were used in experiments on 'semantic memory' and in 'educational psychology', which 'realized' their role in 'learning' (cf. 10.37, 52, 54, 71, 95f, 98ff). 'Extensive work' also brought together 'text linguistics and the psychology of discourse comprehension' (SD 79). Similar trends 'took place in artificial intelligence', where a 'paradigm' was needed for 'the computer-simulated understanding of language' and 'the automatic processing of texts' (SD 3). To be sure, many 'discourse process models' still have 'serious shortcomings', being 'incomplete' and 'focused' on 'problems of representation rather than dynamic aspects of processing', such as 'how textual representations in memory' 'are constructed step by step by a hearer or reader, and what strategies are used to understand a discourse' (SD 61). Also, 'previous models have seriously underestimated the complexity' of 'discourse comprehension', which 'involves processing a large amount of data' (SD 95, 188) (cf. 10.6, 10, 17, 20, 24, 26, 38, 41, 53, 57, 78, 82f, 91, 98).

10.5 Van Dijk and Kintsch now undertake to 'present a broadly based, general, coherent approach to the investigation of discourse phenomena', following the precept that 'contextual information' applies to 'the whole range of communicative behaviour' (SD ix, 238). Their 'programmatic statements' look ahead to 'the future development of an interdisciplinary cognitive science' (SD 19). Though their 'theoretical outline' is not 'a worked-out information processing model', 'fully formalized and explicit', they offer a 'reasonably complete' 'framework for a theory' within which 'such models can be constructed eventually' 'given a particular comprehension situation' (SD x, 95, 346, 351, 383, 385) (cf. 10.21, 44, 90ff; 12.63). Their 'model is general and flexible enough' to be 'later specified', or 'embedded' 'into a broader model of strategic verbal interaction in the social context' (SD 9). This prospect befits the precept that a 'social model should' 'have a cognitive basis' and expound 'strategies' for 'understanding, planning', and 'participating in interaction', e.g., in 'interpreting discourse' (SD 19) (cf. 12.35). We might thus bridge the 'gap between linguistic theory' and 'theory of social interaction' (cf. 9.2, 6f). 'Translating abstract textual structures into more concrete on-line cognitive processes' can suggest how to do the same with 'abstract structures of interaction and social situations'.

10.6 A 'theory' cannot be 'at once specified and general' because 'comprehension' is not a 'unitary process' but 'differs' according to 'situations', 'language users' and 'discourse types' (SD 383f, 9, 26, 259, 364). 'New situations require new and different models', as do particular 'theoretical purposes' (SD 383f) (cf. 9.1; 12.58). So we need 'a framework' for 'discourse comprehension', 'a set of principles' or 'instructions for building specific comprehension models' to fit 'concrete cases' and 'a variety of behaviours' (SD 383, 364, 346f). 'Applications' using 'the same building blocks' lead 'beyond ad hoc, arbitrary miniature models' that, however 'simple' and 'elegant', 'deceive us about the real complexity of comprehension processes' (SD 383). Also, it is easier to 'agree' about 'the outlines of process models', and 'simplicity' enables 'testable empirical predictions at early stages' of a 'model' (SD 293, 46) (cf. 10.90ff; 12.25, 57, 61). When we cannot 'deal with the problem' in its 'full' 'complexity', 'a general framework' keeps us aware of 'where and what' we are 'simplifying' (SD 384).

10.7 At the outset, van Dijk and Kintsch present a list of 'cognitive' and 'contextual assumptions' that 'inspire the major theoretical notions and components of the model' and indicate its 'relationships with other models' (SD 4ff). 'The *constructivist* assumption' is that 'understanding', whether of an 'observed event' or a 'speech-event', 'involves the construction of a mental representation' (SD 4f) (cf. 10.10, 20, 22, 25, 39, 51ff, 72, 100). 'The *interpretive* assumption' is that this 'representation' entails 'not merely' 'visual and verbal data', but 'an interpretation' of them (SD 5) (cf. 10.19, 31, 36, 51). 'The *on-line* assumption' is that 'the construction' 'takes place more or less at the same time as the processing of the input data', not after the latter have been 'first processed and stored' (cf. 10.29, 36, 50, 101). 'The *presuppositional* assumption' is that 'understanding' entails 'the activation and use of internal cognitive information' about 'general knowledge' or 'previous experiences' (cf. 10.51). 'The *strategic* assumption' is that 'processing' is 'flexible' about the 'kind', 'order', or 'completeness' of 'information', and has 'the overall goal' of 'being as effective as possible' (SD 6) (cf. 10.10). 'The *functionality* assumption' is that 'discourse' and 'understanding' are 'functional' in 'a wider sociocultural context', so that 'processing' is both a 'cognitive' and 'a social event' and the 'representation' covers 'the social context' as well as 'the text', which are 'intertwined' 'at all levels' (SD 6f, 221).[3] 'The *pragmatic* assumption' is that 'discourse' is 'social action' consisting of 'speech acts', these too affecting 'interpretation' and 'representation' (SD 7) (cf. 10.8f, 56f, 83f). 'The *interactionist* assumption' is that 'discourse' is 'interpreted' within 'the whole interaction process' among 'speech participants', including 'verbal and non-verbal interaction' (cf. 10.1, 5, 11, 17, 56, 83). 'The *situational* assumption' is that this 'interaction' is 'part of a social situation' wherein 'participants' may have 'functions or roles', and special 'strategies' and 'conventions' may apply (SD 7f) (cf. 10.45, 51, 56f, 66, 74, 76).

10.8 Most importantly, '*cultural information*' and its 'communicative features' 'affect' 'all aspects of discourse understanding' (SD 81) (cf. 3.1f; 12.63). 'Cultural strategies have a very wide scope', involving 'knowledge' about 'geographical areas and locations', 'social structures, institutions, and events', 'speech acts', 'symbolic or ritual values', 'beliefs, opinions, attitudes, ideologies, and norms' – plus a whole 'conceptual ordering of the world and society' (cf. 10.20, 83). Such 'cultural strategies' may be 'speaker- or hearer-oriented', though 'especially in everyday conversation, the two perspectives will coincide' (SD 80). The 'culture' decides what people 'believe to be important, relevant, interesting', or 'prominent' 'in discourse' – for example, whether 'telling a story' is intended to 'amuse', 'reproach', give advice', 'reaffirm' 'norms', or 'teach history' (SD 81, 239) (cf. 10.60ff). For an unfamiliar 'culture', a 'hearer or reader' can apply 'marked strategies' and rely on 'partial understanding', 'limited knowledge', and 'guesses' (SD 81).

10.9 'Cultural strategies provide the basic background' for 'more specific social strategies' relating to 'context' and 'occasion': the 'social structure of a group' or 'institution', and the 'roles or functions of participants', who may be 'young or old', 'rich or poor', have 'more or less power or status', and so on (SD 82f).[4] People know what 'speech acts' should be 'performed' in the 'discourse' of a 'government, a bank, a judge in a courtroom, a student in a class, a friend in a bar, or a child at the breakfast table'. The 'strategies' applied here 'limit the interpretation of many aspects of the discourse to rather restricted sets' and help decide how 'a discourse' is 'understood' as 'aggressive, helping, cooperative', 'obstructive', etc., and how it 'is meant to affect further verbal or non-verbal actions' or 'knowledge, beliefs, opinions, or motivations of the hearer' (cf. 10.8, 20). Indeed, the 'intention of the speech act may be inferred even before we hear' it.

10.10 Van Dijk and Kintsch's 'model' centres 'on the assumption that discourse processing, just like other complex information processing, is a strategic process' 'using both external and internal information' in 'under-standing' (SD 6, ix). '**Strategies** are flexible and operate on many kinds of input' and 'information', even when these are 'incomplete and partial'; they can 'operate in parallel on several levels' and collate the 'results'; and they are 'non-deterministic, often producing a large number of alternative outcomes varying in plausibility' (SD 96f, 6, 10, 15f, 28, 73, 76, 98, 106, 127, 135, 151, 264, 308, 382) (cf. 10.7; 12.52f). 'A strategy' can also be seen as 'a cognitive representation' of 'the means of reaching a goal' or 'of a style' for doing so 'in the most effective way' (SD 65). 'Strategies' themselves are 'cognitive' in that 'they operate on' 'represented information': 'things', 'events, or facts' 'in the world' 'are relevant for a cognitive model only' as they are 'distinguished, understood, and talked about through' their 'representation as concepts in memory' and not as they 'exist in some biophysical' way (SD 80, 88) (cf. 5.68; 10.43, 52f, 61). Still, we should 'make a distinction' whether 'a meaning representation' is 'tied to language' or to a fragment of the world' (SD 88).

10.11 'A strategy involves human **action**': 'goal-oriented, intentional, conscious, and controlled behaviour' that 'establishes' or 'prevents' 'changes in the world' and its 'states of affairs' (SD 62, 264f). 'If the results' in 'the final state' fit 'the intentions of the agent', 'the action is weakly successful', but 'strongly' so if the action 'brings about some goal' or 'far-reaching purpose' (SD 62f, 264). 'Cognitively', 'intentions are representations of doings plus their result', whereas 'purposes' are those of 'wanted consequences'; both 'allow us to monitor' our 'actions' as well as the 'state of the environment (the action domain)' (SD 63). 'Actions are usually complex', composed of 'sequences' in which some may be 'automatized, that is, not governed by conscious intent nor individually' aimed at the 'general purpose' (cf. 10.13, 15, 75, 77, 79, 83, 92, 95). In 'interactions', 'several agents are involved' with their own 'intentions and purposes', though 'goals' can be 'coordinated'.[5]

10.12 The 'notion of strategy' can be 'applied to actions in a strict sense: overt intended doings' of a 'bodily' nature (SD 68, 62) (cf. 5.21ff; 8.24f). But 'overt action strategies' also 'presuppose thinking', e.g., when 'desires' are 'compared' to 'abilities' and 'possible or probable outcomes' (SD 68f). So the 'notion' can apply also to 'cognitive behaviour' and 'mental acts' like 'thinking and problem-solving', which can 'process much information' and can be 'conscious, orderly, and controlled', each 'mental step yielding the information necessary for the next' (cf. 10.25, 51). Even in 'cognitive activities that do not seem' to work this way, such as 'looking at a landscape or at a movie, or reading a text', people have 'the overall goal of comprehending' and 'follow a strategy of good' or 'fast understanding' (SD 69; cf. SD 6, 18, 107).

10.13 These issues bear on how far 'the notion of strategy is appropriate' for 'language use' (SD 70). More than 'problem-solving, the production and comprehension of verbal utterances' is 'automatized' and 'not monitored' unless 'difficult, problematic, or unusual properties' arise, e.g., an 'unknown meaning of a word', or a 'complex' 'sentence structure' (cf. 10.11). 'Language production and comprehension' are 'continuous tasks', made perhaps 'of small-scale problems' but differing from 'problem-solving' in having 'no single' 'well-defined' 'goal' as 'a final state'; and the 'strategies' are seldom 'preprogrammed, intended, conscious, or verbalizable'

(SD 71) (but. cf. 10.51).[6] Nevertheless, van Dijk and Kintsch postulate 'strategies of language use' that entail an 'understanding of an action' 'step by step', 'a rather well-defined' 'starting point', 'alternative routes', and at least a 'fuzzy' 'goal' (SD 70f). These 'strategies' belong to 'the cognitive system' and 'apply to sequences of mental steps' for various 'tasks': 'identifying sounds or letters, constructing words, analysing syntactic structures', or 'interpreting sentences and whole texts'. '**Bottom-up**' strategies are 'data-driven', i.e., based on input, whereas '**top-down**' ones are 'knowledge-driven', i.e., based on the processor's predictions and notions about what is going on.[7]

10.14   So we should appreciate how '*strategic* processes contrast with *algorithmic, rule-governed*' ones (SD 11, 67) (cf. 12.52). The latter 'may be complex, long, and tedious, but guarantee success' if 'the rules are correct and are applied correctly' (SD 11, 28, 67). 'Rules' form 'a closed logical system' which operates by 'blind methodological application' (SD 28, 67). 'An algorithm always works but only in principle, not in real situations' or for 'practical purposes', due to 'human limits on time and resources' (SD 67). In another sense,[8] 'rules' are 'general conventions of a social community, regulating behaviour in a standard way; strategies are particular, often personal ways of using rules' and 'making choices' to suit 'one's goals'. So 'rules' are 'norms for possible or correct action', and 'sanctions' follow if they are 'broken', e.g., in 'games' ('chess') or 'traffic'. 'Similarly, rules of language determine which utterances are correct' in the 'system', e.g., the 'syntactic parsing rules' whereby a 'generative grammar produces a structural description of a sentence' (SD 67, 11) (cf. 7.49). The rules 'represent' in 'idealistic terms what language users in general do or what they implicitly or explicitly think they do or should do' (SD 72) (cf. 9.6). 'Uses of the rules', however, 'depend on 'variable' 'contexts', 'users', and 'goals' (SD 72, 94).

10.15   In contrast, a 'strategy' is 'simpler', 'intelligent but risky', has no 'guarantee' and 'no unique representation', and produces 'effective working hypotheses' and 'fast but effective guesses about the most likely structure or meaning of the incoming data' within 'available' 'resources' in 'real time' (SD 11, 28, 67, 73f). Like 'uses of rules', 'strategies' 'depend on 'characteristics of the language user' ('goals or world knowledge') as well as of the 'text' (SD 72, 11, 7). 'Strategies' are 'part of an open set' and 'need to be learned and overlearned before' being 'automatized'; some, like 'gist inferring, are acquired rather late' or through 'training' with 'new types of discourse' like 'psychological articles' (SD 11). The 'processing features of natural language utterances' make 'strategies' 'necessary': 'language users have limited memory', especially 'short-term'; they 'cannot process many different kinds of information at the same time'; 'production and understanding of utterances is linear, whereas most structures the rules pertain to are hierarchical' (cf. 5.69); and 'production and understanding require' more than 'linguistic or grammatical information' (SD 72f) (cf. 12.44). 'Whereas rules are abstract' and 'formulated a posteriori for complete structures' of 'categories and units', 'strategies allow' for 'production or understanding linearly at several levels simultaneously', using 'different kinds of information' and 'limited knowledge' (SD 73) (cf. 10.7, 19, 26, 32, 35, 38, 58, 77f; 12.53, 57).

10.16 'Although strategic systems are non-deterministic', 'probabilistic', 'open-ended, and highly context-sensitive', 'scientific' 'theories' about them can 'be stated with precision and objectivity' (SD 31, 74). 'Evidence has been compiled showing that people really do operate that way', whereas the 'rule systems that linguists were using to parse sentences were implausible' (SD 28) (cf. 10.3). 'Even if we accept the hypothesis that grammar is a theoretical', 'general, abstract, and idealized reconstruction of the language rules known by language users', we still need 'strategies' for producing or understanding structures' by using the various '**levels**' such as 'grammar, morphology, or syntax', along with 'the communicative context' (SD 73) (cf. 4.71; 5.34f; 7.45f; 8.51f; 9.30; 10.35, 56; 11.82; 12.29). On the other hand, it would be 'uneconomical for the cognitive system' if 'strategies and rules' were 'independent' and 'did not make use of the same units' and 'categories', 'at least in part' (SD 73f; cf. SD 91). When 'strategic' 'guesses' are 'wrong', 'grammatical rules will establish, on second analysis, the correct structure or meaning'. Also, appropriate 'schemas' enable 'interaction' 'between rules and strategies' by 'applying' 'patterns' when 'input data appear to be standard'.[9] Some 'strategies have their counterparts in rules of grammar', though 'other kinds' do not, e.g., those applying to 'the schematic structures of narrative' (SD 91) (cf. 10.60ff).

10.17 'The complexity of action or interaction' requires 'higher organization' by a 'global **plan**', i.e., 'a cognitive macrostructure of intentions, purposes', 'actions', 'consequences', 'goals', and 'strategies' (SD 63, 265). 'A course of action' can be 'represented' by 'a tree diagram' of 'alternative' 'paths' among 'changing' 'states' in 'possible worlds' (SD 63f, 265). 'Paths' differ in 'effort' and 'cost', and may 'involve unwanted intermediary states' (SD 64). 'A rational agent will try to reach an optimal goal along the lowest-cost path', e.g., by 'means–end analysis' ('comparing costs and goals') (SD 64f). Though 'in everyday life, we perform many actions without much of a strategy', 'strategies become necessary' when 'goals' are 'important or the means very costly or risky' (SD 66). 'A **heuristic**' is 'a system of discovery procedures' to 'acquire knowledge about conditions' for 'reaching a goal', especially on 'higher levels' where we cannot 'plan in advance each detailed action' (SD 68) (cf. 9.15, 17). 'A classic example is scientific investigation: to formulate some regularity', we may 'systematically observe' some facts, or 'we may first derive it' and then check it 'with the facts', or we may try both ways (SD 70) (cf. 12.44).

10.18 A 'plan' is 'dominated by a **macroaction**': 'the global conceptual structure organizing and monitoring the actual action sequence' and 'defining global' 'goals' (SD 63, 265). Together, 'plans and strategies' make up 'the content and style of a global action', with the 'strategy dominating the **moves**', that is, the 'functional' ('bound') 'actions' 'in a sequence' (SD 65ff). A '**tactic**' is 'an organized' 'system of strategies' applying to 'large segments or periods of lives and actions' and influencing 'the personality of the agent'; 'bad tactics typically involve conflicting strategies'.

10.19 Therefore, 'linguistic and cognitive theories of discourse' entail 'two sets of related strategies, local and global' (SD 89) (cf. 10.30, 32, 38, 47, 66, 82, 85). 'The **local** strategies establish the meanings of clauses and sentences' and of 'relations between sentences'. The **'global'** ones 'determine' the 'meanings of fragments of discourse' or of the 'whole'. The 'two kinds of strategy must of course interact' in 'text comprehension', possibly in 'hierarchical relations' of 'dominance' (SD 89, 106). 'Global information acts in top-down processing strategies' for the 'local'; and 'local' 'strategies' provide 'constraints for specific meanings' by looking 'forward' for 'meanings to come' or 'backward' for 'meanings' only 'partially interpreted' (SD 106f). In such ways, 'knowledge' can be 'called' by 'all interpretation strategies' to 'provide precisely the relevant information at each point' (cf. Winograd 1972). 'These preparatory, communicative, and contextual strategies' 'specify' 'the overall goal of the reading act' and 'determine the choice' of 'local or global textual strategies of comprehension'.

10.20 The 'role' of **'world knowledge** in production and comprehension' of 'discourse' has been strikingly 'demonstrated' by 'psychology and artificial intelligence' (SD 303, 307; cf. Winograd 1972) (cf. 10.23). 'Large amounts of knowledge' are 'not provided' or 'expressed in the text', but must be 'accessed' and 'retrieved' to 'provide a framework for the text', 'organize' it, 'understand' it, and 'construct' a 'mental representation' in 'memory' (SD 6, 13, 46, 106, 188, 191, 303f, i.r.). Moreover, all this may be 'formed or transformed' during 'discourse-related tasks' themselves (SD 191). Of course, van Dijk and Kintsch cannot 'present a complete representation format for the knowledge' and 'cognitive' and 'contextual information' 'necessary' for the 'semantic operations of discourse understanding' (SD 13, 8f). But we are continually reminded that their strategies and constructs involve or depend on 'knowledge', 'beliefs', 'opinions', 'attitudes', 'ideologies', 'norms', 'conventions', 'evaluations', 'emotions', 'wishes', 'intentions', 'motivations', 'goals', and 'tasks'.[10] Indeed, 'knowledge is everything we know' (SD 312) (cf. 4.14; 5.28).

10.21 Therefore, van Dijk and Kintsch only 'sketch the overall outlines of a knowledge system' with 'many levels' and 'nodes' 'forming overlapping chunks' (SD 311) (cf. 10.75f). Evidently, 'knowledge is well organized' in 'flexible' ways suitable for 'the strategies of knowledge use' (SD 13, i.r.). Instead of 'blindly activating all possible knowledge', these 'strategies' work from 'the goals of the language user', the 'available knowledge from text and context, the level of processing, or the degree of coherence needed for comprehension'. 'Knowledge' can be broken down into (a) *'episodic'*, i.e., 'construed' or 'inferred' from 'previous experience', versus (b) *'conceptual'* or *'semantic'*, i.e., 'derived' through 'abstraction, generalization, decontextualization, and recombination', and therefore 'general, stable', and 'useful' for many 'cognitive tasks' (SD 303, 13, 308, 312; cf. SD 11f, 106, 135, 151, 160, 273, 337, 344) (cf. 10.31, 51, 58, 74ff).[11] Thus, the '"knowledge system"' runs both on 'context-embedded unique personal experience' and on 'decontextualized generalized information', and uses them 'in comprehension' in 'multilevel' ways (SD 312) (cf. 10.10, 13, 39f). One prominent way is '**spreading activation**', which travels 'automatically' among 'nodes' associated in a 'network' (SD 24, 96, 167, 316; cf. Collins and Loftus 1975). A more controlled way is making '**inferences**', i.e., adding 'necessary, plausible, or possible' 'information' to the 'discourse' (SD 49; Rieger 1977) (cf. 10.25). '*Bridging* inferences' are 'required for coherence', while '*elaborative*' ones only 'fill in additional detail' (SD 49, 51; cf. Kintsch 1974; Kintsch and van Dijk 1978).[12]

10.22 In the past, most researchers in 'philosophy', 'psychology', and 'linguistics' have designed 'associative networks' or considered 'how general concepts are abstracted from concrete instances', e.g., via a 'summary description' stating 'necessary and sufficient properties for class membership' (SD 305, 307, 310). This approach works all right for 'artificial concepts', but not for 'natural' ones (SD 305; cf. Bruner, Goodnow and Austin 1956; Smith and Medin 1981). Today, 'psychologists' are 'developing models' providing for 'non-essential features or dimensions' or even for 'concepts entirely characterized by exemplars' (SD 305, 310). Or, 'concepts' are 'defined' 'by their position in the semantic network and their mutual relations', which 'vary' in 'quality' as well as 'strength' (SD 307) (cf. 10.69). But for 'a model' of a 'knowledge system' in 'discourse comprehension', all this is still 'too narrow', too preoccupied with 'categorizing' and 'classifying objects' (e.g., 'animals', 'kinship'). Using 'concepts' for 'constructing text representations' during 'language use' entails much 'fuzziness' of the kind usually 'ignored or ruled outside linguistics' (SD 306) (cf. 5.47; 9.29; 10.26, 34, 39; 12.22, 59).

10.23 Recent research has turned to entire 'knowledge structures' – termed '**schemas**', '**frames** or **scripts**'[13] – for 'information in memory', having 'a label' and 'slots' ('variables') within a 'prearranged relation', and 'accepting information of a given type' via 'instantiation' (SD 307, 47, 13). Here, 'classifying knowledge structures' is done not just 'by content area', but by 'packets' that 'can function as wholes' (SD 47) (cf. 10.27). Such 'schemas are descriptions, not definitions', and vary from 'concrete' to 'abstract' (SD 47). Their 'information' 'is normally valid', but specifies 'no necessary and sufficient conditions' (SD 47f). 'Instead, normal conditions from many different content areas are combined', including 'goals, consequences', 'implications', and so on. 'Although knowledge' is 'socio-culturally variable', its 'generality' evidently suffices 'for intersubjective language use and communication' (SD 303) (cf. 10.16, 37; 12.58). 'Without this general picture of the world' no one could 'understand words' in 'meaningful combinations' within or among 'sentences' or in 'a discourse as a whole', or 'make sense of the facts' (cf. 10.20).

10.24 'Many unsolved problems' remain in 'building a knowledge structure' and getting 'a knowledge base to deliver nicely packaged schemas' yet to 'retain flexibility and context sensitivity' (SD 48, 311). 'In each new context', 'a subtly different complex of information' may be 'relevant' (SD 48) (cf. 4.16; 5.76). 'The meaning of a concept cannot be specified for once and for all by some small set of semantic elements' but 'requires' 'a large, open set of complex statements' (SD 311) (cf. 5.76; 7.77; 12.59). Hence, 'problems of schema use' may arise for both 'identification and application' (SD 48). Also, 'misrepresentation' and 'distortion' can arise when 'readers' 'supply' 'knowledge' left 'implicit' by 'a text' about 'causal relations in the physical world and the goals, plans, and intentions of human actors' (cf. Stevens, Collins and Goldin 1979; Graesser 1981) (SD 46, 304). The 'naive action theory' and the 'causal model people use' is not 'the unambiguous, contradiction-free system of science'; 'even experts' may 'reason at multiple, mutually inconsistent levels' (SD 46f) (cf. 12.24).

10.25 Moreover, 'most discourses' and the 'actions and events' they refer to are 'new' and 'interesting' 'in some respects', and 'pre-established knowledge' may 'not fit' 'precisely' (SD 304). To deal with 'new' material, 'background information' must 'accommodate many variations' and 'contextual demands' by adjusting, combining, etc. 'Schematic structures often occur in a transformed way' in 'actual discourse', and the 'reader' must 'determine' the current 'schematic function' 'from the global content' (SD 92).[14] For such reasons, van Dijk and Kintsch do not equate the 'instantiated frame or script' or schema 'with the textual representation' (SD 307f). Instead, the 'use of general knowledge' involves 'two steps': (1) '*activation*' and '*instantiation*' of a 'schema, frame, or script' via 'some input'; and (2) '*construction*' of 'the knowledge base for understanding the text'. 'Once selected, a schema' 'provides readers with a basis for interpreting the text', and a 'conceptual skeleton' to which they can 'bind the semantic units derived from the textual input' (SD 48). 'Schemas' 'also provide a basis for more active, top-down processes', such as 'inferences' that supply 'missing information' or 'assign default values' (cf. 10.21). 'Deviations' may be 'registered and accepted' or may trigger 'problem-solving' 'to account for them'.

10.26 Since these 'knowledge systems', like other 'concepts', are 'fuzzy', 'flexible, and context dependent', we encounter 'difficulties in designing' 'representations' for them (SD 310, 71). 'Neither concepts nor schemas can be defined in the strict sense', and 'dynamic, flexible systems' are much harder to envision than 'definitional' ones (SD 311). There may be 'no end to special tracks', and special versions 'can be generated on demand' (SD 310). We must 'work with complex, messy interactions' in a 'multi-levelled system' of 'features, concepts, propositions, and schemas' (SD 311). We must inquire if 'knowledge representations are abstract and propositional or if they involve imagery'; 'how we can identify the internal structure of a knowledge system from behavioural data'; and so on.

10.27 Despite such worries, 'the schema notion' now figures in 'theories' ranging from 'letter perception' to 'macrostructure formation' (SD 48). This accord may lead to 'a truly general, comprehensive theory of discourse perception and comprehension' (cf. Adams and Collins 1979). 'Good evidence' indicates 'schema-based knowledge systems are real or at least psychologically plausible', i.e., able to 'function as psychological units' or 'chunks in memory' (SD 309f) (cf. 10.75). Experiments show that people 'cluster' or 'list the actions of a script together or make recognition errors among them'; if 'presented out of order', 'the actions' get 'reordered' (Black, Turner, and Bower 1979) (SD 309f). A 'script is retrieved as a unit', the 'speed' of retrieval depending not on how many 'actions' it has but on 'how close the actions are to each other and how central they are to the script' (Anderson 1980; Smith, Adams and Schorr 1978; Galambos and Rips 1982). Apparently, 'scripts' serve 'both as cognitive cueing structures and as guides for the allocation of attentional resources' (SD 310). 'Evidence' also reveals 'substructures in scripts': 'subjects' 'distinguish fixed scenes' and 'mark them linguistically with a single word' (i.r.). And 'hierarchical' 'structures' appear when 'actions' 'in a narrative activate their superordinates' (Abbott and Black 1980) (cf. 10.62).

10.28 'Linguistics' too has 'widely' postulated knowledge structures, often called '*verb frames*' with '*case roles*' for 'agent, patient, instrument', 'goal', 'source', etc. (SD 308, 114; cf. Fillmore 1968; J.M. Anderson 1971; Dik 1978) (cf. 7.63; 10.48, 61). These 'frames' can form a 'hierarchy' and 'inherit properties' from 'superordinate' 'frames', e.g., a 'transitive act' being assigned 'agent and patient slots' (SD 309). We need not decide 'how many cases there are'; beside 'a few general' ones, many 'specialized cases' can appear with certain 'verbs' and do not form 'a closed set', just as a 'schema' need have no 'finite, fixed set of slots' but may add 'special-purpose' ones – yet another obstacle to 'formal theories' (cf. 10.26).

10.29 Knowledge patterns are managed through 'a system of strategies as used by speakers and hearers to establish, construct, discover, or recognize' '**coherence**' (SD 79, 151). 'Extensive work in text linguistics and psychology' has already explored 'the conditions for discourse coherence' 'in terms of semantics, pragmatics', and 'world knowledge', but largely with a 'structural approach' looking for 'abstract relations between sentences' or 'propositions' 'relative to some possible world' (SD 79, 150f) (cf. 10.40). In contrast, 'language users establish coherence as soon as possible, without waiting for the rest of the clause', 'sentence', 'sentence sequence', 'paragraph', or 'discourse' (SD 15, 154, 205, 44, 237, 285) (cf. 10.7, 50, 101). They must do so 'in real time and with a limited short-term memory capacity', so 'propositions are constructed on-line' when 'information is available' (SD 44, 373, 186; cf. SD 19, 134, 138, 143, 166, 245, 351). Hence, we need to find out how the 'strategies' 'handle the information involved' in 'textual coherence', 'what memory resources and mechanisms are involved', and so on (SD 151).

10.30 For 'language users', 'coherence intuitively means' a 'unity' and 'a normal, possible, understandable, or correct continuation' for the 'ongoing discourse' (SD 79) (cf. 3.25; 9.93). 'These intuitive notions can be theoretically represented' via 'local and global semantic properties of a discourse', and 'reformulated as strategies' for handling 'surface structure' and using 'knowledge' and 'contextual information' (SD 80). 'Whereas an abstract linguistic semantics will formulate' a 'general and abstract definition of coherence', 'a cognitive model' should deal with 'cultural, cognitive, and personal' 'contents' of 'coherence' (SD 150). Yet this mix of 'objective' and '(inter)subjective' does not mean that 'coherence is arbitrary'; some 'properties' 'remain constant', e.g., 'relations between denoted facts' and 'fact elements' (cf. 10.16, 23; 12.58).

10.31 Though 'coherence' can also be 'syntactic', 'stylistic', and 'pragmatic', van Dijk and Kintsch focus on '*semantic* coherence' (SD 149).[15] They see 'two fundamental types': '*conditional*' (or '*extensional*', i.e. 'referential') based on 'cause', 'consequence', and 'temporality', versus '*functional*' (or '*intensional*') based on 'example', 'specification, explication', 'contrast', 'comparison', 'generalization', 'conclusion', and so on (SD 149f, 159, 182, 184f, 204).[16] 'Functional' 'links' dominate in 'typical expository' 'texts', and 'conditional links' in 'narrative ones' (SD 183, i.r.). A 'distinction' is also made between 'three *levels* of coherence' gauged by 'depth of interpretation: *superficial*' if two 'propositions' are 'in the same frame or script'; '*normal*' if the two also 'instantiate a direct conditional or functional connection', and '*full*' 'if further information is inferred from semantic or episodic memory' (SD 160) (cf. 10.21). 'The reader' pursues one or more of these levels 'depending on the type of text' and 'context (tasks, goals, interests, time, etc.)'.

10.32 But by far the most crucial distinction falls between 'local' and 'global coherence' (SD 11f, 13, 80, 150, 308, 337) (cf. 10.19, 47, 56, 66, 77, 83, 85).[17] '**Local** coherence strategies' 'establish meaningful connections between successive sentences in a discourse' 'or between constituents of sentences' (SD 14f, 150, 189). '**Global** coherence' 'organizes' and 'orders' 'predicates', 'referents', 'properties', and so on, around the 'central' ones, and imposes 'unity' and 'sequence' (SD 151). 'Schematic structures' (as in 10.27) apply to 'the organization of discourse' both 'locally' to the 'morphological, syntactic, and semantic levels' and 'globally' to 'the macrolevel' (SD 92, 204f, 308). Against much of linguistics, van Dijk and Kintsch assert that 'the strategy types of the largest scope' are the 'most fundamental to understanding' 'language' and 'semiotic practices', as well as 'interactions, events, and objects' (SD 80) (cf. 12.57). 'Local coherence strategies' need 'guidance' and 'constraints' from the 'global' to relate to the 'discourse as a whole', to surmount 'discontinuities', and so on (SD 188f, 233) (cf. 5.19, 38; 10.19, 35; 12.32). 'Local coherence strategies operate both bottom-up' with 'words and phrases' and 'top-down' with a 'schema, frame, script, or macroproposition' (SD 159) (cf. 10.13). Even when the 'local is minimal' or 'degenerate', 'adequate macrostructures are formed', e.g., in 'skimming newspaper reports' (Masson 1979) (SD 233). Therefore, we should 'investigate' the 'interaction of local and global' for 'easy and difficult texts, stories and essays, skimming and memorizing', and so on.

10.33 These precepts lead to a special view of '**linguistic parsing**' (cf. SD 8, 19, 27, 59, 134, 385) (cf. 7.49; 10.14, 16, 77, 79). In that view, '**phrases**' and 'sentences' are addressed not because they are the central units of an abstract grammar, but because 'psychological evidence' indicates 'readers and listeners are sensitive' to them as 'functional psychological units' for 'processing' and 'chunking' (SD 28, 37) (cf. 12.31). Evidently, 'readers segment at phrase boundaries' (Garrett, Bever and Fodor 1966) and 'hold the final phrase in short-term memory, dumping it' 'at a clause boundary' (Jarvella 1971); also, 'most errors in learning a sentence occur at major clause boundaries' (Johnson 1965) (SD 28).[18] So 'clause boundaries are important' because many 'strategies deal with constituents no larger than the clause' when 'local information' is 'sufficient' (SD 36). But 'whether the clause boundary' actually is 'a decision point' depends on what 'information' is needed for a 'semantically complete' 'unit'.

10.34 Some theories hold that 'people' 'rely on **linguistic rules**' 'applied when parsing a sentence', e.g., those for 'phrase structure' or 'transformations', within a 'closed system' (SD 28) (cf. 7.49; 10.3, 16, 81, 92; Winograd 1983). In contrast, '**strategy** theories of sentence comprehension' hold that 'parsing' runs on an 'open non-deterministic fuzzy system' (cf. 10.14f). Sample 'strategies' might be: 'whenever you find a function word, begin a new constituent' (e.g., a 'determiner' to start a 'noun phrase', or 'a relative pronoun' to 'begin a new clause');[19] or 'attach each word to the constituent that came just before' (again, as with 'relative clauses') (SD 29f). For longer stretches, we might have: 'select the grammatical subject of the previous sentence as the preferred referent for a pronoun' in the next 'sentence'; this 'strategy' makes 'reading times faster' (Frederiksen 1981), but is less 'dominant' than assigning 'role' (e.g., 'agent' of an action), 'recency', and 'topicality' (cf. 10.28, 45, 63f, 68, 79, 86). Even less rule-bound (in Chomsky's sense) is the 'strategy' of 'using semantic constraints to identify syntactic function', which 'in extreme cases allows the construction of propositional representations directly from the sentence, bypassing syntactic analysis'; young 'children' seem to do this (SD 30) (cf. 9.11; 10.3; 12.53).

10.35 'Many models of language' in 'linguistics and psychology' postulate '**levels** of morpho-phonology, syntax, semantics, and pragmatics' (SD 10) (cf. 10.16). Yet such a 'description' is 'not particularly relevant' for 'processing models', where the 'levels interact in an intricate way' (cf. 10.7, 15, 19, 26, 32, 38, 58, 77f; 12.28). 'The strategic approach' stresses 'close cooperation' among 'phonological, morphological, lexical, syntactic, and semantic strategies' (SD 272, 282). This befits 'functional approaches to grammar', which explore the 'dependence of surface structures upon underlying semantic and pragmatic representations and their cognitive and social processing' (SD 283) (cf. 9.22f).

10.36 Accordingly, 'semantic interpretation does not simply follow full syntactic analysis but may already occur with an incomplete surface structure input', and 'syntactic analysis may use information from semantic and pragmatic levels' (SD 10) (cf. 10.7, 100). Nor must we uphold the 'fundamental principle of linguistic and logical semantics that the interpretation of a unit' rests on that of its 'constituent parts' (SD 190; cf. SD 126) (cf. 5.64, 67, 75ff; 6.47f; 7.82; 11.27, 93; 12.18, 59).[20] The principle was convenient when 'linguistic semantics' considered 'the meaning of expressions' 'abstract, stable', and 'intersubjectively invariant', 'belonging to the language system as opposed to actual language use'; thus, meaning could be 'specified independently of contextual and personal variations, which were left to psycho- and sociolinguistics' (SD 192) (cf. 12.55). 'Psychology' too sought 'abstract and generalized models of language understanding' and 'principles followed by all language users' (SD 193) (cf. 10.3).

10.37 Again, such 'abstract accounts' are 'insufficient for cognitive models', which should 'define the actual processes by which **macrostructures** are derived', 'the strategies' for 'handling' the 'information' ('macrostrategies'), 'the memory constraints' and 'representations' for 'macrostructures', the 'knowledge types' needed, the 'retrieval and (re)production of discourse', and the tasks (like 'summarizing, question answering, problem-solving, or learning') that involve 'macrostructures' (SD 191f, i.r.) (cf. 10.29f, 82). Yet insofar as 'the understanding of a discourse depends on variable features of language users and contexts' (cf. 10.6, 14f, 21, 24, 47, 58, 66), 'each language user assigns his or her own macrostructure' and 'finds different meanings prominent, important, relevant, or interesting' (SD 193). Still, 'individual differences presuppose' 'common information', and 'macrostructures' cannot be 'completely arbitrary or disparate' (cf. 10.23; 12.58).[21]

10.38 Van Dijk and Kintsch's own 'model operates' on 'complex chunks', and works 'from the word units on the lower levels up to the units of overall themes or macrostructures', with each end helping to 'construct' or 'understand' the other (SD 10) (cf. 10.19, 21, 26, 32, 35, 47, 58, 77f). The 'model is not *level*-oriented but *complexity*-oriented', with 'understanding' applying to 'words', 'clauses', 'complex sentences, sequences of sentences, and overall text structures', and sharing 'feedback between less' and 'more complex units'. 'The function of a word in a clause' 'depends on the functional structure of the clause as a whole' – a further reason to 'operate with a strategic model', not a 'conventional structural' one (cf. 10.33ff). Thus, van Dijk and Kintsch adopt a semantic approach for both local and global structuring.

10.39 'Ideally', an 'explicit processing model would take text as its input and derive a **semantic representation**', as some 'parsers' do for rather 'restricted domains' of 'English' (SD 38). In 'discourse comprehension models' and 'cognitive semantics', 'the **proposition**' is the 'fundamental' 'cognitive unit' and the 'intensional' or 'conceptual representation' 'assigned to sentential surface structures' (SD 109, 112f, 124) (cf. 3.36, 44f; 8.55; 9.72, 9[24]). Van Dijk and Kintsch also 'take propositions for granted as theoretical units of a cognitive model' and 'formulate' 'typical psychological operations' and 'strategies for (re)constructing' them (SD 125). The 'theory assumes' that during 'comprehension', 'verbal input is decoded' into 'propositions, which are organized into larger units on the basis of knowledge structures to form a coherent textbase' (SD x, 109) (cf. 10.50). 'Complex propositions' 'are expressed by clauses and sentences' and 'represent facts in some possible world' (SD 109, 125). That is, 'propositions' 'represent possible facts' but during 'understanding' are 'instantiated' to 'refer' to 'specific facts'; and a 'structured but fuzzy set of categories may be associated with the proposition' (SD 125). In this way, both the 'general and specific meaning' (or both 'context-free and context-sensitive meaning', or both 'sentence meaning and language user's meaning') 'are cognitively relevant' for 'strategic processes of understanding'; and 'a model of subjective understanding' gains 'a more objective, intersubjective component accounting for general abstract knowledge' (cf. 10.21, 23; 12.58).

10.40 Some 'milestones' are reviewed in the early 'literature on propositions' (e.g., Ogden and Richards 1923; Carnap 1942, 1947; Russell 1940; Reichenbach 1947; Quine 1960) (SD 126, 110ff). Despite 'intricacies', 'disagreement', and 'confusion', the main idea of a 'proposition' emerges as 'the meaning of a declarative sentence' (its *'intension'*) having some 'truth value' (its *'extension'*) (SD 110ff) (cf. 3.35f; 6.22; 9.72; 10.31). Due to 'positivism', this meaning was claimed to be 'not subjective' (not 'a "mental occurrence"'), but 'an objective conceptual structure' or even a property of '"eternal sentences"' free of all 'contextual factors' (SD 109f, 125) (cf. 7.73, 79; 10.36). But in 'more recent theories', this 'truth value' is made 'relative' to 'possible worlds' (cf. Cresswell 1973; Montague 1974). In 'linguistics', meanwhile, 'the influence of behaviourism' 'precluded a systematic study of meaning' 'until the sixties', when 'sentence meanings' and 'semantic interpretations' came under discussion, and 'the seventies', when 'logical semantics' was prominent (SD 111f) (cf. 12.17f). 'Although it is wise in general not to introduce uncritically notions from philosophy, logic, or linguistics into psychological theories of language understanding', we may, by using 'propositions', tap 'a long tradition' and formulate 'constraints of surface structure expression' as a 'direct manifestation' of 'abstract or underlying theoretical units' (SD 126). Just as we can 'couple lexemes with words', we can 'couple' 'complex semantic units' 'with clauses or sentences'. Besides, the 'proposals from philosophy and logic' 'have undergone serious revision in the last ten years from linguists and psychologists' to accommodate more 'intuitions about meaning' (cf. 10.2ff).

10.41 For van Dijk and Kintsch, the 'proposition' is a 'composite unit' of 'concepts': 'a **predicate**' for 'properties or relations' and 'one or more **arguments**' for 'individuals such as things or persons' (SD 113). 'It would be nice if natural language would respect this distinction in surface structure' with 'predicates expressed by verbs and arguments by nouns'. Instead, 'sentences are usually much more complex', with 'not only verbs' and 'nouns' but 'adjectives, adverbs, modal expressions', 'connectives', and so on (SD 113, 125). The 'logical analysis' of these 'categories' and 'structures' 'has met with extremely difficult problems' and become too 'complex' to use for 'representation formats' 'in a cognitive model' (SD 113) (cf. 12.17). If we want to 'account for the so-called *semantic roles* or *cases*' in the 'structure of a sentence' (cf. 10.28), we find they are often 'implicit in the ordering of the arguments' and must be given 'ad hoc labels' in the absence of an 'explicit formal semantics' (SD 113f).

10.42   All the same, 'psychological research in the last few years' shows that 'propositions' as 'semantic units devised' for 'linguistic considerations' can indeed 'function' as 'processing units' (SD 38). 'Lines of converging evidence' include: *'cued recall* studies', where 'words from the same proposition are more effective' in cueing memory 'than words from different' ones; *'free recall* studies' (i.e., without cues), where 'propositional units' are 'recalled as wholes', even without the aid of 'preformed associations, familiarity', or 'semantic plausibility'; *'recognition time'*, where 'how fast people read' and what they can recognize afterwards depend 'on the propositional structure of sentences'; and *'priming'*, where 'recognition latencies' between words are less when 'two words come from the same proposition', irrespective of 'closeness' 'in the surface structure' (SD 38–41).[22] When 'textual input' seems 'unrelated to the propositions' 'in the short-term buffer', 'the reader searches episodic memory' to 'reinstate' some 'proposition' 'sharing an argument' with the 'input', or else makes 'a bridging inference' (SD 45) (cf. 10.21, 48, 65, 70, 76, 95, 100). That both 'operations' are 'resource-consuming' is shown by 'experimental evidence' for 'reading difficulty' (Kintsch and van Dijk 1978) (SD 45) (cf. 10.95f). In sum, 'the evidence for the psychological reality of proposition units is overwhelming' (SD 41).

10.43   Though 'problems' and 'arbitrariness' beset any 'system' for 'representing meaning' in 'propositions', the 'analyses have worked very well in practice' 'for many purposes, such as scoring recall data' or 'representing the semantic level' in a 'processing model' (SD 37f). Researchers 'learn to propositionalize texts quickly, and the interjudge reliability' is 'high' (cf. 12.51). Of course, such 'representations' are not 'all-purpose', but only 'rather primitive' 'tools', and must be tailored to each 'branch of science'. Since van Dijk and Kintsch 'do not hold the view that "meanings" or "concepts" are inherently tied to natural language', 'propositions' can also 'figure more generally in models of comprehension' for 'real or pictorial images', 'scenes, sequences of events, pictures', or 'other semiotic systems' (SD 113, 62) (cf. 10.10, 52f, 61; 12.22). But the 'discussion' in SD is 'limited' to 'natural language' (SD 113).

10.44   'For simplicity' at any rate, 'a representation' is adopted that is 'far from complete' or 'adequate' for 'linguistics' or 'logical semantics' 'but is 'cognitively relevant' (SD 114, 116). It does not cover 'all expressions in surface structure', but 'only semantic properties', as compared with 'pragmatic, stylistic, rhetorical, cognitive, interactional, or social' ones; for example, no entry is made for the 'definite article "the"' 'expressing that an individual' is 'known or identifiable' (SD 114) (cf. 7[39]; 10.86). The 'representation' is 'a *propositional schema*' in which 'semantic categories of the meaning of a sentence are represented as the nodes in a tree-like structure' made of 'atomic propositions' as 'terminal elements' (SD 113f, x). 'Each category may have a subordinated modifier category' ('adjectives and adverbs', etc.) for 'circumstances' and 'modals' that 'localize the complex proposition' (SD 116) (cf. 9.66, 79f).

10.45 'Interpreting the verb phrase as the proposition predicate' 'sets up the propositional schema', with 'the topic noun phrase' being 'assigned to the agent participant' and other 'roles' being made 'ready to receive their content', e.g., 'time and place' (SD 158) (cf. 7.63; 9.57). Filling these roles to 'bind' the 'free variables' or to 'substitute constants' makes 'the action part of the schema' into a genuine 'proposition' which can be 'true or false' (SD 116) (cf. 9.72; 10.40). 'Overall coherence' among 'propositions' is established as 'relevant information' is picked via 'the knowledge schemas activated by the first proposition interpretation' 'about possible facts in the world' and 'situation' (SD 158). Insofar as 'the possible links between facts' and 'propositions are limited', 'the language user can apply a ready-made strategy': 'match the proposition' with a *'conditional* or *functional'* 'category' (SD 158f) (cf. 10.31). 'The language user searches' for 'potential links among facts', e.g., via 'identical referents' ('objects, persons', etc.) or 'related' 'predicates, participants, or circumstances' (SD 15, 150, 157, 183) (cf. 10.39). Thus, a 'proposition' can 'activate expectations' and 'hypotheses' about the 'continuation' based on some 'coherence link', and can set up a 'local coherence goal' of 'establishing a relation' (SD 157). 'Predicates belonging to the same semantic class', for instance, yield 'an obvious semantic link' (cf. 9.93).

10.46 In 'our earlier work' (Kintsch and van Dijk 1978), the chief 'strategy' was to look for 'repeated', 'shared', or 'co-referring' 'arguments among propositions'; but this is only an 'attractive' 'oversimplification' and 'reduction', and is just one 'by-product' or 'example' of the 'more embracing strategy' of 'relating whole propositions or facts' (SD 15, 43, 46, 154, 183).[23] Still, 'relations' based on 'argument repetition' are 'quite predictive of recall', particularly 'in short paragraphs' (Kintsch and Keenan 1973) (SD 43). And 'the psychological importance of shared reference has been demonstrated', e.g., allowing 'sentences to be read more rapidly' (Haviland and Clark 1974). But 'readers' also build 'a *hierarchical* structure of coherence relations' that 'is not based on argument repetition'; and 'hierarchical textbases' with 'superordinate' and 'subordinate propositions' 'predict free recall rather well', the higher ones being heavily favoured (Kintsch, Kozminsky, Streby, McKoon and Keenan 1975; Meyer 1975) (SD 58, 44).

10.47 We thus return to van Dijk and Kintsch's major concern, namely the **'global coherence'** imposed by a 'theme, topic', 'gist, upshot, or point', all 'theoretically reconstructed as **macrostructures'** (SD 15, 52, 104, 150f, 170, 189f, 193f, 224, 237) (cf. 10.18f, 25, 30, 32). 'A central component of the model is a set of **macrostrategies'** for 'inferring **macropropositions'** 'from the sequence of propositions expressed locally by the text' (SD 15). The 'macropropositions may' in turn be 'organized into sequences' or 'levels', leading to 'the macrostructure of the text'. The 'macrostrategies' too are 'flexible and heuristic', since 'the language user' does 'not wait until the end' of a 'sequence of sentences' or of 'a paragraph, chapter, or discourse before inferring' the 'global' content, but 'guesses' 'with a minimum of textual information from the first propositions' (SD 16, 205) (cf. 10.29). 'Titles, thematic words, first sentences', 'settings', and 'information from context' can all contribute (SD 16, 54, 89f, 92, 107, 144, 203, 221f, 361). 'In some discourse types', however, e.g., 'literary or everyday stories, rhetorical devices' may 'delay' such 'indications' to 'arouse interest or suspense' (SD 221) (cf. 10.58, 84).

10.48 'Macropropositions may be directly expressed' and may have their own 'connectives' e.g., 'conjunctions or adverbs' ('"however", "moreover"') for indicating 'conditional' or 'functional' 'coherence structures' (SD 204ff) (cf. 9.87; 10.31). Or, they may be 'inferred from underlying representations', 'organized world knowledge', and 'schematic or superstructural' 'information', e.g., about the 'normal' 'ordering' in 'a narrative' (whereas 'literary texts' may present 'propositions' that are 'abnormal and interesting' or may use 'abstractness' to impede 'the derivation of a macroproposition') (SD 205f, 207f). In general, 'if a sentence' cannot be 'subsumed under the current macroproposition', several options are open: (a) 'setting up a new' one; (b) 'reinstating' one from 'memory'; (c) using 'a wait-and see strategy'; (d) being content with 'only local coherence'; or (e) just 'deleting' the material (SD 204, 206, 208, 221f).

10.49 'In the 'semantics of discourse, macrostructures are defined' via the '*macrostrategies*',[24] which 'map' 'propositions' or 'sequences' of them on to those of 'a higher level' and create a 'hierarchical' structure (SD 190, 236). These 'macrostrategies' include: '*deletion*' of a 'proposition that is not an interpretation condition for another'; '*generalization*' to 'substitute' 'a proposition' for 'a sequence', 'each of whose propositions' 'entails' it; and '*construction*' of a 'proposition' 'entailed' by 'the joint set' of a sequence as a whole (SD 190). These 'rules' 'reduce' materials, but at 'higher levels' they may also 'assign further organization to the meaning of a discourse'.

10.50 'The coherent sequence of propositions' 'formed' 'during comprehension' is called 'the **textbase**' (SD 11, 44f, 51, 109, 342ff, 371). This 'textbase' too is 'constructed' 'in real time' ('on-line'), as 'the reader accumulates semantic units' and 'adds' them 'level by level' 'to the fragment' in 'short-term memory' (SD 44, 373) (cf. 10.7). To stay within 'limited short-term memory', a 'leading-edge strategy' carries 'superordinate propositions' 'from cycle to cycle'; if none are 'available in short-term memory', one is 'chosen from the current input' (SD 44). 'Superordinate' units are 'processed more' and therefore 'recalled more', as studies have shown: 'the level of a semantic unit in the textbase hierarchy determines the likelihood of its recall' (SD 44f, 226, 241) (Kintsch and Keenan 1973; Kintsch and van Dijk 1978). We have here an exemplary 'processing explanation for a structural effect' (SD 44) (cf. 12.31).

10.51 'In parallel' with the 'textbase', 'a **situation model** is elaborated' – a 'cognitive representation of events, actions, persons' – which 'integrates the comprehender's existing world knowledge with information derived from the text' and thus supports 'interpretation' (SD x, 337f, 11f, 51, 163f, 308, 340ff, 348). 'The main semantic and pragmatic function of a text is to enrich this model'; unless we 'imagine a situation', 'we fail to understand'

(SD 337f). 'The situation model' subsumes 'relevant' 'knowledge' 'left implicit' or 'presupposed' by the 'text', both 'general' ('semantic') or 'specific' ('episodic'), and 'may incorporate previous experiences' or 'textbases' (SD 337f, 344, 12) (cf. 10.21). We may be 'reminded of past situations' and 'experiences' in 'clusters', which may offer some 'analogy' whereby 'ill-fitting models are transformed'; 'in this respect, discourse comprehension is a problem-solving task' (SD 337f, 245, 346) (cf. 10.12f, 25).

10.52 Numerous 'linguistic and psychological arguments' are given why the 'situation model' is 'necessary to account for' 'discourse comprehension and memory' (SD 338).[25] It 'fills the gap' 'between "meaning" and "reference"' (cf. 10.10, 43, 61). It provides a 'perspective' or 'point of view' from which 'the facts' – not 'real facts' but 'representations of them' – are 'seen, interpreted', 'talked about', and 'connected' (SD 339). It handles 'parameters' of 'possible world, time, and location in discourse', often 'inferred'. It supplies the 'individuals' to which 'expressions in discourse refer' in 'co-reference' (rather than to 'other expressions') (SD 338) (cf. 9.89, 9[42]). It 'functions' in 'updating and relating' 'general knowledge and personal experiences' in 'memory', e.g., when 'an existing model is modified on the basis of a new text' (SD 342). It can be 'remembered' without the 'text representation' (e.g., if the latter is 'difficult to construct' or entails 'minimal distinctions'), whereas 'the textbase' is 'rarely reactivated' (SD 340f, 344).[26] It accounts for 'individual differences in comprehension' of 'the same information', whence the 'debates about what a classical text "means"' (e.g., in 'literary' studies) (SD 339f). It 'forms the basis for learning' and for taking an 'action' after reading a text (as in 'problem-solving' and 'formal reasoning' in 'mathematics and logic') (SD 344, 341) (cf. 10.98ff).[27] It is 'reconstructed' in 'retelling a story' and encourages people to put 'events' in the 'canonical order' (SD 341) (cf. 10.27, 55, 94, 10[14]). It provides a 'link' for 'cross-modality integration' from 'textual and non-textual sources' (SD 341). It 'relates text representations' in the 'source' and 'target language' during 'translation', particularly when 'the languages' 'differ widely' in 'cultural code' (SD 339).

10.53 This many 'reasons why a situation model is needed' might suggest we 'throw out' 'the text representation' and have 'just words on the one hand and the situation model on the other' (SD 342). But 'text representations' are 'necessary' too, because 'discourse expresses meanings or refers to facts' 'in a specifically linguistic way', and may be 'stored' this way in 'memory' (SD 343). So we need the 'intervening' 'text representation', and theories which dispense with it 'introduce some notational variant through the back door'. 'Cognitive scientists' should be 'clear about what they attribute to text' or 'to the world' and not 'confuse the two' (SD 344) (cf. 10.10). Van Dijk and Kintsch recommend 'limiting the textbase to information expressed or implied by the text', while other 'activated knowledge' goes into 'the situation model with which the textbase is continuously compared' (SD 12).

10.54 Like 'scripts or frames', the 'situation model also has a *schematic nature*' with 'variable terminal categories', which it 'can instantiate' and 'fill', or can 'form' by 'learning' from 'one's own experiences' and 'abstracting' out 'details' during 'frequent use' (SD 344f, 172) (cf. 10.44). 'The model' may have 'a structure' of 'propositions' with 'predicates' and 'participants' 'ordered' by 'recency', 'relevance' etc. (SD 344f, 361). This 'format' 'can be easily retrieved' via 'reminding', and 'information chunks from the current text' can be 'inserted' into the 'categories' (SD 345f). As 'a flexible schema', the 'situation model' helps in 'collecting' and 'grouping together' 'similar experiences' and thus in 'organizing' 'memory'.

10.55 Van Dijk and Kintsch further postulate '**superstructures**': 'typical schemas' for 'conventional text forms', which 'consist of conventional categories, often hierarchically organized', 'assign further structures' and 'overall organization to discourse', and 'facilitate generating, remembering, and reproducing macrostructures' (SD 16, 54, 57, 92, 104f, 189, 222, 236f, 242, 245, 275, 308, 336, 343).[28] We are assured that 'superstructures are not merely theoretical constructs of linguistic or rhetorical models' but also 'feature in cognitive models' as 'relevant' 'units' (SD 237). 'During comprehension', they are 'strategically' 'assigned on the basis of textual' 'information, i.e., bottom-up', yet also create 'assumptions about the canonical structure' and applicable 'schema', i.e., 'top-down' (SD 237, 105) (cf. 10.13). The 'superstructures provide the overall form of a discourse and may be made explicit' as 'categories defining' the 'type' (SD 189, 235f). They are 'acquired during socialization' with 'discourse types'; 'language users know' the 'categories' and 'schemas' 'implicitly' or even 'explicitly' and 'make hypotheses' about them 'when we read' (SD 57, 92).

10.56 These 'additional organizational patterns' may apply to 'the discourse as a whole', e.g., 'narrative' or 'argumentation', or to 'segmented paragraphs', or to 'specific' 'levels', e.g., the 'morphological, syntactic, and semantic' (SD 235f, 241, 105, 92). 'Participants in a given situation may expect a range' of 'discourse types' and make 'strategic guesses' about a 'probable superstructure' 'according to the culture', as 'experiments' and 'ethnographic' 'studies' show (cf. Bartlett 1932) (SD 238).[29] People can use a 'discourse as a whole' to 'perform a global speech act', or can use the 'interactional context' to make 'inferences about possible speech acts being performed' (SD 239). These 'acts' and their 'sequencing' have 'systematic links' to 'global semantic content' and to 'schematic categories' with a certain 'ordering'. Hence, 'text types' are 'defined in pragmatic terms', not merely by 'surface structure style or semantic content and schemas'. In 'argumentative discourse', for example, 'premises and conclusions' 'are linked through a semantic chain of implication, entailment', and 'inference', and through 'speech acts of asserting, assuming, drawing conclusions', and so on. A 'global request' or 'recommendation' might appear not 'in the introduction category', but in a later 'evaluation or coda'.

10.57 'Superstructures' also include 'metrical or prosodic patterns' in 'literary, aesthetic' or 'ritual' texts, e.g., 'meter', 'rhyme, alliteration, repetition, and figures of speech' like 'metaphor and irony' (SD 92f, 241f). Thus, van Dijk and Kintsch's model is much concerned with 'stylistic and rhetorical' aspects (SD 18, 57, 81, 83, 92, 94, 104, 114, 197, 221, 235ff, 241f, 254, 275f, 278, 282, 285, 292, 343). 'The **style** of a discourse' is defined as its 'variation of grammatical', 'schematic, or rhetorical rules or devices' (SD 94) (cf. 3.69; 5.82; 6.52; 8.83; 9.102; 10.10). 'In principle, stylistic variation' correlates 'alternate ways of expression' with an 'underlying identity or similarity' of 'theme', 'semantic representation' ('meaning, referent', etc.), or 'speech act', 'under the controlling scope of text type and context' (SD 94, 17).[30] This 'variation' has 'highly complex effects', such as 'signalling' 'the relationship of speaker to hearer' or of 'discourse' to 'social context' (as 'formal, friendly', etc.), or regulating 'ease of decoding' and 'understanding' (SD 94, 18). The 'language user has the task' of 'selecting words' from a certain 'register' and providing 'indicators' of the 'personal or social situation' by 'strategic use of style markers' (cf. Sandell 1977) (SD 17f) (cf. 9.105).

10.58 'Rhetorical operations' are 'communicative devices to make the discourse more effective' (SD 343) (cf. 10.47, 86, 94f). 'Rhetoric in classical times' studied 'effective' or 'correct manners of speaking', especially for 'persuasion' (SD 92). But 'in principle, any kind of discourse' 'exhibits' 'rhetorical structures, even everyday conversation' (SD 93). So 'understanding discourse implies' some 'recognition of rhetorical devices', and a 'processing model' needs to 'specify what strategies a language user applies' to do this and how they 'interact with the semantic and pragmatic representation of the discourse' (SD 92f). We should examine the 'additional processing' whereby the devices attain 'effectiveness', 'assign' 'additional structure', and 'facilitate semantic comprehension', 'organization', and 'recall' (SD 93, 18, 241). Or, 'rhetorical devices' may 'relate the semantic representation to personal experiences, or to episodically or emotionally relevant information', e.g., by 'vividness'; or may 'signal the macrostructures of a text' by 'pointing to what is important' and 'highlighting the theme' (SD 93, 18; cf. SD 254–59). Similarly, 'representation' may be 'connected' 'with an evaluation' by 'an assignment of additional structures' leading to an 'aesthetic effect', e.g., in 'literature' (cf. Dillon 1978; Groeben 1982) (cf. 3.68f).

10.59 Hence, 'rhetorical form' gets used in SD alongside 'superstructure' to designate types like 'argument, definition, classification, illustration, and procedural description' (SD 254). Although 'forms' 'rarely' appear in 'pure examples' and may be 'combined' 'in multiple, unpredictable ways', they help 'readers' to 'organize the text' and to apply 'top-down processing'. By 'using rhetorical forms' in the normal 'order' or 'signalling' the 'categories' 'clearly', 'writers' can convey their 'intentions', so that 'the right rhetorical schema is triggered' for 'the reader's' 'organization'. If 'the rhetorical structure' is 'hidden', however, 'the reader' may 'still comprehend', but 'miss' the 'point' or 'intention'. This aspect has in fact been demonstrated by 'experiments' with 'texts' (for 'classification, illustration, comparison–contrast and procedural description') in which 'content' was 'identical' but 'rhetorical organization' either did or did not 'conform' to the proper 'schema' (Kintsch and Yarbrough 1982) (SD 254f, 259). 'Effects' showed up 'at the macrolevel' (probed by questions about 'main ideas'), not in 'local processing' (probed by 'cloze test', cf. 10.94) (SD 254f, 257). Moreover, 'rhetorical form' did not seem to 'interact' with 'complexity', being 'just as helpful with simple texts as with complex ones' (SD 257f). When the 'rhetorical form' was 'concealed', however, the 'complex' versions were 'almost unintelligible to our college student subjects', who either 'did not form macropropositions' or formed 'inappropriate ones' based on 'some salient detail' instead of 'the main idea' (SD 259). Data on 'free recall' also reveal a major 'dependence on macrostructure' (Meyer, Brandt and Bluth 1980), though 'micro- and macroprocesses are confounded' there, as are 'textual structure' and 'the structure of the content itself' (SD 259f).

10.60 'The form' 'most widely explored' so far is the '**story**' or '**narrative**', with a 'schema' or 'superstructure' for 'forming macrostructures' whose 'categories' are 'the main events' (SD 55, 92, 235f, 251). A 'story' centres on 'actors' and 'major actions' that 'change' the 'states'; the 'goals and actions' fill 'the story schema' (SD 55) (cf. 10.11).[31] Each '*episode*' consists of 'actions falling into the categories of *exposition*', which 'introduces the actors and the situation'; '*complication*', which 'brings in some remarkable, interesting event'; 'and '*resolution*', which 'returns' 'to a new stable state' (SD 55, 57f, 16, 55, 236, 240, 275). This 'form can be elaborated' by 'embedding' or 'concatenating episodes', or 'overlapping' the 'categories' (SD 55).

10.61 'Recently', a 'fierce debate' arose whether 'story grammars' (inspired by Chomskyan notions) are merely 'theoretical artifacts' for factors better 'explained' or 'modelled in terms of the structure of actions', e.g., 'motivation, purpose, intention, and goal' (SD 55).[32] Following 'available data', van Dijk and Kintsch 'compromise' by 'arguing that narrative schemas and action structures are both necessary for story processing'; 'not all superstructures can be reduced to action-theoretical categories' (SD 56f). 'Stories' are just 'a subset of action discourses' dealing with 'plans', 'purposes', and 'goals', and thus cannot be the only concern of a 'general' 'cognitive account' for 'a variety of tasks'. Also, 'stories' need to be modelled not within 'a theory of action' but within a theory of the 'cognitive representation' and 'description' of 'action', taking account of 'completeness, level', 'ordering, style, perspective, or point of view, etc.' (SD 57, 264). 'Semantic and pragmatic constraints' 'conventionalized' in the 'culture' decide which 'aspects of actions' should be 'told', e.g., the 'unknown, interesting', 'funny, dangerous, unexpected, uncommon' ones; and 'the actions' may be told out of their sequential 'ordering' (SD 56f). Moreover, 'not all action discourses are stories, e.g., police protocols, ethnographic studies, or manuals for repair'.

10.62 'Evidence' has accrued that 'episodes function as psychological units in story comprehension' and 'recall' (SD 57). 'The hierarchical structures' foreseen in 'story grammars predict recall': 'superordinate nodes' fare 'better than subordinate' ones, but 'semantic content' may 'override' this effect, e.g., 'actions' being 'more salient than states' (SD 58) (cf. 10.27f, 46, 50). Also, 'beginning, attempt, and outcome are usually recalled better than goal and ending'.[33] When 'the same sentence' was put 'in different parts of the story', 'subjects took longer to read it' if it was situated to fit an 'important narrative function' (Cirilo and Foss 1980) or to fall at an 'episode boundary' (Haberlandt, Berian and Sandson 1980).[34] Still, since 'narrative categories tend to be confounded with action schemas', we need also to 'investigate texts whose semantic content and rhetorical form are less interwoven', i.e., 'non-narrative' ones (SD 59) (cf. 10.97–100).

10.63 The ' "topic" ' is another key factor 'in the cognitive processing of textual information at the semantic level' (SD 182) (cf. 5.34, 59; 10.34, 45, 47, 86f, 89, 96). 'Topics function both as instructions to search the text representation' and as 'indicators of how and where to connect propositions of the textbase' (SD 156, 171). If we had a 'theory of the internal *relevance* structure of sentences', we could specify 'degrees of topicality and focus' on a 'schematic' basis (SD 171, i.r.). This could capture 'the general cognitive (and hence universal) property that some semantic information is linked with the previous' and is 'more relevant for the continuation of the discourse' and its 'coherence' (cf. 10.30). The 'relevance structure' could 'assign functions such as "topic" or "focus" to nodes in the semantic representation', could be 'scanned' for 'antecedents' to be 'retrieved', and so on. Presumably, 'the favoured positions for relevant antecedents' are (1) 'last occurring, (2) main clause/main proposition, (3) first position, (4) subject, (5) agent/person, and (6) topical noun phrases, in this order of increasing importance' (cf. 10.28, 34, 45, 64, 68, 79, 86).

10.64 Several 'functions' or 'levels of topicality' are 'differentiated' for 'information' ' "in focus" ' (SD 169f, 181). 'The *sentential topic*' in the 'vast' 'linguistic and psychological literature' is 'a function assigned to a part of the semantic representation', 'often marked in surface structure', e.g., by 'initial position in English' (as in 'the first noun phrase', 'especially a definite' one or a 'pronoun', cf. 10.34, 68) (SD 169f, 156) (cf. 7.63; 9.46, 57). So far, though, no 'explicit representation format' or 'adequate formal definition' has been given for 'topic functions' based on 'intuitions and linguistic data from various languages', e.g., 'word order phenomena and topic markers' given by 'morphemes' (SD 155, 167, 171, 182). As 'a cognitive definition' for this level of 'topicality', van Dijk and Kintsch consider 'the "topic" ' 'a discourse function of the sentence', 'exhibiting partial coherence with the (con)textual representation of the previous part' (SD 155). This 'function' 'selects an element (a subtree)' to use in 'constructing the next propositional schema' – an 'account for the overlap defining semantic relatedness' and 'continuation', as found in 'the stereotypical manner of discourse production' (SD 155, 170) (cf. 10.87ff). Thus, 'sentential topic' flows into '*sequential topic*', which 'represents a participant' 'for a sequence of sentences', even 'discontinuous' ones (SD 169f, 181).

10.65 Just as 'macropropositions control processing in short-term

memory' (cf. 10.32, 47f), '*macrotopics* lead to expectations' and 'interpretations' for 'sentence topics' (SD 170). Here, 'topic functions' are assigned to
'complex semantic elements' in the 'cognitive process of expanding and
linking information in discourse representations' and of 'keeping or
reinstating concepts in short-term memory' while integrating 'new information' (SD 181). 'Readers' may 'maintain macroparticipants' and 'sequential
topics' as 'central referents' with 'the strongest claim for local topicality'.
Experiments where readers had to 'write a likely continuation' for a short
'paragraph' showed them 'basing their expectations' on 'topic' rather than
on 'local sentence properties', but 'reverting' to the latter if no topic was
'available' (Kintsch and Yarbrough 1982) (SD 325, 328).

10.66 'Sets of possible topics' are constrained by 'discourse type',
'communicative context or situation', 'culture or subculture', 'social' 'roles',
or even by 'sex, age, or personality of speakers' (SD 197ff, 200). Such a
topic 'set may be ordered' in 'a hierarchy' of likelihood or acceptability' and
may have 'degrees of freedom or boundedness'. Thus, 'contextual
information' for 'possible topics' can be 'reduced to a manageable size'
(SD 200). Yet so far, 'topic sets' and their 'precise forms, order', and
'constraints' have received little 'systematic research in linguistics, sociology,
or anthropology' (SD 197). We still need 'a cognitive theory of discourse
understanding' that 'incorporates a model of language users' applying
'macrostrategies' to 'decide which topics are functional' in 'the global or
local context' (SD 200f).

10.67 Although 'macropropositions' can readily be 'inferred from
semantic interpretations', '*topical expressions*' can also be indicated in
'surface structure': they can 'precede or follow a discourse' (e.g., 'titles',
'summaries'), or be 'expressed in independent sentences', or be signalled by
'type styles', 'highlighting', and 'paragraph indentation' in 'written discourse'
or by 'intonation, stress', and 'pausing' in 'spoken discourse', and so on
(SD 201–05) (cf. 10.85). 'Major cues' for 'macropropositions' range from
'purely grammatical features' and individual 'key words' to 'sequences of
sentences' (SD 205, 202f, 182). 'Syntactic signalling' can 'indicate' 'local
importance' and focus' with a 'passive' or 'cleft sentence structure', and can
'foreground information' by means of 'super-' versus 'subordinate' or 'first'
versus 'final' 'clauses' (SD 203) (cf. 9^{22}, 9^{24}; 10.85). 'In English', 'final,
stressed position' is 'preferred' for 'newness' and 'focus', but 'deviations'
from this can 'mark contrasts' or 'breaches of expectations' (cf. 9.69f).

10.68 In all these ways, 'the syntactic structure and meaning of the
current sentence' get 'analysed' for 'topical function' (SD 170). 'If the
discourse referent is a human being, first its role as an agent will be
preferred': 'hence sentence topics' are often 'subjects of sentences' and
'agents or causes of predicates'; if not, 'a different role is specifically
signalled' (SD 281) (cf. 9.46, 57). For instance, if a 'first-position pronoun'
triggers a 'search for an antecedent' with 'topical function', the 'strategies'
'operate more reliably and faster' when the 'topic' also has 'agent function'
(SD 170f, 181f, 157) (cf. 10.28, 34, 45, 63f). This 'co-topicality strategy'

'operates whether or not a pronoun is structurally ambiguous' (SD 170). Sometimes, the 'strategy assigns only partial' 'provisional coherence', pending a 'definitive interpretation' based on a 'whole clause or sentence' and on 'links with previous sentences' (SD 171). As usual, the most crucial 'criterion' 'is the accessibility in short-term memory' of such 'information' as 'frames, scripts, situation models, and macropropositions' (SD 172) (cf. 10.23).

10.69 As we see again, van Dijk and Kintsch believe 'the process of comprehension cannot be understood' without considering 'current **memory theory**' – fortunately an 'advanced' 'field of research' with a 'consensus' about 'the major phenomena' 'studied in the laboratory' (SD 60). 'Memory' has been found to depend both on *'strength of encoding'* and on *'retrieval operations'* (SD 357). The current 'consensus model of memory', proposed by Raaijmakers and Shiffrin (1981), 'is sufficiently formalized', 'accounts for standard laboratory phenomena', and 'incorporates the major features of memory models of the past decade' (SD 295, 297). 'The model assumes an associative *network* with complex *nodes* containing sensory, semantic, and associative information', e.g., 'word concepts' or 'propositions' (SD 298). 'The probability' of a 'retrieval' depends on 'the relative strength of the association'. During 'retrieval', 'a probe' with 'an array of cues' for 'context', 'task', or 'topic' is 'held in short-term memory'; 'retrieved' 'items' get 'added to the probe', possibly 'displacing others'. So 'retrieval dynamically changes the memory structure itself' (the 'cue' or 'probe' or the 'associative strength'), possibly creating 'output interference' (SD 296, 298). 'Implicitly', 'the *retrieval* operation is always successful' but 'the item' may not be actually *'recovered* and *produced'* if 'strength is too low' (SD 298). The 'primary concerns' are 'the number of retrievals' or 'failures' 'before stopping' or else 'purging the probe', plus 'the strength increment between a cue and a retrieved item'.

10.70 **Memory constraints** are of two types. First, 'short-term memory capacity is limited to about four chunks', or less when 'resources' are in heavy demand (SD 335) (cf. 10.76, 94). Second, 'retrievability' is 'limited' because 'the retrieval cue must match, at least partially, the encoded item', which is then 'reinstated in short-term active memory' (SD 335f). 'Effectiveness' is raised by 'operating within a retrieval system' that supplies 'integrated memory episodes', not 'isolated' 'traces' – an aspect in which 'unorganized word lists as used in classical studies' differ from 'discourse' (cf. 10.93f; Beaugrande 1986).

10.71 It would be ideal to 'get at memory retrieval in its simplest, purest form' and decide if this is 'identical' with the 'retrieval studied in laboratories for the last two decades' (SD 295). Provisionally, van Dijk and Kintsch suggest that 'memory is a by-product of processing' and 'recovers' things according to the 'depth' and 'elaboration' of this 'processing' (SD 335). 'Memorability' depends on 'semantic, meaningful encoding, and embedding experiences in a rich accessible matrix' – just what occurs in 'discourse comprehension' (SD 335f). In the 'usual episodic memory task, the subject is presented with some items' and 'later asked to recall them', and 'learning the items consists in associating them with an experimental context' that serves as a 'retrieval cue'; in discourse memory, however, the 'cue' is 'an association with some topic' (SD 295).

10.72 'Most discourse processing models assume that during comprehension a language user gradually constructs a representation of the text in episodic memory', including 'surface, semantic, and pragmatic information', and 'schematic superstructures' (SD 336) (cf. 10.9, 29, 31, 35f, 58, 86). Of course, 'all the information' 'processed' in 'discourse comprehension' does not make it into 'short-term memory', nor is it 'conscious' (SD 335) (cf. 2.35, 2^{16}; 12.49). For usual 'purposes', 'comprehension' aims at 'memory not for the discourse' but 'for what the discourse is *about*' (SD 336). So, 'the problem is': 'how many' 'knowledge elements' 'become part of the text representation' for 'memory'? To keep it 'relatively uncontaminated', van Dijk and Kintsch allow only what's 'necessary to establish coherence', as opposed to 'much richer text representations' (e.g., Graesser 1981) (SD 336f).

10.73 'The propositional structure' and 'macrostructure', by yielding a 'coherent, interrelated network', 'form an effective retrieval system' (SD 348). 'Retrieval' 'follows' the arrangement of 'the textbase' and 'the situation model', working from a given 'text element' to those 'directly connected', which in turn become 'starting points' for new 'operations' (SD 357) (cf. 10.50f). In this way, many 'paths' among 'nodes' arise, and 'if a textbase is fully coherent', 'all elements can be retrieved in principle' by 'starting anywhere'. In 'top-down' 'recall', though, 'retrieval' 'starts at the top node and proceeds to lower nodes in the text representation', favouring 'propositions' that 'fill a slot in the schema'; and if 'operation is probabilistic, retrieval failures accumulate as the number of nodes' 'traversed along a path increases'.

10.74 To run their whole model van Dijk and Kintsch postulate an 'overall **control system**' 'fed' by 'information about the type of situation', 'discourse', 'plans', 'goals', and 'schematic superstructure' or 'macrostructure' (SD 12). 'This control system will supervise processing in short-term memory', 'guide effective search' in 'long-term memory', 'activate' 'episodic' and 'semantic knowledge' and 'situation models', collate 'higher' and 'lower order information', 'coordinate' 'strategies', and so on (SD 12, 350). Thus, 'the control system' manages 'strategies' for 'producing information' and 'representations' that are 'consistent with the overall goals of understanding', and for 'incorporating all the information' which 'the short-term buffer' 'cannot keep in store' (SD 12). For example, 'the most recently constructed macroproposition' and 'situation model' are kept 'directly available' to 'influence ongoing processing at other levels' (SD 350).

10.75 The total scheme (Figure 10.1) foresees three 'interacting memory systems': 'the *sensory register*, which briefly holds incoming perceptual information and makes it available to the central processor'; '*text memory*', which includes the 'surface memory, the propositional textbase', 'the macrostructure' and 'the situation model'; and *long-term memory*', which includes 'general knowledge and personal experience' (SD 347f) (cf. 10.21, 31, 51, 58).

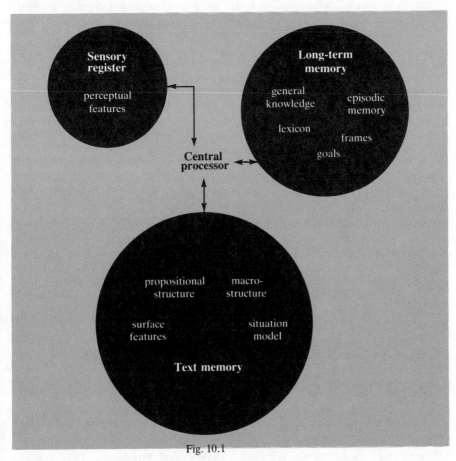

Fig. 10.1

'Surrounded' by these three 'memory systems' and linked to them via the 'control system' is the *'central processor'*, where 'all cognitive operations take place' (except 'retrieval') (SD 348). Here, *'resource limits'* constrain 'the amount of processing', but can be 'circumvented by *automatizing*', whereas *'data limits'* constrain the amount of 'information' and can be offset by *'chunking'* (SD 349, 334f) (cf. 10.27, 33, 38, 70). And since the 'control system' itself is 'not directly conscious' or 'limited', 'many more elements' can 'participate in discourse processing' than would fit into the 'active, conscious' and 'capacity-limited core' and can thus be included 'in the model' when testing its 'predictive power' (SD 350f).

10.76 'Short-term memory' 'maintains' 'the current *chunk*' (a 'complex proposition' often 'corresponding to some phrase or sentence' or to several 'simple' ones), 'plus some carry-over from the previous chunk to establish coherence' (SD 349). Thus, the buffer might hold 'the surface representation of the most recent' 'sentence' and 'the atomic propositions derived from it' as well as some 'stripped-down version' and 'main slots' of 'previous' ones. 'At this point', 'operations' are 'strategically controlled and differ' by 'situation', so they are hard to stipulate 'precisely' (cf. 12.52). 'Previous work' suggests 'the buffer is limited to three atomic propositions', e.g., the 'top slots in the complex proposition', while 'surface expressions' like 'modifiers' for 'time and location', etc. are 'discarded' 'from short-term memory' as soon as 'propositional information is computed'. When 'needed', 'information' can be got back by a 'reinstatement search' of 'text memory' (cf. 10.42, 48, 65, 70); the 'resources' for this would vary by how many 'sentences away' the search travels (SD 350).

10.77 Despite 'the emphasis' on '*higher order*' 'processes', van Dijk and Kintsch do not overlook '*lower order*' ones, such as the 'graphic analysis' of 'letters' and 'words' (SD 59, 22) (cf. 12.33). Like memory, the 'perceptual processes' involved also are addressed by 'a well-developed field of research with a rich empirical database and a history of instructive theoretical controversies' (SD 59, 21). We may find 'analogues at this level' for the 'higher level' 'processes', and the 'theoretical framework' from the lower may 'form the basis' for the higher (SD 21).[35] 'The most basic result' from studies of '**letter identification** and **word recognition**' is that 'the perception of letters is influenced by knowledge about words', and 'the recognition of words' by 'the sentence context' (SD 22) (cf. 10.33ff). 'Thus, recognition is not simply a sequence' of 'bottom-up processes' 'starting with feature detection and letter identification and continuing through word recognition and sentence parsing to more global discourse processing'. 'Interacting' with such activities is a 'top-down' 'process', with 'higher levels' 'affecting the lower ones' (SD 22f) (cf. 10.13; 12.32). For example, 'words are easier to retain than random strings of letters', especially 'if perception is fragmentary'; indeed, 'being part of a word makes the letter easier to see' (Reicher 1969). Similarly, 'words are easier to perceive' 'in a meaningful sentence' or 'text' (Tulving and Gold 1963; Wittrock, Marks and Doctorow 1975). Such 'context effects' are due both to 'automatic facilitation of perception' and to more 'controlled hypothesis testing' (Stanovich and West 1981).

10.78 'Theories of word recognition' are accordingly 'interactive models' with 'bottom-up' and 'top-down processing' on several 'levels': even 'word identification is not a single process or unitary skill', and 'overwhelming' 'evidence' rules out 'the traditional view of reading as extricating information from text' (SD 25f) (cf. 10.13). Because 'perception works' by 'processing all kinds of information' rather than 'filtering out everything that is not relevant at the moment',[36] 'word identification' 'works as a parallel system that fully analyses the input for all possible interpretations and picks out what it needs' (SD 34). 'All the information' is used at 'the cost' of 'brute force calculation', but in return, 'decisions' are 'fully informed' – a 'respect' in which 'perception' starkly 'differs' from 'higher mental processes' (SD 35). The whole 'system' has 'the form not of a strict hierarchy' but of 'a cascade' in which 'output' from one 'level feeds not only into adjacent levels up or down' but also into 'more distant' ones (SD 25). Yet a 'completely interactive system' might attain 'horrendous' 'complexity'; the actual degree of interaction must yet be determined by 'empirical' means or by 'theoretical simulations' on 'feasibility and efficiency' (cf. 10.88f).

10.79 If *'understanding sentences'* operates like 'perceiving words' (and 'there are no a priori reasons' why it should), people might 'work on many possible parsings in parallel', contrary to what 'introspection suggests' (SD 34f). But the two operations 'differ' because words 'are relatively fixed chunks in memory and their retrieval is highly automatized', whereas people 'do not automatically retrieve sentences, let alone discourse meanings; rather, we construct them'. Also, 'irrelevant alternatives' for a whole sentence could lead to 'combinatorial explosion' (cf. Woods 1970). All the same, 'parsing' may entail 'extensive calculations', as has been argued from 'a computational standpoint' (Woods 1980). Either 'one alternative is explored, information' about 'others being carefully stored' for possible 'backtracking'; or 'several' are 'followed up in parallel' ('virtual processing') 'until a choice' can be made by a 'higher-level plausibility judgment'. For instance, 'evidence' suggests that 'people compute all possible referents for a pronoun': 'sentences with an ambiguous pronoun' (like ' "The city council refused to grant the women a parade permit because *they* advocated violence" ') 'take much longer to read' (Frederiksen 1981). But 'even if computations are cheap, there must be limits', e.g., making 'clause boundaries serve as decision points' for 'selecting' some things and 'discarding' others (SD 35f) (cf. 10.33ff). Experiments indicate that 'completing ambiguous phrases' is harder than 'unambiguous' only if no 'clause boundary' occurs before the point for making the completion' (Bever Garrett and Hurtig 1973). 'Sharp breaks' in 'verbatim recall' also 'establish' 'the relevance of sentence and clause boundaries' (Jarvella 1979) and 'indicate that the syntactic structure of sentences is used' in 'scheduling' 'short-term maintenance' of 'discourse' (SD 353).

10.80 In various 'experiments', 'simple sentences' 'appeared to function much like' 'single words in traditional list-learning' (SD 353f) (but cf. 10.70; 12.28). The usual 'interference' 'effects' were found for 'discourse', e.g., that 'reading' takes 'longer times' if interrupted by 'doing addition' or 'counting' (Glanzer, Dorfman and Kaplan 1981). These 'laboratory' findings were confirmed by 'observations' in a 'naturalistic situation', namely 'how shopkeepers' 'answered simple questions' 'over the telephone': 'the wording of the answer' 'reflected' that of 'the question' unless 'short-term memory' encountered 'interference' (Levelt and Kelter 1982).[37]

10.81 So far, 'most work in psycholinguistics is about **comprehension**', using 'the structure of utterances' as an 'independent variable' subject to 'adequate control' (SD 261ff).[38] For many years, 'structuralism and behaviourism favoured the analysis of observable phenomena', such as 'surface structures'. Also, 'generative transformational grammar', 'despite its claims' to be 'neutral', was 'biased toward analysis' (cf. 7.83f). But 'a complete discourse processing model should include **production**' as well, and van Dijk and Kintsch treat at least 'some problems' and 'strategic aspects' (SD 16). One main 'insight' is that 'production is not simply the reverse of comprehension' (SD 261, 16) (cf. 7.83; 10.85; 11.47; 12.57). 'The initial data and the goals differ', as do 'the strategies' (SD 262, 16). Yet the 'processes' can hardly be 'completely separate', since 'comprehension' too is 'constructive' (SD 262, 17).

10.82 So we should 'specify which structures and principles' work 'in either direction' and which do not (SD 262). 'Insights' about 'general or comparable cognitive mechanisms', e.g., 'episodic and short-term memory, help us to specify' the 'initial internal representation' and 'the constraints in production' and thus to 'develop' 'hypotheses and experimental techniques' (SD 264). Since 'a language user' cannot 'construct a long sequence of propositions' as 'input to the surface structure formulators', 'strategic', 'fast', and 'flexible' processes are needed to handle an 'enormous' 'amount of information' for 'constructing semantic representations, lexical expressions, and syntactic and phonological structures', while 'taking into account' 'goals, local and global constraints', and 'fluctuating' 'contextual information' (SD 264, 267) (cf. 10.10, 20, 53).

10.83 Clearly, 'the production' of 'utterances' is 'a complex task which needs planning' – a factor 'neglected in the sentence production literature' (SD 263, 17, 265). 'Whereas at the sentence level this planning may be' 'automatic', it may be 'conscious' for a 'complex' 'discourse', especially a 'written' one (cf. Miller, Galanter and Pribram 1960; Clark and Clark 1977; Hayes and Flower 1980) (SD 263, 272; cf. 10.11).[39] For van Dijk and Kintsch, 'the actual production of discourse begins' with a '**plan**' that has both 'pragmatic and semantic representations' (SD 265f, 17, 272, 276, 279, 289, 293) (cf. 10.17). The plan foresees 'a series of preparatory, component, and terminating speech acts', and 'the ultimate **goal**' is to 'say something about reality', give 'new information', or apply 'persuasion', in order to 'change' 'the knowledge, beliefs, or opinions of the hearer' (SD 266f, 269f, 277) (cf. 10.20). So a 'macro speech act' has 'a global propositional content' (a 'macrostructure', 'macroproposition', 'theme, or topic') 'derived from the interaction context and its cognitive counterparts' (SD 266, 272ff, 279f, 284, 289ff). 'The overall speech act may be indirect', leaving 'interpretation to the hearer' who can 'draw other conclusions' without seeming 'uncooperative' (SD 269). Also, 'monological discourse, such as a lecture, scholarly article, or a news story', allows less 'interaction', though 'implicitly taking it into account'; and 'planning may be more conscious and explicit, and its execution better controlled'.

10.84 The 'principles and strategies' of 'production' must 'leave a lot of freedom in the actual formation of a textbase' (SD 291). 'The basic strategy for textual meaning production consists in the selection of one or more arguments' (e.g., 'discourse referents such as persons or objects'), 'to which a series of predicates is systematically applied', e.g., to supply the 'properties and relations' 'associated' in a 'schema' or 'frame' (SD 281f) (cf. 10.23). Then, 'production' undergoes 'linearization' by following 'an appropriate order', e.g., 'a natural order' 'parallel to the temporal or conditional order of facts' or going from 'general to particular' (SD 275, 281) (cf. 7.3). Or, 'deviations' can arise from 'cognitive reordering' to fit 'perceptions, understanding', etc., or from 'rhetorical', 'interactional', and 'pragmatic reordering' for 'effective execution of speech acts' or for 'aesthetic functions' and 'suspense' (SD 276f, 282) (cf. 10.47). To gain 'cooperation', we may 'delay' 'information' that would be 'difficult' to 'accept', or may 'give' 'conclusions first', and so on (SD 277) (cf. 10.56).

10.85 To work down from 'global information', van Dijk and Kintsch propose 'the inverses' of their 'macrostrategies' for 'comprehension' (in 10.49): *'specification, addition'*, and *'particularization'* (SD 267, 274, 278). The resulting 'distribution' depends on 'complexity', 'importance', and 'relevance', high degrees of which call for 'independent' units like 'clauses' or 'sentences' rather than 'dependent' ones like 'modifiers' or 'relative clauses' (SD 282f, 202) (cf. 9^{24}; 10.67). A common 'strategy' is to 'start from given information' (e.g., in 'the first noun phrase functioning as subject and topic' of a 'sentence') and go on to the 'new' (e.g., in 'a predicate phrase, functioning as the comment' (SD 279ff, 283) (cf. 9.51, 57; 10.28, 34, 46, 63f, 68). In such ways, the 'global plan' or 'representation' again 'controls the local, linear' ('lower') 'levels of discourse production' in 'sentential structure' (SD 266, 283) (cf. 10.19). The 'plan' may not be 'conscious and orderly' but 'sketchy' and 'general' (or, in 'literary prose', 'well hidden') (SD 266, 17) (cf. 10.47, 84). Or, 'control' may be 'data driven' and 'episodic', following only 'the plan' to 'keep up the conversation'; or, 'plans may be changed during speaking' (SD 266f, 269, 17, 273).

10.86 Finally, 'propositions' must be 'given to the sentence formulation mechanism', where 'syntactic form is constructed' from 'semantic and pragmatic information' plus 'lexical and phonological expressions' (SD 278f) (cf. 7.67; 9.20). 'The process of lexicalization will select appropriate lexical items to express the concepts of the propositions', keeping within the 'bounds' of 'style, register', 'text type, and communicative context' (e.g., 'metaphor, irony', etc.) (SD 292). As in comprehension, 'coherence conditions' can call for 'explicit' 'surface structure signals' that 'depend on and determine textual structures', such as 'boundaries' of 'sentences, clauses' and 'episodes', 'word order', 'semantic roles (cases)', 'topic–comment', 'connectives, pronouns', 'adverbials', 'definite articles', 'demonstratives', or 'tense and location markings' (SD 279f, 282–85, 292) (cf. 10.35, 40, 48, 64, 67, 75f). Or, 'control' may be exerted by 'feedback from the surface structure' or from concurrent 'non-verbal' events ('gestures, facial expressions', etc.) (SD 279, 266). So again, a 'sentence not only expresses its own meaning but also the multiple links' 'with the whole text and communicative context' (SD 285) (cf. 5.56f; 9.16; 10.91). 'On full analysis', 'few surface structure items' do not 'signal a semantic, pragmatic, cognitive, social, rhetorical, or stylistic function' (cf. 10.35). Hence, 'little is left of the old Saussurian arbitrariness in the relation between expressions (signifiers) and their meanings (signifieds)' (cf. 2.28; 4.27; 9.13, 32, 36; 12.27).

10.87 In tests carried out by Donna Caccamise (1981) applying the 'model of memory' of Raaijmakers and Shiffrin (1981), 'subjects' were given 'topics' and told to 'talk about' them, 'saying everything that came to mind, without regard to organization or repetition' (SD 293). The 'topics' were varied between (a) 'familiar' or 'unfamiliar' ('"education"' vs '"energy"') and (b) 'general' or 'specific' (e.g., '"energy"' vs '"nuclear energy"') (SD 296). Because 'subjects' 'generalized the specific topics', only the first variation led to 'large and regular differences': 'familiar topics produced twice as many ideas' and so more 'chunks', while the 'unfamiliar' ones elicited 'five times as many' 'unrelated ideas' ('relatedness' being gauged by 'argument overlap', cf. 10.46). When told to speak as if to 'children', subjects proved 'surprisingly poor at taking audience constraints into account'; instead, the 'ideas' merely showed 'less complexity' and 'interrelatedness', and the 'process took twice as long', broken by 'random' 'pauses' (SD 297). Apparently, some 'special editing process' 'destroyed the orderly flow of ideas'.

10.88 'A computer simulation of idea generation' was also performed by William Walker (1982), following 'a straight episodic list-learning model' and assuming 'an associative net' ('100 nodes') which did 'not model any specific semantic field' but in which 'connections' had 'high or low average strength values' and were arranged in 'clusters' (SD 297, 299). 'Efficient idea generation' seems to 'operate' between 'inflexible' 'probing of memory' with 'the initial topic' and 'flexible' 'guidance' by 'items already recovered' (SD 299). So we need to examine 'how many items are in the probe', or are 'changed' or 'replaced', either (a) at 'random', (b) via 'recency' (as in a 'pushdown stack', where 'new elements' 'push older ones' down and must be taken back off before them), or (c) via some 'intelligent' 'strategies' 'focusing' on the 'least' or 'most interrelated' 'array' (SD 300, 348). Walker's 'simulation model' did 'mimic the response patterns' in the empirical 'idea generation' test by Caccamise (SD 299). 'Clusters' were treated in much the way 'people retrieve information from semantic memory', which is 'highly structured' and has many 'overlaps'; 'nodes often pertain to more than one script or frame', 'yet people rarely get confused', because 'different associations are produced' and the 'network' gets 'sliced' 'in various ways'. 'Thus, the model' succeeded in 'mimicking qualitatively' 'what happens when people generate ideas'. Such simulations are an 'important guide' and 'theoretical frame', because 'experimenting with the model' is 'easier than' 'with people' and 'gives readily interpretable results' (SD 299, 301) (cf. 10.78).

10.89 As we see once more, van Dijk and Kintsch are particularly concerned with following up 'predictions' about 'textually based comprehension strategies' (SD 221). For example, we can predict that 'if more contextual/textual signals are available', 'comprehension' should be 'easier, and hence faster' (SD 222). Or that 'local information strategically subsumed under a macroproposition' should be 'retrieved' and 'recalled longer and better'. Or that 'initial sentences' should 'take longer to process' if they are used for 'deriving' a 'macroproposition'. Or that 'texts' with 'unexpected' 'topics' should be 'initially more difficult to process'. And all these predictions have been confirmed by 'experimental investigation'.

10.90 Still, van Dijk and Kintsch readily concede 'the difficulty of evaluating a theory as complex as ours', which is 'not stated formally and explicitly in all the necessary detail' (SD x) (cf. 10.5). 'Our model cannot possibly deal with every component of discourse comprehension'; it must be 'selective' but must 'not contradict current knowledge', and must be 'constructed' so it can be 'extended' to further 'components of discourse processing' or remain 'compatible with other models' (SD 59f, 383) (cf. 5.9; 11.55; 12.63). As we have noticed, 'the emphasis' falls on 'higher order discourse comprehension' 'rather than lower order' 'processes', but similar 'principles', such as 'strategy' and 'schema', should 'also apply' to all levels (SD 59f) (cf. 10.7, 10, 27, 31).

10.91 Admittedly, 'experimental confirmation' of 'hypotheses' about 'strategies or schemas for the production' or 'understanding' of discourse is 'notoriously difficult' and may lead to 'conflicting results' (SD 74). 'Strategies' are not 'generally conscious or intentional'; they may vary between 'controlled (i.e., slow, sequential, resource-demanding) and automatic (fast, parallel, effortless)' (cf. Shiffrin and Schneider 1977) (SD 31; cf. 10.11, 13, 15, 75, 77, 79, 83, 96). Or, 'the child acquiring a strategy may use it differently than does the mature speaker'; or, 'smooth operation may be blocked (as in the garden path sentence)'[40] and 'controlled' 'processes' must take over. Also, 'we must beware of taking for granted the relevance of sentence grammars and psychological experiments using sentence lists' (SD 32) (cf. 10.2f, 14, 16, 40, 61, 81). It is 'different' to 'understand sentences in discourse', where they need to be 'well integrated semantically' (Haviland and Clark 1974) (cf. 10.86). 'Context' can affect 'how fast we can read a sentence' (Sanford and Garrod 1981); how well 'children' can surmount 'difficulties' with 'syntactic forms' (Lesgold 1974); and so on.

10.92 The 'experimental set' is itself a context that can 'easily bias subjects' (SD 31) (cf. 12.47). We must 'beware' of drawing 'wrong conclusions' from 'psychological experiments' set up in an 'idealized', 'artificial, underdetermined situation' 'new to the subject' and requiring 'tasks quite unlike "real reading"', e.g., 'recognizing' 'words' flashed on a 'tachistoscope' (SD 32, 267, 26).[41] 'Normal strategies' from daily life may not work when 'experimental material' is so 'well controlled' and 'the usual redundancies' 'have been removed from the text' (SD 32) (cf. 12.55). Then 'subjects fall back on general problem-solving strategies and devise an on-the-spot procedure' or 'response' that 'reflects task demands' (SD 32, 259) (cf. 7.35). But an 'entirely task-specific' 'procedure' may hold 'no general interest' for modelling 'normal discourse processing' and may lead to giving 'wrong advice to educators, textbook writers, etc.' (SD 32).

10.93 None the less, 'useful explanatory concepts' for 'discourse processing' can be derived from 'laboratory studies with non-discourse', e.g., 'traditional memory experiments' with 'word lists' (SD 352, 356, 46) (but cf. 10.70). Studies on 'classical short-term memory' draw 'our attention' to requirements of 'capacity limits' and 'quick access' (SD 352) (cf. 10.69ff). As 'the term *working memory*' suggests, both 'storage' and 'processing' occur inside it, where they 'compete for capacity' and 'resources'. 'In a memory-span test', 'processing is minimal' and 'storage' can hold up to '7 + 2 items', but only 'around 2 items' in tasks like 'free recall', where much 'encoding' is being done (cf. 10.70, 76). This 'competition' might explain why 'adults', who are 'more efficient processors', 'can maintain more items in short-term memory than can children' (Chi 1976; Huttenlocher and Burke 1976). The account can also apply to 'good versus poor readers', who show 'no significant differences' on 'memory-span' tests but large ones in 'reading' 'comprehension scores'. 'We do not yet know' what 'information' 'is being held in short-term memory': 'the literature suggests an acoustic coding bias' is 'preferred', but 'imagery or abstract semantic information may be retained' as well (SD 354). Usually, only 'verbatim memory' is 'examined', emphasizing 'surface structure', rather than postulating 'a propositional representation of a discourse fragment' as a major 'retrieval structure' (SD 354, 356) (cf. 10.39ff).

10.94 Such issues raise 'important implications for comprehension testing', which needs a 'clearer idea of what aspect' is being 'evaluated' (SD 259). '**Readability**' – 'the relative ease with which texts can be read and remembered' – has usually been gauged by 'superficial' aspects, as in 'word frequency and sentence length', or by purely 'local context' as in 'cloze tests' where 'every fifth word' is 'deleted' and 'subjects have to guess' it (SD 45, 259, 255, 257). A more 'detailed understanding of the psychological processes involved in comprehension' would enable 'separate measurement instruments for macroprocesses, knowledge integration', 'rhetorical form, coherence, parsing', and so on (SD 259f). We might 'predict readability' by consulting 'reading time per proposition recalled on an immediate test', and by estimating 'the number of bridging inferences' and 'memory reinstatements' made in 'constructing' and 'processing' 'a coherence graph' (Kintsch and van Dijk 1978) (SD 45; cf. 10.21, 42, 48, 65, 70, 76). But we should also distinguish 'varying' 'types' of 'readers' and 'inferences', or 'good or bad rhetorical form', or 'the effects of canonical ordering' (SD 46, 255) (cf. 10.52, 55). Even 'ordinary readers are experts' 'at remembering simple, familiar texts' but not when they 'lack the proper knowledge base' or 'strategies', e.g., for 'technical discourse' or 'poetry' (SD 359f) (cf. 10.59). 'Discourse memory, at least under ideal conditions' is by 'nature' an ' "expert" memory', and thus 'better than what we normally observe under laboratory conditions in list-learning experiments' (SD 363f).

10.95 'Educational research too readily assumes that good readers' 'exploit the regularities and redundancies' to save on 'laborious bottom-up processing' (cf. Smith 1973; Goodman 1976) (SD 23). Experimental 'evidence' does show that good readers use 'relevant information', 'higher-order constraints', and 'rhetorical structure' (Perfetti and Roth 1981; Meyer *et al.* 1980). But in addition, 'good readers fixate almost every content word' (Just and Carpenter 1980) and 'are better' at 'detecting misspellings and visual irregularities in a word' (McConkie and Zola 1981). Indeed, 'the best discriminators between good and poor readers' are 'simple letter and word identification tasks' (Perfetti and Lesgold 1977) (SD 23f). And 'paradoxically', 'context effects are most pronounced in poor readers', as revealed by 'substitution errors' (Kolers 1975) or 'facilitation of word recognition' (Perfetti, Goldman and Hogaboam 1979). Such 'context effects are only symptoms' for the real 'issue': 'the speed and accuracy' of 'word recognition operations'. 'Poor readers' 'recognize isolated words inaccurately and too slowly' and 'compensate' 'with context dependent guessing or hypothesis testing', whereas 'good readers' 'form' 'sophisticated hypotheses' and don't need to 'guess' and 'test' so much. When 'context is only weakly constraining', 'a priming effect' is found only 'for good readers'; 'poor readers' may be producing 'lexical items via a slow, controlled serial process', whereas 'good readers' use 'a parallel automatic process' to 'produce a much greater pool' (Frederiksen 1981). Though 'both good and poor readers rely on' 'spreading activation' (cf. 10.21), the 'good readers' can 'devote more resources', whereas the 'poor ones' are 'exhausted by the decoding process'.

10.96 Despite its avowedly empirical orientation, SD features a *Newsweek* article about 'Guatemala' – 'chosen' to 'enhance ecological validity' over 'the tradition of using simple stories' or 'descriptive paragraphs' (SD 98) – printed inside the front cover and analysed stage by stage (SD 133–44, 182–88, 209–19, 242–51, 286–93, 319–24) but never used in empirical tests. The 'sample analysis' only 'hand-simulates' the 'structures', 'processes', and 'representations' 'assigned by an imaginary reader', 'an ideal average reader' (to be exact, a 'middle-class American' 'student of psychology' with 'average knowledge' 'about political affairs') (SD 98ff). Since the article was intended to 'form and change political knowledge', this 'reader' is said to pursue 'the general goal of acquiring relevant information about the world' for possible 'use' in 'conversation' or in 'making political decisions'. 'General strategies' are postulated: 'read the headline', 'establish' the 'topic', 'activate' 'knowledge', gauge 'interest', 'estimate length and reading time', and make a 'decision' whether to 'read the text' (SD 101). All this is straightforward enough, but the purely speculative basis jars with the rest of the book.

10.97 However, van Dijk and Kintsch do provide a thorough empirical demonstration for 'a specific complete process model', namely for 'understanding and solving word arithmetic problems' (cf. Kintsch and Greeno 1982) (SD 364–83). This domain is 'ideally suited' for showing how 'simple, but realistic comprehension' can be modelled by applying 'the general principles' they have 'presented' (SD 364). 'The reader's purpose' in gaining 'information from the text is unambiguous', thus 'restricting the range of strategies'; the latter are 'specialized' and 'unusual', acquired in 'school', where they are less often 'taught explicitly' than 'left to be discovered by the student' during 'trial and error' (SD 364f). Thus, 'the strategies are very distinct and easier to describe' than those 'in our general theory', being 'extremely bottom-up, data driven' and causing 'planning and goal-setting to happen right away' (SD 365, 382). Future 'generalizations should introduce more top-down processing, a deeper semantic analysis of the problem situation', and 'more complex, flexible strategies' (SD 382). Still, this 'model', though not offered as the 'correct' or 'only' one, 'follows straightforwardly from the general theory of comprehension' and 'problem-solving', 'predicts rather well problem difficulty', has 'empirical support', and 'raises interesting questions' about 'teaching methods and educational practice' (SD 383). When 'alternative theories and models' 'reach comparable stages of development', we can 'decide among them' (cf. 12.57).

10.98 Besides, the model 'builds on a large amount of research and theory' on 'problem-solving', though such 'models do not start directly from text, but with a problem representation derived intuitively from text' (cf. Riley, Greeno and Heller 1982) (SD 366). 'The first step is to derive a propositional textbase from the verbal input, in this case' 'a few sentence frames', and build 'set schemas' with 'a label' and 'slots for a specification', 'an object, a quantity, and a role' – 'a start set, a transfer set, and a result set' using such 'schemas' as 'MORE/LESS THAN' (SD 367, 369ff, 377, 380f). So 'the situation model' 'mirrors the textbase' in being 'a set structure' for the 'problem representation' to which 'arithmetic operators' are applied (SD 371). 'A superset is established' 'requesting appropriate subsets' either from 'linguistic cues' or from 'inferences' to get 'missing values' (SD 375, 372).[42]

10.99 Sample tests 'demonstrate' 'that the model works' here: we can 'specify comprehension strategies' and 'schemas' for 'constructing a text representation and a situation model' to fit the 'task' and 'tell why some problems are harder to solve' (SD 377). However, the 'examples' do not 'do justice to the full power of the model' because 'problem difficulty also hinges on 'the order in which information is presented' and on 'the constraints' imposed by the 'limits of the human information processing system' (SD 379). 'The most important' factor is 'memory load', 'related' to the current 'chunk' in 'short-term memory', the chunks needing to be 'reinstated', the 'dangling propositions' being 'carried along', and 'the number of' 'inferences' and of 'active requests for missing information' (SD 380f). Such factors may seem minor when the texts are 'so short', but become crucial for 'longer texts' like those studied by Miller and Kintsch (1980). Children may be 'familiar with the requisite knowledge structures and strategies' and yet have 'trouble' because of 'memory load' (SD 382). Thus, success depends on 'whether a problem is expressed in a way' 'friendly to short-term storage requirements', and we can 'make problems easier by rewording' them and giving useful 'linguistic cues' (SD 381).[43]

10.100 I shall wind up the chapter by surveying some major differences between the other approaches we have examined so far and that of van Dijk and Kintsch. In their view, such approaches need revision because they were designed to analyse completed linguistic structures after the fact, whereas a processing model must work 'on-line' 'in real time' (cf. 10.7, 29, 50). People cannot wait until the end of a structure (clause, sentence, discourse, etc.) before setting the processes to work (SD 10, 14ff, 17, 44, 84, 148, 151f, 154, 164, 166, 205, 237, 285). Moreover, the linguistic materials actually uttered or heard should not be seen as ends in themselves, let alone as free-standing codes or strings of minimal units apart from mental and social processes. However, frequent reference is made to the ways 'surface structure' can indicate or even directly express the various cognitive entities of processing (SD 61, 76f, 84, 86, 92, 94f, 121, 126, 129f, 133, 135, 144f, 157, 159, 165, 169, 171, 182, 194, 202, 204, 241, 251, 268, 272, 279f, 282f, 285, 334) (cf. 10.35, 40, 48, 64, 67, 75f, 86) – ironic when we recall Chomsky declaring that 'surface structure is in general almost totally irrelevant to semantic interpretation' (AT 162) (7.82; cf. 12.47).

10.101 But the most important difference is that van Dijk and Kintsch seek 'the main criterion for the success' of a 'general theory' in its power to 'derive fruitful situation- and task-specific models' and 'experimental tests' of 'principles and implications' (SD 384) (cf. 12.25, 49, 61). Tests done so far have shed new 'light on difficult and controversial issues in discourse comprehension' and shown how the 'general principles of textually based comprehension strategies' lead to 'general predictions' (SD x, 221). Van Dijk and Kintsch set an example themselves by assigning a central role to 'reports of psychological experiments that were performed to test various aspects of our theory' (SD x) (cf. 10.42, 59, 65). Some 'processes' foreseen by 'the theory can indeed be observed under appropriate, carefully controlled laboratory conditions' (SD 384). Further 'experiments' can be devised with a more 'exploratory' nature, sifting 'the theory' for 'indications' of 'potentially interesting phenomena' that may aid 'a more systematic mapping' (SD 385).

10.102 'This use of experiments as tools for theory-guided exploration complements the more traditional' 'tests of predictions' and gains 'importance as theories in cognitive science become more complex' (SD 385).[44] Thus, 'experimental psychology can provide an empirical evaluation' in an 'unconventional way': the 'theory as a whole is too general' for 'direct experimental tests, but the accumulation of observational and experimental evidence' on certain 'points will eventually verify or disconfirm the theory' (SD 384). 'We arrange experiments' with 'texts' and 'tasks' such that 'theoretically interesting behaviours can be observed in relatively clear form; such experiments demonstrate' 'our knowledge' about 'comprehension processes' via 'the control we are able to exercise over subject–text interaction' (SD 384f). The conclusion is clear: 'a general theory of comprehension strategies' 'belongs neither to linguistics nor psychology' alone (SD 383). 'The empirical-experimental background' is 'just as important' as 'the theoretical-linguistic' (SD 60).

Notes

1. The key is only SD: *Strategies of Discourse Comprehension* (1983). The style of the two authors, as we know from their solo works, is rather disparate. Van Dijk reasons and writes less carefully than Kintsch, and some of this carries into SD. Terms are formally announced and defined, but then either (a) not used again (e.g., 'tactic'), (b) used informally despite the definition (e.g., 'rule'), or (c) used interchangeably with common-sense quasi-synonyms (e.g., 'macro-structure' versus 'theme', 'topic', 'gist', 'upshot', 'point', etc.). Also obtrusive are repetitious programmatic listings of factors that processing and processing models should involve, but about which nothing substantive is said: the list of 'beliefs, opinions, attitudes, ideologies' and the like, documented in Note 10, appears over forty times in the book. On these various terms and problems, see 10.8f, 20, 83 and Notes 3, 8, 11, 13, 14, 15, 24, and 28.
2. 'Sentoid' was not used by Chomsky in SS or AT, but his followers postulated 'underlying sentoids of the deep structure' (e.g., Fodor, Bever and Garrett 1974) (SD 75) as idealized sentence-like units. The 'canonical sentoid' was of course 'noun phrase, verb phrase and (optional) noun phrase' ('NP–VP–(NP)') (cf. 7.81).
3. Like a number of terms in SD, 'functional' has several disparate meanings besides that suggested here. Compare 10.11, 18, 31, 35, 38, 45, 66 and Note 31.
4. 'Participant' versus 'observer' is seen in analogy to 'general' versus 'specific' (SD 82f), but, as Pike indicated, the former pair of conceptions is much more intricate than this (see 5.4, 9, 11, 16, 89; 11.27). The reliance on experiments, as van Dijk and Kintsch realize (cf. 10.91ff), is a further complication, because test subjects are keenly aware of being observed and their participation is seldom fully spontaneous.
5. 'Playing chess' is given as an example (SD 63, 66f, 70, 337, 359); on other uses of this game by linguists, see 2.80f, 6.51, 9[49].
6. Herbert A. Simon (personal communication, February 1989) rejects this argument. He told me that problem-solving has no express relation to consciousness, and the seeming ill-structuredness of language processing and its goals probably reflects our lack of knowledge about its well-structured component subprocesses.
7. See SD 22f, 25, 31, 48, 92, 97, 134, 159, 181, 196, 202, 240, 254, 262, 321, 382; and cf. 10.19, 25, 32, 55, 59, 73, 77f, 95, 97; 12.44. 'Pure top-down models have never really existed', being 'psychologically absurd' (SD 25).
8. In fact, the term 'rule' is often casually used disregarding the distinctions drawn here (e.g., SD 7, 18, 79, 90, 126, 127, 159, 190, 203, 237, 287, 317); compare Notes 1 and 24.
9. Like Chomsky, van Dijk and Kintsch say 'all or most of our sentences will be unique, especially if they are long' (SD 74) (cf. 7.90). But unlike him, they do not use this factor as a pretext to reject probabilistic models (cf. 12.59).
10. See SD x, 5, 8f, 12, 17, 19, 47f, 61, 77, 81ff, 85, 89, 99f, 125, 133f, 144, 151, 155, 174, 188, 192f, 196, 263f, 265f, 269f, 273, 277, 279, 292, 322, 334, 342, 348; and compare Note 1. 'Hot cognition' is a current term for much of this material and it too is not included in any SD 'representation model' (cf. Abelson 1979; Wegman 1981) (SD 13, 385).
11. This distinction is complicated, however, by situating the whole ongoing text representation in 'episodic memory' (SD 11f, 45, 88, 93, 98, 101, 139, 151, 163, 200, 218, 336, 347f); 'working memory' would be a less confusing term and is also used (see 10.94). Later, no 'clear distinction' is deemed necessary between 'general knowledge' and 'personal experience': 'they differ only in the

conditions under which they are retrievable, not in the way they are used in comprehension' (SD 348). I don't agree.

12. That the 'bridging' kind are made during comprehension is well established by experiments (e.g., Haviland and Clark 1974); when and how richly the 'elaborative' ones are made is in dispute (cf. Kintsch and van Dijk 1978); and 'restructuring' 'inferences' may be 'a third category' (cf. Schnotz, Ballstaedt and Mandl 1981) (SD 49–52).

13. Van Dijk and Kintsch say 'the basic idea is the same' for these three terms, but they 'prefer the fairly traditional term "schema"' (SD 307). Sometimes they use the three terms fairly interchangeably or side by side (SD 13, 47, 96, 139, 159f, 172, 195, 203f, 245, 291, 307f, 310, 323, 344f, 357, 366) (see Note 1). My own impression from the relevant literature is that a frame is any knowledge array, a schema is an ordered one and a script a highly familiarized and routine one (Beaugrande 1980).

14. For the 'normal' or 'preferred' version of a schema or knowledge pattern, van Dijk and Kintsch expropriate the term 'canonical' (SD 203, 206, 56, 178, 226, 237, 240f, 251f, 254f, 275, 280, 341) (cf. 10.52, 55, 94; Note 2). The term is inherited from formal grammars but its original technical sense by no means applies to ordinary world knowledge. Compare 'n-tuples of sentences' where we could say 'several sentences' (SD 79f, 124).

15. For this reason, not much is made of the 'distinction' 'between coherence and cohesion', the latter designating the 'specific grammatical manifestations underlying semantic coherence' (SD 149). In Halliday and Hasan (1976) and Halliday (1985), 'lexical cohesion' absorbs some of 'coherence', but much is left out (cf. 9.93, 95f).

16. The usual distinction between 'intension' and 'extension' is that made in 10.40: what something 'means' versus what it 'refers to' . Philosophers have painstakingly devised examples where the distinction is clear, e.g., 'Morning Star' and 'Evening Star', but it is much less so in real discourse.

17. Van Dijk and Kintsch suggest that for short texts, the two coincide (SD 52, 370). If so, then their model might be less urgent for studies of isolated sentences. However, even short texts are normally part of some large-scale (i.e., 'macro') activity (cf. Halliday, IF 372–77).

18. Fodor and Bever's (1965) 'famous click studies' showed people believing clicks to occur at such boundaries, no matter where the clicks actually appeared in the recorded sentences (cf. SD 28, 130). This finding was taken to support Chomsky's theorizing (people consulting deep structures, etc.). Johnson's (1965) findings were, in contrast, taken to support immediate constituent analysis as a processing model. But surely *any* model of syntactic processing has to assume that clause boundaries serve some constructive purpose – though probably not the same purpose as when linguists analyse sentences.

19. Tests were done by Fodor and Garrett (1967) with 'self-embedded sentences' like ' "The pen the author the editor liked used was new" ' versus ' "The pen which the author whom the editor liked used was new" ' and 'the relative pronouns were clearly helpful to subjects' in 'paraphrasing' (SD 29). The findings seem ecologically questionable: people hardly ever utter such sentences precisely because neither type is easy to manage.

20. But van Dijk and Kintsch also claim that 'a cognitive model' can work on 'the principle' that 'the interpretation of composite expressions is a function of the interpretation of component expressions' (SD 112). The claim certainly does not hold for *their* model, in which the interpretation of text meaning adds, restructures, or discards local meanings (cf. 10.49).

21. 'The speaker's intention as expressed by the text or reasonably ascribed to the

speaker by the hearer' 'will play a normative role' here (SD 193). But this statement offers no principled solution until we have empirical tests to discover the status of a 'speaker's intention'.

22. By a very exact measuring of 'latency', i.e., of the time between the presenting of an item and the test subject's reaction, 'priming' is a good tactic for telling what's active in the mind (cf. SD 22, 24, 51, 129, 227, 232, 320, 385). Priming tests 'flatly contradict intuition' by showing that 'when people read a lexically ambiguous word, they retrieve all the meanings, contextually appropriate or not', then make 'a choice' and 'deactivate' the 'inappropriate' ones (SD 33) (cf. Swinney 1979; Kintsch and Mross 1985; Kintsch 1988, 1989).

23. Aside from this issue of argument overlap, the earlier version is faulted for being 'too structural rather than strategic'; for lacking the 'concept of situation model' to 'separate textual processes from the use' 'of information conveyed by the text'; for 'bypassing' 'knowledge use' 'with statistical approximations'; and for falling back on 'intuition' to decide what 'superordinate units' are 'chosen from current input' (SD 4, x, 44).

24. Out of loyalty to van Dijk's earlier work (e.g., 1977), SD usually calls these 'macrorules'. Yet they are precisely *not* rules, but strategies in the very senses SD stresses (cf. 10.14f; Note 8). So I use only the term 'macrostrategies' that is eventually substituted anyway (SD 267).

25. Van Dijk and Kintsch say at one point that 'besides the properly "semantic" situation model, we also need a *communicative context model*, representing speech acts and their underlying intentions', but they do not 'further explore' the idea (SD 338). Perhaps we just need a broader concept of what is 'semantic' (Beaugrande 1988b).

26. Far less often, people 'remember the text but have no situation model', e.g., in religious 'chanting'; but usually 'long-term memory is poor' in such cases, because 'retrieval' works best with the aid of a 'larger structure' or 'system', e.g., those in which 'situation models' 'tend to be embedded' (SD 341, 346).

27. Since 'language merely provides the cues' about 'what sort of model needs to be constructed', 'logic' is 'not an appropriate formalism for representation of language' (SD 341) (cf. 10.14, 36, 41; 12.17). Earlier, van Dijk (e.g., 1977) placed great faith in logic, but in those days his work was not empirical and he didn't analyse much extended text.

28. The distinction between 'super' and 'macro' (originating with van Dijk, e.g., 1980) is too fine for comfort. The prefixes are very similar in meaning, and the entities are closely linked, in that 'macrostructures' can be 'the semantic content for the terminal categories' of 'superstructures' (SD 189). And in fact, SD falls back on the term 'schematic structure' alongside 'superstructure' (SD 16, 55, 57, 104, 189, 206, 222, 239, 241, 245, 251, 275, 336, 369), though this too has drawbacks, because 'the term schema is much more general' (SD 236).

29. Bartlett's results were controversial because he used 'an American Indian story' at a time when psychology had no interest in cultural differences among 'narrative schemas' (cf. SD 238).

30. Halliday, for whom 'there are no regions of language in which style does not reside' (EF 112) (cf. 9.102), would resist the views that 'style' is a matter of 'variation in surface structure', and 'rhetoric' a matter of 'grafting' 'on to surface structure' (SD 94, 235). And these views don't fit SD's own stress on the interaction among levels.

31. Propp (1928) believed story episodes (he called them ' "functions" ') to be 'fixed and limited, but later investigators noted their flexible nature' (SD 55). Compare Note 32.

32. As I have shown in detail (Beaugrande 1982), the real issue in the debate was not whether 'narrative structures have processing reality' (cf. SD 55) (no one denied they do), but whether they can properly be called a 'grammar'. In the research literature, terms and notations were borrowed from transformational grammar in empty, arbitrary, and inconsistent ways.

33. In a study where 'young children' were to describe 'pictures which told a story' but which were sometimes presented 'in scrambled order' (Poulson, Kintsch, Kintsch and Premack 1979), the 'resolution' was recalled much better from 'the proper order', since 'depicted states' are 'not very exciting' as such. The 'crucial role' of mental 'imagery' in processing is acknowledged (SD 336, 52, 113, 311, 354, 360, 364), but its relation to language is not clarified.

34. The experimenters were careful to separate this 'effect' from effects due to 'serial position', 'frequency of content words, rated importance of the sentence', and 'the number of words in sentences' or of 'propositions' and 'new arguments' (SD 59). Such meticulous work indicates the enormous labour in testing predictions about one specific factor.

35. Although this model is *not* inspired by phonology (cf. 12.31f), some well-structuredness is borrowed from lower levels over to higher, simply because psychological research studied letters and words before sentences, and whole texts or discourses only quite recently. Elsewhere, van Dijk and Kintsch remark that 'most studies' 'discussed here were concerned with reading, but similar arguments could be made about listening' (SD 22n) (cf. 12.33). The literature on 'list-learning' 'suggests an acoustic coding bias' is the 'easiest', though not the 'necessary' tactic (cf. Glanzer *et al.* 1981) (SD 354) (cf. 4^{13}; 10.94).

36. Current 'models' of perception postulate 'a place' 'where evidence' (in units called 'logogens or word demons', etc.) 'regarding a word is accumulated' (e.g., Morton 1969; Selfridge and Neisser 1960) (SD 25). 'Input activates in parallel a number of letter and word' units or 'features' which can 'both inhibit and facilitate' 'recognition'.

37. 'Control experiments ruled out the possibility that the congruence was not a true memory phenomenon, but the result of plausible reconstruction' (SD 353). Research on text memory has not always been so careful on this point.

38. In much research, 'production' appeared as 'reproduction', e.g., in 'recall experiments' (SD 261). The recalled text was insouciantly taken as direct evidence of comprehension and memory, not as an entity shaped by the tasks of production (cf. Beaugrande 1984a). Recently, 'protocol analysis' of material uttered by test subjects 'thinking aloud' while they are performing a task has become a highly regarded instrument (cf. SD 179, 226f, 263, 285, 361f), but the full complexities of text production have not been appreciated there either.

39. Miller *et al.* are criticized for relying on 'transformational generative grammars', Hayes and Flower for underestimating the 'complexity' of 'planning' and 'neglecting the issue of levels' (SD 263, 289, 293).

40. The classic example of the ' "garden path" sentence', which 'sets up expectations' and then breaks them, is ' "The old man the boats" ' (SD 29; cf. SD 31, 36).

41. This machine shows that 'a word needs to be seen only for 30–40 msec [milliseconds] for a full semantic activation', although 'responses' take '500–1500 msec'; 'fixations during reading typically last for about 200–300 msec', since 'a lot more' is going on there besides 'word identification' (SD 26).

42. The term 'productions' was coined by Newell and Simon (1972) for a 'condition-action' (or 'antecedent-consequent') pair – a misleading term, but by now well entrenched by high quality work in artificial intelligence (e.g., Langley, Bradshaw, Simon and Zytkow 1987), and used in SD as well, 'no

other formalism being nearly as completely worked out' (SD 97, 69, 95f, 371).
In the arithmetic problems, the 'condition' is a 'constellation of sets' and the
action is to 'compute the unknown quantity' (SD 371).

43. The job won't be easy. Van Dijk and Kintsch are dissatisfied with 'degenerate,
     prepared school problems', where 'the macro-operation of generalization'
     'strips the names and objects of all individuality and treats them merely' as
     'sets' – but admit this is a 'crucial' 'abstraction' for all 'formal reasoning'
     (SD 370f). Besides, if 'embedded' into 'a longer text' with 'irrelevant
     information' (e.g., 'an interesting story'), 'word problems' might be 'made
     much more difficult' and 'task-specific macrostrategies' might be devised
     running 'counter to normal reading'.

44. Van Dijk and Kintsch worry about having 'a vacuous supertheory that explains
     everything' and thus 'nothing' (SD 27). 'The problem is that people' do 'diverse
     and contradictory things: indeed', 'everything and its opposite, given the right
     conditions' (cf. 12.52). So the theory must be 'complex but not arbitrary' and
     must 'specify the precise conditions'.

Chapter 11

Peter Hartmann[1]

11.1 Though rarely available in English, the work of Peter Hartmann has been highly influential in the re-establishment of linguistics in Germany after World War II. To present his ideas, I shall translate from the German, contending with his dense, complicated style and his meticulous, specialized use of terms.[2] His book *Theory of Language Science* (*Theorie der Sprachwissenschaft*)[3] (1963a) offers 'not an introduction to the science of language nor to the history, representatives, methods, and results of linguistics, but a fairly abstract *theoretical* argument, intended to be useful for theory, i.e., for a scientific treatment and estimation of the concern for language' (TS 3) (cf. 6.1).

11.2 Hartmann's resolve to cover language study at large does not serve the ambition – detectable in the surveys of Saussure, Bloomfield, Pike, Chomsky, Firth, and Halliday – of validating the scientific credentials of one particular approach over others. Instead, he is the most balanced, syncretistic, neutral, and thorough of all the theorists in my survey. I thus saved him for the last because he organizes and sums up the issues in the widest way. Throughout his career, he advocated 'a truly encompassing theory of linguistics' to 'take account of *all* forms of concern for language', with 'scientific linguistics' 'situated among them and distinguished from them' (TS 5, 13). Though his overview is 'just a specimen' of that 'wide-ranging' 'project' and indicates 'only some basic trends', he is convinced that 'higher theoretical insight can best be achieved if the framework is chosen to be *as wide as possible*', probing 'the various statements about language in all cultures' (TS 5, 50, 6) (cf. 6.20). 'The goal in seeking a theory of linguistics is to subject to theoretical scientific contemplation the procedures which engender and control all concern for language and hence all statements about this object' (TS 7, 168).

11.3 Because 'representations of the object phenomenon' 'can differ according to the direction of research', we should use 'more than just linguistics to characterize the work of the language researcher' (TS 167, 136; cf. Kainz 1960; Ullmann 1957) (cf. 12.35). 'The linguist must recognize that his manner of research pursues just one mode among others, and only in

combination with them constitutes the totality of knowledge about language'
(TS 5f). We might hope not merely to 'characterize and understand
linguistics', but to 'further it as a group' of 'research methods' whose
'scientific quality' depends on 'discovering the specialness of its object' and
on '"being explicit about the primary data on which our statements are
based; these data are human utterances"', which '"in every instance"'
'"must be interpreted by a linguist, with the unavoidable interposition of a
subjective element, and they must be related to the context and situation
from which they sprang"' (TS 6, 160f; cf. Reid 1960: 23) (cf. 1.9; 12.24).

11.4 Being **'scientific'** is depicted as 'demanding insights', 'producing
knowledge', pursuing a 'concern for formality', and 'attempting to
interrelate different modes of characterization within a determining context'
(TS 3f, 159). 'The word **science** [*Wissenschaft*] designates the activity that
results in knowledge [*Wissen*], the knowledge produced, and the totality of
such knowledge' (TS 13f). To decide 'what kind of knowledge science
seeks', we should follow John Dewey (1910) rather than Plato by stipulating
that 'science must have a genuine purpose', and that 'the knowledge must be
operationally usable' for 'analysing, constructing, concluding, etc.' (TS 15f)
(cf. 12.58). Also, the knowledge must be *'intersubjective*, i.e., usable' for
'everyone who proceeds according to it' (TS 16, 19, 59, 157). So the
'cognitive' 'side' should be 'democratic' in respect to the 'practical side': that
the 'practice' be 'accessible to everybody' (TS 16). Equally broad is 'the
main requirement' proposed for 'science': 'to achieve all that can be known
about a field; to strive for a totality of possible determinations; to notice as
many facts as possible; to vary the standpoint' and 'intention' 'in hopes of a
later' 'epistemological' 'unification'; and 'to work through the manifestations
in as many directions as possible' (TS 129f). 'The history of language
research shows that progress comes from shifting and enriching the
problematics' (cf. 12.1).

11.5 Hartmann's 'deliberations' belong to 'second-order science' or
'metascience', 'the science of language science' (TS 3, 168). As signalled by
'the prefix "meta-"', this domain has 'primary sciences as objects', including
their 'elements, forms, structures, and methods' (TS 3).[4]. Within this
'"higher" order of generality and abstractness', where 'naiveté' is 'reduced',
there 'arises a new level of criteria for forms' of 'elements, procedures, and
relations' (TS 3f, i.r.). 'What might otherwise occur "unconsciously" or
come about "on its own"' is made 'the object of treatment'. 'A second-
order science' can attain 'higher-level formal and controlling insights' from
'a scientific reflection and deliberation on a particular science' – here,
'a theory of what people do when they work in linguistics' (TS 168, 4f)
(cf. 11.84; 12.36).

11.6 'Such a theory can assist the whole circle of research directions'
involving the 'functioning of language' (TS 168). The 'linguist assumes the
role of an important member of research communities' when 'research
moves from registering data' over to 'understanding facts according to
transfactual rules or laws' (TS 110) (cf. 11.93, 95f; 12.21). 'Since we don't

know how far the influence of language extends' or 'how much is "only" language', it is 'advisable for research and knowledge to be of the greatest possible breadth' (TS 137f). 'Bound to data and mainly empirical, yet primarily interested in forms and structures', 'linguistics is the neighbour of three general theories dealing with signs, sense, and being' (cf. 12.22). But it is 'self-sufficient thanks to the data placed at its disposition, and probes the structures in statements made about all possible objects by means of signs that have or rather acquire[5] sense' (i.r.). 'To have scientific force', 'linguistics needs a theory as free as possible' of 'extralinguistic theorems' and not subordinated to a 'philosophical or psychological system' (TS 52; cf. TS 135) (cf. 12.10f, 14, 16f).[6]

11.7 'The difficulty for a specifically linguistic theory lies in two facts' (TS 51). 'First, a plausible science of language gains its intersubjectivity and general validity by de-theorizing' its 'object', i.e., by 'dispensing with all categories which are not appropriate to the object or which add something to it'. 'Second, every researcher tends to follow a latent position or "philosophy" that can best be neutralized by moving into the totality of all possible positions'. 'But it would be practicable for only a few people' to 'study all possible standpoints with the intent of transcending and setting them aside', i.e., to 'confront a set of systems (theories) of transcendentals only to totally dissolve their transcendent status' (TS 51f) (cf. 6.5f).

11.8 'Still, this would be a path of **inductive** theory, in accord with the usual maxims of inductive science' 'attending to factual features of phenomena' (TS 52, 120) (cf. 4.7, 67, 76; 5[28]; 6.16f; 7.6f; 11.16, 95f; 12.44). 'In addition, a **deductive** way is permissible for conducting research free of theory, e.g., by immediately recognizing every theory or theoretical entity' and 'allowing only statements that expressly "say nothing" beyond the actual phenomenon' (TS 52) (cf. 6.17, 33). 'Terminology' would be kept 'free of metaphors', and 'every formulation would stipulate how it is meant, e.g., as description, interpretation, explanation', 'evaluation', 'introspection', 'motivation', 'experience', etc. (cf. 11.98)

11.9 A further obstacle lies in 'language being such a familiar, important, and central phenomenon for humans that it is hard to even notice all its basic features and their significance' (TS 21f) (cf. 2.8; 3.1; 4.2; 6.6; 12.1). 'It is a peculiarity of humans to interpret, i.e., to use something to indicate something', and to 'appropriate the world by interpreting it'. 'Humans are highly hermeneutic, dependent on and predisposed toward signs'; and 'human freedom'[7] includes 'using and understanding signs freely within certain limits' (TS 161; cf. TS 62). 'Most human achievements are decisively influenced by the use of language' as 'an interpersonal medium of communication, a practice of using and presenting signs' (TS 262, 20) (cf. 12.22). 'The elements, forms, structures, and practices discoverable in language' are 'open to the most general membership, subsumption, or identity' and thus 'have a normative exemplary value for semiotic procedures in general' (TS 161, 262) (cf. 2.8; 6.53; 12.21).

11.10 'Sign theory' is accordingly situated at 'the beginning of all language study' (TS 70) (cf. 2.8, 30; 6.50–56). 'The sign is a typically human product': it 'arises from an *intent* to mean, indicate, etc.', and the 'communal inventing and using of means for variation and "free" combination are found only among humans' (cf. Hockett 1958: 570ff) (TS 173f) (cf. 3.15; 4.28; 7.35; 8.27; 11.56; 12.12). 'The sign vehicle [*Zeichenträger*]° is the perceptible manifestation' 'bound' to 'the intelligible manifestation' in a 'functive relation' (TS 174) (cf. 11.54; 2.25; 6.25f). Though 'vocal language' 'is the largest and most important area of sign use', 'the broader sense includes every kind of sign' in 'communication', e.g., 'gesture' and 'mimic' (TS 171, 177f) (cf. 2.8; 3.10; 4.25; 5.12, 14; 6.50–55; 8.22; 9.11; 10.86; 11[29]). 'The narrower sense' includes 'only "the linguistic sign"' as 'a special kind' 'not found elsewhere', arising from 'its own constellation of means and intent' (TS 176ff). 'Perhaps influenced by the term "speech"', 'language science' has, 'until recently', 'usually studied' only the narrower domain of signs (TS 178, 171).

11.11 Against Saussure, who treated the sign in dualities like 'sound' and 'idea', or later 'signifier' and 'signified' (cf. 2.25), Hartmann argues that '"four entities must be distinguished: sound and phoneme, abstract meaning and intended referent"' (TS 176n; cf. Lohmann and Bröcker 1942: 2). '"Saussure did not draw this consequence"' of his '"emphasis on the two abstract, inner formal components"', in part because he '"neglected the referential"'. Moreover, 'if a sign can be whatever is not the final purpose of an utterance, then the contents of language elements can be signs' (TS 172). Thus, if 'the signified can be a further sign for another, we can postulate various layers of sign quality: direct and indirect' (TS 172f). 'Generally, however, signs with more than two layers', as in complex 'metaphors', are left 'outside linguistics' and assigned to 'stylistics and literary studies' (cf. 6.54).[9]

11.12 A prominent tactic of Hartmann's is to draw frequent parallels between science and language (cf. 12.48). They both 'depend on symbols' to render 'intersubjective knowledge accessible in a communicative form', and on 'procedures' for 'determining, designating, discussing, and making statements about objects or situations' (TS 17f). 'Science is a language in the sense of being communicable (e.g., in terminology), existing in an intersubjectively valid system of knowledge "above the things" it classifies, and operating with systemic–functional units attained by analysis and usable for basic discourse about something' (TS 146; cf. TS 16, 21n, 159). Therefore we might view 'language science' as 'research attaining inter-subjectively usable insights into structure-creating' 'forms, relations, and functions within a phenomenon that itself consists in utilizing intersubjec-tively valid relations for the purpose of communication' by 'everyone, at all times and places' (TS 165, 16) (cf. 12.48). 'Language science' 'shares the borderline status of language, compelled to run on multiple tracks, combine standpoints and results, and adopt a general outlook', whereby it becomes 'superior to sciences whose object domain has only one sort of manifestation' (TS 168, 39). More specific parallels compare the 'relation' between 'formality' and 'primary science' to the 'relation' between 'grammar' and 'actual language'; and portray a 'theory of language science' as the 'langue' of the linguistic 'parole', i.e., as 'a system of rules for making conclusive or classifying statements about language as the object of research' (TS 4, 135). We'll see more parallels later (cf. 11.40, 44, 46, 48, 69, 87, 93, 98).

11.13 Yet Hartmann notes divergences between science and language too. 'The scientific treatment of language is unlike language in being concerned with the constitution of its object' (TS 146). In 'language', we use a 'relatively unconscious kind' of 'knowledge' and 'communicative value', which is 'more vague and variable' and 'not constructed according to scientific principles', but 'fairly empty' until being 'further interpreted and utilized' (TS 21, 255, 17) (cf. 2.35, 2^{16}; 11.27, 42, 45, 53, 57f; 4.22; 12.49). 'Science *is* a language vis-à-vis its object in the sense of characterizing and foregrounding from a distance, and *has* a language as expression of its activity; its terminology is the language of a special' 'determining context', whereas the 'determining context' of 'ordinary language' is 'not based on some real states or distinctions of things', but 'enables communication and discourse about any correlates whatsoever, including ones unknown as facts' (TS 159) (cf. 11.60f, 63). In this manner, 'language science applies a highly rigorous, intersubjectively valid procedure to a less rigorous intersubjective procedure which is however never without rules' (TS 21, 165). Hence, 'language science represents the scientific analysis of a non-scientific analytic practice' (cf. 3.14; 6.58; 11.64, 86f). 'Language could be aphoristically described as a pre-scientific type of intersubjective knowledge', or as 'a pre-science of everything humans encounter' (TS 17, 21) (cf. 12.24).

11.14 'Science thus needs more than just knowledge of names and terms' and 'approaches language in a non-linguistic, practical way' (asking 'what happens when . . ., what to do such that . . ., why it happens that . . .'), which 'in other domains enables technical construction' or 'prediction' – a possible 'parallel to natural science' (TS 146f) (cf. 2.13; 4.8, 18; 7.11; 9.112; 11.12, 49, 80, 99; 12.11, 58). At one point, Hartmann indeed suggests that 'by virtue of its multilevel object, language science is able to register forms of mental procedure such that they can be largely treated with the exactness of natural science' (TS 39), but he doesn't elaborate.

11.15 'Throughout history, all directions in linguistics have been attempts and results of various representations and transpositions into other' 'determining contexts' 'that were supposed to explain the constitution or so-called essence of language' (TS 159) (cf. 6.22). 'Linguists' can 'suddenly find themselves in the midst of broad and ancient research which can be useful to know', since the same 'issues' still form the 'background' for 'linguistics' (TS 51) (cf. 1.5; 10.1; 12.64). We can 'join with earlier and often more general theories and measure ourselves against them', though they were 'naturally not all equally scientific by today's standards' (TS 51, 5). So Hartmann acknowledges all kinds of prior sources, both 'pre-scientific or scientific', and both 'extralinguistic or linguistic' (TS 113f) (cf. 11.94).[10]

11.16   One major source is 'the ancient concern for language in **philo-sophy**', dealing with 'knowledge in general, correct determination', 'valid conclusion', and so on (TS 8) (cf. 12.11). Here, 'language' is treated as 'a means or indicator', a domain whose 'commonalities' reflect the ' "deeper" causes' presumed to be the 'basis for interpreting language and its manifestations', e.g., 'logical forms' (TS 122, 115) (cf. 12.17f). 'The statements' of 'philosophy' 'should properly be attained via inductive linguistics, but may be usable for more general statements about language', e.g., for 'founding a general grammar' or a 'linguistic semantics' (TS 164, 137). We find many 'statements about constitutive motives [or grounds, *Gründe*] for language in general' and 'speculations about its essence' (TS 32). 'How sense is constituted' is 'the main question' in 'language philosophy' (witness the notion of ' "senseless" ' for 'disallowed, inappro-priate, or misleading combinations of words'), but is an 'antecedent' issue merely 'presupposed' for the 'data' in 'linguistics' (TS 137; cf. TS 185) (cf. 8^7, 8^{14}). Also, linguistics is not expected to search for the 'essence of language' (TS 116, 145f, 156, 165f, 198) (cf. 8.19; 9.1), though Hartmann doesn't exempt the question from other types of inquiry (TS 122, 128, 143, 147, 149, 167) (cf. 11.15, 38f).

11.17   'The attempt to understand the fact of meaning' led philosophers to contemplate 'the origins of language', variously seen as 'a product of human "intellect" ' (Leibniz, Herder, Humboldt), 'divine spirit' (Hamann), or 'natural development' (Darwin) (TS 122, 122n, 114f). The plan to explain language from its 'mutual relation to the intellect [*Geist*]', a 'phenomenon' on 'another level', gave 'impetus' to 'the Romanticist search for knowledge about primordial times', following a 'less historical than philosophical orientation' (TS 122f). Herder (1772) envisioned a 'spontaneously uttered' 'signal' which 'the intellect binds to a judgment of an object and thereby makes into a sign for the object' (TS 123n). Humboldt (1836) believed ' "language was indispensable" ' for the ' "subjective activity" ' of ' "synthesis" ' whereby a ' "representation becomes objective" ' and a ' "concept is formed" ' (TS 123f). The ' "sound" ' of language ' "makes the internal and evanescent activity" ' become ' "external and perceptible to the senses" ' (TS 124n). So in Humboldt's opinion, ' "language is the formative organ of thought" ' and enables it to ' "objectify impressions" ' and ' "attain clarity" ', thanks to the ' "sharpness and unity of the sound" ' (cf. 2.32; 3.3, 10ff; 6.2, 31).

11.18   Humboldt separated 'technical forms', as in 'grammar', from the 'so-called *"inner forms"* ' of a 'semantic and combinatory nature' (TS 124f) (cf. 7^3). The 'inner forms' 'originate in the "intellect of a people" ' in order to 'establish meaningful connections to the world'. Hence, scholars used 'language forms' 'to infer the "world view of the people" ', 'concentrating on semantics' or 'assigning syntactic facts a semantic value' – claiming for instance that 'Amerindians depict a situation as exactly as possible with polysynthetic expressions; that Chinese don't recognize simple connectives and demand more powers of decision'; and so on. Such speculations influenced Sapir's belief in the 'diagnostic value' of 'linguistic forms' for 'the psychology of thought' (SL iii; TS 125n) (cf. 3.10).

11.19 Leo Weisgerber (1929) in turn based his conception of 'native language' or 'mother tongue [*Muttersprache*]' on Humboldt's idea of 'language as "*energeia*" (activity) interacting with 'the intellect', and on Cassirer's (1923–29) 'theory of the artificial sign required to fixate impressions' (compare Saussure's 'arbitrary' sign, cf. 2.28) (TS 126). 'Inner form' was claimed to 'reveal itself' in 'recreating the world as the property of the intellect'. 'Language "radiates its effects on the life of the community"' and is 'hence a "force"' 'in cultural events and historical life', just as 'real as the reality of things'[11] (another idea of Herder's) (TS 126f, 115). 'The world divides into the outer world of "being" [*Sein*], the inner world of human cogitation, and the intermediate world' ('cosmos of content and meeting-ground of forces') wherein 'a mental image [*Bild*] arises from natural conditions and the work of the intellect' (TS 126f, n). ' "The whole human being" is always contained in the sense of signs': 'the sign value unites naming (denotation) with sensation (connotation), reason with feeling, thing with human being' (cf. 8.20). If 'content is not just meanings but "transformative" forms of the effects of language', then 'word formation' and 'sentence patterns' can be 'investigated for their content values', and 'certain cultural forms' can be seen as 'traces of the power of language'. This 'peculiarly German trend', though ominously implying 'one's native language is "better" than a foreign language which allows only "foreign thinking"', 'was welcomed by pedagogy, which is, to an amazing degree, oriented toward tradition and habit, and decisively hostile to structuralism' (TS 127f, 78n) (cf. 4.5f, 85).

11.20 Another major source is '**traditional grammars**', 'the oldest and best-known form of description', circulated 'since antiquity' (TS 63) (cf. 2.5f; 3.36; 4.4f; 6.5; 7.4; 8.5, 7f; 12.7). 'The concept of "grammar" was at first very broad' and 'led to general contemplations of language': 'in various philosophic schools', such as 'the stoics'; 'in rhetoric as the doctrine of language formation', and thus as 'the foundation of later normative grammar'; and finally 'in philology', which 'turned to "outer forms"' and 'coined the first neutral terms like "medium"'. 'The Greek inheritance' with its 'multiple roots' can be traced in 'Latin grammar' and in 'its effects on the Middle Ages' (TS 63f). In contrast, 'Sanskrit grammar' 'consulted only the actual functioning of the language, though from a decidedly normative standpoint, as was also the case among theoreticians of written Arabic: no conscious use of language form without conscious grammar'. 'Sanskrit grammar alone' 'coined artificial and fully unambiguous terms' 'for language practice, i.e., for the combinability of elements', in contrast to the Western drive to 'reinterpret terms' 'in a logical or ontological perspective' (e.g., Harris 1751) (TS 64f; cf. SB 131f) (cf. 2.5; 4.4, 40; 12.17f).

11.21 Like our other theorists, Hartmann notes the drawbacks in earlier grammars (cf. 2.5f; 4.4f; 8.5, 7f; 12.4). They are 'often charged with lacking purity', 'usefulness' and 'unity' (TS 63f, 235). '*Constitution*', i.e., 'operational' 'production', 'was considered a secondary, merely accidental aspect' reserved for 'specialized research' (TS 223, 210). 'Correctness' was attributed to 'grammatical form' rather than, say, to 'units of designation', because 'a feel for formal characteristics and differences arose quite early' among 'grammarians' of 'Greek, Sanskrit, Assyrian, Japanese, and so on', and all these 'model languages demand formal correctness' (TS 210f, 218). 'The Indo-European language type' with its 'formal requirements', although not the only 'godfather', was 'naturally influential' (TS 210n). Many 'grammars' and 'descriptions' were 'oriented toward Latin', which was not too 'disadvantageous because Indo-European languages belong to a shared type' (TS 63ff, 70) (but cf. 2.5; 3.50; 5.24; 6.5; 8.5; 9.25).

11.22 Hartmann dates the modern period of 'language science' proper from the late eighteenth century. He sorts the 'themes' in early 'language science', which failed to adopt a 'metascientific' viewpoint, into five groups in roughly chronological order (cf. 2.5): '(1) language in its peculiarity as a changing and hence "living", "organic" manifestation' (Friedrich Schlegel, Bopp, etc.); '(2) language as a typical phenomenon of human beings' and the 'precondition and expression of thought' (Humboldt); (3) 'the lawfulness in observable changes of language', whereby 'individual manifestations (language forms)' are 'partial, temporally conditioned states, related to others and formed by the same tendencies'; (4) 'the general linguistics' 'proposed by Saussure as research devoted directly to language as such', and still 'fruitful today'; and '(5) subsequent schools staying within the methods of linguistics (phonology, structuralism)' and 'based on theoretical delibera- tions about language' (TS 7f). Scholars in (3) postulated 'sound laws' and 'applied them to etymology' while neglecting the 'language system' in regard to 'word formation and syntax': 'sound analyses reach far back, while syntax was postulated roughly as it is found in historically documented times' (TS 79). Whereas those scholars held 'statements to be incontrovertible as long as they refer' to 'historically attested language forms', scholars in (4) (notably Saussure) argued 'how little' such statements were 'really laws' and 'how little such research takes account of language itself' (TS 7f) (cf. 2.13f, 38).

11.23 These 'themes' demarcate a shifting epistemology, with 'older forms of language science' being **'transcendent'** ('language as a means of knowledge, belief, correct expression', etc.), and 'recent' ones **'immanent'** ('language as a phenomenon of its own – what its nature is and how it works') (TS 54, 9) (cf. 6.6, 8, 10, 20f). 'In contrast' to previous work, 'the modern linguistics of form directly explored the functional mechanism' (TS 32, 139). Saussure's 'new' 'synchronic and descriptive' 'outlook' treated 'forms' as 'indexes of constitution and relation, as well as signals of achieved possibilities' (TS 139n, 218).

11.24 Of course, **'formality** had been emphasized much earlier' (e.g., by Humboldt), and 'the naive linguistics of form is as old as the study of grammar itself' (TS 32) (cf. 11.41, 88). Indeed, 'no study could dispense with formality', though the latter may not be as 'thematic' or 'intentional' as it was in 'the relational linguistics of Saussure, the oppositional linguistics of phonology, or the dependency linguistics of structuralism'. 'Methodological deliberations' were 'relatively difficult and late', 'not until the start of the twentieth century' (TS 55). 'Recent linguistics' became more 'rigorous' and 'theoretical', 'based on insight, not accidental knowledge', and undertook to 'describe languages already described in other ways' (TS 65, 105, 139, 165, 235, 70). 'Progress in linguistics' consisted in 'discovering new objects', 'unknown languages', and 'new forms of description' that 'presupposed a certain theory inquiring into the validity of descriptive methods' (TS 65).

11.25 'The schools of recent linguistics' in the 'descriptive direction' agree that '**difference** is the contribution of any relevant characteristic', and seek 'relations among sounds, sound functions (phonology), forms, form functions (morphology), words, word functions, and so on' (TS 67f; cf. TS 201ff, 216) (cf. 2.26; 11.50, 82; 12.26). This direction 'clearly contrasts with' 'comparative', 'unifying', and 'totalizing' ones (TS 68). 'Recent' work 'bypasses the definition of totality and yet delivers the structures that compose the "totality"' (cf. 11.95, 98). According to the 'underlying epistemological theory' ('discussed by Hjelmslev'), an entity is 'seen only in confrontation and relation with others' 'with which it tends to co-occur' (cf. 5.20; 6.44f). 'The language forms being investigated exist only to indicate relations'. Here Hartmann hails 'one genuine theoretical and methodological change' that was 'not dictated empirically' (TS 68f).

11.26 Despite their 'divergences and controversies', 'the schools of Geneva, Prague, Copenhagen, and so on' were 'close in goals and methods' (TS 69). Their 'quarrels' were chiefly about 'the *relevance* of emphases and the *purity* of description, i.e., the categories being applied'. In 'the Saussurian "system"', 'the basic structure' emerged from 'the tasks, possibilities, and necessities of elements' (cf. 2.27). '"Langue" was circumscribed' with 'the question: what can occur as factual language ("parole") and yet enable and control it as a system?' (cf. 2.20; 12.36). 'In order not to transcend the phenomenon' (cf. 11.23), 'descriptive linguistics did not move beyond technical functions'. 'The epistemological position that the single entity is registered through the multiplicity[12] surrounding it was joined by the methodological position that a phenomenon may be described only from within its own domain'. An extremely 'strict' consequence was to 'consider meaning' an 'extralinguistic' 'effect of expression signs' and to 'leave it aside' (cf. 4.15, 26; 5.61f; 7.56f). Yet this 'position' will not serve for 'discussing the total phenomenon of language', whose 'peculiar property' is its 'relation to the aspect of sense' (Hjelmslev's '"content plane"', cf. 6.24, 29, 42) (TS 69f) (cf. 11.65).

11.27 'The special nature' of 'linguistic treatment lies in demonstrating 'issues' or 'structures' that 'need not be grasped by non-scientific acceptance [*Hinnehmen*] nor become conscious during the naive production of language' (TS 162, 72n) (cf. 11.13, 42, 45, 53, 57f; 12.49). 'The major practice of language research consists in isolating, characterizing, and determining language manifestations according to issues that are structurally latent in the handling of language, yet relevant for constitution': the 'constant forms within the functioning' (TS 167, 163f) (cf. 11.31f; 12.54). Since 'linguistic formalization is an observational procedure' that 'emphasizes forms where none would be noticed by a different method', 'the observer regularly discovers more forms than the language user' (the 'participant' in Pike's scheme, cf. 5.16f) (TS 132; cf. TS 227; SB 133) (cf. 12.49). 'In the observer system', 'even the occurrence of manifestations is described in abstraction from realization', including whatever 'other aspects are involved for participants' (TS 131). 'In general practice, in contrast, forms (structures) are obeyed, but not as conscious formalizing' (TS 132). So 'scientific treatment' 'makes an issue out of functional forms that are normally not an issue, and foregrounds them' with the aid of 'specialized' 'concepts and terms' (TS 162f) (cf. 12.38).

11.28 'A methodological problem arises: the systematic, "automatic" methods of formalizing linguistic objects can lend an "unnaturally" high importance to formal items in expressions', until 'the analyst' 'readily believes that formality is the "essential" and that form is the vehicle of all discourse' (TS 131) (cf. 12.49). Yet a 'formal level of representation' can be 'language only in a derivative, expanded sense', containing merely 'forms of formality'; the 'terms cannot be freely applied elsewhere' (TS 158). Still, 'it is understandable and justifiable' that the 'scientific' 'interest' of 'formal linguistics' 'isolated and objectified' 'forms' and postulated 'new properties' resting on 'basic features abstracted away from real material' (TS 208, 263, i.r.) (cf. 12.54). 'Though the features emerge only during a certain kind of analysis, they can clarify *the ways and forms whereby language functions*' (TS 263).

11.29 'The forms of language' have three 'indexical values' for 'the formation of expression', namely to 'indicate': (1) 'a mode of proceeding' in '*constitution*'; (2) 'a basic precondition' in '*relation*', and (3) 'potentiality', 'regularity', and 'freedom' in '*possibility*' (TS 209). 'Forms in languages' have been 'conceived as manifestations that can change in respect to others they co-occur with' – whence 'the conception of form as transformation [*Abwandlung*]', as 'accident within the domain of non-accident' (TS 208) (cf. 2.13, 6.16). Thus, 'discussions' of 'substance and accident, content and form, inner and outer' reflect 'two kinds of classification' that are both 'interdependent and yet opposed': 'for *constants* and for *variables*' (TS 208f, 211). Hartmann proposes a somewhat Hjelmslevian four-part scheme of 'relative instantiations': (1) 'between constant and another constant (e.g., between word-stems)'; (2) 'between constant and variable (e.g., between word stem and suffixes)'; (3) 'between variable and constant (e.g., between endings and the cases, persons', etc. they signal)'; and (4) 'between variable and another variable (e.g., in paradigms)' (TS 212f) (cf. 6.25, 29, 33f). The first is 'represented in the lexicon', and the other three in 'word-formation and grammar'.

11.30 For Hartmann, 'the **content-form** distinction is largely given in language' and is thus 'legitimate' (TS 212) (but cf. 6.24, 47, 50; 9.38).

'Befitting the demand for the greatest possible variety of standpoints' (cf.
11.2), 'the linguist' must 'deal with form and content' in 'every manifestation
of language', even where 'only one side' appears to 'dominate'; we 'always
need to determine how far form "carries" content and what kind' (TS 131).
Nevertheless, 'chiefly form is encountered in language science proper, firstly
because it alone *emerges* from comparable entities that hold manifestations
together; secondly because scientific insight is directed to *what remains the
same* within all factual change' and can thus be 'reliably communicated and
intersubjectively used'; and thirdly 'because analysis' 'does not collect
undivided manifestations, but *systematizes* them'. In this framework,
'innerlinguistic forms are *facts*'; and 'formal inventories' are 'more constant
than the non-forms they must enter to occur within a phenomenon' (TS 131,
163f) (cf. 12.54).

11.31 Yet Hartmann acknowledges the wide variety of 'claims about
how language unites the semantic content with the non-semantic form'
(TS 130). He conjectures that 'form classes are more stable over time' 'than
meanings' (cf. 11.66), and that 'the semantic domain' is complicated by
'connotative differences in content' and by the 'non-factual, but projected
sameness' in 'metaphor and analogy' (TS 205, 119, 28). He depicts 'forms'
to be 'relatively constant characteristics' whose 'principled invariance'
'guarantees intersubjective usability' and 'a relative permanence of languages
as communicative systems used by communities' (TS 132, 25). Against the
backdrop of '*invariance* needed' for 'utterances to be understood by several
partners', '*variance*' appears when 'different kinds of things are combined'
(TS 25). Evidently, both form and content can be seen as either constant or
variable, depending on how we collate them (cf. 6.24; 11[18]).

11.32 A related problem is where to draw the line around forms. They
'can be "asemantic" only as long as they are kept distinct from the
motivation of discourse', and even then they can have an 'instrumental
semantic value' (TS 132) (cf. 5.62). 'When we evaluate a formal, asemantic
or combinatory symbolic mechanism, a semanticizing usually occurs,
because language is generally used that way' (TS 244). And 'motivation' is
not so easily 'left aside by science' or 'linguistics' (TS 221, 137). 'A structural
description may, for certain limited purposes, work with just one aspect'
such as 'formal inventories', as 'Hjelmslev tried to show' (TS 130). But
'linguistics as a whole cannot ignore the semantic-content side', 'because the
use of language in real events can't be separated from motivations' which,
on 'the level of sense', may be 'more significant than structural issues' – one
reason why 'structuralism failed to attain pure formality' (TS 130, 221).

11.33 None the less, scholars have hoped for a 'handbook of linguistic
statements, formulated as formally as possible' and 'prescribed for valid
work in linguistics' (TS 136) (cf. 5.2, 12ff; 7.7; 8[3]). 'Linguistics' might be the
model for 'formalization in all sciences' if it attained a 'highly accurate
division between form and non-form' (TS 136f) (cf. 2.8; 5.7; 6.9f; 8.16; 11.6,
12; 12.21, 49). 'Examples include: constancy and relevance of grammar
versus innumerable possibilities of expression'; 'constancy of logical

syllogisms versus variable content of the premises'; 'formality in transcendental philosophy' (compare 'Kant's a priori "before all perception"'); 'formal displacements in the metaphoric' (compare 'recent English philosophy since Wittgenstein'); and 'numerical and relational modes in mathematics' (TS 136n). And the claim in recent physics that 'the electron is nothing but its properties' can be compared to Hjelmslev's vision of the 'language element' as 'nothing but the intersection of bundles of dependences' (TS 137n; cf. TS 62n, 251, 256; SB 131) (cf. 6.45, 62).

11.34 One way to promote formality might be a '**mathematicized** treatment of language' (TS 52) (cf. 4.21; 12.15). 'Mathematics' is the mode that most 'appears to be free from standpoints and universally applicable, and to have a terminology and determinacy that falsify the least' (TS 160). 'Mathematics' 'works exclusively with relations that can be calculated, i.e., treated, described, and reconstructed via commensurate operations within the framework of the multiplicity of quantities'. 'Almost every manifestation' 'can be subjected to quantitative manipulation' in terms of 'form or documentation', including 'language' and 'many products of the human use of symbols' (TS 160f; cf. TS 155).

11.35 On the other hand, 'mathematics applies only partially to language', chiefly to 'what is constant' and 'documented' in 'a fixed form or an unambiguous concept', and thus not to 'matters of a continually varying nature, such as assignment, naming, value', 'hermeneutic interpretation', and 'claims about identity' (TS 167, 160, 163, 262, 264).[13] 'In respect to' the 'freedom' of sign use (cf. 11.9, 29, 58), 'quantification is largely "powerless" and irrelevant' (TS 161). Also, 'statistical questions about how many, when, where, can seldom be answered exactly, even though natural limits obtain in principle for the structural givens of the reality of language' (TS 160). Even such 'quantities' as 'sets of similar elements' 'are not decisive' (TS 161). 'Instead, language consists' (1) of '*mixed sets* from several levels at once, e.g., the semantic and the operational'; and (2) of '*domains*, e.g., of validity, appropriateness, and membership within a subjectively variable radius, such that people (a) can talk imprecisely, without addressing the essence (or the "*Ding an sich*"), (b) can talk in detachment from and outside the phenomenon, without considering science and its characteristics, and (c) can characterize things in idiosyncratic and subjective ways, with individualized expressions' (TS 161f, 166) (cf. 11.60f; 12.41). 'Semantic classes have a hermeneutic value, range, and applicability' that can 'always be widened or narrowed' (TS 205) (cf. 11.57). For all these reasons, 'mathematics cannot be the ideal method'.

11.36 Moreover, Hartmann does not favour the solution of 'tying language to **logic**' (TS 29) (cf. 12.17). He does conjecture that 'the units whereby language transcends the merely physical result from a logical capacity'. But he reminds us of the 'contrast between linguistic' and 'logical form' (cf. Flew [ed.] 1951–53) (TS 138n). 'Logical forms need not coincide with forms of sense or meaning in language', e.g., when 'uniform expressions' in language 'mask logical' 'differences' (TS 261, 138n). 'Logic' is limited to inquiring 'how far an expression has sense or meaning when investigated "only from a grammatical standpoint"' (as in 'the Vienna Circle', Carnap, Wittgenstein, Neurath, etc.) or to using 'syllogisms' to 'draw correct conclusions without knowing what one is talking about'; and so on (TS 137n, 145) (cf. 6.56, 64).

11.37 Language science faces the further 'difficulty' of 'finding a method' that can 'unite the factual with the necessary' (TS 121). When we renounce 'seeing language manifestations as effects of logical grounds', we must seek 'general and necessary traits *in the language facts themselves*'. These traits can be 'taken as structural a prioris or as the most general structural laws "in" factual manifestations', and can be 'designated with concepts like sociality, differentiation, reference, determination, identity, assignment, arrangement, elementarity', 'combination, complication, complementation', '(in)variance, opposition', 'abstraction, applicability', 'translatability', 'redundance', and so on (TS 121, 22). 'Ideally', these would 'emerge from the commonalities of specific facts in all languages' (TS 121). Though 'science can use everything in the representation of facts that contributes to comprehending the occurrence of the manifestations in question', 'a general method' does not 'ask about functional forms in realizations of language', 'but about typical ways of functioning' in 'the phenomenon linguists must address' (TS 166, 164).

11.38 In 'method and terminology we should distinguish between registering language as a phenomenon and scientifically treating' 'language as an object' (TS 139) (cf. 12.58). The '**phenomenon**' appears in 'its *suchness*', whereas the '**object**' is 'treated' in its '*otherness*' (TS 140). The 'pure phenomenon' is 'not linked to others, either proximate or remote'; it is 'characterized with its own means' (TS 142). 'Understanding is attained if we can relate our terms to certain states of affairs within the phenomenon'. This direction was pursued in 'language philosophy' (e.g., by Heidegger 1959) using 'subjective methods' (TS 142, 144). 'Statements' were 'usually metaphoric on purpose', e.g., '"language speaks"' (TS 142f). 'Words of the language' were 'interrogated for their deeper, ambivalent sense', wherein language should 'declare itself'. Hoping thus that 'the phenomenon would reveal itself,' philosophers took 'the basic stance that the original experience should not be disturbed by dividing or combining' it, or by 'forcing language into predecided representations' (TS 142f, n) (cf. 6.4; 11.87). We must now consider whether such 'strivings for a trans-scientifically true essence', such a 'passive attitude waiting for the self-revelation of things', are to be 'dismissed' as 'mere thought-experiment' or 'Romantic enthusiasm', or are a 'result of the same justified striving for pure experience that is also at the base of all science' (TS 143f). Although the 'scientific linguist' wants to 'control or prevent' 'the danger' of 'hearing one's own thoughts', 'science' can 'investigate this approach' in order to explore 'what happens when so-called language-internal characteristics' are 'taken seriously' (TS 144, 142) (cf. 11.5, 84; 12.36). This strategy could meet the 'criticism' of 'scientific attitude' 'for limiting the experiential aspect' (TS 144).

11.39 The reproach that 'science covers up the phenomenon with classifications in order to "put it aside" has no force because the classifications never need to cover the whole phenomenon, but only to bring to awareness a partial domain or characteristic' (TS 144). 'Language science need hardly be concerned to state what language 'actually', 'really' is "in its essence"', but can still 'take note of such statements to judge the plausibility of its own statements pursuing a more limited intention' (TS 144f) (cf. 8.19; 9.1; 11.15f). The 'image' of 'language' 'in linguistics' is after all *'incomplete'* because it 'must allow the right set or combination of features' to 'emerge from the progress of research and insight' 'by means of *successive correction through new findings*' (cf. 12.63).

11.40 In contrast to ' "language as **phenomenon**" ', ' "language as **object**" is treated by being interpreted, analysed, characterized', and 'factored' (TS 147).[14] It is 'reasonable' to 'treat language ' "only as an object" ' if 'the cited characteristics allow a truly scientific exploration of language' and a 'foregrounding of formal features' (TS 149, 162). 'Further links' can be established' by means of 'comprehension', 'attribution', 'confrontation with other knowledge', and 'identification' of 'the whole and the parts' (TS 147–50). Again, we do 'not encompass the whole phenomenon, but the manifestations do receive formal names; and the foregrounded structures do belong to the phenomenon' (TS 162). Hartmann sees another parallel, namely to the way 'language' 'assigns symbols and arranges by means of an arsenal of classes (vocabulary)' (TS 149) (cf. 11.12).

11.41 We can also distinguish between 'structural' and 'non-structural' approaches, where '**structure**' is 'a term for a collection' of 'forms in a limited phenomenal domain', or for 'a similarity of types'; 'no grouping is without structure' (TS 141, 49, 154, 45).[15] 'Higher-level formality' requires a 'shift from available achieved facts over to the structures that can be grasped in them' (TS 4). The 'non-structural' mode (the 'main one in earlier language science') 'registers', 'accepts', 'interprets' in 'general terms' (e.g., 'expression, activity'), and 'analyses' into 'units of chiefly semantic kinds' (e.g., 'meanings, motifs') (TS 141). The 'structural' mode (the main one in modern 'linguistics') 'analyses formally' and 'interprets' according to a 'formal typology'. In between, 'traditional grammar' has its 'formality' 'distributed across several levels, each with its own structure'; these can now be subjected to 'a rigorous structural treatment' to 'decide whether or not structure and grammar correspond' and thus how far 'the grammatical analysis was structurally adequate' (TS 235, 237) (cf. 2.6; 6.49; 7.4, 75; 8.38; 11.88, 90; 12.7).

11.42 'The structure' of 'sets of signs' in an 'expression' can be attributed to *'obeying rules of formation'* that 'constitute a higher-order system' (TS 33, 97, 222). 'Insights into structure' are 'attained by a survey of discoverable forms and functions in such a system' (TS 97). The 'rule-governed' 'practice' of 'language' appears in the 'occurrence of an element with something else' and in 'the regularity' of 'constituting sign sequences' (TS 225). ' "**Rules**" ' is 'the typical designation' for such 'observable interdependence' and hence a tool for 'description' (TS 225, 148). Just as 'people speak without noticing grammar', they also 'follow rules without knowing them' (TS 148) (cf. 11.13, 27; 12.49). So 'rules' may function with 'zero consciousness' and no 'actual motivation', in contrast to the 'semantic consciousness' about what is to be 'communicated' and 'achieved' (TS 34, 223). Still, Hartmann concurs with Wittgenstein that 'rules of language are ways to use language' (TS 222f) (cf. 8.47; 12.36).

11.43 'A language expression is multiply structured', and its 'usefulness for communicative purposes rests on simultaneous utilization of all the structures encountered in it' (TS 234f). Hartmann lists 'four main structures': in the 'arrangement' 'within a spoken chain'; in 'the dependence between elements' 'uniting in groups'; in 'the semantics of the element' whose 'components' 'are already signs'; and in 'the semantics of the expression' 'being a sign, a combined totality formed, used, and understood' as such (cf. 9.34, 37; 11.72). 'The circle of possible objects' is 'open wherever new objects can emerge from a new formation of structures', or wherever we can 'discover objects with a new structure' (TS 18). Hartmann suggests that 'the smaller the structural sectors to which we are limited, the easier it is to find commonalities'; 'the more we move toward the total extent of the text, the harder' this becomes (TS 236) (but cf. 12.39). This 'proportion' holds for research in both 'morphology' and 'syntax' (TS 236f). In contrast, 'the full consideration of semantic coherence leads toward powerfully individualized stylistic objects, whose comparability diminishes' as 'the extent of the evidence' increases (but see 12.39). Here, too, content seems less constant than form (cf. 11.29ff).

11.44 Structures appear both in the research and in its objects (cf. 11.12). 'Language science proves to be structural research about an object that itself works by means of continual structuring' (TS 45) (cf. 11.12). 'Structure' is 'the possibility of possibilities', 'the image of possible constitutions' (TS 223f). 'Structuration is the epistemological product' of 'scientific factoring', whereas 'grammaticality' and 'grammar' are the 'product' of a 'historical structuration according to naively discovered relations' (TS 237, 233). In contrast, 'the structure of an expression, in each case, is a fact of "parole"', in that it 'can be done wrong without causing damage'; 'right consciousness' is unaffected by 'occasional distortions of the system' (TS 49) (cf. 7.12).

11.45 'The relative firmness of structure' lies in being 'realized relatively automatically as semantic sentence components' (TS 49) (cf. 10.11). 'Structures can remain unconscious' and be 'followed' through mere 'imitation' (TS 44n; cf. TS 26) (cf. 11.13, 27, 42, 53, 57f). Indeed, 'treatment' is more likely to be 'objective' and 'free of interpretation' when 'the object is normally situated below the threshold of consciousness' (SB 134). 'Structural research' can show 'necessities' without involving 'the motivation for people using elements' (TS 45n; cf. TS 132, 158, 221) (cf. 11.32, 42, 76, 79; 2.28). We 'think of structures only when discrepancies are consciously *noticeable*'; otherwise, 'we do things the way we know how, and do not ask how we *can* know' (cf. 9.6).

11.46 'Language science' therefore pursues 'research intending to gain knowledge about structures inherent to language, independent of time', 'place, and space' (TS 20, 28) (cf. 12.43). Correspondingly, 'as a manifestation of signal values', 'language' itself 'proceeds by suspending (neutralizing) characteristic differences of the designated' 'physical' 'world' (TS 29). It 'suspends space in the typical unity of the name'. It 'suspends time' in the 'conceptuality of class formation'. And it 'suspends motion' in the ' "rigid" form of the idea or the concept'.

11.47 Time is highly relevant here because, due to the 'relation' between 'vehicle and sense' (or ' "signifiant" and "signifié" '), 'the sign' can be depicted as 'a duality bound in **simultaneity**' (TS 175) (cf. 5[16]). 'Simultaneity' also 'applies to the fact that elements' in both 'systems', 'the virtual ("langue") and the actual ("parole"), are given' at once (TS 91) (cf. 12.39). The idea of 'simultaneously available possibilities in the virtual system' (TS 91, 95, 96) is familiar from 'Saussure's *état*' (state), postulated as 'a research category' for 'systemic linguistics' in order to 'detach itself from all aspects of non-simultaneity, like historical development' (TS 91) (cf. 2.40). But the idea applies to the actual system in more complex and less familiar ways. In addition to the 'spatial, temporal relations among sign vehicles in a sequence', Hartmann postulates 'simultaneous', 'non-spatial, non-temporal relations among sense units' (TS 214, 183, 91f) (cf. 9.34, 48, 103; 12.33). 'The speaker' 'converts' the mode wherein 'sense elements are with and for each other' into a mode wherein the 'vehicles are one after another'; 'the hearer' goes the other way, working 'serially' in 'small steps, often in twos', up to 'the simultaneously conscious determination' (TS 93, 176; cf. TS 27, 43) (cf. 7.83; 10.81, 85; 12.57). When 'thoughts are formulated', 'the total intention comes first (like a bridge), and then comes the local filling and shaping'; when 'thoughts are understood', the 'reverse' occurs (TS 92n). In the latter case, 'the sequence is given and needs little notice, except when unclear or erroneous; the hearer "assumes" that the chosen form will work for communicating the thoughts' (TS 92fn). Still, this 'simultaneity of sense relations is only a *functional mechanical background* for the relations being formed', and a perspective for '*insight*' into 'relations outside time and space' (TS 93).

11.48 In a comparable vein, 'language science' is required to 'seek **immateriality** in structures of relations' (TS 20, 19, 45) (cf. 2.17, 20).[16] Only 'by accounting for immaterial modes of constitution can science attain intersubjective validity' (TS 19). Hartmann sees yet 'another parallel to language': 'language science' is 'research leading to intersubjectively usable results and knowledge according to structure-creating immaterialities – forms, relations, structures, functions – with respect to a phenomenon that also consists of using intersubjectively valid structurations for the purpose of communication for everybody, everywhere, always, and about everything' (TS 20) (cf. 5.23; 11.12). 'The term "immateriality" designates a purely analytic contrast' between the 'occurrence' and the things that 'do the occurring', or between 'structuration' and what gets 'structured' (TS 47f).[17] 'Immateriality obtains in arrangements, relations, forms'; it is 'the structure of the form and is thus formal to the second degree' (TS 198, 48). 'Immateriality applies to various facets', such as: 'determination', 'distinctiveness', 'rule application', 'interchangeability', 'combination', and 'grammaticity' (TS 33f, 42).

11.49 If 'immaterial relations are revealed only in structures that determine and control the material', we might ask 'how far the material and the immaterial' are 'symmetrical' (TS 19, 265). Though Hartmann doesn't give an answer (the question comes at the very end of TS), he ponders 'the curious fact that humans express their intellect in language by producing structured material'; 'why does the structuredness of matter, extending from the inanimate to life forms, even constitute the medium that seems to be the least "given in nature"?' (TS 264; cf. TS 262). On the other hand, 'all sciences are "intellectual"' in that they 'deal with immaterial relations'; 'differences between physical and non-physical sciences, natural and humanistic sciences, are due to the structures they address and the methods they use' (TS 19f) (cf. 11.14, 99). In any case, the 'parallel to the binding forces of matter is not pervasive, and is useful only for the material side of language' (TS 264) (cf. 4.8; 6.62; 7.16, 36; 11.59; 12.43).

11.50 To say that 'immateriality is revealed in **distinctiveness**' is to 'address the fact' that 'elements must differ' and to recognize 'not the *processual*, but the *real structure* of language' (TS 42) (cf. 2.26; 12.27). 'Distinctiveness' is 'an elementary structure in the most rigorous sense'; 'elements' 'must be distinctive' in order to be subject to 'disposition and combination'. So 'differentiation is the basic precondition for language', 'communication', and 'analysis', and therefore 'a legitimate domain of research for linguists' (TS 181f, 42) (cf. 2.26; 11.25; 12.26). 'The sign vehicle' consists either of 'one unit differing from units not uttered' or of 'several differing units' into which it 'can be divided' (TS 182). The 'a priori' 'unit' of 'language always occurs where others are either present' or 'merely possible' – 'potential existence has the same effect as real' (TS 182f). Or, 'the unit' may 'emerge from continuation or from non-continuation' (e.g., a 'pause'). Or, 'the same' unit can occur 'twice but with a different function each time', as in a 'tautology' (TS 42).

11.51 The upshot is that 'all languages' have 'elements – words, word-parts, sentences' – which 'are normally present in a shared multiplicity and arranged in a speech sequence divided by differences' (TS 24f) (cf. 2.58; 12.28). 'To the degree' that 'an element' 'is identical to itself, it is also different and special' 'in its environment' (TS 26). 'Language relations are rendered a bit opaque in that difference can appear either in the modification of one type (a constant) or in the opposition between types'. 'The combined expression consists of otherness as well as of elements', the more so if 'the element is what is other than the others' (TS 26, 181).

11.52 'The conception of **system**' is pertinent 'both for the functioning in (or of) structures and for the application or construction of procedures' (TS 83). 'Recognizing functions in structures and using the procedures for structures go together like theory and practice' (TS 83n). We should thus expand the familiar conception of 'system' as 'a union characterized by the co-occurrence of single entities whose basic function is to form this union' (TS 82f). 'The system allows a more dynamic interpretation' than 'the static, set-theoretical view of whole' and 'parts'. Still, 'language research might use set theory for certain problems, such as quantities, relations between quantities, and the constitution and description of sets' (TS 83n) (cf. 11.34).

11.53 'Function' 'designates the dependency of elements that jointly organize a system' (TS 84) (cf. 3.16, 22, 24, 33; 4.47, 49; 7.63; 8.49f, 58, 61; 9.3, 11, 18f, 28, 33; 11.42, 50). ' "Function" can be seen as the complement of "whole", "system", or "set" ', and is 'closely related to value' (TS 85). 'An element *acquires* (not *has*) a value by virtue of the function in which it is used' (TS 86). 'The properties of an element are determined by which functions it receives, while the structure of the system rests on which functions an element can receive' (TS 89). Hence, ' "function" designates the "performance" of form' (TS 88). 'The structurally same form' can 'have different consequences' 'in different data, e.g., the same forms in declensions of both adjectives and nouns or predicate nominatives' (TS 140f). We might 'ascribe a "functional effect" to the element', though it would be 'intransitive' and 'automatic'; we should 'be wary of metaphoric "activities of language" ' or ' "responsibilities of elements" ', which after all can occur only 'in consequence of a schema' (TS 86, 89) (cf. 11.57). The 'schema' has a 'predecided, yet open set of possibilities', and thus 'forms the background for functions' involving 'unconventional uses of elements, e.g., for emphasis and affect' (TS 87).

11.54 'Linguistics must consider various functions on the levels of sign vehicle', 'sense elements, vocabulary, and sentence' (TS 85). To distinguish 'the functions' of 'levels', Hartmann proposes the terms ' "**opposition**" on the sound level and "**determination**" on the sense level' (TS 85, 90) (cf. 12.59). 'In the material of signs, only such functions occur as are compatible with the physical aspect of language', e.g., 'collocation in a rhythmically bound linear realization' (cf. 8.66; 11.49, 80). 'The functions of sense elements are essentially different, despite some traces of the sequential character of language, e.g., mental steps' (cf. 6.47f; 11.47, 76; 12.30).

11.55 When 'elements from a **virtual system**' are 'activated', they form a 'factual or **actual system**' – a transition like that between ' "langue" and "parole" ' (TS 87) (cf. 11.47; 12.39). 'In principle, the virtual system is open, whereas the actualized system is closed, finite, smaller, and formed for the sake of determination' (TS 87f).[18] 'In the virtual system' we have 'not static fixed unions of elements' in 'functions' but 'sets of variable groupings and hence a variability of functions' (TS 99). 'Static description' serves to reveal '**structure**', whereas 'operational production' is the basis of '**constitution**'

(TS 223). Also, 'the scientific description of a language manifestation, e.g., a discourse or a text', 'puts it' into a 'static' 'form' by 'detaching it from its original or direct status' (TS 157) (cf. 2.36; 3.54; 5.31, 33; 6.33; 8.30; 9.95; 12.31).

11.56 The 'autonomy of the system' as a 'set of functions' 'possible in a domain' enables 'creative individuality': 'the individual person uses, builds up, and changes the system' while 'forming actual partial systems' (TS 87, 89) (cf. 7.44; 11.58; 12.41). No such process could occur if 'the system' were 'firmly bound to self-sufficient elements' (TS 90). Yet 'the autonomy is relative' in that 'certain elements' 'demand other elements be situated in certain ways and thus predetermine actualizations', e.g., the case of the 'object' of a verb or preposition (TS 90, 99n).[19] So 'possibilities are conceivable' that cannot be 'realized' or 'considered valid' 'on closer examination' (cf. 6.11): 'combination' is expected to 'follow some system' based on '**compatibility**' (TS 99). Still, if 'everything is combinable except where a definite system of requirements (fixed usual bindings) applies', then a 'virtual system' comprises chiefly 'domain-building functions'; 'complexes can be formed in which virtual elements and possible bonds converge'. Such a 'system has the total domain of possible combination, where possible functions' can form 'commensurate' or 'fuzzy sets' [*unklare Mengen*] (TS 100, i.r.).

11.57 'Functions' can be classed into 'domains' by their capacity 'for forming *names* (associations in name sets, e.g., synonyms, word-fields)' and 'for forming *statements* of an additive or alternating kind (schemas)' (TS 100). 'Name domains create functions that are difficult to determine' because 'words can be reinterpreted to widen or reduce a domain' (cf. 11.35); 'so we can postulate variable structures within changeable sets'. Because 'a continual drifting among concepts alternates with the actualizing of factual givens', 'we live among continual possibilities of combination': 'not among words and sentences but among meanings that can but need not be actualized via words' (TS 101). Thus, 'functions appear coupled with a continual activity of deciding' – 'seldom a conscious one', because 'language is mainly used through imitation' (TS 100) (cf. 11.45; 12.49). 'Due to the speed' and 'familiarity of discourse, a process is experienced only for longer expressions produced consciously, e.g., discerning discussions or public speeches' (cf. 10.83). Hence, we cannot 'expect the effects of functions' to be 'felt by any speaker', and we must take care not to 'ascribe to functions such meaning-creating tasks as they could only have if someone really used them as signs' (TS 100nf). 'Discursive consciousness can be viewed as a ceaselessly running mechanism for identifying and representing [*Vorstellung*]'; only in such cases as 'dreams' and 'illnesses' does it 'overstep the limits of the combinable' (TS 101, 98n) (cf. 11.73).

11.58 '**Classification**' is a similar 'interesting and important aspect' 'permeating the whole phenomenon of language', and must be addressed in any 'structural description' or 'scientific treatment of language' (TS 201, 207) (cf. 2.26, 59; 3.40; 11.12, 29, 39, 64, 86). 'Nobody intends merely to classify when speaking, but we cannot speak except via classification' (TS 196). 'Meaning has class properties in that (1) a word can be used' to 'select an object, designate it as special, and make it the representative of a class (a group of similar objects)'; and (2) 'meaning' is 'at least potentially an instance of grouping similar things' (TS 35). 'The forming of classes in all discourse remains unconscious and latent', 'but the fact is plain' wherever 'manifestations (or their parts and features') reveal 'regularity, similarity, and limitation' (TS 201; cf. TS 259). The 'similarity' of 'functions' within a 'class' complements the 'difference of manifestations' within the 'perceptible side of a language', as seen for instance in 'sounds', 'syllables', 'suffixes', and 'sentence formations' (TS 201f, 204, 206).[20] 'The individual can discover possible classifications just as functions can vary in forming domains'. 'Decisions and trials include language creativity, such as the poet's', and the freedom to 'expand the lexicon' and 'form metaphors' (TS 102) (cf. 12.41). Paradoxically, 'the most abstract mechanism allows the individual personality the surest chance to perform' (cf. 11.55).

11.59 Moreover, 'a new production of "more fitting" classifications and names is always in progress' in response to changes in 'knowledge' of 'the forms of **reality**', e.g., those in 'physics, energy, intention, logic, "thought"', and so on (TS 252, 257). 'The more a designation refers to the real' and 'the more a change in knowledge about the latter is expected, the more likely unfitness is to appear' (TS 258) (cf. 9.67). But though 'further exploration of the real' 'can show earlier designations to be unfit', we cannot 'bypass language' 'except by not speaking of the matter at all'; and 'improved knowledge does not change the fundamental character of language' (TS 258, 256). 'Inadequacy appears' when we need to 'speak of' a 'new object of discourse' 'for which a language has no "fitting" expression', such as the 'new discoveries in the natural sciences' expounded by Heisenberg (1960) (i.e., uncertainty relations and quantum phenomena in physics) (TS 62) (cf. 11.33).

11.60 We needn't be distraught if 'natural language is not adequate for reality in many ways', especially not for 'the reality accessible to natural science' (cf. MacDonald 1951) (TS 151, 150n) (cf. 3.23; 4.22; 5.68; 9.14f, 44, 112; 10.83; 11. 63, 76, 11[30]; 12.11). 'Language' may, for example, 'simplify, or encourage errors through metaphors and analogies' (TS 151). Yet 'communication requires no "exact correspondence" of an expression to what is meant' (cf. 4.15). 'Language does not have the task of containing or reflecting "the essence of things"; if tied entirely to language, thought' would have 'no capacity to recognize any such essence, because language is not a *repetition* of correlates, but their *designation*' (TS 151; cf. TS 57, 145, 149, 151, 166, 198, 255) (cf. 3.10ff). At most, 'language contributes to determinability', which is what 'leads to reality by making everything into something determinate' (TS 252).[21] But 'existence does occur before a mode of determining it has been found', and 'other forms of understanding, insight, and reaction elude designation and classification'. 'Statements about reality are made and understood by means of experience beyond language';

'humans live only partly in a world of language' and 'have the option of more direct experience' (TS 257; cf. TS 36) (cf. 12.24).

11.61 'Debates about language and thought' might be clarified by distinguishing among 'types of knowing' (TS 146n) (cf. 4.9; 5.10; 10.20–29). Though 'the access to language depends in practice on factual knowledge about things', 'knowing what a discourse is about' 'need not include knowing how the things under discussion are constituted' (TS 166) (cf. 11.35). The 'real nature' of a thing does not 'appear in language' except insofar as 'what is known about it' is 'mentally added and understood' 'via the act of naming' (TS 253f). 'Speaking inexactly is the rule in spontaneous discourse and is sufficient; imperfection is only detected when we need to determine something more exactly by means of a formulation alone' (TS 151). 'Reality is falsified only if the form of naming is the only source of information about the "essence" of what is named'; or when 'inappropriate values' and 'false associations' intrude (TS 57).

11.62 We should therefore keep in mind that 'the sign basis of language' is 'merely a specialized and limited consequence' and a 'communicable expression' of 'the overall unity of understanding, knowledge, and volition' (TS 254). 'The assumption that different language communities think differently' 'is "correct"' only 'if thinking is taken to be the constitution of insight with the aid of sense forms' (TS 188) (cf. 3.11f; 9^2; 11.19). 'Senses are aids to the understanding' and 'communication' of 'knowledge, wants, and insights'; 'people don't actually understand sense, but *by means of* sense'. 'Language is not the vehicle of understanding or knowledge' 'but their mediator, and the arranger of the ideal elements' that 'assist comprehension' (TS 256).

11.63 Since 'reality' – when it is 'spoken about, designated, objectified or meant' – 'is a collective term' for 'facts' of many 'very different kinds', and 'language is related to reality' 'in multiple ways', 'we can formulate the question' more simply: 'how is language' related to 'types of *correlates* spoken about?' (TS 251f) (cf. 12.24). The term ' "correlate" ' covers whatever 'people intend or understand' an 'utterance' to 'indicate' (TS 23f). 'All manifestations of language of any extent are assigned to correlates': 'the isolated language element' in a 'simple' way, and 'multiple expression or groups of elements' in a 'complex' way (cf. 11.78f). Hartmann distinguishes three types: the 'external correlate', a 'real thing'; the 'internal correlate, a meaning'; and the 'ideal[22] correlate', a 'classification' (TS 257ff). 'Yet the meaning relation is the same for both ideal and real correlates'; 'the difference lies in the form of existence'. 'Sign-units are in principle independent of real correlates, to which they correspond by virtue of a referential [*Bezug*] intention', yet which they must 'take into consideration' (TS 253). 'The language type decides which forms' are assumed by 'signs for ideal' or real 'correlates' (TS 259) (cf. 3.32). Often, those for the ideal 'correlates are of a special kind', ('non-lexical, non-inflected, etc.'), as in 'polysynthetic languages' like 'Eskimo' (TS 258, n) (cf. 3.53; 4.64; 11.18).

11.64   To fully explore the role of meaning, Hartmann 'contemplates a comprehensive research project that might place all concern for language under the main heading of **semantics**', including not merely 'language science' but 'scholastics', 'philosophy', 'psychology', and 'logic' (TS 50, 130) (cf. 6.50, 53). Again, he notes that 'the semantic side' of language is 'not prefigured in "nature"', though related to correlates to the degree that classifications correspond to givens outside language' (TS 36) (cf. 11.58f; 12.24). 'Once present, analytic signs exist by virtue of referring to correlates despite the principled arbitrariness of labelling (e.g., in semantic fields)'.

11.65   Equally prominent is Hartmann's insistence that 'since no sign could exist without **sense**', and 'the potential for sense is the purpose of the sign', 'linguistics' must be 'concerned with sense', at least 'as far as sense appears in the form of sign-value' (TS 185). The old claim that 'sense' is not 'a legitimate object' for 'linguistics' (cf. 11.26) was just a protest against 'research concerning itself too early or exclusively with sense' (TS 185, 186n). 'That signs in language have sense appears' in their 'constitution', 'use', and 'achievement' (TS 186). But since 'linguistic utterances reflect mixed sets' (cf. 11.35), 'we can expect different kinds of sense', as indicated by 'numericals, pronouns, verb forms, and so on' (TS 187).

11.66   Again like Wittgenstein, Hartmann stresses that 'sense values result from usability' (TS 189) (cf. 11.42). 'Sense' is what 'the individual forms in an utterance' 'take on' when they 'mediate comprehension'. 'The meaning of a word is what appears when a unit of comprehension is decomposed, and what contributes to building such units' (TS 190). 'Sense types are formed' when they 'appear in various positions in an utterance'. Besides, 'translation reveals that sense can be independent from the forms of elements'; and history reveals that a 'sense type need not change' when 'the word forms it subsumes are changed' (TS 187; cf. TS 194f) (cf. 3.58; 8.48; 11.31). However, the idea of 'fixed' 'independent sense-units' and 'meanings' (e.g., 4.50) is favoured by the 'treatment of word-meaning' in 'the special-purpose language of linguists', and by their 'standard practice' of trying to 'make sense "visible" by interchanging sign vehicles' and 'noticing what's different' (TS 190, 193, 196) (cf. 4.52; 5.46).[23]

11.67   Invoking once again the '"langue" and "parole"' division, Hartmann proposes to 'distinguish the meaning a sign has as a component of a language system', i.e., the 'usual' and 'potential sense registered in the lexicon', from 'the meaning a sign has as a component of an actual language manifestation', i.e., the 'factual sense' (TS 191, 188n) (cf. 11.55f; 12.39). Each kind should be 'a research domain' of its own, though 'potential senses' always presuppose 'actual manifestations', even if the latter are merely the 'syntax and sentences' within the 'explanations of words glossed in a lexicon' (TS 191, 88n).[24]

11.68   To specify the issues further, Hartmann proposes to 'divide' the 'communicative' or 'informational value' 'into the nominal value and the understood value', 'the nominal' being 'the literal meaning' and thus 'the decisive structural part in linguistic utterances' (TS 254f) (cf. 4.24; 5.66; 7.61; 9.97). 'Speaker and hearer' (or 'encoder' and 'decoder') can 'increase the value far beyond the nominal', and 'what one wants to achieve with an utterance can be very different from what one must say to make it understood'. The 'nominal content of an utterance' is also given a more decisive role than 'purpose', 'emotion', and the 'extralinguistic reactions' elicited by 'intonation, irony, allusion', and the like (TS 172f) (cf. 12.24).

11.69 As we can see, Hartmann goes further than our other theorists in foregrounding and detailing the semantics of language. He is strongly disposed to inquire how far 'grammar', in 'transmitting information', 'may run parallel to the structure of sense', since 'categories' and 'word types' 'differ in accord with the purposes of determination' (TS 240, 232) (cf. 6.24, 26; 9.13; 12.29, 59). Whether 'grammatical' and 'semantic combination' 'are equated depends on whether one finds grammar in the sequences typical of languages or in the sense formation that controls these sequences'; and 'on whether one sees the purpose of the linguistic utterance in its designation or in the form in which it characterizes' (TS 228). 'The structure of a sentence' or 'message' can be seen as a 'second-order sign for its mode of disposition' and 'explication' (TS 49).

11.70 When 'treating grammatical phenomena', 'linguistic analysis' may inquire 'how far descriptive methods can be independent of sense', or, conversely, how far 'technical formality is controlled by sense' (TS 227). We may elect to find 'grammar' in *arrangement* ('the language combinations' that 'generate expressions'), or else 'in *assignment*' ('the combination of material and sense within the sign') – 'two aspects' 'not adequately distinguished' 'in the usual grammars' (TS 226, 200) (cf. 11.76). 'Grammaticity'[25] would be 'the fact that all elements in a given bond stand in determining relations'; 'all statements in grammar' are 'interpretations of types of arrangement' to which 'a firm sense can be assigned, e.g., subject and predicate, noun and verb', etc. (TS 90f). 'Grammar' can designate either 'the operational linkage' of 'language elements or the scientific registration' of this linkage (TS 225) (cf. 12.45).

11.71 'Grammar occurs in language' as 'the analytic demonstration of the constitution of sequences': its 'analytic method corresponds to' 'the combinatory formation of expressions and sets in spoken language' (TS 225f) (cf. 6.59; 11.14, 87). Its 'paradigms' are 'schemas of forms assigned to several elements when placed in an appropriate position' (TS 118). Yet 'grammar' is a 'knowledge of possibilities' and 'deals with' 'facts that are not identical' with 'events or productions' in 'language realizations' (TS 226). So 'grammar is a special sector of the theories of formulation, information, and communication', and is 'antecedent to the decision of whether something forms a sentence (syntax) or a word (morphology)' (cf. 2.55; 3.26, 34f; 4.60; 5.51, 53f; 6.45; 8.56; 9.75, 9[15]; 10.40, 79f; 11.75, 77; 12.28).

11.72 In the same spirit, 'grammar' can be 'found in the different positions within a series of language elements that must differ from each other', and is thus 'an indicator of **difference**', a 'metalinguistic' 'symbolism' of 'role, position, and form' (TS 229, 231) (cf. 2.57f; 11.43). This stipulation fits the notions that 'linguistic sequences consist of positions standing in **opposition**'; that 'grammatical gestalts' are composed of 'non-identical mutual determiners'; and that although 'grammar' is 'based on recurrence', 'multiple repetition of one kind of element' is 'excluded' (TS 44, 233, 229f). But unlike most structuralists, Hartmann asks: 'how far does one think about oppositions when forming expressions?' (TS 45) (cf. 2.57). Is '"opposition"' only 'a concept from structural analysis' (TS 44n)?

11.73 'To underlie the practice' of 'spoken language', 'grammar' must 'presuppose some ability' among 'speakers and communities' (TS 228) (7.12, 14; cf. 12.49). 'Grammar is an aid to understanding semantic statements and must be articulated because every partner expects the aid'; yet 'the intended meaning is still recognizable within limits' when grammar is 'inadequate or incorrect' (TS 148) (cf. 11.44). Normally, though, 'there is nothing ungrammatical in the human practice of language', except in 'what does not yet fully belong to the language' (speech of 'children or foreigners') or no longer belongs (speech of the 'mentally ill') (TS 230) (cf. 11.57).

11.74 'Since the earliest times, grammar has been an interpretation' of 'language-internal' 'connected forms described in a functional, deterministic, or set-theoretical manner' (TS 90). Now, Hartmann is still searching for ways to circumscribe the notion of 'grammar', as attested by his largest volume, *Theory of Grammar* (*Theorie der Grammatik*) (1963b), which 'probes the general motives for structural elements like opposition, formality, relation, etc.' 'well beyond the frame of usual linguistics' (TS 32f). For example, he abstractly circumscribes 'grammar' as 'the assembly of usual indicators of combinatory possibilities'; or the 'system' 'containing whatever keeps appearing as the same in the formation of sentences', thus 'uniting commonality, sameness, form, and recurrence' (TS 218, 118). 'Grammar' seems 'difficult' when it 'demands' 'numerous possible bonds' (e.g., in 'Amerindian languages') or 'varied indicators for the same form' (e.g., in 'declensions of Indo-European languages') (TS 218f) (cf. 11.18).

11.75 'Grammar' is closely allied to 'the special province of **syntax**', i.e., 'sign formation' and 'arrangement'; '"syntax" is the application of "grammar"', the two being on 'different levels', with 'grammar' 'one level deeper in consciousness and relevance' (TS 245, 213, 36; SB 136f). 'Appearing together' is 'characteristic of all original, natural, spontaneous language' and 'counts' as a 'group with a determining intention' (TS 216, 240); 'things can be actually unconnected only through deliberate isolation, as in science' (TS 216) (2.40; cf. 3.25). 'The necessarily syntactical character of all discourse' 'emerges wherever syntagmation, determined chiefly by semantics, appears in language formations' (TS 245). 'Several symbols of different value are needed' unless 'one of the determining elements is clear or understandable by itself' so that 'an expression' can consist of 'just one word' (TS 239; cf. TS 59).

11.76 Since 'the fundamental practice in assignment and referral to correlates' lies in 'the formative element (word, affix), in the formulation (sentence, expression), and in the formulative sequence (argument), the basis of language manifestations is *assignment in arrangement*' (TS 24) (cf. 11.70). 'Both semantic assignment' and 'syntactic arrangement' are 'arbitrary'; but 'the syntactic aspect' 'is far more independent from any forms of reality', and its 'motivation' is 'internal to language', namely, to 'symbolize the mode of combination' (TS 36f). So 'a second-order arbitrariness appears in sentence formation', in both the 'application' and the 'disposition of symbols' (but cf. 2.29). The 'sign character of sentence formation' therefore entails 'two levels of signage', such that 'one-dimensional syntactic bonding joins multilevel units' (TS 37, 60). 'The syntactic aspect of words "converts" certain object phenomena into contexts' by 'varying the determining *role* of these words' (TS 61f). 'The contexts of words and syntax' in 'language in no way disturb a fact by following their own structure' (TS 61). The 'linear', 'sequential character' of 'arranged parts' cannot be 'parallel' to the 'non-linear structure of content' (TS 39f) (cf. 11.53).[26] 'Syntagmation disposes by comprehensively positing relations': 'in the semantics of **words**, a delimiting opposition *by means of* neighbouring elements'; 'in the semantics of **syntax**, however, a constraining disposition (determination) *among* neighbouring elements' (TS 37).

11.77 Due to syntax, 'one finds a fixed definite structure' in 'actually uttered **sentences**'; 'a sentence *has* a given structure' '"always" and "everywhere" to the degree that it occurs by virtue of a sentence pattern' (TS 97) (cf. 3.38; 4.68f; 5.40, 58; 7.51, 90f). 'The *obligatory* variation in the sentence vis-à-vis the *potential* variation in the word demands that a sentence consist of more than one word' (TS 26) (but cf. 4.67; 5.58; 6.45; 11.75). So 'as far as the linguist is concerned, syntax is to be approached *operationally*, as the production of sentences in combinatorial groupings', and '*descriptively*, as the discovery and analysis of such groupings' (TS 245) (cf. 12.45). 'How far word formation or morphology is included is left to the practices of each individual language, e.g., when sentence formation is expressed in word formation' (cf. 11.71).

11.78 'The sentence' can also be viewed as 'the manifestation of a communicative and judgmental form' (TS 61) (cf. 3.35; 4.68; 5.57f; 8.56). Whereas 'in the lexicon' the 'assignment to correlates is found' 'between word and meaning, signal and concept, idea and thing, and in grammar' it is found 'between form and functional meaning, in the sentence' it is found 'between sentential sign and determining situation' (TS 24). The 'constellation of names in a sentence corresponds to a communicable object that exists' 'primarily as a mode of determination'; 'determination is the structural object of sentence expressions' (TS 246, i.r.).[27] The 'predication' is a 'complete determination', whereas the 'attribution' is a 'partial' one (TS 238). 'If we rank predications by the quantity of determining parts', we find that 'the more gets included in an expression, the less a known correlate needs to be given; the less gets included, the more must "go without saying"' (TS 239). We must also acknowledge 'redundance': 'the multiple grounding of sense in the sign material', in that 'an utterance usually has more elements than are necessary for understanding' (TS 26).[28]

11.79 'The distribution of determining values among elements of the same ranks, such as subject and predicate, is not that the first is "known" and the second is "new"', but that 'the second supplies a role or function of the first' (TS 241) (but cf. 9.49). 'Verbs' are 'predicate words' 'bracketed with subjects' and have a 'structural, not ontological class meaning' of 'expressing a functional position' or 'role' for 'a "subject" or "agent"', such as 'activity, state', 'motion, action, and the like' (TS 242f) (cf. 9.46). This can be 'joined by typical verbal adjunct formations' like 'voice', 'tense', 'aspect, and mood'. But these formatives are 'properly' – i.e., structurally and without recourse to 'content' – 'language-internal reflexes of class formation'; 'only secondarily' are they 'designations for forms of the real contexts' that are 'primary for motivation and content' (cf. 11.32). Still, 'factual, mainly anthropomorphic activities have crept into definitions of the class meaning' of verbs.

11.80 Again unlike our other theorists, Hartmann does not devote much attention to language sounds, precisely because they present the fewest theoretical difficulties – no doubt the very reason why 'the phonological scheme dominated' and 'shaped recent linguistics' and why 'language science sometimes stopped in the domain of sound structures' (TS 44) (cf. 12.27). He makes the standard referral of the 'physically perceptible' 'material' of 'language' back to 'a differential set of sound variances' (TS 40) (cf. 2.70f; 3.14, 18, 21; 4.29; 5.42; 8.70; 12.26). Here, too, 'language functions by exploiting commonalities' rather than 'unique and individual facts': in this case the '"purely phonetic" vocal sound' which 'belongs in the domain of so-called natural science' and is treated by 'phonetics' (TS 118, 40). 'Important is not the produced succession, but the structure in the sequence according to which mere sounds become phonemes', i.e., 'sound-classes' for 'the smallest basic components' (TS 40f, 46) (cf. 2.69; 4.29f, 33; 5.42f; 6.43; 8[35]; 12.26). 'By entering relations', 'sounds' serve 'certain functions made possible' via 'otherness, opposition, arrangement, combination, distinction, complication, system, etc.' (TS 46, 41). So 'phonology works with systems of possibilities', and 'language is also in its sound basis a varying phenomenon composed of invariants' (TS 136n, 44) (cf. 11.29).

11.81 However, 'the sound of the sign vehicle depends on the organs producing it', and 'its presence and duration' depend on 'an irreversible linear sequence', 'a spoken chain of mutually differing vocal tones', the 'differences appearing in sound type, tempo, rhythm, grouping, part-wholes, etc.' (TS 183, 41f) (cf. 2.57f; 11.51). 'The mechanism of difference' works not merely with 'opposition' but with 'alternation', e.g., between 'opening and closure' in 'vowel and consonant', respectively (TS 44, 183f) (cf. 4.34f; 8.68).

11.82 Hartmann portrays the extrapolation from sounds to other levels as a projection based on 'whole' versus 'parts': 'sounds as repeatable vocal realizations'; 'syllables as repeatable sound groups'; 'roots, stems', and 'affixes' in words; and words in 'sentences' (TS 105f) (cf. 2.62; 3.27; 4.50; 6.45; 9.30, 9^{16}; 11.58). To use the same 'terms' in phonology and 'syntax', we must 'assume that: (1) certain basic forms of signs, such as opposition, permeate the whole of language, so that words in a sentence can be seen like phonemes in a word; and (2) a separation between the formation of sound, word, and sentence is not justified: the differences lie in content' and 'can be arranged in steps or levels' (TS 41). Although 'even in the "smallest" manifestation of language we find a surprising complexity of connections in several levels', this 'complexing "neutralizes" the divergence of levels by combining them all' into 'new wholes' (TS 264) (cf. 12.57). Therefore, 'it does not matter if seemingly incompatible things are combined, e.g., inner and outer, content and form'.

11.83   Significantly, Hartmann sees the levels as a 'visual representation' and 'imagistic interpretation', not as an 'explanation' (TS 41). They are devised because 'the first real manifestations we find in all languages' are 'sounds' we 'actually hear', and 'the sign vehicles' 'have no visible manifestation' (TS 39).[29] It should follow that 'all terms and descriptions suited for the visible must be non-essential and metaphoric' (TS 40) (cf. 12.33). However, 'writing is a special derivative stage of visible mediation and preservation of language, materialized in relatively constant forms' (TS 39). Writing allows 'vocal sign vehicles' to be 'transposed' into an 'independent', more 'permanent' 'medium', and 'represented' in 'varying degrees of precision' (TS 178). 'Pictorial writing' and 'ideograms' are the 'closest to content', whereas 'syllabic or phonetic writing' are 'closer to the sign vehicle'; but 'direct', 'reproducible' 'conservation of sound', as on 'tape recording', is 'the only fully satisfactory mode for investigating the sign vehicle in phonetics and phonology'. Historically, of course, 'a major part of the work in linguistics had to rely on language conserved in the "imprecise" secondary symbolism of writing' (TS 178f) (cf. 2.23; 4.43f; 6.50; 8.72ff; 9.42f; 12.33). 'This limitation was not particularly noticed' as long as there was no other 'form of the data' and the main concerns were 'semantics (content, philology)' and 'the categories of grammar'. Even 'the sound laws' 'could only be determined from the regular attestation' of 'correspondence and change' in 'written form'.

11.84   As we can appreciate by now, Hartmann's major 'line of argument is directed not to the structures of language, but to the *structure in the procedures* of treating language' (TS 4) (cf. 11.5). Its 'type of structural forms' yields 'the best means for bringing a science into a system with others' (TS 175). He accordingly proposes a scheme for the various 'general linguistic methods' (TS 53), which can be explored or combined in many ways (see Table 11.1 below).[30] The two main headings are '**obtaining data** and **evaluating data**'. The four modes of 'obtaining data' are 'descriptive', 'analytic', 'comparative', and 'explanatory'; the two modes of 'evaluating data' are 'generalizing' and 'interpreting'. Alongside his two main headings he places the 'metalinguistic study of methods, the theory of language science' and cites Hjelmslev as 'the main representative', though his own work certainly goes here as well. I shall briefly survey each of his six 'modes', beginning with those for 'obtaining data'.

11.85 'Descriptive research' is concerned with 'documentation' and 'designation': it 'assembles and systematizes discovered language data' and 'tells what belongs to what' (TS 53, 59). 'Pure description' 'means discovering a formulation' which 'describes something as such' 'without adding anything to what was found' (TS 58). This is 'the hardest problem of research' and 'the central question of science', though 'the idea of pure description is as old as philosophy itself', and 'countless descriptive statements have always been made' (TS 62). 'How can an object be represented so as to remain "itself" with nothing added' (TS 56)? It would be possible if we have 'a method whose categories' 'indicate only relations inherent to the phenomenon'. 'Description' can examine language in terms of its 'inherent basic features', 'structure-giving immaterialities', 'analytic procedures', and 'the factual gestalt of manifestations', in that order (TS 23).[31]

11.86 'Analytic research' is 'the chief method' of all and provides 'access to formality' and 'intersubjectivity', 'the central criteria of science' (TS 15, 19) (cf. 11.4, 7, 12, 14, 33, 48, 97; 12.54). 'Science' does not 'contemplate a unitary phenomenon', but 'analyses everywhere' in order to 'investigate characteristic partial domains' (TS 17f). So 'analytic treatment' is 'the proper domain of language science', although 'the analyst knows the manifestations being investigated are only a part of language' and 'do not have their own purpose' (TS 167, 156). The resulting 'representation', though 'not proper to the postulatable pure phenomenon', 'is relevant and useful', because 'the forms' it 'extracts and classifies' are the ones that 'result in the observed phenomenon' (TS 167). 'Linguistic analysis' 'divides into multiples in order to make statements about unities'; or 'specifies an exponent in order to characterize a solidarity' (TS 18, 37) (cf. 6.41).

11.87 In yet another of many parallels, 'the functional analysis of systems as the mainstay of language science' is said to investigate 'the procedures that create language and are themselves analytic in both semantic and communicative ways' (TS 103; cf. TS 18, 34–38, 203) (cf. 11.12). 'Linguistic analysis is based on the actualized and creative semantic–grammatical analysis or factoring in language, which operates by decomposing contexts or situations' in order to 'communicate' them (TS 104).[32] 'Systemic analysis is directed to the factual events of language and their preconditions' and is 'prior to all "applications"' (TS 103). 'Yet analysis is just an auxiliary method' and becomes 'an object of research in its own right only when questions are posed about knowledge and its results'. 'For instance, the analytic method in language research has been criticized on epistemological grounds by those who insist on the "unity of the phenomenon"' (cf. 11.38). In this 'remnant of earlier philosophy', the 'justified emphasis on the unity of thought was unjustly carried over to the elements of phenomena' (TS 104n). The traditional 'opposition' makes 'the real (the thing)' 'divisible', and 'the ideal (the concept)' 'indivisible'; 'but in practice the real can be indivisible (e.g., when dividing a thing makes it into something else), and the ideal can be divisible' (e.g., when 'classifying' 'decomposes unity into partial insights').

11.88 Since 'analysis' 'occurs everywhere where scientific results are sought', it is used in 'comparative, historic, functional, and descriptive language research' (TS 102). Being also 'presupposed by every grammar', 'analyses have been made since earliest times', and 'recent' ones are only more rigorous and scientific'; we need to 'inquire whether older analyses (grammars) are usable for systemic linguistics' (TS 107, 105) (cf. 11.41, 90). Whereas 'recent work consciously proceeds from the system', 'earlier works' may 'retain their value' via 'restatements' that 'trace back their results to elements and relations in a systemic union' (TS 107).

11.89 According to 'Hjelmslev's work' (engaged in detail in TG), 'every language utterance made of signs' is 'realized' in a 'complex whole whose parts' are 'evident' (TS 105). Thus, 'language elements can be called partial types' whose 'main role' is to 'be special and to stand in opposition, function, or non-function' 'relative to each other'. By 'dividing the partial types' into 'those having semantic sense and those making it possible to have sense', 'we can define the means of language in a precise and general way' (TS 106). '"Words" are parts of an expression that "contain" a semantic class to the degree that they are elicitable signals for classes' whose 'range is not within language itself, but in what is talked about' (cf. 12.24).[33] 'Affixes' are parts of an expression which contribute to forming a semantic class' yet which are 'non-elicitable signals for classes' whose 'range is a form, e.g., a position'. '"Phonemes", finally, are parts of semantic signs and are usually meaningless (indicate no semantic class)', 'but help the sign to be meaningful'; by themselves they 'designate their distinctiveness' (TS 106f) (cf. 12.26). In this regard, Hartmann suggests they could be 'formal signs' 'with no extent'. But his remarks on 'immateriality' and abstraction from 'time and 'space' (cf. 11.46ff) might suggest that *all* forms may have no extent *as forms*. If so, the descriptive methods defining units and levels in terms of the size of segmentable units would signal a partial relapse into substantialism (cf. TS 31) (cf. 2.16; 12.26).

11.90 'Comparative research' was 'for a long time' equated with 'language science', 'especially in Germany', 'the classic form' being 'Indo-European studies' (TS 71, 73) (cf. 2.5, 10, 52, 63; 3.19f; 4.1, 73). For Hartmann, 'comparing is a typical human[34] performance' that 'asks not about the object, but its sameness or non-sameness', and is given most 'clearly' in 'the structure of utterances making comparisons'; but 'every formulation' offers 'structural testimony' of a 'comparative' 'concern for fitting things together' (TS 71f, 81, 73). We can 'infer an underlying comparison wherever multiplicity has become a fact, e.g., in all syntax as a complementarity' of 'comparing and differentiating' (TS 72). So Hartmann sees 'comparing' as a part not merely of 'comparative language research' but of 'description', 'explanation, (e.g., Indo-European studies), interpretation (e.g., Humboldt), analysis (e.g., etymology)', and 'generalization' (e.g., 'general linguistics') (TS 73). The modern 'structural view' might make 'older research' 'useful by delineating not the elements, but the structures for whose sake the elements are present' (TS 74nf) (cf. 11.41, 88; 12.27).

11.91 After 'about 1800', 'historic' 'comparison' treated 'similarities as evidence of original unity', unless they could be 'proven to originate in local creation, convergence, or assimilation' (TS 74) (cf. 2.5; 4.73). 'Sameness' was thought 'typical', whereas 'deviations were due to historical conditions'. 'Languages of the same type were called "related"', 'stemming from an original unified form'. The project of stating 'what manifestation is the same, similar, or related to what other' led scholars to postulate 'a basic form rather than a basic language', because 'the typical always appears' in a 'form', and 'the basic language is not reconstructable as a fact' (TS 74f). This 'basic form allowed one to renounce reality and notice only formal' 'structures that are "repeated" in individual languages'. The question, "how did the ancient Indo-Europeans speak?", was deflected to the level of the language system': a 'formal schema reconstructed' from the 'features' 'left after a process of abstracting, unifying, and rarefying' (TS 75f). Yet 'only an exact inventory' of 'credible evidence can decide' 'how likely it is that the older language form was in principle more abstract and less diverse'. 'It would also be important to know what chances the basic form' had to 'spread' from its 'native place'; the 'spread' need not entail 'real events like war, conquest, or migration' (TS 77n, i.r.). Or, we could 'investigate why one form was "stronger"', e.g., 'absentmindedness, compulsion, economy, simplicity, cultural superiority,' or greater 'abstractness or clarity' (cf. Tauli 1958) (TS 77, 79n).

11.92 'Explanatory research' seeks to 'find reasons for discoverable manifestations' and say whether 'accidental conditions' or 'effective rules' are involved' (TS 80). 'Explanation' can be either 'internal' or 'external to the phenomenon', as exemplified by 'systemic' and 'historical research', respectively. Even the 'systemic' approach deploys 'means of description on a different level than the forms to be characterized', namely 'the metaphenomenal level that determines phenomena', as when we state that 'all higher life-forms function' by means of 'comparison and differentiation' (TS 81, i.r.). 'The goal of explanation is reached when states given by a system or structure are furnished as reasons' (TS 82). In contrast, the historical approach can be 'an etymological search for connections between word and thing, can emerge from a specialized interrogation foreign to language, and can deal only with primal words which are expressly "similar" to the thing or correlate, e.g., in onomatopoeia' (TS 151) (cf. 8[43]).

11.93 The research methods for '**obtaining data**', which we just reviewed, are presupposed by those for '**evaluating data**', to which we now turn (TS 108). Hartmann admits that the 'border' between these two is 'fluid' and 'soon crossed', but he sees 'a clear difference in the treatment of facts': only in 'evaluation' are 'the facts' or 'data' 'understood as a representation, realization, or sign of something' 'transfactual and interphenomenal', rather than as 'a goal in themselves' (TS 109ff) (cf. 11.6). 'Viewing data as an indicator of states of affairs, relations, or laws' is likely to be 'favoured wherever the data are well known or no longer interesting in themselves'. Still another parallel between science and language (cf. 11.12) is suggested: 'the word is related to the sentence as the single fact is to the multiplicity of facts: the single word allows no interpretation, and can at most name a thing'; 'the multiplicity in the word-context of a sentence' 'results in' 'an insight or interpretation that is more than the parts' (TS 109n) (cf. 2.27; 5.64f, 67, 75ff; 7.82; 10.36, 10^{20}; 12.59).

11.94 'As befits the many-sidedness' of 'evaluation', it 'necessarily unites several levels' and gains 'more general' 'superior' 'knowledge' (TS 111f). In its full form, such 'research' 'ideally' 'demands a combination of sciences' (Hartmann calls it 'syntactic'), which may be 'hardly attainable' (TS 112f). And we should 'ideally evaluate from all languages' and seek out what is 'general' or 'universal' (TS 121, 118).[35] At least 'the demand for multiple determination' can be 'fulfilled' by 'dealing with the whole phenomenon, not just parts of it, in its dependencies, oppositions, and relations to others' (TS 112). Alongside the older 'pre-scientific' and 'extralinguistic' 'evaluation' in 'philosophy, psychology, theology', and 'history' of 'language', Hartmann focuses on 'formal' 'evaluation' and subdivides this domain into 'generalizing' and 'interpreting' (TS 113f, 116, 53).

11.95 '**Generalizing** research discovers shared basic types (as in typology), establishes factual similarities (as in Saussure's general linguistics)', or 'demonstrates generally necessary features (as in a priori grammar)' (TS 53). 'The goal is to pursue insights into language facts by seeking commonalities' and 'unity in all realizations' (TS 116). In 'seeking formal commonalities' and 'features', 'modern research' remains 'inductive' 'even though it entails abstraction into transphenomenal contexts' (TS 115f, 118, 120). 'Individual facts in their totality' are 'unique', but may reveal 'partial coincidences': what makes 'facts' 'partially comparable' is 'necessarily something formal' that 'receives a special new *value* detached from uniqueness' (TS 117) (cf. 11.30f). In this 'non-totalizing' outlook, 'what is factually incomparable now figures only as the carrier of this special form' and hence is 'limited to the extent needed to be confronted with another fact'.

11.96 '**Interpretive** research' looks for 'a "deeper" cause [*Wirksames*]' than does 'generalizing', and is 'chiefly concerned' with 'judgments of language as a phenomenon' (TS 122) (cf. 11.38). 'The interpretive direction still belongs to science' insofar as it 'depends on the results of fact analysis'. And 'interpretation' need not be 'unlinguistic, because introducing trans-factual relations may lead to a better description of language facts' (TS 128). 'The interpretive predisposition of the researcher' to 'determine language' can be gauged in 'inductive or experimental ways, e.g., the "performance" of language observed by psychology'. Here also, 'not the standpoint but the degree of formality is decisive for being scientific and useful' (cf. 11.4, 14, 33, 86).

11.97 Because 'language interprets and is used for interpreting', 'language science' is 'the analysis of the material [*Stoff*] that plays the main role in the hermeneutics of ordinary life' (TS 22, 138) (cf. 11.9, 35). Yet 'language science proper' 'explores the structures of language as such, not the further structures of meaning or the effects of language' 'arising from intersubjective interpretation' (TS 22) (but cf. 12.58). The latter 'become important only when they influence the intersubjective phenomenon of language'. Still, 'interpretation is a legitimate meeting place for adjacent disciplines' and seeks to 'unite insights from different quarters' (TS 154) (cf. 8.16). This factor suggests why 'interpretation is near typology', as when 'languages' are treated as instantiations of 'possible types'.[36] Also, 'etymology' is a 'form of interpretation' 'supplying motives' 'abstracted from the facts', e.g., 'sound laws' and 'analogy' (TS 192) (cf. 11.90, 92; 2.75).

11.98 Implying one last 'parallel between science and language', Hartmann finds it 'practical to reduce each mode of language research to the basic form of its statements' (TS 66, 129n). For the modes just reviewed, his 'forms of statement' are as shown in Table 11.1 (TS 128f; cf. TS 58, 60, 66f, 82, 111, 119, 123).

TABLE 11.1

Description: something called 'A' is/does/acts as something called 'B'	
Comparison (neutral):	A corresponds to B
Comparison (historical):	A comes from/becomes/is related to B
	A is such because/if B is such
Analysis and explanation:	A is systematically conditioned by the context B
	A shows the function B under analysis
Evaluation (formal):	The general structural element A corresponds to the necessary structural requirement B
Evaluation (interpretive):	A, B can be represented as realizations of X

These 'different forms' indicate the 'different epistemological intentions and forms' of 'methodological stances' (TS 129). 'Each pattern is appropriate to its respective goals' and 'has its own full value' according to 'what can be grasped with it in practice'. Like 'words and sentences', 'methods are not false in principle' but 'only in an unacceptable application' (TS 129n) (cf. 11.61). Hartmann's concern for the 'value' and 'intentions' of 'statements' befits his vision of 'science' 'striving for a totality of possible determinations' (TS 129) (cf. 11.2; 12.63).

11.99 In sum, the wide expanse of 'research' Hartmann surveys, wherein 'language' is 'classified and systematized' in order to attain 'an abstract and incomplete but scientifically useful picture' of 'its functioning', undeniably justifies his plea that it 'commands our interest' (TS 166, 263). 'Only today' have we 'reached the phase where language knowledge and language critique interact on a broad level and might merge into a general theory of formulation' (TS 9; cf. TS 79n). Now, 'linguistics is not just a substitute for the philology of languages long past, but special research' 'applying all productive perspectives to the instrumental object "language"' (TS 263). 'Linguistics falls in between the sciences dealing only with the real, and those dealing only with the ideal, and thus oscillates between the natural sciences and the humanities' (TS 39) (cf. 11.14). 'Like the natural sciences, linguistics has a non-temporal *enduring* object and can draw *generally valid* conclusions' – in 'marked contrast to research on past objects or cultures or on fairly unique manifestations' (TS 263). In the humanities, we can address the role of 'language in literature, poetry, tradition, information, conversational contact, processes of understanding, and so on'. We can now confront such 'promising questions' as 'what is "in" a text?' Or, 'what is the role of additions, the things people know or believe without being told?' Or even, 'is a universal formula conceivable and in what sense?' (TS 265). 'Here, the linguist can contribute facts that are limited, but perhaps instructive.' 'If we can grasp what makes language what it is for human beings, this object will lend great significance to its science' (TS 263).

Notes

1. The key for Hartmann citations is: SB: *Syntax und Bedeutung* (1964); TG: *Theorie der Grammatik* (1963b); and TS: *Theorie der Sprachwissenschaft* (1963a). TG and SB, which I cite here only in cross-references, are high-level studies of grammar and syntax in general, not just in language (cf. 11.74).
2. Of course, the placement of quote marks cannot be so strict as when I am working from an original English text. Some major terms I consistently used in translating are: being: *Sein*; communicate: *verständigen/mitteilen*; concern: *Beschäftigung*; contemplation: *Anschauung*; context: *Sachverhalt*; deliberation: *Überlegung*; designation: *Bezeichnung*; domain: *Bereich*; essence: *Wesen*; evaluate: *auswerten*; image: *Bild*; indicate: *hinweisen*; Indo-European: *indogermanisch*; intellect: *Geist*; issue: *Tatbestand*; level: *Ebene/Schicht*; manifestation: *Erscheinung*; object: *Objekt/Gegenstand*; obtain: *gewinnen*; pattern: *Bauplan*; procedure: *Verfahren*; process: *Vorgang*; quantity: *Anzahl*; representation: *Vorstellung*; sense: *Sinn*; statement: *Aussage*; utterance: *Äusserung*. I include the German term in the text or make special notes wherever the English term might be misleading (see Notes 8, 11, 12, 22, 25, 30, 32). When I needed a neutral noun for a German nominalized attribute, I used 'entity'. Note also that German has many pairs with a native term alongside a roughly equivalent foreignism. Here are some pairs Hartmann seems to equate: *Auswertung* vs *Interpretation* (TS 52, 113; but cf. TS 109 and Note 30); *Bestimmung* vs *Determination* (TS 93); *Intention* vs *Absicht* (TS 25); *kombinieren* vs *zusammenstellen* (TS 25); *Mitteilung* vs *Kommunikation* (TS 92); *Motiv* vs *Grund* (TS 158); *Relation* vs *Verhältnis* (TS 93, but cf. TS 217); *Verwendung* vs *Applikation* (TS 57).
3. In German usage, '*Sprachwissenschaft*' ('language science') is broader than '*Linguistik*', the latter usually designating twentieth-century structuralist and generativist work (cf. TS 71). I therefore preserve the distinction in English.
4. 'Linguistics', Hartmann suggests, might contribute to a '*"mathesis universalis"*', i.e., a formal scheme for as many facts as possible from several or all sciences' (TS 89n, 136f, 262) (cf. 11.99). The Latin term pays tribute to Leibniz's scheme for a universal foundation of scientific reasoning.

5. On the important question of whether language elements 'have or acquire' sense, see 11.54, 66f, 11^{24}, and TS 188f.

6. Elsewhere, though, Hartmann emphasizes the value of psychological methods for exploring language (e.g. TS 128, 130) (cf. 3.10; 12.10f, 14).

7. In 'language', 'interpretive freedom appears alongside formal compulsion, and the two require different treatment' (TS 161) (cf. 2.44, 61; 3.38f; 4^6; 11.29, 35, 58).

8. In order not to blur the abstract quality and the duality of the sign as a relation (cf. 2.25ff), Hartmann follows semioticians like Charles Morris (1946: 251) in using 'sign vehicle' for the manifest element (cf. 11.47, 50, 54, 66, 81, 83).

9. 'Intentional metaphors' are of course prominent in 'poetic language'; a 'special concern' of philosophers is with 'poets who hope the world will reveal itself' through language, whence Heidegger's (1959) interest in Hölderlin, Trakl, and Rilke (TS 143, n). But a 'poetic disposition' might 'reject analysis in both science and language' (TS 18) (cf. 11.38).

10. The 'extralinguistic' domains include 'contemplations of language as a whole in philosophy, psychology, and theology' (TS 144ff, 8f) (cf. 11.38, 94). The listing in TS 7f suggests that everything before Schlegel, Humboldt, and Bopp was pre-scientific (cf. 11.22, 94). Moreover, the 'historical search for the "primordial"' (presumably among 'Romantics'), and Humboldt's 'reciprocation between language and intellect' are given as examples of 'prior views later found erroneous' (TS 113) (cf. 7.3, 12, 32; 11.17ff).

11. An untranslatable pun is made here between '*Wirkung*' (effect) and '*wirklich*' (real) (TS 126). Compare Note 32.

12. The German term '*Mehrheitlichkeit*' merely indicates the quality of being 'more than one' and does not necessarily imply the numerousness often associated with 'multiplicity'.

13. 'At most', these matters can be 'grasped via quantitative oppositions', whose 'extreme values are one-to-one and one-to-infinity' (TS 160) (cf. 2.22; 3.32; 5.48, 64; 6.27; 9.39).

14. Like Saussure and Hjelmslev, Hartmann stipulates that 'language' is to be 'characterized without recourse to substance' (TS 38, 156) (cf. 2.16; 6.13, 28ff, 44). Also, 'substance' is equated with 'non-form'; and 'the linguistics of substance' is reproved for its 'simple model of language as object', with the 'sentence as a sequence of sense-bearing building-blocks, which may themselves be made up of smaller (or older) pieces' (TS 48, 31) (cf. 9.75; 11.88).

15. Hartmann wonders what a 'pre-grammatical stage' (Tauli 1958) or a 'pre-syntactical stage' (Sandmann 1954) could have 'looked like: maybe just holophrases' (TS 46n) (cf. 8.56, 65; 9.11).

16. 'The opposition between outer (sign base) and inner (sense)' 'indicates that however indispensable the real factuality of perceptible language may be, *non-perceptible forms*' 'are the supporting frame' (TS 265). The role of schemas in perception helps to explain how the forms are none the less generated (cf. 10.27, 77).

17. 'If we follow Wittgenstein's theory', 'immateriality' is open 'not to *description*, but only to *insight*' (TS 47). Hartmann vows this 'immateriality' is 'not a level of platonic ideas'; 'the materialities themselves give each other their respective forms merely by being present together' (TS 48).

18. Contrast Hartmann's portrayal of 'form' as 'the open, infinitely practicable mode', 'the possibility of all realizations', and of 'content' as 'the closed, fixed extract delimited' 'in every actualization' (TS 88), with his view of form as constant and content as variable (cf. 11.30f).

19. A category like 'accusative' depends not merely on 'suffix', 'ending', or 'case', but on a 'syntactic relation' – an instance of how 'older research' might be given

a 'structural interpretation' (TS 74nf) (cf. 11.41, 88).

20. 'Non-analysed language seldom descends below the syllable'; 'the individual sound', not being 'connected to a specific formal part', is 'discovered only under special circumstances' (TS 216) (cf. 4.35; 5.36, 44, 55; 6.39, 45; 8^{32}; 9.30, 9^{16}; 11.82).

21. Heidegger (1959) even suggests that 'statements' 'produce being' because only 'words' can say what '*is*' (TS 138n). On the theological overtones here, compare Note 36.

22. The German term is '*ideel*' (pertaining to ideas), not '*ideal*' (conceived in the best possible way).

23. Though 'the total value' and 'applicability' are 'changed' by this tactic, 'some fragments of the complex are preserved' (TS 197). At least, the supposition that the tactic is the simplest possible now seems questionable (cf. 5.14, 61, 65).

24. 'Because words are not listed in groups according to sense, no form arises in the lexicon or dictionary [both *Lexicon* in German]' (TS 88n). We might prefer a 'formulation' that 'does not say whether elements have their own sense', or 'where they get sense' such as that 'appearing in the dictionary'; 'do they have sense only because they are used without thinking?' (TS 189fn).

25. Unlike Anglo-American linguists, German ones often maintain the distinction between 'grammaticity' (*Grammatizität*) as the fact that grammar underlies language, and 'grammaticality' (or 'grammaticalness', cf. 7.41f, 60) (*Grammatikalität*) as the status of some sample allowed by the grammar. Failing to distinguish the two may have encouraged American linguists to imagine that grammaticity must fully and definitively determine the borders of grammaticality.

26. 'Predications' are included under 'non-linear' (TS 40), despite the close associations they are often assigned with sentences (cf. 4.69).

27. Of course, 'most determining elements can correspond to several manifestations' in 'the "world"' (TS 248). 'The quantity of sentence-internal information sites is also not parallel to reality; people are more likely to make reality parallel' to 'the sentence' (TS 246) (cf. 12.24).

28. Examples include '"superfluous" infixes for relations or sentence roles; or clarification of the predicate through personal endings' (TS 27).

29. 'The production of language involves visible motions' and is often 'accompanied by gestures', but 'the decisive role belongs to entities independent of being seen' (TS 39) (cf. 11.10).

30. 'In practice, there is seldom a strict division' between '*registering*', '*interpreting*', and '*analysing*' language (TS 139). Even the schematic tables (TS 53f) have many mixed types (and cf. 11.88, 90, 93). I have rearranged the tables for the purpose of exposition ('analysis' appears there as a part of 'explanation', but he consistently gives it a more general status elsewhere). I use 'data' for '*Materien*' because he is clearly not concerned with 'the material aspect of language' (as depicted in 11.49, 53). '*Auswertung*' does not have as much accent on value as 'evaluation' ('*Bewertung*'), and might be rendered with 'interpretation' (e.g. TS 53), had he not made the latter a subtype.

31. His demonstration uses the German suffix '-*heit*/-*keit*': as 'sounds', a 'construction' of 'phonemes'; as 'formation', a 'morpheme'; as 'grammar–syntax', a means for 'forming substantives'; as 'set–syntax, an element added to existing repertories' to 'provide a possible role'; as 'partial system', 'a metaclassification' and 'a component to fixate a partial domain of expressions so that they can be used in several ways (in a subject, attribute, or predicate)'; as 'virtual system, a component of langue' and a 'form for expressions' that 'presuppose a judgment'; and as 'semantics, an abstractive derivation of adjectives, and meaning something is a state of affairs' (TS 94ffn). Oddly, Hartmann omits the regular criteria (preceding phonemes) for using the '*h-*' or the '*k-*' form.

32. A pun is made here between *'teilen'* (decompose) and *'mitteilen'* (communicate).
33. 'Proof can be obtained in that false application of such classes' engenders 'different responses', e.g., to 'commands' (TS 106n).
34. 'The typically human' is mainly conceived as 'the contrary of typically animal', as if 'animal abilities' 'encroach' on ours (TS 70fn). 'Humans differ from animals' in 'speed of decision', 'consistency', 'freedom not to react', and 'decomposition of manifestations, even of one's self' (TS 72, 105n) (cf. 12.12).
35. Cf. 2.10; 3.67; 4.4, 71f, 74; 5.44; 6.5, 10, 34; 7.19f, 22, 29, 33f, 45, 55, 62, 65, 71, 78f, 91, 93, 7^{10}, 7^{32}, 7^{39}; 8.19, 60, 86; 9.3, 25, 60; 12.18.
36. Hartmann also cites the 'theology' of the 'Christian' or 'Biblical typology', with 'the human as a typos for God', and its influence on Hamann and Heidegger (TS 154nf).

Chapter 12

Linguistics versus language: retrospects and prospects[1]

12.1 We have now surveyed the discourse of 'theorizing' in some major works in this century attempting to establish the foundations of linguistics. Focusing on the works as discourse helps to see them not just as documents, but also as 'performances' with characteristic 'discourse moves' (cf. 1.11). These moves include claiming scientific status for linguistics; estimating the state of the discipline with its strengths and weaknesses, and situating it in respect to other disciplines; selecting certain aspects for investigation and rejecting others; proposing criteria for constructing theories or discovering data; setting degrees of precision or delicacy; determining what counts as the same or different within one language or among several; deciding how many levels of structure should be postulated for language sequences; presenting and justifying terms or notations; and so on. Many theoretical steps involve trade-offs, where some advantage is gained by accepting a disadvantage elsewhere in the theory (cf. 9.111; 12.20, 52, 55). But local losses and gains can still add up to a global increase in insight: 'the history of language research shows that progress comes from shifting and enriching the problematics' (11.4). We can thereby move beyond the ordinary awareness wherein 'language is such a familiar, important, and central phenomenon' 'that it is hard to even notice all its basic features and their significance' (11.9; cf. 2.8; 3.1; 4.2; 6.6). Yet linguists also are continually in danger of understanding the data too readily and underestimating their involvement in producing them (cf. 1.9; 2.66; 3.11, 50; 4.4, 31, 72; 5.9, 11, 24, 78; 8.14; 12.36, 49).

12.2 My survey hardly resembles the 'textbook' sketched by Thomas S. Kuhn (1970: 137ff). Because 'the scientist's contemporary position seems so secure' and because they are 'pedagogic vehicles for the perpetuation of **normal science**', Kuhn says, 'textbooks' get 'rewritten in the aftermath of every **scientific revolution** and then disguise not only the role but the very existence of the revolutions that preceded them' (cf. 1.4). 'Textbooks thus begin by truncating the scientists' sense of their discipline's history and then proceed to supply a substitute for what they have eliminated'. They 'refer only to that part of past work which can easily be viewed as contributions to the statement and solution of the textbook's **paradigm** problems'. So 'instead of forgetting' their 'founders', 'scientists are able to forget' 'or revise their works'.

12.3 By restaging the founders' works in a complex fabric of individual voices, my survey hopes to dissolve the complacent idea that past trends have been inexorably leading up to some culmination in the present. Indeed, I do not see any obvious current 'normal science paradigm' in linguistic theory.[2] Nor is there currently one general theory capable of subsuming and integrating the available alternatives (cf. 5.9; 6.18; 8.35), which is scarcely surprising given the widespread accentuation of divergences (cf. 12.6). Basic works in linguistics typically controvert the Kuhnian 'textbook' by their express intent to inaugurate 'revolutions', and thus find it strategic to criticize the state of the discipline and to propose new projects in declared opposition to past research.[3]

12.4 This intent favoured the impression that 'revolutions' in linguistics have been 'frequent and radical in throwing away all that came before' (Winograd 1983: 8). On closer inspection, the progress of the discipline reveals a more interesting and complicated pattern we might call 'ancestor-hopping': repudiating one's immediate precursors while reaching further back for sources. Time and again, our theorists directed their sharpest criticism against the more recent segments of prior research, which they no doubt viewed as the nearest competitors. Suppose we made a roughly chronological chart:

1. Traditional grammar (classical, medieval, school grammar)
2. Philology (historical or comparative grammar, phonetics of sound change)
3. Mentalist descriptive linguistics (continental European structuralism)
4. Physicalist descriptive linguistics (American and British structuralism)
5. Logical linguistics (algebra, calculus, generative or transformational grammar)
6. Systemic or functional linguistics (British functionalism)
7. Computational research (artificial intelligence)
8. Cognitive research (cognitive science and psychology)

We can often see an approach dissociating itself from the one(s) just before it, while approving one or more earlier ones. The mentalist descriptive linguistics of continental European structuralism spearheaded by Saussure turned against philology so emphatically that 'traditional grammar', though admittedly 'unscientific', was judged more 'correct' and 'less open to criticism' (2.6). The physicalist descriptive linguistics of American structuralism inaugurated by Bloomfield repudiated mentalism, which 'still prevailed' 'among men of science', and which he grouped together with the outlook of 'grammarians' in 'our school tradition'; in exchange, philology was lauded as 'one of the most successful' 'enterprises' 'of European science in the nineteenth century', one that 'replaced speculation' 'with scientific induction' (4.4f, 8, 73, 76). In turn, Chomsky rebuked Bloomfieldian descriptive structuralism as 'fundamentally inadequate' and gave a high appraisal both to 'mentalism' and to 'traditional grammar', which he also associated with each other (cf. 7.5, 7, 34, 37, 10, 4). His own 'generativism' was in its turn reprimanded by van Dijk and Kintsch's cognitive approach, which in exchange saluted linguistic 'Structuralism' and 'Formalism', along with 'classical poetics and rhetoric', and even 'literary scholarship' (10.1f, 58).[4]

12.5 On the British scene, Firth, like Bloomfield, excoriated both mentalism and current school grammar; but he also mistrusted 'philology' and reached far back to ancestors in phonetics, grammar, and orthography from the Elizabethans down to Henry Sweet (cf. 8.24, 37, 41, 6f, 15, 8[13]). Halliday's 'systemic' or 'functional' approach purported to be an elaboration of Firthian linguistics, and an alternative to both American structuralism ('chain grammars') and Chomskyan generativism ('formal' and 'transformational' grammars) (cf. 9.3–6, 9[20]).[5] In fact, his approach entailed extensive revisions of Firth's, particularly by incorporating the Prague school's 'functional' strand of European structuralism dealing with communicative topics and focus, which Firth would probably have considered mentalistic (9.47, 56, 9[10], 9[19]; cf. 8.25). Only Hartmann seems to have genuinely appreciated *all* his predecessors, and even he, in doing so, was revising a preceding tradition, namely the isolationist 'mother-tongue' linguistics that held sway in Germany before and during World War II (cf. 11.19) – and of course the general fractiousness of the discipline.

12.6 These patterns of 'ancestor-hopping' indicate that linguistics did not so much deny its global history as accentuate its local discontinuities, censuring the more recent or dominant past and commending the more remote or marginal past. Hence, each 'revolution' in linguistics overthrew and supplanted the currently ruling paradigm, which could again be hailed as a source after a later revolution, when it would no longer pose a threat of competition. Paradigms in linguistics have thus proven more resilient and resurrectable than those in many other disciplines. Admittedly, the acute emphasis on local discontinuities can foster an image of linguistics as a contentious field with more periods of 'crisis' than of 'normal science'.[6] If we totalled up all the criticism raised at some time against theories and methods (cf. 12.3), few if any would remain unscathed.

12.7 Of course, explicit discontinuities did not preclude implicit continuities. Despite declared antagonism, our theorists retained some contact with traditional grammar and at times raised the prospect of recycling it into linguistics (cf. 2.6, 15; 6.49; 7.4, 75; 8.38; 11.41, 88, 11[21]). A case in point is the embattled 'parts of speech' schemes often subjected to 'muckraking' (5.72ff; cf. 2.65; 3.23; 4.51; 6.49; 8.37, 43, 58f; 9.13, 34, 9[13]). Theorists concurred that the criteria for defining these 'parts' had been inconsistent, diffuse, vague, and unreliable, but did not agree which new criteria should replace the old. Recourses included: not presenting one's own parts-of-speech scheme at all (Saussure, Sapir, Firth, Hartmann); proposing an entirely new scheme (Hjelmslev); or, most often, maintaining and revising the traditional scheme with added or substituted criteria drawn from fieldwork on lesser-studied languages (Sapir, Bloomfield, Pike), formal logic (Chomsky), communicative contexts (Halliday), or cognitive psychology (van Dijk and Kintsch). The popularity of maintenance and revision suggests a general belief that a totally new scheme wouldn't be accepted, and that the old criteria were not such a serious liability because they could be easily used and because they reflected the fuzziness of the categories themselves (cf. 2.33; 12.59). Linguists can usually agree on what to classify as a 'noun' or a 'verb', however intuitive their criteria might be, whereas brand-new terms like Hjelmslev's 'plerematic syntagmateme' and 'nexus-conjunction' for those categories (6.59) lack that advantage, unless they are taken to mean exactly the same as the old terms, which would defeat the purpose. Ironically, it was Chomsky's proposal to create a 'purely formal basis' for 'grammatical theory' (cf. 7.56) that relied most heavily on traditional, very *non*-formal grammars, and set up English as the model of 'underlying' formality in place of Latin with its explicit formality (cf. 12.30, 42).[7]

12.8 Continuity also obtained when structuralists borrowed from philological methods and materials, although they reversed the earlier emphasis by foregrounding the formal diversity of languages rather than the comparison and classification into families based on genetic commonalities (cf. 2.5, 10; 3.40, 45ff; 4.72ff; 5.26, 5[6]). The generativists borrowed the materials and methods, now much expanded by the structuralists, and (though generally ignorant of philology) returned to an emphasis on commonalities – not genetic but arising from 'universals' – while devaluing formal diversity as a 'surface' issue (cf. 7.19). All these far-reaching but implicit continuities made the history of the discipline far less cataclysmic, whence Halliday's wry remark that 'twentieth-century linguistics' 'has tended to wrap old descriptions' inside 'new theories' instead of seeking genuinely 'new descriptions' (9.24).

12.9 An equally intriguing pattern of alliances and antagonisms appears in the shifting relations between linguistics and the other disciplines. The latter often provided strategic frameworks, the more so when linguists were anxious to dissociate themselves from the prior or current paradigms in their own discipline. So 'linguistics' conspicuously illustrates how the 'scientist looking for a new paradigm is strongly affected by the other sciences currently enjoying successful development' (Winograd 1983: 8). The pressure to borrow is reinforced when the object domain is too complex to suggest any obviously appropriate theory, and when the scientific climate is too austere to favour entirely novel theories. On the other hand, linguistics sometimes showed a drive to go its own ways and remain aloof from its neighbours (cf. 2.7; 6.6; 8.17).

12.10 Of all the disciplines, **psychology** had the most varied fortunes as a model. In the early decades of the twentieth century, when Saussure and Sapir were working out their conceptions (and the young Bloomfield was writing his 1914 *Introduction to the Study of Language*), mentalistic psychology was well established, particularly in Europe. It therefore seemed plausible that 'the concrete object of linguistic science is the social product deposited in the brain of each individual', and that language is a medium for coordinating discoverable forms (words, word-parts, 'signifiers', etc.) with their communally assigned content ('ideas', 'thoughts', 'concepts', 'signifieds', etc.) (cf. 2.16, 83; 3.1, 17). For Sapir, 'language' represented 'a fully formed functional system within man's psychic or "spiritual" constitution', and 'linguistic forms' 'had the greatest possible diagnostic value' for 'understanding' 'problems in the psychology of thought'; 'perhaps psychologists of the future would be able to give us the ultimate reasons' for the 'fundamental form intuitions' of language (3.9f, 55; cf. 2.7, 17, 32, 35; 3.12, 20, 37, 62; 6.6). Certain affinities for mechanism and physicalism were detectable (cf. 2.31, 83, 2^3; 3.20, 3^{11}) but were not felt to disturb the mentalist scenario (cf. also 7.16, 93).

12.11 The dramatic swing from mentalism to the 'mechanism' or 'physicalism' roundly espoused by Bloomfield, Pike, and Firth, however, transformed the scientific climate and the prospects for cross-disciplinary interaction. Psychology lost its model status to ostensibly 'harder' disciplines. Bloomfield hopefully suggested that 'the methods of linguistics' 'resemble those of a **natural science**, the domain in which science has been the most successful' (BL 509) (4.8; cf. 2.13; 4.18; 7.11; 9.112; 11.14, 49, 99). Whereas Sapir had declared that 'languages' were in no way 'explainable' by 'the laws of **physics** and **chemistry**', Bloomfield now declared that the constitution of 'speech' follows 'cause-and-effect sequences exactly like those we may observe, say, in the study of physics and chemistry' (3^{10}; 4.8; cf. 2.82; 5.66). Henceforth, all mentalist terms, like ' "mental images" ', "feelings" ', "thoughts" ', "concepts" ', ' "ideas" ', or ' "volitions" ', were deemed 'merely popular names for various bodily movements' (4.9; cf. 8.22ff).

12.12 Although Bloomfield's 'stimulus-response' model came not from physics or chemistry but from animal-conditioning research, he nowhere expressly proposed **biology** as a model science. Instead, he usually mentioned 'biological' factors as a contrast to language, and averred that 'the effects of language' 'distinguish man from the animals' – a view aired also by Sapir, Chomsky, Firth, and Hartmann (cf. 4.34, 75, 2; 3.15; 7.35; 8.27; 11.10, 11^{34}; 12.18), though semioticians reject it today. Perhaps biology seemed unhelpful because Bloomfield realized that an explanation of language would not readily come from 'the working of the nervous system', which 'is not accessible to observation from without', nor even by one's own 'sense-organs' (4.18; cf. 8.21). Another, more powerful reason may have been that nineteenth-century language study had drawn elaborate parallels to such biological conceptions as 'organicism' and 'evolution' (cf. 3.2; 8.6; 11.17). An emergent science might later find it old-fashioned to advertise its reliance on biology.

12.13 Despite having been a pupil of Sapir's (cf. 5.69), Pike made similar moves to Bloomfield's. Pike's 'particle', 'wave', and 'field' scheme was more elaborately modelled after physics than was Bloomfield's sketch of speech as 'sound wave' transfer (cf. 5.31f; 4.10); in return, Pike's 'Unified Theory' made no explicit appeals to biology. Firth attacked 'philology' for its 'biological analogies', but drew some of his own, e.g., advocating the study of 'linguistic behaviour' as a way of 'maintaining appropriate patterns of life' in analogy to 'the study of the whole man by biologists, anatomists, physiologists', 'neurologists, and pathologists' (8.6, 20).

12.14 The fortunes of psychology in linguistics also alternated with those of **social research**. For the early mentalists, 'language' was 'exclusively psychological' (cf. 2.31). In return, 'society' and 'social' aspects were treated only episodically, chiefly as a regulatory factor that disseminates language and imposes uniformity upon it (cf. 2.16, 28, 33, 67; 3.1, 3, 55), and sometimes as a devisive or irrelevant factor, a move repeated by Hjelmslev (cf. 2.9, 44; 3.64f; 6.14).[8] Later, the physicalists and behaviourists declared their disdain for 'mentalistic psychology' and for 'psychological doctrine', theory', 'explanations', or 'analysis' (cf. 4.8, 19, 80, 4^1, 4^{26}; 8.17, 24, 28, 54f).[9] In return, much attention was given to the 'social' aspects of language, the latter being 'the most fundamental of our social' 'activities' (4.16; cf. 4.9f, 25, 82, 84f, 88; 5.65, 85; 8.10, 16, 28, 47; 9.8f, 18, 40). Firth and Halliday suggested that 'sociology' exerted priorities conflicting with 'psychology', which they considered too dependent on (non-observable) mental states and individual dispositions (cf. 8.17, 25, 28; 9.6f, 9^9). Van Dijk and Kintsch finally signalled a balanced synthesis: their methods are mainly psychological, but social factors are prominent also (cf. 10.1), notably in such concepts as 'schemas' of shared world knowledge, and in the appeal to large experimental test populations rather than to themselves, single readers, or 'ideal speaker–hearers'.[10]

12.15 The relation between linguistics and **mathematics** has also had a peculiar history, being upheld more often in name than in deed. Saussure and Sapir betrayed a taste for 'formulas' and envisioned some parallels between 'language' and '**algebra**' (cf. 2.70, 82; 3.72f), but made no attempt to work out a full theory or representation on that basis. Bloomfield wistfully admired 'mathematics' as the 'ideal use of language' and a 'specially accurate form of speech', and introduced some of his own 'formulas' and 'equations' (4.21, 4^{20}), but he too went no further. Firth dourly conjectured that 'a linguistic mathematics' would 'become a dead technical language' (8.31). Hjelmslev, however, declared the 'main task' of 'linguistics' to be the creation of 'an immanent algebra of language', and his *Résumé* executed such a system in relentless detail (cf. 6.8, 29, 42, 59). He also advocated a '**logical** theory of signs' based on 'the metamathematics of Hilbert', whereby we could 'consider the system of mathematical symbols' without 'regard for their content, and describe its transformation rules' 'without considering possible interpretations' (6.56; cf. 11.36). In return, Hjelmslev made no appeal to biology or chemistry, and placed physics, sociology, and psychology firmly outside the scope of his proposed discipline (cf. 6.7, 12, 14, 32, 43, 54, 62).

12.16 Logic played an influential role too in the unsettled relation between linguistics and **philosophy**. Having been a chief ancestor of linguistics, philosophy was a common target of censure from many theorists except the inclusive Hartmann (cf. 11.16f, 20, 33, 38, 94). Saussure's brief overview of the prior 'stages' of his 'science' omitted language philosophy outright, even its offshoots in philology, e.g., via Humboldt (cf. 2.5; 11.16f, 20). Sapir grouped 'philosophers' with 'romancers' as people concerned with 'what lies beyond the demonstrable' (3.67). Bloomfield blamed 'philosophy' for the disarray and confusion in 'traditional grammar', and derided the 'metaphysics' in such conceptions as 'universal forms of speech or of human "thought"' (4.4ff, 51, 72). Firth similarly chided the 'philosophically pretentious' nature of 'traditional grammatical categories', the reliance on 'logic and metaphysics', and the notion of 'universals'; he cheerfully forecast that 'during the next fifty years general linguistics may supplant a great deal of philosophy', Hjelmslev's work being one foretaste (8.5, 19, 16).

12.17 And Hjelmslev's deliberations did demarcate an important shift, abetted by the continuing march of 'positivism' and 'unified science' (Vienna Circle, Carnap, Neurath, Morris, Hempel, etc.).[11] For Bloomfield and Firth, 'logic' had been just a part of 'philosophy' and as such a baleful influence on traditional grammar (4.4f; 8.5, 17; cf. 3.23). Hjelmslev too occasionally gave 'logical' a negative sense by associating it with 'psychological', and strongly rejected 'metaphysics', a domain in which he surprisingly included 'realism', 'objects', and 'substance' (cf. 6.3, 7, 12ff, 28, 32, 39, 44). Yet he envisioned a new 'semiotics' as a 'logical theory of signs', inspired by the work of 'logicians' (Tarski, Carnap) (6.56). Evidently, formal logic was one branch of 'philosophy' free from all suspicion of 'metaphysics' and suited to offer a prestigious example for linguistics, as occasionally signalled also by Firth, Halliday, van Dijk and Kintsch, and Hartmann (cf. 8[7]; 9.59; 10.40; 11.64). Still, we find a more widespead undercurrent of scepticism in linguistic theorizing about the usefulness of models from logic.[12] Pike, for instance, was nonplussed by Hjelmslev's 'general, logical "grid"' of relations of a quasi-mathematical type', and by proposals for 'a theory' as 'a set' of 'postulates, definitions, transformation rules and theorems' (Olmstead 1954: 106), or for 'a scientific theory' 'constructed' upon a 'relevant mathematical system' (Peterson and Fillmore 1962: 477), and so on (LB 285, 71f) (cf. 5.86).[13]

12.18 In Chomsky's *Aspects*, the reverence for logic was coupled with the admission of philosophy at large, including areas once classed under metaphysics, e.g., 'universals', which are much less likely to emerge from empirical findings.[14] At that point, philosophy was set up as a full-fledged framework in opposition to the sociological and anthropological ones favoured by both structuralist and systemic-functional approaches (cf. 9.3f), thanks above all to the famous 'idealization' about the 'completely homogeneous speech community' (cf. 7.12, 7.96). Regarding other disciplines, Chomsky was syncretistic, even opportunistic, appropriating symbols and notations from mathematics and algebra, and comparing his own theory to 'a scientific theory' in 'physics', and his 'grammar' to a 'chemical theory' that 'generates all physically possible compounds' (cf. 7.16, 33, 36, 40, 7[18]). Or, he brought in biology by appealing to such notions as 'evolution' and 'neural organization' 'grounded in physical law' and by referring to 'animal learning', even though he elsewhere dismissed 'comparisons with species other than man' and asserted that 'language' is 'a human creation' (cf. 7.33, 35; 12.12). Still, Chomsky's invocations of 'natural science' (7.11) were not reflected or pursued very far in his actual proceedings. For example, his treatment of sentences was more elementary than a chemist's treatment of compounds: whereas compounds have emergent properties unlike those of the parts extracted by analysis (e.g., water vs oxygen and hydrogen), the sentences were supposed to be treated by the grammar as the sum of invariant parts and features (cf. 7.82; 12.59).

12.19 Chomsky's revitalized mentalism brought renewed attunement with psychology, but not with its then current paradigm. In effect, he envisaged a revolution in psychology to be steered by remote control from his new linguistics, which rejected the behaviourist inductive–experimental methods in favour of elaborate conceptions of 'intrinsic cognitive capacities' responsible for language acquisition (cf. 7.10f, 30–35). This intervention helped to hasten the decline of the stagnating behaviourist paradigm within psychology and to lend fresh momentum to the field of 'psycholinguistics', which provided new ways to test linguistic claims and, ironically, later uncovered the flaws in Chomsky's own paradigm, consumed so to speak by the outrunners of its own revolution (cf. 10.2f, 34, 40, 81).

12.20 By a curious symbiosis, contact with linguistics seems to cause other disciplines to undergo fractionation. Just as philosophy got polarized into 'bad' metaphysics and 'good' formal logic by Hjelmslev and the positivists, so also was psychology split into 'bad' behaviourist empiricism and 'good' innatist rationalism by Chomsky and the generativists. The counter-trend, namely an openness to cross-disciplinary currents despite inner-disciplinary rivalries, has been fairly rare and appears most clearly in Hartmann's synthesis, e.g., when he respected the philosophical approach of 'registering language as a phenomenon' rather than 'treating' it 'as an object' because 'the original experience should not be disturbed by dividing or combining' it, or by 'forcing language into predecided representations' (11.38).

12.21 The reverse side of this indebtedness to other disciplines was the remarkable eagerness of linguistics to present itself as the model or theoretical centre (cf. 2.7f; 4.88; 5.7, 84; 6.9f, 22, 32, 41, 53; 7.8; 8.16, 29, 35; 11.6, 9, 12, 33, 64; 12.59). Even Hjelmslev, whose theorizing remained in the most expressly preliminary stage, felt 'led to regard all science as centred around linguistics', and foresaw a perspective in which 'no object is not illuminated from the key position of linguistic theory' (6.10, 53). His reasoning may have resembled Firth's, who claimed that 'linguistics' as 'a social science' was 'ahead of the others in theoretical formulation and technique of statement'; or Pike's, who said that 'formal studies in the linguistic area' offer 'a base which' 'is easier to build on' (8.16; 5.7). Evidently, the abstractness, generality and rigour of linguistic theorizing were construed as advantages over sciences with more concrete empirical methods and more tangible objects (cf. 11.99; 12.60).[15]

12.22 Or, the key argument in claiming model status could be the centrality of language, which our theorists enjoy emphasizing (cf. 1.9; 2.8; 3.1, 3; 4.2, 10, 82; 6.2, 20; 8.12, 18; 11.9). Though language is not the only mode of human understanding, it is undeniably the most readily shared and documented mode, and thus ought to be a key domain in a general enterprise of exploring communication, epistemology, and social interaction.[16] However, as the shifting interdisciplinary scene indicates, the centrality of language does not necessarily establish the centrality of linguistics. For one thing, a house divided against itself or under continual reconstruction hardly offers an inviting haven for neighbouring enterprises that already have greater unity and continuity. For another thing, all the factors contributing to the centrality of language comprise too broad an expanse for linguistics to incorporate with any methods prevailing so far (cf. 8.39; 9.1, 24; 12.63). Some of the main issues that make language central to human understanding tend to be considered 'non-linguistic'.[17] Even the most conspicuous counter-example, Pike's foray into the 'non-verbal', brought along a markedly linguistic groundwork (cf. 5.8, 84).

12.23 Decisions about what factors to include or exclude significantly shape every linguistic school or approach and endow it with its peculiar glory and misery. The history of the field indicates that major issues can be left in the background only so long before they exert uncomfortable pressure on the conceptions and practices situated in the foreground. In consequence, linguistics has been prone to undergo 'gestalt' switches wherein foreground and background change places. For instance, the social and situational contexts of language use marginalized by Saussure were resolutely brought to centre stage by Bloomfield, Pike and Firth, later pushed behind the scenes again by Chomsky and his school, and then restored again to prominence by Halliday and van Dijk and Kintsch (cf. 12.14).

12.24 If language seems highly central at some times, it can also seem marginal or derivative at others. Much, though by no means all, of the apparent organization of language, including some of the traditional 'parts-of-speech' scheme and large areas of semantics, comes second-hand from the organization of a language community's world-model of 'reality'.[18] This 'reality' factor is reflected in the common-sense belief that language is primarily a means of 'representing' things and conveying 'information' (cf. 3.15; 8.47; 9.15, 11.68). But the factor has received very diverse treatment by linguists, from refusing to address it on grounds of 'arbitrariness' (Saussure) plus 'metaphysics' (Hjelmslev), or 'autonomous syntax' (early Chomsky), over to attacking it head-on in terms of behavioural 'hierarchies' (Pike), semantic 'universals' (later Chomsky), 'experiential' organization of clauses (Halliday), and finally actual 'world' models (van Dijk and Kintsch).[19] Gradually, everyday knowledge has been recognized as a cogent and powerful resource, not an unmanageable hodgepodge vastly inferior to scientific knowledge (cf. 4.22 and 8^7; 8^{14} vs 10.24). It cannot have a solely objective relation to language because objective knowledge is not appropriate or even possible for many domains that language must deal with; but language is the major means wherewith the subjective is negotiated into the intersubjective (cf. 11.12f; 12.58).

12.25 If we insist, as Saussure and Hjelmslev in particular did, on addressing only the organization 'in' language and not 'in' the external world (cf. 2.9; 6.64), we face the perennial problem of how to uncover the 'internal reality' of language (cf. 2.15; 6.12). Hjelmslev adopted the most startling recourse, abjuring reality altogether as a 'metaphysical' factor, vowing that 'linguistic theory cannot be verified (confirmed or invalidated) by reference to any existing texts and languages', and offering no 'discovery procedure' (cf. 6.12, 19, 61). His notion of 'theory' seems to have had an exceptional sense, i.e., 'formal system' or 'notation', which are indeed not verifiable but merely more or less insightful and appropriate. Yet to assume that a formal system or notation already *is* a theory or an explanation would set linguistics outside mainstream science, where theories must be testable (cf. 2.82; 7.86; 9^{12}; 10.6, 75, 99, 101f; 12.14, 19, 49, 57, 61). Evading this issue leads to such unusual senses of the term 'empirical' as those contrived by Hjelmslev and Chomsky (cf. 6.13, 7.85).

12.26 A more moderate and popular recourse for locating the reality in language has been to take the spoken sequence – the 'chain', 'string', 'utterance', 'sentence', etc. – and segment it into '**constituents**' until we obtain the '**minimal distinctive units**'.[20] This solution enjoyed exemplary success with language **sounds**: the smallest units were those that could make a **difference** between two speech events, usually uttered words (cf. 2.69f; 4.29ff, 34; 6.43; 7^{27}; 8.64f, 70; 11.80, 89). These 'distinctive' sound-units both constitute and are subsumed by an '**underlying**' (not directly 'manifested') system organized on a small number of criteria. However, these criteria were derived from the reality of **articulation**: not how the units in fact distinguish words or utterances but where and how they are formed by the speech organs (cf. 2.70, 73; 3.14, 18, 21; 4.29, 34; 5.42, 5^{12}; 6.43; 7.20; 8.66, 70; 11.80).[21] This derivation persisted despite the theoretical division between '**phonology**' (or 'phonemics') versus '**phonetics**', and remained the most reassuring backdrop for Saussure's vision of pure 'differences' ostensibly 'abstracted' away from 'substance' yet moored in the 'concrete' (cf. 2.16f, 26, 68; 6.13, 28ff; 11.25, 50). The concrete events (explosion, implosion, etc.) and sites (dental, labial, etc.) of articulation guaranteed the reality of the abstract system that preserves the identity of sound units ('phonemes') against the multitude of variations and accidents involved in acts of utterance, such as loudness, pitch, inflection, tone and quality of voice, emotional colouring, and so forth (cf. 2.68, 70; 3.20; 4.3, 45; 5.42f; 6.42f; 7.43; 8.23, 70; 11.80, 89). The correlation between phonemes and written letters was also reassuring, though usually rejected in theory (cf. 2.69; 3.19; 4.38, 45; 6^8; 8.71)

12.27 Buttressed by these implicit supports, phonology could afford a high abstractness – above all in its focus on pure 'difference', 'distinctiveness', 'opposition', and 'relation' – and its purportedly clean-cut separation between system and event, without seeming unrealistic or vague. Also, the phonemic system clearly showed the cogency of the notion of 'linguistic level' (cf. 4.71; 5.35; 7.46; 8.67; 9.30; 10.35; 11.82). Impressed by this feat, theorists aspired to project the methods and conceptions of phonology (often with phonetics in its wake) over to other domains of language (cf. 2.17, 67, 69ff; 3.18, 58f; 4.30; 5.42, 44, 5^{12}; 7.20, 71; 8.66f; 11.80, 82). 'Morphology' postulated its own minimal units of form, again those capable of differentiating utterances, and, in the early stage at least, suggested that these 'morphemes' were composed of phonemes (cf. 4.50; 5.36, 45; 7.46, 61; 11.82). Admittedly, neither the organization nor the inventory of morphemic systems could be as tidy and compact as those of phonemes, and articulatory criteria could no longer offer any concealed guarantee, though writing was still helpful (cf. 4.42). Even the familiar 'paradigms' like noun declensions and verb conjugations in conventional grammar seemed to some theorists rather diffuse and artificial, in part because they don't form sequences or chains (cf. 4.57ff, 86; 5.74; 6.34; 7.75f; 8.57, 59; 9.31, 9^{11}; 11.29, 71). I suspect the 'arbitrary' quality diagnosed in language is enhanced by the 'arbitrary' decisions and classifications linguists must increasingly make as they go beyond language sounds, the more so if communicative contexts are discounted.[22] An additional strain was exerted by the demand to keep the 'levels' separate, again doubtless inspired by the seeming independence of the phonemic level (cf. 5.34f; 7.20, 46; 8^{23}). And separating levels provided an argument for keeping them free of 'semantics' or 'meaning', which was, ironically, an original criterion in recognizing phonemes (cf. 4.14ff; 5.61; 6.43, 56, 60; 7.56ff; 8.31, 46, 56, 69).

12.28 The state of affairs became still more unsettling when linguistics moved on toward the 'levels' of description 'above' morphemics. There, neither constituency nor relative size offers fully reliable criteria, and each unit of a sequence differs from those before and after it in diverse, complex ways (cf. 2.58; 11.51). If we discount forms identifiable only through etymological derivation, many 'words' appear to consist of just one 'morpheme' (cf. 4.53; 5.40, 46, 53; 6.45). Also, although a 'phrase', 'sentence', or 'utterance' usually contains several words, some consist of just one word, and some consist of several words which none the less function as a self-sufficient unit (a 'fixed phrase') (cf. 2.55, 61; 3.34; 4.60; 5.32, 54; 7^{34}; 9.93; 10.80). In addition, the capacity of larger units for being subjected to interruption or interpolation implied 'discontinuous constituents', and the absence of a unit where one appeared in parallel forms implied 'zero' elements (cf. 4.10, 60; 5.6; 7.39; 8.61; 10.32, 64; 2^{26}; 4^3; 5.46, 5^{12}; 6^{16}; 7.75, 90). For such reasons, many diverse conjectures were made about how phrases, clauses, or sentences might form a system, and which types an inventory should list (cf. 3.37f; 4.68f; 5.57f, 5^{29}; 6.49; 7.50–53; 9.46, 54, 57f, 61–64, 74; 10.40, 67). Also, the border-line between morphology and syntax has remained problematic, due mainly to analogies between morphemes in words and words in phrases; and 'grammar' is generally construed to include both.[23]

12.29 These perplexities indicate that data should be distinguished not merely by the constituency and size of units, but by the aspect of language placed in focus. In American linguistics, the term '**level**' was somewhat indiscriminately defined both by size and by aspect, whereas the British proposed the term '**rank**' for sizes and 'level' for aspects (cf. 4.71; 5.34f; 7.45f; 8.51f; 9.30, 33ff, 75, 83; 10.16f, 35, 56; 11.82). The distinction is important because a 'higher level' may not always have 'larger' units than a 'lower one' (cf. 5.41), and because in theory, the levels should be natural and common to all human languages (cf. 4.71; 5.34f; 7.45; 8.51f; 9.30). In practice, 'rank' and 'level' would correspond roughly like this:[24]

Ranks	Levels	Units
sound, vowel, consonant	phonology	phonemes
word, stem, prefix, suffix, infix	morphology	morphemes
word, fixed phrase	lexicon	lexemes
word-part, word, phrase, clause, sentence	syntax	syntagmemes
proposition, predicate, argument	semantics	sememes
utterance, speech act, text, discourse	pragmatics	utteremes

These correspondences are conspicuously untidy, especially regarding the '**word**'. Hence, theorists were frequently uncertain about the status of the word, even though it is the entity ordinary people probably consider most obvious in language (cf. 2.18, 55, 2[7]; 3.31, 73; 4.54, 60; 5.53; 6.23; 7.70, 7[19]; 8.53f; 11.69, 71, 77; 12.32).

12.30 It was therefore predictable that the paradigm shift from **structuralist** toward **generative** approaches would involve a fundamental reorientation away from the minimal units obtained by inductive segmentation of utterances and placed in complete inventories (cf. 7.6). In the new paradigm, units could be postulated deductively and situated in more 'abstract', 'underlying' configurations of words and morphemes appearing alongside symbols (e.g., '"the + man + Aux + V + the + book"', SS 39) (cf. 12.51). The notations for 'rules' freely mixed items that correspond to discoverable, segmentable units together with items that only describe or classify units (e.g., 'V → [V + [+ Abstract] − Subject, + [Animate] − Object]', AS 114) (cf. 7.74). Words were treated in terms of 'lexical entries' of 'formatives' in which most 'features' did not fit segmentable units at all (e.g., 'boy, [+ Common, + Human, + Count, . . .]', AS 166), the plus sign now indicating mere presence, not concatenation (cf. 7.70ff; 12.33). This treatment circumvented the problem, latent in Hjelmslev's proposals, of how to handle semantics ('the content plane') by a progressive, exhaustive partition of text (the 'expression plane') even though meaning is not really linear or isolatable by segments (6.24, 42, 47f; 11.54; cf. 5.76; 7.71f). In return, the new freedom to postulate abstract items fostered an explosion of ad hoc constructions when the description became fairly detailed. No system of 'sememes' or 'semantic features' could be as neat and complete as the system of 'phonemes' anchored in articulation (cf. 12.26, 59).

12.31 This rising need to impose more control on non-manifest items and structures and on explosive, ad hoc inventories created an auspicious setting for computational and cognitive processing approaches. In the computational one, items, structures, and inventories were selected and organized in terms of computability, and the explosion inherent in a generative approach was confined by the development of new programming techniques as guides and heuristics for search and construction (cf. Winograd 1972, 1983). In the cognitive approach, items, structures, and inventories were justified by showing plausible effects of their presumed utilization during tasks like recognition or recall of discourse (cf. 10.27, 33, 42, 46, 50, 58f, 62, 77, 89, 94). Both approaches saw immediate advantages in studying realistic text and discourse, where controls are the most elaborate and semantics becomes more tractable.[25] However, the full status of the text will be appreciated only when we overcome the tendency, inherited from 'static' linguistics, to treat it as a stable configuration, and can see it as a dynamic process (cf. 2.36; 3.54; 5.31, 33; 6.33; 9.43, 95; 11.56). That step would in turn help in finding 'a more dynamic interpretation' of the 'system' than 'the static, set-theoretical view of whole' and 'parts' (11.52; cf. 12.36). If language is **action**, then the system is a potential for action, and the theory a mode of 'meta-action' (cf. 4.88; 5.7ff, 12, 26f, 50; 8.20ff, 26f, 46; 9.7ff; 10.5f, 11f; 12.58).

12.32 As we'd expect, this progression of paradigms drifted steadily away from phonology as the basic model. Hjelmslev's glossematics already proposed an 'analysis' of both 'the content plane' and 'the expression plane' into 'an inventory' of 'virtual elements' leading to 'essentially different results from the phonemic analyses hitherto attempted' (PT 99) (cf. 6.42, 49); one big difference would come from postulating *only* 'relations' and 'dependences', not 'units' (6.25, 28, 44f; cf. 5.20; 11.25). Despite their appeal to 'universal phonetic features', again grounded in articulation, generativists relegated phonological aspects to an after-the-fact 'interpretation' of strings 'generated' by the 'syntactic component', which was declared the 'sole creative' one because it alone could arrange and move things (cf. 7.20, 71, 67; 12.41). From a computational or a cognitive standpoint, language sounds are of interest only insofar as they assist processing in a 'bottom-up' manner, whereas the 'top-down' controls are more likely to be applied to higher levels and larger ranks (cf. 8.52; 10.13, 19, 25, 32, 55, 59, 73, 77; 12.44). In effect, sounds were now regarded not as a simplification but as a complication that could be postponed by assuming the input or output to consist of written character strings made of separate words (cf. 10.34, 10[35]). Here at least, the obvious heuristic value of the 'word' for both machines and people easily compensated for its troublesome role within purely segmental and classificatory sound-based schemes (cf. 3.31f; 12.28f).

12.33 Again predictably, the status of **written language** fluctuated in inverse proportion to the status of phonology. For strongly sound-oriented theorists like Saussure, Bloomfield and Pike, writing was merely derivative, if not misleading (cf. 2.21; 4.37, 45; 5[48]). But for theorists more interested in the 'higher levels', like Firth, Halliday, and van Dijk and Kintsch, writing was a major medium in its own right for both theory and practice (8.72ff; 9.42f; 10.67, 77, 93; cf. 3[26]). Firth still accepted language sounds as the procedural base and phonology as a model, but also advocated the investigation of corpuses of written texts, which can be strategically selected to exemplify a 'restricted language' (cf. 8.33, 65, 72ff, 81). Halliday treated sounds only in terms of the 'intonation' of longer stretches of utterance and their communicative intent or impact, not of their minimal differential units, and ranked speech over writing in terms of complexity (cf. 9.52, 42). Both Firth and Halliday hoped for a really new 'grammar of spoken language', but were content to compromise by revising the traditional one, which they admitted was centred on writing (especially in regard to the 'sentence') (8.58, 67, 73; 9.24, 43, 82, 9[41]; 12.7; cf. 2.21; 4.39; 7.61). Later, formalist approaches relied directly (albeit metaphorically) on the spatial quality of written representations as sentences or symbol chains with 'left' and 'right' sides, etc., and discounted the unfolding of utterances in time (cf. 2.17, 60, 72; 5.27; 6.50; 7.48; 11.47, 83; 12.33). Even Chomsky, the champion of underlying order, once called for 'a general theory of linguistic structure' whose 'notions' like 'phrase' and 'transformation' 'are defined' 'in terms of physical and distributional properties of utterances' (SS 54).

12.34 For an empirical, experimental approach, the modalities of spoken versus written language must be handled as a concrete factor in tasks such as production, perception, recognition, and recall. Most research for longer stretches of discourse has centred on reading, while listening has been addressed chiefly in phoneme or word-recognition tasks in very limited contexts (cf. 10[35]; cf. Beaugrande 1980, 1984a, 1986b). Some research indicates that reading involves phonological recoding, but whether this is obligatory or exhaustive has been questioned (cf. 4[13]; 4[15]; 10[35]) (references in Beaugrande 1984a: 224). Van Dijk and Kintsch did not try to resolve the issue of recoding, which does not decisively affect the overall comprehension of discourse in terms of knowledge structures, and they saw a continuity between their own research and the ethnographic work on oral narratives and folktales (cf. 10.1, 60ff).

12.35 The foregoing sketch suggests overall that when linguistic theory moves away from language sounds, alternative controls are introduced, such as the frameworks of formal logic or operational processing. Also, the greater the concern for extended realistic communication, the more evident it becomes that exhaustive analysis into minimal, fully distinctive units is a specialized concern, useful for some tasks, such as preliminary discovery of otherwise uninvestigated languages, but by no means an account of language as a human phenomenon, a processing medium, or an interactional domain (cf. 3.24; 7.6, 30; 8.31). However, recent trends also indicate a widening awareness that such an account is unlikely to emerge out of any 'pure' linguistics isolated from other disciplines, particularly from sociological, anthropological, and psychological issues (5.7f; 8.16; 9.2; 10.1, 4f, 100, 102; 11.3; 12.14, 53). Saussure's famous demand for a 'linguistics' whose 'unique object' 'is language studied in and for itself' (2.9) ultimately means taking language as a given and abandoning the project of explaining it.

12.36 This recent awareness sends us back to the 'uses' of language that Saussure so emphatically set aside, and to a re-examination of his division between 'langue' and 'parole'.[26] It now seems more productive to view the two not as a *static dichotomy*, but as a *dynamic dialectic* that can be suspended or abstracted out only by lowering control over both theory and practice. Either we investigate how the knowledge of language influences the uses of language and vice versa, or we leave the dialectic as a hidden step within the linguists' own discovery and analysis and have few real guarantees of consistency or reliability from case to case (cf. 1.9; 12.1, 49; Beaugrande 1984b, 1987a, b, 1988b, 1989b). A study of people using language is also the best foundation for a comparative study of linguists analysing language (cf. 5.9, 13f, 16, 18, 20, 36, 46; 6.58; 8.36, 83; 11.5, 39, 84).

12.37 The dialectic can be pictured as a bi-directional complementarity, wherein each side *controls* the other by *limiting its indeterminacy* (Figure 12.1).

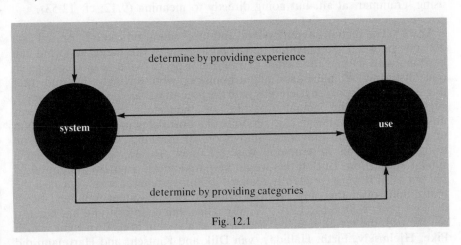

Fig. 12.1

On the one hand, the 'system' of the language as known to the communicative participants determines what items, relations, and significances they assign to any instance of language in use. On the other hand, the steadily accruing body of experience with language use is both the source of that knowledge and a continual influence upon it.

12.38 Presumably, language acquisition involves some stage at which the system assumes a *'critical mass'* in the sense that it can be effectively applied to most instances of use without undergoing any further radical

revisions (cf. 1.9). How the system might be organized prior to that stage is
among the most difficult questions for linguistics. The structuralists left the
question aside and constructed their own 'grammars' of remote languages
from the ground up, though with an enormous head start over the native
child, namely their knowledge about other language systems and about
language as a cultural factor (cf. 5.26).[27] They were unfairly attacked by the
generativists, who openly claimed that language acquisition operates the
same way as the linguist's grammar-constructing process, for having created
an implausible acquisition model (cf. 7.24f, 88). But Chomsky's *Aspects*
offered no account either about what an infantile language system might
look like prior to critical mass, nor indeed about how linguists should
construct a grammar (cf. 7.9). He merely invoked 'the best information now
available', without saying what it was, as proof that 'children cannot help
constructing' a 'transformational grammar' (cf. 7.89). He skipped over the
details of this process by adopting an 'idealized "instantaneous" model'
where 'successful language acquisition' happens in one 'moment', and by
declining to 'consider' the 'order and manner' in which 'linguistic data' 'are
presented', or the 'series of successively more detailed and structured
schemata corresponding to maturational stages' (cf. 7.89). Finally, Halliday's
'systemic' approach postulated a 'proto'-stage in which children are not yet
using 'grammar' at all, but going directly to meaning (9.12; cf. 12.53).

12.39   The dichotomy of 'system' and 'use' can also be reinterpreted as a
dialectic between the **potential** or **virtual** aspects of the language (what can
be done with it) and the **actual** or **realized** aspects (what is in fact done in
real discourse).[28] Saussure and Chomsky, who strongly insisted that
linguistic theory concern itself only with the potential ('langue', 'competence'),
suggested that the actual ('parole' or 'langage', 'performance') was
unsystematic (cf. 2.19f; 7.12). Bloomfield's postulates of 'infinite' variation
of circumstance and universal 'innovation' of meaning, with 'every person
using speech-forms in a unique way' (cf. 4.14, 16, 31, 75, 78), carried a
similar suggestion. But all this would be paradoxical: a virtual system could
not persist if it were frequently realized in non-systematic ways, because the
realizations offer the only tangible evidence that a system is indeed being
deployed (cf. 2.20; 8.61; 11.67, 77, 83). Thus, the counter-trend has been to
see the use, the actual realized discourse, as a system in its own right, which
Pike, Hjelmselv, Firth, Halliday, van Dijk and Kintsch, and Hartmann did
(cf. 5.7f; 6.34–37, 45, 6[11], 6[12]; 8.43ff, 49f, 52, 65, 70, 76, 80; 9.22, 24, 26, 41,
55, 102, 109; 10.19, 23, 32, 56, 86; 11.47, 55f). Most recently, computational
and cognitive approaches have undertaken to develop explicit models for
the systematic quality of actualization processes, whether simulated or
human (cf. 10.13, 16, 21f, 26f, 29, 34, 74f, 78) (cf. Winograd 1972, 1983).
Despite the longstanding limitation of linguistics to the sentence (cf. 12.54),
longer stretches of discourse are evidently not unmanageably higher in
complexity; on the contrary, sentences in context are easier to process,
whereas isolated ones will seem more indeterminate or 'ambiguous' (cf. 5.56f;
7.14, 61, 82; 9.16; 10.2f, 86, 91; 11.43). Similarly, 'context-free grammars'
may look clearer and easier to write but prove more awkward and effortful
to apply to realistic samples (cf. 7.48, 73f; 10.40).

12.40 Bloomfield's 'innovation' postulate and Chomsky's 'uniqueness' argument (cf. 4.16, 61; 7.90f) signal a pervasive discomfort about language being open and flexible, allowing even modifications of the system itself. To minimize the issue, linguists typically preferred 'clear cases' that were either obviously acceptable or totally bizarre, and discounted the effects of 'far-fetched' contexts (cf. 4.67; 7.21, 41f, 58). Rules and formalisms were neatly constructed by postponing the stage of diminishing returns where we move beyond the core of clear cases and structures into areas where the controls are more variable and may be due to factors other than language (cf. 8.43, 52; 9.2, 40; 10.3; 12.43f). Distressingly, native speakers have proven unskilled in deciding what sentences or utterances do or do not belong to their language or 'grammar', no doubt because this decision seldom arises in real discourse. What is or is not produced or accepted as an utterance depends on the participants' 'intentions', a factor whose relevance for linguistic theory was in dispute (cf. 2.20, 80; 3.15 and 8.63 vs 5.65; 10.11, 10^{21} and 11.10). It also depends on parameters of 'style', another disputed factor (cf. 3.69; 5.82; 6.52; 7.41, 53; 8.83; 9.102; 10.57). For these reasons, no secure empirical basis is likely to be found for a 'purely formal' account of 'degrees of grammaticalness' (cf. 7.42; 9.102) – an ominous prospect for theories which rest on a firm opposition between 'grammatical' and 'ungrammatical' (cf. 7.36, 41f; 12.59).

12.41 Yet linguistics cannot indefinitely ignore creative uses of language not foreseen by the system (cf. 7.44; 11.35, 56, 58). A conspicuous instance is modernist poetry, which violates the conventions both of ordinary discourse (including grammar) and of traditional poetry, yet can be appreciated by focusing on relations among events and choices within the newly emerging pattern (Beaugrande 1979, 1986a). But more modest examples of creativity can be found in much 'ordinary' discourse, where unusual but appropriate usages are readily produced and accepted (cf. 9.42; Beaugrande and Dressler 1981). Such creativity can hardly be accounted for in terms of the 'recursive processes' developed in 'mathematics' (which only repeat embedded structures), nor of any purely 'syntactic component' (which only reshuffles formal sequences) (cf. 7.44, 67; 12.32).

12.42 The dialectic described between the knowledge and the use of language has a useful analogy in the dialectic between '**theory**' and '**data**' in linguistics, again with each side 'controlling' the other by limiting its indeterminacy (Figure 12.2) (cf. Beaugrande 1987a; Yates and Beaugrande 1990). On the one hand, the 'theory' of language controls what items, relations, and significances linguists will assign to any instance of language data. On the other hand, the 'data' control what theoretical constructs are likely to be postulated, especially when the language under investigation has a markedly different organization than do the languages for which the theory had been designed. The organization of familiar languages tends to pervade the theory in less noticeable ways, whence the urgent need for defamiliarization (cf. 2.32; 3.5, 50; 8.14; 12.7).

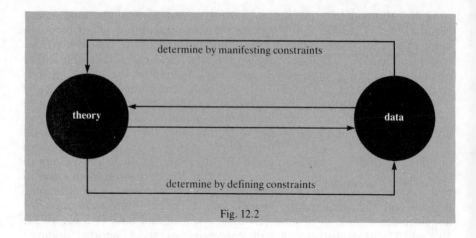

Fig. 12.2

12.43   This dialectic entails complex dilemmas because the determination may be too low or too high. Theory is *underdetermined* by actual data in that (a) several theories are usually possible for the same data; and (b) the data sample can never be complete (cf. 2.12; 4.67; 7.23, 43). Linguists must rely on their intuitions about when a 'critical mass' is attained such that the data sample can be judged sufficient and representative for a theoretical account of a 'whole system', and high-level frameworks can be applied to detailed analysis (cf. 3.4, 6; 4.16, 23, 29, 67, 78; 5.2, 37f; 6.20; 8.44, 65, 70, 76; 9.19, 26; 11.94). Ideally, the theory itself might supply explicit criteria for such a judgment, but in practice we have been content so far with approximations. Theory is also *overdetermined* in that (a) it sets up criteria and categories with standards for rigour and formality to which at least some data do not conform; and (b) the native speakers producing the data never have a full consciousness of its theoretical organization. Reciprocally, data are *overdetermined* in that (a) their occurrence always involves at least some circumstances that are merely accidental but necessary, such as exact time and place of utterance; and (b) other factors, such as speakers' personality traits or emotional states, control the data besides the relation to an underlying language system. And data are *underdetermined* in the sense that (a) collected data are finite, but the data that could belong to language are infinite; and (b) specific choices are often significant in respect to others that were *not* made, but could have been, according to varying degrees of probability or 'markedness'.[29] Due to the diverse pressures of under- and overdetermination, linguistic theory remains uncomfortably compelled both to enrich and to rarefy its theories and its data. We enrich by constructing theoretical categories too complex to be explicitly taught or learned by ordinary speakers, and rarefy by classifying large numbers of distinct data events as being, for our purposes, the 'same' or 'different'. And we also enrich our data by adding 'underlying' organization and formality, and rarefy by discounting 'superficial' organization and fuzziness, often without explicit criteria for deciding what to add or detract and where to start or stop.

12.44 The complementary dialectic between theory and data strongly recommends a concerted interaction between **inductive** 'models of data' abstracted from empirical instantiations, and **deductive** 'models on theory' specifying the theory under given conditions (Yates 1986) (cf. 10.17; 11.8; 12.19, 31). Such an interaction plainly occurs during the use and comprehension of language: inductively taking into account the elements and structures (e.g., words and phrases) we judge to have been selected ('bottom-up' processing), while deductively constructing and testing hypotheses about what is being said or will be said, and what it probably means for us ('top-down' processing).[30] Like acquisition, comprehension attains a 'critical mass' whereby the discourse can be understood without major revisions (cf. 12.38), but this usually occurs so readily and rapidly that little is known about the inductive and deductive operations involved. In all probability, the knowledge being applied extends well beyond language (cf. 10.15; 11.10, 32, 36; 12.40).

12.45 Surprisingly, however, linguistic theory has tended to argue for just one outlook at the expense of the other, notably Bloomfield for induction, Hjelmslev and Chomsky for deduction (cf. 4.7, 76; 6.16f; 7.5ff, 25, 30, 34). These imbalances created predictable blind spots and vagaries in both argument and method. The inductivists' heavy reliance on 'observation' of 'manifest activity' entrained them in a potential explosion of data for the 'infinite' variety of situations, while their theories remained parsimonious (e.g., based on 'constituency' or 'minimal units') (cf. 4.8, 13f, 31, 61; 5.19, 25, 28, 38, 52, 80f, 85; 8.42; 12.26). The deductivists' reliance on 'intuition' left them uncertain about how data can be gathered and matched against theoretical constructions, which became luxuriant and highly technical (cf. 6.25, 59; 7.81). Moreover, the match between theory and data was often prematurely built right into the deductive terminology, e.g., by 'using the term "**grammar**"' both for 'the native speaker's internally represented "theory of his language"' and for 'the linguist's account of this' (7.15; cf. 7.28, 78). Applying the same terms to a set of events and to one's analysis of it stems from a long non-operational and non-empirical tradition (cf. 11.70, 77), which ultimately must be replaced by detailed demonstrations that the two indeed do match (cf. 12.57).

12.46 Although it is still far from settled what the relationship between language and linguistics is or should be, we can imagine at least five scenarios (Figure 12.3) (Beaugrande 1987b). (i) *Language contains linguistics* (1a): the activity of 'doing linguistics' is just one more instance of language being used, not essentially different in kind from other instances. (ii) *Linguistics contains language* (1b): the activity of 'doing linguistics' has language as one domain within its larger, more abstract study of the general formal, combinatorial, and organizational properties of sign systems. (iii) *Linguistics and language overlap, but neither contains the other* (1c): the two

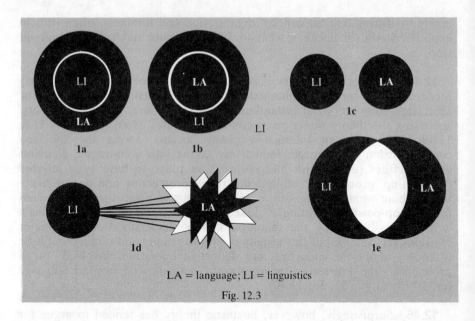

LA = language; LI = linguistics

Fig. 12.3

domains share some aspects, but neither can be fully subsumed by the other. Linguistics studies language in relation to other aspects, such as social organization; and yet linguistics never gets the entirety of language into its scope of vision. (iv) *Linguistics disturbs language* (1d): the activity of 'doing linguistics' suspends the normal operation or function of language in order to scrutinize, generalize, objectify, formalize, and so on, perhaps in the way that 'doing biology' entails starving, injuring, or killing living organisms. (v) *Linguistics is independent of language* (1e): the activity of 'doing linguistics' is independent from language, perhaps in the way that 'doing biology' is separate from the coding and decoding of enzymes.

12.47 These five scenarios form a rough continuum between two extremes: complete mutual containment at one end versus complete independence at the other. The extreme scenarios are virtually impossible to maintain in an absolute sense, and none of our theorists does assert that doing linguistics is just a typical use of language, or that linguistics and language are fully independent. Nor did they maintain that linguistics ought to embrace the whole of language plus other sign systems, but reserved that enormous expanse for 'semiology' or 'semiotics' (cf. 2.8f; 6.10, 50–56; 9.110; 10.43; 11.6). The theorists usually opted for some version of the 'overlap' scenario, pushed in one direction or the other. Interactive approaches that acknowledged the role of the linguist as language understander and communicative participant (Sapir, Pike, Firth, Hartmann) tended toward the 'containment' scenario, whereas formalizing, logic-based approaches that discounted the linguist's role (Hjelmslev, Chomsky) tended toward the 'independence' scenario. The 'disturbance' scenario has been recognized by both fieldworkers like Pike and experimentalists like van Dijk and Kintsch, who air the prospect that their investigations can be intrusive on normal language operations (cf. 5.13; 10.92, 10^4). Conversely, the generativists ironically implied that *language disturbs linguistics* due to 'degenerate performance', 'irrelevant' and 'unrevealing surface structure', and so on (cf. 7.24, 62, 82, 84; 9.5; 10.100).

12.48 The 'overlap' scenario offers the best framework to explore how the investigation *of* language is carried on to a great degree both *in* and *by means of* language (cf. 1.8f; 5.23; 6.55, 58; 8.33–36, 39; 9.27; 11.12f; 12.50). Reciprocally, we can inquire how the traits of language may parallel those of a science, as Hartmann has done, e.g.: 'language science' 'shares the borderline status of language, compelled to run on multiple tracks, combine standpoints and results, and adopt a general outlook' (11.12; cf. 11.40, 44, 46, 48, 69, 87, 93, 98). The conspicuous specialized terminologies in linguistics indicate a widespread ambition to create a 'metalanguage' whose application and force are not of the same order as ordinary language. This ambition falls under the general strategies for founding a 'discipline' or 'science' by setting it apart from the pre-scientific practice it proposes to describe, and supplying theoretical concepts and terms to supplant 'pre-theoretical' ones. But the new terms must both reliably relate to their definienda and form a coherent system among themselves, and so far such demands have been only provisionally engaged.[31]

12.49 Moreover, our theories must in some way take into account the presumed language knowledge of ordinary 'speakers'.[32] Some of our theorists have cautioned that such speakers would either not make any analysis or would make an inadequate one.[33] But most theorists compromised by arguing that their account addresses knowledge which speakers do have but of which they are not 'conscious'; the linguist approaches the same data, but with higher 'awareness'.[34] This argument puts the linguists in the awkward stance of claiming powers of reasoning and insight not open to normal people, much the same stance criticized for traditional grammarians (cf. 4.5; 8.7f). The best grounds for such claims would be results showing that one's insights generate predictions confirmed by empirical tests. Other solid grounds would be a thorough knowledge of numerous languages with extremely diverse organizations (cf. 2.10). To base the claims only on having a theory or formalism is less compelling, since the theory increases 'the danger' of 'hearing one's own thoughts' (cf. 11.38), especially when formalisms receive more attention than the data do, and when having a notation is equated with having a 'theory' (cf. 12.25, 49).

12.50 In any event, attempts to create a completely independent 'theoretical' apparatus without *any* grounding in ordinary language are unlikely to succeed. The normal business of any discipline, including the bulk of theoretical argumentation and practical demonstration, must be conducted in discourse, and no discourse, however many formalisms we deploy, can be fully separated from ordinary language. An artificial formal language can be a revealing construct only if we pay close attention to how it is made and used, and do not allow it to take on a life of its own by dictating to us what we can label and classify or by erasing the vital characteristics of natural data (cf. 8.31; 9.5). For example, the multiple structurings of a clause as a syntactic pattern, a transitivity configuration, and an information slope were often collapsed into a single one because most formalisms are syntactically oriented (cf. 5.40; 9.46, 55, 75, 109). Evidently, formal 'algorithms' are a two-edged sword for both discovering and concealing potential data (cf. 5.62, 86; 9.110; 10.14).

12.51 In recent linguistics, the balance between theory and data has been weighted by a large number of alternative non-language representations, such as 'symbols', 'bracketings', 'trees', 'matrices', and so on.[35] Such formalisms suggest generality, since each representation can 'stand for' numerous possible 'realizations' in language material. However, the further a representational mode is indeed removed from language, the more fresh problems can arise in providing reliable, intersubjective methods for translating between actual data and formal representation, and the more quarrels can come up about results, thus imperilling generality. The problems have been sidestepped somewhat by allowing actual words to appear as well in symbol strings or trees, and by treating actual sentences as if they were the underlying structures themselves (cf. 12.30; 7.80). A truly exhaustive conversion of language examples into formal representation would soon become explosive and opaque (for illustrations, see the structuralist approach of Koch 1971, or the generative one of van Dijk, Ihwe, Petöfi and Rieser 1972). A more workable and pragmatic approach would be to select a fairly language-like representation for ranking and measuring data (such as a proposition structure), which different researchers can apply with reliable agreement (cf. 10.43).

12.52 A disquieting trade-off seems to be at work here. 'General linguistics' naturally wants to construct a metalanguage that does not inherit the same degrees of complexity, variety, and indeterminacy characteristic of ordinary language, but instead meets the aspirations of science for simplicity, unity, and determinacy. Yet an unduly forceful attempt to squeeze the complexity, variety, and indeterminacy out of the theory and its metalanguage simply tends to relocate it all in the relation between the theory and its domain of data (Figure 12.4). The more we strive for rigour in theory, the harder it may become to decide exactly how the theory relates to natural language data. This would strongly apply to a fully formalized theory with a completely new and precise metalanguage, as attempted most radically by Hjelmslev, who also provides the least data for illustration. Chomsky hoped that formality could be combined with simplicity, and his 'grammar' was claimed to meet both standards; but his theory grew steadily more complex anyway, despite his tactic of moving complexities out of the grammar into the lexicon (cf. 7.36f, 50, 70, 73). A 'realistic' approach, in contrast, acknowledges the great variety of possible discourse events, which even controlled experiments cannot eliminate, but also the effectiveness of discourse strategies (not strict 'rules' or 'algorithms') for managing

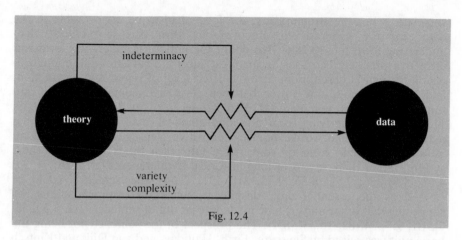

Fig. 12.4

complexity and imposing determinacy on many kinds of 'input' and 'information' (cf. 10.6, 14).

12.53 A promising solution, and one finally gaining ground in science (cf. Bohm 1980; Prigogine and Stengers 1984; Bohm and Peat 1987; Gleik 1987), is to seek order in apparently accidental or uncontrollably complex domains by revising our conventional conceptions of 'science' and its clean-cut divisions into areas and disciplines with well-fenced problems. In linguistics, this strategy would mean that new models with an interdisciplinary basis can assist the treatment of more data which are 'realistic' in quality, large in scale, sensitive to context and goals, and controlled also by non-language aspects. Among the 'strictly linguistic' approaches to date, Halliday's has pursued this direction the furthest, and perhaps as far as could be done while still maintaining an applicability to the whole of English, and maybe to other languages as well (cf. 9.25). Wider contexts have been addressed heuristically from both the outside of the clause or sentence and the outside of linguistics proper by van Dijk and Kintsch, using knowledge structures ('frames', 'schemas', etc.) as controls on text processing (cf. 12.14, 24, 34). No claims were made here that the synthesis and analysis of language sequences entails an exhaustive segmental or classificatory treatment on each separate level; instead, people are presumed to use a mixture of cues and clues from all levels and to be content with a fuzzy, but reasonably adequate result (cf. 2.33; 5.34f, 53; 7.46; 8^{23}; 9.34; 10.15, 35; 11.82; 12.27, 57). It has indeed been argued that where appropriate, people circumvent syntactic analysis altogether (cf. 9.39; 10.4, 34; 12.38), a prospect linguists might not relish.

12.54 Still, the leitmotiv in linguistics until Halliday has been the accentuation of form over content and function. Categories, distinctions, and meanings have usually gained recognition only if they had some formal correlate.[36] For the structuralists, the forms had to be discoverable in the data; for the generativists, discoverable form was less crucial than underlying form (cf. 12.28ff). No doubt the notion of underlying form was attractive precisely because the manifest substrate isn't 'formal' enough to enable structural descriptions at the desired level of rigour and abstraction, and because one-to-one ratios between form and content or form and function are not predominant (cf. 3.16, 32; 4.17, 26, 50; 5.48, 64; 6.27; 9.39; 11.14). Also, underlying form provided an ideal level for supposing that manifest forms, like words, phrases, or whole clauses and sentences, are mutually derivable from or convertible into each other within the same system, rather than, say, over long historical developments (cf. 3.26, 34, 39; 4.65; 5.54, 56; 7.52; 8.56; 9.75, 81f, 101). Thus, the 'sentence' could be treated as the essential unit, despite its uncertain empirical status, by supposing that other units can be made into or out of sentences (cf. 5.30, 56; 7.51ff; 9.5, 34, 82; 10.33f, 85f). The prospect of the sentence *not* being the basic unit was raised by Saussure, Firth, Halliday, and van Dijk and Kintsch (2.61; 8.55; 9.82; 10.2f, 16), but they all (except Saussure) worked with it anyway.

12.55   And yet this very striving for abstraction and formality entailed the trade-off I described between a gain and a loss of control. The same contextual factors carefully reasoned out of the theory can be the actual means whereby people control their own operations when they use language (cf. 2.85; 5.57; 10.3, 92). An artificial vacuum was created when whatever did not seem properly abstract and formal was deemed 'non-linguistic' (cf. 12.22). What was left seemed extremely rarefied, and an increasingly large part of the discovery, preparation, and analysis of the data had to be done behind the scenes (cf. 12.36). The famous concept of 'transformation', originally introduced to gain control by compacting many structures into a few, also had the opposite effect by proliferating undesirable structures (cf. 7.50ff; Woods 1970).

12.56   For the same reason, the issue of how to choose between alternative 'grammars', now rated as 'theories' (cf. 7.8f, 37–40, 92), became more convoluted as the linkage to data became more mediated and abstract. The structuralists had typically made their 'grammars' out in the field and saw no special motive to justify them on any other grounds than the heuristic derivation (cf. 12.38). Chomsky correctly foresaw that his new approach could lead to a substantial number of competing 'grammars' for one and the same language, which would not have been such an imminent scenario for practising fieldworkers. He deployed this new plurality to develop complex arguments about criteria for choosing a grammar without regard to how it might have been constructed, and asserted that 'evaluation' and 'decision' should take precedence over 'discovery' (cf. 7.8). The structuralists were totally unprepared for such debates; they could only point to the hundreds of grammars they had in fact constructed, an achievement Chomsky refused to recognize (cf. 5.2, 89; 7.5, 87).

12.57   I see no principled abstract solution to these longstanding controversies over how to balance theory and data, knowledge and use, potential and actual, and so on. Our problems may after all have been aggravated by premature aspirations to find and enforce such solutions. A concrete empirical analysis and testing of ordinary language communication seems to me the only recourse for a multitude of issues which cannot be resolved by introspection or intellectual judgment; the greater the body of findings, the easier it will be to rate competing theories (or 'grammars') by criteria such as 'psychological' and 'social reality'.[37] For example, it seems intuitively plausible, and congenial for linguistics as well, that when an utterance is produced and then comprehended, the same operations run first in one direction and then in the reverse: the producer goes from deeper (or 'higher') levels to the 'surface structure' (or 'lower' levels), and the comprehender goes back again, both working thoroughly and independently through each level in terms of its own proper constituents (cf. 7.83; 11.47). But empirical research proves that this appealingly reversible scheme does not fit the actual operations people perform: the two process groups run partly in parallel, and various levels are consulted throughout (cf. 5.32, 34f; 10.15, 81; 12.53). Evidently, 'the strategy types of the largest scope' are the 'most fundamental to understanding' 'language' (10.32; cf. 5.19). Leaving them aside exaggerates the impression that the relation between signifier and signified is 'arbitrary' (cf. 2.85; 12.27).

12.58   I would have to agree with Halliday that 'a theory being a means of action', we must consider what 'action' we 'want to take' 'involving' 'language' so we will know what is 'relevant' and 'interesting' for 'the investigation or the task at hand' (9.1; cf. 1.11; 10.6; 11.4; 12.31). Until we determine our goals, we do not have adequate criteria or controls either for designing a theory or for selecting a set of manifestations as evidence of a general system, pattern, or consensus within the language. Though our theorists may argue for a disinterested 'objective' viewpoint, the 'subjective' aspects cannot be fully eliminated but at best negotiated toward an intersubjective viewpoint – just what language itself is so well suited for doing (cf. 11.12; 12.24).[38] If 'other sciences work with objects that are given in advance' while in 'linguistics' 'the viewpoint' 'creates the object' (cf. 2.9), then we need to probe the commonalities and divergences of our viewpoints.

12.59   Inevitably, an intersubjective grounding cannot be fully stable. The approaches built close to large amounts of data, such as Sapir's, Pike's, Halliday's, and van Dijk and Kintsch's, can expect to encounter substantial 'indeterminacy' and 'fuzziness' in categories, concepts, and boundaries.[39] But apart from Pike's notion of 'waves' (cf. 5.31, 87), few provisions were made for representing this factor in an explicit part of the theory, and 'probabilistic' models and 'statistical' methods were often rejected with questionable arguments (cf. 4.27, 77; 6.62; 7.90f, 7^{30}, 7^{42}; 8.31; 10^9; 11.35). Many linguistic theorists seemed to believe it devolved upon *them* to postulate and reconstruct some definitive determinate order or taxonomy. This aspiration may pass in phonology, where 'opposition' is the major factor, but makes superhuman demands in semantics, where 'determination' must be performed from case to case (cf. 11.54), where no set of ultimate 'minimal units' can be found, and where the idea of meaning as a sum of parts is ultimately unworkable.[40] The abstraction away from ordinary contextual controls magnifies the task still more, as does the demand to write a rule system explicitly excluding all disallowed utterances or sentences (cf. 7.41; 12.40). Many idiosyncrasies within usage are probably specific to a small area or even a single locution; but the proposals to pack them all into the 'dictionary' or 'lexicon' is not helpful as long as the organization of such a lexicon has not been explained in detail (cf. 2.29, 2[21]; 4.46, 48f, 52, 59; 6.48; 7.70f; 10.3). And even the most comprehensive lexicon could not be expected to store *all* the information and instructions for all possible uses of the entries. Thus, both lexicon and grammar must be designed to allow for fuzziness, indeterminacy, and probability (cf. 12.7, 54).

12.60 The ambition for a 'general linguistics' may encourage the notion that a prior statement of goals is unnecessary, perhaps even restrictive. In consequence, when Hjelmslev calls for a linguistic theory to cover not merely all existing languages but all possible ones, the only goal he raises is to establish 'linguistics' as the 'centre' of 'all science' (cf. 6.10). Similarly, when Chomsky says 'the main task of linguistic theory must be to develop an account of linguistic universals', he offers no goal except 'explanatory adequacy' relating 'an explanation of the intuition of the native speaker' to 'an empirical hypothesis about the innate predisposition of the child', and thereby conveniently excluding demands for application by showing that 'one cannot really teach language' (cf. 7.19, 23, 32). Perhaps the ambitions to make linguistics the very model of theory (cf. 12.21) filled the place of more tangible goals, especially for the more formalized theories, which are inherently hard to apply to social or educational needs (cf. 9.2).

12.61 For van Dijk and Kintsch, 'the main criterion for the success' of a 'general theory' lies in its power to 'derive fruitful situation- and task-specific models' and 'experimental tests' of 'principles and implications' (10.101). This is still a self-directed goal: using theory to keep the usual methods moving along. However, they go on to suggest that 'our knowledge' about 'comprehension processes', derived from such 'experiments', enables better 'control' 'over subject–text interaction' (10.102). Wide prospects for applying empirically anchored theories to communication are indicated here, such as methods to make reading and learning more efficient, or to teach native or foreign languages, including 'restricted' ones (cf. 4.85–88; 5.89; 8.9f, 12, 14, 65, 89; 9.111; 10.94f). The more direct and detailed our applications, the broader our empirical base has to be.

12.62 Whatever their declared motives, our theorists certainly had expansive moods and evoked vast panoramas. For Saussure and Sapir, 'linguistic questions interest all who work with texts' (2.87), including the 'outside public' (3.2). For Bloomfield, 'the study of language may help us toward the understanding and control of human events' (4.88). Pike hoped for 'a theory, a set of terms, and an analytical procedure' to make 'intelligible' not merely 'language behaviour and overt physical activity' but 'all human overt and covert activity', 'all psychological processes', all 'responses to sensations, all of thinking and feeling' (5.89). Hjelmslev saw 'linguistic theory' 'reaching its prescribed goal' by 'recognizing' 'man and human society behind language, and all man's sphere of knowledge through language' (6.64). For Firth, 'general linguistic theory' should undertake 'a serial contextualization of our facts, context within context, each one a function' 'of a bigger context, and all contexts finding a place' in 'the context of culture' (8.91).[41]

12.63   Whether linguistics can attain such scope and significance remains to be seen. We must concede, without much surprise, that the outcome to date falls far short of these panoramas. As is typical for would-be founders, our theorists themselves often stress the incomplete or provisional character of their models.[42] And in principle, the 'image' of 'language' 'in linguistics' remains 'incomplete' because it 'must allow the right set or combination of features' to 'emerge from the progress of research and insight' 'by means of successive correction through new findings' (11.39).

12.64   Still, linguistics has already been influential in language education and language policy-making, as well as psychology and social science. And computation and cognitive research show linguistic contributions being put to work in broad new ways, notably under the interdisciplinary aegis of 'cognitive science' (cf. 10.1, 5, 102). It might therefore not be unduly sanguine to expect further uses and influences in the future. Conditions will be most favourable if we can keep the richness of our past firmly in mind and view our total achievements within a concerted assembly, not within a set of rotating and disputatious fragments. With so much still to discover, we must strive to remain aware of *all* our options. If this book can aid such an awareness, I will be most content.

Notes

1.   In this section I use the abbreviations listed at the front of the book or, where relevant, cross-references to particular paragraphs in the preceding chapters. Bulky lists of cross-references are given in these Notes. Individual terms can also be traced through the Index.
2.   A revealing contrast to surveys like mine can be found by seeing how recent Kuhnian textbooks invest steadily greater effort and hyperbole in making the development of linguistics fit one 'normal' paradigm. Newmeyer's (1980) *Linguistic Theory in America* makes only the merest mention of Sapir, Bloomfield, and Pike, and directly equates both 'theory' and 'science' with Chomsky's standard model, touted on the jacket as 'the world's principal linguistic theory'. For Newmeyer, 'no viable alternative exists', and 'the vast majority' of 'linguists' 'who take theory seriously acknowledge (explicitly or implicitly) their adoption of Chomsky's view of language' (1980: 249f). At the conclusion, we are asked to believe that 'on the basis of [Chomsky's] idealization, more has been learned about the nature of language in the last 25 years than in the previous 2500' – calling to mind Firth's words: 'to dismiss two thousand years of linguistic study in Asia and Europe' 'is just plain stupid' (P1 139). But read carefully, Newmeyer's book reveals, against the author's

will, how heavily his acclaimed 'revolution' relied not on insights into language but on charisma and polemics (cf. 7.2).

3. Compare 2.3ff, 10, 36, 39; 3.2; 4.3; 5.2f, 5, 37, 62f; 6.3, 26, 49; 7.2–5, 7, 37ff, 62; 8.2, 4, 6ff, 10, 17, 19f, 25, 46, 87; 9.2–6; 10.2f, 34, 40.

4. The more usual disaffection with literary language and its study (cf. 2.24; 3.4; 4.41; 6.4) had its own political motives: the largest body of language study had been expended on literature and, for a time at least, many linguists had to occupy uneasy positions in departments of literature (cf. 5.56).

5. What might be 'transformations' or 'transforms' in a formal grammar appear in Halliday's grammar as 'variants', 'close parallels', 'different analyses', 'interpretations', 'expansions', and so on (cf. IF 61, 93, 225, 223, 165, 175). Whereas Chomsky's grammar sticks so close to the wording that it cannot handle the 'relation' between ' "I liked the play" ' vs ' "The play pleased me" ' (AT 162), Halliday's relations are flexible enough to link 'pairs of clauses' that are 'representations of same state of affairs' such as ' "Mary liked the gift" ' vs ' "the gift pleased Mary" ', which are not merely 'active' vs 'passive' (IF 107) (cf. 9.62). Still, Halliday concedes that 'we can hardly explain' a 'clause by saying that it is doing duty as a replacement for' another (cf. 12.54).

6. Especially in the eyes of other disciplines. I have heard this view expressed in conversation both by psychologists like Walter Kintsch and by computer scientists like Robert F. Simmons.

7. On English as a model, see 3.28, 53, 3^{14}, 3^{20}; 4.5, 27, 56ff, 68, 70, 4^9, 4^{22}; 5.54, 73; 7.5, 18, 41, 61, 66, 79, 81, 7^{39}; 8.12, 15; 9.24–27, 42, 52f, 58f, 61, 63f, 66ff, 82f, 87f, 91, 107, 9^{13}, 9^{16}, 9^{20}, 9^{30}, 9^{33}, 9^{41}; 10.64, 67. On Latin, see 2.5; 3.27, 50, 53; 5.24; 6.5; 8.5, 8; 9.25; 11.20f.

8. And Sapir blamed the 'social sciences' for 'the evolutionary prejudice' that has been 'the most powerful deterrent of all to clear thinking' (3.2).

9. Pike was more even-handed in considering psychology (cf. 5.23, 27, 42, 89), probably because by that time 'psycholinguistics' had attained some success (cf. 5.10, 31; 12.19).

10. Van Dijk's recent work has now taken on a primarily sociological orientation, addressing such issues as 'prejudice' and 'racism' (e.g., van Dijk 1984, 1987).

11. Compare 4.7; 5.86, 5^1; 6.56, 64; 8^7, 8^{14}; 10.40. For political motives, Chomsky denounced positivism (cf. 7.10) despite relying on logic more than any other linguist.

12. Compare 3.23, 37; 4.4f, 4^2; 5.73, 86, 89, 5^{28}; 8.5, 17, 31, 55; 9.3, 5, 59; 10.14, 36, 41, 10^{27}; 11.36f.

13. However, Pike acknowledged formal 'approaches to language and logic' and the 'contribution of transformational grammar' (LB 496f). He even stated a 'feeling that tagmemics and transformational grammar should ultimately merge in the mainstream of linguistics'. He argued, for instance, that 'transformation tests underlie our early methodology', and deployed 'transforms' for describing structures (LB 223n, 67, 441, 459). Yet he was 'unable to match' Chomsky's (1961: 14) 'disclaimer' of having no 'model of speaker or hearer' 'against the current work of some transformationalists', e.g., when Lees (1959: 1) says 'speakers, both in producing and understanding sentences, make use of the "generation" ' 'by the grammar' (LB 281, 495) (cf. 7.83). Pike also 'believes' 'the dream of mechanical generation of all and only the well-formed linguistic units is hopeless', partly because there are 'linguistic units' 'beyond the sentence', and partly because some texts, such as 'poems', 'deliberately exploit departures from well-formedness' (LB 494) (cf. 12.41). He agrees with Chomsky that 'mechanical discovery procedures' are not 'possible', but 'vigorously rejects' the dismissal of ' "practical discovery procedures" ' on those grounds (LB 225n, 492f; cf. 7.7ff; SS 56).

14. For a wide range of views about what is or is not 'universal', see 2.10; 3.67; 4.4, 72; 5.44, 84, 5^2; 6.5, 10, 34, 44; 7.1–4, 19f, 27, 31, 77; 8.19, 27, 60, 86; 9.3, 18, 25, 47, 60; 10.63; 11.94. Many of these passages suggest that the 'universal' aspect is not 'in' language, and certainly not in its grammar; presumably, a language can have a grammar at all only as a self-contained system (cf. 2.10; 8.60; 9.19). What seemed 'universal' to Chomsky was merely due to the worldwide uniformity of the articulatory apparatus and the familiarity of his grammatical notions.

15. I can make nothing of Firth's claim that it should be 'easier' for 'linguists' to 'acquire sufficient psychology and sociology' than for 'a psychologist or sociologist to acquire the necessary linguistic technique' (cf. 8.16). The remark is unusually glib, even for Firth, since the other disciplines had far more substance at that time than linguistics did, at least in Britain.

16. Compare 2.32; 3.1, 10; 4.10; 5.7f, 69, 84; 6.9, 54; 7.10, 30f, 35; 8.10, 14, 28; 9.1f, 7, 14, 27, 38, 111f; 10.1, 5, 43; 11.6, 9. Compare also Bloomfield's Sibylline remark that the 'features' 'appearing in every language' may 'exist' as 'realities either of physics or of human psychology' (4.71).

17. See 2.7, 9, 19; 3.12, 15; 5.8, 68; 6.8, 10, 29, 32f, 49; 9.23, 39, 59, 72; 10.22; 11.14; 12.55.

18. Compare 2.15, 65; 3.23, 46; 4.24, 27, 55, 70; 5.68, 5^{10}, 5^{13}, 5^{34}; 6.12, 29f, 54; 7.69, 71; 8.43; 9.14f, 27, 44, 60, 112; 10.8, 10, 53, 83; 11.13, 18, 60–64, 76, 89.

19. See 2.28f; 5.7f; 6.12, 15, 31; 7.57, 69, 71; 9.60f, 68, 77; 10.10, 17, 20, 23f, 45, 51, 53.

20. On 'constituents' and 'minimal distinctive units' see 2.17; 3.33; 4.33, 45, 48, 52, 59–62, 64f; 5.21, 28, 34, 51f, 58, 62, 5^5; 6.23f, 39, 42; 7.6, 30, 36f, 40, 45, 49f, 68ff, 81; 8.31, 36; 9.33f, 75, 9^{15}, 9^{16}; 10.32, 10^{18}.

21. The oddest offshoot of this derivation was the notion, quite fashionable for a time, that 'thought' should be viewed as silent articulation and studied through the speech muscles (3.10, 3^7; 4.9; 5.39; 8.22, 8^{17}). Even if the two operations reliably concur, which they do not (cf. 8^{17}), we could detect only when a person is thinking, but not what or why.

22. On this kind of 'arbitrariness', see 2.59, 85; 3.13; 4.27, 49, 82; 5.17, 22, 30, 51, 60, 87; 6.15, 18, 24, 29, 31f, 60; 9.32, 35f; 10.41, 43; 11.64, 76; 12.57. An intriguing case is the intuitive disposition to see the central category of a grammar in the noun like Sapir and Halliday seemed to do (cf. 3.36; 9.81, 9^{40}), or in the verb like Firth seemed to do (cf. 8.61) Of course, the organization of a given language may encourage such views, witness the heavy predominance of verbs in Yana (cf. 3^{16}).

23. On this 'border' see 2.55; 3.26, 34f; 4.61f, 65; 5.51, 53f; 6.45, 49; 7.75f; 8.57; 9.31, 34, 75, 9^5, 9^{15}; 10.35, 40; 11.71, 75, 77; on the inclusion of 'morphology' and 'syntax' in 'grammar', see 2.55; 4.62–65; 7.46ff, 76; 9.31, 34; 11.71, 77.

24. Halliday claimed the 'text' is a 'semantic unit', but did not implement the argument in his analyses (cf. 9.86, 95f). Perhaps he made the claim to fend off demands that his grammar be extended more fully to texts, since he fears that 'the organization of text is' 'much looser than that of grammatical units' (cf. 9.96).

25. See 10.1f, 86, 91; 12.53; and compare 2.87; 3.31; 5.5, 15; 6.37f; 8.35, 44; 9.1, 3, 8, 16, 38, 41f, 107, 111, 9^{19} as well as Note 24 to this chapter.

26. On the need to study (or not to study) the 'use' of language, see 7.4, 10, 12, 59, 82ff, 84, 87f, 90, 97; 8.5f, 27, 33, 40, 47, 8^7; 9.26; 10.1, 13, 21ff, 36; 11.9, 20, 31f, 35, 42f, 53, 58, 65, 11^{31}. On Saussure's division, see 2.20; 5.7; 6.33, 46; 7.12; 8.30; 9.5, 22; 11.12, 26, 47, 55, 67.

27. According to Halliday's portrayal, however, the child surpasses the adult analyst in having multiple language models, which later get reduced or

neglected in favour of 'informational' (or 'representational') and 'ritual' models (cf. 9.14f).

28. On these four terms, see 3.20, 40; 5.27, 29f, 49, 54, 70, 5^9; 6.11, 15, 33, 35, 38, 42, 57, 63; 7.10, 12f, 25, 31, 48, 62, 66, 75, 85, 94, 97; 8.70; 9.6, 8ff, 19, 28, 9^3; 10.83; 11.12, 29, 47, 50, 55ff, 67, 71. Compare van Dijk and Kintsch's concepts of 'activation' (10.7, 21, 25, 27, 45, 53, 74, 96, 10^{36}, 10^{41}) and 'instantiation' (10.23, 25, 31, 39, 54).

29. On 'finite' vs 'infinite', see 3.3, 6, 70, 75; 4.13, 29, 31, 61; 5.25, 29; 7.16, 26, 43ff, 64, 69, 7^3, 7^8; 8.42; 9.24f, 34; 10.29; 11.55, 11^{18}. On 'marked choices', see 9.6, 43, 45.

30. On 'bottom-up' and 'top-down' processing, see 10.19, 25, 32, 55, 59, 73, 77f, 95, 97, 10^7; 12.44.

31. See 2.3; 3.66; 4.22, 50; 5.1, 6, 38, 51; 6.3, 9, 59, 61; 7.18; 8.34, 37–40; 9.29; 11.8, 13, 27.

32. On 'speakers', see 2.40, 42, 44, 47, 53, 59, 63, 66, 83, 2^{15}; 3.11, 19, 38, 57, 64, 3^{22}; 4.13, 15, 17, 19, 54, 61, 66, 75, 4^{20}; 5.10, 20, 47, 75ff, 82, 88; 7.7, 10, 12, 14f, 21ff, 28, 38, 42, 44, 62, 78, 84, 87, 95f; 9.6, 9, 50, 71, 77ff, 105; 10.29, 10^{21}; 11.73.

33. On potential problems, see 2.33f, 46f, 63; 3.31; 4.6, 19, 53f; 5.5, 13–16, 75, 5^4, 5^{47}; 7.11, 14f, 62; 11.57, 73.

34. On matters of 'consciousness' and 'awareness', see 1.9; 2.33, 35, 40, 47, 52, 59, 71, 2^{16}; 3.3f, 10ff, 13, 38, 40, 55ff, 62f, 69, 72; 4^{20}; 5.11, 13f, 16, 18, 22, 46, 48, 71, 88; 6.3, 6f; 7.15, 22, 89; 8^{30}; 9.4, 27, 38, 9^{15}; 10.13, 72, 75, 81, 83, 91; 11.5, 13, 25, 27, 39, 42, 45, 53, 57, 75.

35. On 'symbols', see 7.71–74, 86, 7^{11}, 7^{22}, 7^{35}, 9^{35}. On 'trees', see 7.81; 9.33, 109; 10.3, 17, 44, 64. On 'brackets', see 7.86; 9.33. On 'matrices', see 5^{15}; 7.71, 7^{37}.

36. On the centrality of 'form', see 2.17; 3.16, 22ff, 33, 36, 38, 40f, 58; 4.17, 27, 31, 49–52, 54f, 4^8, 4^{17}; 5.58, 73, 85f; 6.12, 15, 22, 24, 27ff, 33, 47; 7.20, 56, 60, 69, 7^{31}; 8.37, 43, 46, 58, 62; 9.3f, 22, 31f, 36, 39, 62, 95; 11.27f, 30, 33, 40, 74, 79, 86.

37. On these modes of 'reality', see 2.15, 36, 63; 3.31, 37; 4.71; 5.23; 6.12, 16; 7.10, 71, 84; 8.24, 33, 41, 45, 49f, 8^{21}; 10.27, 42, 97, 10^{32}.

38. On the various estimations of 'objective', 'subjective', and 'intersubjective', see 2.24; 3.15, 20; 5.10, 15, 18, 50, 70; 6.3, 44; 7.7, 11, 90; 8.25, 81, 8^{26}; 9.6, 77f, 100, 110; 10.16, 23, 30, 36, 39f; 11.3ff, 7, 17, 30f, 35, 38, 45, 48, 97; 12.24, 51.

39. On 'indeterminacy' and 'fuzziness', see 2.33, 61; 3.22, 42, 46, 57, 64, 66; 4.20, 45, 74, 83; 5.16, 34, 36f, 39, 45, 49, 53, 70, 72, 77, 87, 5^{25}; 6.62; 8.39, 42; 9.19, 29, 35, 88, 9^{32}, 9^{38}; 10.22, 34, 36, 39; 12.7.

40. On units of 'meaning' and 'sum of parts', see 2.27, 85f; 5.31, 64f, 67, 75ff; 7.68, 82; 10.24, 36, 10^{20}; 11.27, 53, 69, 93; 12.18, 30; and Beaugrande 1988b.

41. On the import of 'culture', see 3.1f, 9, 13, 20; 4.24, 41; 5.8, 12, 17, 19, 26, 44, 57f, 60, 65, 79, 5^2, 5^4; 8.26, 42, 44; 9.1f, 6ff, 18, 22, 107; 10.1, 7ff, 30, 56, 61, 66.

42. Such reservations are raised in 2.3; 3.51; 5.1, 51, 72; 6.61; 7.80, 85, 94; 9.21; 10.5, 20f, 44, 90; 11.2.

References

Wherever the theorists were not specific, I followed my best guess about which works they were referring to. Where relevant, original dates of authorship or publication are supplied in square brackets.

ABELSON, ROBERT, 'Differences between belief and knowledge systems', *Cognitive Science* 3, 1979, 355–66.

ABBOTT V. and BLACK, JOHN, *The Representation of Scripts in Memory*, New Haven: Yale University Dept of Psychology Technical Report, 1980.

ADAMS, MARILYN and COLLINS, ALLAN, 'A schema-theoretical view of reading. In Roy Freedle (ed.), *New Directions in Discourse Processing*, Norwood, NJ: Ablex, 1979, 1–22.

ANDERSON, JOHN M., *The Grammar of Case*, London: Cambridge University Press, 1971.

ANDERSON, JOHN. R., *Concepts, Propositions, and Schemata: What are the Cognitive Units?*, Pittsburgh: Carnegie-Mellon University Psychology Dept Technical Report, 1980.

ARNAULD, ANTOINE and NICOLE, PIERRE, *La logique, ou l'art de penser*, Paris: Charles Savreux, 1662.

ASCHAM, ROGER, *The scholemaster, Or plaine and perfite way of teachyng children, to vnderstand, write, and speake, the Latin tong*, London: Ione Daye, 1570.

BAIN, ALEXANDER, *Mind and Body*, New York: Appleton, 1873.

BAR-HILLEL, YEHOSHUA and SHAMIR, ELI, 'Finite-state languages: Formal representations and adequacy problems', *Bulletin of the Research Council of Israel* 8/3, 1960, 150–66.

BARTLETT, FREDERICK, *Remembering*, Cambridge: Cambridge University Press, 1932.

BAUDOUIN DE COURTENAY, JAN IGNACY NIECISŁAW, *Otryvky iz' lektsii po fonetike i morfologii russkago iazyka*, Kazan: Kazanskom Universitet, 1882.

——, *Skice językoznacze*, Warsaw: P. Laskauera, 1904.

BAZELL, CHARLES, 'On the problem of the morpheme', *Archivum Linguisticum* 1, 1949, 1–15.

——, 'Phonemic and morphemic analysis', *Word* 8, 1952, 33–38.

——, *Linguistic Form*, Istanbul: Istanbul Üniversitesi Edebiyat Fakültesi Yayinlarindan No. 574, 1953.

BEATTIE, JAMES, *Theory of Language*, London: A. Stahan, 1788.

BEAUGRANDE, ROBERT DE, 'Toward a general theory of creativity', *Poetics* 8, 1979, 269–306.

——, *Text, Discourse, and Process*, Norwood, NJ: Ablex, 1980.

——, 'The story of grammars and the grammar of stories', *Journal of Pragmatics* 6, 1982, 383–422.

——, *Text Production*, Norwood, NJ: Ablex, 1984a.

——, 'Linguistics as discourse: A case study from semantics', *Word* 35, 1984b, 15–57.

——, 'Schemas for literary communication', In László Halász (ed.), *Literary Discourse*, New York: de Gruyter, 1986a, 34–68.

——, 'Psychology of language: A field in transition', *Gavagai: Revista Interdisciplinar en Filosofia de los Lenguajes* 2/1, 1986, 75–104.

——, 'Determinacy distribution in complex systems: Science, language, linguistics, life', *Zeitschrift für Phonetik, Sprachwissenschaft und Kommunikationsforschung* 40, 1987a, 145–188.

——, 'Special purpose language and linguistic theory', *LSP–ALSED Newsletter* 10/2, 1987b, 2–11.

——, *Critical Discourse: A Survey of Contemporary Literary Theorists*, Norwood, NJ: Ablex, 1988a.

——, 'Semantics and text meaning: Retrospects and prospects', *Journal of Semantics* 5, 1988b, 89–121.

——, 'Quantum aspects of perceived reality: A new engagement of science and art', *Journal of Literary Semantics* 18, 1989a, 1–49.

——, 'Special purpose language as a complex system: The case of linguistics'. In Christer Laurén and Marianne Nordman (eds), *Special Language: From Humans to Thinking Machines*, Philadelphia: Multilingual Matters, 1989b, 3–29.

——, and DRESSLER, WOLFGANG, *Introduction to Text Linguistics*, London: Longmans, 1981.

BECK, CAVE, *The Universal Character*, London: William Weekeley, 1657.

BELL, ALEXANDER MELVILLE, *Visible Speech*, Tribune, NY: Simpkins Marshall and Co., 1867.

——, *The Science of Speech*, Washington, DC: The Volta Bureau, 1897.

BENFEY, THEODOR, *Geschichte der Sprachwissenschaft und orientalischen Philologie in Deutschland*, Munich: G. Cotta, 1869.

BENVENISTE, ÉMILE, *Problems in General Linguistics*, Coral Gables: University of Miami Press, 1971.

BERNSTEIN, BASIL, 'Aspects of language and learning in the genesis of the social process', *Child Psychology and Psychiatry* 1, 1961, 251–63.

——, *Class Codes and Control*, Routledge & Kegan Paul, 1971–72.

BEVER, THOMAS, GARRETT, MERRILL and HURTIG, RICHARD, 'The interaction of perceptual processes and ambiguous sentences', *Memory and Cognition* 1, 1973, 277–86.

BJERRUM, ANDERS, *Fjoldemålets lydsystem*, Copenhagen: E. Munksgaard, 1944.

BLACK, JOHN, TURNER, TERRENCE and BOWER, GORDON, 'Point of view in narrative comprehension, memory, and production, *Journal of Verbal Learning and Verbal Behavior* 18, 1979, 187–98.

BLANCHARD, WILLIAM, *A complete system of short hand, Being an improvement upon all the authors whose systems have yet been made public*, London: Blanchard, 1787.

BLOCH, BERNARD, 'A set of postulates for phonemic analysis', *Language* 24, 3–46.

—— and TRAGER, GEORGE, *Outline of Linguistic Analysis*, Baltimore: Waverly, 1942.

BLOOMFIELD, LEONARD, *An Introduction to the Study of Language*, New York: Holt, 1914.

——, 'Linguistics as a science', *Studies in Philology* 27, 1930, 553–57.

——, *Language*, Chicago: University of Chicago Press, 1933.

——, *Outline Guide for the Practical Study of Foreign Languages*, Baltimore: Waverly, 1942.

——, *Linguistic Aspects of Science* [*International Encyclopedia of Unified Science* I/4]. Chicago: University of Chicago Press, 1949.

BOHM, DAVID, *Wholeness and the Implicate Order*, London: Routledge & Kegan Paul, 1980.

—— and PEAT, DAVID, *Science, Order, and Creativity*, New York: Bantam, 1987.

BOLINGER, DWIGHT, 'Rime, assonance, and morphemic analysis', *Word* 6, 1950, 117–36.

——, 'Syntactic blends and other matters', *Language* 37, 1961, 366–81.

BOPP, FRANZ, *Über das Conjugationssystem der Sanskritsprache*, Frankfurt am Main: Andrea, 1816.

BRAUNE, WILHELM, *Althochdeutsche Grammatik*, Halle: Niemeyer, 1886.

——, *Beiträge zur germanischen und romanischen Etymologie*, Berlin: Pormetter, 1894.

BRIGHT, TIMOTHE, *Characterie, An art of short, swift and secret writing*, London: I. Windet, 1588.

BRUGMANN, FRIEDRICH KARL CHRISTIAN, *Zum heutigen Stand der Sprachwissenschaft*, Strassburg: K.J. Trubner, 1885.

—— and DELBRÜCK, BERTHOLD, *Grundriss der vergleichenden Grammatik der indogermanischen Sprachen*, Strassburg: K.J. Trubner, 1886–1900.

BRUNER, JEROME, GOODNOW, JACQUELINE and AUSTIN, GEORGE, *A Study of Thinking*, New York: Wiley, 1956.

BÜHLER, KARL, *Sprachtheorie: Die Darstellungsfunktion der Sprache*, Jena: G. Fischer, 1934.

BULLOKAR, WILLIAM, *Booke at large, for the amendment of orthographie for English speech*, London: H. Denham, 1580a.

——, *Bref grammar for English*, London: Edmund Bollifant, 1580b.

BURTON, RICHARD and BROWN, JOHN SEELY, 'Toward a natural language capability for computer assisted instruction'. In Harold O'Neil (ed.), *Procedures for Instructional Systems Development*, New York: Academic, 1979, 273–313.

BUTLER, CHARLES, *The English grammar, or the institution of letters, syllables, and woords in the English tung*, Oxford: W. Turner, 1634.

BYROM, JOHN, *A catechism of shorthand*, London: Limbird, 1834 [*ca* 1750].

CACCAMISE, DONNA JEAN, *Cognitive Processes in Writing*, Boulder: University of Colorado dissertation, 1981.

CARNAP, RUDOLF, *Logische Syntax der Sprache*, Vienna: J. Springer, 1934.

——, *The Logical Syntax of Language*, London: Paul, Tench and Trubner, 1937 [transl. and expansion of 1934].

——, *Introduction to Semantics*, Cambridge, MA: Harvard University Press, 1942.

——, *Meaning and Necessity*, Chicago: University of Chicago Press, 1947.

——, *Foundations of Logic and Mathematics* [*International Encyclopedia of Unified Science I/3*]. Chicago: University of Chicago Press, 1955 [1939].

CARROLL, JOHN, *The Study of Language*, Cambridge, MA: Harvard University Press, 1953.

CASSIRER, ERNST, *Das Erkenntnisproblem in der Philosophie und Wissenschaft der neueren Zeit*, Berlin: B. Cassirer, 1906–07.

——, *Philosophie der symbolischen Formen*, Berlin: B. Cassirer, 1923–29.

——, *Determinismus und Indeterminismus in der modernen Physik*, Göteborg: Elanders Boktryckeri, 1937.

——, *Language and Myth*, New York: Harper & Brothers, 1946.

——, *Philosophy of Symbolic Forms*, New Haven: Yale, 1953 [transl. of 1923–29].

CHI, MICHELENE, 'Short-term memory limitations in children: Capacity or processing deficits?', *Memory and Cognition* 4, 1976, 559–80.

CHOMSKY, NOAM, *Morphophonemics of Modern Hebrew*, Philadelphia: University of Pennsylvania MA thesis, 1951.

——, 'Systems of syntactic analysis', *Journal of Symbolic Logic* 18, 1953, 242–56.

——, *The Logical Structure of Linguistic Theory*, Cambridge: MIT dissertation, 1955.

——, *Syntactic Structures*, The Hague: Mouton, 1957.

——, Review of *Verbal Behavior*, by B.F. Skinner, *Language* 35, 1959, 28–58.

——, 'On the notion "rule of grammar"'. In Roman Jakobson (ed.), *Structure of Language and Its Mathematical Aspects*, Providence, RI: American Mathematical Society, 1961, 6–24.

——, *Aspects of the Theory of Syntax*, Cambridge: MIT Press, 1965.

——, *Cartesian Linguistics*, New York: Harper & Row, 1966.

——, *Topics in the Theory of Generative Grammar*, The Hague: Mouton, 1966.

——, 'Deep structure, surface structure, and semantic interpretation'. In Danny Steinberg and Leon Jakobovits (eds) *Semantics*, Cambridge: CUP, 1971, 183–216 [1968].

——, *Studies in Semantics in Generative Grammar*, The Hague: Mouton, 1972.

——, *The Logical Structure of Linguistic Theory*, New York: Plenum, 1975.

——, 'Conditions on rules of grammar', *Linguistic Analysis* 2, 1976, 303–51.

——, 'On wh– movement'. In Peter Culicover, Thomas Wasow and Adrian Akmajian (eds), *Formal Syntax*, New York: Academic, 1977, 71–132.

—— and HALLE, MORRIS, *The Sound Pattern of English*, New York: Harper & Row, 1968.

——, —— and LUKOFF, FRED, 'On accent and juncture in English'. In Horace Lunt (ed.), *For Roman Jakobson*, The Hague: Mouton, 1956, 65–80.

CIRILO, RANDOLPH and FOSS, DONALD, 'Text structure and reading time for sentences', *Journal of Verbal Learning and Verbal Behavior* 19, 1980, 96–109.

CLARK, HERBERT and CLARK, EVE, *Psychology and Language*, New York: Harcourt Brace Jovanovich, 1977.

COFER, CHARLES, 'A comparison of logical and verbatim learning of prose passages of different length', *American Journal of Psychology* 54, 1941, 1–20.

COLES, ELISHA, *The Complete English Schoolmaster*, London: Peter Parker, 1692.

COLLINS, ALLAN and LOFTUS, ELIZABETH, 'A spreading-activation theory of semantic processing', *Psychological Review* 82, 1975, 407–48.

CORDEMOY, GERAUD DE, *Discours phisiqve de la parole*, Paris: A. Lambert, 1668a.

——, *A Philosophicall Discourse Concerning Speech*, London: J. Martin, 1668b [transl. of 1668a].

COREN, STANLEY and GIRGUS, JOAN, *Seeing is Deceiving*, Hillsdale, NJ: Erlbaum, 1978.

CROCE, BENEDETTO, *Estetica come scienza dell'espressione e linguistica generale*, Milan: R. Sandron, 1902.

CRESSWELL, MAX, *Logics and Languages*, London: Methuen, 1973.

——, *Aesthetic as a Science of Expression and General Linguistic*, London: Macmillan, 1922 [transl. of 1902].

CURTIUS, GEORG, *Grundzüge der griechischen Etymologie*, Leipzig: B.G. Teubner, 1858–62.

——, *Zur Kritik der neusten Sprachforschung*, Leipzig: S. Hirzel, 1885.

DALGARNO, GEORGE, *Didascolocophus*, Oxford: Halton, 1680.

DANEŠ, FRANTIŠEK, 'A three-level approach to syntax', *Travaux Linguistiques de Prague*, 1, 1964, 225–40.

DESCARTES, RENÉ, *Les méditations métaphysiques*, Paris: I. Camusat & Pierre le Petit, 1641.

——, 'Notes directed against a certain programme published in Belgium in 1647'. In Elizabeth Haldane (ed. and transl.), *The Philosophical Works of Descartes*, Cambridge: Cambridge University Press, 1931, 429–50.

DEWEY, JOHN, *How We Think*, New York: D.C. Heath, 1910.

DIDEROT, DENIS, *Lettre sur les Sourds et les Muets*, Paris: [publisher unknown], 1751.

DIEZ, FRIEDRICH CHRISTIAN, *Grammatik der romanischen Sprachen*, Bonn: E. Weber, 1836–44.

DIJK, TEUN VAN, *Some Aspects of Text Grammars*, The Hague: Mouton, 1972.

——, *Text and Context*, London: Longmans, 1977.

——, *Macrostructures*, Hillsdale, NJ: Erlbaum, 1980.

——, *Prejudice in Discourse*, Amsterdam: J. Benjamins, 1984.

——, *Communicating Racism: Ethnic Prejudices in Thought and Talk*, Newbury Park, CA: Sage, 1987.

——, IHWE, JENS, PETÖFI, JÁNOS and RIESER, HANNES, *Zur Bestimmung narrativer Strukturen auf der Grundlage von Textgrammatiken*, Hamburg: Buske, 1972.

——, and KINTSCH, WALTER, *Strategies of Discourse Comprehension*, New York: Academic, 1983.

DIK, SIMON, *Functional Grammar*, Amsterdam: North Holland, 1978.

DILLON, GEORGE, *Language Processing and the Reading of Literature*, Bloomington: Indiana University Press, 1978.

DIXON, ROBERT, *Linguistic Science and Logic*, The Hague: Mouton, 1963.

DUMARSAIS, CÉSAR CHESNEAU, *Logique et grammaire*, Paris: Braissol, 1729 [*ca* 1730].

DUPONCEAU, PETER. 'Dissertation on the nature and character of the Chinese system of writing', *Transactions of the Historical and Literary Committee of the American Philosophical Society 2*, 1838.

EDGERTON, FRANKLIN, 'Notes on early American work in linguistics', *Proceedings of the American Philosophical Society 87*, 1942, 25–34.

ELLIS, ALEXANDER JOHN, *The Alphabet of Nature: A More Accurate Analysis and Symbolization of Spoken Sounds*, London: S. Bagster, 1845.

FILLMORE, CHARLES, 'The case for case'. In Emmon Bach and Robert Harms (eds), *Universals in Linguistic Theory*, New York: Holt, Rinehart & Winston, 1968, 1–88.

FIRBAS, JAN and GOLKOVÁ, EVA, *An Analytic Bibliography of Czechoslovakian Studies in Functional Sentence Perspective*, Brno: Pyrkyn University, 1976.

FIRTH, JOHN RUPERT, *Speech*, London: Benn, 1930.

——, *Tongues of Men*, London: Watts, 1937.

——, *Papers in Linguistics 1934–1951*, London: Oxford, 1957.

——, *Tongues of Men and Speech* (ed. Peter Strevens). London: Oxford, 1964 [reissue of 1930 and 1937].

——, *Selected Papers of J.R. Firth 1952–1959* (ed. Frank R. Palmer), London: Longmans, 1968.

FLEW, ANTHONY GARRARD NEWTON (ed.), *Logic and Language*, Oxford: Blackwell, 1951–53.

FODOR, JERROLD and BEVER, THOMAS, 'The psychological reality of linguistic segments', *Journal of Verbal Learning and Verbal Behavior 4*, 1965, 414–20.

——, BEVER, THOMAS and GARRETT, MERRILL, *Psychology of Language*, New York: McGraw Hill, 1974.

—— and GARRETT, MERRILL. 'Some syntactic determinants of sentential complexity', *Psychological Review 2*, 1967, 289–96.

FOERSTER, HEINZ VON (ed.), *Cybernetics: Transactions of the Seventh Conference, 1950*, New York: Macy Foundation, 1951.

——, *Cybernetics of Cybernetics*, Urbana: University of Illinois Biological Computer Laboratory, 1974.

FREDERIKSEN, JOHN, 'Sources of process interaction in reading'. In Alan Lesgold and Charles Perfetti (eds), *Interactive Processes in Reading*, Hillsdale, NJ: Erlbaum, 1981.

FREGE, GOTTLOB, *Funktion, Begriff, Bedeutung*, Jena: H. Pohle, 1891.

FRIES, CHARLES CARPENTER, *The Structure of English*. New York: Harcourt & Brace, 1952.

——, 'Meaning and linguistic analysis', *Language* 30, 1954, 57–68.

——, *Linguistics and Reading*, New York: Holt, Rinehart and Winston, 1962.

GALAMBOS, JAMES and RIPS, LANCE, 'Memory for routines', *Journal of Verbal Learning and Verbal Behavior* 21, 1982, 260–81.

GARDINER, ALAN, *The Theory of Speech and Language*, Oxford: Clarendon, 1932.

GARRETT, MERRILL, BEVER, THOMAS and FODOR, JERROLD, 'The active use of grammar in speech perception', *Perception and Psychophysics* 1, 1966, 30–32.

GLANZER, MURRAY, DORFMAN, DAVID and KAPLAN, BARBARA, 'Short-term storage in processing text', *Journal of Verbal Learning and Verbal Behavior* 20, 1981, 656–70.

GLEIK, JAMES, *Chaos: Making a New Science*, London: Cardinal, 1987.

GLINZ, HANS, *Die innere Form des Deutschen*, Bern: Francke, 1952.

GODEL, ROBERT, *Les sources manuscrites du 'Cours du linguistique générale' de Ferdinand de Saussure*, Geneva: S. Dorz, 1957.

GOLDING, WILLIAM, *The Inheritors*, London: Faber & Faber, 1955.

GOLDSTEIN, KURT, *Language and Language Disturbances*, New York: Grune & Stratton, 1948.

GOMBRICH, ERNST, *Art and Illusion*, London: Phaidon, 1960.

GOODMAN, KENNETH, 'Reading: A psycholinguistic guessing game'. In Harry Singer and Robert Ruddell (eds), *Theoretical Models and Processes of Reading*, Newark: International Reading Association, 1976, 259–72.

GOODMAN, NELSON, 'On likeness of meaning', *Analysis* 10/1, 1949, 1–7.

——, 'On some differences about meaning', *Analysis* 13/4, 1953, 90–96.

GRAESSER, ART, *Prose Comprehension beyond the Word*, New York: Springer-Verlag, 1981.

GRASSLER, RICHARD, *Vom Sinn der Sprache*, Lahr in Baden: Schauenburg, 1938.

GREENBERG, JOSEPH, 'Some universals of grammar with particular reference to the order of meaningful elements'. In Joseph Greenberg (ed.), *Universals of Language*, Cambridge, MA: MIT Press, 1963, 58–90.

GRIMES, JOSEPH, *The Thread of Discourse*, The Hague: Mouton, 1975.

——, (ed.), *Papers on Discourse*, Arlington: Summer Institute of Linguistics, 1978.

GRIMM, JACOB LUDWIG KARL, *Deutsche Grammatik*, Göttingen: Dieterichsche Buchhandlung, 1819–37.

GROEBEN, NORBERT, *Leserpsychologie*, Münster: Aschendorff, 1982.

GURNEY, THOMAS, *Brachygraphy, Or short writing made easy to the meanest capacity*, London: Gurney, 1752.

HAAS, WILLIAM, Review of A.A. Hill, *Introduction to Linguistic Structures*, *Word* 16, 1960, 251–76.

HABERLANDT, KARL, BERIAN, CLAIRE and SANDSON, JENNIFER, 'The episode schema in story processing', *Journal of Verbal Learning and Verbal Behavior* 19, 1980, 635–50.

HALDEMAN, SAMUEL STEHMAN, *Report on the Present State of our Knowledge of Linguistic Ethnology, Made to the American Association for the Advancement of Science*, Philadelphia: Lovering, 1856.

——, *On the Relations between Chinese and the Indo-European Languages*, Philadelphia: Lippincott, 1877.

——, *Outlines of Etymology*, Philadelphia: Lippincott, 1878.

HALLIDAY, MICHAEL ALEXANDER KIRKWOOD, *A Study of the Language of the Chinese Version of the 'Secret History of the Mongols'*, Cambridge: Cambridge University dissertation, 1955.

——, *Intonation and Grammar in British English*, The Hague: Mouton, 1967.

——, 'Notes on transitivity and theme in English', *Journal of Linguistics* 3, 37–81, 3, 199–244, and 4, 179–215, 1967–68.

——, 'Some notes on "deep grammar"', *Journal of Linguistics* 5, 1969, 57–67.

——, 'Functional diversity in language as seen from a consideration of modality and mood in English', *Foundations of Language* 6, 1970, 322–61.

——, Review of *Selected Papers of J.R. Firth 1952–59*, *Bulletin of the School of Oriental and African Studies* 34, 1971, 664–67.

——, *Explorations in the Function of Language*, London: Arnold, 1973.

——, *Learning How to Mean*, London: Arnold, 1975.

——, *Language as a Social Semiotic*, London: Arnold, 1978.

——, 'On the language of physical science'. In Mohsen Ghadessy (ed.), *Registers of Written English*, London: Pinter, 1988, 162–78.

——, *An Introduction to Functional Linguistics*, London: Longmans, 1985.

—— and HASAN, RUQAIYA, *Cohesion in English*, London: Longmans, 1976.

—— and ——, *Language, Context, and Text*, Victoria: Deakin, 1985.

——, MCINTOSH, ANGUS and STREVENS, PETER, *The Linguistic Sciences and Language Teaching*, London: Longmans, 1964.

—— and MARTIN, JAY (eds), *Readings in Systemic Linguistics*, London: Batsford, 1981.

HARRIS, JAMES, *Hermes, Or a philosophical inquiry concerning language and universal grammar*, London: Nourse & Vallian, 1751.

HARRIS, ZELLIG SABATTAI, *Methods in Structural Linguistics*, Chicago: University of Chicago Press, 1951.

——, 'Discourse analysis', *Language* 28, 1952, 1–30 and 474–94.

——, 'Distributional structure', *Word* 10, 1954, 146–62.

HART, JOHN, *An Orthographie, conteyning the due order and reason, howe to write or paint the images of mannes voice, most like to life or nature*, London: William Seres, 1569.

HARTMANN, PETER, *Theorie der Sprachwissenschaft*, Assen: van Gorcum, 1963a.

——, *Theorie der Grammatik*, The Hague: Mouton, 1963b.

——, *Syntax und Bedeutung*, Assen: van Gorcum, 1964 .

HASAN, RUQAIYA, *Grammatical Cohesion in Spoken and Written English*, Harlow: Longmans, 1968.

HAVILAND, SUSAN and CLARK, HERBERT, 'What's new? Acquiring new information as a process of comprehension', *Journal of Verbal Learning and Verbal Behavior* 13, 1974, 512–21.

HAYES, JOHN RICHARD and FLOWER, LINDA. 'Identifying the organization of the writing process'. In Lee Gregg and Edwin Steinberg (eds), *Cognitive Processes in Writing*, Hillsdale, NJ: Erlbaum, 1980, 3–30.

HEIDEGGER, MARTIN, *Sein und Zeit*, Halle: Niemeyer, 1927.

——, *Unterwegs zur Sprache*, Pfullingen: Neske, 1959.

HEISENBERG, WERNER, 'Sprache und Wirklichkeit in der modernen Physik', *Wort und Wirklichkeit* 1, 1960, 32–62.

HEMPEL, CARL, *Fundamentals of Concept Formation in Empirical Science* [*International Encyclopedia of Unified Science II/7*]. Chicago: University of Chicago Press, 1952.

HERBERT, EDWARD, LORD OF CHERBURY, *De Veritate*, Paris: Zaehnsdorf, 1624.

HERDER, JOHANN GOTTFRIED, *Abhandlung über den Ursprung der Sprache*, Berlin: C.F. Voss, 1772.

HILBERT, DAVID, *Grundlagen der Geometrie*, Leipzig: Teubner, 1899.

——, *Grundlagen der Mathematik*, Leipzig: Teubner, 1928.

—— and ACKERMANN, WILHELM, *Grundlagen der theoretischen Logik*, Berlin: Springer, 1928.

HJELMSLEV, LOUIS, *Prolegomena to a Theory of Language*, Madison: University of Wisconsin Press, 1969 [1943].

——, *Essais linguistiques*, Copenhagen: Sprog- og Kulturvorlag, 1970.

——, *Essais linguistiques II*, Copenhagen: Sprog- og Kulturvorlag, 1973.

——, *Résumé of a Theory of Language*, Copenhagen: Sprog- og Kulturvorlag, 1975 [1941–42].

HOCKETT, CHARLES, 'A system of descriptive morphology', *Language* 18, 1942, 3–21.

——, 'Problems of morphemic analysis', *Language* 23, 1947, 321–43.

——, 'A formal statement of morphemic analysis', *Studies in Linguistics* 10, 1952, 27–39.

——, *A Manual of Phonology*, Bloomington: Indiana University Publications in Anthropology and Linguistics 11, 1955.

——, *A Course in Modern Linguistics*, New York: Macmillan, 1958.

HOLDER, WILLIAM, *The Elements of Speech*, London: J. Martyn, 1669.

HUMBOLDT, WILHELM VON, *Über die Verschiedenheit des menschlichen Sprachbaus*, Berlin: Akademie der Wissenschaften, 1836.

HUME, ALEXANDER, *Of the orthographie and congruitie of the Britan tongue*, London: Trubner & Co. facsimile, 1865 [*ca* 1610].

HUTTENLOCHER, JANELLEN and BURKE, DEBORAH, 'Why does memory span increase with age?', *Cognitive Psychology* 8, 1976, 1–31.

JAKOBSON, ROMAN, 'On the identification of phonemic entities', *Travaux du Cercle Linguistique de Copenhague* 4, 1949, 205–13.

——, 'Linguistics and poetics'. In Thomas Sebeok (ed.), *Style in Language*, New York: Wiley, 1960, 350–77.

——, 'The phonemic concept of distinctive features', *Proceedings of the Fourth International Congress of Phonetic Sciences*, 1962, 440–54.

—— and HALLE, MORRIS, *Fundamentals of Language*, The Hague: Mouton, 1956.

—— and LOTZ, JOHN, 'Notes on the French phonemic patterns', *Word* 5, 1949, 151–58.

JARVELLA, ROBERT, 'Syntactic processes of connected speech', *Journal of Verbal Learning and Verbal Behavior* 10, 1971, 409–16.

——, 'Immediate memory and discourse processing'. In Gordon Bower (ed.), *The Psychology of Learning and Motivation*, New York: Academic, 1979.

JESPERSEN, OTTO, *The Philosophy of Grammar*, New York: Holt, 1924.

——, *A Modern English Grammar on Historical Principles*, Copenhagen: Ejnar Munksgaard, 1940–49.

JOHNSON, ALEXANDER BRYAN, *A Discourse on Language*, Utica, NY: William Williams, 1832.

JOHNSON, NEAL, 'The psychological reality of phrase structure rules', *Journal of Verbal Learning and Verbal Behavior* 4, 1965, 469–75.

JONES, DANIEL, *An Outline of English Phonetics*, Berlin: Teubner, 1914.

——, *The Pronunciation of English*, Cambridge: Cambridge University Press, 1912.

JONES, WILLIAM, *Discourses Delivered Before the Asiatic Society*, London: Arnold, 1824.

JOOS, MARTIN, *Readings in Linguistics*, Washington, DC: American Council of Learned Societies, 1957.

——, 'Semiology: A linguistic theory of meaning', *Studies in Linguistics* 13, 1958, 53–70.

JØRGENSEN, JØRGEN, *Traek af deduktionsteoriens udvikling in den nyere tid*, Copenhagen: B. Lunos, 1937.

JUST, MARCEL and CARPENTER, PATRICIA, 'A theory of reading', *Psychological Review* 4, 1980, 329–54.

KACHRU, BRAJ, '"Socially realistic linguistics": the Firthian tradition', *International Journal of Social Language* 31, 1981, 65–89.

KAINZ, FRIEDRICH, *Psychologie der Sprache*, Stuttgart: F. Emke, 1941; second revised edition, 1960.

KATZ, JERROLD and FODOR, JERROLD, 'The structure of a semantic theory', *Language* 39, 1963, 170–210.

KINTSCH, WALTER, *The Representation of Meaning in Memory*, Hillsdale, NJ: Erlbaum, 1974.

——, *Memory and Cognition*, New York: Wiley, 1977.

——, 'The role of knowledge in discourse comprehension: A construction–integration model', *Psychological Review* 95/2, 1988, 163–82.

——, 'The representation of knowledge and the use of knowledge in discourse comprehension'. In Rainer Dietrich and Carl Graumann (eds), *Language Processing in Social Context*, Amsterdam: North Holland, 1989, 185–209.

—— and DIJK, TEUN VAN, 'Toward a model of text comprehension and production', *Psychological Review* 85, 1978, 363–94.

—— and GREENO, JAMES, *Understanding and Solving Word Arithmetic Problems*, Boulder: University of Colorado Dept of Psychology Technical Report, 1982.

—— and KEENAN, JANICE, 'Reading rate and retention as a function of the number of propositions in the base structure of the text', *Cognitive Psychology* 5, 1973, 257–74.

——, KOZMINSKY, ELY, STREBY, WILLIAM, MCKOON, GAIL and KEENAN, JANICE, 'Comprehension and recall of text as a function of content variables', *Journal of Verbal Learning and Verbal Behavior* 14, 1975, 196–214.

—— and MROSS, ERNEST, 'Context effects in word identification', *Journal of Memory and Language* 24, 1985, 336–49.

—— and YARBROUGH, CRAIG, 'The role of rhetorical structure in text comprehension', *Journal of Educational Psychology* 74, 1982, 828–34.

KOCH, WALTER ALFRED, *Taxologie des Englischen*, Munich: Fink, 1971.

KOLERS, PAUL, 'Pattern analysing disability in poor readers', *Developmental Psychology* 11, 1975, 282–90.

KORZYBSKI, ALFRED, *Science and Sanity: An Introduction to Non-Aristotelian Systems and General Semantics*, Lakeville, CT: International Non-Aristotelian Library, 1933.

KROEBER, ALFRED and KLUCKHOHN, CLYDE, *Culture: A Critical Review of Concepts and Definitions*. Cambridge, MA: Peabody Museum at Harvard University, 1952.

KRUSZEWSKI, MIKOŁAI HABDANC, *Über die Lautabwechslung*, Kazan: Kazanskom Universitet, 1879.

KUHN, ADALBERT, *Beiträge zur vergleichenden Sprachforschung auf dem Gebiete der arischen, celtischen und slawischen Sprachen*, Berlin: F. Dümmler, 1858–76.

KUHN, THOMAS, *The Structure of Scientific Revolutions*, Chicago: University of Chicago Press, 1970.

KURYŁOWICZ, JERZY, 'La notion de l'isomorphisme', *Travaux du Cercle Linguistique de Copenhague* 4, 1949, 48–60.

LABOV, WILLIAM, 'The reflection of social processes in linguistic structures'. In Joshua Fishman (ed.), *Readings in the Sociology of Language*, Mouton: The Hague, 1968.

——, *Language in the Inner City*, Philadelphia: University of Pennsylvania Press, 1972.

LAMB, SIDNEY, *Outline of Stratificational Grammar*, Berkeley: University of California Press, 1962.

——, 'Linguistic and cognitive networks'. In Paul Garvin (ed.), *Cognition: A Multiple View*, New York: Spartan, 1970, 195–222.

LANCELOT, CLAUDE and ARNAULD, ANTOINE, *Grammaire générale et raisonnée*, Paris: Pierre le Petit, 1660.

LANGLEY, PATRICK, BRADSHAW, GARY, SIMON, HERBERT and ZYTKOW, JAN, *Scientific Discovery: Computational Explorations of Creative Processes*, Cambridge, MA: MIT Press, 1987.

LEEPER, ROBERT, 'Cognitive processes'. In Stanley Smith Stevens (ed.), *Handbook of Experimental Psychology*, New York: Wiley, 1951, 730–57.

LEES, ROBERT, 'Automata and the generation of sentences', *Anthropological Linguistics* 1, 1959, 41–44.

LEIBNIZ, GEORG WILHELM, *Neue Anschauungen über den menschlichen Verstand*,

Berlin: B. Heimann, 1873 [1702–03].

LESGOLD, ALAN, 'Variability in children's comprehension of syntactic structures', *Journal of Educational Psychology* 66, 1974, 333–38.

LESKIEN, AUGUST, *Die Deklination im Slawisch-Litauischen und im Germanischen*, Leipzig: S. Hirzel, 1876.

LEVELT, WILLEM and KELTER, STEPHANIE, 'Surface form and memory in question answering', *Cognitive Psychology* 14, 1982, 78–106.

LI, CHARLES and SANDRA ANNEAR THOMPSON, *Mandarin Chinese: A Functional Reference Grammar*, Berkeley: University of California Press, 1981.

LOHMANN, JOHANNES and BRÖCKER, WALTER, 'Von der Intentionalität des sprachlichen Zeichens', *Sprachkunde: Zeitschrift zur Pflege und Förderung des Sprachstudiums*, 1942, Nr 6, 1–3.

LONGACRE, ROBERT, *Grammar Discovery Procedures*, The Hague: Mouton, 1964 [1958].

LOUNSBURY, FLOYD, *Oneida Verb Morphology*, New Haven: Yale University Publications in Anthropology 48, 1953.

MACDONALD, MARGARET, 'The philosopher's use of analogy in logic and language'. In Flew (ed.), vol. I, 85–106.

MACNEILAGE, PETER, 'Motor control and serial ordering of speech, *Psychological Review* 77, 1970, 182–96.

——, 'Speech production', *Language and Speech* 23, 1980, 3–23.

MALINOWSKI, BRONISLAW, 'The problem of meaning in primitive languages'. In Ogden and Richards 1923, 296–336.

——, *Coral Gardens and their Magic*, London: G. Allen & Unwin, 1935.

——, *Freedom and Civilization*, New York: Roy, 1944.

MANN, WILLIAM and MATTHIESEN, CHRISTIAN, 'Nigel: A systemic grammar for text generation'. In James Benson and William Greaves (eds), *You and Your Language*, Oxford, Pergamon, 1984.

MARR, NIKOLAI ĪAKOLEVICH, *Izbrannye raboty. Gosudarstvennīa akademīa istorii material'noĭ kul'tury*. Leningrad, Sofsialno-ekonomicheskoe izdatel'stvo, 1934.

MARTIN, SAMUEL, Review of Charles F. Hockett, *A Manual of Phonology*, *Language* 32, 1956, 675–705.

MARTINET, ANDRÉ, 'Linguistics today', *Word* 10, 1954, 2–3.

MASSON, MICHAEL, 'Cognitive processes in skimming stories', *Journal of Experimental Psychology: Learning, Memory, & Cognition* 8, 1982, 400–17.

MCCONKIE, GEORGE and ZOLA, DAVID, 'Is visual information integrated across recessive fixations in reading?', *Perception and Psychophysics* 25, 1979, 221–24.

—— and ZOLA, DAVID, 'Language constraints and the functional stimulus reading', in A.M. Lesgold and C.A. Perfetti (eds), *Interative Processes Reading*, Hillsdale, NJ: Erlbaum, 1981.

MCCORDUCK, PAMELA, *Machines Who Think*, San Francisco: Freeman, 1979.

MCINTOSH, ANGUS, 'Saying', *Review of English Literature* 6/2, 1965, 9–20.

MEAD, GEORGE HERBERT, *Mind, Self and Society*, Chicago: University of Chicago Press, 1934.

——, *The Philosophy of the Act*, Chicago: University of Chicago Press, 1938.

MENCKEN, HENRY LOUIS, *The American Language*, New York: A.A. Knopf, 1919.

MESHCHANINOV, IVAN IVANOVICH, *A New Theory of Linguistics*, Moscow: Akademia Nauk SSSR, 1945.

MEYER, BONNIE, *The Organization of Prose and its Effects on Memory*, Amsterdam: North Holland, 1975.

——, BRANDT, DAVID and BLUTH, GEORGE, 'Use of top-level structure in text', *Reading Research Quarterly* 16, 1980–81, 72–103.

MILLER, GEORGE ARMITAGE, *Language and Communication*, New York: McGraw-Hill, 1951.

——, GALANTER, EUGENE and PRIBRAM, KARL, *Plans and the Structure of Behavior*, New York: Holt, Rinehart & Winston, 1960.

MILLER, JAMES and KINTSCH, WALTER, 'Readability and recall of short passages', *Journal of Experimental Psychology: Human Learning and Memory* 6, 1980, 335–54.

MONTAGUE, RICHARD, *Formal Philosophy*, Cambridge, MA: Harvard University Press, 1974.

MORRIS, CHARLES, *Foundations of the Theory of Signs* [*International Encyclopedia of Unified Science I/2*]. Chicago: University of Chicago Press, 1938.

——, *Signs, Language, and Behavior*, New York: Prentice Hall, 1946.

MORTON, JOHN, 'Interaction of information in word recognition', *Psychological Review* 76, 1969, 165–78.

MOULTON, WILLIAM, 'Juncture in Modern Standard German', *Language* 23, 1947, 212–26.

MULLER, FRIEDRICH MAX, *The Science of Language*, London: Longmans-Green, 1864–66.

MURRAY, LINDLEY, *English Grammar*, York: Wilson, Spence & Mawman, 1795.

NADEL, SIEGFRIED FREDERICK, *The Foundations of Social Anthropology*, Glencoe, IL: Free Press, 1951.

NEGUS, VICTOR EWINGS, *The Mechanism of the Larynx*, London: Heinemann, 1949.

NEISSER, ULRIC, *Cognition and Reality*, San Francisco: Freeman, 1976.

NEURATH, OTTO, *Le développement du Cercle de Vienne et l'avenir de l'empirisme*, Paris: Hermann & Co., 1935.

NEWELL, ALLAN and SIMON, HERBERT, *Human Problem Solving*, Englewood Cliffs: Prentice-Hall, 1972.

NEWMEYER, FREDERICK, *Linguistic Theory in America*, New York: Academic, 1980.

NIDA, EUGENE, 'The analysis of grammatical constituents', *Language* 24, 1948, 414–41.

——, *Morphology: The Descriptive Analysis of Words*, Ann Arbor MI: University of Michigan Press, 1949 [1946].

——, 'A system for the description of semantic elements', *Word* 7, 1951, 1–14.

——, 'Problems of semantic equivalents'. Paper at the Meeting of the Linguistic Society of America, 1955.

OGDEN, CHARLES and RICHARDS, IVOR ARMSTRONG, *The Meaning of Meaning*, London: Paul Trench and Trubner, 1923.

OLMSTEAD, DAVID, 'Toward a cultural theory of lexical innovation: A research design', *Georgetown University Monograph Series on Languages and Linguistics* 7, 1954, 105–17.

OPLER, MORRIS, 'Some recently developed concepts relating to culture', *Southwestern Journal of Anthropology* 4, 1948, 107–22.

OSGOOD, CHARLES, 'On understanding and creating sentences', *American Psychologist* 18, 1963, 735–51.

—— and SEBEOK, THOMAS (eds), *Psycholinguistics: A Survey of Theory and Research Problems*, Bloomington: Indiana University Publications in Anthropology and Linguistics 10, 1954.

OSTHOFF, HERMANN and BRUGMANN, KARL, *Morphologische Untersuchungen*, Leipzig: S. Hirzel, 1878–1910.

OTT, HUGO, *Martin Heidegger: Unterwegs zur seiner Biographie*, Frankfurt am Main: Campus, 1988.

PANCONCELLI-CALZIA, GIULIO, *Das 'als ob' in der Phonetik*, Hamburg: Stromverlag, 1947.

PAINTER, CLARE, *Into the Mother Tongue: A Case Study in Early Language Development*, Oxford: Frances Pinter, 1984.

PARETO, VILFREDO, *The Mind and Society*, London: Jonathan Cape, 1935.

PAUL, HERMANN, *Prinzipien der Sprachgeschichte*, Halle: Niemeyer, 1880.
——, Principles of the History of Language, New York: Macmillan, 1889 (transl. 1880)
PAVLOV, IVAN, *Conditioned Reflexes*, London: Oxford, 1927.
PERFETTI, CHARLES, GOLDMAN, SUSAN and HOGABOAM, THOMAS, 'Reading skill and the identification of words', *Memory & Cognition* 7, 1979, 273–82.
PERFETTI, CHARLES and LESGOLD, ALAN, 'Discourse comprehension and the sources of individual differences'. In Marcel Just and Patricia Carpenter (eds), *Cognitive Processes in Comprehension*, Hillsdale, NJ: Erlbaum, 1977, 141–83.
PERFETTI, CHARLES and ROTH, SARAH, 'Some of the interactive processes in reading'. In Alan Lesgold and Charles Perfetti (eds), *Interactive Processes in Reading*, Hillsdale, NJ: Erlbaum, 1981.
PETERSON, GORDON and FILLMORE, CHARLES, 'The theory of phonemic analysis', *Proceedings of the Fourth International Congress of Phonetic Sciences*, 1962, 476–89.
PIAGET, JEAN, *The Origins of Intelligence in Children*, New York: International Universities Press, 1952.
——, *Biology and Knowledge*, Chicago: University of Chicago Press, 1967.
PICKERING, JOHN, *A Vocabulary or Collection of Words and Phrases which have been Supposed to be Peculiar to the United States*, Boston: Hilliard & Metcalf, 1815.
——, *An Essay on a Uniform Orthography for the Indian Languages of North America*, Cambridge MA: Hilliard & Metcalf, 1820.
PICKETT, VELMA, *The Grammatical Hierarchy of Isthmus Zapotec*, Glendale, CA: Summer Institute of Linguistics, 1960.
PIKE, KENNETH, 'On tagmemes *née* grammemes', *International Journal of American Linguistics* 24, 1958, 273–78.
——, *Language in Relation to a Unified Theory of the Structure of Human Behavior*, The Hague: Mouton, 1967.
—— and PIKE, EVELYN, *Grammatical Analysis*, Huntington Beach: Summer Institute of Linguistics, 1975.
PIRSIG, ROBERT, *Zen and the Art of Motorcycle Maintenance*, New York: William Morrow, 1974.
POSTMAN, LEO, 'Towards a general theory of cognition'. In John Rohrer and Muzafer Sherif (eds), *Social Psychology at the Crossroads*, New York: Harper and Row, 1951, 242–72.
POTT, AUGUST FRIEDRICH, *Das physiologische und psychologische Moment bei der sprachlichen Formenbildung*, Berlin: C Habel, 1879.
——, *Einleitung in die allgemeine Sprachwissenschaft*, Leipzig: J.A. Barth, 1884.
POULSON, DOROTHY, KINTSCH, EILEEN, KINTSCH, WALTER and PREMACK, DAVID, 'Children's comprehension and memory for stories', *Journal of Experimental Child Psychology* 28, 1979, 379–403.
PRIGOGINE, ILYA and STENGERS, ISABELLE, *Order out of Chaos*, London: Heinemann, 1984.
PROPP, VLADIMIR, *Morfologia skazki*, Leningrad: Akademia, 1928.
PULGRAM, ERNST, 'Statics and dynamics of linguistic subcodes', *Lingua* 10, 1961, 305–25.
QUINE, WILLARD VAN ORMAN, *From a Logical Point of View*, Cambridge, MA: Harvard, 1953.
——, *Word and Object*, Cambridge, MA: MIT Press, 1960.
RAAIJMAKERS, JEROEN and SHIFFRIN, RICHARD, 'Search of associative memory', *Psychology Review* 88, 1981, 93–134.
REICHENBACH, HANS, *Elements of Symbolic Logic*, New York: Free Press, 1947.
REICHER, GERALD, 'Perceptual recognition as a function of the meaningfulness of stimulus materials', *Journal of Experimental Psychology* 81, 1969, 274–80.

REID, THOMAS BERTRAM WALLACE, 'Linguistics, structuralism, philology', *Archivum Linguisticum* 8, 1956.

——, *Historical Philosophy and Linguistic Science*, Oxford: Clarendon, 1960.

RIBOT, THÉODULE, *English Psychology*, New York: Appleton, 1874.

RICHARDS, IVOR ARMSTRONG, *Mencius on the Mind*, London: Paul Trench & Trubner, 1932.

RIEGER, CHARLES, 'Spontaneous computation in cognitive models', *Cognitive Models* 1, 1977, 315–54.

RILEY, MARY, GREENO, JAMES and HELLER, JOAN, 'The development of children's problem-solving ability'. In Herbert Ginsberg (ed.), *The Development of Mathematical Thinking*, New York: Academic, 1982, 153–96.

ROBINS, ROBERT H, *Ancient and Mediaeval Grammatical Theory in Europe, with Special Reference to Modern Linguistic Doctrines*, London: Bell, 1951.

——, 'Malinowski, Firth, and the "context of situation"'. In Edwin Ardener (ed.), *Social Anthropology and Language*, London: Tavistock, 1957.

——, 'John Rupert Firth', *Language* 37/2, 1961, 199–200.

ROSENBLOOM, PAUL, *The Elements of Mathematical Logic*, New York: Dover, 1950.

RUSSELL, BERTRAND, *An Inquiry into Meaning and Truths*, New York: Norton, 1940.

SANDELL, ROLF GUNNAR, *Linguistic Style and Persuasion*, London: Academic, 1977.

SANDMANN, MANFRED, *Subject and Predicate*, Edinburgh: Edinburgh University Press, 1954.

SANFORD, ANTHONY and GARROD, SIMON, *Understanding Written Language*, New York: Wiley, 1981.

SAPIR, EDWARD, *Language*, New York: Harcourt, Brace & World, 1921.

——, *Selected Writings on Language, Culture, and Personality* (ed. David Mandelbaum), Berkeley: University of California Press, 1949.

SAPORTA, SOL, Review of Colin Cherry, *On Human Communication*, *International Journal of American Linguistics* 24, 1958, 326–29.

SAUSSURE, FERDINAND DE, *Mémoire sur le système primitif des voyelles dans les langues indo-européennes*, Leipzig: B.G. Teubner, 1879.

——, *Cours de linguistique générale* (ed. Charles Bally, Albert Sechehaye and Albert Riedlinger), Lausanne: Payot, 1916.

——, *Recueil des publications scientifiques de Ferdinand de Saussure*, Geneva: Dorz, 1921.

——, *Course in General Linguistics* (transl. Wade Baskin), New York: McGraw-Hill 1966 [transl. of 1916].

SCHLEGEL, FRIEDRICH VON, *Über die Sprache und Weisheit der Inder*, Heidelberg: Mohr & Zimmermann, 1808.

SCHLEICHER, AUGUST, *Compendium der vergleichenden Grammatik der indogermanischen Sprachen*, Weimar: H. Böhlau, 1861.

SCHNOTZ, WOLFGANG, BALLSTAEDT, STEFFEN-PETER and MANDL, HEINZ, 'Prozesse beim Zusammenfassen von Lehrtexten'. In Heinz Mandl (ed.), *Zur Psychologie der Textverarbeitung*, Munich: Urban & Schwarzenberg, 1981.

SECHEHAYE, ALBERT, *Programme et méthodes de la linguistique théorique*, Paris: H. Champion, 1908.

SELFRIDGE, OLIVER and NEISSER, ULRIC, 'Pattern recognition by machine', *Scientific American* 203, 1960, 60–80.

SHANNON, CLAUDE and WEAVER, WARREN, *The Mathematical Theory of Communication*, Urbana: University of Illinois Press, 1949.

SHEFFIELD, ALFRED, *Grammar and Thinking: A Study of the Working Conceptions in Syntax*, New York: Knickerbocker, 1912.

SHIFFRIN, RICHARD and SCHNEIDER, WALTER, 'Controlled and automatic human information processing', *Psychological Review* 84, 1977, 1–66 and 127–90.

SIEVERS, EDUARD, *Grundzüge der Phonetik zur Einführung in das Studium der*

Lautlehre der indogermanischen Sprachen, Leipzig: Breitkopf & Härtel, 1881.
——, *Angelsächsische Grammatik*, Halle: M. Niemeyer, 1882.

SINCLAIR, ANGUS, *The Conditions of Knowing*, London: Routledge & Kegan Paul, 1951.

SKEAT, WALTER WILLIAM, *Principles of English Etymology*, Oxford: Clarendon, 1887.

SKINNER, BURRHUS FREDERICK, *Verbal Behavior*, New York: Appleton-Century-Crofts, 1957.

SMITH EDWARD, ADAMS, NANCY and SCHORR, DENNIS, 'Fact retrieval and the paradox of the expert', *Cognitive Psychology* 10, 1978, 438–64.

SMITH, EDWARD and MEDIN, DOUGLAS, *Categories and Concepts*, Cambridge, MA: Harvard University Press, 1981.

SMITH, FRANK, *Psycholinguistics and Reading*, New York: Holt, Rinehart & Winston, 1973.

SMITH, HENRY LEE, 'An outline of metalinguistic analysis', *Report of the Third Annual Round Table Meeting on Linguistics and Language Teaching*, 1952, 59–66.

SMITH, THOMAS, *De recta et emendata linguae Anglicae scriptione*, Paris: R. Stephan, 1568.

SPERBER, HANS, *Einführung in die Bedeutungslehre*, Leipzig: K. Schroeder, 1923.

STANOVICH, KEITH and WEST, RICHARD, 'The effect of sentence context on ongoing word recognition', *Journal of Experimental Psychology: Human Perception and Performance* 7, 1981, 658–72.

STEVENS, ALBERT, COLLINS, ALLAN and GOLDIN, SARAH, 'Misconceptions in students' understanding', *International Journal of Man-Machine Studies* 11, 1979, 145–56.

STÖCKLEIN, JOHANN, *Der Bedeutungswandel der Wörter*, Munich: J. Lindauer, 1898.

SWEET, HENRY, *A New English Grammar, Part I: Introduction, Phonology, and Accidence*, Oxford: Clarendon, 1891.

——, *A New English Grammar, Part II: Syntax*, Oxford: Clarendon, 1898.

——, *The Practical Study of Languages*, New York: Holt, 1900.

——, 'Word, logic, and grammar'. In *Collected Papers of Henry Sweet*, Oxford: Clarendon, 1913 [1875–76], 1–33.

SWINNEY, DAVID, 'Lexical access during sentence comprehension: (Re)consideration of context effects', *Journal of Verbal Learning and Verbal Behavior* 18, 1979, 645–59.

TARSKI, ALFRED, *O logice matematycznej metodzie dudukcyjnej*, Lwów: Ksążnica Atlas, 1935.

TAULI, VALTER, *The Structural Tendencies of Languages*, Helsinki: Finnish Academy of Sciences, 1958.

TEMPLE, RICHARD, 'A theory of universal grammar, as applied to savage languages', *The Indian Antiquary* 28, 1899, 197–208 and 225–35.

THORSEN, AGNES, 'The relation of tongue movements to internal speech', *Journal of Experimental Psychology* 8, 1925, 1–32.

TILL, ROBERT, MROSS, ERNEST and KINTSCH, WALTER, *Time Course of Priming for Associate and Inference Words in a Discourse Context*, Boulder: University of Colorado Institute of Cognitive Science Technical Report 151, 1986.

TOGEBY, KNUD, 'Structure immanente de la langue française', *Travaux du Cercle Linguistique de Copenhague* 6, 1951.

TRAGER, GEORGE, 'La systématique des phonèmes en polonais', *Acta Linguistica* 1, 1939, 179–188.

—— and SMITH, HENRY LEE, 'An Outline of English Structure', *Studies in Linguistics*, Occasional Paper No. 3, 1951.

TRENCH, RICHARD CHEVENIX, *On the Study of Words*, London: George Routledge & Sons, 1832.

——, *English Past and Present*, New York: Redfield, 1855.

TRUBETZKOY, NIKOLAI, *Gründzuge der Phonologie*, Prague: Czechoslovakian

Ministry of Education, 1939.

TULVING, ENDEL and GOLD, CECILLE, 'Stimulus information as determinants of tachistoscopic word recognition', *Journal of Experimental Psychology* 66, 1963, 319–27.

TWADDELL, FREEMAN, 'On Defining the Phoneme', *Language Monographs* 16, 1935.

ULDALL, HANS-JØRGEN, 'The phonematics of Danish'. *Proceedings of the Second International Congress of Phonetic Sciences*, 1936, 54–57.

——, 'Outline of glossematics', *Travaux du Cercle Linguistique de Copenhague* 10, 1957, 1–89.

ULLMANN, STEPHEN, *The Principles of Semantics*, Glasgow: Jackson, 1957.

URBAN, WILBUR, *Language and Reality*, New York: Macmillan, 1939.

URE, JEAN, 'Lexical density and register discourse formation'. In G.E. Perren and J.L.M. Trim (eds), *Applications of Linguistics*, Cambridge: CUP, 1971.

URE, JEAN and ELLIS, JEFFREY, 'Register in descriptive linguistics and linguistic sociology'. In Oscar Uribe-Villegas (ed.), *Issues in Sociolinguistics*, The Hague, Mouton, 1972.

VACHEK, JOSEF, 'One aspect of phoneme theory', *Proceedings of the Second International Congress of Phonetic Sciences*, 1936, 33–40.

——, *A Prague School Reader in Linguistics*, Bloomington: Indiana University Press, 1964.

VAUGELAS, CLAUDE FAURÉ DE, *Remarques sur la langue française*, Paris: J. Camusat, 1647.

VINACKE, EDGAR, 'The investigation of concept formation', *Psychological Bulletin* 48, 1951, 1–31.

VOEGELIN, CHARLES, Review of K.L. Pike, *Phonemics*, *International Journal of American Linguistics* 15, 1949, 75–85.

——, YEGERLEHNER, JOHN and ROBINETT, FLORENCE, 'Shawnee laws: Perceptual statements for the language and for the content', *American Anthropologist* 56/6, 1954, 32–46.

VOGT, HANS, 'The structure of the Norwegian monosyllables', *Norsk Tidsskrift for Sprogvidenskap* 12, 1942, 5–29.

VYGOTSKY, LEV SEMONOVICH, 'Thought and speech', *Psychiatry* 2, 1939, 29–54.

WALKER, WILLIAM H, *Interest as a Function of Knowledge*, Boulder: University of Colorado Institute of Cognitive Science Technical Report 109, 1981.

——, *Retrieval of Knowledge from Memory*, Boulder: University of Colorado dissertation, 1982.

WALLIS, JOHN, *De loquela, sive sonorum formatione tractatus grammaticophysicus*, London: J.A. Langerak, 1727.

WATSON, JOHN BROADUS, *Behaviorism*, New York, Chicago: University of Chicago Press, 1925.

WEGENER, PHILIPP, *Untersuchungen über die Grundlagen des Sprachlebens*, Halle: Niemeyer 1885.

WEGMAN, CORNELIS, 'Conceptual representations of belief systems', *Journal for the Theory of Social Behavior* 11, 1981, 279–305.

WEINER, MELVIN, *The Cognitive Unconscious*, Davis, CA: International Psychological Press, 1975.

WEISGERBER, JOHANN LEO, *Muttersprache und Geistesbildung*, Gottingen: Vandenhoeck & Ruprecht, 1929.

——, *Vom Weltbild der deutschen Sprache*, Düsseldorf: Schwann, 1953.

WEISS, ALBERT PAUL, *A Theoretical Basis of Human Behavior*, Columbus, OH: R.G. Adams, 1925.

WELLS, RULON S., 'Immediate constituents', *Language* 23, 1947, 81–117.

WHITNEY, WILLIAM DWIGHT, *Language and the Study of Language*, New York: C. Scribner, 1867.

——, *The Life and Growth of Language: An Outline of Linguistic Science*, New York: Appleton, 1875.

——, *Language and its Study*, London: Trubner, 1876.

WHORF, BENJAMIN LEE, *Language, Thought, and Reality*, New York: Wiley, 1956.

WILKINS, JOHN, *Essay towards a Real Character and a Philosophical Language*, London: Gellibrand, 1688.

WILSON, THOMAS, *Arte of Rhetoricke*, London: Kingston, 1553.

WINOGRAD, TERRY, *Understanding Natural Language*, New York: Academic, 1972.

——, *Language as a Cognitive Process*, Reading, MA: Addison-Wesley, 1983.

WISSLER, CLARK, 'Material culture'. In Carl Murchison (ed.), *Handbook of Social Psychology*, Worcester, MA: Clark University Press, 1935, 520–64.

WITTGENSTEIN, LUDWIG, *Tractatus Logico-Philosophicus*, London: Routledge.

——, *Philosophical Investigations*, Oxford: Blackwell, 1953.

——, *Preliminary Studies for 'Philosophical Investigations'; Generally Known as the Blue and Brown Books*, Oxford: Blackwell, 1958.

WITTROCK, MERLIN, MARKS, CAROL and DOCTOROW, MARLEEN, 'Reading as a generative process', *Journal of Educational Psychology* 67, 1975, 484–89.

WOLF, FRIEDRICH AUGUST, *Encyclopädie der philologie*, Leipzig: Teubner, 1837 [*ca* 1777].

WOODS, WILLIAM, 'Transition network grammars for natural language analysis', *Communications of the Association for Computing Machinery* 13/10, 1970, 591–606.

——, 'Multiple theory formation in speech and reading'. In Rand Spiro, Bertram Bruce, and William Brewer (eds), *Theoretical Issues in Reading Comprehension*, Hillsdale, NJ: Erlbaum, 1980.

WRIGHT, JOSEPH, *The English Dialect Grammar*, Oxford: H. Frowde, 1905.

WUNDT, WILHELM, *Sprachgeschichte und Sprachphilosophie*, Leipzig: W. Engelmann, 1901.

——, *Völkerpsychologie*, Leipzig: W. Engelmann, 1900–09.

YATES, FRANCIS EUGENE, 'Semiotics as a bridge between information (biology) and dynamics (physics)', *Recherches Sémiotiques/Semiotic Inquiry* 5, 1986, 347–360.

—— and BEAUGRANDE, ROBERT DE, 'Physics and Semiotics'. In Walter A. Koch (ed.), *Semiotics in the Individual Sciences*, Bochum: Brockmeyer, 1990, 318–51.

YNGVE, VICTOR, *A Model and a Hypothesis for Language Structure*, Cambridge, MA: MIT Research Laboratory of Electronics Technical Report 369, 1960.

ZIPF, GEORGE KINGSLEY, *The Psycho-Biology of Language*, Boston: Houghton Mifflin, 1935.

Index of names

Index of terms

These listings are mainly devoted to substantive uses addressing the role, status, or meaning of the term rather than simply mentioning it in passing. For example, the citations of 'word' are those in which the 'word' receives attention as a potential or actual linguistic entity. Numbers in italics indicate passages where the term is defined or explained.